Family Practice: Brief Systems Methods for Social Work

Cynthia Franklin
University of Texas at Austin

Catheleen Jordan
University of Texas at Arlington

Brooks/Cole Publishing Company

I(T)P® An International Thomson Publishing Company

Pacific Grove • Albany • Belmont • Bonn • Boston • Cincinnati • Detroit • Johannesburg • London
Madrid • Melbourne • Mexico City • New York • Paris • Singapore • Tokyo • Toronto • Washington

Sponsoring Editor: *Lisa I. Gebo*
Editorial Assistant: *Susan Wilson*
Marketing Team: *Steve Catalano, Aaron Eden,*
  Kyrrha Sevco, and Jean Thompson
Production Editor: *Mary Vezilich*
Manuscript Editor: *Patterson Lamb*

Cover Design: *E. Kelly Shoemaker*
Interior Design: *Laurie Albrecht*
Cover Illustration: *Diana Org/SuperStock*
Typesetting: *Carlisle Communications, Ltd.*
Printing and Binding: *Webcom*

For more information, contact:

BROOKS/COLE PUBLISHING COMPANY
511 Forest Lodge Road
Pacific Grove, CA 93950
USA

International Thomson Publishing Europe
Berkshire House 168-173
High Holborn
London WC1V 7AA
England

Thomas Nelson Australia
102 Dodds Street
South Melbourne, 3205
Victoria, Australia

Nelson Canada
1120 Birchmount Road
Scarborough, Ontario
Canada M1K 5G4

International Thomson Editores
Seneca 53
Col. Polanco
11560 México, D. F., México

International Thomson Publishing GmbH
Königswinterer Strasse 418
53227 Bonn
Germany

International Thomson Publishing Asia
60 Albert Street
#15-01 Albert Complex
Singapore 189969

International Thomson Publishing Japan
Hirakawacho Kyowa Building, 3F
2-2-1 Hirakawacho
Chiyoda-ku, Tokyo 102
Japan

Printed in Canada

10   9   8   7   6   5   4   3   2   1

Library of Congress Cataloging-in-Publication Data
Franklin, Cynthia.
    Family practice: brief systems methods for social work / Cynthia Franklin, Catheleen Jordan.
      p. cm.
    Includes index.
    ISBN 0-534-16182-0 (pbk.)
    1. Family social work. 2. Family psychotherapy. I. Jordan,
Catheleen, [date-]. II. Title.
HV697.F73 1998
362.82—dc21   98-16953
                    CIP

To my teachers for their dedication, service, and contributions to my success. Especially to my mentor, Dr. John S. McNeil, who helped me become a professor and has supported and nurtured my career. To Dr. Jeanne P. Deschner, who showed me the importance of being a practitioner/researcher. To Ms. Judy Garrett, my 11th grade English teacher, who told me that I was a good writer.

Cynthia Franklin

To Mary Joyce Perdue Jordan for her loving support of her children.

Catheleen Jordan

CONTRIBUTORS

Marjie Barrett, Ph.D., *Associate Professor, University of Texas at Arlington*

Marianne Berry, Ph.D., *Associate Professor, University of Texas at Arlington*

Joan Biever, Ph.D., *Associate Professor, Our Lady of the Lake University*

Monte Bobele, Ph.D., *Professor, Our Lady of the Lake University*

Norman H. Cobb, Ph.D., *Associate Professor, University of Texas at Arlington*

Diana M. DiNitto, Ph.D., *Professor, University of Texas at Austin*

Sophia F. Dziegielewski, Ph.D., LCSW, *Visiting Associate Professor, University of Central Florida*

Cynthia Franklin, Ph.D., *Associate Professor, University of Texas at Austin*

Glen T. Gardner, Ph.D., *Professor, Our Lady of the Lake University*

Darlene Grant, Ph.D., *Assistant Professor, University of Texas at Austin*

Donald K. Granvold, Ph.D., *Professor, University of Texas at Arlington*

Nora Gustavsson, Ph.D., *Associate Professor, Arizona State University*

Dianne Harrison Montgomery, Ph.D., *Professor and Dean, Florida State University*

Catheleen Jordan, Ph.D., *Professor, University of Texas at Arlington*

Ara Lewellen, Ph.D., *Associate Professor, Texas A&M—Commerce*

James I. Martin, Ph.D., *Assistant Professor, University of Texas at Arlington*

Kelly Conroy Moore, MSSW, *Doctoral Student, University of Texas at Austin*

Vicki Vandiver, Ph.D., *Associate Professor, Portland State University*

Keith Warren, MSSW, *Doctoral Student, University of Texas at Austin*

CONTENTS

PART 4

New Directions in Brief and Systems Family Theory and Practice   *395*

CHAPTER FOURTEEN

Advances in Systems Theory   *397*
—*Cynthia Franklin and Keith Warren*

PREFACE

This book is relevant for clinical students in training and practicing professionals in social work, marriage and family therapy, and allied disciplines. Its main audience, however, is undergraduate and graduate social work students in training to be family practitioners. The purpose of the book is to provide an overview of several different practice models in family therapy with a specific focus on preparing social work practitioners to work in today's practice contexts of managed behavioral health care and short-term treatment and integrative services systems. All the approaches covered in the book share a theoretical bedrock in family systems theory, and each approach lends itself to brief treatment. Clinical approaches and issues covered throughout the text address the needs of today's practicing professionals who require effective and time-limited family practice models on which to base their practices. For the most part, the book is a prescriptive "how to" book that provides information on the methods of change offered by each of the family practice models covered.

This book is meant to be an applied text instead of a theoretical treatise on the family therapy models. Several other books provide an overview of the theoretical constructs of family practice (e.g., Becvar & Becvar, 1996; Goldenberg & Goldenberg, 1997; Nichols & Schwartz, 1995). This book distinguishes itself from such texts by its emphasis on preparing practitioners to work in today's practice contexts and its illustration of the methods of brief (time-limited), systems approaches. Although this book does provide an introduction to several family therapy models, including brief explanations of theories, it goes further in case illustrations and explications of methods than other books written as overviews of family theories and models. This applied focus is believed to be especially useful for preparing students to use theory to guide practice.

There are four sections to the text. Part 1, "Introduction," presents one chapter on the current practice contexts in which family practitioners[1] work. Managed behavioral health care and the trend toward integrative service systems are highlighted, and the effects of these practice trends on family practice is examined. Case examples are included to illustrate the points made.

Part 2, "Time-Limited (Brief) Family Practice Models for Social Work Practice," presents seven chapters illustrating family practice models and one integrative chapter illustrating assessment methods. Family practice models reviewed include structural, strategic, behavioral and cognitive-behavioral models, solution-focused brief therapy, postmodern (social construction and narrative models), psychoeducational, and family preservation approaches. Although this is not an exhaustive list of brief family systems practice models, the approaches covered represent important models that have emerged from the perspective of family systems theory.

Each chapter covering a practice model presents a brief introduction, including the history and the development of the practice model and its theoretical basis. There is also information about how well the model works in today's practice contexts of managed behavioral health care, and further information on the specific consistencies with social work practice. Because empirical research is so important to today's outcome-oriented practice environments, each chapter also presents information on the research basis for the model. The chapters are designed to illustrate therapeutic methods a practitioner follows to implement the model in practice. There are lengthy case illustrations, including transcripts from actual practice situations, in each chapter.

The assessment chapter reviews important clinical techniques used across the family practice models and also summarizes several standardized family assessment measures. Managed behavioral health care has created practice environments in which family therapists must use the most up-to-date assessment and measurement procedures to evaluate the effectiveness of their practices. For this reason, we have included this lengthy chapter on rapid assessment that details several measurement approaches that may be used to assess family problems and to document the effectiveness of practice interventions.

Part 3, "Intervening in Larger Systems and the Sociopolitical Context of Family Practice," provides three chapters that prepare practitioners to do clinical work with ethnically and culturally diverse families and one chapter on family policy. Today's family practitioners work in a multicultural world where they come into contact with diverse family types and are expected to know how to work with many different family lifestyles. For this reason, this section includes chapters on practice with marginalized ethnic families (Native American, Latino, and African American), gay and lesbian couples and families, and a chapter that addresses the issue of gender in family therapy. The ethnic diversity chapter provides several case examples demonstrating the effectiveness of differing family models with ethnic families. Work with gay and lesbian clients also includes important case content and methods to help practitioners examine their own biases toward these families. Gender issues are discussed in the context of examining the limitations of family models to provide appropriate theoretical thought concerning gender and the significance of male and female stereotypes in therapy. Covered also is the historic oppression of women and how societal forces influence therapeutic models.

Clinical practitioners need to be knowledgeable about the social policies that affect families, because the larger sociopolitical context cannot be separated from the contexts in which family practitioners serve families. The effects of managed behavioral health care on families and clinical practice is a good example. A chapter has been included on family policy to prepare practitioners

---

[1]The terms *social worker, family practitioner, family therapist,* and *clinical practitioner* are used interchangeably in this book to describe clinicians who work with families.

to influence the macro context in which families exist. There are case examples and materials to assist students and practitioners in their assimilation of this information.

Finally in Part 4, "New Directions in Brief and Systems Family Theory and Practice," the book offers one capstone chapter on advances in systems theory that provides an introduction to the sciences of chaos and complexity and their potential significance for brief family therapy models. Although this chapter is highly theoretical, it updates current theoretical models relevant to understanding the person-in-environment perspectives of social work, and also offers a lengthy section on the practice implications of these theoretical perspectives.

We envision the book to be an important instructional resource for students and practitioners in the beginning stages of training to be family therapists. More advanced practitioners may also find the text useful because it offers interesting updates on assessment methods, family policy, advances in systems theory, and newer practice approaches such as solution-focused therapy, social constructionism, and family preservation.

provided ongoing assistance in typing and editing the book, and we appreciate her able assistance with the glossary and index. We also thank our reviewers: Lupe Alle-Corliss, California State University—San Bernardino; Donald Bardill, Florida State University; Don Basse, Adams State College; LaVonne Cornell-Swanson, University of Wisconsin; Craig LeCroy, Arizona State University; Doman Lum, California State University—Sacramento; Dennis Saleeby, University of Kansas; Emily Scott-Lowe, Student Counseling Center at Pepperdine University; Thomas Edward Smith, Florida State University; Barbara Thomlison, University of Calgary; Stephanie Vaughn, New Mexico State University; and David J. Westhius, University of Southern Indiana.

Additionally, we thank Jim Franklin and Rick Hoefer for their support during the writing. Finally, we would like to thank Christina Mae Franklin for delaying her imminent birth for a few short days while her mother finished the revisions on the manuscript.

Cynthia Franklin
Catheleen Jordan

Acknowledgments

Writing a book is like playing team sports. You count on the work of all involved to make it a winning effort. We would like to thank some of the people who helped us along the way. We thank all the professionals at Brooks/Cole Publishing Company for their help and guidance. We especially thank Lisa Gebo, Mary Vezilich, and Patterson Lamb for their support and help with the editorial process. Amy Dolejs also

References

BECVAR, D. S., & BECVAR, R. J. (1996). *Family therapy: A systemic integration* (3rd ed.). Boston: Allyn & Bacon.

GOLDENBERG, I., & GOLDENBERG, H. (1997). *Family therapy: An overview*. Pacific Grove, CA: Brooks/Cole.

NICHOLS, M. P., & SCHWARTZ, R. C. (1995). *Family therapy: Concepts and methods* (3rd ed.). Needham Heights, MA: Allyn & Bacon.

PART ONE

Introduction

everal trends are changing the way family practitioners do their work. Two trends highlighted in this book are managed behavioral health care and the move toward integrated services delivery systems. Both represent efforts to improve mental health and social services and to increase the use of services, efficiency, and cost effectiveness. These trends also increase the demands for accountability in practice and require practitioners to measure outcomes in their practices. Managed behavioral health care was implemented because of rising health care costs. With the advent of managed care, in most states, there has been a massive restructuring in the way clinical services are financed and delivered. Integrated services delivery systems are a trend within managed care, but they also represent restructuring and reforms in human services systems.

Chapter 1 offers a framework for understanding this book and its contents. Managed behavioral health care and the development of integrated services delivery systems are summarized. Also discussed is the need for family practitioners to use brief, effective, and time-limited family approaches. Chapter 1 also explores the ways the family models covered in this book meet the criteria for brief family practice models and how these models also have a family systems orientation. Further highlighted are similarities across the models that increase their utility for today's practice contexts.

CHAPTER ONE

Cynthia Franklin, Ph.D.
University of Texas at Austin
Catheleen Jordan, Ph.D.
University of Texas at Arlington

Family Practice in Today's Practice Contexts

Family practice is being influenced by the development of alternative mental health and health care funding policies known as managed behavioral health care. Pinsof and Wynne (1995) state, "As never before demands are being made that reimbursable health care services demonstrate their effectiveness and cost effectiveness" (p. 341). Managed care is a way of financing health, mental health, and social services in which the major focus is on containing costs and increasing the quality of clinical services delivered (Strom-Gottfried, 1997). Managed care has become the dominant method of funding for family therapy and other mental health services. Currently, more than 100 million Americans are participating in some type of managed care plan. These numbers are also believed to be escalating (Hoyt, 1995a). The Child Welfare League of America has found that 41 of 49 states are considering some form of managed care for their clients, with the top plan being to contract out services to local providers who will provide services at a set cost to the state government (Hutchins, 1996). Managed care influences use and cost of services and measures the performance of providers. An example of a provider is a family practitioner delivering clinical services. Integration, accountability, effectiveness, and cost efficiency are especially emphasized within managed care systems (Giles, 1991). Chapter 13 further discusses managed care and points out some of its limitations. Here we focus on the effects of managed care on family practice and highlight what practitioners must know and do to work in managed care settings.

Current Trends in Today's Practice Contexts

Before managed care emerged in the 1980s, mental health and other health care systems relied on categorical funding strategies. Through categorical funding mechanisms, funding for clinical services such as family therapy were usually separated into public versus private revenues. Public agencies, such as child protective services and public mental health services, were primarily funded through public tax money. At the same time, private, nonprofit services such as family services agencies and child guidance clinics were primarily supported by money raised through local communities, charities, and foundations, and sometimes businesses or local governments. Finally, private for-profit practices received revenues from private payers and third-party payers such as insurance companies. Of course, there were always exceptions to the categorical funding schema for private and public services; some public and private partnerships were achieved, and funding streams may cross over from one type of service delivery system to another. For the most part, however, these categorical funding mechanisms were responsible for how mental health and social services were funded and subsequently how family practitioners were paid.

Categorical funding arrangements often created a two-tiered system, making sharp distinctions between public and private services and other distinctions between nonprofit and for-profit services. One of the big distinctions was in who came for the services. Most often, poorer clients came to public agencies and richer, middle-class clients came for help in private agencies. The most advantaged clients often came to family practitioners working in private practices. Families seen in private practice were sometimes referred to in the therapy literature as YARVIS clients. YARVIS is an acronym for young, attractive, rich, verbal, intelligent, and successful. Chapter 13 discusses in more detail the two-tiered system and its affects on poor families.

The emergence of managed behavioral health care has changed funding for clinical services. Managed care organizations (often called MCOs) are encompassing all public and private services and changing the way family therapists and other professionals conduct their practices. For example, in the private practice of one of the authors, a psychiatrist has a full case load of public-funded Medicaid clients in a private psychiatric hospital (Franklin & Johnson, 1996). In another example, one of the authors who is a social worker/family therapist worked previously in a group private practice that specialized in treatment with families who batter one another and were referred by the child protective services agency. Almost all the families were low income. Even though the family therapist worked in a private practice, she had a contract with a public agency to offer family therapy services to the public-funded clients. This arrangement brought the practitioner into continual contact with the public welfare bureaucracies, where she was expected to work as a team member with other public social services workers.

A case example reported by Franklin and Johnson (1996) may further clarify how the current practice contexts operate and affect how practitioners work. A family therapist who is a private practitioner received a referral for a family from the state rehabilitation, public-funded agency. The family consisted of a 38-year-old Anglo male and his 11-year-old son. The father was unemployed and receiving workers' compensation for a work-related injury. Presenting problems included a need for evaluation of his prognosis for returning to work, an assessment for a possible mental disorder, and help in managing his son's attention deficit-hyperactivity disorder (ADHD) and behavioral problems. This case, however, was intertwined with very complicated family and social issues. The client had a very unstable work history, for example. In fact, he had never worked anywhere longer than six months in his adult life and had held infrequent jobs, often living with the help of welfare, assistance from community agencies, and other informal support systems. He and his son moved from place to place often to escape conflict with authorities such as schools and police. They had been clients of the child protective services agencies in three other states, but the son had never been removed from the home or placed in substitute care. Currently, the son was not going to school and had not been in a class in the past two years. Because of their frequent moves, the family was not able to maintain relationships with public or community agencies for an extended period of time.

Successful treatment required a full spectrum of community services and coordination of those services between different agencies and practitioners. It meant providing supportive and skills interventions aimed at improving the client's goal-directed behavior, mental health functioning, and parenting skills. The family therapist was often required to leave her office and to attend meetings between the client and community agencies. Many referrals and case management processes had to occur for both the client and the son. Meetings involved individuals and agencies such as a psychiatrist, workers' compensation representative, and workers from a rehabilitation agency, a local public community mental health agency, family preservation services, and child protective services.

Franklin and Johnson (1996) note that the current practice context of managed behavioral health care is blurring the boundaries so that the former public versus private distinction no longer applies. These authors discuss how in many states and communities, private practitioners and private and public agencies are competing for the same dollars and serving the same clients. Private practitioners obtain contracts to provide services to the public agency clients, and public agencies look for opportunities to serve middle-class clients so that they can receive additional funds from the private managed care companies. Capitation of expenditures is a frequent funding method used in managed care. Capitation refers to periodically (usually monthly) paying a practitioner a stipulated per capita rate for services. In other words, practitioners negotiate a pre-set amount of money for taking care of the family and meeting all their mental health needs.

The advent of managed care is having a major impact on the structure of private practice. First, managed behavioral health care affects practice by rearranging the way family practitioners work in private practice. In the context of managed care, the idea of a small or solo private practice is outdated. Across the country, family therapists and other practitioners are organizing themselves into large group practices and entering into contractual arrangements with managed care companies, preferred provider networks, and public agencies (Newman & Bricklin, 1991; Winegar, 1993). Of course, not all practitioners join these types of group practices. Some may opt for more independence and arrange their practices so that they can see all self-pay clients. Most practitioners, however, do feel obligated to join group practices.

Second, group practice arrangements resemble agencies more than private practices, and this structure has several implications for the way family therapists work. For example, group practice yields more paperwork than does private practice. Also, practitioners sacrifice some autonomy in a group practice. Many practitioners work for the practice instead of owning their own business, and this arrangement affects the amount of money they earn. Even if family practitioners are full partners, cost-containment measures employed by managed care mean less money. In addition, the managed care organization puts further constraints on the autonomy of private practitioners because it makes decisions about client treatment that would previously have been made by the practitioner and the client. How long a client may be seen in treatment and whether the goals are being reached in a time-efficient manner are examples of the types of decisions managed care organizations make concerning treatment. These methods bring increased accountability into practice but undermine the professional's role as an autonomous agent of change. They also assume that the managed care organization knows how to make the best decisions for the client. This may not be the case in every situation; managed care organizations are motivated by cost reductions, and this mind-set sometimes may interfere with offering the best care. Of course, family practitioners who work in public services are used to these types of restraints on their autonomy; they know the difficulties in following rigid guidelines concerning eligibility for seeing their clients and facing possible funding removal because of political whim.

Third, because of the preferred provider networks set up by managed care organizations, practitioners work much more in a network of services in collaboration with many other professionals. Of course, this makes all family therapist roles more similar to those discussed in traditional social work practice. Skills like case management, interprofessional collaboration, marketing, community organization, and client advocacy become essential to maintaining a successful clinical practice.

Hoyt (1995a) has identified 12 prevailing trends in managed behavioral health care that have further implications for the future of family practice and how therapists work:

1. More outcomes measurement, particularly assessment of resolution of the presenting complaint and determination of patient satisfaction

2. More treatment planning and more attention to differential therapeutics and the integration of techniques drawn from varying theoretical backgrounds, asking, What would be the best approach with this patient with this problem in this setting at this time?

3. Greater involvement of mental health services in primary care, based on fuller recognition of the connection between physical and mental well-being, following from the many studies that demonstrate that unnecessary medical utilization is reduced when emotional and psychological issues are addressed professionally

4. Increasingly organized, vertically integrated systems of care

5. Fewer and larger managed care companies

6. More group practices and fewer solo practices

7. More care provided by master's-level clinicians, psychiatric nurses, and various certified counselors, in keeping with the managed-care cost saving principle of having the least expensive workers do most of the labor

8. More group therapy, including more psychoeducational programs on a variety of topics (e.g., stress reduction, parenting skills, communication training), which will require administrative and financial support to make group referrals available and attractive

9. Much less inpatient care, with what there is mostly emphasizing rapid stabilization and return to the community as soon as possible

10. Greater reliance on computer technology, with its information processing and research advantages as well as attendant risks to confidentiality

11. Less utilization review, at least in the outpatient arena, as education, certification, and credentialing of efficient preferred providers moves forward

12. More emphasis on constructive therapies, ones that are future oriented, collaborative, and based on patients' competencies and resources (pp. xiii–xiv)

The Importance of Brief Therapy

In today's practice contexts, family therapy and other clinical services are offered by a mix of practitioners working in a diversity of private practices and traditional public agencies, but the trend is toward educationally focused, brief, solution-oriented practice (Corcoran & Vandiver, 1996; Franklin & Johnson, 1996; Franklin & Jordan, in press; Strom-Gottfried, 1997; Winegar, 1993). Current practice environments offer short-term treatment sessions. Clients rarely see practitioners more than six or eight times, regardless of the therapeutic orientation (Koss & Shiang, 1994). Some practitioners have advocated that practice should follow a course of intermittent work similar to a "primary care model." In this type of approach, practitioners would offer fewer sessions spaced over a long period of time (Cummings & Sayama, 1995). Other models are also being used, such as intensive outpatient treatment, where clients are seen two to three times a week for a limited time period. Even single-session therapies are being used (Talmon, 1990).

Managed care systems mandate the development of "best practices." This means that family practitioners are expected to know the most effective methods for addressing family problems. Practitioners may even be put in situations in which they have to defend different family practices before a case manager or review board operated by a managed care organization. For example, a practitioner may have to justify a certain type of treatment or build a case for the reason a client needs additional sessions to improve. This is not an uncommon occurrence in practice situations.

Because managed care is based on a medical model, "best practices" are usually determined by examining the empirical research undergirding particular methods. In addition, in today's practice it is important to use valid and reliable methods for assessing problems. Because there is an increasing emphasis on accountability, it is also important to be able to provide measures for outcomes of cases (Franklin & Jordan, in press). Family practitioners who develop successful practices need to be equipped with a variety of diverse family practice skills that provide brief and effective assessment and treatment (Blackwell & Schmidt, 1992; Corcoran & Gingerich, 1994; Giles, 1991; Lazarus, 1995; Sabin, 1991).

Integrated Services Delivery Systems and the Importance of a Systems Orientation

Current trends in clinical services delivery dictate that family therapy be offered through a service delivery system that integrates health, mental health, and social services (Winegar, 1993; Budman & Armstrong, 1992; Broskowski, 1991; Sabin, 1991). This increases the importance of an open systems approach to intervening into the problems of families because integration of services requires practitioners to work in a collaborative fashion with many community systems in order to help families. Ecological systems theory provides a basis for the open systems approach by helping practitioners develop a philosophical position on the importance of working with the family, community, and larger social structures that may be affecting the family.

Effective practitioners working in integrated services delivery systems must keep in mind the "big picture." Systems theory provides a framework for seeing families as more than a collection of individuals and for viewing their problems as encased in a web of difficulties intricately intertwined with other systems. As one of the basic tenets of systems theory is the belief in the hierarchical nature of systems, families may be viewed as one system among many others, such as neighborhood, community, state, federal, and even world levels. Larger systems may constrain the outcomes of family therapy on some family systems. For example, lack of economic security brought on by a slumping economy can create stressors that increase intrafamily conflicts and disagreements. The emphasis on integrating service delivery systems reminds us of another important systems idea: Every part affects the other parts. This makes it essential for effective linkages and integration to take place across systems and their parts.

Current trends in practice are to integrate health, education, and human services, and these trends are a part of a restructuring effort aimed at improving human services in the United States. Those in the human/social service professions see the trend toward integration as a long overdue strategy for how to serve families better—to reduce duplication of services and to provide a comprehensive network of supports for families (Franklin & Allen-Meares, 1997). Integration of services takes on several different meanings in the literature (Franklin & Allen-Meares, 1997). For some reformers involved in redesigning human services systems, it refers to the total restructuring of human services, including educational systems, to create a new and improved services delivery system. To others, however, it means only initiatives to formulate partnerships to improve working relationships so that practitioners can provide more effective and efficient services (Franklin & Streeter, 1995). According to Hare (1995), the integrationist movement has emerged partially as a response to childhood poverty. Some authors have depicted services integration as a child welfare movement offering important family-centered reforms (e.g., Hooper-Briar & Lawson, 1994; Kirst, 1991; Mellaville & Blank, 1993).

Each system has its own set of reasons for believing in the need for services integration, but access to services, the possibility of cost reduction, and the achievement of greater efficiency and effectiveness in services delivery are major reasons cited (Franklin & Allen-Meares, 1997). These goals are consistent with the type of cost containment and effectiveness objectives mentioned above. In fact, these efforts often converge in different states as funders and policymakers search for cost-efficient ways to provide human services.

According to Franklin and Allen-Meares (1997), the terms *services integration, wrap-around services, comprehensive services, interprofessional collaboration, one-stop shopping, colocated services, school-linked services,* and *full service schools* have been associated with the integrationist movement. Actually, these terms originate in different literatures and converge in philosophy concerning the need for collaboration and services integration (Dryfoos, 1994; Kahn & Kammerman, 1992; Mellaville & Blank, 1993). The terms *services integration* and *wrap-around services* are frequently encountered in the social services and mental health literature, and the terms *interprofessional collaboration, full service schools,* and *comprehensive services* are encountered in the education literature.

New integrated human services systems increase the importance of in-home services, and community-based alternatives advance the idea that it is important to offer services in the natural environment of the client instead of a hospital or a treatment center. Broskowski (1991), for example, advises psychologists that the future opportunities in practice are "embedded in their ability to design cost-effective alternatives, particularly modalities that deliver the care within the patients' natural settings, such as the home or school" (p. 12). These ideas for how to best serve clients are consistent with traditional social work practice. Ecological systems theory provides the guiding framework for understanding social work practice for the past 20 or 30 years. Franklin and Jordan (in press) discuss some of the limitations of systems approaches for practice in managed behavioral health care. Despite the limitations of the systems theories defined by these authors, the historic development of family therapy models within social work and allied disciplines illustrate the continuing ability of family systems approaches to provide helpful methods for working with families. Models coming out of family therapy, for example, provide more than a framework. They provide specific techniques for quick and effective behavior change.

Importance of Systems Theory to Family Practice

Systems theory in social work provides a specific way to think about working with families. Specific practice models, including methods for changing systems, developed within the field of marriage and family therapy. Early in the development of family practice, systems approaches distinguished themselves from other individual perspectives. In particular, systems theory emphasized the social, structural, and interactional bases of behavior. A family practitioner working from this perspective, for example, focuses on how certain communication or social-interactional processes in a family result in a problem pattern rather than focusing on the specific deficits of a family member. Early family systems therapists drew on general systems theory and sociological theories of the family, such as those embedded in structural functionalism, as a basis for the development of practice models. Later theorists wishing to expand these ideas incorporated theoretical notions from cybernetics and ecological theory into family practice. For example, Hartman and Laird developed the "family centered" ecological systems model. Social work practitioners also make use of the "life model" of Germain and Gitterman and Maluccio's "competence-oriented" model (Franklin, DiNitto, & McNeece, 1997).

One of the early major applications of systems theory to social work practice came from Pincus and Minahan (1973), who define social work in the following manner:

> Social work is concerned with the interactions between people and their social environment which affect the ability of people to accomplish their life tasks, alleviate distress, and realize their aspirations and values. The purpose of social work therefore is to (1) enhance the problem-solving and coping capacities of people, (2) link people with systems that provide them with resources, services, and opportunities, (3) promote the effective and humane operation of these systems, and (4) contribute to the development and improvement of social policy. (p. 9)

One of the important elements of their framework was a focus on the inadequacies of the formal, informal, and societal resource systems for meeting human needs. These ideas should sound remarkably up-to-date and consistent with issues addressed through integrated services delivery systems. Another equally important characteristic of the framework was its focus on the *interaction* of people with their network of resource systems. This led them to view problems as attributes of an individual's social situation, not as attributes of the individual. Such ideas are very consistent with how family therapists view problems within a family system. However, early family models put more emphasis on what went on within family systems and less emphasis on how broader societal systems interacted with family systems to create and maintain problems.

Major Concepts from Family Systems Theory

Franklin, DiNitto, and McNeece (1997) review some of the major concepts from family systems theory, and the following discussion is taken from their review.

RECIPROCAL CAUSALITY AND MUTUAL INFLUENCE

Systems are composed of component parts that interact to serve a particular function. Each level of the system adds a new level of analysis, and these complexities interact together to produce specific effects. *Reciprocal causality* and *mutual influence* describe the functioning of systems. In other words, A does not cause B, which in turn causes C. Instead, A and B interact together to cause C, which in turn causes A. "Recursion" is often used to explain how each element in a system mutually influences others in a manner that defies linear causality. In a family situation, for example, when the son has a behavior problem like disobeying the rules or running away, the mother and father may get in "knock down, drag out" fights over the son's behavior. However, this does not mean that the son's behavior started the fights. In fact, the opposite could also be true—that the behavior of the parents precipitates the disobedience of the son. In this way, the parents and son mutually influence one another's behavior. The family gets locked into a vicious cycle that spirals into an endless recursion of difficulties. Family systems therapists make direct interventions into "vicious patterns" to stop those behaviors, and they also work to modify the meanings that families associate with their interactions as a basis for altering future behavior patterns.

AUTOPOIESIS

In recent years, systems theorists in cybernetics have explained the relationships between systems, their environment, and observers in even more complex ways. *Autopoiesis*, or the process of self-generation, is the way parts of systems relate to one another. Whereas it holds true that a boundary between a system and another system is defined by an observer, it is also true that a system becomes distinct from its environment through a dynamic process of its own. This process cannot be understood separate from the environment that participates with this process, nor can it be separated from the observer who defines the process by setting a boundary. In this manner, the boundary between a system (e.g., a family) and the environment does not cause the system, and neither does the system cause the boundary between itself and the environment. They are both responsible for each other and exist together in an autopoietic (self-generating) system. The processes of autopoiesis are made concrete if one thinks about the ongoing reforms initiated in human services and educational organizations. This, of course, may include the current reforms in human services being discussed in this chapter. Reform efforts often bring forth reorganization after reorganization, but finally the structure and processes inherent in these organizations and their relationships with the environment manage to stay the same.

STRUCTURAL DETERMINISM AND STRUCTURAL COUPLING

Two other concepts from cybernetic systems theory build on this idea that systems self-generate and seek to maintain themselves. First is *structural determinism*, a term that defines the autonomy of systems and their abilities to decide how much deviation they can tolerate without losing their identity and integrity. The basic thesis behind this idea is that systems are limited by their own inherent structure, and that whatever effects the environment has on a system will be determined by the system's own properties and not those of the environment. The environment acts to perturb or constrain the system, but the result of this constraining is contingent on the system itself. Becvar and Becvar (1996) use this analogy to explain the concept of structural determinism. Your foot (environment) may kick a ball, and it will roll, but the fact that the ball rolls has to do with its shape (structure), which is round. In this analogy, it could also be said that a ball will always roll unless the environment constrains it in some way, such as if it runs up against a curb. In this way, it is also true that the system will do exactly what its structure dictates unless it is constrained by the environment. Systems just do what they do, and their behavior is perceived as wrong only by an observer.

Structural coupling, a concept from cybernetics, explains how systems coexist with other systems. Systems must constantly transform their structure to meet the demands of the environment if they are to survive. Thus, systems are always interacting together and mutually influencing (changing) one another to be able to maintain themselves in a given context. In a family, for example, if the parents get a divorce, one parent (usually the mother) and the children may suffer economic hardship. That parent may take a job, sell the house and car, and move to an apartment to keep the family together and maintain the child in the same neighborhood and school. Thus, certain concessions are being made with the environment. At the same time, however, the environment is responding as well, because the divorce may be associated with the loss of friends and additional conflicts with other family members.

STRUCTURE

The *structure* of a system is described by the form of the relationships that bind the individual elements or component parts together. Structures may be quite simple or incredibly complex. Complex systems may include *hierarchies,* or ordered levels of other subsystems. The notion of hierarchy is important in systems theory, because for a system to function appropriately across subsystems, the hierarchical arrangements of the system must also be maintained, with each component part keeping its integrity. On a more human level, the family is one type of structure found within the larger social system. We might view the nuclear family as a subsystem of a larger structure—the extended family, for example.

BOUNDARIES

Boundaries serve one universal function: to separate or distinguish the system from its environment. Anything outside the boundary belongs to the environment. A system's boundaries are dependent on the observer's level of inquiry, the intent in drawing the boundary line, and the observer's perception of the functioning of the system. Boundary decisions are essential when one is studying *open* systems, systems that interact with other systems. (We can also conceptualize *closed* systems, systems that become depleted because of a lack of interaction with other systems.) An example from family systems may help clarify the importance of boundaries. A family is a system made up of subsystems of couples, parents, parents/children, and siblings. It is important for each of these subsystems to maintain intact boundaries.

FEEDBACK

Two essential types of feedback are important for system activities: *positive* (amplifying) feedback and *negative* (attenuating) feedback. However, it is important to know that the terms do not mean good or bad but rather describe corrective processes that take place within the system. Negative (attenuating) feedback is corrective and helps maintain the system within a critical operating range or eliminate performance fluctuations around a norm or standard. More of A means less of B. Negative feedback helps maintain the status quo. A woman who calls her husband while she is in a battered woman's shelter and listens to his pleas to return home and give him another chance is introducing negative feedback into their couple system. If she returns home without further intervention, the system will maintain the status quo and a negative feedback loop will be enacted.

Positive (amplifying) feedback corrects the system by reinforcing the operation of the system. There may be a multiplier between input and output so that output increases with an increase in input. In other words, more of A leads to more of B. If a teenager becomes angry and parents also get upset, they are likely to be met with an amplification of the teenager's emotional outbursts and defiance. The family has created a positive feedback loop. Positive feedback may cause system instability whereas negative feedback leads to system control. To further use our example concerning the battered woman from above, the woman in the battered woman's shelter was assaulted by her husband and sought assistance from the woman's shelter. This action initiated a positive feedback loop, in which the output increased proportionally with input from the woman's shelter, forcing the system to adjust itself and change. Had the woman continued her counseling (sharing her relationship problems—output—and receiving the input from the shelter), the system would have become more unstable and made some type of dynamic change or would have ceased to exist (entropy). If the husband comes to counseling at the shelter, the system may find a new balance between output and input that will lead to a new order in the system (negentropy).

EQUIFINALITY AND MULTIFINALITY

Equifinality (equal ending) implies that no matter where one begins with a system, the end will be the same. Becvar and Becvar (1996) explain equifinality in this way:

> People in relationships tend to develop habitual ways of behaving and communicating with one another. We refer to these habits and characteristics processes as redundant patterns of interaction; systems are comprised of patterns and these patterns tend to repeat. Thus, no matter what the topic, the way the members of a given relationship argue, solve problems, discuss issues, and so forth will generally be the same. These redundant patterns of interaction are the characteristic end state referred to by the term "equifinality." (p. 69)

Multifinality (multiple endings), or equipotentiality, means that the opposite also takes place in systems. Different end states may be accomplished through the same beginnings. Therefore, the same intervention may produce very different outcomes at different times and across different families. Both equifinality and multifinality demonstrate that no deterministic predictions or simple cause-and-effect relationships can be accomplished with systems.

FIRST-ORDER AND SECOND-ORDER CHANGE

First-order change refers to changes or small adjustments in systems within the parameters of the system's own rules and structure. *Second-order change,* on the other hand, requires a major transformation within the system's rules and structure. Both types of change are important to systems, but for systems to grow dynamically and developmentally, second-order changes are usually required. For example, as children grow, parents have to make adjustments in the way they set rules to govern the children's behavior. When a child is 5, for example, a bedtime of 8 P.M. is not unreasonable; but when the child is 10, the parents may raise the bedtime to 9 P.M. or even 10 P.M.. This type of adjustment is a first-order change, because the structure and rules of the family system keep operating the same with this change. The parents keep setting the rules and expecting the child to obey. When a child is 14 or 15, however, this type of structure may cause problems, because the adolescent seeking autonomy within the system may desire to set his or her own bedtime. If the parents continue to set and enforce a bedtime autocratically without input from the child, adolescent rebellion may ensue. What is needed is a second-order change in which a change occurs in the way the rules are set for bedtime. In this situation, the bedtime may be negotiated between the adolescent and parents. (See Chapter 14 for a fuller explanation of systems theories, including current updates in the field.)

The Clinical Utility of the Family Practice Models Presented

We have been discussing current trends in family theory and practice that affect the way family therapists conduct their practices. To be successful in today's practice contexts, a family therapist must pay attention to the work environment and be prepared with an armament of family therapy skills that match the demands of the work. Skills needed to conduct clinical sessions successfully include the following:

1. Ability to make contact and establish rapport
2. Ability to communicate clearly the specific purpose of a family meeting
3. Acumen for orienting and instructing the client effectively in how to use therapy within the few sessions allowed
4. Skills that allow practitioners to create an open environment in which the client has the opportunity to express feelings, thoughts, and behaviors
5. Skills at rapid assessment of the client's problems, strengths, motivations, and expectations
6. The ability to establish behaviorally defined (specific, measureable) treatment goals that are obtainable in a short time frame
7. Skills at making quick treatment interventions, assessing the outcomes of those interventions, and making adjustments when needed
8. Ability to construct appropriate tasks and homework assignments and to assign them to the client immediately
9. Business and marketing skills that allow practitioners to attend to business matters such as future appointments and fees (Hoyt, 1995c, p. 289)

The family practice approaches in this book were selected because they are believed to provide useful methods for working in today's practice contexts. Practitioners following the schools of therapy reviewed in this book will find that the approaches will help them develop skills for conducting clinical sessions similar to the prescriptions described earlier. For this reason, the family therapy models covered share similarities that make them suitable alternatives for use in managed behavioral health care and integrated services delivery systems. By making this claim, we are not suggesting that other types of family therapy may not be useful in current practice contexts. We are only suggesting that the approaches covered in this book lend themselves to effective practice in a brief context. The practice approaches reviewed here meet the following criteria that we believe offer suitable alternatives for preparation for today's practice environments:

Family therapy approaches in this book are all based on family systems practice. The influence of systems theory varies with each model, but all the models were significantly influenced by the systems orientation and developed within family systems traditions in therapy. We include a broad array of practice models that may be linked to systems approaches to therapy. These approaches provide an environmental focus concerning change, which we also believe is consistent with social work practice. Some models, such as structural, strategic, and family preservation models, are clearly associated with systems models. Others, such as the behavioral and cognitive-behavioral and the psychoeducational models, have distinct origins in learning theories and base their environmental changes on this perspective. Social learning models, however, took on aspects of the systems theory as they were translated into family practice. Solution-focused and social construction perspectives have as their historical progenitors influences of the family systems models such as the Mental Research Institute (MRI) brief therapy model and the Ericksonian approaches. However, solution-focused and social construction models currently distinguish themselves from systems theories. These models retain historic ideas about the importance of the effects of the social environment on family system functioning. Models covered in this book share in common a focus on systems change in one of three areas:

- Cognitive-interpersonal. Focusing on changes in meanings or in the ways clients think about their social environments. These types of cognitive changes are illustrated in the postmodern, cognitive-behavioral, and strategic-Milan perspectives.
- Behavioral-interactional. Focusing on changes in repetitive behavioral patterns and social interactions. These types of changes are illustrated in the solution-focused, cognitive-behavioral, and strategic therapies.
- Structural changes in social relationships. These types of changes are illustrated through approaches such as structural family therapy and the family preservation models.

Family practice models covered in this book to a greater or lesser extent emphasize all three of these areas as bases for change. The book further offers chapters emphasizing the importance of systems understanding from the perspective of changing the institutional and societal relationships—such as ethnicity, alternative family lifestyles, and gender relations—in which families exist.

The practice methods all qualify as brief therapy approaches.   By brief therapy, we do not refer to any specific model of therapy but rather to the model's effectiveness for use in a time-limited or brief context. Each approach covered in this book begins to implement changes right away from the first session. Brief therapy approaches assume that long-term therapy has no advantages over time-limited approaches and in fact may not be as effective as using the present moment and life circumstances to facilitate changes (Hoyt, 1995b; Hoyt, Rosenbaum, & Talmon, 1992; Koss & Shiang, 1994). This does not mean, however, that some clients may not require longer term therapy. In fact, some clients, such as those with chronic and persistent mental disorders, do require ongoing services or longer term therapy. What it does mean, however, is that practitioners do not automatically assume that a client needs a lot of therapy to improve. In fact, in most cases changes are possible in a short period of time because each case is individualized, and the therapist uses a pragmatic approach in helping clients change as quickly as possible.

All family practice approaches covered in this book focus on the rapid resolution of presenting problems.   Each therapy works primarily in the present and does not belabor lengthy histories or unnecessary details about problems and their background. In managed behavioral health care and other brief practice settings, it is important to work in the present to help the client discover options for coping, new learning, and different behavior. It is assumed that change usually happens outside the therapy session and that the practitioner serves as a catalyst. It is also assumed that once change is started in therapy, it will continue forward and gain momentum even without the aid of the therapist (Hoyt, 1995b; Hoyt et al., 1992). All the approaches in this book make similar assumptions about change.

Each approach discussed is nonpathological and takes a strengths perspective. The natural process of life in interactions with social systems is assumed to be important for the main force of change. For the most part, approaches discussed emphasize social-interactional changes, developmental processes, life circumstances, faulty attempts at solutions, and the effects of the social environment as a basis for family difficulties rather than individual psychopathologies. Perhaps the one exception is the psychoeducational model, which acknowledges the importance of a biologically based deficit that creates the circumstances causing family difficulties in functioning. Even this model, however, emphasizes family strengths and resiliency as a basis for work with families.

Approaches are action-oriented, goal-directed, and interventive.   They present specific methods for how to help clients change, and in every model there are well-defined procedures to follow in facilitating changes. We believe that goal-directed approaches are important for today's practice context of brief therapy. It is important to target specific goals and help clients reach those goals. An interventionist approach, however, has become a controversial idea in family therapy because it has been associated with the power, mystique, and autocratic preferences of the therapist, or with the therapist acting as an "expert" who takes primary responsibility for the change without consulting the client (Andersen, 1987; Anderson & Goolishian, 1992; Hoffman, 1985; Laird, 1995). However, we do not mean intervention in this way. What we mean by intervention is that the therapist and the client work together toward a purposeful solution that meets the client's goals. From this definition, interventions are collaborative. Even family practice approaches that emphasize the power and responsibility of the therapist to bring forth changes, such as strategic interventions, do not do so without finding out what specific goals the client has for change. In our view, social construction and narrative models as well as solution-focused therapy, which takes a nonexpert nonintervention stance, are also highly interventive. It is impossible for a therapist not to be interventive, and we believe the models in this book offer an excellent assortment of intervention methods that help clients quickly reach their goals.

The diverse models discussed are flexible and capable of responding to a variety of client problems and situations. It is important for practitioners to be trained in a variety of models that can address different family situations. Although it is often necessary in today's practice environments for family practitioners to specialize, we believe that the best practitioners have a diversity of skills to call on. If one approach does not work with a client, practitioners can quickly move to another approach.

Family practice approaches covered are researchable because their methods are well defined. Research is important because managed care companies are interested in outcomes and "best practices." Many companies are willing to pay only for treatments that have been demonstrated to be effective. Each approach covered in this book can bear the scrutiny of efficacy and effectiveness studies that examine the outcomes of its methods with different problems and populations. Each family approach covered is further capable of comparison to other approaches for helping clients change. All approaches discussed have at least some research that supports their effectiveness, and other research studies are forthcoming.

Summary

This chapter offers an introduction and a framework for understanding the contents of this book. Prevailing trends were highlighted concerning the context of clinical services delivery and how these trends affect family practitioners. In particular, managed behavioral health care was discussed. The chapter further highlighted the need for family practitioners to use brief, effective, and time-limited family interventions in their practices. Trends toward services integration and the use of systems theory in family practice were further summarized. Finally, the chapter discussed the ways the models stem from a systems orientation and meet the criteria for brief family practice models.

Process Questions

1. Managed behavioral health care is changing the way family practitioners work. What is managed care and how is it affecting practice?

2. Why are brief therapies important approaches to treatment in today's practice contexts?

3. Systems theory has influenced family practice since its inception. What are some of the major ideas of systems theory?

4. What skills does a therapist need to know in today's practice contexts? What specific knowledge do the practice models covered in this book emphasize that provides important preparation for work in managed care and integrated services delivery systems?

References

ANDERSEN, T. (1987). The reflecting team: Dialogue and meta-dialogue in clinical work. *Family Process, 26,* 415–428.

ANDERSON, H., & GOOLISHIAN, H. (1992). The client is the expert: A not-knowing approach to therapy. In S. McNamee & K. J. Gergen (Eds.), *Therapy as social construction* (pp. 25–39). Newbury Park, CA: Sage.

BECVAR, D. S., & BECVAR, R. J. (1996). *Family therapy: A systemic integration* (3rd ed.). Boston: Allyn & Bacon.

BLACKWELL, B., & SCHMIDT, G. L. (1992). The educational implications of managed mental health care. *Hospital and Community Psychiatry, 43,* 962–964.

BROSKOWSKI, A. (1991). Current mental health care environments: Why managed care is necessary. *Professional Psychology: Research and Practice, 22,* 6–14.

BUDMAN, S. H., & ARMSTRONG, E. (1992). Training in managed care settings: How to make it happen. *Psychotherapy, 29,* 416–421.

CORCORAN, K., & GINGERICH, W. J. (1994). Practice evaluation in the context of managed care: Case recording methods of quality assurance reviews. *Research on Social Work Practice, 4,* 326–337.

CORCORAN, K., & VANDIVER, V. (1996). *Maneuvering the maze of managed care.* New York: Free Press.

CUMMINGS, N. A., & SAYAMA, M. (1995). *Focused psychotherapy: A casebook of brief, intermittent psychotherapy throughout the life cycle.* New York: Brunner/Mazel.

DRYFOOS, J. G. (1994). *Full-service schools: A revolution in health and social services for children, youth, and families.* San Francisco: Jossey-Bass.

FRANKLIN, C., & ALLEN-MEARES, P. (1997). School social workers are a critical part of the link. *Social Work in Education, 19*(3), 131–135.

FRANKLIN, C., DINITTO, D. M., & MCNEECE, C. A. (1997). In search of social work theory. In D. M. DiNitto & C. A. McNeece (Eds.), *Social work: Issues and opportunities in a challenging profession.* Needham Heights, MA: Allyn & Bacon.

FRANKLIN, C., & JOHNSON, C. (1996). Family social work practice: Onward to therapy and policy. *Journal of Family Social Work, 1*(3), 33–47.

FRANKLIN, C., & JORDAN, C. (in press). Assessment in managed care: The clinical utility of models and methods. In B. Compton & B. Galaway (Eds.), *Social work processes* (5th ed.). Pacific Grove, CA: Brooks/Cole.

FRANKLIN, C., & STREETER, C. L. (1995). School reform: Linking public schools with human services. *Social Work, 40,* 773–782.

GILES, T. R. (1991). Managed mental health care and effective psychotherapy: A step in the right direction? *Journal of Behavior Therapy and Experimental Psychiatry, 22,* 83–86.

HARE, I. (1995). School-linked services. *Encyclopedia of social work.* Washington, DC: NASW Press.

HOFFMAN, L. (1985). Beyond power and control: Toward a "second order" family systems therapy. *Family Systems Medicine, 3,* 381–396.

HOOPER-BRIAR, K., & LAWSON, H. A. (1994). *Serving children, youth, and families through interprofessional collaboration and service integration: A framework for action.* Oxford, OH: Danforth Foundation and Institute for Educational Renewal, Miami University.

HOYT, M. F. (1995a). Preface. In M. F. Hoyt (Ed.), *Brief therapy and managed care* (pp. xi–xv). San Francisco: Jossey-Bass.

HOYT, M. F. (1995b). Brief psychotherapies. In A. S. Gurman & S. B. Messer (Eds.), *Essential psychotherapies: Theory and practice* (pp. 441–487). New York: Guilford.

HOYT, M. F. (1995c). Brief psychotherapies. In M. F. Hoyt (Ed.), *Brief therapy and managed care* (pp. 281–387). San Francisco: Jossey-Bass.

HOYT, M. F., ROSENBAUM, R., & TALMON, M. (1992). Planned single-session therapy. In S. H. Budman, M. F. Hoyt, & S. Friedman (Eds.), *The first session in brief therapy* (pp. 59–86). New York: Guilford.

HUTCHINS, J. (1996). Managing managed care for families. *NAFBS News, 5*(2), 102–113.

KAHN, A. J., & KAMMERMAN, S. B. (1992). *Integrating services integration: An overview of initiatives, issues and possibilities.* New York: Columbia University School of Public Health, National Center for Children in Poverty.

KIRST, M. W. (1991). Improving children's services. *Phi Delta Kappan, 72,* 615–618.

KOSS, M. P., & SHIANG, J. (1994). Research on brief psychotherapy. In A. E. Bergin & S. L. Garfield (Eds.), *Handbook of psychotherapy and behavior change* (4th ed., pp. 664–700). New York: Wiley.

LAIRD, J. (1995). Family-centered practice in the postmodern era. *Families in Society, 76,* 150–162.

LAZARUS, A. (1995). Preparing for practice in an era of managed competition. *Psychiatric Services, 46,* 184–185.

MELLAVILLE, A. I., & BLANK, M. J. (1993). *Together we can: A guide to crafting a profamily system of education and human services.* Washington, DC: U.S. Department of Education and U.S. Department of Health and Human Services.

NEWMAN, R., & BRICKLIN, P. M. (1991). Parameters of managed mental health care: Legal, ethical, and professional guidelines. *Professional Psychology: Research and Practice, 22,* 26–35.

PINCUS, A., & MINAHAN, A. (1973). *Social work practice.* Itasca, IL: F. E. Peacock.

PINSOFF, W. M., & WYNNE, L. C. (1995). The effectiveness and efficacy of marital and family therapy: Introduction to special issue. *Journal of Marital and Family Therapy, 21,* 341–343.

SABIN, J. E. (1991). Clinical skills for the 1990s: Six lessons from HMO practice. *Hospital and Community Psychiatry, 42,* 605–608.

STROM-GOTTFRIED, K. (1997). The implications of managed care for social work education. *Journal of Social Work Education, 33,* 7–18.

TALMON, M. (1990). *Single session therapy.* San Francisco: Jossey Bass.

WINEGAR, N (1993). Managed mental health care: Implications for administrators and managers of community-based agencies. *Families in Society, 74,* 171–177.

PART TWO

Time-Limited (Brief) Family Practice Models for Social Work Practice

Students and practitioners need to learn brief and effective models of family practice. Chapters 2 through 8 provide an introduction to several different family therapy models with a specific focus on preparing social work practitioners to work in today's practice contexts of managed behavioral health care and short-term treatment. All the models reviewed emerged from or currently use systems theory. Each approach lends itself to brief treatment and practice in today's practice contexts. Family practice models reviewed include structural, strategic, cognitive-behavioral, solution-focused, social construction and narrative, psychoeducational, and family preservation. For the most part the chapters in this section are prescriptive and provide information on the methods of change offered by each of the family therapy models.

Each chapter presents a brief introduction, including the history of the development of the practice model and its theoretical basis. There is also information about how well the model works in today's practice contexts of managed behavioral health care, and further information on the specific consistencies with social work practice. Since empirical research is so important in today's outcome-oriented practice environments, each chapter also presents information on the research basis for the model. The chapters are designed, however, to illustrate therapeutic methods a practitioner follows to implement the model in practice. There are lengthy case illustrations, including transcripts from actual practice situations, in each chapter.

Chapter 9 provides an overview of several family assessment methods. Rapid assessment and its importance for today's practice contexts is discussed. The chapter further provides practitioners with important assessment and measurement tools that can be used to measure the outcomes and the effectiveness of their practices. These tools are believed essential for practice in managed behavioral health care and integrated services delivery systems.

CHAPTER TWO

Catheleen Jordan, Ph.D.
University of Texas at Arlington
Cynthia Franklin, Ph.D.
University of Texas at Austin

Structural Family Therapy

Structural family therapy is an action-oriented, directive family therapy that works to effect quick changes in family functioning. This makes it especially suitable for today's practice contexts, such as managed behavioral health care and integrated services delivery systems. Based on systems theory, structural family therapy developed from the work of psychiatrist Salvador Minuchin. Elements of ecological systems theory, general systems theory, network therapy, and other approaches give structural family therapy its uniqueness. Embedded in the structural family therapy are the structural-functional understandings found in early sociological theories. The goal of structural family therapy is to change the structure, including subsystems, boundaries, hierarchy, and transactions in the family. Structural family therapy has recently evolved to emphasize the need for changes in other social systems as well (Aponte, 1994). Consistent with the ecological systems theory, Minuchin and his colleague Harry Aponte (a social worker) began to propagate the idea that the structure of families is not the only dysfunctional social structure that needs to be changed. In fact, family dysfunction is often influenced and maintained by the dysfunctional medical and welfare systems of which families are a part. This is especially true for poor families. (See Chapter 13 on family policy for a discussion of these larger systems issues and how they affect families.) Structural theory contends that the properties of systems and their functioning, described in this chapter as they relate to families, also apply to the larger social systems.

The chapter describes the history of structural family therapy, its theory, and its therapeutic methods. The consistency of structural family therapy with social work practice is also examined. A number of research studies support the effectiveness of structural family therapy with different populations, and some of these studies are described here. Cogent critiques of the structural model are highlighted. The usefulness of structural family therapy in today's practice contexts of managed care and integrated services delivery systems is further highlighted. Finally, a case is presented that illustrates the practice of structural family therapy.

History

Salvador Minuchin was born into a Jewish family in rural Argentina in the 1920s and trained in pediatrics (Colapinto, 1991b; Fenell & Weinhold, 1989). Minuchin served as a physician in the Israeli army and trained in psychiatry in the United States. He then returned to Israel to work with children. On his later move to New York City, Minuchin worked with delinquent minority boys and their families.

The Wiltwyck School for Boys in New York was Minuchin's training ground for development of structural family therapy in the early 1960s (Colapinto, 1982; Goldenberg & Goldenberg, 1991). The boys at the school, not helped by traditional insight-oriented therapies, were largely from poor families. Minuchin found that action-oriented, concrete techniques were more successful with these families. Braulio Montalvo's influence at Wiltwyck contributed to the development of Minuchin's approach, as did the work of Harry Aponte. Aponte contributed ideas about how the client's resources can be used to organize disorganized families (Colapinto, 1991b; Aponte, 1976). The structural model that developed was based on the presumption that social and family context are more important to the understanding and treatment of families than are isolated individual problems (Colapinto, 1991b). Montalvo moved with Minuchin from Wiltwyck to Philadelphia, where they were joined by others, including one of the developers of the strategic family model, Jay Haley (see Chapter 3) from California.

As director of the Philadelphia Child Guidance Clinic and in collaboration with the Children's Hospital of Philadelphia, Minuchin applied his structural family therapy to clients with diabetes, anorexia nervosa, asthma, and other types of family problems. Haley emphasized that family power struggles and hierarchies contribute to family problems and must be assessed (Colapinto, 1991a). Though Minuchin and Haley diverged in theory, each influenced the work of the other. Haley helped to develop the clinic's therapy training program, which focused on use of live supervision and videotaping (Colapinto, 1991a). In 1975, Minuchin devoted himself to training and theory development at the Family Therapy Training Center (Colapinto, 1991a). The center's goal is to refine the theory and add to the body of clinical information collected by the structural group over the years. Dr. Minuchin is currently retired but is active in his practice and development of the structural model.

Theoretical Basis for the Practice Model

Structural family therapy is a unique family practice model that focuses on the family system rather than on the individual. In the structural approach, the family is described as a system—change in one part causes the rest of the system to change as well. Systems concepts such as family structure, boundaries, and subsystems are unique to structural family therapy. The family structure consists of the predictable family patterns that govern family members' interactions (Minuchin, 1974). Boundaries are invisible borders that separate the family from the outside environment as well as borders that separate the family subsystems. Subsystems, formed by generation, sex, interest, or function, form the subunits of the system. Examples are the parent-child subsystem and the sibling subsystem.

Structural family therapists view families as living, open systems (Minuchin, 1974; Rosenberg, 1983). Family members are interdependent and move through normal developmental stages together (Colapinto, 1982; Minuchin, 1974). Healthy families are able to adapt to changing internal and external conditions and to encourage the growth and development of family members (Minuchin, 1974). Symptoms of individual family members stem from family transactions and from a dysfunctioning family structure (Colapinto, 1982; Goldenberg & Goldenberg, 1991).

Major Assumptions

The basic assumptions of structural therapy have been reviewed by Laird and Vande Kemp (1987). They found that power is an important concept, and families are seen as hierarchically organized, with parents having the authority to manage their children. Rules govern interactions across and within family subsystems and may be overt or covert. Symptomatic behavior may be maintained by faulty hierarchies and boundaries; therefore, a goal of therapy is to improve the subsystem's boundaries. Boundaries between family subsystems and between the family and external systems should be clear and firm.

Social relationships have problem potential. Individuals are members of the family as well as members of other groups and social contexts. Wife, mother, friend, and worker may all be roles that one family member undertakes at different times and in different settings. The family social system responds to internal and external changes from family members as well as from changes in the social environment. When the mother returns to work after taking several years off to stay home with the children, her new role as worker may create problems and necessary adjustments for family members.

Normal developmental transitions may also be problematic for the family. For example, the birth of the first baby may create new problems for the young family. Change in the structure of the family or in family rules and roles may be required. Within the family, members develop a preferred degree of emotional proximity/distance toward each other. Whereas a young child may want to be close to the mother at all times, the teenager usually requires more distance from the parents. Relationships occur in patterned ways repeated over time.

Individual family members are viewed positively, as competent and resourceful. Interactional problems between members may affect individual functioning. Family conflict should not be avoided, however, but used as an impetus toward change. Families are viewed as having the resources needed for change.

Key Constructs

Key constructs of family structural therapy are these: (1) The family is a basic human system; (2) subsystems serve a function within the family system; and (3) system and subsystem boundaries have unique characteristics (Brown & Christensen, 1986; Colapinto, 1991a).

THE FAMILY AS A BASIC HUMAN SYSTEM

Family structure is the organized pattern in which the members interact; it is created by the repetition of family transactions. Change in one part of the system will create the impetus for change in other components. Transactional patterns are expectations or rules that determine the limits of family members' behavior. These structural rules are either generic or idiosyncratic. Generic rules, common to all families, relate to the mutual interdependence of members or the hierarchical nature of relationships between members. For example, parents are generally believed to have authority over their children. Idiosyncratic rules differ from family to family and define expectations about members' behavior on a day-to-day basis. For example, a family may believe that a child must perform certain duties in order to earn an allowance.

Subsystems refer to the joining of members to perform various functions within units based on different characteristics. Each family member may be a part of several different subsystems. A woman may be a member of the parental, spousal, and parent-child subsystems, for example.

SUBSYSTEM FUNCTIONS

Subsystems are units within a family bound together by characteristics such as sex, age, or interest. A coalition refers to an alliance between two members, sometimes against a third member. Triangulation occurs when a member of a coalition requires the other member to side with him or her against someone else. A typical triangle is parent and child against the other parent. The child, expected to side with one or the other parent, may feel helpless. Detouring occurs when the conflict between two family members is redirected through another member. Often the conflict between spouses is redirected through a child. This allows the conflicted subsystem to pretend to healthy functioning.

Complementarity describes the process whereby family members accommodate each other by developing traits that complement each other. For example, one parent is strict, the other lenient; or one sibling is quiet whereas the other is talkative.

Hierarchies describe the power relationships in the family. In a traditional, high-functioning family, the parents are the leaders of the children, and therefore have a higher hierarchical position than the children. A dysfunctional family might include a child serving in the role of co-parent to replace a nonfunctional, absent, or alcoholic parent.

SYSTEM AND SUBSYSTEM BOUNDARIES

Boundaries are invisible lines of demarcation in a family. Family structural therapy aims to define, strengthen, loosen, or change them. Boundaries are described as ranging from rigid to diffuse, with clear boundaries being the goal of therapy.

Boundaries are permeable; they regulate contact between family members. Enmeshed families are so interdependent that autonomy is difficult; their boundaries are generally diffuse. Conversely, disengaged families have rigid boundaries. Members are so separate they don't recognize the effects of their behavior on other family members. Rigid boundaries discourage closeness, yet encourage independence. Structural family therapy aims to clarify boundaries. Generational boundaries are invisible lines of demarcation between generations. Healthy generational boundaries allow members to fill appropriate roles. For example, parents' and children's roles should not overlap but should remain distinct. A typical problem seen in therapy is a parental child who has the power of a parent.

Therapeutic Methods

Structural family therapy relies on an understanding of the family structure. Its unique assessment methods, behavior change procedures, and change techniques are described next.

Assessment Methods

History taking in structural family therapy is not as important as the family's current functioning and presenting problem. Therefore, therapy from the structural perspective is short term, time limited (brief), and goal directed. The assumption is that if the boundaries and hierarchy of the family subsystems are improved, the positive changes will generalize to the functioning of the family members.

Nichols (1984) described the therapy process as (1) the therapist joining and leading the family; (2) the therapist observing and mapping family patterns; and (3) the therapist intervening to alter family structure. Structural therapists join with the family to create and modify transactions between family members. Minuchin and Fishman (1981) recommended that the therapist enter the family system and experience its characteristics. The therapist interacts with the family at different levels, both proximate and distal. In addition to interacting with the family, the therapist also observes family processes, particularly the way members behave and organize themselves. Also important is noticing which members talk and which ones are ignored. Individual family members' perceptions of the interaction are also important. This observation process reveals information not only about family problem areas but family strengths as well. The structural family therapist, using interaction and observation, acts and reacts to the system.

The therapeutic process is painful, and the therapist is prepared for resistance. Observation of family dynamics is important, not just members' descriptions of family interactions. Each individual family member is validated by the therapist's obtaining everyone's perception of the problems. Therapy is present-focused, and problems are seen as systemic. The therapist assumes families are competent and can be helped to depend on their own resources.

Steps of the assessment process have been defined by Colapinto (1991b): (1) preplanning, (2) tracking, (3) staging enactments, (4) searching for strengths, and

(5) reframing the problem. Preplanning refers to the initial visit or telephone call. Enough information is obtained to allow the therapist to make an initial hypothesis about the family structure and the family's strengths and weaknesses. Tracking is the continuation of collecting information about the family interaction. The therapist listens, observes, and clarifies verbal and actual family transactions. By staging enactments, the therapist further learns about the family. The therapist may introduce new information, change the transaction, change the seating arrangement of the members, or create some additional stress in order to observe the family interaction. The search for strengths is the therapist's way of redirecting the focus away from negative labeling of family behavior. Instead, the therapist looks for and encourages displays of family member strength. By reframing the problem, the therapist helps the family to have a new, broader perception of the problem, or to refocus on the complementarity of behaviors. For instance, a rebellious teenager's acting out behavior may be relabeled as misguided efforts toward the positive goal of becoming an independent, mature adult.

FAMILY MAPPING

Family mapping is the diagramming of a family's organizational structure, boundaries, and patterns of interaction. (See case example at the end of this chapter for an illustration of this technique.) It is useful in hypothesizing family functioning and forming goals for structural change. The map answers questions such as number of people in the family and their relationships with other family members. Maps may be given descriptive names such as "a blended family" or "an out-of-control family" (Colapinto, 1991a).

Change Techniques

The structural family therapist seeks to help families learn new skills, make structural changes, and operate differently. Therapists use family diagnosis, direction, confrontation, interpretation, reframing, and feedback, among other techniques, to help families make constructive changes. The therapist may use joint sessions with the whole family together, or concurrent sessions with different family members present.

Change is facilitated by the therapist joining together with the family. That is, the therapist becomes a part of the family system when working with a family. Restructuring of the family system is the therapist's goal (Minuchin, 1974). Also, the structural family therapist helps the family to anticipate constant growth and change. The focus of change is on family structure rather than on the intrapsychic growth of family members (Colapinto, 1982; Minuchin, 1974). Insight alone cannot move the family toward change. Therefore, the therapist's role is as an active participant who guides the family's restructuring. However, the therapist's participation is aimed at moving the family to find its own resources for change and growth. Structural family therapy is goal oriented and short term. Typically, therapy averages three to seven months (Rosenberg, 1983).

Structural family therapists choreograph a session by physically rearranging the members, reinforcing or reorganizing family structure, or constructing new interactional patterns (Aponte & Van Deusen, 1981). Minuchin, Montalvo, Guerney, Rosman, and Schumer (1967) recommend that the structural family therapist uncover the unique set of techniques that matches each family's interactional patterns. Also, therapists are advised to select techniques compatible with their own comfort level and ability. The techniques described here are categorized under three subheadings: joining, activating family transactional patterns, and transforming the family structure (Okun & Rappaport, 1980).

JOINING

Joining, the process of establishing a relationship with each family member, allows the family to feel at ease with the therapist. Spending time getting to know each person, asking about interests and hobbies, facilitates the client-therapist relationship. It is critical that the therapist establish this relationship with family members early so that members will feel confident enough to share feelings and problems with the therapist. Also, joining facilitates family members' motivation to change later in the treatment process. Elements of joining are tracking, maintenance, and mimesis.

Tracking.   The therapist uses the words, symbols, history, and values of the family in communicating with them. For example, the therapist might use the pet names of family members during sessions. The two goals of tracking are for the therapist to think and feel like a family member and for the family to feel more understood.

Maintenance.   The therapist shows respect for the family by acknowledging their current rules and roles. If the father is believed to be the head of the household and in charge, the therapist may speak to him first. The goal of maintenance is to help the family feel respected and therefore more willing to participate in therapy and move toward change.

Mimesis.   The therapist imitates family members' moods, tones of voice, postures, communication, and behavior. For instance, the therapist might talk slowly or more animatedly, depending on the style of the family. The goal is for the family to feel more accepting of and accepted by the therapist.

ACTIVATING FAMILY TRANSACTIONAL PATTERNS: ENACTMENT

To understand the family structure, the therapist uses enactment, asking the family to act out the problem. This allows the therapist to observe the family in action as they interact and display the problem situation to the therapist. Enactment also may occur spontaneously during a session. The therapist may then give alternatives for change or model more positive behaviors. Piercy and Sprenkle (1986) recommend using enactment in the beginning sessions to avoid reinforcing unproductive problem solving. The therapist can intervene early to introduce more effective problem-solving strategies. Enactment helps the therapist view families' problem behaviors and better understand family structure.

Boundary making is a type of enactment in which the therapist encourages interactions of some members but closes the interaction to others (Colapinto,

1991a). For example, one sibling is encouraged to stay out of conflicts between the mother and a second sibling, leaving the two to negotiate their own relationship without help or interference. The therapist might even sit between the interfering sibling and the other two members as a way of making the point. The therapist might also physically move members of the family to make symbolic boundaries. For instance, the triangulated child sitting between his parents is moved so that parents sit together, side by side.

TRANSFORMING THE FAMILY STRUCTURE

Once therapists understand the family structure by enactment techniques, they move to restructure those maladaptive patterns. Restructuring may be approached in three ways: system recomposition, symptom focusing, and structural modification.

System Recomposition. System recomposition occurs when the therapist chooses to add or eliminate a subsystem. This action may be profitable if existing subsystems do not meet the needs of the family. An example is a mother-daughter alliance that excludes the father. The therapist may give the parents a homework assignment to go on a date together alone, the goal being to create a parental subsystem. The unhealthy mother-daughter subsystem may then be targeted for elimination. The daughter may be assigned to go shopping with both parents together, or to go with peers to a movie.

Symptom Focusing. In structural family therapy, symptoms displayed by individual members are viewed in the context of the total system functioning. Symptom-focusing techniques aim to affect family functioning by focusing on the symptom itself. Here are some examples of symptom-focusing techniques.

Relabeling the Symptom (Reframing): In reframing, the therapist redefines the symptom. The new definition should be one that helps the family have a new or more positive understanding of the behavior. Typically, a rebellious child is relabeled as seeking autonomy, or a distant father is relabeled as overwhelmed by his emotions. Of course, the definition must be plausible, and it must help the family move forward.

Altering the Affect of the Symptom: Rather than altering the definition of the symptom, this technique alters the feelings associated with the symptom. Angry feelings may be relabeled as feelings of sadness, or even fear.

Expanding the Symptom: To expand the symptom, the therapist identifies family members' symptom-maintenance behaviors. For instance, the mother's role in overprotecting the child and contributing to the child's fear of new situations might be discussed. This helps family members recognize their contributions to the problems attributed to the identified patient (Fenell & Weinhold, 1989).

Exaggerating the Symptom: Increasing the intensity of or exaggerating the symptom is a paradoxical technique used to emphasize the undue attention given to the symptom (Fenell & Weinhold, 1989). For example, the therapist might suggest that all the family gather to watch specifically at six o'clock every evening as the teenage daughter throws a tantrum.

Deemphasizing the Symptom: Conversely, deemphasizing the symptom requires the family to ignore it (Aponte & Van Deusen, 1981; Fenell & Weinhold, 1989). The parents may be instructed to ignore their child's tantrums. This technique is used when families are too reinforced by focusing on the symptom.

Focusing on a New Symptom: Another technique, sometimes used with deemphasizing the symptom, refocuses the family on the behavior of a family member other than the identified patient (Aponte & Van Deusen, 1981). For example, parents who are unhappy with the rebellious teenager's behavior are asked to come to an agreement about the rules for acceptable teenage behavior.

Structural Modification. Another set of restructuring techniques encourages structural modification of the family system (Aponte & Van Deusen, 1981; Fenell & Weinhold, 1989; Minuchin & Fishman, 1981). Five types of structural modification are discussed here.

Challenging the Current Family Reality: The family's reality can be explored by encouraging the members to look at alternative explanations that challenge their rigid thinking about the problem. For example, parents who feel hurt and abandoned because their son is going far away to college may be told that their son is trying to make them proud and to honor the family name by selecting such a prestigious school.

Creating New Subsystems and Boundaries: Creating new structures may help the family function more appropriately. The therapist may assign homework to encourage new healthy alliances. For example, father and son may be instructed to go bowling together regularly.

Blocking Dysfunctional Transactional Patterns: The therapist blocks dysfunctional patterns by preventing the family from interacting in their typical fashion. The therapist may stop an emotional interchange between family members in process, for example.

Reinforcing Patterns: The therapist reinforces healthy interactional patterns of family members. An enmeshed family may be reinforced for their love and support for each other as they are being taught new, more appropriate ways to be independent.

Educating and Guiding: Education and guidance are used by the therapist to teach the family members how to maintain and support each other, as well as how to maintain the positive gains of therapy. For example, the therapist may teach the parents more effective ways to communicate or to parent their children.

OTHER TECHNIQUES

Other techniques used by structural family therapists include intensity and intervening isomorphically (Piercy & Sprenkle, 1986). Intensity refers to the degree of impact of a therapeutic message. The therapist achieves intensity by increasing the length of a transaction or by repeating the same message in different transactions. For instance, a young man who decides to move out of his parents' home and then does not, is asked repeatedly (80 times!) during the session, "Why didn't you move?" (Colapinto, 1991a). To intervene isomorphically, the therapist may point out the similar meaning of events that appear to be dissimilar. For example, a teenage boy may break his curfew, shave his hair off, and fail all his subjects in school. The therapist may point out that these are indications of his striving for independence.

Termination

Termination may be initiated by the therapist, the family, or by agreement of both (Minuchin et al., 1967). The termination process should help clients to look forward and recognize that the family will continue to experience changes and normal transitions. These changes may be related to normal developmental and transitional stages, changes in roles of family members, or a changing social context. The therapist may invite the family to return for continued therapy in the future if needed.

Consistency with Social Work Practice

The structural family therapy concepts and methods have been used by social workers to describe family functioning. This influence has come into the present as is witnessed by a review of major social work practice texts such as Hepworth and Larsen (1994). These authors, for example, borrow extensively from the structural theory in their descriptions of family processes. Structural family therapy considers the family as an interacting system rather than focusing on individual family members' pathologies. This approach supports social work's contextual view of human behavior and the strengths perspective, partly accounting for the popularity of the model in social work. Structural family therapy also supports an open systems view in which family systems are not seen in isolation but are viewed in other systemic contexts. This is also consistent with social work practice.

Historically, social workers have subscribed to the notions of developing healthy social systems in which people can thrive. This type of ideology is also embedded in structural family therapy. In addition, this type of therapy has been demonstrated to have clinical utility for work with poor families, a concern consistent with the historic mission of social work practice. The therapist's relationship with the family is also important, and therapists seek to understand and support the family. This purpose reflects the humanitarian values of social workers who have been actively involved since the inception of the profession in strengthening and supporting families.

Research Support for the Model

Relevant research reviews and meta-analyses have found research support for systems therapies such as structural family therapy. Systems family therapies are more effective than no-treatment control groups and are just as effective as individual therapies with a variety of populations (e.g., Kazdin, 1987; Markus, Lange, & Pettigrew, 1990; Shadish et al., 1993; Shadish, Ragsdale, Glaser, & Montgomery, 1995). Structural family therapy has been used in families with problems related to low socioeconomic status, delinquency, psychosomatic illness, school issues, drug abuse, mental retardation, and specific symptoms such as elective mutism and encopresis (Colapinto, 1982). Todd (1986) suggests that structural family therapy, first designed for work with lower socioeconomic status families, is most successful with that population.

Support has been found for the effectiveness of structural family therapy with drug abusers (Stanton & Todd, 1979). Szapocznik, Kurtines, Foote, Perez-Vidal, and Hervis (1983, 1986) and Szapocznik et al. (1988) also found support for the effectiveness of structural family therapy with adolescents who use drugs. There is considerable support for the effectiveness of structural family therapy with conduct-disordered and delinquent youth (Chamberlain & Rosicky, 1995). Recently, structural family therapy has been integrated with other approaches and used in a family preservation model (known as multisystemic therapy) to treat juvenile offenders. Outcome research on the multisystemic model has demonstrated its effectiveness with this population (Henggler, Melton, & Smith, 1992).

Earlier studies indicated, however, that disengaged families may not be helped as much as those assessed as enmeshed. Aponte and Van Deusen (1981) reported that the highest success rates appear in studies of psychosomatic families. Campbell and Patterson (1995), for example, noted that structural family therapy has research support for work with families with a variety of medical problems and disorders. Other populations reported to be helped by structural family therapy are children of divorce, families of handicapped children, families with a member who has schizophrenia, and single-parent families (Schaefer, Briesmeister, & Fitton, 1984). It has also been used with families with unresolved mourning issues (Fulmer, 1983) and with families of pregnant teenagers (Romig & Thompson, 1988).

Sykes (1987) found that structural family therapy works with all ethnic groups, and is especially potent with African-American youth. The structural concept of joining the family during therapy helps young African-Americans with their problems of mistrust, anger, and fear in psychotherapy. Other key factors in therapy with African-Americans include the therapist's willingness to process feelings regarding working with African-Americans and to confront his or her own stereotypes and prejudices. Research has also supported the effectiveness of structural family therapy with Hispanic youths and their families (Szapocznik et al. 1989). (See Chapter 10 for a more detailed discussion of structural family therapy as a useful approach with ethnic families.) Minuchin and colleagues (1967) reported positive outcomes related to family structure. Enmeshed families have better outcomes than disengaged families. Also, the model works best with families in some degree of crisis and those who are motivated (Colapinto, 1982).

Overall, structural family therapy helps with families who do not communicate effectively, have dysfunctional boundaries, and have difficulties in social functioning, as with drug abuse and delinquency. Structural family therapy is also especially effective with psychosomatic families (Aponte & Van Deusen, 1981). There is also research support for the clinical utility of the structural model with low-income families (Todd, 1986). Brown and Christensen (1986) suggest that further research on structural family therapy should use different types of families and presenting problems. Also, more research comparing structural therapy with other types of family approaches is needed.

Empirical Support for Key Concepts

Minuchin and his colleagues (1967) at the Wiltwyck School studied the concepts of enmeshment and disengagement with 12 patient families and 11 nonpatient control families. Minuchin used the term *enmeshment* to describe families whose members are overly involved with one another, lack boundaries, and experience high degrees of bonding. *Disengagement* is descriptive of families whose members are emotionally distant from one another, have tight boundaries, and lack connection. Patient families were reported improved after treatment. Data that indicated the clustering of patient families at extremes in their transactions before treatment support the argument for enmeshed versus disengaged family patterns. (See Chapter 9 for a review of measures that assess the degree of enmeshment and disengagement in a family system.)

Davis, Stern, and Van Deusen (1977) studied enmeshment in alcoholic families and control families. Speaking patterns in the alcoholic families were cited as evidence of disengagement in those families. Support for the concept of subsystems also was indicated. Minuchin, Rosman, and Baker (1978) studied 53 psychosomatic families. The results indicated that normal families were less enmeshed than patient families, and that normal families had clear subsystem boundaries whereas patient families did not.

Outcome Evaluations

FAMILIES WITH LOW SOCIOECONOMIC STATUS

In Minuchin's 1967 study of family functioning, structured interaction tasks and the family interaction apperception technique were used with 12 patient families and 11 control families. Pre- and post-measures assessed changes in family characteristics, including leadership, behavior control, and guidance statements. Post-treatment, enmeshed families showed clearer boundaries; however, disengaged families showed no improvement.

FAMILIES WITH PSYCHOSOMATIC MEMBERS

Minuchin and his colleagues (1978) studied psychosomatic families and found positive post-treatment results on patients' psychosomatic symptoms and psychosomatic behaviors. Reduced rehospitalizations were reported as well. Harkaway's (1987) study of obese adolescent girls found their family patterns to be similar to those of Minuchin's psychosomatic families. Rosman, Minuchin, and Liebman (1977) measured the weight gain of eight anorexic patients. Patients were reported improved after structural treatment.

Rosman, Minuchin, Liebman, and Baker (1978) summarized the research findings in 20 cases of labile diabetes, 53 cases of anorexia, and 17 cases of intractable asthma. One hundred percent of the labile diabetic patients were reported to be either improved (88%) or moderately improved (12%). Of the anorexic cases, psychosocial functioning and anorexia symptoms were improved in 86% of cases. Ninety-four percent of asthmatics achieved recovery (82%) or improved moderately (12%).

FAMILIES WITH ADDICTIONS

Zeigler-Driscoll (1979) compared conjoint family structural therapy of addicts and their families to an inpatient program for individuals. No group differences were found in abstinence or recidivism. The author concluded that family structural therapy improved the family's coping ability when the addict member returned to drug use. Stanton and Todd (1979) compared structural/strategic family therapy with two groups: a placebo group and a group receiving structural/strategic family therapy treatment. Sixty-five families with a heroin-addicted son, and 25 control, nonaddict families were studied. The structural/strategic group was reported to be significantly affected. Prior to treatment, addict mothers used inappropriate statements; after treatment, addict families were more expressive, increased their numbers of agreements, and increased solidarity during task completion. Better subsystem boundary maintenance was also noted.

Critiques of the Model

Limits of structural family therapy include decreased effectiveness when a family member is hospitalized or a member is on medication. Additionally, feminist critics suggest that structural family therapy perpetuates a patriarchal family system, thus contributing to the oppression of women. This is because of the notion of hierarchy and the fact that the structural approach emphasizes the normative nature of an orderly family system with a clear authority structure instead of the more egalitarian relationship patterns that feminist theorists prefer. (See Chapter 12 for a more detailed discussion of feminist approaches to family therapy and the limitations of family therapy models in addressing women's issues.)

Structural Family Therapy and Managed Behavioral Health Care

Structural family therapy is a significant approach for work in today's practice contexts, such as managed behavioral health care environments and integrated services delivery systems. As noted by Aponte (1992), structural family therapy lends itself to a brief therapy approach because the model works "in the here and now, through direct positive action, and for palpable outcomes" (p. 324). Structural family therapy is action oriented. Therapists working from this orientation begin changing family structure right away from the first session. The introduction of enactments and other directive approaches by the therapist is an example of immediate change strategies. In addition, the therapist is focused and directive and does not allow the clients to venture too far from presenting problems and the goals that brought them to treatment. Though therapists may have their own agendas for modifying the family structure, they always keep in mind the necessity of changing the presenting problems. The structural model also offers a strengths orientation that sees distressed families as going through a life transition. In this regard, families are quite changeable. They only need some modifications in structure and functioning to get through difficult times. All these assumptions are a good match for managed care settings.

In addition, the structural model has demonstrated itself to be a useful model when applied with other approaches and in work with multiple systems. This makes the structural family therapy a promising approach for work in integrated service delivery systems that require interprofessional collaborations and cooperation between systems to help clients change.

Case Example[1]

Identifying Information

Name: Jennifer Jones and family

Address: 1111 C Street, Arlington TX 76000 Telephone: 555-1234 (home)

Family members living at home: John, 46, father, plant foreman; Ann, 42, mother, substitute teacher; Jennifer, 16, identified patient, student (11th grade); Sarah, 13, sister, student (8th grade); Kevin, 11, brother, student (6th grade)

Income: $45,000 per year

Race: Anglo

Religious affiliation: Methodist

Presenting problem: Jennifer has been referred to therapy by her physician. He has treated her for asthma since she was 3 years old. But in the past several years the frequency of her asthma attacks has increased (almost tripled in the past year). The doctor can find no physical reason for the increase in episodes. He suspects "stress" to be part of the problem and referred her to therapy. The therapist requested the entire family to be present in the therapy session.

Jennifer and her mother report that her asthma attacks appear to be occurring more frequently as she becomes older. As a result, she has missed a number of days at school. She has been hospitalized several times in the past year. When she is hospitalized, her mother Ann usually stays with her at the hospital. Often she has a homebound teacher work with her before she returns to school. Jennifer's grades have dropped from the A and B level (range of 94 to 83) to the B and C level (range of 88 to 72) during the past school year. Jennifer states that she is con-

---

[1] Assessment and Intervention Plan prepared by Mary Lou Workman at the School of Social Work, the University of Texas at Arlington.

cerned about her dropping grades. She reports that she would like to take driver's education, like most of her friends, but her parents will not allow her to drive because of her frequent illnesses. Jennifer reports being very worried about her mother because her mom has to stop everything she is doing when Jennifer is ill.

Jennifer was diagnosed as asthmatic at age 3. Her first hospitalization was at age 4. According to her mother's report, Jennifer was hospitalized on the average of one time a year, usually in the spring, until 1988. That year Jennifer was hospitalized four times. Neither Ann nor Jennifer could explain the increase in hospitalizations. Jennifer reported being in the eighth grade in 1988. She said she liked her teachers and friends, and she won an award in science that year. Ann reported that her husband was promoted to foreman in 1987, and she stopped teaching in 1988 to care for Jennifer.

No member of the family has ever been referred for psychological help. Efforts to deal with Jennifer's asthma have been medical in nature. The mother questioned how psychotherapy would benefit Jennifer's medical problem, and the social worker offered an explanation of emotional stress and changes in breathing patterns. He also suggested that an asthmatic child might forget to take medications or have problems following a treatment plan. Ann assured him that she was always there to see that Jennifer complied with her treatment plan. She added that she was still unsure of how family therapy would help Jennifer, but she would do anything she was told to try. This indicated motivation to attend therapy, even though Ann questioned its value.

Related Problems: The interview revealed other areas of stress in the family. The mother indicated several areas of worry, including jobs and finances. Sarah has also seen some drop in her math grades. Kevin has been involved in some minor vandalism with some of his neighborhood friends. Family functioning and structural problems are suspected to be major contributors to Jennifer's problem. The mother appears to care for Jennifer to the exclusion of other family members. The father is concerned about the family functioning that seems almost lost because of Jennifer's predominant illness. Enmeshment and boundary problems appear to be issues for this family. On the surface, the family appears to function as a typical middle-class family, but further investigation reveals possible job and financial stress. The mother indicated that the family can attend therapy sessions together.

Goals: Ann and Jennifer prioritized the problems, moving from the most to the least severe as (1) Jennifer's health problems, (2) Jennifer's missed days from school, (3) financial worries, and (4) Kevin's involvement in neighborhood vandalism. The goals of the structural family therapist working with this family are based on research suggesting that families of psychosomatic children display characteristics of (1) enmeshment, (2) overprotectiveness, (3) rigidity, and (4) lack of conflict-resolution. The mapping would appear like this:

$$
\begin{array}{c}
\underline{\qquad \text{J} \qquad} \\
\text{M} \qquad \underline{\quad \text{F} \quad} \\
\underline{\text{SK}}
\end{array}
$$

The goals are to (1) define clearer boundaries in the family thus strengthening the parental unit and decreasing the enmeshment between mother and Jennifer, and (2) increase flexibility in the family. The resulting family map should look like this:

$$\frac{\text{F} \qquad \text{M}}{\text{J} \qquad \text{K} \qquad \text{S}}$$

Intervention and Treatment Plan

SESSION 1

The first session of the treatment phase will include the entire Jones family and the structural family therapist. The primary goals of the therapist at this point will be joining the family system and reframing the problem from that of the identified patient to that of the family system. The structural family therapist often joins with the family through the children. As the therapist moves from child to child soliciting information about the problem, he or she is also building rapport with the family members.

The therapist will also encourage an enactment of the Jones family's communication that fosters the problems. This helps him continue to assess the family problems and gives him an opportunity to reframe the problem.

SESSION 2

Again the therapist and the entire family will meet together. The goals of the therapist in this session are to continue challenging the family's symptoms. He may still be joining with the family and reframing problems, but he will be focusing on one family issue, thus challenging the family interaction. The therapist also works toward achieving intensity by repeating the same message over and over for the family. He may focus on the enmeshment between Jennifer and her mother by asking questions such as "Does your mother always speak for you?" Then, as he asks this question of other family members, the special relationship between Jennifer and her mother is seen more clearly by all the family. He continues to clarify and challenge this special relationship by repeating the message several times: "Is this how you two run your lives together?" "You activated your mother."

SESSION 3

The therapist will meet with the entire family. The family will now begin to view him as part of their system. The goals of this session will be to continue to challenge the family symptoms and to introduce challenges to the family structure.

The therapist will again encourage enactment, looking for subsystems in the family. He may be ready at this point to work with the boundaries within the subsystems, reinforcing appropriate subsystems and establishing new ones. He can physically place family members in new positions in the therapy circle to demonstrate new boundaries.

The therapist may use the technique of deemphasizing the symptom to ignore unhealthy channels of communication in favor of new communication patterns. This is seen when he ignores Jennifer's attempts to distract her parents' conversation when it becomes threatening to her. Instead, he directs Jennifer to care for herself and the parents to continue their interaction.

SESSION 4

The therapist may meet with the entire family or may consider meeting with parents only at this point. The goals of this session are to continue to strengthen the new family boundaries, thus challenging the family structure and challenging family realities.

He may help the parents develop new cognitive constructs, such as having the parents make family decisions instead of Jennifer and her mother making family decisions. He may use reframing to emphasize strengths in the family. He will continue to challenge problems with boundaries and relationships while teaching the concept of complementarity, the idea of individual behaviors interlocking like puzzle pieces in a family, thus illustrating that family interaction goes beyond the behavior of one individual family member.

Transcript

THERAPIST: Who would like to tell me why you are here today?

MOTHER: [To oldest daughter] Shall I explain?

JENNIFER: Go ahead, Mom. You tell her.

MOTHER: Well, Dr. Smith sent us to see you. You see, Jenny's asthma is getting worse. She has had it since she was 3. Dr. Jones has treated her most of her life, but she seems to be getting worse and worse, and Dr. Smith can't see any reason why. [Mother moves closer to Jennifer and pulls her closer in a protective way.]

THERAPIST: [To Jennifer] Is this how you two run your lives together, protecting each other?

MOTHER: Of course I have to protect Jenny. She really needs me. She gets so sick.

THERAPIST: [To Jennifer] Does your mother always answer for you?

JENNIFER: Well, sometimes. Not all the time, but a lot.

THERAPIST: Sarah, what about you? Does your mother answer for you?

SARAH: Not too much. I can answer myself.

THERAPIST: Kevin, does your mother answer for you?

KEVIN: Maybe, sometimes. But I talk for myself a lot.

MOTHER: He talks a lot!

THERAPIST: But you emphasize what he has to say. [To John] What about you? Does your wife speak for you?

FATHER: I usually speak for myself.

THERAPIST: [To Jennifer] So, your mother answers for you a lot.

JENNIFER: Yes.

MOTHER: [Nods her head, yes]

THERAPIST:	You see? You activated your mother. So you're together in this. [To Jennifer] You have an invisible thread that weaves you and your mother together. This helps you activate her when you need her?
JENNIFER:	I guess so.
MOTHER:	[Nods her head again]
THERAPIST:	You activated her again. [Family all laughs at this]
THERAPIST:	You are very involved in your daughter's health.
MOTHER:	Yes.
SARAH:	You got that right.
THERAPIST:	Sarah, what is your idea about your mom and Jennifer's asthma? You seem to have an opinion here.
SARAH:	Mother worries about Jennifer a lot. She has to take care of her.
KEVIN:	Yes. Mom takes care of Jennifer all the time. She's real busy.
THERAPIST:	Mom takes care of Jennifer? They are close?
KEVIN:	Real close.
THERAPIST:	Are you and mom close?
KEVIN:	Sometimes, when she is not busy with Jennifer.
SARAH:	Mother spends a lot of time with Jennifer. Sometimes we wish she would spend more time with us.
THERAPIST:	What does Jennifer think about this?
SARAH:	I don't know.
THERAPIST:	Well, ask her.
MOTHER:	I don't think they can answer all this.
THERAPIST:	[To mother] Let's let them try to work this out themselves. Jennifer, you come over here with Sarah and Kevin, and you three decide how you feel about being in this family together and how you want to get along with your mother. [Therapist moves Jennifer to be with her siblings and moves mother by father] [Kids start talking to each other]
MOTHER:	[To children's group] Now, Jennifer, you know that I have your inhaler if you feel an attack coming on.
THERAPIST:	Mother, are you trying to talk for that group? Earlier Sarah and Kevin said that you let them talk for themselves. Let them talk for themselves now. Let Jennifer talk for herself now too, all right?
MOTHER:	I don't want them to gang up on Jennifer; she might have an attack.
THERAPIST:	Dad, see how hard a time your wife is having? Let's try this, you take her over there and see if you can keep her attention so she can be relieved of talking for this group. [To the children] Now how are you doing?
JENNIFER:	I didn't know that Sarah and Kevin were feeling left out when I'm sick. They want Mom too.
THERAPIST:	So you three figured this out for yourselves.
SARAH:	Yes, we all want to share Mom.
THERAPIST:	Good. Jennifer, I see you really care about your brother and sister. When you really care about people you help them get what they

would like. They want some of your mom's attention. How long are you going to make them wait for it?

JENNIFER: I don't know.

THERAPIST: How long are you going to need your mother's care? Until you are 30? 40?

JENNIFER: I don't know.

THERAPIST: Ask your mother how long you will need her.

JENNIFER: How long, Mom?

MOTHER: As long as your health is poor. As long as you need me.

THERAPIST: Sounds like your mom needs you, Jennifer. Some families may need someone to be sick for a long time. But Jennifer, whose lungs are those?

JENNIFER: Mine.

THERAPIST: And who breathes for you?

JENNIFER: I do.

THERAPIST: So who can take care of your lungs?

JENNIFER: I can.

THERAPIST: Yes, you can [pause]. You don't need to be sick for your family to keep the family together. [To mother] You were saying you stopped working to care for Jennifer. How did you come to this decision?

MOTHER: I taught the fourth grade. I loved the classroom and I miss it, but Jenny needed my attention.

THERAPIST: How did you come to the decision to stop working?

MOTHER: John and I talked about it. He didn't want me to stop.

FATHER: We are just like everybody else these days. We need two incomes to make it.

MOTHER: John! Don't start that again here in front of the children.

FATHER: [Raises his voice] I'm sorry my income doesn't go far enough, but let's face it, three children are expensive.
[Jenny starts to sit up, and her body gets tense. She looks toward mother].

MOTHER: Jenny, do you need some help? Here I have your inhaler. [Digs in purse to find inhaler]

THERAPIST: [Takes inhaler and gives it to Jenny] Here, Jenny. Use your inhaler when you need it. Sarah, you help your sister if she needs you. [To the parents] Now John, finish your conversation with your wife.

FATHER: This is so hard for me to talk about. I worry so much about making ends meet with three children and one of them sick. I don't seem to be going anywhere on my job. I have been passed over for the last two promotions. I just don't know what's going to happen to us.

MOTHER: I had no idea you felt like this. We never see you at home. I thought work was going great for you. I had no idea you were so unhappy on your job. I've been paying so much attention to Jenny, I just didn't notice what's happened to you, and to us.

THERAPIST: I see Mom and Dad working together here. Maybe this family doesn't need someone to be sick after all. Jenny can care for herself. You two can talk to each other like the majority of families where the adults make the important decisions. This will free both of you to attend to all your children in a healthy, supportive way.

Summary

This chapter described the history of structural family therapy, its theory, and its therapeutic methods. The consistency of structural family therapy with the values of social work practice was explored. A number of research studies support the effectiveness of structural family therapy with different populations, and some of these studies were presented. Cogent critiques of the structural model were highlighted as well as the usefulness of structural family therapy in today's practice contexts of managed care and integrated services delivery systems. Finally, a case was presented that illustrates the practice of structural family therapy.

Process Questions

1. Identify the specific structural techniques used in this transcript.
2. What function(s) does Jennifer's asthmatic behavior serve in maintaining the family structure?
3. Suggest some other ways the social worker might reframe Jennifer's asthmatic behavior to the family.
4. To strengthen the marital dyad, what techniques might the social worker use?

References

APONTE, H. (1976). Underorganization and the poor family. In P. Guerin (Ed.), *Family therapy: Theory and practice.* New York: Gardner Press.

APONTE, H. (1992). The black sheep of the family: A structural approach to brief therapy. In S. H. Budman, M. F. Hoyt, & S. Friedman (Eds.), *The first session in brief therapy* (pp. 324–344). New York: Guilford.

APONTE, H. (1994). *Bread and spirit: Therapy with the new poor: Diversity of race, culture, and values.* New York: Norton.

APONTE, H., & VAN DEUSEN, J. (1981). Structural family therapy. In A. Gurman & D. Kniskern (Eds.), *Handbook of family therapy* (pp. 310–360). New York: Brunner/Mazel.

BROWN, J., & CHRISTENSEN, D. (1986). *Family therapy: Theory and practice.* Monterey, CA: Brooks/Cole.

CAMPBELL, T. L., & PATTERSON, J. M. (1995). The effectiveness of family interventions in the treatment of physical illness. *Journal of Marital and Family Therapy, 21,* 545–584.

CHAMBERLAIN, P., & ROSICKY, J. G. (1995). The effectiveness of family therapy in the treatment of adolescents with conduct disorders and delinquency. *Journal of Marital and Family Therapy, 21,* 441–460.

COLAPINTO, J. (1982). Structural family therapy. In A. Horn & M. Ohlsen, *Family counseling and therapy* (pp. 112–140). Itasca, IL: F. E. Peacock.

COLAPINTO, J. (1991a). Structural family therapy. In A. Horne & J. L. Passmore (Eds.), *Family counseling and therapy* (2nd ed., Chap. 4). Itasca, IL: F. E. Peacock.

COLAPINTO, J. (1991b). Structural family therapy. In A. Gurman & D. Kniskern (Eds.), *Handbook of family therapy* (Vol. 2, Chap. 13). New York: Brunner/Mazel.

DAVIS, P., STERN, D., & VAN DEUSEN, J. (1977). Enmeshment-disengagement in the alcoholic family. In F. Seixas (Ed.), *Alcoholism: Clinical and experimental research.* New York: Grune & Stratton.

FENELL, D., & WEINHOLD, B. (1989). *Counseling families: An introduction to marriage and family therapy.* Denver: Love Publishing.

FULMER, R. (1983). A structural approach to unresolved mourning in single parent family systems. *Journal of Marital and Family Therapy, 9,* 259–269.

GOLDENBERG, I., & GOLDENBERG, H. (1991). *Family therapy: An overview.* Belmont, CA: Wadsworth.

HARKAWAY, J. E. (1987). *Eating disorders.* Rockville, MD: Aspen.

HENGGELER, S. W., MELTON, G. M., & SMITH, L. A. (1992). Family preservation using multisystemic therapy: An effective alternative to incarcerating serious juvenile offenders. *Journal of Consulting and Clinical Psychology, 60,* 953–961.

HEPWORTH, D. H., & LARSEN, J. (1994). *Direct social work practice: Theory and skills* (4th ed.). Pacific Grove, CA: Brooks/Cole.

KAZDIN, A. E. (1987). *Conduct disorders in childhood and adolescents.* Newbury Park, CA: Sage.

LAIRD, H., & VANDE KEMP, H. (1987). Complementarity as a function of stage in therapy: An analysis of Minuchin's structural family therapy. *Journal of Marital and Family Therapy, 13,* 127–137.

MARKUS, E., LANGE, A., & PETTIGREW, T. F. (1990). Effectiveness of family therapy—A meta analysis. *Journal of Family Therapy, 12,* 205–221.

MINUCHIN, S. (1974). *Families and family therapy.* Cambridge, MA: Harvard University Press.

MINUCHIN, S., & FISHMAN, H. (1981). *Family therapy techniques.* New York: Harvard University Press.

MINUCHIN, S., MONTALVO, B., GUERNEY, B., ROSMAN, B., & SCHUMER, F. (1967). *Families of the slums.* New York: Basic Books.

MINUCHIN, S., ROSMAN, B., & BAKER, L. (1978). *Psychosomatic families: Anorexia nervosa in context.* Cambridge, MA: Harvard University Press.

NICHOLS, M. (1984). *Family therapy: Concepts and methods.* New York: Gardner Press.

OKUN, B., & RAPPAPORT, L. (1980). *Working with families: An introduction to family therapy.* North Scituate, MA: Duxbury.

PIERCY, F., & SPRENKLE, D. (1986). *Family therapy sourcebook.* New York: Guilford.

ROMIG, C., & THOMPSON, J. (1988). Teenage pregnancy: A family systems approach. *American Journal of Family Therapy, 16,* 133–143.

ROSENBERG, J. (1983). Structural family therapy. In B. Wolman & G. Stricker (Eds.), *Handbook of family and marital therapy* (pp. 159–185). New York: Plenum.

ROSMAN, B. L., MINUCHIN, S., & LIEBMAN, R. (1977). Treating anorexia by the family lunch session. In C. E. Schaefer & H. L. Millman (Eds.), *Therapies for children: A handbook of effective treatments for problem behavior.* San Francisco: Jossey-Bass.

ROSMAN, B. L., MINUCHIN, S., LIEBMAN, R., & BAKER, L. (1978, November). *Family therapy for psychosomatic children.* Paper presented at the annual meeting of the American Academy of Psychosomatic Medicine, Atlanta, GA.

SCHAEFER, C., BRIESMEISTER, J., & FITTON, M. (Eds.). (1984). *Family therapy techniques for problem behaviors of children and teenagers.* San Francisco: Jossey-Bass.

SHADISH, W. R., MONTGOMERY, L. M., WILSON, P., WILSON, M. R., BRIGHT, I., & OKWUMABUA, T. (1993). Effects of family and marital psychotherapies: A meta-analysis. *Journal of Consulting and Clinical Psychology, 61,* 992–1002.

SHADISH, W. R., RAGSDALE, K., GLASER, R. R., & MONTGOMERY, L. M. (1995). The efficacy and effectiveness of marital and family therapy: A perspective from meta-analysis. *Journal of Marital and Family Therapy, 21,* 345–360.

STANTON, M., & TODD, T. (1979). Structural family therapy with drug addicts. In E. Kaufman & P. Kaufman (Eds.), *The family therapy of drug and alcohol abuse.* New York: Gardner Press.

SYKES, D. (1987). An approach to working with black youth in cross cultural therapy. *Clinical Social Work Journal, 15*(3), 260–270.

SZAPOCZNIK, J., KURTINES, W. M., FOOTE, F. H., PEREZ-VIDAL, A., & HERVIS, O. (1983). Conjoint versus one person family therapy: Some evidence for the effectiveness of conducting family therapy through one person. *Journal of Consulting and Clinical Psychology, 51,* 881–899.

SZAPOCZNIK, J., KURTINES, W. M., FOOTE, F. H., PEREZ-VIDAL, A., & HERVIS, O. (1986). Conjoint versus one person family therapy: More evidence for the effectiveness of conducting family therapy through one person with drug-abusing adolescents. *Journal of Consulting and Clinical Psychology, 54,* 395–397.

SZAPOCZNIK, J., PEREZ-VIDAL, A., BRICKMAN, A. L., FOOTE, F. H., SANTISTEBAN, D., HERVIS, O., & KURTINES, W. (1988). Engaging adolescent drug abusers and their families in treatment: A strategic structural systems approach. *Journal of Consulting and Clinical Psychology, 56,* 552–557.

SZAPOCZNIK, J., RIO, A., MURRAY, E., COHEN, R., SCOPETTA, M., RIVAS-VANQUEZ, A., HERVIS, O., POSADA, V., & KURTINES, W. (1989). Structural family versus psychodynamic child therapy for problematic Hispanic boys. *Journal of Consulting and Clinical Psychology, 57,* 571–578.

TODD, T. (1986). Structural/strategic marital therapy. In N. Jacobson & A. Gurman (Eds.), *Clinical handbook of marital therapy* (pp. 71–105). New York: Guilford.

ZEIGLER-DRISCOLL, G. (1979). The similarities in families of drug dependents and alcoholics. In E. Kaufman & P. Kaufman (Eds.), *The family therapy of drug and alcohol abuse.* New York: Gardner.

CHAPTER THREE

Catheleen Jordan, Ph.D.
University of Texas at Arlington
Cynthia Franklin, Ph.D.
University of Texas at Austin

Mental Research Institute (MRI), Strategic, and Milan Family Therapy

Change is the focus of strategic family therapy, a systems approach in which the family's interactional sequences are assessed and systematically altered to help clients achieve their therapeutic goals. Strategic therapy is directive, time limited, and focused on the present, not the past. Other names for this therapy approach are brief therapy or systemic therapy. In this chapter, we use strategic family therapy as a general name to discuss three different approaches: the Mental Research Institute's (MRI) brief therapy approach, Haley/Madanes strategic, problem-solving model (currently referred to as the Washington model), and the traditional Milan therapy approach. These models were some of the first to advocate a radical constructivist viewpoint (Watzlawick, 1976). Bateson's (1972) concept that the "map is not the territory" points to the multiple ways that clients may construct their reality and is used as a metaphor by strategic models to explain the idiosyncratic ways clients perceive the world. Strategic approaches emphasize the importance of understanding clients' reality and how these individuals conceptualize the world around them. Strategic therapists assume that people behave in ways consistent with their cognitive constructions and beliefs concerning the world. Strategic approaches also share in common a sensitivity to the beliefs and meanings families construct concerning their problems—constructions that may inadvertently constrain them from seeing all their options.

All strategic approaches have in common a focus on strategic interventions, or specific strategies used by therapists to convince families to alter the dysfunctional interactional patterns believed to maintain their presenting problems.

Important contributors to the development of strategic approaches include Gregory Bateson, Milton Erickson, John Weakland, Don Jackson, Jay Haley, Cloe Madanes, Paul Watzlawick, and Mara Selvini-Palazzoli.

This chapter describes the history of strategic family therapy, its theory, and its therapeutic methods. Each model—MRI, brief therapy, Haley/Madanes, and the Milan team—is covered in separate discussions about its history, theory, and methods. The consistency of strategic family therapy with social work practice is explored, and the research basis for strategic family therapy is summarized. Important critiques of the strategic model are discussed. The usefulness of strategic family therapy in today's practice contexts of managed care is further highlighted. Finally, a case is presented that illustrates the practice of strategic family therapy.

History

Strategic therapy developed from communication theory, cybernetic systems theory, and constructivist theory, and from the early work of Gregory Bateson and his research group at the Mental Research Institute in Palo Alto, California (Shilson, 1991). Norbert Wiener wrote *Cybernetics* in 1948, introducing the idea of homeostatic systems. The system's feedback processes were described as allowing for system self-correction. These ideas were integrated by the Bateson group into their work with families. *Toward a Theory of Schizophrenia* (Bateson, Jackson, Haley, & Weakland, 1956) was the seminal work from this group and introduced the idea of the double-bind communication patterns of families. That is, family communication is contradictory across levels; for example, verbal and nonverbal messages do not match. The goal for family therapy was for family communications to be more direct and honest. Others involved in this early developmental stage of strategic therapy were Jay Haley, interested in analysis of fantasy, and John Weakland, a chemical engineer interested in anthropology.

Don Jackson, a psychoanalytic psychiatrist, served as a supervisor of psychotherapy with schizophrenic patients. Jackson was responsible for introducing into family theory seminal concepts such as family homeostasis and quid pro quo relationships. He was also the first clinician to advocate a higher order cybernetics view in systems theory and the constructivist orientation. The psychiatrist William Fry also worked with Jackson and colleagues and was interested in the use of humor in therapy. Milton Erickson was another influence in the early development of strategic therapy, contributing paradoxical interventions and hypnosis. Strategic family therapists have chosen to apply the basic principles in somewhat different ways, giving rise to three practicing groups. The history of these groups will be reviewed here. Though the three groups share some commonalities, controversy exists as to whether their approaches should be considered together as strategic therapies.

Mental Research Institute: Brief Therapy

Brief therapy was conducted at the Palo Alto Veteran's Administration Hospital with schizophrenic patients and their families. Later the model was applied to clients with other problems as well. Bateson, Haley, Weakland, and Fry believed that schizophrenic behavior developed in response to a dysfunctional family system. The strategic approach was furthered with the development of the Mental Research Institute (MRI) in 1959. The brief therapy project was introduced in 1967. John Weakland, Paul Watzlawick, Richard Fisch, Arthur Bodin, Carlos Sluzki, and Virginia Satir were involved with this early development of the MRI. The techniques of Milton Erickson, such as hypnosis and paradoxical instructions, contributed significantly to the development of this approach. At MRI, Jackson integrated Bateson's ideas about cybernetics and general systems theory with his understanding of family processes. Satir was director of training. Jay Haley, at MRI from 1962 to 1966, contributed to the work of Milton Erickson. John Weakland, Paul Watzlawick, and Richard Fisch developed their brief therapy approach, commonly called the MRI approach, as part of a research project involving new directions for therapy.

Haley/Madanes Model: Strategic Therapy

In 1967, Haley left Palo Alto and joined Salvador Minuchin and Brulio Montalvo at the Child Guidance Clinic in Philadelphia. Haley's collaboration with Minuchin produced shared features between Haley's strategic problem-solving model and Minuchin's structural model. However, Haley's model also retained the cybernetic communication influences of the original MRI group. Haley was particularly interested in the power aspects of communication. Haley's approach is a blend of the MRI brief therapy model and Minuchin's focus on hierarchies and coalitions. Cloe Madanes, Haley's wife and colleague, also contributed her ideas about family metaphors and pretend techniques. In 1976, Haley and Cloe Madanes moved to the University of Maryland Medical School and established their own family therapy institute (Stanton, 1981; Foley, 1989). Later they moved their institute to Washington, D.C. At the Washington Institute of Family Therapy, Haley and Madanes practice their unique brand of strategic family therapy.

Milan Group: Systemic Therapy

Meanwhile, Mara Selvini-Palazzoli in Milan, Italy, had begun treating anorexia nervosa cases and focused on treatment of the entire family. The Milan Institute for Family Study opened in 1967, the same year the MRI brief therapy project began. Both groups defined themselves as research clinics that would concentrate on methods to help difficult-to-treat families. The Milan group, including Mara Selvini-Palazzoli, Luigi Boscolo, Gianfranco Cecchin, and Giuliana Prata, began to borrow family techniques from a strategic perspective. The Milan colleagues were frustrated with their lack of success in individual treatment of anorexic patients. They began to reach out to family therapists in the United States, seeking to incorporate their ideas. As a part of this thrust, they invited Watzlawick to come to Milan to train the team. Watzlawick originally guided the team's work in family systems ideas. The group further shifted toward the work of Haley and Bateson and developed their own model, focusing on Bateson's circular epistemology. They were also influenced by Lynn Hoffman and Peggy Penn from the Ackerman institute, who visited the Milan team in Italy. Hoffman has been particularly influential by chronicling and integrating the diverse perspectives across clinics.

Theoretical Basis for the Practice Model

Strategic family therapy is an action-oriented brief therapy model that focuses on change versus insight. Strategic therapy focuses on the presenting problem or symptom, but a distinction is made between identifying a problem presented in therapy and creating a problem by applying a diagnosis or by characterizing an individual or a family in a certain way (Madanes, 1991). Traditional psychiatric diagnosis is not believed to be helpful in the change process.

Major Assumptions

All the strategic approaches discussed share certain common assumptions. In all three models, the presenting problem is the focus of change (Duncan & Parks, 1988). Directive or paradoxical interventions are aimed at adding new information or changing perceptions of old information. Change, rather than growth or insight, is the focus. The family's present functioning is more important than the family's past, as healthy families are believed to be more successful at negotiating or coping with normal family developmental stages. Dysfunctional families do not adapt to the changes that occur in these transitional periods and continue to solve problems using old, unsuccessful patterns or solutions (Stanton, 1981). Other problems may occur when the family has dysfunctional hierarchies resulting from confused generational boundaries. Dysfunctional family patterns are described as cyclic behaviors, and one member's behavior is a manifestation of a dysfunctional family communication pattern. Treatment is focused on the entire family.

Nelson, Fleuridas, and Rosenthal (1986) cite some of the assumptions about communication that are important to the strategic model. Both verbal and nonverbal communication are important, as is the context in which the communication occurs. The intervention should focus on what causes people to change rather than the reasons they change. The processing of information is important as it affects functioning of family members. Members perceive and evaluate their environment in idiosyncratic ways. Rules and norms govern family interaction patterns. Families maintain organizational functioning and equilibrium through both verbal and nonverbal information exchanges.

Communication theory is the unifying idea that brought the strategic family therapy group together (Nelson et al., 1986). The study of communication as related to the family focused on information processing between family members as well as information processing from environmental systems outside the family. Information is processed by family members based on their unique perceptions and evaluations of the information received. The therapist's responsibility from this perspective is to offer new information or to help family members process and evaluate information in a new way.

Key Constructs

Piercy and Sprenkle (1986) review the key constructs of strategic family therapy. A primary concept, circularity, refers to cyclical explanations of behavior that occur in the context of the family. This view differs from linear cause-and-effect explanations of behavior, which are believed to be oversimplistic. In the context of circularity, an adolescent's acting-out behavior would be considered in the family context as opposed to other explanations, such as labeling her behavior conduct disordered.

Homeostasis is the system's tendency to resist change and maintain its status quo. The addition of a new baby to the family may require adjustments in role performance of the parents. However, if one or both of the parents is inflexible and attempts to maintain the earlier patterns of functioning, problems result.

Negative feedback is a process that reestablishes a previous state of equilibrium. For example, the death of a family member brings distant family members closer together.

Positive feedback activates change in the system. This includes any event or intervention that challenges family homeostasis with a resultant change of behavior. Families' attempts at intervening with the problem may sometimes exacerbate the problem rather than eliminate it: The parents ground their teenage son for bad grades, and he responds by running away from home.

Analogical messages are communications between family members that have symbolic meaning. For example, when spouses argue over who will drive the car, they may really be having a battle for control.

Error amplification is the result of a dysfunctional family's repeated attempts to solve their problem. These repeated solutions actually exacerbate the problem rather than solve it. Error amplification may be used as an intervention when the therapist "prescribes the symptom," or asks the family to increase the dysfunctional behavior, with the aim of eliminating it.

Metacommunication is communication about communication—that is, any verbal or nonverbal cues as to how the actual message is to be interpreted. Meaning may be given to a message by body language, voice inflection or tone, or other explanations about the message. For example, "I'm listening" may not be well received if the speaker is hiding behind a newspaper when he says it.

Punctuation refers to the interactional qualities of relationships and the importance of attributions to the significance of the interactions. For example, if a mother's rejecting attitude and her teenage daughter's rebellious behavior occur in a cyclical fashion, the mother might say, "I reject my daughter because she is rebellious," but the daughter would say, "I rebel because she has always rejected me."

Therapeutic Methods

Techniques discussed first are those used by all three groups, followed by techniques associated with the particular strategic groups; MRI brief therapy, Haley/Madanes therapy, and Milan team therapy are presented in separate discussions of each model.

Techniques Used by All Strategic Models

Relabeling is used to relabel or redefine the situation or behavior in order to give the family a more positive perspective (Goldenberg & Goldenberg, 1991). For instance, the runaway teenager's behavior is relabeled as a misguided attempt at the normal developmental process of separating and gaining more independence from his parents. Also, positive motives may be ascribed to client behaviors (Stanton & Todd, 1979). Dad is not home because he is working so hard to maintain the family. In the strategic approach, this alteration of meaning is seen as a precursor to change.

Paradoxical techniques give the client information or instructions that are contradictory to what the client expects (Goldenberg & Goldenberg, 1991). For example, the therapist may *prescribe the symptom,* or ask the family to continue or exaggerate their current behavior. An interfering mother-in-law might be instructed to interfere regularly, every night after dinner for exactly 10 minutes. The underlying belief is that this new awareness of the family members' control over their own behavior gives them the freedom to discontinue it if they wish. *Restraining the symptom* is used to discourage change (Stanton, 1981). The family is told to go slow, or the therapist may express doubt about the likelihood of change. *Positioning* is used to side with one family member who expresses a negative view of change (Stanton, 1981). The therapist may exaggerate the client's negative predictions.

Hypothesizing is the therapist's attempt to understand the family's problem behavior and is referred to as the "core reality" of the family interactions (Nelson et al., 1986). For instance, a mother may nag her children and her husband. The children may respond by poking fun at their mother and by using sarcasm. The father may respond by being overprotective of the mother and overdisciplining the children. A working hypothesis for this family might be that the family attempts to encourage intimacy with each other by nagging, joking, overprotecting, and overdisciplining. The hypothesis is not communicated to the family (Nelson et al., 1986); however, the family may be given the following explanations for their behavior based on the hypothesis. The mother nags the children out of her love and concern for them; the children love her and express their love by joking with her. Their sarcasm is their misguided attempt to get her attention. The husband is simply trying to protect his beloved wife, maybe a little too zealously at times when he overdisciplines the children.

Circular questioning is used to obtain information with which to develop a hypothesis (Selvini-Palazzoli, Boscolo, Cecchin, & Prata, 1978). (Circular questioning is described and illustrated in Chapter 9.) The focus of circular questions is to elaborate on the interactions and connections between family members. All are questioned; members may be asked the same question to get each individual's perception of family relationships. For example, each member is asked to tell about the family problem. *Triadic questions* ask members to tell about relationships between other members of the family. For instance, a sister may be asked to tell about the relationship between her mother and brother.

Neutrality may be used in the circular questioning process. By remaining neutral, the therapist remains an ally of all the family members (Goldenberg & Goldenberg, 1991).

Mental Research Institute (MRI) Brief Therapy Model

The MRI approach assumes that problems result when the family's solutions fail (Duncan & Solovey, 1989). Additionally, families continue to attempt to solve their problems by applying more of the same solution that has failed. Problems arise as a part of the natural course of life circumstances and developmental transitions. It is assumed that the process of continually applying a faulty solution to these normal life difficulties will result in maintaining a problem or making the problem worse. In other words, problems are like the proverbial "vicious cycle." The reason that families continually apply faulty solutions is partly because of their beliefs about a problem. For example, a parent repeatedly punishes (applies the same solution) to an adolescent who stays out past curfew even though these punishments do not work. This interaction may evolve into a vicious cycle: The more the adolescent stays out late, the more the parent punishes—and the more the parent punishes, the more the adolescent stays out late. This type of interaction is known as a recursive feedback loop (Keeney, 1983).

In a recursive feedback loop, there is no specific cause or effect. Each sequence of behavior feeds on the other. In this example, the attempted solution to a normal adolescent rebellion may be maintained or escalated into an even larger power struggle between parent and child. The parents in our example probably have the mistaken belief that this class of behaviors (punishment) should be effective in changing the behavior of their child. Unfortunately, the parents become constrained by their own rigid belief systems about the situation. Even though the solution is not working, they often have difficulty giving up the behavior patterns in favor of alternate solutions that may not be in accordance with their "common-sense" (constructed) beliefs. The MRI group also notes the reinforcing aspects of dysfunctional behavioral patterns. The vicious cycle is self-reinforcing and maintains itself through a type of positive feedback loop. Intervention is described as any strategy that can stop the faulty attempted solutions that maintain the problem and start the family in a more productive direction.

The MRI model was the first family therapy model to propose the idea for therapists to work in teams behind a one-way mirror. Therapists work with the clients in one room while a team of therapists observes the therapeutic dialogue from behind a one-way mirror. Therapists behind the one-way mirror are not simply passive observers. The team frequently sends in messages to help the therapist interviewing the family. Messages from the team are communicated to the therapist by a tap on the door allowing other team members to enter the room, or by calling into the therapy room via a telephone. The therapist and team also briefly meet following the session, and the team helps the therapist devise an intervention to help the client solve the presenting problems.

Another important contribution of the MRI model is their conceptualization of the differing positions—*customer, complainant,* and *visitor*—that clients take when they enter therapy. It is important for a therapist to assess who is the customer because this is the person who is motivated to change. Complainants on the other hand are most usually not motivated to change themselves but come to therapy to complain about another person and his or her problems. Their investment is in seeing changes in others. An example of a complainant is a parent or a spouse who is disgruntled about a child or partner. A visitor is someone who comes to therapy but is not invested in the change process. Visitors are the most difficult to engage in any type of therapeutic change.

The MRI is a pragmatic therapy that subscribes to a parsimonious approach to therapeutic change. According to Weakland and Fisch (1992), "Problems are defined as consisting of 1) observable behavior, which 2) is characterized as undesirable (deviant, difficult, distressing, dangerous) either by its performer or by some other concerned person, but which 3) persists despite efforts to alter or get rid of it, therefore 4) the concerned person seeks help from a professional" (p. 308). The model focuses totally on changing behavioral interactions between people. The steps of change include assessing who is doing what to whom and how it is a problem. A part of this process is to determine who are the customers and complainants. A second step is to track the attempted solutions to the problem. What has the client done to try to solve the problem? What has worked and what has not worked? Third, a therapist will have the client describe what would be a first noticeable sign of improvement for that person. Therapists are looking for a very small, concrete, behaviorally defined example. Fourth, therapists note what the client's beliefs are concerning the problem and how it can be resolved.

Fifth, based on knowledge of the attempted solutions and beliefs of the client about the problem resolution, therapists determine what interventions need to be avoided so they do not get trapped into feeding into the vicious cycle of the client's attempted solutions. For example, if we were trying to help the parents who were repeatedly punishing the adolescent who was staying out late, we would not want to suggest another type of punishment because this would represent the same class of behaviors that had failed, and we would be feeding into the problem. Instead, we might suggest something counterintuitive to these parents who believe that punishment should work: Lock the door and ignore the adolescent. Such a strategy is likely to interrupt the attempted solution sequence. Sixth, as in our example, therapists strategize about what intervention they can suggest to the family to help them give up the attempted solution and try something different. Here, therapists usually come up with homework assignments and tasks they direct family members to perform between sessions. Some of these tasks, as mentioned, are paradoxical or counterintuitive, but all tasks are designed to get families to give up the attempted solutions and do something different to interrupt the dysfunctional behavioral pattern. Finally, therapists evaluate progress and change their intervention strategies as needed (Ray, 1996; Fisch, Weakland, & Segal, 1982; Weakland & Fisch, 1992).

THERAPEUTIC TECHNIQUES USED IN THE MRI MODEL

The MRI model recommends *directed behavior change*. This technique is used when the therapist directly asks that an instruction be followed. The therapist is aware that clients are often resistant. Therefore, therapists believe that the instruction should be framed in an indirect manner and "played down" to appear insignificant. The therapist may suggest an instruction and then back off, stating that it is too early in therapy for the client to undertake such a task, or the therapist may suggest some instruction that appears insignificant but really is a big first step.

Homework assignments may be used to facilitate behavior change. One example of this type of intervention involves a client who always avoids making demands of others in his personal relationships. He is instructed to go to a gasoline station and to ask for one gallon of gasoline and each of the usual free services.

Another intervention technique is *danger of improvement/predicting a relapse*. For example, when a family comes into the session reporting an improvement, the therapist will caution them not to be too optimistic and will predict a relapse. This enables the family not to feel pressured to continue to improve; paradoxically, this often causes more rapid improvement. An example is "You would like to be a better parent, but are you prepared to face your wife's jealousy of your relationship with your daughter?"

The *go slowly* technique is similar to the danger of improvement techniques described above. Clients are encouraged to move slowly in terms of change. Later, when clients report progress, the therapist suggests that the clients may be moving too fast and encourages them to slow down.

HOW TO CONDUCT AN MRI SESSION

Ray (1996) outlined the steps of a MRI, brief therapy model, as described here.

Define the problem. Who is the customer? Who is complaining? Who is most interested in seeing the problem resolved? Describe the problem in concrete terms: Who is doing what to whom, and how is it a problem? Get recent examples: What made you call us now? You have mentioned these difficulties [list them]. Prioritize: What problem do you want to fix first?

Establish the goals of therapy. What would be a small, concrete sign that would let you know that the problem has not yet been resolved, but you are heading in the right direction?

Explore attempted solutions. What have you done in your best efforts to solve the problem?

Determine the main theme of the attempted solutions. What is the main theme of the attempted solutions?

Design an intervention. Avoid more of the same (i.e., suggestions that are consistent with solutions that have been tried and have failed). The aim is to get the person to drop the attempted solutions. The best way to do this is to propose interventions that are 180 degrees from the main thrust of the attempted solutions.

Elicit the client's cooperation. What is the client's position? What is your best guess as to why the problem is occurring? (We are not interested in why, but only in ascertaining the client's position.) Use the client's position to sell your intervention.

Monitor progress and terminate. Has progress been made in the problem? Suggest change is more enduring when it happens slowly, so go slowly.

Haley/Madanes Model

In Haley's strategic problem-solving model, the therapist clearly defines the presenting problem but also emphasizes the social context of the problem (Haley,

1976). Symptoms are viewed in operational terms. Rather than being seen as residing within the individual, such symptoms as depression and anxiety are seen as the result of interactions between people. Like Minuchin, Haley was interested in the hierarchies within families. He thought that many symptoms emerged as a result of the power dynamics inherent in relationships. He theorizes that family relationships were characterized as symmetrical and that members have equal power, or complementary, one-up and one-down positions. Thus, the power distribution, operating norms, and rules in families could be discovered by observing the family communication patterns and behaviors.

Haley (1976, 1980) described therapy as a power struggle between client and therapist. The therapist's role is to find interventions that will change the power balance, break up coalitions, and rearrange dysfunctional hierarchies. Haley theorized that clients maintain their control in therapy by continuing to have symptoms and not improving in spite of the therapist's attempts to change client behavior. He further believes that putting clients in a therapeutic paradox by asking them to continue their symptoms has the opposite effect. In such a therapeutic paradox, therapists are in a win-win situation in terms of helping the client change. If clients resist the therapist, they change their behavior in a desired position. On the other hand, if they decide to do what the therapist says, they have surrendered their power and will become more amenable to following the directives of the therapist for changing their behavior. It is most likely, however, that clients will resist symptom change because to stay in control, clients must give up their symptomatic behavior (Haley, 1976). Haley and Madanes use paradox along with other strong directive techniques to get clients to change their dysfunctional patterns.

Madanes has also contributed techniques that soften the strong directive orientation to Haley's approach. She most often uses drama to help clients act out the problem sequences and solutions to problems. She also uses pretend techniques so that clients can act out the directives given through drama, making it easier for them to make changes in the family patterns. Madanes (1984) describes a case that illustrates the use of the pretend strategy. A primary care physician referred a daughter who had diabetes and her mother to Madanes. The presenting problem was the daughter's noncompliance with the medical treatment. This led to frequent trips to the emergency room because she had not taken her insulin. In investigating this case, Madanes discovered that the mother also had diabetes, for which she never got any treatment except when the daughter and she came to the emergency room. The presenting problem of the daughter's noncompliance with the medical treatment was interpreted as a *metaphor* (to be explained in more detail below) for the mother's lack of medical care. In this context, there was also a dysfunctional hierarchy as the daughter was refusing treatment to protect and take care of her mother. Madanes used a pretend strategy with the mother and daughter to intervene and change the inverted hierarchy. She had the mother dress up like a nurse and act out administering the insulin to her daughter. As a nurse, she also had to administer insulin to herself, which corrected the problem that brought the two into therapy.

Therapy teams are used in Haley's strategic problem-solving approach but not to the same extent as in the MRI model and the Milan model. Whereas

Madanes and other therapists use the team approach, Haley does not prefer this method except for supervising a case.

In contrast to the MRI brief therapy model, which concentrates completely on changing behavior, Haley's strategic problem-solving model focuses on the meaning and function of symptoms. Symptoms or presenting problems are believed to hold meaning for relationship issues and dynamics going on in the family, such as the power issues mentioned earlier. Other common relationship issues whose symptoms alert therapists are dysfunctional hierarchies, such as a child taking care of a parent, and *perverse triangles,* as when one spouse has not resolved issues in his or her family of origin and is still carrying on secret power alliances across generations. Haley and Madanes believe that symptoms carry a message or serve as a metaphor for other problems that exist in a family. According to Madanes (1984), family symptoms can "tell a story about their patterns of interaction" (p. xi). Haley and Madanes also believe that symptoms serve a function that helps maintain and regulate the family relationship patterns. For example, a child may become symptomatic to decrease a conflict between her parents.

An example of what is meant by relational metaphors is cited by Madanes (1984). A father comes home from work upset because he has lost his job. While he is receiving comfort from his wife, his son develops an asthma attack. The father then focuses his attention on his son, comforting the son in the same way that he was being comforted by his wife. In this sequence, one metaphorical sequence replaces another. The balance of power has shifted. This same sequence may be applied by the family to a variety of situations. To understand family patterns, it is important to mind the process instead of the content of patterns. Processes tend to repeat themselves regardless of what content is being discussed or acted out.

Another example from one of the authors' cases may further define how symptoms of one family member may serve as a metaphor for other relational patterns. One of the authors saw a couple who complained that they were having behavioral problems with their 10-year-old son. In the process of the interview, it became apparent that the father was aligned with the son against the mother (power coalition), and there were considerable disagreements between him and his wife about the way the wife treated the son. However, when the therapist asked what the mother could do differently for the son, the father began to list things such as pay more attention to him and bring him a sandwich when he wanted it. At that point, it became apparent that the father was really describing what he wanted from his wife, and that the issues of the son were only a message signaling the presence of the marital relationship patterns. In this situation, the relationship pattern between the mother and son can be described as being *isomorphic* to the relationship pattern of the husband and wife. By displaying behavioral problems, the son served a function of regulating the conflict between his parents, allowing them to focus on his problems instead of their own.

Another aspect of Haley's strategic therapy was the development of ordeal therapy (Haley, 1984). The idea of the therapeutic ordeal first came to Haley in the 1950s. An ordeal is intended to get clients to give up their dysfunctional patterns and to adopt a new way of relating. The therapist approaches this by asking them to do something that is difficult and unpleasant and that requires considerable effort. Giving up the symptom becomes easier for the family than continuing the ordeal. In his work in the 1950s, Haley successfully treated an insomniac with a short-term ordeal strategy. He directed the sleepless client to catastrophize while trying to go to sleep. The insomniac, when given a choice, preferred sleeping to catastrophizing, and his insomnia immediately disappeared. Haley consulted Milton Erickson about the quick success with this case. Erickson explained that he had cured patients using similar strategies. In 1984, Haley postulated that all change processes include some type of ordeal that pushes people to change.

THERAPEUTIC INTERVENTIONS USED IN HALEY/MADANES MODEL

The Haley/Madanes strategic model is more directive than the brief or Milan models and takes a "one-up" approach. Family hierarchy incongruities are believed to be the basis for most clinical problems (Haley, 1980). Haley describes the appropriate hierarchical structure as parents being in control of their children. This is similar to Minuchin's structural view, described in Chapter 2. Haley also describes issues of control and power struggles between two or more members of the family and between the family and the therapist. Haley describes the therapist as needing to be in control of the session.

Directives may be direct or indirect, and give precise instructions to the individuals (Goldenberg & Goldenberg, 1991). A direct directive is a straightforward assignment of something to be done outside therapy. Its accomplishment depends on the motivation of the individual and is hard to enforce. The direct directive may be advice, coaching, homework assignments, or direct suggestions. An example is the therapist's advice that a sister stop interfering when her mother and younger sister are trying to resolve an issue. An indirect directive is deliberately planned and paradoxical as a way to encourage change. The indirect directive may be used with resistant clients (Madanes, 1981). Two types of indirect directives are the prescriptive paradox and the descriptive paradox (Madanes, 1981). The prescriptive paradox asks the family members to do more of the problem. For example, siblings who fight are instructed to fight and keep a diary about the fights. The descriptive paradox relabels the problem, giving it a positive connotation. For example, an absent workaholic father may be described as working hard to support his family.

Madanes's contribution to strategic therapy includes her pretend techniques, paradoxes based on fantasy, play, and humor (Madanes, 1981). The context of a problem may be changed by having family members pretend to exhibit their symptoms and then pretend to help solve the problem. For example, a tantrum-throwing child may be instructed to pretend to throw a tantrum, and the parents are instructed to pretend to help the child get her behavior under control. Pretend techniques were discussed earlier.

HOW TO CONDUCT A SESSION OF THE HALEY/MADANES MODEL

The strategic problem-solving model is a very structured therapy. Haley (1980) describes the initial interview as following four stages: the social stage, when the family gets acquainted with the therapist; the problem stage, when the therapist learns about the presenting problem from every family member's perspective; the inter-

action stage, when the therapist explores the power issues and relationship patterns around the presenting problems; and the *goal-setting stage,* when the therapist sets and prioritizes goals for change. At the end of the first interview, the therapist gives the client a homework assignment or some type of strong directive to get the change started.

Milan Team Model

Milan family therapy originated from the work of a team of four psychiatrists from Milan, Italy: Mara Selvini-Palazzoli, Luigi Boscolo, Gianfranco Cecchin, and Guilliana Prata. The team published *Paradox and Counter Paradox* in 1978, which discussed the theories and techniques of their strategic work with families who had a member with schizophrenia. In 1980, the original team split apart and began to pursue different paths. Selvini-Palazzoli and Prata have continued their research on strategy-based techniques similar to the ones discussed by the original team. Boscolo and Cecchin spent their time in training. As their training techniques evolved, Boscolo and Cecchin's ideas about therapy greatly diverged from the strategy-based methods of the original team. Currently, their therapy is more similar to the social construction and narrative approaches discussed in Chapter 6. At present, describing the "Milan team" is difficult because the original members of the team hold different perspectives. This chapter, however, focuses on the original strategic model the team developed and some of the work that Selvini-Palazzoli did following the breakup.

The original Milan team was influenced by cybernetics, communication, and systems theories (Selvini-Pallozoli, Boscolo, Cecchin, & Prata, 1978). Their interventions aimed to identify and break dysfunctional family rules, give positive connotations to each member's motivation, and find tasks that encourage change (Foley, 1984). The focus of the therapy was on the here-and-now interactions of the family and how the interactions related to the presenting problem of the individual family member. Problems were not seen as being created or maintained in an individual but as the results of interactions among other people.

The original Milan team was especially influenced by Bateson's ideas concerning the need for a "circular epistemology" (Bateson, 1972). Bateson saw the family as a self-correcting system that was constantly evolving. At times, a family would appear "stuck" in a dysfunctional repetitive pattern. They get stuck because of their beliefs or the meanings that they make, which Bateson called "epistemology." The term *epistemology* was used to indicate that the knowledge a person has about the world is constructed within his or her own mind and through unique social interactions and does not represent the "reality" of the situation. "The map is not the territory" was a metaphor used to describe this phenomenon. As a part of the strategic approach of the Milan team, special attention was given to differentiating meaning and action, and interventions were geared to introduce new connections between the two (Tomm, 1984a).

The therapist acted as a facilitator for the release of new information in the family that could connect the discrepancies between family members' beliefs and behaviors (Tomm, 1984b). Changes happened through different interventions that altered meanings and allowed families to get "unstuck." In this way, repetitive behavioral patterns were interrupted and people could accomplish the move forward that Bateson wrote about.

Strategic interventions of the Milan team involved therapists' moving beyond the linear view of families to a truly systemic understanding of how all the family members' interactions fed into one another to maintain meanings and patterns. (See Chapter 9 for an example of a Milan-style interview for a family. This interview illustrates the meaning of symptoms for the family and the embedded interactions around the problem sequences.)

The Milan approach shares with Haley's approach an emphasis on the meaning and function of symptoms. All presenting problems are viewed as serving a broader function within a family system than first appears. Selvini-Palazzoli (1986), for example, described dysfunctional family patterns involving a psychotic child as "psychotic games." Five stages of the game are (1) the parents reach a stalemate; (2) the child's behavior becomes problematic in an effort to control the parents; (3) the parents misinterpret the child's behavior and side against the child; (4) the child feels rejected and reacts with psychotic behavior; (5) the family game continues, maintained by the psychotic behavior of the child. Strategic interventions devised by the Milan team were aimed at disrupting these "games." The majority of interventions such as reframing and circular questions (described later) were aimed at directly changing meanings and thus helping the family move beyond the game. Other interventions, such as prescribing rituals for families to follow, were meant to indirectly stop the behavioral patterns associated with the game.

The Milan team described their method of working with families as the long brief therapy because of the influence of the MRI brief therapy model. It was called long brief therapy because they would see a family once a month for five to 10 sessions. The reason they saw families once a month is because the families in Italy had to travel long distances to get to the research center. Eventually, the Milan therapists begin to think that these long intervals between sessions were needed to provide an opportunity for the family to process the information given by the therapists and for the intervention to take full effect (Selvini-Palazzoli et al., 1978).

THERAPEUTIC INTERVENTIONS USED IN THE MILAN MODEL
The Milan team observed that families try to solve their problems in repetitive, redundant patterns; therefore, change efforts were focused on changing the repetitive pattern (Tomm, 1984a, 1984b). However, the pattern presented by the family may be paradoxical, because families come to therapy saying they must change while at the same time resisting change. Family belief systems are seen as contributing to the problem and are a focus of intervention. The therapist's goal is to introduce new information to the family system to change or create new beliefs. *Directives* are given to family members and are focused on behaviors that occur in the families' home environment. In addition to directives, restraining techniques such as "go slowly" and the "be aware of the dangers of improvement" may be used. Subsequent sessions are used to explore the effectiveness of the intervention. Unlike the confrontive techniques of Haley/Madanes, Milan therapy espouses neutrality on the part of the therapist (Selvini-Palazzoli et al., 1980). This neutrality separates the therapist from the family and keeps him or her on a dif-

ferent level. From this position, the therapist uses circular questioning to understand the complexities of the family system (Selvini-Palazzoli et al., 1980). Cecchin (1987) defines circular questions as "a method by which a clinician creates curiosity within the family system and therapist system . . . whereby the family itself may become somewhat neutral toward its own hypotheses" (p. 412). Circular questions also provide therapists with valuable information that they could use to construct a working hypothesis about how the family interacted. Basic to circular questioning is the use of the verb *to be* (e.g., Does your dad tend to be angry when you yell at your mom?). Another way to structure a circular question is to orient it to a future context or use the word *if*. (See Chapter 9 for a transcript dialogue in which a therapist uses circular questions.)

The Milan therapist uses *relabeling* to add information to the family belief system or to give new meaning to a belief system. Also similar to Haley/Madanes, the Milan therapist uses directives in either a direct or indirect manner. *Ritualized prescriptions* are described as a way of giving clients directives (Selvini-Palazzoli et al., 1978). For example, the therapist may prescribe that parents take turns disciplining the children. The parent not "on duty" is instructed to keep a diary recording the spouse's compliance with the prescription. The *invariant prescription* is used to break-up enmeshed families involved in a psychotic family game (Selvini-Palazzoli, 1986). This prescription is called *invariant* because the directive is exactly the same for each family. In the invariant prescription, parents are told to do something together, in secret, without the children. Parents keep a diary in which they record the children's reactions.

In yet other interventions, the Milan team recommends prescriptions such as even/odd days, when families are instructed to follow the preferences of one family member on even days and the other family member on odd days of the week. This is a helpful technique for cases in which couples are in a power struggle and may have difficulty seeing the usefulness of each other's ideas. The Milan therapist may also *unbalance the family system* by joining with one member to the exclusion of other members (Stanton, 1981). The purpose may be to strengthen generational boundaries or to avoid power struggles with family members.

HOW TO CONDUCT A SESSION OF THE MILAN MODEL

Pre-session. In the pre-session, all four therapists meet to read the referral data or to report on the previous session. Therapists develop hypotheses for what relational issues may be maintaining the presenting problem. These hypotheses, however, are only tentative and are meant to be checked out in the interview. As a part of the checking-out process, a therapist asks questions that could both confirm and disconfirm the hypothesis generated.

The Session. The actual therapy session lasts about an hour during which co-therapists (two members of the team) interview the family for the purposes of checking out hypotheses and formulating new hypotheses. The other two therapists watch the session from behind a one-way mirror.

Inter-session. Therapists take a break to plan a strategy. All four members of the team meet to discuss what happened in the interview and to decide which intervention to use with the family.

Delivery of the intervention. Therapists return to the therapy room and deliver the intervention to the family while the other two members continue to observe.

Post-session. The team meets to process how the family reacted to the intervention and to make plans for future sessions.

Consistency with Social Work Practice

The strategic therapy model has characteristics that make it compatible with social work practice. Proponents of this approach believe people have the ability to solve their own problems with therapist input. Also, goals of the therapist are negotiated between the therapist and the client, a practice that supports the social work philosophy of client self-determination. Strategic models promote both a social and a systemic understanding of human behavior. These views are also held by social work practitioners, who have a long history of emphasizing the social basis for behavior. The interventionist aspect of the model is also compatible with social work's emphasis on social planning and targeting systems for influence and change. The idea of neutrality is emphasized in social work practice. To represent differing client interests, the social worker learns to listen to and support different viewpoints.

Research Support for the Model

The unconventional methods of strategic therapy approaches are justified by applied research reported from the strategic schools. The literature supporting strategic therapy includes reports of descriptive studies as well as single-subject reports of success. Those reported to be most helped by strategic therapy include families with a member with anorexia, schizophrenia, encopresis, agoraphobia, anxiety, or psychosis. Resistant families are also believed to be helped by strategic techniques (O'Connor & La Sala, 1988). Similarities and overlap between strategic and behavior therapy are noted in the literature (Madanes & Haley, 1977; Michelson & Ashcher, 1984). The use of paradoxical intentions in the cognitive-behavioral research literature supports this controversial technique. For example, the strategic interventions of "dangers of improvement" and "go slowly" were combined with cognitive-behavioral techniques to intervene with stress management problems (Duncan, Parks, & Rock, 1987).

Cooper and Erickson (1954) studied the use of Ericksonian directives, tasks, and paradox in relation to time distortion, recovering material from the unconscious, creative thought, motor and nonmotor learning, and facilitation of mathematical mental activity. Suggestions related to time distortion, recovering material from the unconscious, creative thinking, and nonmotor learning appeared to be successful according to self-report of participants. Duncan and Solovey (1989) discussed the role of insight in strategic therapy. They studied commonalities and differences between therapist-ascribed and client-ascribed meaning, interpretation, and insight. They argued that insight is important in strategic therapy.

Outcome Evaluations

Case examples have been used by strategic therapists to validate outcomes. For example, Selvini-Palazzoli (1986) reported that 19 families had been treated with the invariant prescription. Although only 10 families followed the prescription, she reported excellent results. The identified patients were believed to be cured. Criteria for successful outcomes, however, were not specified.

Paradoxical techniques were studied by Wilcoxon and Fenell (1986). Ninety-six clients at three mental health centers were divided into two treatment condition groups. The clients each were attending therapy alone, though the spouses' attendance was desired. Nonattending spouses were sent either a linear letter or a paradoxical letter requesting their attendance. Sixty-nine percent of spouses receiving the linear letter attended therapy versus 37% of those receiving the paradoxical letter.

Stanton (1981) identified and summarized seven research articles on the effectiveness of strategic interventions. Langsley, Fairbairn, and DeYoung (1968) studied 300 patients at a psychiatric emergency center. Half were assigned to outpatient family crisis therapy utilizing strategic techniques and the other half were treated as inpatients. At 18-month follow-up, only one-half the strategic therapy group required hospitalization versus the inpatient group.

Alexander and Parsons (1973) compared strategic family therapy with client-centered family therapy, eclectic-dynamic therapy, and a no-treatment control group for treatment of delinquent behavior. Recidivism rates of the strategic family therapy group were half that of the other treatment conditions. Also, siblings of the strategic group members showed fewer problems over a three-year period.

The MRI school (Weakland, Fisch, Watzlawick, & Bodin, 1974) reported a 72% improvement rate on 97 clients versus a 61% to 65% improvement rate for nonfamily individual therapies (Bergin, 1971). No control groups were studied.

Garrigan and Bambrick (1975) administered strategic family therapy to adolescent, emotionally disturbed boys and then compared them with a no-treatment group. Although behavior of the two groups was not significantly different, the therapy group boys showed a higher perception of family adjustment than the no-treatment group. In a later study, Garrigan and Bambrick (1977) enlarged their sample, including females and older children. Half the sample received brief family therapy, whereas half received parent group discussions and seminars. Symptoms and family perception were significantly improved in the brief family therapy group at one- and two-year follow-ups.

Garrigan and Bambrick (1979) studied strategic therapy with oldest male siblings. One-third of the males were from single-parent families. The authors blamed lack of significance on the effects of the single-parent family structure. Mothers of intact families perceived the therapy as more effective than did single mothers.

Nugent (1989a) reported success on seven case studies treated with Ericksonian suggestion. Follow-up on six cases showed no relapse in five cases. He also reported on a single-case study of Ericksonian techniques, suggesting a strong causal relationship between intervention and outcome (Nugent 1989b).

Stanton and colleagues (1978) employed a structural/strategic approach with drug addicts in a methadone program. Black and white lower-class males under 36 years of age were randomly assigned to three groups: a paid family therapy group, a nonpaid family therapy group, and a group that received methadone and individual counseling. The paid family therapy group had the highest number of days free from various drugs at six-month follow-up. Also, reduced drug use was correlated with changes in the behavioral interactions of family members.

Critiques of the Model

Specific strategic techniques, especially paradoxical techniques, are integrated into other family models such as the cognitive-behavioral model (Duncan & Parks, 1988). In particular, paradoxical methods are reported to serve as helpful methods in behavioral therapy when clients are reluctant to change. Other authors have found that paradoxical techniques are especially helpful with resistant clients (O'Connor & La Sala, 1988). Paradoxical techniques, however, are believed by some to be deceitful (Duncan & Solovey, 1992). Other criticisms of strategic therapy are that it is controlling, manipulative, disrespectful, and too superficial (Wilner, 1988).

The premise underlying these criticisms is that manipulation is bad. Jay Haley has responded to ethical issues involved in his approach, particularly manipulation. Haley contends that all therapeutic approaches involve interpersonal influence and manipulation, whether acknowledged or denied (Levant, 1984). Haley suggests that a more cogent ethical issue is whether a therapeutic approach resolves the problems of the client. In the mind of Haley and many other strategic therapists, if families change in therapy and improve their level of functioning, the therapeutic strategy must be justified.

Most criticisms are brought against the strategic model because of its pragmatic focus and tendency toward highly directive therapeutic interventions. Feminists have also critiqued strategic models for the same reason that they object to Minuchin's structural model (Chapter 2)—because they believe it is overly authoritarian and promotes a patriarchal view (Luepnitz, 1988). The authoritarian and directive nature of strategic models has come under question in recent years and has spawned a backlash of criticisms of family therapy models based on therapeutic strategy. The development of social construction and narrative models that are more collaborative, nondirective, and "not knowing" in their approach is partly a reaction against the strategic models. (See Chapter 6 for a review of social construction and narrative models.)

Despite favorable appraisals of the clinical utility of strategic family therapy, the outcome research is weak (Anderson, 1986). Most frequently, supportive data is of a single-case or descriptive nature. Palazzoli's work is criticized, in particular, because of lack of clarity about population, hypothesis, treatment, and results (Anderson, 1986). Other concerns are the absence of proper scientific inquiry and sound methodological research. Another ethical concern is that the Milan group's negative labeling of families as playing "games" raises questions about the group's lack of neutrality and respect for families.

Strategic Therapy and Managed Behavioral Health Care

Strategic models are directive, brief, and action oriented. From the inception of the MRI brief therapy approach in 1967, strategic therapists have believed that clients with a variety of difficulties could be successfully treated in 10 to 14 sessions. In this regard, strategic models are forerunners of the current emphasis on time-limited therapies. The goal-directed and interventionist approaches used in the therapies are also good matches for managed care.

Interventions used in the strategic models are extremely pragmatic, focusing practitioners on the quick resolution of presenting problems. The brevity and practical emphasis on change promises to be a cost-effective alternative for work in today's practice settings. The Milan team's intermittent work of seeing families only once a month is also cost effective and consistent with ideas promoted in managed care of spacing sessions for the purpose of allowing longer contact between therapists and clients and at the same time promoting cost savings.

The use of teams that has been emphasized in strategic therapies, however, is not a cost-effective method and will likely need to be modified for use in managed behavioral health care settings. Even so, some of the ideas, such as hypothesizing, strategizing, and receiving supervision of one's work, may be preserved. For example, many managed care companies, in their quest to develop accountability, are mandating that practitioners receive clinical supervision. The best aspect of the team concept may be utilized through live supervision models.

Case Example[1]

Identifying Information

Name: Kay Smith

Address: 212 S. Uter, Ft. Worth TX 78888, phone 555-2323

Family members living at home: Joe Smith, 42, father, 14 years of education, sales manager, good health; Mary Smith, 38, mother, 16 years of education, unemployed, good health; Billy Smith, 18, brother, 13 years of education, student, good health; Kay Smith, 14, client, 8 years of education, student, health guarded

Religious affiliation: Protestant

Family income: $56,000

Presenting problem: Kay has developed eating problems over the last year. Her parents report that they became aware of the seriousness of the problem about six months ago when Kay started losing weight. She was hospitalized for two months, but there was no change in her condition. She has been out of the hospital for five weeks. About three weeks ago, Kay's parents became aware that she was eating large amounts of food, then forcing herself to vomit. Reportedly, this happens three to four

---

[1] Presented by Janet Sonier at the University of Texas at Arlington, School of Social Work, Summer 1991.

times a day. They consulted with their physician, who referred them to a hospital with a treatment program for eating disorders. Kay was discharged because the treatment program was not effective; her parents wished to seek other help. She is holding her weight at the present time. Her condition is not currently life threatening, but without appropriate interventions this status could change. Kay's parents were warned to seek hospitalization if her weight began to drop. During hospitalization, Kay was involved in individual and group therapy and family therapy with her parents and brother. Antidepressants and minor tranquilizers were tried and discontinued when they proved ineffective. Since her discharge, the family has consulted with various mental health/eating disorder specialists, but outpatient treatment has been ineffective.

Related problems: Mrs. Smith is very concerned over Kay's, eating and weight loss. She sees this problem as a reflection of her parenting skills. For Kay, problems with her parents have served to increase her anxiety level. Mr. Smith is angry about Kay's problems, as they have interfered with his work. He realizes there is a problem but has trouble understanding why Kay has an eating disorder. Billy is concerned over Kay's health.

Mr. and Mrs. Smith report that Kay's illness has caused a strain on their marriage and financial situation. Mr. Smith believes that Kay would not have this problem if her mother had handled her "correctly." He is unable to say what "correctly" would be. Mr. and Mrs. Smith both report that the problem has caused a strain in their relationship and with Mrs. Smith's parents (Tom and Carla Jones). Mrs. Smith's parents are reported to interfere occasionally in the Smith's family matters. The in-laws generally focus on how ineffective the Smiths are as parents.

Family communication is a problem. The parents have trouble communicating with each other and with the children. Kay denies that her behavior is a problem, and the parents are afraid to confront her about it. Kay does not appear motivated to change or to control her eating disorder. Kay does appear to receive secondary gains from her bulimia in the form of increased attention and control in the family. Kay has excellent family support; the parents are concerned and state that they will do anything to help, although the father does appear detached from the situation. He holds Mrs. Smith responsible for allowing "things to get out of hand." Mrs. Smith is rather passive and overwhelmed by the present situation.

Intervention and Treatment Plan

SESSION 1
The presenting problem and family dynamics are assessed. For homework, the parents were assigned to be responsible for making Kay eat the proper foods and to monitor her purging. This is an attempt to put the parents in charge of Kay. The therapist believes that Kay has taken away power and control from her parents with her eating problem. This intervention is designed to return control to the parents and unite them in helping Kay.

SESSION 2
The family reports no improvement in Kay's eating disorder, and the parents are frustrated with their inability to control the problem. The problem with Mrs. Smith's

parents (Tom and Carla Jones) is worse. The Joneses call and attempt to bribe Kay into "eating right"; meanwhile, they berate the Smiths as incompetent parents.

During the session, a call is made to the Joneses. Before the telephone call, the Smiths are given instructions about what to tell the grandparents. Mrs. Smith is to tell her parents that she loves them and is sorry for anything she has done to hurt their feelings or to cause them pain. Mr. Smith is to do the same. They are instructed to tell the Joneses that they (the Smiths) are ineffective parents and do not know what to do about solving Kay's eating problems. They are to ask the grandparents if they could spend a week with the Smiths. The Smiths agree to let the grandparents have complete control over Kay's bulimia and general behavior.

The Smiths are to request that the grandparents teach them how to be effective parents. Billy eagerly agrees to let the grandparents have control of his behavior. The Smiths agree that the grandparents will not be allowed to do anything but discipline the children around the house. If the grandparents get involved in other activities, the Smiths are to tell them that their only responsibilities are the children's behavior and teaching the Smiths parenting skills.

The grandparents readily agree to the project. The therapist also outlines the procedure with the grandparents. The Smiths are to report on progress during the week at the next session. It is requested that the grandparents also come for the next session.

Strategic therapy uses any resources available to the therapist and often involves extended family members. With involvement of the grandparents, several things are being accomplished. First, the natural hierarchy including the extending family is reestablished. The grandparents are put in the position of experts in child care.

The parents are positioned as students of the parents and temporarily relieved of the continued stress of dealing with the eating disorder. It is unlikely that Kay will completely stop her behavior, but she may reduce it. The inability of the grandparents to control the problem will raise their opinions of the Smiths as parents. This realization will align the parents and grandparents in control positions while diminishing Kay's control of her behavior.

SESSION 3

Present are the Smith family and the grandparents, the Joneses. The grandparents discuss the frustration they feel because they are unable to stop Kay's eating problems. They discuss how overwhelmed and confused they are about the problem and the many activities that concern the children. The grandparents report that they are not sure how the Smiths manage as well as they do.

Homework for the next week is for the family to arrange so that one of the members is constantly with Kay. Mr. Smith's parents are called during the session and agree to take shifts with Kay. The family is instructed that at no time is Kay to be alone. Everyone is assigned shifts that fit around their schedules. Shifts are assigned around the clock. Someone is to accompany her to the bathroom and to stay in the room while she showers. Kay can leave the house only in the company of one of the relatives. If she wishes to go somewhere with friends, a family member is also required to go. Kay is to eat only nutritional food, only at the times when the family is eating, and only in normal quantities. This rule is to be enforced if she goes out with friends or family. The family is to report on the results of the assignment during the next session. Mr. Smith's parents are encouraged to attend the next session.

This strategy is another step toward placing the adults in control, while reducing Kay's control. By involving both sets of grandparents, the competition that might occur between them has been decreased. Kay's control continues to be diminished and has started to limit her behavior in the outside world.

SESSION 4

In attendance are the Smith family and both sets of grandparents. They report that the bulimia is still a problem but that Kay's purging has dropped to only one or two times a week. Kay complains that she has no time to herself and is never alone. It is explained to Kay that she has a very serious, life-threatening eating disorder. Because she has no control over the problem, we have given her some help. Her family loves her very much and wants to do anything they can to help her. They are willing to give up their time and rearrange their schedules to help her with her problem.

For the next week, the family is again put in charge of Kay's eating patterns. As there is a reduction in the incidence of behaviors associated with bulimia, the around-the-clock vigil will be reduced. The family is assigned to be with Kay during meals to encourage her to continue eating in a more normal manner. They are to stay with her for three hours after meals. The grandparents agreed that they can be called in to assist if needed by the parents. Otherwise, the Smiths feel that they can manage the task. By now the hierarchy of the adults has been established. Kay's self-destructive behavior has been reduced and is expected to continue to decline. Although Kay is allowed more freedom, she is still subject to parental control.

SESSION 5

The Smiths report fewer problems with Kay's eating disorder during the recent week. She still is not gaining weight, but her eating has become more normal and the parents are unaware of any purging. Kay reports that she purged two times during the last week.

For the next week, the family is instructed to use the Gandhi technique. If during the next week Kay resorts to bulimic behavioral patterns, the family must stay home for 24 hours. This means that during this 24-hour period, Mr. Smith will not go to work or leave the house. Mrs. Smith will not leave the house, either; any engagements will have to be canceled. If something is needed that cannot wait, the family can call the grandparents or neighbors; otherwise, the phone will not be used. Billy and Kay will also not be able to leave the house. All outside activities will be suspended for the 24-hour period if Kay demonstrates bulimic behavior.

Transcript

Kay has been in a psychiatric hospital for two months for bulimia nervosa. Her status is not life threatening at the present time. To date there has been no progress in treatment. This is the first session in family therapy.

THERAPIST:	[to family] I'm glad you could come today. Dr. Blankenship [Kay's physician] gave me a little background information when he made the referral, but I'd like to get to know you better. Mr. Smith, can you tell me a little about your family. This will help me understand what's going on.
FRANK:	Well, Kay just got out of the hospital a little over a month ago. She was in there for two months. It didn't seem to help. Dr. Blankenship sent us here. We've gone to groups and meetings. Seen everyone and done everything, and nothing has worked!
THERAPIST:	[to Kay] Kay, if I asked your mother why your family was here, what would she say?
KAY:	I don't know. [twists in chair, no eye contact]
THERAPIST:	Well, just try to imagine. [silence to the point of discomfort]
KAY:	I guess she would say that I'm sick. [silence] I guess she would tell you that I'm not eating like I should.
THERAPIST:	Kay, what is it about your eating has everyone so upset?
FRANK:	Kay eats a bunch of food and then throws it up! I can't believe it! She cleans out the icebox, and then just vomits it up!
THERAPIST:	[to Frank] I know you want to help Kay, but it's very important that Kay answer for herself. [to Kay] What is it about your eating that has everyone so upset?
KAY:	Like he said . . . [says this fast and softly]
THERAPIST:	I'm sorry, I didn't understand.
KAY:	[angry] They say I'm bulimic. [pause] I eat and then throw up sometimes. [pause] I'm overweight and . . . it's just to lose a few pounds. I don't understand why everyone is so upset.
THERAPIST:	[to Kay] How long has this been going on?
FRANK:	About six months. Heaven only knows how long before her mother noticed it!
THERAPIST:	[to Frank] Mr. Smith, I'd really like Kay to answer for herself. [to Kay] How long has this been going on?
KAY:	I don't know. [silence] I guess I started about a year ago, but it was just once in awhile when I really pigged out. I guess it got worse about seven or eight months ago.
THERAPIST:	How much weight have you lost?
KAY:	[softly] About 20 pounds.
THERAPIST:	Excuse me?
KAY:	[louder] About 20 pounds.
THERAPIST:	[to Mary] Mrs. Smith, do the children's grandparents live close by?
MARY:	My parents live nearby; we see them pretty often. Frank's parents aren't close. We don't see them as often.
THERAPIST:	How do you get along?
MARY:	We got along pretty well until all of this. They don't understand why we're having this problem. They keep saying all we

	have to do is to make her eat. [tearful] They don't understand. [pause] It's not that easy. I've tried; I don't know what I've done wrong.
THERAPIST:	[to Mary] Maybe we need to put the grandparents in charge if they feel like they could do the job better. I don't know about their doing any better. I see parents here who love their daughter and want to help her.
FRANK:	Kay has the problem—she's the one we need to talk about. We've tried everything we can think of to help her, but she just won't eat right. I don't know what to do about her. We give her everything she could want. I don't know what to do with her. I'm a busy man and don't have time for this. I don't understand why she just won't do what she is supposed to do.
THERAPIST:	[to Mary] Mrs. Smith, what kinds of things does Kay like to do?
MARY:	Regular girl things. I try not to interfere with her activities. She's always going somewhere with friends. She's always gone.
THERAPIST:	[to Mary] What are her friends like?
MARY:	Well, I guess I really don't know. They don't come over often. They always have someplace to go and are in a hurry.
THERAPIST:	[to Frank] Mr. Smith, what type of work do you do?
FRANK:	[frustrated] I don't see how this will help. Why are you asking about me? Kay is the one having trouble. I shouldn't even be here. I need to be at work.
THERAPIST:	[to Frank] I can understand that it's hard for you to take time off to come in for family therapy, but it sounds like other things haven't worked. I need to find out what is happening. It's important for me to get to know you as a family. That will help me work with Kay and make things better. Mr. Smith, it sounds like you're really busy, but I know you love Kay and want to help her.
FRANK:	[still frustrated] Yes, I'll do anything. I'm a regional sales manager for Acme. I do a lot of traveling. I guess I'm gone most of the week, but I'm at home almost every weekend.
MARY:	No, you're not!
THERAPIST:	Mrs. Smith, it sounds like you disagree with your husband when he said he was home every weekend.
MARY:	He's in town but not at home! He's always working.
FRANK:	[to Mary] I have to make the money for all this mess. What do you expect me to do, just let the bills pile up?
KAY:	Would you two just stop it! [pause] Is this all you two can do? [catches herself and looks down]
THERAPIST:	Kay, sounds like this is pretty common to you. Is this what happens at home?
KAY:	I guess so.
THERAPIST:	You guess so? [silence]

KAY:	Yes! That's what they do all the time at home. Fuss and argue. It makes me sick. They think it's all my fault. If I got well, then everyone would be happy.
THERAPIST:	I'm sure your parents will be happy when you get well. I know they love you very much or they wouldn't be here. But I don't think that you cause all the problems. I wonder, if you got better what would your parents talk about? [pause] Kay, how do you like school?
KAY:	Pretty good, I guess.
MARY:	She always makes A's, even as sick as she's been. Kay is a good student. She's always been a good girl. I just don't understand what is happening. It doesn't make any sense.
THERAPIST:	Sometimes things get pretty confusing and don't make a lot of sense.
MARY:	I just don't understand. Everything was so nice. Kay is in the Beta Club, and a cheerleader. Everyone likes her; she has so many friends. She's always made excellent grades. No trouble at all and now this. We were so proud. It's awful, just terrible. Who knows what our friends think.
THERAPIST:	[to Mary] Your husband is gone a lot, and Kay is in school. Do you work outside the home?
MARY:	No, I'm a housewife.
THERAPIST:	Well, that's an around-the-clock job. Tell me about your day.
MARY:	Well, I get up and get Kay up and get her stuff together for school. If Frank is home I get him off to work. Then I do the things around the house that need to be done. Not very exciting.
THERAPIST:	But very important. Sounds like you're the hub of the family and do for everyone. [to Kay] Kay, you have a lot of activities. Do you have a boyfriend?
KAY:	Guess I stay busy. I'm in some clubs at school and do volunteer work at the senior citizen center.
THERAPIST:	That's wonderful. Do you date?
KAY:	[looks down] No, I don't date; a bunch of us go out together, but I don't date.
THERAPIST:	I have an idea that I think will help Kay, but I don't know if you'll be able to do it.
FRANK:	We'll do anything if we can get some help with this mess. We've tried everything we could think of and haven't had any luck.
THERAPIST:	I know you really feel you and your family would be willing to do anything, but, I don't know. This is pretty unusual.
FRANK:	[starting to get mad] I said we'll do anything! Nothing you come up with will be as unusual as what's already going on in this family. We're willing to try anything!
THERAPIST:	[to Kay] Kay, are you willing to try something different?

KAY:	I guess so.
FRANK:	What do we need to do?
THERAPIST:	[hesitates] Well, if you're sure you can do it. Mr. and Mrs. Smith, I would like you to be in charge of Kay all week and responsible for what she eats. Also, you will be responsible for seeing to it that she eats only healthy food, no junk food. Also, both of you will be in charge of monitoring her purging and reporting back to me.
FRANK AND MARY:	Well, we can try it.
THERAPIST:	Good. I'll see you all next week and you can tell me how it went.

Summary

This chapter describes the history of strategic family therapy, its theory, and its therapeutic methods. Each mode—MRI brief therapy, Haley/Madanes, and the Milan team—was covered in separate discussions about history, theory, and methods. The consistency of strategic family therapy with social work practice was discussed. The research basis for the strategic family therapy was also summarized. Important critiques of the strategic model were further highlighted. The usefulness of strategic family therapy in today's practice contexts of managed were highlighted. Finally, a case was presented that illustrates the practice of strategic family therapy.

Process Questions

1. Identify the specific strategic techniques used in the manuscript.
2. What is the social worker's role in this type of family therapy?
3. Suggest several possible hypotheses to explain Kay's bulimia.
4. Explain the "Gandhi" technique and how it is used in this case example.

References

ALEXANDER, J., & PARSONS, B. (1973). Short-term behavioral intervention with delinquent families: Impact on family process and recidivism. *Journal of Abnormal Psychology, 81,* 219–225.

ANDERSON, C. M. (1986). The all-too-short trip from positive to negative connotation. *Journal of Marital and Family Therapy, 12,* 351–354.

BATESON, G. (1972). *Steps to an ecology of mind.* New York: Ballentine.

BATESON, G., JACKSON, D., HALEY, J., & WEAKLAND, J. (1956). Toward a theory of schizophrenia. *Behavioral Science, 1,* 251–264.

BERGIN, A. (1971). The evaluation of therapeutic outcomes. In A. Bergin & S. Garfield (Eds.), *Handbook of psychotherapy and behavior change: An empirical analysis.* New York: Wiley.

CECCHIN, G. (1987). Hypothesizing, circularity, and neutrality revisited: An invitation to curiosity. *Family Process, 26,* 404–412.

COOPER, L., & ERICKSON, M. (1954). *Time distortion in hypnosis.* Baltimore: Williams & Wilkins.

DUNCAN, B. L., PARKS, M. B., & ROCK, J. W. (1987). Strategic-behavioral therapy: A practical alternative. *Journal of Psychotherapy, 24*(2), 196–201.

DUNCAN, B. L., & PARKS, M. B. (1988). Integrating individual and systems approaches: Strategic-behavioral therapy. *Journal of Marital and Family Therapy, 14*(2), 151–161.

DUNCAN, B. L., & SOLOVEY, A. D. (1989). Strategic-brief therapy: An insight-oriented approach. *Journal of Marital and Family Therapy, 14*(2), 151–161.

DUNCAN, B. L., & SOLOVEY, A. D. (1992). Ethics and strategic therapy: A proposed ethical direction. *Journal of Marital and Family Therapy, 18*(1), 53–61.

FISCH, R., WEAKLAND, J. H., & SEGAL, L. (1982). *The tactics of change: Doing therapy briefly.* San Francisco: Jossey-Bass

FOLEY, V. D. (1989). Family therapy. In R. J. Corsini & D. Wedding (Eds.), *Current psychotherapies* (4th ed.; pp. 447–490). Itasca, IL: Peacock.

GARRIGAN, J. J., & BAMBRICK, A. F. (1975). Short-term family therapy with emotionally disturbed children. *Journal of Marriage and Family Counseling, 1,* 379–385.

GARRIGAN, J. J., & BAMBRICK, A. F. (1977). Family therapy for disturbed children: Some experimental results in special education. *Journal of Marriage and Family Counseling, 3,* 83–93.

GARRIGAN, J. J., & BAMBRICK, A. F. (1979). New findings in research on go-between process. *International Journal of Family Therapy, 1,* 76–85.

GOLDENBERG, I., & GOLDENBERG, H. (1991). *Family therapy: An overview.* Monterey, CA: Brooks/Cole.

HALEY, J. (1976). *Problem solving therapy: New strategies for effective family therapy.* San Francisco: Jossey-Bass.

HALEY, J. (1980). *Leaving home.* New York: McGraw-Hill.

HALEY, J. (1984). Marriage or family therapy. *American Journal of Family Therapy, 12*(2), 3–14.

KEENEY, B. P. (1983). *Aesthetics of change.* New York: Guilford.

LANGSLEY, D. G., FAIRBAIRN, R. H., & DEYOUNG, C. D. (1968). Adolescence and family crisis. *Canadian Psychiatric Association Journal, 13,* 125–133.

LEVANT, R. (1984). *Family therapy: A comprehensive overview.* Englewood Cliffs, NJ: Prentice Hall.

LUEPNITZ, D. A. (1988). *The family interpreted: Psychoanalysis, feminism, and family therapy.* New York: Basic Books.

MADANES, C. (1981). *Strategic family therapy.* San Francisco: Jossey-Bass.

MADANES, C. (1984). *Behind the one-way mirror: Advances in the practice of strategic therapy.* San Francisco: Jossey-Bass.

MADANES, C. (1991). Strategic family therapy. In A. Gurman & D. Kniskern (Eds.), *Handbook of family therapy* (Vol. II). New York: Brunner/Mazel.

MADANES, C., & HALEY, J. (1977). Dimensions of family therapy. *Journal of Nervous and Mental Diseases, 165*(2): 88–98.

MICHELSON, L., & ASHCHER, L. M. (1984). Paradoxical intention in the treatment of agoraphobia and other anxiety disorders. *Journal of Behavioral Therapy and Experimental Psychiatry, 15*(3), 215–220.

NELSON, F. S., FLEURIDAS, C., & ROSENTHAL, D. M. (1986). The evolution of circular questions in training family therapists. *Journal of Marital and Family Therapy, 12*(2), 113–127.

NUGENT, W. R. (1989a). Evidence concerning the causal effects of an Ericksonian hypnotic intervention. In S. R. Lankton (Ed.), *Ericksonian hypnosis: Application, preparation and research* (pp. 35–53). New York: Brunner/Mazel.

NUGENT, W. R. (1989b). A multiple baseline investigation of an Ericksonian hypnotic approach. In S. R. Lankton (Ed.), *Ericksonian hypnosis: Application, preparation and research* (pp. 69–84). New York: Brunner/Mazel.

O'CONNOR, J., & LA SALA, M. (1988). Unified services for children and adolescents. *Journal of Strategic and Systemic Therapies, 7*(3), 53–66.

PIERCY, F., & SPRENKLE, D. (1986). *Family therapy sourcebook.* New York: Guilford.

RAY, W. (1996). MRI Brief Therapy. Workshop presented at the American Association for Marriage and Family Therapy (AAMFT) 54th Annual Conference, The Value of Family Therapy, October 17–20, Toronto, Canada.

SELVINI-PALAZZOLI, M. (1986). Towards a general model of psychotic family games. *Journal of Marital and Family Therapy, 12*(4), 339–349.

SELVINI-PALAZZOLI, M., BOSCOLO, L., CECCHIN, F. G., & PRATA, G. (1978). *Paradox and counter paradox.* New York: Jason Aronson.

SELVINI-PALAZZOLI, M. S., BOSCOLO, L., CECCHIN, G., & PRATA, G. (1980). A ritualized prescription in family therapy: Odd days and even days. *Journal of Marriage and Family Counseling, 4*(3), 3–9.

SHILSON, E. A. (1991). Strategic therapy. In A. Horne & L. Passmore (Eds.), *Family counseling and therapy* (2nd ed. Chap 6). Itasca, IL: Peacock.

STANTON, M. D. (1981). Strategic approaches to family therapy. In A. S. Gurman & D. P. Kniskern (Eds.), *Handbook of family therapy* (Vol. II). New York: Brunner/Mazel.

STANTON, M., & TODD, T. (1979). Structural family therapy with drug addicts. In E. Kaufman & P. Kaufman (Eds.), *The family therapy of drug and alcohol abuse.* New York: Gardner Press.

STANTON, M. D., TODD, T. C., HEARD, D. B., KIRSCHNER, S., KLEIMAN, J. I., MOWATT, D. T., RILEY, P., SCOTT, S. M., & VAN DEUSEN, J. M. (1978). Heroin addiction as a family phenomenon: A new conceptual model. *American Journal of Drug and Alcohol Abuse, 5,* 125–150.

TOMM, K. (1984a). One perspective on the Milan systemic approach: Part I. *Journal of Marriage and Family Therapy, 10,* 253–271.

TOMM, K. (1984b). One perspective on the Milan systemic approach: Part II. *Journal of Marriage and Family Therapy, 10,* 113–125.

WATZLAWICK, P. (1976). *How real is real?* New York: Random House.

WEAKLAND, J., FISCH, R., WATZLAWICK, P., & BODIN, A. M. (1974). Brief therapy: Focused problem resolution. *Family Process, 13,* 141–168.

WEAKLAND, J., & FISCH, R. (1992). Brief therapy: MRI style. In S. H. Budman, M. F. Hoyt, & S. Friedman (Eds.), *The first session in brief therapy* (pp. 306–323). New York: Guilford.

WILCOXON, S. A., & FENELL, D. (1986). Linear and paradoxical letters to the non-attending spouse: A comparison of engagement rates. *Journal of Marital and Family Therapy, 12,* 191–193.

WILNER, R. (1988). In defense of strategic therapy. *Contemporary Family Therapy—An International Journal, 10*(3), 169–182.

CHAPTER FOUR

Catheleen Jordan, Ph.D.
University of Texas at Arlington

Norman H. Cobb, Ph.D.
University of Texas at Arlington

Cynthia Franklin, Ph.D.
University of Texas at Austin

Behavioral and Cognitive-Behavioral Family Therapy

Behavioral family treatment (BFT) and cognitive-behavioral family treatment (C-BFT) are based on social learning theory principles, including respondent and operant conditioning, modeling, reciprocal determinism, and expectancy of reinforcement. Family members' interactions with each other and with the environment are believed to be most important in describing family functioning, though intrapersonal factors, such as depression, may place limits on an individual's performance. As behavioral models were translated into family therapy practice, they also took on aspects of systems theory, in that the mutually reinforcing influences of different family members' behavior are understood to follow a reciprocal pattern of behavior that is interactional and repetitive. In fact, in some models, such as the functional family therapy model discussed in this chapter, the behavior patterns are also viewed as serving a particular function or purpose for the family system. The techniques of cognitive-behavioral family treatment focus on helping families learn new skills, modify surfeits or deficits in functioning, and reframe or alter cognitive perceptions. This approach is action oriented rather than insight oriented. Many of the techniques to be described have been integrated into other uniquely social work approaches, such as family psychoeducation and family preservation, described in Chapters 7 and 8.

The behavioral and cognitive approach is time limited (brief) and based on empirical research supporting its efficacy and effectiveness with various problems and populations, thus making it a compatible approach in today's managed care environment. This chapter reviews the history of cognitive-behavioral family therapy, followed by a review of the theory, methods, research, values, compatibility with managed care, and a case example.

History

Important contributors to the development of cognitive-behavioral family theory and treatment are I. Pavlov, B. F. Skinner, Joseph Wolpe, Albert Bandura, Arnold Lazarus, Albert Ellis, and Aaron Beck. Skinner (1974) identified the role of reinforcement and punishment in operant conditioning for determining behavior. Wolpe (1958) specified respondent conditioning as key to understanding and changing behavior. Bandura's social learning theory (1977) introduced the role of covert behaviors and vicarious learning; Lazarus (1981) contributed his multimodal assessment model. Irrational or negative thinking was the central ingredient of cognitive-behavioral therapy for Ellis (1970) and Beck (1976).

In social work, Bruce Thyer's 1989 book on behavioral family therapy brought together behavioral social workers including Eileen Gambrill (1983, 1997) (social work practice), Richard Polster and Richard Dangel (1989) (behavioral parent training), and Sheldon Rose (1989) (behavioral group therapy). Edwin Thomas's contributions (1977) to behavioral methods in social work were groundbreaking, followed by Don Granvold in cognitive behavioral methods (1994) and Richard Stuart on behavioral marital therapy (1980). Other important contributors to BFT include Neil Jacobson and Gail Margolin (1979) (marital therapy), James Alexander and Bruce Parsons (1982) (functional family therapy), I. R. Falloon (1988a) (family psychoeducation), and Robert Liberman (1970) (imitative learning in families).

Theoretical Basis for the Practice Model

Behavioral family therapy developed out of behavioral theory and social learning theory. As a result, behavioral family therapists are committed to the scientific method and to measurement and evaluation. This treatment method uses social learning theory and the five behavioral principles to help families achieve their goals. Social learning theory (Bandura, 1977) explores the relationship between behavior (both overt and covert) and the environment. Operant conditioning describes how individuals learn from environmental consequences. Respondent conditioning describes how individuals learn when environmental cues are associated with other things in an individual's world, such as new behaviors or neutral objects. Additionally, individuals learn vicariously by observing how others behave and the consequences of their behavior.

Major Assumptions

The assumptions of behavioral family therapy and cognitive-behavioral family therapy relate to how behavior is acquired and maintained, and, therefore, how it can be treated in the natural or therapeutic context. Both treatment methods are focused on the present and on interpersonal environments that maintain behavioral patterns. Behavior is assumed to be learned, and unconscious processes are eschewed. Likewise, problematic behavior is learned and maintained by controlling conditions in the environment. Contemporary behaviorists also acknowledge the role of genetic predisposition as it relates to developmental stages. Because maladaptive behavior is learned, it can be modified, unlearned, or replaced by new adaptive behavior.

Therapeutic procedures are action oriented rather than relying on clinical insights. Behavioral family therapy and cognitive-behavioral family therapy both emphasize a scientific approach, which makes assessment strategies and interventions rather easily manualized and replicated. They frequently contain validated, structured measurement and evaluation methods. Assessment is considered an ongoing process monitored throughout the treatment phase, so treatment can be altered to increase its effectiveness. The BFT and C-BFT therapist is more directive than insight-oriented therapists. The therapist is seen as teacher and trainer, with a responsibility to design a treatment program that will motivate the family to change. Rose (1977) identified the following assumptions of the behavioral model:

> Cognition is recognized as a consequence of behavior; problems and treatments are believed to be multidimensional; problems should be viewed operationally; internal and external events are equally important; anything worth doing is worth evaluating; generalization and maintenance of change, not change itself, is the focus of treatment; maximum involvement of the client in everything that happens to him or her is encouraged; the therapeutic relationship with the client must happen first if change is going to occur. (p. 19)

Key Constructs

Key principles are in two categories: behavioral principles and tenets of social learning theory. In this section, the five behavioral principles are followed by four key elements in social learning. In the behavioral and cognitive-behavioral perspective, overt and covert behaviors are viewed as learned according to overlapping or interacting components.

BEHAVIORAL PRINCIPLES

Positive reinforcement is a procedure or mechanism that tends to increase the future rate of a behavior because the behavior has been followed by a positive stimulus (a positive event, reward, desirable object, or other positive consequence). For example, when a spouse gives flowers, and the partner responds to the gift in a positive way, the rate of "flower giving" will most likely go up. Positive reinforcement is said to occur if the rate actually increases. The flower giver's behavior has been rewarded.

Punishment operates in a similar way. For example, instead of the positive response to flowers, the partner could have responded negatively. The partner might have been a radical conservationist and said, "I do not know why an adult would kill a living organism to give it as a sacrificial symbol of affection!" The rate of flower giving would most likely decrease. The flower giver's behavior has been punished.

Operant extinction is a procedure or mechanism in which a previously reinforced behavior is no longer followed by the reinforcer. Extinction is a common and effective response to stop children from throwing tantrums. A tantruming child behaves to get reinforcers or attention, whether positive or negative. A parent may institute extinction by no longer responding to the child in a characteristic way. For example, the parent may discontinue a practice of giving in to a request for candy at the grocery store or responding to the child's calls for parental attention at bedtime even though the parent knows that the child is fed, clean, and safe. Typically when a parent first uses extinction, the child's behavior escalates in an attempt to elicit a response from the parent. If the parent gives in, the child is reinforced for even worse behavior. If the parent continues with extinction, the behavior begins to decline in frequency, and extinction has occurred.

Response cost focuses on the removal of a positive reinforcer following the occurrence of a problem behavior. Parents have used this method for years and called it "grounding." For example, an adolescent with a new driver's license takes a friend for a drive in the family car. When the adolescent returns an hour past the agreed time, the parent takes away the car keys or privileges to use the family vehicle. The grounding, or removal of the positive reinforcer, follows the principle of response cost. The rate of future late arrivals is expected to decline.

Negative reinforcement is surprisingly common in human life, but is frequently misunderstood and confused with punishment. The term *reinforcement* refers to an increase in the desired behavior (just the opposite of punishment). In punishment, a negative act or event follows a behavior; however, in negative reinforcement, a negative or aversive condition is terminated. For example, we learn to terminate the darkness of a room by turning on the light. As we develop the habit of turning on the light (even when sufficient light exists in the room), negative reinforcement accounts for the learning. A further example is the termination of a child's whining in the grocery store by parental reinforcement with candy. The child has been positively reinforced and will likely continue to whine for candy. The parent has been negatively reinforced; that is, she will likely terminate the child's whining (an aversive stimuli) by giving candy.

SOCIAL LEARNING PRINCIPLES

Behavioral theorists such as Bandura became interested in the reality we often learn from watching others act or from hearing or reading about their actions. The dilemma Bandura faced was the ability of persons to reenact the behavior long after seeing the modeled actions. In essence, the behavior was learned without being actually reinforced; therefore, cognitive mediation played a considerable role in the learning of behavior. These observations of vicarious learning were molded into what is now termed social learning theory.

Bandura developed four key principles that have significant implications for family therapy. The first, *expectancy of reinforcement*, refers to the association of reinforcement with an action. A father may offer a hug to a child because he associates the hug with a warm affirmation. The learned expectancy—the relationship between the behavior and the consequence—developed according to the classical conditioning paradigm that would have made Pavlov proud. In reality, many behaviors are learned through classical conditioning; however, the more typical examples are fears and phobias.

As people build a set of expectancies of reinforcement, they gain an increased sense of *self-efficacy.* This second principle is the degree to which people believe or expect they can accomplish various tasks. The expectations may derive from previous successful actions, vicarious experiences (seeing others perform the task), persuasion from others, or sheer emotional commitment to making changes in the family. In therapy, family members can be involved in change efforts if they believe they have power to make real differences or hope that change will help the situation.

The third social learning component, *reciprocal determinism,* accounts for the way people influence their environment and, in turn, are affected by it. For example, a woman makes a statement to her partner and watches for reactions to her words. The partner hears the information, processes the message according to learned rules or perceptions, and replies to the message. The woman, in turn, is affected by her partner's response, and she processes the message and responds. Through this interactive exchange, each person affects the environment and is affected by it.

Modeling is at the core of social learning. People learn how to behave by watching others. They see others' actions and the consequences of the behavior. Through cognitive mediation, they reproduce images of the event and can rehearse the behavior. Later, they reproduce the behavior toward someone else and expect to receive the same or similar reinforcer. Television plays a significant role in modeling behavior. Children who watch war movies tend to be more aggressive than those who prefer nature shows. Family members learn how to treat each other because vivid or salient TV scenes display "the way life is supposed to be."

Therapeutic Methods

The behavioral family therapy and cognitive-behavioral family therapy models are perhaps the most operationalized of the family therapy approaches because of their focus on empirical validation. This section reviews cognitive-behavioral family therapy assessment, behavior change procedures, and behavior change techniques.

Assessment Techniques

Jordan and Franklin (1995) reviewed assessment from a behavioral perspective. In empirically based assessment, the assumption is that judgments are based on observation and measurement rather than solely on social worker intuition. Clinical judgment is also important but requires substantiation by empirical observations and documentation. For example, clinician judgments are supported by information gathered by the client who has been trained to monitor and collect valid information.

Bloom and Fischer (1982) described the scientist-practitioner model as a problem-solving experiment in which the client is viewed objectively, case activity is monitored and evaluated using single-subject design or other methods, and clinicians continually monitor the empirical literature and choose interventions based on empirical support. The cognitive-behavioral family therapy model assumes that the clinician is familiar with the empirical literature supporting various treatment modalities.

Gambrill (1997) lists the characteristics of contextual assessment from the behavioral perspective:

> Individually tailored assessment (each person, group, family, organization, or community is viewed as unique); a preference for testing inferences; a focus on the clients' assets rather than their deficiencies; a focus on the present; an emphasis on contingencies on interrelated system levels; a preference for observation (seeing for yourself); a clear description of problems and desired outcomes; a clear description of assessment methods; the use of valid assessment methods; a close relationship between assessment and intervention. (pp. 212–213)

In the context of collecting information for assessment, problems are prioritized and stated in measurable terms. This type of concrete behavioral definition of problems and their interventions is consistent with the way clinicians are expected to specify treatment plans in managed care settings. For example, depression would be broken down into components that more clearly indicate how it affects people's lives and what is needed to help people function more effectively. Clinicians would behaviorally describe the client's problem with depression in ways such as "stays in bed three days a week and does not go to work, cries five times a day, sleeps only two hours a night." These particular problems are very specific and objective and can be easily monitored to make sure the client is improving. For example, it is easy to see whether the client's sleep is increasing or he or she starts working every day.

The clinician's role in C-BFT is as teacher and facilitator of change (Falloon & Liberman, 1983). Once the initial assessment is completed, the clinician reviews the findings with the client; client and clinician together set the therapeutic goals. Assessment and intervention are intimately linked, and the therapeutic goals are well defined and specific before the initiation of any intervention.

Change Techniques

A variety of specific interventions are clustered under the category of behavioral and cognitive-behavioral family therapy. Rarely does the literature report on one technique with one family. Family therapy is usually a cluster of components designed to effect change in a particular family. The following sections describe some of the frequently used approaches, but the "magic" of the model evolves from the clinician who combines truly effective methods to fit the particular needs of a specific family.

BEHAVIORAL CONTRACTING

Various methods are used in the context of parent training, but they can also be used with the entire family. Behavioral contracting is an agreement that specifies the behavior to be performed and the consequences. For generations, parents have successfully negotiated with children for specific behaviors and rewards. Similarly, adult partners may negotiate mutually acceptable behaviors. Several steps, however, are crucial to the process. In parent-child situations, for example, parents should limit the number of behaviors to be contracted at any one time. Next, they need to be sure their children have the ability to perform the behaviors. If children do not have the necessary skills, parents must be prepared to teach them. Parents also should anticipate the difficulties the child will have. For example, some parents negotiate for lawn mowing, but they sometimes underestimate the problems with fueling and starting the mower. Next, parents should clearly identify or negotiate the rewards and penalties. All participants in the contract should respect individual preferences for reward; what is a reward to one person may not be so to another. A next and crucial step is to identify the person who will help keep track of the behavior and give rewards and penalties. Unfortunately, many contracts are short-circuited, because the rewards are not delivered in the correct amount, not delivered in a reasonable time, or never delivered. Frequently, these and other problems can be headed off by writing down the details of the contract and posting it in a prominent place. Finally, the contract should be tried out, evaluated for effectiveness, and altered when necessary.

Parents may use less formal contracts with younger children. Parents determine a behavior that they want to occur more often. They begin to give the child reinforcers, such as words of encouragement, pats on the shoulder, opportunities, food, or any of a million other things the child likes. When the consequence is desirable to the child, the child will usually respond again and again. The professional literature documents the extreme effectiveness of positive reinforcement. In the private lives of families, however, parents can point to the living truth of behaviors that were reinforced and continue, even such socially unattractive behaviors as tantrums.

Finally, couples can use behavioral contracting to negotiate various behavioral exchanges. Many modern couples negotiate housekeeping chores on the basis of three strategies: assigning jobs based on an individual's personal expertise or interest (cooks cook and gardeners garden), assigning some jobs on the basis of time and availability ("you take and I'll pick up"), and assigning less-than-rewarding jobs (cleaning the toilet and mowing the lawn) on an equal basis. In all the examples, couples assume and assign behaviors and rewards. The expert cook is assumed to gain self-reinforcement and family praise from great meals. The sharing of some chores signals negative reinforcement (one spouse is partially freed from a responsibility if he or she does half the task). Finally, couples can agree to reinforce themselves positively by cleaning the house in exchange for the mutual reward of a special dinner, back rub, movie, or quiet time at home (in a clean house).

COGNITIVE RESTRUCTURING

Because thinking and behaving are intimately related, rational and irrational beliefs, perceptions, and expectations affect how people behave. Satir (1972) described how families name children in ways that connote personality characteristics or expectations for behavior. The daughter named Mary, after the beloved "Grandma," will be treated differently from her brother, who was named after the infamous boxer Mike Tyson.

Cognitive restructuring begins when people accept the notion that their beliefs and thoughts affect their behavior. Next, clients need to recognize that their beliefs and assumptions are creating some aspect of the problem. For example, the son's name affects how family members treat him or expect him to act. Furthermore, they look for confirming information to validate their beliefs about him. In response, he behaves to "do what he is supposed to do," but unfortunately, his behavior is disruptive or too aggressive.

After family members have accepted the possibility that their beliefs affect their actions and contribute to the problem, they can identify when and where the problem occurs. They may then be given words, phrases, suggestions, or images that substitute for the troublesome beliefs. For example, the family might discuss the image of boxers as strong but gentle giants, such as George Foreman. Consider the persona of Tyson a few years before his legal battles. Perhaps Mike should be referred to as "Mike, our gentle giant." The family members could redirect their attention to Mike's interests in basketball, music, or history. Who is named Mike in these fields, and what new images are helpful?

Finally, clinicians may support family members for making significant efforts to change a problem in their world. They can be encouraged to examine other areas of beliefs and assumptions to see what changes can be made.

THOUGHT STOPPING

A remarkably simple and effective tool to control thoughts goes by the unimaginative name of thought stopping. People frequently think about events, images, or self-directed phrases that are negative and destructive. Negative images or critical thoughts influence how people think about themselves. Saying "I'm a fraud" or "I can't do statistics" is very damaging and leads to the familiar self-fulfilling prophecy. Marks (1973) validated this technique with obsessive-compulsive patients. He taught them to reduce their obsessive thoughts by forcefully saying "stop" in their minds. Then clients can switch thoughts to images or words that are more attractive and valid. For example, the jealous husband who feared that his wife would have an affair, was told to "yell 'Stop' in your mind" and switch his thoughts to images of him and his wife sharing a tender moment.

ANGER CONTROL

Deschner (1984) formulated a strategy to help couples handle potentially violent interactions. The 10-week group intervention has considerable applicability to all family members. Parents can use it to teach their children anger control. The first sessions begin with information about the biological mechanisms of anger. Next, members are made aware of how anger can escalate through the reciprocal interactions of family members. The third step is getting family members to agree to a method for handling angry interactions. Specifically, family members must agree to recognize and acknowledge when disagreements are escalating into anger. Next, they must agree to give each other an acceptable signal that indicates "I am getting too angry to continue this discussion, and I need to take a break and cool off." After the signal is given, the discussion stops for an hour or so while things cool, but the family must agree to come back together and negotiate a time to discuss and resolve the problem. If things escalate again, the time-out period is reinstituted.

The method is educational in focus and requires family members to agree to new rules about interpersonal relationships. The behavioral principles are active at every turn. The signal terminates the aversiveness of the argument, and family members are reinforced by a sense of control. The previous pay-off for losing control is extinguished. All participants (and observers) gain a new perspective on family members' willingness to solve family problems.

AVERSIVE CONSEQUENCES

Aversive control or punishment continues to be a hot topic for client families. Using physical punishment with children appears to work because children usually stop what they are doing to focus their attention on the part of the body that hurts. Such redirecting of attention could be better served in a more humane way. For example, the child who wants to touch the hot stove can be redirected into another room that contains the child's favorite doll, car, food, TV, playmate, pet, or any other object that appeals to that child.

A child management method such as time-out is much more effective, and it avoids the serious side effects of punishment. These potentially negative side effects include adults' modeling the use of violent means to get what they want, children's avoidance of the punisher, and the adult's loss of opportunity to teach something positive. Any delay in the punishment runs the risk of punishing the wrong behavior. As a final note, stepparents' use of physical punishment is very risky. As the child does not have a strong emotional bond with the adult stepparent, the child experiences physical punishment as being hit by a stranger, and worse, he or she sees the biological parent condoning it.

Punishment is defined not only as physical punishment. Whatever is aversive to a particular person may act to decrease a prior behavior. For example, a family may have a rule that dinner is served at 6 P.M.; those who are late will need to reheat the food, eat it cold, or make other arrangements. This approach is effective if the consequences are aversive to the late person. Similarly, a punctual spouse may say to the habitually late spouse, "Because we have two cars and the party has already started, I think I'll go on to the party and you can come later. I'll tell the host you have been detained." Again, if the consequence is aversive, the slower spouse may take deadlines more seriously in the future.

Numerous additional techniques and packages of techniques are available in the behavioral and cognitive-behavioral literature. The reader may survey various sources, such as Falloon (1988a), Falloon and Liberman (1983), Gurman and Kniskern (1981), Jacobson and Margolin (1979), Jordan, Cobb, and McCully

(1987), Liberman (1970), Patterson (1971, 1982), Ruff (1985), Stuart (1980), Thyer (1989), and Wells (1994).

How to Conduct a Session of Behavioral Family Therapy and Cognitive-Behavioral Family Therapy

Behavioral family therapy and cognitive-behavioral family therapy emphasize an educational perspective and changes in behavior. Questions about family problems are worded to focus on specific behaviors and situations where the behavior occurred. Clients must become aware that behavior is greatly affected by consequences, and cognition triggers behavior. Therefore, the initial stage of family therapy begins with a description of problems, and the clinician directs family members' attention to the antecedents and consequences of behavior and cognitions that trigger behavior. This awareness gives family members new ways to conceptualize behavior and how changes in the environment can result in behavior changes.

> *Goal I: Family problems are defined in behavioral terms.*
>
> *Social worker's task:* Workers must ask questions that focus on behavior: "What did you do?" "What happened next?" "Who" did what? Questions like, "How did you feel" are appropriate to the extent that the answers provide an understanding of the family's mood or motivation and establish rapport.
>
> *Goal II: Educate family members about the role of antecedents, consequences, and cognitions affecting behavior.*
>
> *Social worker's task:* When family members describe problematic behavior, the worker focuses attention on the controlling conditions: "What happened immediately after" the behavior occurred? "What happened before" the behavior occurred? "What thoughts went through your mind when" you were behaving in such a way?
>
> *Goal III: Teach intervention methods.*
>
> *Social worker's task:* Workers must teach behavioral and cognitive interventions. Parents must be taught how to use reinforcement to increase children's behavior that is desired and how to use negative consequences appropriately to decrease undesired behavior. Everyone should learn how to direct attention, restructure perceptions, and evaluate the irrational nature of individual or commonly held beliefs. Role-plays and behavioral rehearsals are helpful tools.
>
> *Goal IV: Act and evaluate.*
>
> *Social worker's tasks:* Family members can be assigned tasks and exercises to change behavior in the home environment. For example, they may begin behavioral contracts to increase children's prosocial behaviors or to increase the quality and frequency of partners' interpersonal exchanges. They should be taught how to evaluate changes in behavior to help the family and clinician learn how to continue the assignments or alter them to make more effective changes in behavior.

Functional Family Therapy: An Example of a Specific Behavioral Family Therapy Model

The functional family therapy model developed by James Alexander and colleagues (e.g., Alexander & Barton, 1976; Alexander & Parsons, 1973) integrates concepts from systems theory, behavioral therapy, and cognitive therapy. It is one of the better researched family therapy models, having developed in the process of a research project into the communication processes of families in which a child is a juvenile offender (Alexander & Parsons, 1973).

The systems theory components of functional family therapy include a focus on the family, not the individual, and an emphasis on circular causality. Circular causality is an idea from systems theory which suggests that an individual's behavior is understood within the familial context, and one person's behavior is a reaction to and influences the behavior of others. The functional model also emphasizes homeostasis—the family system's attempt to maintain the status quo.

As a behavioral model, functional family therapy subscribes to the notion that behaviors are learned within and perpetuated by the family. Consistent with cognitive theory, a person's perceptions are viewed as stimuli that affect behaviors and responses to stimuli. The functional model operates on several assumptions:

1. Behavior is not good or bad, but rather efficient or inefficient.
2. A specific behavior does not lead to a specific outcome.
3. All behavior is adaptive and represents the best presently available means to attain interpersonal functions.
4. The three functions of behavior are merging, separating, and midpointing.
5. The function of a behavior can be determined by examining the outcome of the behavior rather than the behavior process.

The functional family therapy model defines therapy as the preparation of the family to be receptive to learning new skills and behaviors. Functional family therapists see therapy as only one part of intervention. Therapy mostly serves to help families become open to change. The real work of change takes place in educating the family toward new behaviors. All behavior within a family system serves three basic interpersonal functions: merging, separating, and midpointing. Merging is an interpersonal need to make contact, come together, and be close. Separating means distancing and coming apart. Midpointing is staying stuck, maintaining the status quo, and neither coming close nor coming together. Alexander and Parsons (1973) suggest that problem behaviors in families can be understood by examining these interpersonal functions of behavior. Therapists are to pay attention to the outcome and function of a behavior rather than its process. For example, what outcome does Johnny's behavior of running away serve in a family system? What is the end result? Does the family end up pulling together and having a big family conference and long weekend together instead of maintaining their usual separateness? If this were the case, it would be assumed that the behavior was serving the interpersonal function of merging. In this case, the family would be taught ways to come close without having the running away ordeal. In other words, the functional family therapists would work on helping the family get what they want in a more appropriate and socially acceptable manner. On the other hand, if the result of the running away behavior was that complacent and acquiescent parents confronted their own conflicts and began arguing, the situation would be viewed as serving the interpersonal function of separating.

Assessment in functional family therapy is ongoing (see Figure 4.1). The therapist needs to understand how the family works as a system. The functional model is an early example of a family therapy model that uses assessment as a part of intervention. To facilitate assessment as intervention, the therapist must illustrate how each family member's behavior, feelings, and thoughts are interdependent and necessary for those of the others. Assessment as intervention should make order out of crisis and help family members see how to think about themselves and each other in different ways. A relationship focus is created by content and process, which tie family members together. It causes change because it shakes

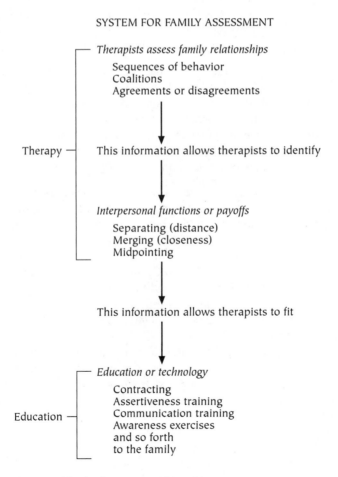

SYSTEM FOR FAMILY ASSESSMENT

Therapy

Therapists assess family relationships
Sequences of behavior
Coalitions
Agreements or disagreements

↓

This information allows therapists to identify

↓

Interpersonal functions or payoffs
Separating (distance)
Merging (closeness)
Midpointing

↓

This information allows therapists to fit

↓

Education

Education or technology
Contracting
Assertiveness training
Communication training
Awareness exercises
and so forth
to the family

FIGURE 4.1   *Conceptual levels of assessment shown in sequence.*

family members' perceptions that the problem the family is experiencing is caused by a faulty individual (Alexander & Parsons 1982).

Therapy interrupts interactional patterns that create a need to develop new ways to meet functional ends. Techniques often used to make this happen include relabeling (see Figure 4.2) and refocusing. Education helps families learn new process skills and maintain changes in behavior. Skills important for families to learn include communication skills such as brevity, specificity, directness, and congruence, acceptance of responsibility, and active listening. Specific behavioral change programs (technical aids) are used to help families make changes. These involve techniques such as contingency contracting, relaxation exercises, token economies, and time-outs. When families have learned new, more efficient ways to interact that are congruent with the family system's functional ends, it is time to terminate therapy.

The therapist's interpersonal skills are emphasized in the functional model. In their early research, Alexander and Parsons (1982) identified two important sets of skills: relationship skills and structuring. Therapists with good relationship skills are able to make families feel understood and accepted. They have good active listening skills and possess warmth, humor, and a nonblaming attitude. More

---

Relabel: Verbal portrayal of any "negative" family or individual behavior in a benign or benevolent light by describing "positive" antonym properties of the behavior and portraying family members as victims rather than perpetrators. Relabeling casts problems in a new way and facilitates behavior change by helping families stop automatic responding and break out of old behavior chains.

Steps for Establishing Positive Relabels

1. Create **plausible relabels** of client behavior that match the worldview of clients (e.g., if a family values independence and assertiveness, relabel the delinquent behavior of an adolescent member as just a way the youth is trying to become independent and establish his own place in the world.)
2. Create relabels that **suggest benign or benevolent motives** (e.g., relabel the distancing, workaholic behavior of a father as his way of protecting the family from his job stresses and negative emotions).
3. Create relabels that **point out the benefits of symptomatic behavior** (e.g., relabel sibling fighting as developmentally normal behavior that manages to get a lot of attention from the parents).

Three Levels of Relabeling

1. **Interactional/Interpersonal**—Provides benign description of the impact of interpersonal behavior (e.g., so Mom, when Dad gets discouraged and starts throwing things, you calm him down by leaving the room).
2. **Motivational**—Recasts motives in a benign or benevolent manner (e.g., you really care for your son and by grounding him you are trying to protect him).
3. **Systemic level**—Emphasizes the similarities between people or family themes (e.g., you are such a close family that it seems you are all trying to get some space and figure out who you are as individuals. It seems that all of you are trying to develop this space by doing something you have never done before, something risky and exciting. Dad is trying to get his space by taking a job promotion that will mean living away from the family a good part of the time in another city. Mom is trying to get her space by seeing her old boyfriend, and Karen is trying to get her space by experimenting with drugs and skipping class).

F I G U R E   4 . 2   *Creative relabeling.* SOURCE: Morris, S. B., Alexander, J. F., & Waldron H. (1988). Functional family therapy. In I. R. H. Falloon (Ed.), *Handbook of behavioral family therapy.* New York: Guilford.

structured therapists are those who set goals, are directive, and push families to move along in the therapy. They keep families focused on interaction and control and direct the session. Alexander and Parsons found that the most effective therapists are those who possess both sets of skills.

Integrative Couples Therapy: An Example of a Specific Behavioral Family Therapy Model

Behavioral and cognitive-behavioral family therapies have proved to be some of the most effective approaches for getting quick changes in couples and family problems. However, over the years, developers of behavioral therapy models have identified limitations to the models and have attempted to improve them. Neil Jacobson and Andrew Christensen developed integrative couples therapy (ICT) in response to the difficulties found in maintaining long-term changes in behavioral couples therapy. Research on behavioral family therapies had shown that the relational exchange model used in behavioral therapy produced quick change but that the changes did not last. To correct the deficits in the model, therapists/researchers added communication/problem solving to therapy. The results indicated that the new model had a 50% success rate in terms of lasting change (Jacobson & Christensen, 1996).

A 50% rate of change, however, was still not satisfactory, and Jacobson wanted to improve the model further. He began by reevaluating the behavioral therapy methods. During this period, he examined more closely the writings of Skinner—in particular, Skinner's distinctions between naturally occurring contingencies and rule-governed behavior. Jacobson was also influenced by Sue Johnson, a student of Les Greenberg who pioneered emotionally focused therapy. Emotionally focused therapy is an experiential therapy in which therapists help clients focus on emotional changes. Therapy critic Dan Wile was further influential in helping Jacobson update traditional behavioral couples therapy by adding the dimension of acceptance to therapy. Acceptance becomes a primary vehicle for change and for maintaining the changes achieved through traditional behavioral therapy techniques.

Having its roots in traditional behavior therapies, ICT shares many of the same practice methods, such as contracting, communication skills training, and problem-solving methods. The distinguishing feature of ICT is its focus on the construct of acceptance. Acceptance means that couples can have an improved relationship because of problems, not in spite of them. Acceptance also means letting go the struggle to change one's partner. Jacobson borrowed this method from the Mental Research Institute's (MRI) brief therapy model (see Chapter 3). This method helps therapists make powerful contextual shifts as a way of changing cognition (meanings) and behavior. Acceptance in ICT is understood as a change in a couple's emotional reaction to a behavior and is divided into two components. The first is a vehicle for converting relationship problems into opportunities for intimacy building; the second is a tool for freeing couples from the highly difficult and unlikely task of changing each other (Jacobson & Christensen, 1996). The ICT approach is "integrative" in that it combines the emotional change of acceptance with behavioral change strategies. Acceptance is hypothesized to be an extremely effective behavioral intervention for bringing about lasting change in marital therapies.

Jacobson also integrated into the new behavioral couples model the idea of first-order and second-order change as discussed in the MRI and other systems therapies. This is a good example of how behavioral family therapies have increasingly integrated the concepts of other systems therapies. Traditional behavioral couples therapy exchange techniques are considered to solicit first-order change, and newer acceptance techniques promote second-order change.

ASSESSMENT

Integrative couples therapy uses several assessment techniques that are similar to those used in the functional family therapy model discussed earlier. In addition, it incorporates systemic techniques much like the ones in MRI brief therapy (see Chapter 3). Other techniques include the use of self-report questionnaires before the start of the initial session and face-to-face interviews of the clients. The initial session in ICT is dedicated to assessment, and the change process does not begin until the second session (Jacobson & Addis, 1993).

CONDUCTING THE FIRST SESSION

The initial session consists of a short conjoint interview followed by individual sessions with the clients. Individual interviews may take place on the same day or be spread out over time. Observation of a client's body language and other nonverbal cues is important to the assessment process; therefore, information is rarely collected over the telephone.

Some of the self-report instruments used by Jacobson and Christensen (1996) include the Dyadic Adjustment Scale (Spanier, 1976), Marital Satisfaction Inventory (Snyder, 1979), Marital Status Inventory (Weiss, 1980), Conflict Tactics Scale (Straus, 1979), Areas of Change Questionnaire (Weiss, 1996a), Areas of Change and Acceptance Questionnaire (Jacobson, 1996), and Spouse Observation Checklist (Weiss, 1996b). See Jacobson and Christensen (1996) for a more detailed discussion of how these measures are used.

During the first couples interview the presenting problem is usually not discussed in detail. Instead, the therapist focuses on obtaining background information on relationship strengths and the couple's courtship history. Also in the initial session, the ICT therapist lays out the format of the therapy sessions and requests that the clients "evaluate" the therapist and decide whether they want to continue therapy (Christensen, Jacobson, & Babcock, 1995; Jacobson and Christensen, 1996).

Some of the questions asked during the interview to assess client strengths include these:

- How did the couple get together?
- What was their courtship like? What was the relationship like before the problems began?
- How is the relationship different *now* on days when the partners are getting along?

- How would the relationship be different if the problems that currently exist were no longer a problem?

Throughout the assessment phase the ICT therapist is gathering information to answer the following six questions:

- How distressed is this couple?
- How committed is this couple to this relationship?
- What are the issues that divide them?
- Why are these issues such a problem for them?
- What are the strengths holding them together?
- What can treatment do to help them?

Answers to these questions help the ICT therapist to identify themes, polarization processes, and mutual traps that are specific to the couple that has come into therapy. Once the therapist formulates an evaluation regarding these areas, a feedback session is held with the couple. The therapist requests feedback from the clients regarding how closely the therapist's descriptions match the clients' perceptions of their relationship. In the feedback session the therapist works toward a mutually agreed-on set of problems that the couple can work on with the therapist.

As mentioned above, ICT employs all the traditional behavioral therapy methods. In addition, there are four techniques used in ICT to enhance emotional acceptance. These include promoting emotional acceptance through empathic joining around the problem, promoting acceptance through detachment from the problem, enhancing emotional acceptance through tolerance building, and enhancing emotional acceptance through greater self-care. In the first two, the therapist enhances acceptance by helping the couple experience the problem in a different way. In the last two techniques, acceptance is enhanced by reducing the aversiveness of the partners' actions.

Empathic joining around the problem   is the first intervention by the therapist during the initial feedback session with the couple at which time the therapist reformulates the problem in terms of common "differences" between partners instead of as the fault of a "bad" partner's behavior. The therapist may say something like this: "It seems you have different ideas about how to solve this problem with Billy." The therapist makes this statement instead of accepting the couple's definition that each is a bad parent. Therapists will also guide couples in a different way of talking about their problems. This "language of acceptance" emphasizes talking about one's own experiences rather than talking about each other. This approach frees the listener from having to make defenses and counterattacks, and he or she is able to listen and understand the other's position. When clients talk about their feelings, the therapist encourages "soft" feelings and thoughts instead of "hard" ones. Hard feelings and disclosures reveal the self in a stronger, more dominant position vis-à-vis the partner. Soft disclosures, in contrast, reveal the self as vulnerable, reflecting feelings of hurt, fear, or disappointment (e.g., "I wasn't sure he cared about me" instead of "I told him off when he did not come home on time"). Soft disclosures help the partners find empathy and listen to each other.

Emotional acceptance through detachment   from the problem works toward the same goals by promoting a detached, meta-cognitive, and descriptive view of the problem. The therapist helps the clients to discuss the problem as an "it" they share, rather than as adversaries. At times, the therapist may bring out a chair and say, "Let's put the problem in the chair and talk about it. But whenever you refer to it, talk about it as an 'it' sitting in this chair" (Christensen, Jacobson, & Babcock, 1995; Jacobson & Christensen, 1996). Detachment techniques are similar to the method known as "externalizing the problem" used in narrative therapy and discussed in Chapter 6. Although similar in therapeutic strategy, "detachment" and "externalizing the problem" developed independent of one another.

Enhancing emotional acceptance through tolerance building   involves a number of specific techniques. One of these is finding positive features of negative behaviors. The therapist, for example, may reframe a couple's differences in terms of the difference, creating a positive balance in the relationship so that it can function more smoothly. Another tolerance-building technique involves role playing or behavior reversal of negative behavior so that couples can gain a greater acceptance of one another's reactions to the difficulties as they experience them.

Integrative couples therapy has an interesting method of responding to relapse prevention. ITC therapists give couples the message that no matter how effective they are in making changes, they will encounter occasional slip-ups. This method helps couples with relapse prevention by focusing on more tolerance building and acceptance of one another's behaviors that each does not like. The therapist prepares the couple for such lapses into old behavior by having them rehearse a relapse during the session. During these rehearsals, the therapist helps the couple discuss the feelings and thoughts that arise in them or might arise if the episode occurred in real life. This exercise exposes couples to likely scenarios without the destructive forces of attack, defense, and counterattack. Faked incidents of negative behavior are also used as a technique to enhance tolerance. Therapists ask couples to fake incidents of negative behavior at times when they are really not inclined to do that behavior. The faker's calm state of mind allows him or her to observe clearly the partner's pain in these instances. Also, the partners are instructed to reveal the "fake" almost immediately so as to prevent escalation.

Emotional acceptance through greater self-care   The ITC therapist promotes greater independence and self-reliance in members of couples so they can better manage times when their partner is unavailable to them. The idea of personal responsibility and the importance of need satisfaction are introduced to the couple. Couples are taught to take responsibility for their own need satisfaction instead of relying on the partner to meet all their desires.

Other common means of protecting and caring for oneself in the face of stress include assertively altering the situation, defining the situation differently, leaving the situation, and seeking solace from others. With greater self-care, partners may experience less pain, greater tolerance, and greater acceptance.

Consistency with Social Work Practice

Behavioral family therapy and cognitive-behavioral family therapy both value an approach that is direct, negotiated with the client family, and focused on the family's environment. It is time limited, and termination is based on objective, measurable indicators. Numerous authors (Acosta, Yamamoto, & Evans, 1982, for example) have advocated behavioral approaches for social work clients because of these characteristics. Furthermore, family therapy in general has developed through the last few years as an alternative to more traditional therapies (Bergin & Garfield, 1994). As described in the literature, family therapy models are likely to be described as family therapy "with a schizophrenic family member," "with divorcing parents," "with conduct disorder children," "with drug abuse issues" (see the October, 1995, issue of *Journal of Marital and Family Therapy*). This trend is coherent for social workers who traditionally have focused on special populations (e.g., child abuse, drug abuse, mental illness) in the environmental context of social work. The behavioral and cognitive-behavioral models combine the population-at-risk perspective with clusters of the most effective therapeutic techniques.

Research Support for the Model

As early as 1898, researchers, particularly John Thorndike, empirically established the effectiveness of operant conditioning. Skinner (1953) refined Thorndike's presuppositions, and from this work, the understanding of human behavior focused on the learning process and the complexities of the specific task (Thorpe & Olson, 1990). Pigeons perform behaviors to get food; humans learn to speak the language of their caregivers. Positive reinforcers consistently outperformed punishers in making long-term changes in behavior (Kazdin, 1994). In modeling studies, Bandura (1969, 1977) found that children exhibit behaviors shown to them in films and classroom demonstrations. In fact, he emphasized the life-saving necessity of learning vicariously.

The examples fill legions of books and monographs. As Kazdin (1978) underscored, research into operant and classical conditioning and social learning principles present the best established documentation on how humans acquire and discard behavior.

Outcome Evaluations

The overall evaluations of cognitive-behavioral family therapy are derived from a diversity of sources; however, the results are consistently positive. In 1987, Szykula, Morris, and Sayger compared strategic therapy and behavioral family therapy when the focus was changing children's behavior. Although both methods showed comparable effectiveness in reducing problem behavior and family satisfaction, the behavioral method produced more consistently favorable results. Similarly, Klein, Alexander, and Parsons (1977) found behavioral family treatment superior to client-centered models in reducing recidivism and improving the quality of family processes.

Falloon (1988b; Falloon et al., 1985) demonstrated the versatility of family behavioral treatment by treating 36 families with members previously diagnosed with schizophrenia. When this method was compared with traditional, clinic-based psychotherapy, clients showed a low 6% rate of symptom exacerbation compared to the 44% rate for traditional treatment. In addition to other gains, the rate of return to hospitals dropped to 11% for clients in behavioral family therapy versus 50% for the traditional model. Treatment focused on education about schizophrenia, problem-solving methods, and communication skills. Additionally, the behavioral family model costs less to provide.

Similar to Falloon's studies, Randolph and colleagues (1994) compared behavioral family therapy to traditional family therapy with 41 families of schizophrenic clients. Only 14% of the clients experienced exacerbated symptoms, compared to 53% of clients in traditional family treatment.

A growing body of empirical studies has evolved around the management of parent and child issues. In the Oregon Social Learning Center, programs have used the methods of Patterson, Reid, Jones, and Conger (1975). They combined various cognitive and behavioral methods to treat families with troublesome children. As Wells (1994) reported, treated families improved 30% or greater from baseline information on troublesome behavior. The success of their methods has persisted in studies with wait-list and placebo control groups. To further document the success of their work, Patterson, Chamberlain, and Reid (1982) used random assignment of families to protect their successful results from criticism of selection biases. Families reported a 63% reduction in problem behavior, compared to 17% reduction in the control group.

Baucom, Epstein, and Rankin (1995) provided a very reasoned assessment of the effectiveness of cognitive restructuring to enhance acceptance of couples' relationship standards and assumptions. When couples are the focus of treatment, cognitive restructuring enhances how couples view their relationship and their marital adjustment. Baucom, Epstein, and Rankin emphasized that their findings also demonstrate the effectiveness of behavioral marital therapy (see also Baucom & Lester, 1986; Huber & Milstein, 1985).

In summary, the research on behavioral family therapy is very positive. The components of treatment vary from study to study and with a variety of populations. Fortunately, the variety has not clouded the overall positive results for families and various types of "identified patients." Each component in the behavioral and cognitive-behavioral repertoire is related to the behavioral and social learning principles that have received consistent empirical support.

Research on Functional Family Therapy

Functional family therapy (FFT), a systemic behavioral model, is one of the best researched of the family therapies. A particular area of interest for researchers has been delinquency (Alexander & Parsons, 1973; Alexander, Barton, Shiavo, & Parsons, 1986; Barton, Alexander, Waldron, Turner, & Warburton, 1985; Klein, Alexander, & Parsons, 1977; Parsons & Alexander, 1973). Functional family therapy shows a consistently replicated lower recidivism rate (26%) in juvenile delinquents, compared to much higher recidivism rates in other therapies (Alexander et al.,

1986; Barton & Alexander, 1981; Gordon, Arbuthnot, & McGreen, 1983). Barton and colleagues (1985) discovered a significant difference in recidivism rates for functional family therapy used with hard-core delinquents. At the end of a 15-month follow-up, delinquents undergoing FFT had a 60% recidivism rate, compared to 93% recidivism in comparison treatments.

Barton and colleagues (1985) found that functional family therapy is generalizable to the entire family system, promoting such changes as increased talking and clarification of feelings, increased supportiveness, and decreased defensiveness. Klein and associates (1977) reported similar findings, noting that far fewer siblings of delinquents in FFT engaged in delinquent activity than did siblings of families undergoing other therapies.

Case examples show that functional family therapy may also be useful in treatment for inhibited sexual desire (Regas & Sprenkle, 1984). This method, through the use of relabeling, allows the focus to be moved from intercourse to the relationship in general.

A very important aspect of functional family therapy is the therapist's commitment to the model and willingness to work within it for family change. Therapists must be able to blend good relationship skills with structuring skills for the best possible effect (Alexander et al., 1986). Though some critics speculate about the effectiveness of this approach with individuals (Torgenrud & Storm, 1989), it has proven to be an effective model for use with families, including individual family members.

Research on Integrative Couples Therapy

When removed from the context of behavioral therapies, integrative couples therapy does not have a tremendous amount of research supporting its efficacy. This is because the therapy is relatively new and there has been insufficient time for careful experimentation. Nevertheless, ICT can be evaluated to a certain extent from studies that have examined its precursor, behavioral marital therapy (BMT). BMT, the core of ICT, has been well researched and has proved an effective means of intervention for couples therapy. The use of BMT for family therapy, however, has not been widely researched.

Babcock and Jacobson (1993) reviewed research testing BMT's usefulness across a wide range of couple populations, including marriages in which one of the spouses was depressed or suffering from schizophrenia. For these populations there was a 67% success rate. As can be expected, for populations suffering from less severe problems, the rate of success was approximately 83%. Another study by Fals-Stewart, Birchler, and O'Farrell (1996) examined the use of BMT for couples in which the male was a substance abuser. Results of this study indicated that BMT was effective in improving the couple's satisfaction with their marriage and also helpful in reducing the male's drug-using behavior.

Often missing in the research literature on behavioral family therapies is the evaluation of the newer methods used in therapy. Many techniques, such as relabeling and acceptance, for example, are crucial to the functioning of contemporary behaviorally based interventions such as functional family therapy and integrative couples therapy. Indispensable to Jacobson's integrative couples therapy is the idea of "acceptance" (Jacobson & Christensen, 1996). Acceptance is considered to be an important element of change because it shifts the couple's attention away from one another's behavior and onto the problem. It is the concept of acceptance that distinguishes integrative couples therapy from traditional behavioral marital therapies.

Jacobson did a pilot study to initiate research on the effectiveness of the techniques of acceptance (Jacobson & Christensen, 1996). Findings from that study indicate that behavioral exchange and communication training are significantly more effective when accompanied by a focus on acceptance. At a one-year follow up, 50% of the couples receiving traditional behavioral interventions alone continued to be satisfied with their marriage. In contrast, 75% of the couples whose therapist emphasized acceptance reported high levels of satisfaction (Jacobson & Christensen, 1996). Although this research is preliminary, it does lend support to the addition of the concept of acceptance in behavioral interventions.

One limitation of this research on the effectiveness of ICT for social work practitioners and other family therapists is the lack of diversity in the sample. Because of the homogeneity of the sample, conclusions must be drawn cautiously about the effectiveness of the therapy with a diversity of couples that therapists may encounter in practice. Nevertheless, Jacobson and Christensen (1996) believe that ICT will be useful in assisting African-American couples because of its emphasis on expressing vulnerability within the relationship. In contrast, Jacobson and Christensen (1996) do not believe that ICT will be as helpful to Asian-American couples because many Asian-Americans have a strong tradition of patriarchal families in which egalitarianism is not emphasized. ICT, like its predecessors, will probably be most effective when applied to couples who are relatively young in age, have a strong degree of commitment, are emotionally engaged, value egalitarian relationships, and have similar goals (Jacobson & Christensen, 1996).

Research evaluating BMT and ICT is promising, but one serious limitation remains. Gains achieved in BMT have been demonstrated to decrease significantly within two years (Jacobson, Schmaling, & Holtzworth-Munroe, 1987). Studies evaluating the effectiveness of maintenance techniques have found them to be of questionable value for extending the gains of BMT intervention (Babcock & Jacobson, 1993). Because ICT is new, the research is not complete enough to show whether these newer techniques have addressed the long-term maintenance issues found in the model.

Behavioral Family Therapy, Cognitive-Behavioral Family Therapy, and Managed Behavioral Health Care

According to Hutchins (1996), almost every area in social work and services to families will be affected by managed care. The driving theme is the management of costs; therefore, services are restricted to the most needy. Currently, health services are the primary focus of management companies. Hutchins, however, cited a recent development in child welfare services. The Child Welfare League of America found that 41 of 50 states were considering some form of managed care for their clients. The leading plan is to contract out services to local service providers who will assume the responsibility of providing services at a set cost to the state government.

Other agencies and services that provide family therapy will probably be controlled with managed care techniques. These will likely include time limits, frequent review of services to verify progress and evaluate the necessity for additional care, and ideally, coordinate services for children and families.

In the unsettled atmosphere of managed care, the behavioral and cognitive-behavioral principles hold considerable promise. With the focus on changes in behavior, practitioners can easily verify whether target behaviors have changed in the desired directions. Time-limited services are not in opposition to time limits in family therapy; however, professionals and managed care administrators have differed over how long services should last. Finally, by focusing on documented behavioral change and measuring change with scales and data collection methods, clinicians will be able to document the successfulness of various components of behavioral and cognitive-behavioral therapy. The documented evidence can be used as a meaningful source of data to help managed care administrators evaluate time limits. Similarly, practitioners can better estimate how long services must continue to be effective. This information is crucial before practitioners make informed decisions about capitated contracts, in which agencies agree to see so many clients for a set period of time and at a set price.

Critiques of the Model

The effectiveness of changing behavior by manipulating the environment may lead some people to overlook the human aspect of work with families. Too much reliance on reinforcers, punishers, modeling, and so forth may undercut the dire predicament of some of our families. For example, many of our families have significant emotional pain over the loss of dreams. Parents realize that their children may not fulfill all their expectations. Children all too frequently face the humanness of their parents and experience the consequences of their mistakes. Neil Jacobson and Andrew Christensen (1996) point out the limitations of behavioral couple therapy, for example. Research indicated that the quick effects achieved in the behavioral model did not always last. There are certain limitations to a strict educational model that emphasizes skills training and the learning of new behavior but does not give much attention to the emotional aspects of behavior. The behavioral couple therapy model is especially limited for couples who do not accept egalitarian relationships, because it assumes a give-and-take approach to learning and changing oneself. Jacobson and Christensen have made corrections to the model by researching an approach that emphasizes acceptance of partners instead of change. Models like functional family therapy also correct for neglect of emotional issues by attending to the interpersonal functional meaning of behavior. However, functional therapy does not address important aspects of behavior, such as the normative aspects of functions at different levels of development. For example, the functional family therapist does not consider the importance of separating over too much merging in adolescents. A therapist would not consider a family's desire to merge as developmentally inappropriate. Rather, families would be helped to find other ways to merge, even if that might be viewed as developmentally inappropriate by some therapists.

Similarly, scientific support for the principles and assumptions may obscure the necessity for clinicians to administer or direct treatment artfully. They must teach parents and children how to assess overt and covert behavior and how to match individual needs with reinforcers, models, and formulations for more rational thoughts (and actions).

Clinicians, therefore, are cautioned to formulate interventions carefully with particular family members in mind. They are urged to see emotions as indications of motivation and level of desire for change. Additionally, they are required to maintain their knowledge of effective methods and techniques.

Feminist and Developmental Critiques

Avis (1985a) approaches functional family therapy from a feminist perspective, arguing that the practice of this method of not altering a family's functions, even if they are oppressive to women, reinforces sex-role stereotypes and tacitly approves them. Avis calls for a revision of functional family therapy, in which therapists can acknowledge a family's behavior roles while still challenging the underlying belief system. Alexander, Warburton, Waldron, and Mas (1985) disagree, stating that it is not family functions that maintain sexual stereotypes and that prompting a family to change functions based on a political agenda may be unethical. Avis (1985b) contends, however, that discussing family belief systems is the therapist's ethical responsibility.

> Wetchler (1985) asserts a different criticism of functional therapy: The functional family therapy model as it exists now creates a static view of the family as it exists at one point in time. In order to better assess and treat the family, the clinician/researcher must add another level to the process, that of the family life cycle. (pp. 41–42)

Assessing the family from the life cycle perspective should provide the therapist a better understanding of family behaviors, especially helping development of a treatment plan that takes into account family members' developmental processes.

Case Example[1]

THERAPIST: Last week we discussed the need for your husband to suffer the consequences for his drinking. In the past, Karen, what would you have done when your husband had driven home after having too much to drink?

[1]Linda Loveless, Barbara Smoler, and Gail Hartin (1997) at the University of Texas at Austin provided this case example.

KAREN:	Well, I'd go down and literally drag him out of the car and up the stairs to our second-story bedroom. Then I would undress him and put him to bed.
THERAPIST:	How do you feel about doing this?
KAREN:	Well, I'm mad as hell, because it is the only thing I can do.
THERAPIST:	The only thing you can do?
KAREN:	Yes, what else is there to do?
THERAPIST:	Let's talk about some other things you could do. We talked about Bill's being responsible for his own actions. Keeping this in mind, what is another way you could behave in this situation?
KAREN:	Well, I couldn't just leave Bill in the car for the night.
BILL:	I wish you would leave me in the car, so I wouldn't have to listen to complaining all the next day about how hard it is to get me upstairs and into bed.
THERAPIST:	Karen, how would you feel about leaving Bill in the car overnight?
KAREN:	Well, I would worry about him. What if he was hurt or something?
THERAPIST:	One option is that when you hear his car drive up you can wait and see if he comes in on his own.
KAREN:	But what if he doesn't come in on his own?
THERAPIST:	Then you can go down to check to be sure that he is not injured. If Bill is all right, you return to the house, leaving him there, and not check on him again. Also, go to bed at your regular time. Do you think you could do this, Karen?
KAREN:	[Looking at Bill] What would you think if I did that?
BILL:	I told you; it would be better than hearing you complain.
KAREN:	I think I probably could do that.
THERAPIST:	How about if we practice your going through this process in your mind?
KAREN:	O.K.
THERAPIST:	Karen, get comfortable in your chair and close your eyes. Imagine it is late and you hear Bill's car pull in the driveway. You wait to see if he comes up. When he doesn't come up in 10 minutes, you go down to be sure that he isn't injured. You find that he is asleep in the front seat of the car. You return to the house and back to the task you were doing. You get ready to go to bed at your regular time. Open your eyes. How did you feel when you did this?
KAREN:	I felt a little awkward.
THERAPIST:	Any time we do something new it feels awkward. Often with practice we feel more comfortable. Would it help to repeat this exercise?
KAREN:	Yes, I think it would.
THERAPIST:	[Repeats exercise with Karen.] How did it feel this time, Karen?

KAREN:	That was much better. I could actually feel myself doing it.
THERAPIST:	It will become easier and feel more natural each time you practice this exercise, Karen. For your homework this week I would like you to practice the exercise several times per day for a week. Will you be able to do this, Karen?
KAREN:	Yes, I think this will help.
THERAPIST:	Bill, I have noticed that often when Karen is talking you make faces or roll your eyes. Why do you do this when Karen is talking?
BILL:	I do it when I don't agree with what she says.
THERAPIST:	Well, you just made faces when Karen said that she felt the exercise would help her.
BILL:	It might help her, but she'll still be on my back for the drinking.
THERAPIST:	You remember, we practiced three-part assertion last week. Remember how we rephrased messages in three parts: I feel, when you, because.
KAREN AND BILL:	[Nod heads yes.]
THERAPIST:	Bill, you stated that Karen is always on your back. I'd like you to put your feelings into three-part form. [prompts] When you . . .
BILL:	When you are on my back about drinking, I feel frustrated because I have been trying and have cut way back on my drinking.
THERAPIST:	That is really good, Bill. Now, Karen, do you remember how to do the reflexive listening to someone who has just made the three-part assertion?
KAREN:	I think so.
THERAPIST:	[Prompts] When I . . .
KAREN:	When I am on your back about your drinking, you feel frustrated because you have been trying and have cut back on your drinking a lot.
THERAPIST:	That was very good. You both did a good job with that. Have you been practicing?
KAREN AND BILL:	[Look at each other and shake their heads, yes.] We've been trying.
THERAPIST:	Let's go back to the feelings that you have, Bill, about Karen's nagging about your drinking. Could you give me an example? What is usually going on when this happens?
BILL:	Whenever I come home even a little bit late, Karen assumes I've been out drinking. She starts yelling and accusing me of stuff.
KAREN:	What else am I supposed to think? Whenever you are late, I just know you must be drunk or hurt or dead from some accident.
THERAPIST:	Have there been any times during your marriage, Karen, that Bill has been late for any other reason?
BILL:	Sometimes, I work late you know.

KAREN:	Yeah, I know, and sometimes he has stopped by his mother's on the way home, but you haven't called to let me know you're going to be late.
BILL:	Sometimes I can't call—remember that time I stopped to help the lady with her tires?
THERAPIST:	So there can be other reasons for Bill's being late besides staying out to drink? Is that correct, Karen?
KAREN:	Yes, I guess there have been times when Bill was late and he wasn't out drinking.
THERAPIST:	It may help you to think of the other reasons the next time Bill is late. Bill, what do you think you can do to help Karen change her thinking the next time you are going to be late?
BILL:	When I can, I guess I could give her a call and let her know I'm going to be late.
THERAPIST:	Would this help you, Karen?
KAREN:	Yes, it would.
THERAPIST:	Karen, I would like for you to monitor your thoughts when Bill is late. Here is a form that might make that easier for you. [Therapist goes over form with Karen.] I just want you both to know that from my observations and the Marital Satisfaction Scale you both completed, you have a lot of positive feeling for each other and really care about each other. A fun thing to do that might bring you closer is to contract for pleasers from each other. Between now and next week you can be thinking about five positive things that you can do for each other. Karen, you think of five things you would like Bill to do for you and five things you would be willing to do for Bill. Bill, you think of five things you would like Karen to do for you and five things you would be willing to do for Karen. These things don't have to be big things. It could be something like a back massage, a love note, or a phone call during the day. These pleasers must be positive. These pleasers must be specific, and they must not have been the subject of recent conflict. Do you two think you can do this?
BILL:	I'm going to like this exercise.
KAREN:	This is going to be fun.
THERAPIST:	Karen, last time we met, we talked about your not feeling good about yourself.
KAREN:	Well, I've really felt pretty low lately. I don't know why. For such a long time I wished for Bill to stop drinking, and now he's really trying to do that. I should feel good about myself, but for some reason I don't.
THERAPIST:	Can you tell me what you are feeling when you are low?
KAREN:	I feel lonely. Now that Bill has his support group and everything, it's like I don't really count any more. For all these years I've

	protected him and kept his drinking a secret; now it's like I don't have as much meaning in his life any more.
THERAPIST:	It seems to me, Karen, that you spent so much time taking care of Bill, that you haven't had time for your life. What were the things you used to enjoy?
KAREN:	I used to enjoy reading. And I used to sing. I used to love to sing. In fact, I used to be in our church choir, years ago. I was pretty good, too. There were four of us who made up a quartet. We even went to sing at church banquets and meetings.
THERAPIST:	Would you have an opportunity to be involved with your music again?
KAREN:	As a matter of fact, the church choir director called a couple of weeks ago and asked if I would be interested in being a member of the choir again.
THERAPIST:	What did you say?
KAREN:	I told him I really didn't have time for it. After talking about it with you, though, I've changed my mind. I think I'm going to call him back and tell him I'll join the choir after all.
THERAPIST:	I feel that's a good idea, Karen. You'll be doing something you enjoy and it will also help you to feel better about yourself. Have you thought any more about the assertiveness group at the clinic I told you about?
KAREN:	I still have the number of the woman to get in touch with. I'm just not sure that I want to join a group right now. I want to be sure which night choir practice will be, first.
THERAPIST:	That's fine, Karen. There are some things that you can do for yourself even before you decide to be part of a group. Do you remember when I asked you to think of five things that you liked about yourself?
KAREN:	Yes. I had a hard time thinking of five of them, but I finally thought of all of them.
THERAPIST:	Can you tell me those five things, Karen?
KAREN:	Well, I am a generous person, and I'm energetic.
THERAPIST:	Good!
KAREN:	And I'm a good wife.
THERAPIST:	Now, I'm sure you are, but that's a role you play for someone else. Can you think of other things that just concern you?
KAREN:	I'm a good singer.
THERAPIST:	Good!
KAREN:	I have a good sense of humor.
THERAPIST:	One more.
KAREN:	I'm brave. I've had to face a lot in my life, and I've always been able to do it.
THERAPIST:	Those are five good things, Karen. Now, I'd like you to write these things on five index cards and carry them with you in your purse

	each day. Once every hour, pull out one of your cards and read it to yourself. That will be your homework this next week. You'll find that you really begin to believe these good things about yourself. How do you feel about this assignment?
KAREN:	An assignment that calls for me reading nice things about myself every hour? I think I can handle that. As a matter of fact, I'll look forward to it.
THERAPIST:	You also mentioned that you like to read. I'd like to recommend a couple of books to you. One is *The Assertive Woman, A New Look,* and the other is *Your Perfect Right (A Guide to Assertive Living).* I'll write down the titles and the names of the authors for you before you leave.
KAREN:	Good! I'll be going by the bookstore on the way home.

This example highlights some of the key issues in family therapy. Karen reported feeling responsible about taking care of Bill when he came home drunk. The therapist helped her evaluate the irrational nature of her ideas and develop a way for her to respond. Bill was protected from suffering some of the consequences of his drinking; therefore, the therapist encouraged him to take more responsibility. Both partners believed that they were unimportant or not cared for. The therapist validated their level of caring for each other and helped them devise a plan to give and receive positive attention. The therapist also helped them acquire important rewards or reinforcers. The typical nature of this case underscores the degree to which people develop and maintain unnecessary and unhealthy patterns of interactions, personal behaviors, and beliefs. Behavioral and cognitive-behavioral therapy is a proven resource for troubled families.

Summary

Behavioral and cognitive-behavioral family therapies were documented as effective tools for social work practitioners. This chapter reviewed the historical significance of behavioral and cognitive perspective for treating families. The five behavioral principles and the key precepts of social learning theory were presented as the foundation for successful work with families. The central assumptions emphasized changing overt and covert behavior through changes in the social environment and in the cognitive behavior of family members, such as beliefs, perceptions, and cognitive rules. Specific techniques were presented because of their effectiveness with families. These included cognitive restructuring, thought stopping, anger control techniques, and aversive consequences. One specific behavioral family therapy model, functional family therapy, was highlighted as an example. Finally, a case example depicted behavioral and cognitive-behavioral components. The case surveyed a variety of interventions that assisted a typical family. The example described an effective approach in the context of a time-limited, managed care environment.

Process Questions

1. Identify the specific behavioral or cognitive behavioral techniques used in the transcript.

2. Practice making three-part assertion messages (I feel . . . when you . . . because . . .) that Karen and Bill might use to communicate their feelings to each other.

3. Respond to the three-part assertion statements you make (question 2) with appropriate reflexive listening statements.

4. Develop a simple form that Karen might use to monitor her thoughts when her husband is late.

References

ACOSTA, F. X., YAMAMOTO, J., & EVANS, L. A. (1982). *Effective psychotherapy for low-income and minority patients.* New York: Plenum.

ALEXANDER, J. F., & BARTON, C. (1976). Behavioral systems therapy with families. In D. H. Olson (Ed.), *Treating relationships.* Lake Mills, IA: Graphic Publishing.

ALEXANDER, J. F., BARTON, C., SHIAVO, R. S., & PARSONS, B. V. (1986). Systems-behavioral intervention with families of delinquents: Therapist characteristics, family behavior and outcome. *Journal of Counseling and Clinical Psychology, 44*(4), 656–664.

ALEXANDER, J. F., & PARSONS, B. V. (1973). Short-term behavioral interventions with delinquent families: Impact on family process and recidivism. *Journal of Abnormal Psychology, 51,* 219–225.

ALEXANDER, J. F., & PARSONS, B. V. (1982). *Functional family therapy.* Monterey, CA: Brooks/Cole.

ALEXANDER, J. F., WARBURTON, J., WALDRON, H., & MAS, C. H. (1985). The misuse of functional family therapy: A non-sexist rejoinder. *Journal of Marital and Family Therapy, 11*(2), 139–144.

AVIS, J. M. (1985a). The politics of functional family therapy: A feminist critique. *Journal of Marital and Family Therapy, 11*(2), 127–138.

AVIS, J. M. (1985b). Through a different lens: A reply to Alexander, Warburton, Waldron, and Mas. *Journal of Marital and Family Therapy, 11*(3), 127–138.

BABCOCK, J. C., & JACOBSON, N. S. (1993). A program of research on behavioral marital therapy: Hot spots and smoldering embers in marital therapy research. *Journal of Social and Personal Relationships, 10,* 119–135.

BANDURA, A. (1969). *Principles of behavior modification.* New York: Holt, Rinehart and Winston, Inc.

BANDURA, A. (1977). *Social learning theory.* Englewood Cliffs, NJ: Prentice-Hall.

BARTON, C., & ALEXANDER, J. F. (1981). Functional family therapy. In A. S. Gurman & D. P. Kniskern (Eds.), *Handbook of family therapy* (pp. 403–443). New York: Brunner/Mazel.

BARTON, C., ALEXANDER, J. F., WALDRON, H., TURNER, C., & WARBURTON, J. (1985). Generalizing treatment effects of functional family therapy: Three replications. *The American Journal of Family Therapy, 13*(3), 16–26.

BAUCOM, D. H., EPSTEIN, N., & RANKIN, L. A. (1995). Cognitive aspects of cognitive-behavioral marital therapy. In N. S. Jacobson & A. S. Gurman (Eds.), *Clinical handbook of couple therapy* (pp. 65–90). New York: Guilford.

BAUCOM, D. H., & LESTER, G. W. (1986). The usefulness of cognitive restructuring as an adjunct to behavioral marital therapy. *Behavior Therapy, 17,* 385–403.

BECK, A. (1976). *Cognitive therapy and the emotional disorders.* New York: International Universities Press.

BERGIN, A. E., & GARFIELD, S. L. (1994). *Handbook of psychotherapy and behavior change* (4th ed.). New York: Wiley.

BLOOM, M., & FISCHER, J. (1982). *Evaluating practice: Guidelines for the accountable professional.* Englewood Cliffs, NJ: Prentice-Hall.

CHRISTENSEN, A., JACOBSON, N. S., & BABCOCK, J. C. (1995). Integrative behavior couples therapy. In N. S. Jacobson & A. Gurman (Eds.), *Clinical handbook of marital therapy* (pp. 29–70). New York: Guilford Press.

DESCHNER, J. P. (1984). *The hitting habit.* New York: Free Press.

ELLIS, A. (1970). *The essence of rational psychotherapy: A comprehensive approach in treatment.* New York: Institute for Rational Living.

FALLOON, I. R. (1988a). *Handbook of behavioral family therapy*. New York: Guilford.

FALLOON, I. R. (1988b). Behavioral family management in coping with functional psychosis: Principles, practice, and recent developments. *International Journal of Mental Health, 17*(1), 35–47.

FALLOON, I. R., BOYDE, J., MCGILL, C., WILLIAMSON, M., RAZANI, J., MOSS, H., & GILDERMAN, A. (1985). Family management in the prevention of morbidity of schizophrenia: Clinical outcome of a two-year longitudinal study. *Archives of Behavioral Psychiatry, 42*, 887–896.

FALLOON, I. R., & LIBERMAN, R. (1983). Behavioral therapy for families with child management problems. In M. Textor (Ed.), *Helping families with special problems* (pp. 121–147). New York: Jason Aronson.

FALS-STEWART, W., BIRCHLER, G. R., & O'FARRELL, T. J. (1996). Behavioral couples therapy for male substance abusing patients: Effects on relationship adjustment and drug using behavior. *Journal of Consulting and Clinical Psychology, 64*, 959–972.

GAMBRILL, E. (1983). *Casework: A competency-based approach*. Englewood Cliffs, NJ: Prentice-Hall.

GAMBRILL, E. (1997). *Social work practice: A critical thinker's guide*. London: Oxford University Press.

GORDON, D. A., ARBUTHNOT, J., & MCGREEN, P. (1983, October). *Short-term family therapy and school consultation with court-referred delinquents*. Paper presented at the Society of Police and Criminal Psychology, Cincinnati, OH.

GRANVOLD, D. (Ed.). (1994). *Cognitive and behavioral treatment: Methods and applications*. Pacific Grove, CA: Brooks/Cole.

GURMAN, A. S., & KNISKERN, D. P. (Eds.). (1981). *Handbook of family therapy*. New York. Brunner/Mazel.

HUBER, C. H., & MILSTEIN, B. (1985). Cognitive restructuring and a collaborative set in couples' work. *American Journal of Family Therapy, 13*(2), 17–27.

HUTCHINS, J. (1996). Managing managed care for families. *NAFBS News, 5*(2), 102–113.

JACOBSON, N. S. (1996). Areas of Change and Acceptance Questionnaire. Center for Clinical Research, Department of Psychology, University of Washington, Seattle, Washington.

JACOBSON, N. S., & ADDIS, A. E. (1993). Research on couples and couple therapy: What do we know? Where are we going? *Journal of Consulting and Clinical Psychology, 61*, 85–93.

JACOBSON, N. S., & CHRISTENSEN, A. (1996). *Integrative couple therapy: Promoting acceptance and change*. New York: Norton.

JACOBSEN, N. S., & MARGOLIN, G. (1979). *Marital therapy: Strategies based on social learning and behavior exchange principles*. New York: Brunner/Mazel.

JACOBSON, N. S., SCHMALING, K. B., & HOLTZWORTH-MUNROE, A. (1987). Component analysis of behavioral marital therapy: Two-year follow-up and prediction relapse. *Journal of Marital and Family Therapy, 13*, 187–195.

JORDAN, C., COBB, N. H., & MCCULLY, R. (1987). Clinical issues of the dual-career couple. *Social Work, 34*(1), 29–32.

JORDAN, C., & FRANKLIN, C. (1995). *Clinical assessment in social work: Quantitative and qualitative methods*. Chicago: Lyceum.

KAZDIN, A. E. (1978). *History of behavior modification: Experimental foundations of contemporary research*. Baltimore: University Park Press.

KAZDIN, A. E. (1994). *Behavior modification in applied settings*. Pacific Grove, CA: Brooks/Cole.

KLEIN, N. C., ALEXANDER, J., & PARSONS, B. (1977). Impact of family systems intervention on recidivism and sibling delinquency: A model of primary prevention and program evaluation. *Journal of Consulting and Clinical Psychology, 45*(3), 469–479.

LAZARUS, A. (1981). *Multimodal therapy*. New York: McGraw-Hill.

LIBERMAN, R. (1970). Behavioral approaches to family and couple therapy. *American Journal of Orthopsychiatry, 40*, 106–111.

LOVELESS, L., SMOLER, B., & HARTIN, G. (1997). Case example. Unpublished manuscript. Austin: University of Texas.

MARKS, I. (1973). New approaches to the treatment of obsessive compulsive disorders. *Journal of Nervous Mental Disease, 156*, 420–426.

MORRIS, S. B., ALEXANDER, J. F., & WALDRON H. (1988). Functional family therapy. In I. R. H. Falloon (Ed.), *Handbook of behavioral family therapy*. New York: Guilford.

PARSONS, B. V., & ALEXANDER, J. F. (1973). Short-term family intervention: A therapy outcome study. *Journal of Consulting and Clinical Psychology, 41*(2), 195–201.

PATTERSON, G. (1971). *Families: Applications of social learning to family life*. Champaign, IL: Research Press.

PATTERSON, G. R. (1982). *A social learning approach: Coercive family process* (Vol. 3). Eugene, OR: Castalia.

PATTERSON, G. R., CHAMBERLAIN, P., & REID, J. B. (1982). A comparative evaluation of a parent-training program. *Behavior Therapy, 13*, 638–650.

PATTERSON, G. R., REID, J. B., JONES, R. R., & CONGER, R. E. (1975). *A social learning approach to family intervention: Families with aggressive children*. Eugene, OR: Castalia.

POLSTER, R., & DANGEL, R. (1989). Behavioral parent training in family therapy. In B. A. Thyer (Ed.), *Behavioral family therapy* (pp. 31–77). Springfield, IL: Charles C. Thomas.

RANDOLPH, E. T., ETH, S., GLYNN, S., PAZ, G. B., LEONG, G. B., SHANER, A. L., STRACHAN, A., VAN VORT, W., ESCOBAR, J., & LIBERMAN, R. P. (1994). Behavioral family management in schizophrenia: Outcome from a clinic-based intervention. *British Journal of Psychiatry, 164*, 501–506.

REGAS, S. J., & SPRENKLE, D. H. (1984). Functional family therapy and the treatment of inhibited sexual desire. *Journal of Marital and Family Therapy, 10*(1), 63–72.

ROSE, S. D. (1977). *Group therapy: A behavioral approach.* Englewood Cliffs, NJ: Prentice-Hall.

ROSE, S. D. (1989). *Working with adults in groups: Integrating cognitive-behavioral and small group strategies.* San Francisco: Jossey-Bass.

RUFF, M. (1985). Behavioral family therapy symposium. *The American Journal of Family Therapy, 14*(2), 171–174.

SATIR, V. (1972). *Peoplemaking.* Palo Alto: Science and Behavior Books.

SKINNER, B. F. (1953). *Science and human behavior.* New York: Free Press.

SKINNER, B. F. (1974). *About behaviorism.* New York: Knopf.

SNYDER, D. K. (1979). Dyadic Adjustment Scale: Multi-dimensional assessment of marital satisfaction. *Journal of Marriage and the Family, 41*, 813–823.

SPANIER, G. B. (1976). Measuring dyadic adjustment: New scales for assessing the quality of marriage and similar dyads. *Journal of Marriage and the Family, 38*, 15–28.

STRAUS, M. A. (1979). Measuring intrafamily conflict and violence: The conflict tactics (TC) scales. *Journal of Marriage and the Family, 41*, 75–88.

STUART, R. B. (1980). *Helping couples change: A social learning approach to marital therapy.* New York: Guilford.

SZYKULA, S. A., MORRIS, S., & SAYGER, T. (1987). Child focused behavior and strategic therapies: Outcome comparisons. *Psychotherapy, 24*, 546–550.

THOMAS, E. J. (1977). *Marital communication and decision making: Analysis, assessment, and change.* New York: Free Press.

THORNDIKE, E. L. (1898). Animal intelligence: An experimental study of the associative processes in animals. *Psychological Review* (Monograph Supplement), *2*(8), 1, 16.

THORPE, G. L., & OLSON, S. L. (1990). *Behavior therapy: Concepts, procedures, and applications.* Boston: Allyn & Bacon.

THYER, B. A. (Ed.). (1989). *Behavioral family therapy.* Springfield: Charles C. Thomas.

TORGENRUD, J., & STORM, C. L. (1989). One person family therapy?: An analysis of family therapy schools. *The American Journal of Family Therapy, 17*(2), 143–154.

WEISS, R. L. (1980). *Marital Status Inventory.* Oregon Marital Studies Program, Department of Psychology, University of Oregon, Eugene.

WEISS, R. L. (1996a). *Area of Change Questionnaire.* Oregon Marital Studies Program, Department of Psychology, University of Oregon, Eugene.

WEISS, R. L. (1996b). *Spouse Observation Checklist.* Oregon Marital Studies Program, Department of Psychology, University of Oregon, Eugene.

WELLS, K. C. (1994). Parent and family management training. In L. W. Craighead, W. E. Craighead, A. E. Kazdin, & M. J. Mahoney (Eds.), *Cognitive and behavioral interventions.* Boston: Allyn & Bacon.

WETCHLER, J. L. (1985). Functional family therapy: A life cycle perspective. *The American Journal of Family Therapy, 13*(4), 41–48.

WOLPE, J. (1958). *Psychotherapy by reciprocal inhibition.* Stanford, CA: Stanford University Press.

CHAPTER FIVE

Cynthia Franklin, Ph.D.
University of Texas at Austin

Kelly Conroy Moore, MSSW
University of Texas at Austin

Solution-Focused Brief Family Therapy

Solution-focused therapy is a strengths-based therapy model developed at the Brief Family Therapy Center in Milwaukee, Wisconsin, by Steve de Shazer (de Shazer, 1985, 1988, 1991, 1994; de Shazer et al., 1986) and Insoo Kim Berg (Berg & Miller, 1992; Berg, 1994; Berg & De Jong, 1996) and associates (Miller, Hubble, & Duncan, 1996; Walter & Peller, 1992) over the past 15 years.

The growth and wide dissemination of solution-focused therapy has resulted in many different variations of the solution-focused model. Aside from some differences in style and technique, therapists seem to have a uniformity in treatment philosophy used across fields of practice. The growth of solution-focused therapy has also led to a differentiation between practitioners who are *solution oriented* versus those who are *solution focused* (Becvar & Becvar, 1996). Solution-focused practitioners are associated with the progenitors and follow the original model developed by de Shazer and Berg. Solution-oriented therapists apply a broader range of techniques and innovations, resulting in deviations from the original model.

This chapter follows closely the solution-focused model developed by Steve de Shazer and Insoo Kim Berg and those who were trained by them at the Brief Family Therapy Center in Milwaukee. The chapter describes the theoretical basis of solution-focused therapy and its major assumptions and techniques, including a discussion of how to conduct a solution-focused therapy session. The developing research basis of the solution-focused therapy model is further highlighted, and its values base and consistency with social work theory and practice are examined. Elements of the therapy that make it compatible with managed behavioral health care are discussed. Finally, the methods of solution-focused therapy are illustrated with a therapy transcript from a session conducted by Insoo Kim Berg.

History

Both Steve de Shazer and Insoo Kim Berg were originally educated as social workers and trained as systemic family therapists; they were heavily influenced by the Mental Research Institute (MRI) brief therapy model that originated in Palo Alto, California, in 1967. (See Chapter 3 for a review of the MRI brief therapy model.) Solution-focused therapy retains aspects that make it similar to the MRI model but has also incorporated several changes and innovations (Berg, 1994).

Solution-focused therapy was developed by clinical practitioners who studied its uses and effectiveness using idiographic, qualitative methods such as case study analysis (de Shazer & Berg, 1997). Because there is often a wide gap between the experimental methods employed by clinical researchers and the case study methods used by practitioners, the model did not evolve out of the use of experimental research designs. Practitioners, however, found solution-focused therapy to be a useful model, and this has led to its wide use in clinical practice. In particular, solution-focused therapy, or solution-focused brief therapy as it is sometimes called, is a model useful in behavioral health care and other brief therapy settings where practitioners have limited time to work with clients toward developing coping strategies and quick resolutions of their presenting problems.

Theoretical Basis for the Practice Model

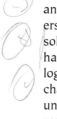

Solution-focused therapists espouse a set of philosophical beliefs about clients and their inherent capacities for strength, resiliency, and self-change. Practitioners using this model hold a deep regard and respect for clients' own capacities to solve their problems. The role of the therapist is to create a context where this can happen. From this philosophical basis, solution-focused therapists are nonpathological in their approach. They do not see problems as being enduring or unchangeable. Essential to solution-focused therapy is the idea that clients have untapped strengths and resiliencies that may be utilized to help them develop workable solutions. One such set of strengths encompasses the personal strategies and contexts that have helped clients avoid the problem in the past. Solution-focused therapists identify and amplify the naturally occurring social support systems and personal and social behaviors of clients that have helped them to overcome past difficulties. The therapist works very hard to help clients realize what those strengths are and to use them in the present and future situations.

Solution-focused therapists, like narrative therapists (see Chapter 6), use a not knowing or "Colombo" (the television homicide detective) approach to relationships with clients. The practitioner is client-centered, and clients are treated as experts on their problems and lives. This does not mean that the practitioner has no expertise, but rather that he or she does not know as much about clients and their resources as clients do. Solution-focused therapists build expectancy and seek to establish a future orientation. This does not mean that they ignore problems. Solution-focused therapists, for example, ask questions to assess how much the clients identify with their problem roles and how invested clients are in their own explanations about their problems. Solution-focused therapists specifically assess how motivated clients are to change and how well they are coping with their problems, instead of spending most of their time on problem identification, as in the problem-solving model. Solution-focused therapists examine previous problem-solving successes and are more interested in exceptions to the problems. Solution-focused therapists believe there are many ways to achieve goals and that change is inevitable. They seek to build on changes in a way that helps clients accomplish their goals (Berg, 1994; De Jong & Berg, 1997).

Major Assumptions

The focus of solution-focused therapy models is on the strengths and competencies of the client. Personality and other individual characteristics are not static; they can change, but insight and awareness are not needed to produce this change. There is no need to know the cause, function, or meaning of the complaint (unless organic in nature). The practitioner's responsibility for treatment is to create an atmosphere for change, especially for behavior change outside the session. A client's past experiences do not limit present or future behavior. Clients have resources that can enhance solution building. If the practitioner listens closely to the client, he or she will know how to utilize those resources (O'Hanlon & Weiner-Davis, 1989).

Franklin (1996) applied a meta-framework to understand the change processes involved in solution-focused therapy. From this research, she argued that the therapy focuses on getting clients to change behavior patterns and social interactions in ways that comprise a perceived solution to the presenting problems. Behavior therapists Jacobson and Christensen (1996a) characterized solution-focused therapy as primarily relying on a behavioral exchange model whereby clients are asked to increase the frequency of positive behaviors and social exchanges in ways that will increase rewarding interactions. Others, such as Pinsoff (1996), have also described solution-focused therapy as centering on a behavioral approach to change. Carpenter (1997) further acknowledges that "others observe that its similarities to aspects of the cognitive behavior therapy remain unexplored" (p. 117).

For the most part, identification of the solution-focused model with a behavioral approach to change has primarily been by academics who categorize treatment models based on the way they match the theory and methods of other models and connect to a spectrum of explanatory social science theories that have been developed to promote change. From this viewpoint, the major techniques and change strategies proposed by solution-focused therapy are behavioral and cognitive in nature.

The actual theory base of the solution-focused model, however, has been evolving and has changed during the course of its development. In the 1980s, for example, solution-focused therapy was identified with a range of social science theories, including behavioral theory, ecological theory, general systems theory, and constructivist theory. One reason the theory base for the model has been discussed in such diverse ways may be that the main focus of the solution model is on developing viable change strategies and not on the empirical grounding of the therapy in social science theory. Practitioners who developed the model focused on detailing successful change strategies, and metaphorically borrowed from theories to explain what they were doing. Much like the MRI brief therapy discussed in Chapter 3, solution-focused therapy presents methods for rapid behavior change with little attention to a formal theory of human behavior. For example, de Shazer (1988) directs people away from trying to understand an etiology of a behavior or from seeking answers to why the behavior exists. These things do not matter as much as how the behavior can be changed.

More recently, the developers of the solution-focused model (de Shazer, 1994) have defined changes in language (the way clients and others talk about a problem) as being essential to changing clients' conceptions and actions. Because solution-focused therapy seeks to change language, narratives, and cognitions in a process that leads to behavior change, it has been closely associated with the social construction theory. Links with social construction theory, however, remain tenuous, as the theoretical base of solution-focused therapy has evolved through the years. The model was developed by practitioners and not researchers, so systematic analysis of the theoretical constructs of the model have not been completed. The focus instead has been on development of the therapeutic techniques for generating change in clients. Most of the theoretical analysis of the model has been articulated by Steve de Shazer, one of the developers of the model. De Shazer (1988, 1994) has written extensively about the basis of solution-focused therapy, but these writings are philosophical, not empirical. Therefore, the links with social construction theory have been used as one way to describe how the model works.

Consistent with social constructionism, solution-focused therapists believe that a client's interpersonal and social reality evolve out of a social context, or interactions with other people. Social interactions are defined and maintained through language. For this reason, solution-focused therapists work to get clients and those involved in clients' social contexts to talk differently about the client and the problem. Talking differently helps clients to think differently and act differently, leading to the resolution of presenting problems. For example, by using a miracle question (described below), a client may for the first time begin to talk through what the solution to a problem is and what changes can be made. Clients may not have been aware of what they wanted before they heard themselves answer the question. Others answering the question or listening to each other answer the question may also become aware of the solution for the first time. The process of describing a solution in detail begins to create a new perceptual and social reality that clients may act on. Along with these notions is the idea that clients do not know what they think until they speak. Changes in language and cognitions are used as a means to define and generate the behavioral changes that are needed to develop an agreed-on, socially constructed solution.

From the viewpoint of changing language to change behavior, it is not helpful and may even be counterproductive for a therapist to spend a lot of time talking about the problem or taking lengthy histories about past problem behaviors. The work of the solution-focused therapist is directed toward co-constructing with the client a set of solution-oriented future behaviors. Therefore, the therapist works on what the client will do and on what is going to be different instead of focusing on the problem behavior. The only relevant past history relates specifically to the future solution, such as times when the client successfully mastered the presenting problem (called an exception). This does not mean that solution-focused therapists will not listen to the problem stories that clients bring to therapy. Solution-focused therapists are not "problem phobic" (de Shazer, 1994). Listening carefully is important for validating clients' feelings and personal reality as well as for establishing rapport. Solution-focused therapists, however, listen with a type of "third ear" approach. That is, they listen for things not emphasized by the client, such as times that the client's life is going well and the problem is absent. They also listen for strengths and resiliencies clients may not notice in themselves. They then proceed to direct the conversation toward strengths and solutions.

Key Constructs

Over the past five years, social constructionism has become an important theory influencing family practice (Franklin, 1995), and one that is increasingly being identified with solution-focused therapy. Chapter 6 discusses narrative and postmodern approaches, practice models that use as their theoretical base the social construction theory. Here we discuss some of the main theoretical assumptions of social constructionism.

Gergen (1985) describes social constructionism (SC) as being concerned with the social processes by which people come to describe, explain, and account for their world. Inquiry is invited concerning social artifacts, social situations, and the historical and cultural understanding of world construction. Social constructionism uses historical, cultural, and contextual analysis to deconstruct social processes. Such "sacred cows" as logical positivism and all psychological theories are understood as socially constructed, essentially social myths (Gergen, 1982). Berger and Luckman's (1966) famous treatise on the sociology of knowledge, *The Social Construction of Reality,* describes how humans are biologically predestined to construct and to inhabit a world with others: "This world becomes the dominant and definitive social reality. Its limits are set by nature, but once constructed, this world acts back upon nature. Man produces reality and thereby produces himself" (p. 183). Social constructionism is remarkably similar to Alfred Schutz's (1962) phenomenological sociology—a branch of sociology in which subjectivity is paramount and adherents focus on how social experiences are made meaningful. Harold Garfinkle's (1967) radical approach to research, ethnomethodology (a research methodology that studies how people create, sustain, and manage their sense of everyday reality), is also very similar. Similarities between these approaches should come as no surprise, however, as Peter Berger was a student of Schutz, as was Garfinkle (Wallace & Wolf, 1991).

Berger and Luckman (1966) believed that the sociology of knowledge must concern itself with whatever passes for knowledge. As sociologists, they also believed that all human knowledge is developed, transmitted, and maintained in social situations and through social institutions (Berger & Luckman, 1966, p. 3).

They hoped to develop a type of "sociological-psychology" that could explain knowledge development. Because of their emphasis, they believed that the sociology of knowledge must give attention to the sociology of language. They were particularly interested in socialization processes such as the legitimization of knowledge and how humans reify social structures that subsequently construct their realities.

Social constructionism is appropriately discussed as a method of postmodern discourse (McNamee & Gergen, 1992; Hoffman, 1990). Lax (1992) contends that "all postmodern discourses are basically deconstructive because they seek to distance us from and make us skeptical about beliefs concerning truth, knowledge, power, the self, and language that are usually taken for granted, and serve as legitimization for contemporary western culture" (p. 71). McNamee and Gergen (1992) believe that social constructionism may serve as a meta-framework in which all critical perspectives, including those embodying literary criticism, critical theory, and social action, may gather. Doise (1989) states that constructionism is a "grand theory [that] adheres to a new kind of nominalism, according to which the ultimate foundation of our understanding is not to be found in objective reality itself but in language" (p. 390). Language is self-referential and self-contained. Although all ideas are social conventions, it is the act of being and talking with others in a social context that defines our social reality. Gergen and Kaye (1992) are explicit about this belief when they define the "self" as an interpersonal or socially constructed phenomenon. Similar to social construction theory, solution-focused therapy emphasizes the narrative basis of reality and the interactional and social contextual basis for behavior (Becvar & Becvar, 1996).

Social construction theory, however, is neither a clinical practice theory nor a model; it was historically adopted into social work—and more recently, into family therapy—as a meta-framework for practice (Hoffman, 1990; Richan & Mendelsohn, 1973; Saleeby, 1992; Witkin, 1991). As social constructionism was used as a guiding framework for social problems theory in the discipline of sociology, it was integrated into social work practice in accordance with this view. Its usage in family therapy is related to a growing discontent with systems theories by some practitioners and a desire to return to a more cultural or anthropological basis for understanding families. Ideas associating the solution-focused therapy with social construction theory parallel these developments in the broader field of family therapy (Franklin, 1995).

Therapeutic Methods

Solution-focused therapy is a behavioral and goal-directed, strengths-based therapy model. Solution-focused therapists, for example, use a set of behaviorally and cognitively oriented therapy techniques to amplify positive behaviors and reinforce the use of effective coping strategies. Solution-focused therapy is different from other prescriptive approaches because of its emphasis on process and its total focus on the future behaviors that will help clients accomplish their goals. For this reason, solution-focused therapists do not spend very much time exploring problems but instead are more interested in working with the client to construct a set of behavioral tasks that lead to a rapid solution.

The major tasks of the solution-focused therapist have been described by Kral (1995), who discusses a 5-D model. The therapist is to *develop* an image of a realistic solution. The job of the therapist is to help clients develop a clear picture of what their world would be like without the presenting problem. What will be different when the presenting problem is no longer a problem? *Discover* how and in what ways the solution is already occurring in the client's life. *Determine* small, measurable steps (goals) toward the solution. *Describe* those thoughts, actions, or feelings that can help obtain the goals. This includes recognizing possibilities for using differing aspects of the client's life such as hobbies, fantasies, and competencies in other areas to promote change (often called the utilization principle). The therapist also identifies applications by thinking about the client's life and some similar set of difficulties he or she has solved. It is then possible to come up with a set of interventions in which the client is competent and which he or she can use in solving the problem. The therapist also provides connections between the client's competencies and skills and the possible resolutions for the problem. This helps clients think of ways already in their repertoire of mastery and skills to approach the problem differently. Last, *do* something to make a difference. The therapist either focuses the client on doing more of the same behaviors that have worked in the past or on doing something totally new and different in the situation. The new behavior is often counterintuitive and is directed toward changing repetitive behavioral patterns.

Methods of the solution-focused therapist include a set of process stages or sequences that the therapist carries out in a session. However, these sequences may not be serial, in that therapists sometimes change the order of the sequences from the ones presented below. For example, the miracle question may be asked before scaling questions. The use of at least three main process sequences in a session is necessary for a therapy to be considered solution focused (Berg & de Shazer, letter and personal communication, January 2, 1997). These three sequences are (1) therapist used the miracle question; (2) therapist used scaling questions; (3) therapist gave clients compliments, sometimes followed by "homework" tasks at the end of the session. The last step usually comes after the therapist has taken a break to plan the compliments and tasks.

Conducting the First Session of Solution-Focused Therapy

Franklin and Biever (1997) describe the process steps that may be followed in a solution-focused therapy session and the major techniques used:

FINDING OUT ABOUT THE CLIENT'S LIFE

Paying special attention to interests, motivations, competencies, and beliefs, the therapist asks about the client's life. This is accomplished in a social, conversational manner by "chatting" with clients about their work, hobbies, vocations, interests, and commitments. Special attention is given to metaphors and the use of these to access the client's beliefs and to assist the client in changing existing beliefs and behaviors. This sequence is ongoing in that the therapist is always learning about the client, but a short time—usually 5 to 10 minutes—is allotted in the first session to get the sequence started. At the end of this sequence the therapist should be able to answer questions such as these: What does the client like to do? What are some major hobbies or interests of the client? How does the client use language to describe himself or herself and others? Can any important key words or metaphors be used to communicate with the client? What is known so far about the client's worldview or beliefs?

GATHERING A BRIEF DESCRIPTION OF THE PROBLEM BEHAVIORS

After the solution-focused therapist is acquainted with the client, he or she proceeds to gather a problem description from the client by asking questions such as, "What would have to happen for you to know that it was worth your time to come and see me today? If we were successful in making progress in solving the problem that brought you here today, what would need to be different?" The client will usually begin to volunteer information about the presenting problem. The therapist asks follow-up questions to gain a sense of the problem, context of the problem, and exceptions to the problem. However, the questions may be phrased in different ways to accommodate individual clients. The therapist should come out of this sequence having asked and been provided answers to the following questions: What is the problem? How long has the problem been going on? How often does the problem occur? Where or in what situations does the problem occur? Who is there when the problem happens, or who is involved in the problem? What each person does in a sequence (What does your teacher do? What do your classmates do? When the principal comes, what does he do?). Whose idea was it for you to come for help with the problem? Why did you come or get sent for help now and not before? What is your explanation for why this problem is happening? What have you tried so far to solve the problem?

ASKING RELATIONSHIP QUESTIONS

Relationship questions can help the client define the socially constructed nature of the problem. The therapist asks relationship questions such as, "What would your teacher say about your grades? What would your mother say? If you were to do something that made your teacher very happy, what would that be? Who would be most surprised that you did really well on the test? What would that person say about the fact that you are doing so well?" Relationship questions are used throughout the sessions at different points to help the client gain a meta-perspective about the problem and to assess the individual cognitive constructions and social constructions concerning the problem definition and resolution. Relationship questions can be used to help clients discuss their problems from a meta-perspective (third person's point of view), making the problems less threatening to discuss and further drawing on untapped resources from the client.

After asking relationship sequence questions, a therapist should know how the client perceives the problem as well as the client's perceptions about others' perspectives on the problem or problem resolution. The therapist should also know how the problem is being socially constructed. Who, from the client's perspective, makes the problem worse, and who makes it better? What social supports and resources are available to the client and how may these resources be used to solve the problem?

TRACKING SOLUTION BEHAVIORS OR EXCEPTIONS TO THE PROBLEM

The therapist identifies times when the problem does not occur, effective coping responses, and the contexts for the absence of the problem. Therapists using solution-focused therapy are interested in "pre-treatment change." They will ask clients how things have improved between the time they set the appointment and the present. This process is usually carried out throughout the session. The therapist says something such as, "Even though this is a very bad problem, in my experience, people's lives do not always stay the same. I'll bet that there are times when the problem of being sent to the principal's office is not happening, or at least it is happening less. Describe those times. What is different? How did you get that to happen?"

The therapist gathers as many exceptions to the problem pattern as possible by repeatedly asking the client what else . . . what other times . . .? The therapist must be patient and give the client time to construct the exceptions from episodic memory. Because clients are often focused on the problem situations, the exceptions may not be foremost on their minds. Once an exception has been identified by the client, the therapist uses "prompts" such as "Tell me more about that" to help the client describe in detail the exceptions. The therapist also uses his or her own affects, tone, and intense attention to the client's story to communicate to the client that he or she is very interested in those exceptions. Such nonverbal gestures as nodding, smiling, leaning forward, and looking surprised are used. Therapists also may say things such as "How about that! I am amazed! Wow!" as social reinforcement to the client. This encourages the client to talk on and to develop the exceptions story in more detail.

The therapist should come out of this sequence knowing the following: What exceptions to the problem exist? How often have exceptions occurred? When was the last time an exception happened? What was different in the situation when the exception occurred from situations when the problem happens? Who was involved in making the exception happen?

SCALING THE PROBLEM

Using scaling questions, the therapist will anchor the problem and track progress toward problem resolutions. The therapist says, using the prior descriptions of the client concerning the problem descriptions and exceptions, "On a scale of 1 to 10 with 1 being that you are getting in trouble every day in the class, picking on Johnny and Susi, getting out of your seat and being scolded by your teacher, and 10 being that instead of fighting with Johnny and Susi you are doing your work, and that you ask permission to get out of your seat, and your teacher says something nice to you, where would you be on that scale now?" With children, often smiley and sad faces are also used to anchor the two ends of the scale.

Several other uses of the scaling technique in the therapy process include the following: asking questions about where the client is on the scale in relation to solving the problem; using the scaling experience to find exceptions to the problems; employing scales to construct "miracles" or identify solution behaviors. For example, the therapist asks where on the scale (with 1 representing low and 10 representing high) the client is, and how the client will get from 1 to a 3. Or the therapist asks how clients managed to move from a 4 to a 5 rating. What new behaviors did they implement, or what was different in their lives that made the changes? Solution-focused therapists may also express surprise that the problem is not worse on the scale as a way of complimenting the client's coping behavior or as a way to use language to change the client's perception of the intractable nature of their problem. The therapist may use the scale, along with the "miracle question" (described below), by asking the client, "If there were an overnight miracle and you could get to a 9 or 10 on the scale, what would be the first thing you would notice that was different?"

Solution behaviors described by the client through the use of the scaling technique are often used in constructing specific tasks or homework assignments that are prescribed and discussed in future sessions. When the scaling sequence is finished, the therapist should have developed with the client a scale from 1 to 10 that can be referred to in future sessions. Two concrete behavioral descriptions or self-anchors should describe the problem and its solutions: 1 should be anchored as the problem behaviors and 10 the presence of solution behaviors. The therapist uses the client's own words, descriptions, and images to develop the anchors. At the close of the scaling sequence, the therapist should have obtained a rating from the client on where he or she is on the scale today.

USING COPING AND MOTIVATION QUESTIONS

Another set of questions will help the therapist assess how clients perceive they are coping and determine their motivation for change. This step is a variation on the scaling question that helps the therapist assess clients' motivations for solving problems as well as how well clients perceive that they are coping with problems. The therapist says something like, "On a scale of 1 to 10, with 10 being you would do anything to solve this problem and 1 being that you do not care so much for solving it, where would you say you are right now?" Or the therapist may say, "On a scale of 1 to 10, with 1 being that you are ready to throw in the towel and give up ever doing well in school, and 10 being that you are ready to keep on trying, where would you rate yourself right now?" After asking coping and motivation questions the therapist should be able to determine the following: whether the problem is too overwhelming to the client; how much self-efficacy and hope the client possesses for problem resolution; whether the client is committed to working on the problem; and whether the problem that has been defined is the one that really interests the client and is the priority for the client.

If the problem is too overwhelming, it needs to be broken down into smaller steps and redefined for the client. If the client does not believe the problem can be solved, steps must be taken to change this belief. The exception questions are empowering in this regard. If the client is not interested in committing to working on the problem, the problem must be redefined to muster some degree of commitment.

ASKING THE MIRACLE QUESTION TO DEVELOP SOLUTIONS

The therapist says, "Let's suppose that an overnight miracle happened and the problem you are having with your teacher disappeared. But you were sleeping and did not know it. When you came to school the next day, what would be the first thing you notice?" The therapist helps the client envision a new way of behaving and how things could be different. An extreme amount of detail is elicited to help develop a set of concrete and behaviorally specific solution actions.

The therapist should come out of this sequence with a detailed description of what life would be like for the client without the problem. The therapist should also have helped the client develop a specific set of behaviors, thoughts, and feelings that can be substituted for problem patterns. It is important to discover what the client and others will perceive as a solution to the problem. Asking relationship questions along with the miracle question helps confirm this information.

NEGOTIATING THE GOAL FOR CHANGE

From the problem descriptions and the miracle question, the therapist negotiates with the client small concrete and behavioral goals that make up the miracle picture of the client. The ideal goal is important to the client—something the client is motivated to accomplish. Clients should have clearly stated that this goal is something they want for their lives. Goals should also be small and obtainable. Movement should be possible toward the goal immediately and before the next session. To ensure the possibility of immediate movement toward the goal, a goal should be concrete, specific, and behaviorally defined. The therapist and client should be able to describe specifically what the client is to do. The frequency, duration, and context of goal-directed behaviors should be easily described. What, when, how, and with whom is the behavior to happen? Goals should be realistic and achievable within the context of clients' lives. The goal must be a set of behaviors a client can practice in everyday life. It cannot depend on other people to accomplish unless those people have agreed to work on the goal too. The goal should involve something clients are capable of doing on their own.

To be most effective, goals should include the presence rather than absence of a behavior. A goal should describe what a client is to do instead of the problem behavior. Goals should be represented to the client as a beginning to behavior change rather than an end to the process. The therapist may use phrases like, "This is a step" or "This is a beginning." Goals should be understood by the client as hard work, something he or she has to work at constantly to achieve. Action must be taken and tasks must be completed if the goal is to be reached. The therapist may say things like, "I know that this may not be easy, but you have done it before. Are you willing to work to get this going? This will take a lot of effort but is something you can do." The therapist should come out of this sequence having helped the client set realistic goals.

TAKING A SESSION BREAK

Near the end of the session, the therapist takes a 5 to 10 minute break for reflection and to construct the information gained into a behavioral task or homework assignment. It is not absolutely necessary for the therapist to give a homework assignment. He or she may simply offer a set of reflections for the client to think about, but in most instances an assignment is given. Part of the work of the therapist is to formulate as many genuine compliments as possible to deliver to the client. If working with a team of therapists behind a one-way mirror, the therapist may also use this time to consult with the team to develop compliments and homework tasks.

The therapist should come out of the break with a list of compliments to give to the client. Compliments should be based on the exceptions generated from the client, the miracle picture, and the client's strengths and capacities that are assessed in the session. A behavioral task or a set of reflections that requires the client to engage in behavioral exercises, recording behaviors, or reflections aimed at changing behavior, thoughts, or feelings should be assigned.

A helpful end to this sequence is a bridging statement that ties together the content of the session with a rationale for the homework assignment. A bridging statement serves as a transitional sentence that moves the therapist from the compliments sequence back to the session content to the homework assignment. For example, "Because you do so well finishing your homework on the days that you do not ride the bus but your mom picks you up, I am wondering if you can play a pretend game with me that asks you to do something different on the days you have to ride the bus. You do really well when you get home earlier and start your homework right away before you watch TV. I am wondering if on the days you ride the bus, you could pretend that it is an hour earlier when you get home. In fact, I want you to set your watch and clock in your room an hour backward. Prepare the VCR to tape the show you usually watch and spend that hour on your homework."

DELIVERING COMPLIMENTS AND TASKS

The therapist gives four to five genuine compliments to the client. The therapist and client discuss a set of meaningful reflections or a concrete behavioral task for the client to work on between sessions. At this time, the therapist should obtain a commitment from the client to do the task and communicate that they will follow up on successes in the next session. The session is ended by setting another appointment.

Solution-Focused Therapy Process Following the First Session

All solution-focused therapy sessions use a similar process and set of sequences, implemented by the therapist, as in the first session described above, with a few variations. Subsequent sessions follow this process.

WARM-UP

The initial step includes carrying on a social conversation with the client. A therapist should come out of this sequence having established a rapport with the client observed by an ease in communicating and a relaxed atmosphere in the session. The therapist should inquire further about personal attributes and continue learning how clients use language to describe themselves and others. In addition, the therapist should always work toward learning more important key words or metaphors that can be used to communicate to the client and gaining more knowledge about the client's worldview or beliefs.

TRACKING NEW EXCEPTIONS TO THE PROBLEM

To begin the work of the session, the therapist asks the question, "So, what has changed or what is better?" This also includes a review of the client's uses of the homework assignment given in the last session. The therapist should finish this sequence knowing the following: What new exceptions to the problem have occurred over the last week? How often have exceptions occurred? When was the last time an exception happened? What was different in the situation where the exception occurred than in situations where the problem happens? Who was involved in making the exception happen? What were the results of the homework assignment?

USING RELATIONSHIP QUESTIONS

The next step is to track how the client perceives that others have responded to the changes and to amplify the client's belief in the power of the changes. The therapist should ask relationship questions to reinforce the changes and exceptions that occurred. For example, the therapist would ask, "Who was the first to notice that you did your homework on Monday, Wednesday, and Friday? What did Ms. Smith say? How did that make you feel for her to say she was proud of you? Did you tell anyone that this happened to you?"

The relationship questioning sequence will help the therapist learn how the client perceives the problem as well as the client's perceptions about others' perspectives on the problem or problem resolution. This sequence should also show the therapist how the problem and solution are being socially constructed and who from the client's perspective makes the problem worse and who makes it better. The therapist should also find out what social supports and resources are available to the client and how these resources are being used to solve the problem.

ASKING THE SCALING QUESTION

The scaling question is asked to see where the client has moved on the scale and to help the client move ahead even further toward a goal. The therapist should end this sequence by obtaining a new scale rating from the client and asking how the client will move forward another point.

BUILDING MORE SOLUTION BEHAVIORS FOR THE FUTURE

The therapist may ask clients the miracle question or its variations to learn how close they are to the miracle picture or what pieces of the miracle have happened over the past week. Alternatively, the therapist may ask the entire miracle question over in relation to a new goal or different aspect of the goal.

TAKING A BREAK TO FORMULATE THOUGHTS
AND DEVELOP COMPLIMENTS AND TASKS

A therapist should return to the session with a list of compliments to give to the client. Compliments should be based on the exceptions generated from the client, the miracle picture, and the client's strengths and capacities that are assessed in the session. A set of reflections or behavioral tasks should be given to the client that requires the client to continue engaging in behavioral exercises, recording behaviors, or reflections aimed at changing behavior, thoughts, or feelings. This is often a variation on a task co-constructed with the client from the questioning sequences earlier in the session. This sequence can be ended with a bridging statement that ties together the content of the session with a rationale for the homework assignment.

DELIVERING THE COMPLIMENTS AND ASSIGNING THE NEW TASK

In this sequence, the therapist should give four or five genuine compliments to the client. After developing a set of reflections or a concrete behavioral task for the client to work on between sessions, the therapist should obtain a commitment from the client to do the task and communicate that the client will follow up on his or her successes in the next session. Set another appointment.

Examples of Tasks and Therapeutic Maneuvers Used to Change Behavior

Solution-focused therapists use homework assignments, behavioral exercises, and structured tasks to help the client change. Tasks are often formulated through a process of Socratic questioning and co-construction with the client. In other words, the therapist asks curious, reflective, or probing questions, and the client responds. Through this process behavioral tasks emerge. Following are some examples of the types of task and interventions used.

The *first formula task* is an all-around task that is helpful when clients have difficulty developing very many exceptions. The therapist tells the client to keep track (record) of the times when things are going well and the problem is not happening and to notice what is different at those times.

Betting is a method that has proven to be a powerful approach, particularly with children and adolescents who are competitive and respond to challenges rather than to internal drives. The student is challenged with a monetary or "gentlemen's" bet relating to the continuation of an identified change. This method requires that the new behaviors can be described in concrete terms and that there is a notable degree of confidence that the client intends to continue the new pattern. Care should be taken to set the bet in such a fashion that the individual feels challenged while the goal remains within a reasonable range. It is also important for the therapist to communicate some degree of faith in the client's ability to maintain the changes and win the bet (Kral, 1995).

Betting appears to work best when an outside source (e.g., teacher, assistant principal, lunch room supervisor, parent) is given the role of the skeptic. This allows the therapist to take the side of the client and bet against the external force. Thus, the client feels both challenged and supported at the same time.

A *new context* is a co-created task that represents the delineation of the factors that need to be present for the new behavior to continue. Ask the question, "What needs to occur for [the desired behavior] to happen again or more often?" The therapist proceeds to co-construct along with the client how the context and situation can be changed to assure that the desired behavior will keep happening. For example, ignoring people who "bug" you may work in some situations. What situations? How can you create that situation again?

The *prediction task* is one of several formula tasks used at the Brief Family Therapy Center in Milwaukee. It is generally used when three criteria are met: An exception to the complaint pattern is identified, the exception appears to happen in a pattern similar to "good days, bad days" or "up days, down days," and the client appears to cooperate with behavioral tasks. The task is given to predict whether the following day will be a "good day," as defined by the exception. The following day, the individual is to decide whether it is a "good day" or "bad day." If the prediction is consistent over the course of the day ("on target"), then the person is asked to take note. If the prediction is "off-target," that is, "good" on a day that was predicted to be "bad," then this is to be accounted for (Kral, 1995).

Compliments are used at the end of the session to amplify positive behaviors and help the client to feel empowered to change.

Using language to externalize problems is a technique that is aimed at separating the problem from the self and increasing a person's self-agency over the problem behaviors (e.g., "When ADHD [attention deficit-hyperactivity disorder] tries to get you in trouble with your teacher, what does it make you do? When the fears are trying to scare you, what do they whisper in your ears? Are there times that you stand up to ADHD and don't let it push you around?").

Reversal questions involve asking if someone has any advice for anyone else in terms of helping that person. This is a good technique with children. For example, "What advice can you give your teacher about how she can get you to raise your hand before talking out loud? What ideas do you have for your teachers to help you better in school? What advice do you have for me when I work alone with your teacher? What should I work on changing with her?" Then the therapist agrees to take the advice or asks the child to do a task based on the advice.

The Secret Surprise is a technique developed by Selekman (1997) to use with children. Meet alone with the child and have him or her pick two nice surprises that he or she could perform in one week's time to shock the parents in a positive way. The child is not to tell the parents what the surprises were until the next scheduled appointment. The parents will be asked to play detectives and guess what the surprises were.

Do Something Different Task is another Selekman (1977) technique used as a behavioral task for changing the behavior of children. Explain to the parents that their child has got their number because they are too predictable. Instruct the parents as an experiment to do something different when the child engages in the problematic behavior they wish to see changed.

When *The Imaginary Time Machine* is used, the child is given the following directive: "Let's say I have sitting over here an imaginary time machine, and once you enter it, you can take it anywhere in time, in the past or into the future; where would you go? What would you see there? Who would you meet and talk with? What would you talk about? If you and the famous person from the past hopped into the time machine and came back to present, how would the famous person help you out today? What advice would he or she give you at school? How would he or she help you out with your parents? In other time trips, what would you bring back to help you today?" Selekman uses this task with children to help them develop a meta-perspective about their difficulties and to generate solutions.

Flagging the minefield asks the client to identify factors that could result in the "old" pattern. This technique is powerful in two ways. First, it strongly differentiates between "now" (new or desirable behaviors) and the "old" way by encouraging the client to look back at the way things used to be and to consider what would need to happen for that to occur again. In this way the past (which includes the problem) is clearly different from the present (which does not include the symptomatic behavior). Second, the client is forewarned of the possibility of relapse. When signs of potential trouble are identified in advance and possible responses determined, everyone is in a better position to avoid a recurrence of the presenting complaint. The client is instructed to follow the new identified pattern (Kral, 1995).

Using presuppositional language helps clients restructure cognitive meanings about themselves and their problems (e.g., "*when* you start doing better" instead of *if*). Other examples are these: "Twenty-five percent of the time you get sent to the principal's office, but I am amazed that 75% of the time you don't." "Let's just pretend that you do know what to do to get along with your teacher." Instead of accepting "I do not know" from a child, say, "If you did know, what would you say, or what would the X-Men say?" or "If you were Barney how would you make Ms. Smith happy?" Using these types of questions, therapists can construct a behavioral task to follow.

Consistency with Social Work Practice

Although solution-focused therapy is relatively new to the field of social work, its basic tenets are not. The functionalist school movement that began in the early 1900s closely parallels the ideologies and values of the solution-focused model.

History of the Functionalist School Movement

By the time Richmond's *Social Diagnosis* was published, social work had already begun to move away from the person-family environment configuration to a psychodynamic practice model influenced by the medical profession's conceptual framework of disease-diagnosis-cure and its focus on the individual organism. In 1919, Jessie Taft and Mary Jarrett identified the psychiatric base for all social work practice and suggested that all training programs incorporate material on mental hygiene (Austin, 1986; Dore, 1990). By the end of the 1920s, Freudian thought dominated casework teaching in most professional schools.

Kenneth Pray, dean of the Pennsylvania School in 1922, played a role in changing this dominant discourse. He was academically trained in political science and had been a community organizer before joining Pennsylvania School's faculty. He was deeply committed to social interpretations of individual differences.

Another who strongly influenced the functionalist school was Otto Rank, on whose personality theory the functional model was based (Dore, 1990). Rank was trained as a psychoanalyst in Vienna, but began to break away from Freud in the early 1920s. In his book, *Trauma of Birth*, Rank (1929/1973) described the basic human struggle and claimed that the source of most individual problems was the ongoing tension between a desire to realize one's separate and distinct individuality—to move toward growth and change—and the competing wish to remain psychologically connected and dependent on others—to retreat from growth and change. He believed that change took place from a self-asserted Will. The therapeutic task was to strengthen and mobilize the Will, an accomplishment that came through the helping relationship. Relationship, he felt, was central to the helping process. The therapist is to experience the clients as they present themselves, not "knowing" clients through a cognitive or intellectual process. His focus was on the present, not the past.

Rank also presented the idea of time limits to the therapeutic relationship. He believed that placing time limits on the helping relationship would force the therapist and client to focus on separation as a component of the treatment process, an impetus to growth (Rank, 1929/1973). Jessie Taft was a follower of Rank, and the two worked on a way to incorporate Rank's ideas into a practice model. This led to Taft's seminal statement of functional practice in the *Journal of Social Work Process* in 1934.

Functional Model Principles Similar to Solution-Focused Therapy

Functional theory and solution-focused therapy share some basic tenets in their approaches to treatment. Some of them include the role of diagnosis in the intervention process, the client's right to self-determination, the idea of assessment as an ongoing process, and the belief that therapy should be organized around a time-limited structure.

In both solution-focused therapy and functional theory, a diagnosis is not necessary to implement correct intervention (Dore, 1990; Metcalf, 1995). In both models, labels are neither necessary nor helpful for treating a client effectively. In fact, a goal in solution-focused therapy is to reframe the problem. For example, a child would not be called an Attention Deficit-Hyperactivity Disorder child, but instead a child with a lot of energy (Metcalf, 1995). Functionalists rejected the idea that psychopathology was at the root of all problems in a person's life. Therefore, it is possible that a person does not even have a "diagnosis" for a problem.

In both models, the client plays the central role in the change process because the client chooses the problem to be addressed. The social work tenet "starting where the client is" was a functionalist principle (Dore, 1990). It refers to accepting the client's interpretation of the problem and using that interpretation to organize the focus of the intervention. Therapy begins with the presenting problem, as it is assumed this is the most pressing need, not a metaphor or symbolic meaning expressed by the unconscious. These ideas are also reflected in solution-focused therapy. The therapist is instructed to "follow" very closely with the client's story, not make abstract interpretations of what the client is saying (Berg & De

Jong, 1996). The practitioner's understanding of the client grows solely out of the events of their relationship.

Like all brief therapies, the functionalist school introduced a time-limited approach to treatment that included three phases: beginning, middle, and end. These proponents argued that having a time limit on therapy is beneficial because it provides a structure for the client to work through the problem and gives them ownership of it. What may seem like contemporary concepts, such as time-limited therapy, have historical roots. Time-limited therapy can be traced to optimistic beliefs in the self-determination, self-agency, strengths, and resiliencies inherent in clients. These ideas are at the heart of solution-focused therapy and preceded societal changes such as managed care, which is frequently cited as the cause of time-limited therapy.

Research Support for the Model

Currently, solution-focused therapy is being applied to a wide variety of clinical problems and fields of practice such as child welfare and family-based services (Berg, 1994), inpatient psychiatric disorders (Webster, Vaughn, & Martinez, 1994), alcohol abuse (Berg & Miller, 1992), school-related behavior problems (Durrant, 1995; Metcalf, 1995; Kral, 1995; Murphy, 1994a, 1994b), crisis-oriented youth services (Franklin, Nowicki, Trapp, Schwab, & Petersen, 1993; Franklin, Corcoran, Streeter, & Nowicki, 1997), sexual abuse (Dolan, 1991), and spouse abuse (Sirles, Lipchik, & Kowalski, 1993). Practitioners who use the therapy have illustrated the process, methods, and procedures used in solution-focused therapy practice.

Solution-focused therapy was developed through practice wisdom, not through rigorous empirical testing of its constructs or methods. Only recently have practitioners and researchers worked together for the purpose of evaluating the effectiveness of the model (de Shazer & Berg, 1997). Franklin and colleagues (1993, 1997) demonstrated the uses of the therapy and several methods for evaluating its effectiveness with an agency serving homeless and runaway youth. At present, few outcome studies have been conducted on solution-focused therapy, but the ones that have been completed show that the model is a promising approach that deserves further evaluation (De Jong & Hopwood, 1996; Kiser, 1988; Kiser & Nunnally, 1990).

Early studies on solution-focused therapy are limited in that they are mostly nonrandomized, uncontrolled program evaluations conducted on clients at the Brief Family Therapy Center in Milwaukee. Each study involved the use of follow-up questionnaires and the scaling technique as an outcome measure. Some studies have used process measures (Beyebach & Carranza, 1997). The scaling technique developed by de Shazer, Berg, and colleagues at the Brief Family Therapy Center in Milwaukee has emerged as an important outcome measure for solution-focused therapy. With this method, the therapist constructs the client's problems along a 10-point continuum or another ordinal scale. Because the scaling technique is already used in solution-focused therapy, it seems to be a natural approach for collecting outcome data. Practitioners have recently illustrated its use for this purpose (Berg & De Jong, 1996; Franklin et al., 1993, 1997).

Bloom, Fischer, and Orme (1995) describe a "do-it-yourself" scale similar to the scaling technique that may be used as an outcome measure. Scales have been referred to in the literature as self-anchored scales, target complaint scales, individual problem rating scales, and, more recently, individualized rating scales (Bloom et al., 1995, p. 160). As a measurement instrument, these scales serve as ordinal scales. Practitioners using self-anchored scales construct any client problem on a 7-, 9-, or 10-point scale to monitor the effectiveness of their practice interventions.

A wide variety of individualized behaviors, emotions, thoughts, or other experiences may be rated on different metrics on the self-anchored scales. For example, seriousness, intensity, frequency, or importance may be used for the rating dimensions of scales (Bloom et al., 1995). Ratings represent the quantitative dimensions of the scales, but anchors represent the qualitative definitions that give the scale meaning. According to Bloom and colleagues (1995), anchors are important because they define the meaning of the numbers on a rating scale. For this reason, anchors must be collaboratively constructed with the client, using the client's own words and experience. Studies on the psychometric properties of self-anchored scales demonstrate that these scales usually have acceptable validity and reliability. A review of the literature on the validity and reliability of self-anchored scales is provided by Nugent (1992).

Self-anchored scales are a clinically sensitive outcome method compatible with single-case designs. Single-case designs are research designs in which each participant serves as his or her own control by developing a baseline of behaviors that acts as the focus of change. This baseline is developed preferably before the treatment begins but may be developed retrospectively. Clinical researchers have advocated single-case designs as compatible research designs for the evaluation of brief therapies such as solution-focused therapy (Conoley, 1987; Murphy, 1992, 1996; Franklin et al., 1997). The use of single-case designs may greatly improve the existing research and provide practitioners with a useful method for outcome evaluation in managed care settings (Corcoran & Vandiver, 1996; Franklin et al., 1997).

Though single-case designs provide a promising method for outcome evaluation of solution-focused therapy, early studies on solution-focused therapy as a general rule did not use standardized outcome measures, adequate baselines, control groups, or other rigorous experimental procedures. For example, Berg and De Jong (1996) report on a one-group, posttest design study, conducted at the Brief Family Therapy Center, that is typical of the early studies. In this study, 275 clients were tracked for outcomes during therapy and seven to nine months after therapy. Because no experimental procedures were used, results must be viewed with this limited research design in mind. Using scales of 1 to 10, therapists tracked clients' progress. No difference was found in rates of progress along gender or race lines or in terms of the type of problem treated. At follow-up, clients were asked a question with three possible responses: (1) "treatment goal met," (2) "some progress toward treatment goal," and (3) "no progress toward treatment goal." Forty-five percent of the clients said that their treatment goal was met, whereas 32% believed they had made some progress toward their goal. This resulted in a 77% success rate. See McKeel (1996) for other reviews of the early research on solution-focused therapy. Several new studies have just been released, and others are forthcoming (e.g., Franklin & Biever, 1997).

Lee (1997), in a descriptive study using a posttest only design, assessed the outcomes of solution-focused therapy in a children's mental health facility. Fifty-nine families receiving treatment from 1990 to 1993 were included in the study. Each family had an average of 5.5 therapy sessions. A 14-item questionnaire adapted from the one used in previous studies at the Brief Family Therapy Center in Milwaukee was used to explore goal obtainments and outcomes. Families were called six months following the therapy and administered the questionnaire. Findings were similar to those of other studies, including the one described above, indicating a 64.9% success rate. Support was further found for the clinical utility of solution-focused therapy with a wide range of families with diverse backgrounds.

A similar study was conducted by Macdonald (1997), who followed up 36 clients treated with solution-focused brief therapy in a psychiatric setting. Follow-ups were completed one year after treatment. An adaptation of the same questionnaire was used as described above. The questionnaire was administered to the clients and their attendant physicians who had referred them for the treatment. Twenty-three cases (64%) were found to be successful. Findings are similar to the ones reported by Lee (1997).

Lindforss and Magnusson (1997) conducted a randomized, two-group, pretest-posttest experimental design study with an experimental and control group on the effectiveness of solution-focused brief therapy with a serious criminal population in Swedish prisons. A network approach was used, along with the solution model. Prisoner participation was solicited from all who were within two months of release. From those who volunteered for the study, 60 were randomly assigned to experimental and control conditions so there were 30 in each group. One prisoner later died, leaving 29 in the control group. Subsequent analysis of numerous characteristics of participants in both experimental and control groups indicated that the two groups were equivalent, including such important issues as past history of criminal offenses and recidivism rates.

The average number of sessions of solution-focused therapy received by study participants was five. Recidivism at 12 months and 16 months after release from prison was used as an outcome measure, as well as the seriousness of the offenses by those who had experienced recidivism. Results at 12 months indicated that 47% of the experimental group had remained crime free versus 24% of the control group. At the 16-month follow-up, 40% of the experimental group remained crime free versus only 14% of the control group. This result indicated a considerable clinical difference between the two groups. Analysis indicated that these differences were statistically significant as well as clinically significant. Overall, the control group also committed a greater number of offenses (153) than the experimental group (86). In addition, when comparing the two groups on seriousness of offenses committed at a 12-month follow-up, the control group had committed more serious offenses than the experimental group. This was especially true of drug offenses; of these, the control group committed twice as many offenses as the experimental group.

Schindler, Zimmerman, Prest, and Wetzel (1997) conducted an empirical study on the effectiveness of solution-focused therapy groups for couples. A psychoeducational component was also used in the therapy. A pretest-posttest, between-groups, nonrandomized design with a comparison group was utilized. Twenty-three couples participated in the treatment group and thirteen couples in the comparison group. Participating couples received six sessions of solution-focused group therapy. Two standardized measurement instruments were used to measure outcomes: the Marital Status Inventory and the Dyadic Adjustment Scale. Unfortunately, the treatment group and comparison group ended up not being comparable, so researchers could examine the outcomes using only a pretest-posttest, within-groups design. Significant improvements were found from pretest to posttest on the Dyadic Adjustment Scale for the treatment group. Findings were further corroborated from self-reports of the clients.

Despite the limitations of studies, the ones completed have shown that the solution-focused therapy is a promising therapy for a wide variety of behavioral and social difficulties. Solution-focused therapy deserves to be evaluated as a promising model developed by practitioners. Its clinical utility and applicability to managed behavioral health care and wide dissemination and usage across practice fields makes it a good candidate for larger scale outcome evaluations.

Critiques of the Model

Selekman (1996) discusses the solution-focused therapy model's limitations. One critique is that the model is too formulaic and rigid. He implies that the model can, at times, overlook the many differences that exist among families by prescribing roughly the same approach for all of them. He has categorized three case scenarios, in particular, that require additional techniques outside the solution-focused model. The first is when the parents have changed and met their goals, but the child remains symptomatic. The second is when the formulated goals have been achieved by both parents and children, but the change is not deemed significant or exciting by the family—even after sufficient cheerleading and amplification of change has occurred. One reason for this may be that by overemphasizing the positive, the therapist may have "edited the family's story" and not allowed them to talk about problems or painful issues that need to be addressed. Finally, he cautions against being too positive in dealing with a family that has a long history of involvement in multiple systems. By overfocusing on the positive while collaborating with these systems, the therapist may be discounting the efforts already made by other providers and inadvertently creating a situation in which treatment is sabotaged.

Another critique of the model is its overfocus on behavior while minimizing the role of emotions and developmental issues. Kiser, Piercy, and Lipchik (1993) claim that solution-focused therapy does not address emotions and/or feelings adequately and assert that the model can be enhanced by more overtly incorporating emotions into its theoretical framework and therapeutic strategies. This is an important critique and addition to the solution-focused model, because to limit the model's focus to behavioral change may repeat errors of the past. For example, it was found that in other behavioral exchange models developed for couples therapy, the changes accomplished were not lasting for some couples. This required further modifications of the models with more emphasis on emotions and acceptance of behaviors that do not easily change (Jacobson & Christensen, 1996b). (See Chapter 4 for a review of cognitive-behavioral therapy models.)

A further criticism of the solution-focused therapy model is that in its attempt to minimize the role of the therapist as the expert, it may overlook the important relationship between the therapist and the client. This is true especially when dealing with children. Children can become attached to the therapist, and by not addressing the important nature of the relationship, a therapist may be discounting the power of the connection. Not acknowledging the child's feelings about the relationship with the therapist can also sabotage efforts at termination, as a child may want to be able to stay in treatment and thus stay connected.

Another limitation is that solution-focused therapy does not emphasize the biological basis for behavior. The model does not necessarily discount the biological basis of behavior or the use of medications, but it does try to reframe mental disorders as pathologizing labels and focuses on resolving presenting problems through changing social interactions and clearly defined behaviors. This may become a limitation when dealing with persistent mental illness such as schizophrenia. In such cases, it may be necessary to combine the solution-focused therapy with approaches such as the psychoeducational model discussed in Chapter 7. Educational methods may be used in solution-focused therapy. In fact, Insoo Kim Berg (1996) suggests that in some cases (e.g., child abuse) it is necessary. When solution-focused therapists educate clients, however, they first seek to use the Socratic method of learning and may add information as needed. They still maintain their belief in clients' resources that may be tapped through the educational process as the best way to solve problems.

Solution-Focused Therapy and Managed Behavioral Health Care

Solution-focused brief therapy is very compatible with work in managed behavioral health care settings. Insoo Kim Berg reports, for example, that the average number of sessions at the Brief Family Therapy Center is four (Berg & DeJong, 1996). Solution-focused therapy is also what Hoyt (1995) calls a constructive therapy. It is future oriented and goal directed. It works with the strengths of clients and targets specific changes. Hoyt discusses how therapies with these types of characteristics are a good match for managed behavioral health care.

Case Example[1]

The following case example involves a teenage girl who is currently in foster care; for the purposes of this chapter she will be called Keisha. Keisha had run away from the foster home, and this session takes place after she had returned there. Berg had planned on seeing the child alone in an individual session. The foster

[1]The authors wish to thank Insoo Kim Berg for providing this transcript from the Brief Family Therapy Center for use in this chapter.

mother did not know that she was going to be in the interview, and Berg did not know she was coming. The mother was planning to read a book in the waiting room, and, without knowing much about the case, Berg invited the foster mother into the session.

The session takes place with a team watching behind a mirror. "T" will refer to the therapist, "M" to the foster mother, and "K" to Keisha. The name of the client has been changed to protect her confidentiality. The transcript has been edited for readability and is summarized in several sections for brevity.

The first part of the session illustrates the first step of finding out about the client's life. As one will see, even while the therapist is attempting to get the basic information about the clients' lives, she asks exception-finding questions.

T: How long has Keisha been with you?
M: Uh . . . about three years but every time I . . . she act up and I . . . get rid of her.
T: And then she comes back?
M: She end up knocking back at my door. [laughs]
T: She's right back at your door, eh? [laughs]
M: So I told her I would give her another chance providing she try to help her-self . . .
T: Ah.
M: And that is by getting professional help.
T: Ah, so this is the first time for professional help?
M: She made an attempt last year, but she didn't cooperate and, uh, by her not cooperating, you know, nothing became of it.
T: Yeah. I'm glad you're here.

The therapist proceeds to explain the concept of the team approach and the fact that there is a team on the other side of the mirror.

M: Her attendance has been fine because I am on her. That is not a problem. When she was with me before she would get up and go to school. And she would come home on time. And that was not a problem either. But, after her behavior got so bad . . . with the other girls in my home and she started running with the wrong people. Then, uh, when she left my house . . . when I asked her to leave my house.
T: You asked her to leave your house?
M: Oh, yeah.
T: Ah.
M: Because some of the things she was doing, I couldn't tolerate.
T: Yeah. Yeah. So she has been back for how long now?
M: 'Bout two weeks.
T: Two weeks, okay. What made you come back?
K: What made me?
T: Yeah.
K: Cause I missed it and I like it there.
T: You like it there? Ah. What do you call your foster mother?
K: Mama.
T: Mama? Okay. So you like it, you like living with your Mama?
K: Mmm-hmm.

T: What about it?

K: It's just fine.

T: What about it do you like? What about living with her do you like?

K: The environment and . . .

T: The environment is good. Good for you? Tell me more about this . . . what about the environment that you like?

K: It's nice. It's fun to be there.

T: Uh-huh.

K: She . . . she can always be mad at us but we like it when she be mad.

T: [laughs] Yeah?

K: Just fine.

T: So you like her, or so you know she's good for you? What does she do that makes you think that she is doing things that are good for you?

K: She talks to us and she is always on us about . . . um, what is right and what is wrong.

T: So she tries to teach you what is right and wrong.

K: Uh-huh

T: What else? What else do you like about living with her?

K: She is always there for us when we need her and everything.

T: You like that too? Sounds like you have really good feelings for your Mama, lots of good feelings for her. So how do you decide to come back each time?

K: I don't know. It just happens. I was over there visiting and then me and the other girls was talking. And then they started saying, "Well, you should ask Mama if you could come back."

T: Mmm.

K: Then I was going to ask her, but somebody beat me to it.

T: So you like being there and you also know it's good for you. What about being there, living there, is good for you?

K: Oh, we got our own little apartment.

T: Yeah.

K: It's just nice to have it.

T: Okay.

K: Cause most foster, well, other foster mamas don't have that. They don't have it as good.

T: Yeah. What does Mama do that you like?

K: Well, she do everything, I mean . . . she tries to help us out and stuff and talks to us.

T: You like that. Her talking to you. Okay. What else do you like that she does?

K: She cooks pretty good.

T: Oh, she's a good cook, huh? [laughs] Of course, food is important, right? Okay. What else?

K: Everything she do for us like except when she yell and stuff and we have to listen to her. But, it is for our own good.

T: How good *are* you at listening to her?

K: I listen.

T: You do? Oh! [to the mother] She is a strikingly beautiful girl, isn't she?

M: Mmmhmm. She is a sweet girl.

T: Yeah?

M: That is why I let her come back.

T: I imagine.

M: As far as disrespecting *me*, she won't do that. She has enough sense to not do that.

T: Is that right?

M: Because when they start disrespecting me . . . *me*, that is when they know they burned their bridges. But now she won't do that but . . . she has to . . .

T: So she's really respectful of you?

M: With *me*. Yes.

T: How does she show you that?

M: Uh well . . .

T: Does she . . .

M: She doesn't curse back at me. She doesn't rebel, holler back at me. You know. She will sneak out the door in the middle of the night when she thinks I'm asleep.

T: Mmmm.

M: And I will ask her not to do that and she continued doing that. Then there is something else she going to have to work on.

T: Hmmm.

M: Keisha's problem is anger. And I told her that . . . when you, I mean husbands and wives argue. Sisters and brothers argue . . . But you don't try to kill when you do that. And see this is the problem she has.

The therapist continually asks questions about the exceptions to the problem like "What made you decide to come back?" instead of probing further into the problem. The following section illustrates the introduction of the miracle question. Notice how the therapist asks detailed questions that are concrete and behaviorally specific to help develop a set of solution behaviors.

T: Keisha, let me ask you a strange question. Okay. This may sound somewhat strange, but it is going to take some imagination. Uh, let's see, you are 16. That means you are a junior? sophomore?

K: Junior.

T: Junior. Junior in high school. Okay. Um . . . I guess by the time you're a junior you have a pretty good imagination. So let me ask you this. Let's say . . . after we talk today and uh you go home . . . and tonight you go to bed . . . and everybody in the house is sleeping . . . um . . . while you are sleeping some miracle happens and the problem that brought you here . . . is solved just like that . . . wiped out . . .

K: So I go home and go to sleep and whatever made me come here is . . . gone.

T: Is gone! The temper, the problems that make Mama send you back or . . . what she says that you're not doing right of all the problems that brought you here are solved . . . just disappeared. But because you're sleeping and everyone is sleeping, Mama doesn't know that this has happened and you don't know that this has happened. Other kids in the house don't know that this has happened because everyone was asleep. So when you wake up tomorrow morning . . . how would you know this happened?

K: I don't think that I would know until um . . . like somebody made me mad and then I have . . . y'know the way I react . . . or whatever.

T: Okay. So, how would you react?

K: I guess I probably wouldn't have a reaction. I would have a reaction, but if you say everything is, um, my temper has now changed or gone, then I probably really shouldn't have too much to do or anything since all that stuff has disappeared.

T: So somebody makes you irritated. I guess that's going to happen, right?

K: Um-hmm.

T: When you live in the world you are going to get irritated. So what would you do instead of losing your temper?

K: Probably go down and talk to Ma. Go downstairs and talk to her.

In the following excerpt the therapist continues with the miracle question, but she begins to ask relationship questions pertaining to the miracle question. This is done to get a meta-perspective on the problem and track the socially constructed nature of the problem and solutions to the problem.

T: So how would you talk to her that would tell your Mama that "Hmm, something has happened with Keisha. Something's different about her; there must have been a miracle last night."

K: Cause I usually never go down there and tell her . . . like some bad blood upstairs or whatever.

T: Yeah.

K: I, I usually take it into my own hands.

T: Yeah.

K: Which isn't really the good thing to do.

T: Yeah. So, you won't . . . instead of taking it into your hands, you'll talk to your Mama about that.

K: Mmm-hmm

T: And what would you say? How would you say it? That would tell her, "Hmm, something is changed with Keisha."

K: I would say, "So-and-so upstairs done this and done that and instead of getting angry or upset I came and talked to you."

T: Ohh, okay. Just coming and telling her would be a big difference for you. It would be a big change for you. Okay. Uh-huh. Anything else? What about other girls in the house; what would they notice different about you that make them say, "Hmmm, she changed overnight."

K: They really don't bother me, because I, um, they know how . . . my temper. I really don't try to get too mad but . . . if they know they really made me mad, then I don't do nothing, I go downstairs, talk to her . . . they may ask or say there is something wrong with her.

T: Something wrong with her! [laughs] And they'll be wondering, what happened to her? Is that right? Uh-huh. Okay. All right. [to mother] What about for you? What would you notice different about tomorrow, tomorrow morning that would tell *you* that, wow, a miracle must have happened overnight.

M: What would I notice different?

T: Yeah.

M: Well, I would notice when, someone, you know, do something to Keisha to trigger her anger, if she didn't fight, then I would notice that as a difference because . . .

T: So what would she do instead of fighting? [An attempt to track solution behaviors]

M: Come and talk to me.

T: Talk to you

M: Like I urge them to do.

T: Okay.

M: Um, if there is a problem, come and talk to me. We'll talk about it. I will do my best to straighten that problem out.

T: Okay.

M: And I tell them that all the time. But instead of Keisha coming and talking to me, Keisha will fight it out.

T: Right.

M: And I do not want that.

T: Right, so instead come and talk to you.

M: Mm-hmm.

T: Right. And when she talks to you about what happened upstairs, how will she tell you that? After this miracle?

M: How will she tell me what now? You mean that something has happened?

T: Right.

M: Well usually, um, I guess she would just come and say, "Well, Mama I want to talk to you." And then she would come and talk to me.

T: Mm-hmm.

M: And tell me what happened. And, I will in turn go and try and investigate and find out what happened.

T: Uh-huh.

M: That is the way I like to solve problems.

T: Right. So when you go upstairs and investigate what happens, what will she do?

M: She'll probably go with me.

T: Uh-huh. And when she goes upstairs with you, what will she do different that would tell you that . . .

M: She will stand there and watch me handle the situation, instead of fight it out, like she usually do.

T: So, she will let you sort of be in charge.

M: Yes.

T: And handle the, solve the problem.

M: Yes. Yes. Yes.

T: Okay. All right. Anything else? Anything else that would be different around the house? What would be different around the house?

M: You mean what would be different after she changed?

T: Yeah.

M: Well, that's one thing that would be different after she changed, um, they're usually pretty happy around the house already.

After eliciting as many solutions from the miracle question as possible, the therapist attempts to track exceptions to the problem that already exist. That is, she investigates whether there are already times the miracle is happening.

T: [to Keisha] Now, are there times when you are able to handle situations like that, even a little bit?

K: You mean if someone is messing with something of mine?

T: Someone messes with you, are you able to not get into fighting, but somehow sort of handle it like your Mama suggests?

K: It depends on what is done, or how I feel at the time, or what I'm thinking about at the time, or . . .

T: Yeah, tell me about that [Note how the therapist highlights the importance of solution behaviors by focusing her interest on exceptions].

K: Mmm. Like, if I'm in a bad mood, or if I'm not feeling up to, whatever.

T: Yeah. Yeah.

K: If somebody come and, make me upset, then I'm, well, I might be upset, but then . . .

T: But, are there times when somebody come and messes with you, and then you don't lose your temper?

K: It depends on what they do.

T: Tell me about that. What do you mean?

K: Like if a person just come and just do something that really makes me upset, like, I don't know, we, we play, like, around the house upstairs, we all play so much with each other that um, they know when to leave you alone. They know when you're not really ready to play.

T: So, are there times when other kids bug you? And you still leave them alone? Not get into fights?

K: That happens all the time, like if somebody bugs me when I'm not really ready, I just wait two days and I'm really ready and I bug them. But I just don't like people bringing up stuff from the past that happened with me. And try to mess with my things; that's what I really get upset about.

T: Now, other kids messing with your things, that is what bugs you the most. Right. And what about bringing things up from the past. That bugs you too?

K: Uh-huh.

T: What about your school? Are there times when other kids at school bug you?

K: Nobody really bothers me at school.

T: No?

K: No, they really don't bother me. They try to be my friends.

T: They do? So you lose your temper only at home then.

K: No, I lose my temper, um, I don't know . . .

T: [to mother] You're shaking your head.

M: She loses her temper anywhere.

T: Anywhere. In school too.

M: Keisha will lose her temper anywhere with anybody, at certain times. She's not the type of person that would go out here and just be aloof all the time. That is just not the type of person she is.

T: Right. Just to start a fight. Just for the sake of fighting.

M: No. No. She doesn't do that.

T: Uh-huh.

M: She's not that type of person. She has a right to get angry.

T: Mmm.

M: She has a right to express that. But my problem with Keisha is that when she get angry, she doesn't know how far to take her anger.
      [The mother describes many ways in which Keisha has lost control of her temper]

T: So after this miracle happened, she will still get upset?

M: Yeah.

T: But she will handle it more . . .

M: She'll know how to handle it in a more . . . sort of mature way. That is what I would like to see you work for, Keisha.

T: Okay. That makes sense. So it's not like she's turning off her feelings altogether.

M: No!

T: It's just that she will handle them more maturely.

M: Exactly! Exactly!

T: So, are there times when she is a little bit more mature, she acts a little more mature? When she gets upset?

Note how the therapist closely tracks the same language used by the client. She is now referring to controlling anger as handling it more maturely, like Mama said. The session continues, but the mother is having a difficult time coming up with any solutions or exceptions. The team from behind the mirror phones into the session and makes a suggestion. The following is an excerpt of how the session shifts after the call.

T: I think I may not have heard it correctly, or maybe I missed it. She doesn't get upset with you personally? I mean she doesn't come after you with a brick or anything like that.

M: No, you're not crazy are you, honey? No she doesn't do that.

T: She doesn't do that with *you*.

M: No, she doesn't do that.

T: Really? How come?

K: Cause I would . . . she would never . . . I *know* I would never do that to her.

T: You would never do that to *her*.

K: Uh-huh.

T: I mean . . . you know adults do make you . . . make you angry . . . when you're 16. But you would never do that to her?

K: Uh-uh.

T: How come?

K: I would do that to my *real* mother but I wouldn't do that to her.

T: You'd do it to your real mother, but not to her. How come. How do you not, I mean how do you manage that . . . how do you do that?

K: How do I do what?

T: How do you not do that to your Mama?

K: I would *never* think about doing nothing like that.

T: Never think of doing that. How come. How do you do that. There must be a time when she gets, you know, when you get irritated with what she does.

K: Uh-uh, she never done anything that upset me?

T: Really?

K: I mean I be upset but . . . it wouldn't be cause she, like the . . . my real mother, my natural mother she would *hit* me and then *provoke* me to do . . . the things that I would do to *her.*

T: Okay.

K: But she is so little, every time she try to hit me, I *run.*

T: Is that right? Instead of turning around and hitting her . . . you will try to run? Wow. So what's different about . . . I mean, when you're 16, all adults make you mad sometimes. How come you don't do that with her?

K: I don't know; I would never do that.

M: And she doesn't allow anybody else to do that with me either.

T: Really?

M: Uh-huh.

M: She would . . . I don't know. If any of the girls at home disrespect me she would tell them about it.

T: Really?

M: Uh-huh.

T: So *you* are *very* important to her.

M: Apparently. She wanted to beat up a couple of foster girls for talking back to me and disrespecting me.

T: Wow. And she doesn't talk back to you. I think you mentioned that she's not disrespectful of you.

M: No.

T: She is *very* respectful of you. Wow. Where did you learn that?

K: What you saying where did I learn . . .?

T: Where did you learn to be so respectful?

K: I respect everybody

T: Oh, you do?

M: No, you don't.

K: I do. I respect people who will respect me.

T: That's the difference . . . between the two of *you?*

K: I guess.

T: Your foster mother respects you. You know that. Wow. How do you know that she respects you?

K: Cause she show it.

T: How?

K: By the things she do.

T: And you can tell when someone . . . like you real mother, doesn't respect you . . . but your foster mother who respects you, you can tell the difference. That is amazing. And you said you're only 16? At 16 you already know that?

K: Uh-huh.

T: Wow.

The above section exemplifies highlighting the client's strengths. Even though she could not elicit any behaviors that the client engages in to control her anger, the therapist attempts to draw out solution-behaviors that the client is already accomplished at. The therapist elicits further strengths by asking who else Keisha respects and is able to have a positive relationship with. This discussion also includes ways in which Keisha is respectful of her foster mother and helps around the house. The foster mother introduces some additional behavioral problems, including Keisha's involvement with a boyfriend the foster mother doesn't approve of. The following section illustrates the therapist's attempt to re-focus the conversation on solutions and to establish some concrete behavioral goals.

T: Now what will tell you . . . what will she do to let you know that she is chang-ing her way and she is no longer . . . you know, footloose and fancy free.

M: Well, she might not tell me anything, but I will see her behavior around the house. I will see that she is home instead of out in the street somewhere. She might not come to me and say this or that and the other, but . . .

T: Okay. So she'll be keeping a curfew.

M: Yeah.

T: And she'll be home when she should be home.

M: Mmm-hmm

T: That kind of stuff. She won't be running out of the house in the middle of the night . . . that kind of stuff. That would tell you that she is sort of following the rules.

M: Right. I try to stress to Keisha that you know what you're doing for yourself.

T: Right.

M: You're not doing it for me.

T: Sure.

After the rules have been made clear and agreed on, the therapist begins the scal-ing technique to anchor the problem and to track progress toward problem reso-lutions. She also uses scaling questions to track the client's confidence in her abil-ity to change. This is a variation on the scaling question that helps the therapist assess the client's motivation for solving the problem as well as how well the client perceives that they are coping with the problem.

T: Okay. So, how are you going to do all this?

K: Do all what?

T: What your Mama asks you to do.

K: It is not a lot to do. Just . . .

T: Just do it?

K: Yeah.

T: Just do it . . . hmmm. Let me ask you in a slightly different way then. Let's say . . . 10 means you're very confident that you can follow through with all these rules . . . it sounds like quite a change for you. Ten means that you're very confident. And 1 means you're not confident at all that that you're going to be able to follow through with all this. Where would you say you are between 1 and 10?

K: One means I'm confident?

T: Ten means you're confident, 1 means you're not at all.

K: Mmm, I say about 8.

T: Eight! Really? That is pretty good. And you've been there two weeks now?

K: Yeah.

T: Wow. Because that is a big change for you. It's a lot of change for you, isn't it? [to mother] How about for you?

M: What?

T: Knowing Keisha from the past and you know these past two weeks. How confident are you that she will be able to follow through with these rules?

M: Well, I think she can if she wants to . . . and, ah, apparently she wants to because she came back to me and asked if she could come home.

T: Yeah. So how confident are you at this point between 1 and 10 that she'll be able to follow through with all these rules and stick with it and stay in your home with you.

M: Well, I guess I will have to say, knowing Keisha, she will do what she needs to do. She'll stay there. I have that much confidence in her.

T: Really?

M: Because I feel like if she was not going to do that, and if she was not going to try and get her life together, I don't think she would've asked if she could come back home. Because it took a lot for Keisha to ask if she could come back.

T: Really?

M: Yes it did. Because I told her, she's been, I told her she . . . I would never take her back. Because this is the third time I took her back after she mess up. And I told her that I wasn't going to take her back anymore. So it took a lot for her because she knew I wasn't going to take her back. So it took a lot for her to ease around until she, you know, ask the question. So now that she's back in there I feel . . .

T: So she worked very hard to get back to live with you.

M: Oh yeah. I didn't tell her she could come back first time she, you know, asked.

T: Wow.

M: I told her I said I don't know if I can deal with your behavior.

T: Wow.

M: And I said to her you're going to have to change your behavior if you are going to come back here. And that is when she promised me that she would go to school. She promised me that she wouldn't run the street. She promised me she would come see a psychologist. To get some help for herself.

T: Mmmm.

M: So I guess I would say this is the first step. And I feel I would say 7 or 8. You know.

T: You too, huh? Seven or eight! So what would it take to go up to either 8 or 9?

M: I think she is going to have to work on herself. And try to learn how to solve problems in a more positive way.

T: Mmm-hmm. What about you? [to Keisha] What would it take for you to go from 8 to 9?

K: Me working on my behavior.

T: Say more about that.

K: Well, I think it's not really my behavior; it's my temper makes my behavior re-act. Cause if I'm not, if I'm upset, then I'm . . . you know . . . pretty good.

T: Is that right? So as long as you know how to handle your temper, you're okay most of the time. Wow. By the way, how have you learned to do that? How have you learned to be respectful of people, how have you learned to be able to tell the difference between someone who is respecting you, and someone who's not respecting you?

K: By the things they do for you.

T: Yeah? Is this something somebody taught you? To be respectful? Of others who respect you? Or is it something you figured out for yourself?

K: She taught me. [pointing to mother]

T: She taught you! You know what. That is pretty smart. I guess you're right. It's a pretty smart thing for her to figure out . . . that learning something like her teaching you something is good for you . . . I mean that takes a lot to figure it out . . . I'm amazed. How did you know that coming back to live with her is good for you? What told you that?

K: Cause she was always concerned about what we did.

T: And you like that. Well it sounds like you live in a situation where you could've done anything you wanted. Right?

K: Mmm-hmm.

T: You could've gone for days and you . . . nobody would be upset with you. And you knew that wasn't good for you? It is amazing how you knew that. And you're saying you learned all this since you came to live with your foster mother? When you were 13? You did? You learned a lot! In that time. Haven't you? All right. Anything else you think it might be important for me to know? Before I go talk to my team?

M: I guess not, unless you want to know in detail some of the behavior that she has demonstrated.

T: Well, I think I have a pretty good idea. [Note how therapist cuts off problem talk here.] Yeah, I think I have a pretty good idea. And I think you have a right to be concerned. This is the point where I go talk to my team, and we'll put our heads together and think about all of this. Then I'll come back with some feedback.

The therapist takes a short break for reflection and time to construct the informa-tion gained into a behavioral task or homework assignment. Following the break, the therapist returns and delivers compliments to the family along with a behav-ioral task and homework assignment.

T: Well, first I wanted to tell you that I think you did the right thing by coming here. Because you wanted to get started on the right foot.

M: Uh-huh.

T: And to make sure it stays on the right foot. So I think the timing of your being here is excellent. And also, your being involved here is also very helpful because it gives me a much more accurate picture of what is going on. And so again, we really appreciate your being here. I think that we agree with you that it will take time . . . especially given the fact that she is 16.

M: Mmm-hmm.

T: And along with many other things, one of the striking things about Keisha is that we are really impressed by how you knew that living with Mama was good for you, and I think it takes quite a bit of brains and maturity to figure out what is good for you. I think that a lot of kids your age would have said uh, you know staying out all hours and saying you can do anything you want that would have been wonderful, but you know that was not good for you in the long run and you had enough brains to figure that out. The other thing is that when your foster mother treats you with respect, you know that she is treating you with respect. And, uh, also realizing that it is good for you. It sounds like you really worked very hard to get back into that kind of situation. Which is incredible, I mean, when you think about it. It's really really incredible. Um, it seems like you also, when you are talking to her and when you are yelling at her, you must do it in such a loving and respectful way that Keisha knows it.

M: I try to . . . sometimes it's hard.

T: It has gotten through to her. It sounds like she has learned a lot from you. So apparently you taught her a lot more than you realize.

M: I guess so.

T: You guess so?

M: [laughs] Well, I try.

T: You have succeeded. There are lots of things you have done for Keisha. So I guess in a lot of ways, both of you are doing a lot of good things, and we are really glad that you came so that you can get started on the right track and so you don't have to repeat this on-and-off thing. And maybe you can just stay on the right track. We also agree with your idea that maybe her staying with you is your way of preparing her to deal with the world out there. So it sounds like you already got started on that.

M: Mmm.

T: By letting her handle this boy thing in her own way and trusting her enough to give her enough time to figure out what to do about this. So I think once again, you are on the right track.

M: Thank you.

T: We also like the way you lay down the conditions about what she has to do in order to live with you and make it very clear from the outset so that she knows what she has to do to meet those conditions.

M: I try.

T: So since both of you are doing a lot of good things. We need to know more about what these good things are, and it is also our hunch that Keisha must be doing a lot more things to control her temper, but it seems like it is not clear for us and also it is not clear to her.

M: Mmm.

T: Our hunch is that she may be controlling her temper a lot more than she thinks she is. So in order for us to help her, we need to become aware of all those things, even little things that she does. It would be helpful if both of you could pay attention to those things. [Notice how therapist does not take ex-

pert position and instead gives the role of expert to the client and her mother.]
Okay? So how about I see you in a couple of weeks?

M: Mmm

K: Okay.

Summary

Solution-focused therapy is a strengths-based brief therapy developed by clinical practitioners. It provides viable methods and techniques for use in behavioral heath care settings. This chapter discussed the solution-focused model developed by Steve de Shazer and Insoo Kim Berg and those who were trained by them at the Brief Family Therapy Center in Milwaukee. The chapter described the theoretical basis of solution-focused therapy and its major assumptions and techniques used in the therapy, as well as how to conduct a solution-focused therapy session. The developing research basis of the solution-focused therapy model was further highlighted, as well as its consistency with social work theory and practice. Important compatibilties of solution-focused therapy for work in today's practice contexts are also discussed. Finally, the methods of solution-focused therapy were illustrated with a therapy transcript from a session conducted by Insoo Kim Berg.

Process Questions

1. In what way does the therapist use the skill of asking for exceptions to the problem with Keisha and her mother?

2. How are scaling questions used by solution-focused therapists, and how did scaling help with this case?

3. What is the miracle question, and what effect did it have when used with this family?

4. Solution-focused therapists currently use the social construction theory. What is social constructionism and what are some examples of its applications with this case?

References

AUSTIN, D. (1986). *A history of social work education*. In J. Otis, D. M. Austin, & A. Rubin (Eds.), Social Work Monograph Series. Austin: University of Texas, School of Social Work.

BECVAR, D. S., & BECVAR, R. J. (Eds.). (1996). *Family therapy: A systemic integration*. Needham Heights, MA: Allyn & Bacon.

BERG, I. K. (1994). *Family based services: A solution-focused approach*. New York: Norton.

BERG, I. K. (1996). *Making home visits II*. Audiotape. Milwaukee, WI: Brief Family Therapy Center.

BERG, I., & DE JONG, P. (1996). Solution-building conversations: Co-constructing a sense of competence with clients. *Families in Society, 77*(6), 376–390.

BERG, I. K., & MILLER, S. D. (1992). *Working with the problem drinker: A solution-focused approach.* New York: Norton.

BERGER, P., & LUCKMAN, T. (1966). *The social construction of reality.* Garden City, NJ: Doubleday.

BEYEBACH, M., & CARRANZA, V. E. (1997). Therapeutic interaction and dropout: Measuring relational communication in solution-focused therapy. *Journal of Family Therapy, 19,* 173–212.

BLOOM, M., FISCHER, J., & ORME, J. (1995). *Evaluating practice: Guidelines for the accountable professional.* Englewood Cliffs, NJ: Prentice-Hall.

CARPENTER, J. (1997). Investigating brief solution-focused therapy. *Journal of Family Therapy, 19,* 117–120.

CONOLEY, J. C. (1987). Strategic family intervention. Three cases of school-aged children. *School Psychology Review, 16,* 469–486.

CORCORAN, K., & VANDIVER, V. (1996). *Maneuvering the maze of managed care.* New York: Free Press.

DE JONG, P., & BERG, I. K. (1997). *Interviewing for solutions.* Pacific Grove, CA: Brooks/Cole.

DE JONG, P., & HOPWOOD, L. E. (1996). Outcome research on treatment conducted at the brief family therapy center. In S. D. Miller, M. A. Hubble, & B. L. Duncan (Eds.), *Handbook of solution-focused brief therapy* (pp. 272–298). San Francisco: Jossey-Bass.

DE SHAZER, S. (1985). *Keys to solution in brief therapy.* New York: Norton.

DE SHAZER, S. (1988). *Clues: Investigating solutions in brief therapy.* New York: Norton.

DE SHAZER, S. (1991). *Putting differences to work.* New York: Norton.

DE SHAZER, S. (1994). *Words were originally magic.* New York: Norton.

DE SHAZER, S., & Berg, I. K. (1997). What works? Remarks on the research aspects of solution-focused brief therapy. *Journal of Family Therapy, 19,* 121–124.

DE SHAZER, S., BERG, I., LIPCHIK, E., NUNNALLY, E., MOLNAR, A., GINGERICH, W., & WEINER-DAVIS, M. (1986). Brief therapy: Focused solution development. *Family Process, 25,* 207–222.

DOISE, W. (1989). Constructivism in social psychology. *European Journal of Social Psychology, 19,* 389–400.

DOLAN, Y. M. (1991). *Resolving sexual abuse: Solution-focused therapy and Ericksonian hypnosis for adult survivors.* New York: Norton.

DORE, M. (1990). Functional theory: Its history and influence on contemporary social work history. *Social Service Review, 64*(1), 359–374.

DURRANT, M. (1995). *Creative strategies for school problems.* New York: Norton.

FRANKLIN, C. (1995). Expanding the vision of the social constructionist debates: Creating relevance for practitioners. *Families in Society, 76*(7), 395–407.

FRANKLIN, C. (1996). Solution-focused therapy: A marital case study using recursive dialectic analysis. *Journal of Family Psychotherapy, 7*(1), 31–51.

FRANKLIN, C., & BIEVER, J. (1997). *Evaluating the effectiveness of solution-focused therapy with learning challenged students using single case designs.* Unpublished manuscript. Austin: University of Texas.

FRANKLIN, C., CORCORAN, J., STREETER, C. L., & NOWICKI, J. (1997). Using client self-anchored scales to measure outcomes in solution-focused therapy. *Journal of Systemic Therapies, 16*(3), 246–265.

FRANKLIN, C., NOWICKI, J., TRAPP, J., SCHWAB, A. J., & PETERSEN, J. (1993). A computerized assessment system for brief, crisis oriented youth services. *Families in Society, 74*(10), 602–616.

GARFINKLE, H. (1967). *Studies in ethnomethodololgy.* Englewood Cliffs, NJ: Prentice-Hall.

GERGEN, K. J. (1982). *Toward a transformation in social knowledge.* New York: Springer-Verlag.

GERGEN, K. J. (1985). The social constructionist movement in modern psychology. *American Psychologist, 40,* 266–275.

GERGEN, K. J., & KAYE J. (1992). Beyond narrative in the negotiation of therapeutic meaning (pp. 166–185). In S. McNamee & K. J. Gergen (Eds.), *Therapy as social construction.* Newbury Park, CA: Sage.

HOFFMAN, L. (1990). Constructing realities: An art of lenses. *Family Process, 29,* 1–12.

HOYT, M. F. (1995). *Brief therapy and managed care.* San Francisco: Jossey-Bass.

JACOBSON, N. S., & CHRISTENSEN, A. (1996a). Integrative couple therapy. Presentation at the AAMFT Annual Convention, Toronto, CA.

JACOBSON, N. S., & CHRISTENSEN, A. (1996b). *Integrative couple therapy.* New York: Norton.

KISER, D. (1988). *A follow-up study conducted at the Brief Family Therapy Center.* Unpublished manuscript.

KISER, D., & NUNNALLY, E. (1990). *The relationship between treatment length and goal achievement in solution-focused therapy.* Unpublished manuscript.

KISER, D. J., PIERCY, F. P., & LIPCHIK, E. (1993). The integration of emotion in solution-focused therapy. *Journal of Marital & Family Therapy, 19*(3) 233–242.

KRAL, R. (1995). *Strategies that work: Techniques for solutions in schools.* Milwaukee: Brief Family Therapy Center.

LAX, W. D. (1992). Postmodern thinking in a clinical practice. In S. McNamee & K. J. Gergen (Eds.), *Therapy as social construction* (pp. 69–85). Newbury Park, CA: Sage.

LEE, M.-Y. (1997). A study of solution-focused brief family therapy: Outcomes and issues. *The American Journal of Family Therapy, 25*, 3–17.

LINDFORSS, L., & MAGNUSSON, D. (1997). Solution-focused therapy in prison. *Contemporary Family Therapy, 19*, 89–104.

MACDONALD, A. J. (1997). Brief therapy in adult psychiatry. Further outcomes. *Journal of Family Therapy, 19*, 213–222.

MCKEEL, A. J. (1996). A clinician's guide to research on solution-focused brief therapy. In S. D. Miller, M. A. Hubble, & B. L. Duncan (Eds.), *Handbook of solution-focused brief therapy* (pp. 251–271). San Francisco: Jossey-Bass.

MCNAMEE, S. A., & GERGEN, K. J. (1992). *Therapy as social construction*. Newbury Park, CA: Sage.

METCALF, L. (1995). *Counseling toward solutions: A practical solution-focused program for working with students, teachers, and parents*. Englewood Cliffs, NJ: Simon & Schuster.

MILLER, S. D., HUBBLE, M. A., & DUNCAN, B. S. (1996). *Handbook of solution-focused brief therapy*. San Francisco: Jossey-Bass.

MURPHY, J. J. (1992). Brief strategic family intervention for school-related problems. *Family Therapy Case Studies, 7*, 59–71.

MURPHY, J. J. (1994a). Brief therapy for school problems. *School Psychology International, 15*, 115–131.

MURPHY, J. J. (1994b). Working with what works: A solution focused approach to school behavior problems. *The School Counselor, 42*, 59–65.

MURPHY, J. J. (1996). Solution-focused brief therapy in the school. In S. D. Miller, M. A. Hubble, & B. S. Duncan (Eds.), *Handbook of solution-focused brief therapy* (pp. 184–204). San Francisco: Jossey-Bass.

NUGENT, W. R. (1992). Psychometric characteristics of self-anchored scales in clinical application. *Journal of Social Service Research, 15*, 137–152.

O'HANLON, W., & WEINER-DAVIS, M. (1989). *In search for solutions: A new direction in psychotherapy*. New York: Norton.

PINSOFF, W. M. (1996). An integrative biopsychosocial approach. Presentation at the AAMFT Annual Conference, Toronto, Canada.

RANK, O. (1929/1973). *The trauma of birth*. New York: Harper & Row.

RICHAN, W. C., & MENDELSOHN, A. R. (1973). *Social work: The unloved profession*. New York: New Viewpoints.

SALEEBY, D. D. (1992). *The strengths perspective in social work practice*. New York: Longman.

SCHINDLER, K., ZIMMERMAN, T. S., PREST, L. A., & WETZEL, B. E. (1997). Solution-focused couple therapy groups: An empirical study. *Journal of Family Therapy, 19*, 125–144.

SCHUTZ, A. (1962). *Collected papers I: The problem of social reality*. The Hague, Netherlands: Martinus Nijhoff.

SELEKMAN, M. D. (1996). Solution-focused therapy with children. Workshop presented at the AAMFT Conference in Toronto, Canada.

SELEKMAN, M. D. (1997). *Solution-focused therapy with children*. New York: Guilford Publications.

SIRLES, E. A., LIPCHIK, E., & KOWALSKI, K. (1993). A consumer's perspective on domestic violence interventions. *Journal of Family Violence, 8*, 267–276.

WALLACE, R. A., & WOLF, A. (1991). *Contemporary sociological theory* (3rd ed.). Englewood Cliffs, NJ: Prentice-Hall.

WALTER, J. L., & PELLER, J. E. (1992). *Becoming solution-focused in brief therapy*. New York: Brunner-Mazel.

WEBSTER, D. C., VAUGHN, K., & MARTINEZ, R. (1994). Introducing solution-focused approaches to staff in inpatient psychiatric settings. *Archives of Psychiatric Nursing, 8*, 251–261.

WITKIN, S. L. (1991). Empirical clinical practice: A critical analysis. *Social Work, 36*, 158–163.

CHAPTER SIX

Joan L. Biever, Ph.D.
Our Lady of the Lake University

Glen T. Gardner, Ph.D.
Our Lady of the Lake University

Monte Bobele, Ph.D.
Our Lady of the Lake University

Social Construction and Narrative Family Practice

Postmodern family therapies are most associated with narrative, collaborative language systems, reflecting team therapy, and other models that ascribe to social constructionism. Postmodernism refers to a movement in our culture away from the belief in, and search for, fundamental truths. Some have described this movement as a result of the evolving complexity of our view of the world: The "postmodern Mind is one which . . . has come to question whether [reality] is ordered in a way in which man's reason can lay bare" (Smith, 1989, p. 7). Postmodernism has been described as "a linguistic theory that proposes that the social world cannot be treated as an objective system" (Pardeck, Murphy, & Jung, 1994, p. 343). Postmodernism does not reject outright reality, science, or technology. Rather, postmodernism is interested in exploring the ways in which language, power, social factors, and history shape our views about reality, truth, and knowledge (Hollinger, 1994, p. 177). Social work has recently begun to define the importance of this intellectual movement on theory and practice (Franklin, 1995; Pardeck et al., 1994; Saleeby, 1994).

This chapter describes the new and evolving family therapy models that have been influenced by postmodernism. The theory and assumptions of postmodernism are discussed, along with the major therapeutic techniques used. The consistency of postmodern practice perspectives with social work practice are further highlighted. Beginning research studies that hold promise for establishing an empirical basis for postmodern family therapies are also discussed. Some of the promising features of postmodern practice in today's contexts of behavioral health are highlighted. Finally, a case study that illustrates the postmodern practice is presented.

History

Postmodernism has recently influenced family practice models and represents a newer social-cultural orientation to family therapy (Laird, 1995). Family therapies such as those using the social construction theory and narrative approaches have been associated with postmodern practice perspectives. The historic roots of these approaches can be found in the systemic models; however, postmodern family practice models also depart from traditional systemic thinking and practice. The family practice models associated with postmodernism evolved out of systemic perspectives and sometimes in reaction to those models. Most of the progenitors of the models were originally trained as systemic family therapists. Feminist and multicultural critiques of traditional family therapy models are influential in setting the stage for the postmodern perspectives. Some practitioners also became disenchanted with constructivist, strategic models and wanted to explore new ways of conceptualizing and working with families (Hoffman, 1990). Other factors in the development of postmodern family practice include an increasing tendency to see the family as an open system influenced by many other social systems, an increasing awareness of the importance of language in therapy, an interest in postmodern social science theories, and a new interest in including social action and social and cultural critique as part of the therapy process. Therapists such as Michael White, David Epston, and Lynn Hoffman were especially influential in advocating both a sociopolitical view of therapy and the need for social action to change dominant narratives that are present because of the oppressive influences of the larger society and culture (Hoffman, 1992; White & Epston, 1990).

Theoretical Basis for the Practice Model

Kurt Lewin (1951) once observed, "There is nothing so practical as a good theory" (p. 169). A theory orients us to the pragmatics of therapy: how we define problems, how we understand the origins of problems, who we talk with about problems, how we set goals, and how we determine our successes. For the newcomer to postmodern therapies, a theoretical understanding is often facilitated through an exemplification of the practice of postmodern therapies. As David Hunt (1987), rephrasing Lewin, has put it, "There is nothing so theoretical as good practice." We illustrate the practice below, but first we discuss some of the assumptions undergirding postmodernism.

Major Assumptions

Postmodernism assumes that there is no singular, universal reality but many possible understandings of behaviors, interactions, or events and that language serves as the primary vehicle for the transmission of meanings and understandings. These ideas have profound implications for therapists' behavior. Postmodernism can be illustrated through considering the art of the last century. Historically for artists, the fundamental problem was how to accurately represent the three-dimensional world on a flat canvas. Artists mastered the laws of perspective, color, and composition in an attempt to provide the viewer with a near-perfect representation of reality. As we moved into the 20th century, the artist's goal became a presentation on the canvas that would convey the artist's impressions, or interpretations, of the subject, rather than a re-presentation. The artist's goal was to convey the meanings a subject evoked in the artist, how the artist felt about the subject, and perhaps an attempt to evoke in the reader a similar feeling for the subject. Artists became less absorbed in the problem of representing a reality and more fascinated with evoking realities and experiences in the viewer. Similarly, in anthropology, one finds a movement away from the idea that an ethnography accurately portrayed the life and culture of some civilization in an "objective" manner. Instead, ethnographies have come to be understood as resulting from interactions between the anthropologist, the culture under study, and the reader of the document (Clifford & Marcus, 1986). This trend in anthropology is mirrored in popular culture, as exemplified by Paul Simon's *Graceland* album, the increased diversity of ethnic foods in grocery stores and restaurants, and the multiculturalism that pervades society.

Postmodern thinkers are disenchanted with unadaptable norms. The appreciation of context has given rise to notions such as "situational ethics," which depend on circumstances, individuals, and local expectations. This is different from the "engraved in stone" Ten Commandments understanding of ethics. In the criminal justice system, the question is often not "Did he do it?" but "Why did he do it?" If the contextual reason is satisfying, the guilt is mitigated. Although we frequently attribute behavior to the makeup of individual psyches, there is an increasing appreciation for the impact of context on behavior.

Social Constructionists

One important group of postmodernists are the social constructionists (Berger & Luckman, 1966; Gergen, 1985; McNamee & Gergen, 1992). In an attempt to define how we make sense of the world if we abandon the quest for foundational and knowable truths, the social constructionists have turned to our social natures. For them, the world we perceive and the meanings that we create about that world are the result of social interactions—that is, talking with other people and living in a cultural context that transmits meanings to us.

Social constructionism emphasizes a crisscrossing of ideas in our conversations with one another (Anderson & Goolishian, 1988). This does not mean that we exchange ideas like trading cards. Rather, there is a recognition that what we say to you is interpreted in a unique and particular way. The understandings created are shaped by, and will shape, other ideas. We then make a unique interpretation of others' understanding. Rather than exchanging trading cards, we are passing a ball of modeling clay back and forth, each of us squeezing it and shaping it to our own liking before passing it back. The clay changes somewhat with each exchange. The constructionist position is that even though we habitually act on a particular meaning as if it were the only meaning, as if it were the only truth about a problem, it is only one of several plausible meanings or interpretations of the same events or behaviors.

This concept implies that meanings are transitory, changing from moment to moment in the conversation, like the ball of clay. Meanings are constantly "under construction" from this point of view. Ultimate, foundational "Truths" are viewed with a great deal of skepticism by social constructionists.

Therapeutic Methods

Therapists, regardless of theoretical orientation, set the stage for therapeutic interaction by determining the procedures that will be followed. Procedural details include setting, composition of the client system, goals of therapy, role of the therapist, and criteria for termination. These procedural details are somewhat independent from the process of therapy. We briefly discuss the procedures that are characteristic of therapists working within a postmodern perspective and turn to processes and techniques in the next section. It is important to remember that postmodern family therapists are theoretically diverse, and guidelines for working from this perspective are still emerging.

Setting

Many advocates of postmodern approaches (Andersen, 1991; Anderson & Goolishian, 1988; Hoffman, 1990) work in settings that utilize therapy teams. Although most postmodern family therapists practice alone, the influence of working in teams remains. It has been previously argued that the use of teams is a preferred method for training in postmodern therapy (Biever & Gardner, 1995; Bobele, Gardner, & Biever, 1995). Teams can take a variety of forms in postmodern practice, but reflecting teams are most closely associated with this form of therapy. Reflecting teams were developed in Norway by Tom Andersen and his colleagues (Andersen, 1987, 1991). The reflecting team is a departure from the Milan-style team structure (Slevini-Palazzoli, Boscolo, Cecchin, & Prata, 1980) in that clients listen to the intersession team discussion rather than waiting for feedback/messages to be delivered by therapists. (See Chapter 3 for a discussion of the Milan approach.) Reflecting teams allow clients direct access to the team's ideas rather than funneling the team's ideas through the therapist.

The applications of reflecting teams have been expanded by several authors. For example, Furman and Ahola (1992) describe using a joint discussion format in which they extend the sharing of therapists' ideas with clients to all conversations therapists have regarding clients, including consultations, presession conversations, and postsession conversations. Anderson and her colleagues at the Houston Galveston Institute have dispensed with the use of one-way mirrors; the team remains in the room with clients and therapists throughout the therapy session. Therapists who work in co-therapy teams may incorporate the reflecting process by talking with each other. For instance, Madigan (1993) describes the use of "listening therapists." Listening therapists are situated in the room along with the therapist(s) conducting a session (performative therapists) and the clients. During the session, in the clients' presence, questions the listening therapists ask about the questions the performative therapists asked in the therapy session are periodically discussed.

Therapists who work alone may also incorporate a reflecting position into their work. For instance, brief breaks may be taken as "thinking time" for the therapists. Therapists may leave the room or simply ask for a few minutes to reflect on the session up to that point. Clients may be invited to do the same. Therapists and clients then share their reflections. Wangberg (1991) suggests that therapists should differentiate reflecting comments from other therapeutic exchanges by looking at the floor or window while reflecting. Reflecting is talking *about* clients, not *to* them. Reflecting offers the opportunity for a different type of conversation. The reflective stance is discussed further in a later section.

Composition of Client System

Therapists who are influenced by social constructionism think in terms of social and cultural contexts. Thus, they often work with families or larger social systems. Anderson and Goolishian (1988) proposed that the therapeutic system should comprise all who are in conversation about the problem situation or person. Hoffman (in Simon, 1993) prefers the formulation that problems create systems rather than thinking that systems create problems. As such, the client system may comprise family members, extended family, or others involved with them, such as teachers or social service workers. Many postmodern therapists work with individuals and couples, smaller groups of the larger social system, while remaining mindful of the larger context.

Role of the Therapist

Traditionally, therapists were viewed as experts who conceptualize cases and develop treatment plans from their theoretical orientation. In contrast, the role of postmodern family therapists is to facilitate therapeutic conversations, in which the therapist actively attempts to learn about clients' perspectives and understandings. Sluzki (1992) describes this role as facilitating or promoting changes in specific stories or the relationship between stories. Therapists are respectful of clients' understandings and positions regarding their presenting problems. All explanations and descriptions are viewed as viable and are taken seriously. Therapists' understandings of clients' stories are introduced as possibilities or tentative hypotheses rather than as prescriptions for "better" stories or ways of understanding. These ideas are presented with the goal of generating conversation, not providing answers.

Goals of Therapy

Postmodern family therapists generally start therapy by eliciting clients' views of their situation and how it is problematic for them. Clients' self-stated problems are the issues attended to in therapy. Therapeutic goals are not determined by theoretical ideas as to what is "healthy" functioning, nor are the self-stated problems viewed as merely symptomatic of underlying conflicts that can be determined only by therapists. Normative assessment and diagnostic procedures are typically not used to determine the focus of treatment. Diagnostic labels are viewed as just one of many possible descriptions of problems. The danger of using such labels is that such descriptions frequently lead to understandings that are not helpful to clients. The goal of therapy is to expand understandings and possibilities. There is not a particular emphasis on behaviors, feelings, or thoughts. Clients may emphasize one or more of these; however, therapists are more interested in the meanings that are created by the stories surrounding behaviors, feelings, and thoughts.

Termination

Termination of therapy is seen as evolving gradually from therapeutic conversations. Anderson and Goolishian (1988) discuss termination of therapy as the "dissolving" of the problem-saturated story. Therapy ends because behavior, interactions, or the understandings of problem behavior have changed. Clients are assumed to be the better judges of when therapy is no longer needed.

Therapeutic Techniques

As postmodern family therapies evolved from philosophical theories, therapists began rethinking therapeutic techniques. Therapists who incorporate postmodernism into their practices use a variety of techniques. However, the focus is on changing meanings and understanding rather than on changing behaviors. Indeed, some proponents (e.g., Anderson & Goolishian, 1988) argue against deliberate interventions. In contrast, Epston (1993) argues that social constructionist perspectives may become an endangered species of potential practice if the theory is not translated into practices. This idea, espoused by Epston, is especially applicable to the new practice contexts of managed behavioral health care in which we must be able to define our methods and evaluate their effectiveness.

An obstacle in describing the techniques of postmodern family therapies is that these approaches to therapy were developed by a number of different individuals and groups, diverse in geography and culture: Harry Goolishian and Harlene Anderson in Texas, Michael White in Australia, David Epston in New Zealand, Tom Andersen in Norway, and Lynn Hoffman in Massachusetts. Postmodern family therapies have also been described by a number of different names. For example, Michael White and David Epston's model has been called narrative therapy, and Goolishian and Anderson's model, the collaborative language systems approach. Lynn Hoffman's ideas have been referred to as social constructionism. Tom Andersen is best known for the reflecting team therapy. These therapists, however, share a common philosophy. As stated by de Shazer (1993), for every theoretical idea there are at least 40 clinical practices or techniques that can express it. Indeed, practices of postmodern therapy value multiple perspectives and the belief that there are many "right" ways to do anything. With this in mind, we illustrate some of the common emphases of postmodern therapies: therapeutic stance, conversations, meanings, and narratives in therapy.

How to Conduct a Session

THERAPEUTIC STANCE

The postmodern therapeutic stance is characterized by collaboration, not-knowing, curiosity, and reflecting.

Collaborating.   For many, the primary difference between traditional modern and postmodern therapies is the position, or stance, that therapists take in relationships with clients. Therapy from the postmodern perspective is a collaborative effort between clients and therapists. Therapists make active efforts to reduce unhelpful effects of hierarchy rather than adopting a one-up/one-down relationship in which therapists' ideas dominate. There is a sense of being "in this" *with* the client instead of searching for deficits, traumas, or dysfunctions.

Not-knowing.   O'Hanlon (1993) described the therapeutic relationship as one in which

> clients and therapists are both considered experts. Clients are experts on their own experience, including their pain, suffering, and concerns. They also have expertise about their memories, goals, and responses. Therapists are expert at creating a conversational and interactional climate for change and results in therapy. Clients and therapists are partners in the change/therapy process and collaborate on deciding the focus for therapy, the goal to be sought, and when therapy should come to an end. (p. 12)

Anderson and Goolishian (1988, 1992) have called this the "not-knowing position." Therapists who adopt this stance assume that understandings and explanations in therapy should not be bounded by the therapist's previous experience or theoretical knowledge. Therapists ask questions to increase their understanding of the client's world, not to gather data to formulate a conventional diagnosis. Therapists' ideas are viewed as being no more useful or valid than are the client's ideas. Therapists' expertise lies in the conduct of the therapeutic conversation, which generates new ideas and meanings with clients. Therapists may introduce new ideas, explanations, or descriptions, but clients are ultimate judges about the usefulness of the ideas.

Curiosity.   An emphasis on maintaining curiosity is also characteristic of postmodern approaches to therapy (e.g., Cecchin, 1987). Anderson (1995) suggests that therapists display curiosity by learning a little about one thing and then moving on to other areas to avoid giving the impression that they are interested in only one narrow part of clients' experiences. Anderson and Goolishian (1992) suggest that therapists should not "understand" too quickly. When therapists "understand" clients, the possibilities for expanding and creating meanings become limited. The position of curiosity is a different stance from modernist approaches that put therapists in an investigatory stance fixed on discoverable "facts" or ideas.

Reflecting.   The term *reflecting* was introduced by Andersen (1987, 1991) in his descriptions of reflecting teams. The idea of reflecting has been expanded and is now used both to describe a process (reflecting conversations) and a stance (reflecting position) therapists may use whether they work in teams, co-therapy, or alone.

Andersen (1992) described the reflecting process as inner and outer conversations that allow therapists and clients to shift back and forth between talking and listening. He further explained, "These two different positions in relation to the same issues seem to provide two different perspectives, and these two perspectives of the same will most probably create new perspectives" (p. 62). Hoffman (1992) uses the word *reflexive* to describe her similar approach to therapy:

> To me the word implies that there is an equity in regard to participation even though the parties may have different positions or different traits . . . [reflecting conversations] . . . indicate a preference for a mutually influenced process between consultant and inquirer as opposed to one that is hierarchical and unidirectional. (p. 17)

Thus, Hoffman focuses on how the reflecting process influences the nature of the relationships between clients and therapists. Griffith and Griffith (1994) describe the reflecting position as

> a listening position. In its most fundamental aspect, it is a place in a conversation where one can listen to others talk without feeling compelled to respond to what is heard, or listen freely to one's inner talk without feeling compelled to relegate it to total secrecy or total exposure. (p. 160)

MANAGING CONVERSATIONS

The postmodern therapist's expertise is in the management of a special type of conversation, the therapeutic conversation. Therapeutic approaches based on postmodern perspectives depict the nature of therapeutic conversations more often than specific techniques. As social interactions are conducted largely through language, language is viewed as the primary vehicle for the transmission and construction of meanings and understandings. Anderson and Goolishian (1988) explain:

> Therapy is a linguistic activity in which being in conversation about a problem is a process of developing new meanings and understandings. The goal of therapy is to participate in a conversation that continually loosens and opens up, rather than constricts and closes down. Through therapeutic conversation, fixed meanings and behaviors (the sense people make of things and their actions) are given room, broadened, shifted, and changed. There is no other required outcome. (p. 381)

Such conversations open space for change, are tentative, and take a both/and stance.

Opening Space for Change.   The goal of the conversation is the creation of an opportunity for change by introducing new possibilities. Therapists ask questions that extend and expand the conversation while avoiding questions that constrict conversations. Constricting questions are those to which the answer is already known, those that are intended to lead clients to conclusions the therapists believe are correct, and those that elicit answers that support the therapists' theories about the cause of and/or solutions to the clients' problems. Such questions tend to restrict opportunities for the development of new understandings.

Harlene Anderson (1995) suggests that *shared inquiry* is the essence of the therapeutic conversation. Shared inquiry occurs when the therapist's interest and curiosity about the client's view results in a "mutually puzzling process in which therapist and client become engaged in conversation with each other in coexploring the familiar in a manner that leads to codevelopment of the new" (p. 36). Shared inquiry leads to a dialogue in which both people change.

Freedman and Combs (1993) describe questions designed to elicit meaningful experiences for the client. They identify three categories of questions that may be useful in this process: opening space questions, story development questions, and meaning questions. Opening space questions are aimed at generating alternative experiences and knowledge. Therapists may inquire about exceptions to the problem description, explore others' views of the problem situation, or inquire about changes (or potential changes) in the problem over time or in different circumstances. Story development questions and meaning questions are discussed later.

Tentativeness. The presentation of ideas in a nonauthoritarian manner is frequently advocated by postmodern family therapists. Offering ideas in a tentative manner may invite clients to offer their own thoughts and ideas more freely. Harlene Anderson (1995) believes that tentativeness may be conveyed by the use of unfinished sentences or hanging words and phrases such as *wondering, kind of,* or *maybe.* Tom Andersen (1991), in discussing guidelines for reflecting teams, suggests that the team members present "a smorgasbord of ideas" versus correct "interpretations," and offering ideas not as "rigid explanations but as tentative thoughts" (p. 133). Stating ideas tentatively may be a natural consequence of adopting postmodern ideas.

Both/And Stance. Andersen (1987) suggests that therapists adopt a both/and stance in place of an either/or stance. This flows from the postmodern idea of multiple, socially constructed realities and the valuing of diversity. The both/and stance extracts therapists from the position of determining who is "right" in family disagreements. The focus is on understanding how each position came about without choosing which is the best. Often, exploring intents or underlying meanings provides a way out of either/or standoffs. When therapists take this stance, often even logically inconsistent ideas can coexist.

EXPANDING MEANINGS

A postmodern perspective emphasizes that meanings and understandings are fluid and always changing. Psychological theories are viewed as nothing more than agreed-on understandings that have proven useful in one or more contexts (Howard, 1991). As no account or interpretation of reality can be considered more valid than any other, the focus shifts to deciding how and when a theory may be useful rather than trying to prove particular theoretical ideas. Therapists who work from this perspective often begin therapy by exploring the client's understanding of the problems or concerns instead of exploring the client's fit with the therapist's theories about the nature of psychological problems, diagnostic categories, and change. As noted by O'Hanlon (1993), therapy is a balance between acknowledgment of clients' realities and creation of new possibilities. Therapists should always keep the arrival of meaning "on the way" (Anderson & Goolishian, 1992).

Furman and Ahola (1988) describe interviewing techniques that explore clients' causal explanations or their impressions of others' causal explanations. They note that clients often infer therapists' explanations from the kinds of questions that are asked and that agreement leads to cooperation whereas disagreement leads to lack of cooperation. Thus, it is important for therapists to understand both clients' own causal explanations and clients' impressions of the therapists' explanations. Furman and Ahola encourage therapists to display curiosity and avoid expressing agreement or disagreement with the clients' explanations.

One way to explore causal explanations of clients is to ask direct, explanation-seeking questions. It may be easiest to start by asking for clients' impressions of others' explanations, like "What does your son's teacher think caused this behavior?" These types of questions are similar to the "relationship questions" used in solution-focused therapy as described in Chapter 5. If clients hesitate, therapists may need to reformulate the question or ask clients to use their imaginations: "But if you could know the reason, what would it be?" At times, it may be useful for therapists to speculate about alternative explanations to demonstrate that they are not seeking the one "correct" explanation.

Furman and Ahola discuss several advantages of exploring client explanations. Asking for client explanations indicates respect for the opinions of clients and shows that their opinions are valuable. Also, by seeking out the explanations of each person in the system, therapists acknowledge the importance of each person's opinion. This helps therapists avoid unintentional coalitions with some members of the system. Exploring alternate causes of problem behaviors may also have the effect of loosening firmly held explanations and allowing for the exploration of other explanations and new possibilities. Finally, working *with* clients' explanations may lead to efficient and effective change.

Freedman and Combs's (1993) meaning questions may be used to expand or create understandings and to assure that the story that is the focus of therapy is an experience that matters to clients. Such questions invite clients to look at the implications of the content of conversations in therapy. Examples of meaning questions include "What does finding out that your spouse appreciates this about you let you know about your relationship?" or "Now that you see your family this way, what do you know about your relationships to one another that you didn't know before?" (p. 301). Tom Andersen (1991), in discussing reflecting teams, suggests that observing therapists keep two questions in mind as a way of expanding meanings: "How else can this situation/behavior/pattern be described?" and "How else can it be explained?" These questions are useful for therapists who work alone, as well. By asking such questions, therapists will remain open to, and help generate, new possibilities.

Harlene Anderson (1986) suggests that therapeutic impasses occur in conversations when each of the participants believes that his or her description or explanation of a situation is correct and tries to convince the other(s) to adopt this position. This competition of ideas may cause the participants to become increasingly rigid in adhering to their own beliefs. Thus, the conversation becomes "stuck," with little opportunity for the development of new ideas or behaviors.

Such impasses may occur among the various members of the client system or between therapists and one or more members of the client system. This view of impasse reminds therapists to ask themselves "Who is trying to convince whom of what?" when therapy seems "stuck." For her, a therapeutic impasse occurs when meanings cease to be expanded and become constricted.

USING STORIES AND NARRATIVES

A focus on stories or narratives is common in postmodern therapies. Lynn Hoffman (1990) has described problems as stories people tell themselves. The terms *narratives* and *stories* are often used interchangeably. Following the lead of Saleeby (1994), we use *stories* as the descriptions and explanations given to events, interactions, and experiences told in the context of smaller systems, such as families, work groups, neighbors of individuals, families, or other social groups. *Narratives* are used to describe stories based on the norms or expectations of larger cultural groups. Narratives are cultural tales that set parameters for what stories are possible. Therapists work primarily with stories of individuals, couples, and families, though at times it may be helpful to place these stories in a larger context, such as single-parenting narratives or family violence narratives. Generally, postmodern family therapists believe that the presenting problem is one "story" that could be told, and that the story may change with each subsequent telling. Changing the story changes the meanings attached to events, behaviors, and interactions.

Stories and narratives are used in several ways by modern and postmodern family therapists. One way the use of stories varies is the source of the story. Generally, in modern approaches, therapists either generate the story (therapist-created metaphors), transform client stories into what therapists believe are more adaptive stories (e.g., Gardner, 1971), or fit the life stories of clients into a preconceived theoretical structure (e.g., psychodynamic approaches). That is, "the client's narrative is either destroyed or incorporated—but in any case replaced—by the professional account" (Roberts, 1994, p. 169). Postmodern family therapists tend to focus on client-generated stories. However, the amount of direction provided by therapists varies. We view the range of differences among postmodern therapists as falling along a continuum—from correcting or editing stories to facilitating client-generated changes.

Theorists who prescribe more direction from therapists include Michael White (White, 1993; White & Epston, 1990) and those who have built on his work (e.g., Parry & Doan, 1994). White focuses on the ways clients' stories are constrained by dominant social and cultural narratives, such as oppressive stories that develop out of abusive situations. Re-storying often involves the externalization of problems. Problems are externalized (described as some external thing that is affecting the person rather than a part of the person) to separate the person from the problem and/or restraints that maintain the dominant story. Questions are then asked to assess the influence the problems have over clients versus the influence of clients on the problems. Literary devices, including letters, documents, and certificates, become a few of the means by which clients rewrite their relationship with problems.

Another narrative approach focuses on changing the structure of stories independent of content (Sluzki, 1992). Sluzki defines a therapeutic conversation as one in which "a transformation has taken place in the family's set of dominant stories so as to include new experiences, meanings, and (inter)actions, with the effect of loosening of the thematic grip of the set of stories on symptomatic-problematic behaviors" (p. 219). Therapists may facilitate the transformation of client stories by attending to the following dimensions: time, space, causality, interactions, values, and the telling of the story. Sluzki describes a continuum for each of these dimensions along which stories may shift. Where clients' stories fall on the continuum is not important; the job of therapists is simply to help clients shift the position.

Roberts (1994) also focuses on narrative structure in her description of differing styles of storytelling. In *intertwined* stories, events that occurred at one point in time are used to interpret other events in the clients' lives. Such stories may collapse time so that the past is lived in the present. On the other end of the continuum are *distinct/separated* stories. When stories are disconnected, there is no access to meaning-making across contexts. No connections are made, even when there are similar dilemmas. In *minimal/interrupted* stories, there is little access to historical time and few details from which meanings are derived. *Silenced/secret* stories are hidden; meanings are unclear and confusing and may contain hidden alliances or coalitions. Time may appear to be frozen in *rigid* stories, with interpretations remaining unchanged across tellings by different persons. When stories are *evolving*, there is a recognition that stories may change over time.

Roberts suggests that story type influences which therapeutic approaches may be useful. For instance, therapists may explore differences between intertwined stories or the similarities between disconnected stories. With minimal stories, therapists can ask questions to fill in the missing pieces. Likewise, with silenced/secret stories, therapists can work with clients to decide whether, when, where, and how stories may be shared. Therapists may expand rigid stories by inquiring about different perspectives or different possible endings. Evolving stories may be identified by asking questions regarding change over time and how changes affected persons and relationships.

Griffith and Griffith (1994) describe narrative factors that may prevent people from escaping dilemmas: (1) lack of vocabulary or linguistic distinctions needed to articulate life experience in narrative form, (2) life stories that prevent the sharing of some personal experiences, (3) stories that lead to consequences that are too terrible, and (4) social practices (political, cultural, religious, etc.) that prescribe dilemmas but prevent discussion. Griffith and Griffith call these stories *binding*. They suggest helping medical clients expand their bound stories to include the meanings and effects on family members, alternative ways of viewing illness when they are feeling blamed, and the history of encounters with medical personnel.

The least direction is advocated by therapists who focus on developing stories rather than on providing frameworks for changing stories. Therapy is seen as an opportunity for clients to explore a variety of stories while discouraging commitment to any one truth (Gergen & Kaye, 1992). The collaborative languaging approach developed by Anderson and Goolishian (1988, 1992) provides one model for this way of thinking. Asking questions from a not-knowing position leads to "the unfolding of these 'yet-unsaid' possibilities, these 'yet-unsaid' narratives" (p. 34). Further, "the creation of new narrative or knowledge is not standardized; it is realized in the process of conversation and relationship" (Anderson & Swim, 1993, p. 150). Freedman and Combs (1993) are also nondirective in their use of questions to develop the stories brought in by clients. Story development questions are aimed at connecting newly developed possibilities to contexts, people, and the past and future. They suggest that the standard journalist's questions of "Who? What? When? Why? and How?" can be used to expand narratives.

Applications to Specific Problem Areas

ABUSE AND VIOLENCE

Several writers have presented the use of the narrative metaphor with victims of sexual or physical violence. The focus is generally on the types of stories that developed around the abusive experiences. It is noted that some people, but not necessarily all, who have experienced violence and abuse may develop stories about themselves that are limiting. Adams-Westcott, Dafforn, and Sterne (1993) find that problems often develop when people perform oppressive stories about themselves and their relationships. Further, Durrant, and Kowalski (1990) note that persons victimized by sexual assault may develop limiting or constraining stories about themselves as helpless and incompetent.

In working with the perpetrators of family violence, White (1989) suggests that a patriarchal ideology be presented to couples as an alternative explanation of domestic violence. Patriarchal narratives are such

> that women are the property of men and, following from this, the idea that men have the right to do with their property whatever they wish; and the notion of hierarchy as the natural order, of man's unquestionable entitlement to assume the superior position in this natural order, accompanied by a very great emphasis on control of those less entitled beings (women) by "power-over" tactics. (p. 102)

The stories that are told around the behaviors of both partners can then be examined in the context of a cultural narrative. Clients can be asked to explore the differences that would result from challenging the patriarchal narrative.

Jenkins (1990) provides another framework for therapy with men who are abusive to family members. He suggests that the focus should be on factors that restrain men from acting responsibly rather than on factors that "cause" persons to act violently. Examples of factors that may restrain responsible behavior include gender expectations, exaggerated sense of entitlements, preoccupation with sense of personal adequacy and competence, and misguided attempts to control abuse. Explanations of abusive behavior are evaluated according to the extent to which they help perpetrators take responsibility for abusive behaviors, point to plausible and accessible solutions ending the abuse and related problems, and are sensitive to all levels of context (e.g., individual, family, cultural). Jenkins's approach invites men to address their violence, argue for a nonviolent relationship, examine misguided efforts to contribute to the relationship, and externalize restraints such as male ownership, oppressive feelings, patterns of reliance, and avoidance of responsibility. Jenkins then asks clients to consider their readiness for change and facilitates the planning of new actions. New actions to be considered include promoting safety and nonviolence, promoting self-responsibility, demonstrating respect and ownership, and demonstrating responsibility for past abusive behavior. Clients are encouraged to attribute their own meanings to changes.

CULTURAL ISSUES

González, Biever, and Gardner (1994) have described the similarities between the social constructionist and multicultural perspectives in therapy. Both perspectives recognize the importance of social contexts in understanding meanings, behaviors, and relationships. Each perspective challenges therapists to work at understanding clients' worlds without making a priori assumptions. With respectful curiosity, therapists work within the cultural and social frameworks to expand understandings and possibilities.

Waldegrave (1990) argues that therapy that does not address cultural meanings may distance clients from their closest relationships. For him, "Good therapy engages authentically with people's woven pattern of meaning, and then in appropriate ways weaves new threads of resolution and hope that blend with, but nevertheless change, the problem-centered design" (p. 19). He urges therapists to search for "liberating traditions" within each culture. The idea is that some undesirable behavior may reside within larger cultural traditions that have value and that can be used as a positive therapeutic force. For example, when working with clients from cultures with rigid gender roles, therapists may focus on the value and skills involved in the traditional roles. Thus, both/and situations can be created that explore the possibilities of a person's belonging to the culture while having a sense of equity. Working within a postmodern perspective allows therapists to respect cultural variations and to nurture those differences without trying to fit clients into molds shaped by the dominant culture.

Consistency with Social Work Practice

Both Dean (1993) and Franklin (1995) argue that the practice methods used in social construction therapies are similar to the ones used in traditional social work practice. Postmodern therapy's emphasis on engaging systems in conversations that are involved in problem definitions is similar to the larger systems and community approaches found in social work. Franklin (1998) further identifies common ideologies between social work and social construction therapy. Ideologies include but are not limited to (1) supremacy of the social and cultural environment, commonly known as the person-in-environment metaphor; (2) the strengths perspective; (3) collaborative, client-centered orientation; (4) dislike and/or disbelief in the medical model and other types of labeling of the client; (5) belief in "client self-determination" or that people have the right to direct their own lives, including the therapy; (6) belief that problems are contextual, embedded in social situations, and may be resolved through a mutual understanding and coordinated actions between those involved; (This idea has been explained in social work literature as including the "observing systems" of the social worker and other systems in which she works.) (7) use of empowerment as a guiding metaphor; (8) respect for diversity, including multiple meanings and perspectives of clients; and (9) commitment to social action and changing the dominant discourses and narratives that oppress people. Although social workers traditionally have not used the language or "metaphors" of postmodern discourse to explain these views, these linguistic elements have been a part of the social work practice for many years (cf. Compton & Galaway, 1989; Hepworth & Larsen, 1993; Pincus & Minahan, 1973; Smalley, 1967).

Research Support for the Model

To date, the bulk of the research in postmodern approaches to family therapy reflects the postmodern character of the researchers. By this, we mean that research, for the most part, has focused on the processes of therapy rather than outcomes. Overall, there has been a lack of interest in the use of quantitative research methods. Constructionist practitioners seem to prefer qualitative methods such as case studies, ethnography, and discourse analysis (Franklin & Jordan, 1995). Polkinghorne (1992) has eloquently addressed the meaning of research from a postmodern practitioner's perspective. He argues that the process of therapy is different from the phenomena frequently investigated by academic researchers and highlights a number of studies that suggest that psychotherapists rarely find conventional research relevant for practice. Following Polkinghorne's lead, Shotter (1992a) suggests an alternate postmodern methodology of research that involves the researcher in less detached, "objective" stances. Hunsley (1993) provides even more concrete suggestions for the conduct of applicable research informed by a postmodern perspective. Several studies using ethnographic methods have attempted to produce an understanding of how postmodern therapists operate (Todtman, 1990), how clients view the process of therapy (Kassis & Mathews, 1987; Smith, Winton, & Yoshioka, 1993), how therapists themselves value and understand the practice of postmodern therapies (Kassis & Mathews, 1987; Smith, Winton, & Yoshioka, 1992), and speech patterns used in therapeutic settings (Gale & Newfield, 1992; Morris & Chenail, 1995).

Despite the fact that some postmodern therapists and researchers reject conventional quantitative research approaches, there is an empirical basis for many of the ideas found in social construction therapies. Franklin and Nurius (1996) have summarized research that supports constructivist perspectives. According to these authors, the research basis for constructionism exists primarily within the psychological sciences:

> Research into cognitive and social structures and processes such as 1) memory (Brower & Nurius, 1993), 2) social cognition (Fiske & Taylor, 1984), 3) evolutionary epistemology [how humans construct knowledge] (Mahoney, 1991), 4) ecological psychology (Greenberg & Pascual-Leone, 1995), 5) narrative psychology (van den Broek & Thurlow 1991), 6) new social cognitive, applied developmental and learning theories (Aldridge, 1993; Bandura, 1989; Prawat, 1993) and 7) complexity systems theory

(Mahoney, 1995; Warren, Franklin, & Streeter, in press) provide support for many of the tenets discussed in constructionist therapies. Brower and Nurius (1993), for example, review empirical research from cognitive, personality and social psychology, as well as ecological psychology and describe the importance of the constructionist perspectives. (p. 2)

Most of the research that demonstrates the empirical basis of social constructionism is theoretical and comes either from experimental social and personality psychology or process research on cognition and psychotherapy (Richardson & Franklin, 1998). Only recently have practitioners given attention to the evaluation of practice approaches such as the narrative methods discussed in this chapter. For this reason, and also because it is so new, postmodern therapy has few empirical, outcome studies. David Besa (1994), however, did a series of single-case experiments using a multiple baseline design and demonstrated the efficacy of narrative therapy with six families experiencing parent-child conflict.

Though clients generally report favorable perceptions of the reflecting team process, outcome studies on it, too, are rare. Andersen (1995) reports immediate observable differences after a reflecting team was implemented in a therapy session. Griffith and colleagues (1992), using the Structural Analysis of Social Behavior (SASB), compared family interactions before and after a reflecting team intervention. Family conversations showed significant changes, and families exhibited increased trusting, relying, comforting, and nurturing. Sells, Smith, Yoshioka, and Robbin (1994) have completed the most comprehensive study on reflecting teams and clients' perceptions of their effectiveness. Client feedback indicated an appreciation for the multiple perspectives. Other researchers (Biever & Franklin, 1997; Franklin, Biever, & Scamardo, 1997) have replicated these findings, demonstrating that reflecting teams promoted changes in the presenting problems of some cases. Further research is needed on reflecting teams and postmodern therapies in general to explore whether changes in presenting problems accompany the positive perceptions of clients.

Critiques of the Model

Postmodern therapies are not without critics who address important philosophical and moral issues that become evident in emerging practices. In the larger arena of academia, dialogue about postmodern ideas is currently being conducted (Harris, 1992). Several thinkers reject constructivist ideas in favor of modifying familiar concepts of realism. Greenwood's (1992a) scientific realism is an example that has been the object of debate in the psychological literature (Greenwood, 1992b; Parrott, 1992; Potter, 1992; Shotter, 1992b). Some family therapists have questioned the utility of total abandonment of the concept of a knowable reality. Speed (1991) argues for a position she calls "co-constructivism," which takes into account a relationship between the knower and the known. Other family therapists are troubled by the constructionist position around issues of family violence. Bograd (1984, 1992) has argued that the practice of assigning no preference to one position over any other is naïve and dangerous in the treatment of violence situations.

Postmodern Practice and Managed Behavioral Health Care

The researcher facing postmodern therapies is presented with a number of unique problems concerning what is the best way to establish the validity of these therapies. Yet, without establishing the validity of postmodern methods, it will be impossible in the current practice environment for social construction approaches to move beyond an experimental rating to be viewed within a "best practices" framework. A pragmatic concern arises in communicating with colleagues and managed care organizations whose language and understandings may be very different from those of the postmodern therapist. Issues of diagnosis, treatment planning, and outcomes are often described in "modernist" terms that are less useful to the postmodern therapist. Despite these challenges, postmodern practice approaches have several features that make them compatible with managed behavioral health care settings.

One feature is that these approaches use a strengths orientation. They use resources of the client and social system to find agreeable solutions. Using such a client-sensitive approach is likely to lead to high ratings in the area of consumer satisfaction, and this is an important outcomes indicator for managed behavioral health care organizations. Second, social construction approaches also usually focus on the here-and-now in the stories that clients bring to therapy. They move quickly to change these narratives and to help clients to get "unstuck" so they can move on with their lives. This action qualifies postmodern perspectives as a brief therapy approach. Third, postmodern perspectives use social supports and other social resources in resolving problems. Postmodern therapists influence the social networks, both their conversations and beliefs, that surround families and their problem stories. From this vantage point, they move beyond the therapy room into the natural environments in which people live as a method of dis-solving problems and finding solutions. This type of an approach has a high probability to decrease relapse patterns, and this is an important issue for the cost-containment efforts involved in managed care. The contextual approach of the postmodern therapies also makes them excellent therapies for working in integrated services delivery systems. It is a natural match for the methods because they subscribe to the idea that everyone, including human services professionals involved in defining the problem, should be included in a narrative dialogue aimed at dis-solving the problem. The team approach will work well in these settings.

The idea of therapists working in teams, however, may be a foreign idea to some managed care companies who may see this practice as contraindicated because of the lack of cost effectiveness. However, the teams may offer an important solution for training in managed care settings. It is important to managed care companies, for example, always to have a licensed professional with impeccable credentials working with clients. This presents a challenge for how to offer experience to interns and other students who are in training. Teams provide one method for resolving this dilemma in training. As mentioned previously, also, it is not necessary for the team to be present for the therapist to use the postmodern approach. Therapists can use themselves and their clients to maintain the reflexive stance necessary to conduct this type of therapy.

Case Example

The following case example presents a couple seen in San Antonio as part of an ongoing monthly externship, sponsored by the Houston Galveston Institute, focusing on narrative/social constructionist approaches. Two therapists in the externship group were feeling stuck and requested a consultation with a couple they had been seeing. Raheem and Marsha resided in a small West Texas town 200 miles from San Antonio. Marsha,[1] a 17-year-old high school student, and Raheem, a 20-year-old college student employed by a telephone company, were separated after eight months of marriage.

Raheem was originally from India and attended college on a student visa. He had left home at 16 after graduation from high school, traveling in England and the United States before settling in Texas. He was proud of managing without financial help from his parents. About a year earlier, he had been in danger of losing his student visa and being deported. As a result, he lost an attractive scholarship. During this difficult time, he met Marsha, a friend of his roommate's girlfriend. They became friends and began dating about six months later. Marsha had lived all her life in Texas. Until her marriage, she lived with her single mother, a professional in the public schools. Marsha described herself as a normal teenager who enjoyed "hanging out" with her friends and occasionally dating. Approximately three months before beginning to date Raheem, she was date-raped and experienced some difficulties as a result.

Beginning the Session

There are many ways of doing postmodern psychotherapy, and this is an example of *our* version. During the consultation, one of the consultants and one of the original therapists were in the room; the other consultant and original therapist and three externship participants were behind a one-way mirror. We usually begin by explaining the structure of the consultation or therapy session. It is common in our work to see clients with a co-therapist and with an additional team of two to four therapists behind a one-way mirror. We may also see clients with the whole team in the therapy room for the entire session. In that instance, the team members would be invited to comment from time to time but would not interact with the clients other than to observe and listen. We prefer to communicate, as early as possible, that we value a variety of perspectives, particularly those of the clients. We also express, both directly and indirectly, that our clients are the best judge of what ideas fit for them. Raheem and Marsha had been briefed on the structure of the session at the time the original therapists had invited them for the consultation. We added some detail to what they said they had been told. The following excerpt from the beginning moments of the session introduces the idea of the reflecting team.

THERAPIST: Generally, the team comes in here and talks about what they've observed in the first half of the session and we'll generate some ideas.

---

[1]The clients' names and the reflecting teams' names have been changed.

We can do that in a couple of different ways. One is that the four of us can just trade rooms with them so they can come in here and talk about the first half of the session as all of us observe their conversation from behind the mirror. Or we can take a break, and you can go to the waiting area and we'll all talk about their observations. Then you can come back and we'll finish our session. Either way you want to do it. It's very different from what you've experienced before, I'm sure. What's your preference? The first way of doing it is known as a reflecting team, so they will be reflecting on what they heard from all of us as they're listening to us and watching us. Or the other way is to just simply take a break.

The First Half of the Session

Several themes arose out of the conversation with the couple during the first part of the session. We have identified themes that we thought were important in our understanding of their situation.

The Decision to Marry

Marsha's mother was one important factor in their decision to marry. One evening over dinner, after Raheem and Marsha had dated a while, Raheem's predicament with the Immigration and Naturalization Service (INS) came up. Marsha's mother suggested that they get married as a solution to this predicament. This appeared to be an important aspect of the story to develop in order to get a historical context for their current situation. Marsha described the scene:

MARSHA: Well, cause see, he was gonna be deported and we had actually talked about marriage, but we had thought like way after college. And then she [her mother] said [something about] contract marriage. [We thought] she was joking. And so my mother said, "Well, would you marry Marsha?" She goes, "I'm serious!" And we both looked at each other like "yeah, right." It's probably one of those things that a parent says to get your reaction. That type of thing. And we were uh . . .

THERAPIST: You were shocked?

RAHEEM: We were shocked.

MARSHA: Yeah. We just like avoided the question. Then later on we were upstairs. Then I said, "Mom, were you serious?" She said "Yes, Marsha. If it makes you happy. I'll support you in whatever you want to do. If he is deported, I don't want you to blame me for being unhappy."

The Culture Clash

Raheem and Marsha were married in August by a justice of the peace, but did not live together until they had a subsequent church ceremony in October. Raheem's parents came from India to attend the second wedding, a six-week visit that precipitated conflict between Raheem and Marsha. The differences in cultural rituals and expectations, especially concerning the involvement of his mother, resulted in anguish for both of them. The following excerpts illustrate a few of the conflicts. The exploration of cultural themes and implications for the couple are revisited many times throughout the session by the clients and therapists. The therapists maintained a curious, not-knowing stance to allow for the clients' perspectives to prevail. As suggested earlier, it is assumed that stories change with each retelling.

MARSHA: I was really stressed out, like when Raheem's parents were here.

THERAPIST: What was stressful about that?

MARSHA: Well, just different cultures and I mean his parents didn't mean to—but like one day I was supposed to wake up at like five in the morning—well earlier, to meet her really early in the morning and go over there [to the parents' room] and pray and things. I was supposed to fast the whole day. She didn't ask me. She just expected me to do it.

THERAPIST: Who?

MARSHA: His mother—I mean she didn't ask me or anything. She just like expected me to do it. I was just like, oookay.

RAHEEM: But I told Marsha that she doesn't have to go with that. It's a thing for a new bride that they do and they get the new clothes and new jewelry and things like that. It's just that she wanted that basic thing with her new daughter-in-law while she was here.

THERAPIST: I see. That's a tradition that she wanted to carry out?

RAHEEM: Not carry out, just make her aware of. I told Marsha she did not have to do it, and she did not do it, either. It's not that she did it or anything.

MARSHA: Well, I didn't tell his mother that. [that she did not fast]

RAHEEM: It was one of those things my parents would have liked that we have a temple ceremony if we ever found the time. But we never found the time. . . .

THERAPIST: [to Marsha] So you didn't go over, so things got a little tight?

MARSHA: Yeah. And other things she did, like henna on your hands. It stays on weeks and when they wash it off, it looks like orange marker. And I didn't want to walk around school with people who would say "What's that on your hands?" I didn't want to do it in the first place. . . .

A little later in the conversation:

MARSHA: Well, so many times when his parents were here I would go to bed crying. And I was just really upset.

THERAPIST: And so how did that affect the two of you—the relationship during that time?

RAHEEM: Well, I don't know. During that time Marsha's complaint was that I wasn't spending enough time with her. I used to be with my parents a lot. And I know I was because I was seeing them after a long time. And it just doesn't seem right that somebody spend so much amount of time and money to fly across, especially my parents. I mean I just talk to them. It messes your lifestyle. I knew that . . .

Both expressed strong resentment about their experiences during his parents' visit. Both saw it as an impediment to positive change in the relationship.

Resentment Toward Her Mother

As the newlyweds' problems escalated, Raheem became more resentful toward his mother-in-law. According to him, Marsha's mother seemed to add fuel to the fire by her "meddling" in the relationship. On the other hand, Marsha's own story about her mother included an understanding that her mother was only trying to protect her daughter's best interests. Their experience of Marsha's mother was quite different. Our goal was not to favor one story over the other, but to make room for the multiple understandings emerging from our discussion. We accomplished this by asking "who, what, when, where, and how" questions, allowing them to tell their differing stories. We were trying not to "learn too quickly" but rather to hear the different points of view and perhaps to expand their understandings. A few examples might be helpful.

RAHEEM: Can I say something? It's just that I still think her mother interferes a lot. I mean right from the basic decisions it seems like she's always there.

THERAPIST: At her place?

RAHEEM: Yeah, well, Marsha would be there. I mean she wasn't going there once a week. Let's face it. [To Marsha] Were you going there once a week?

MARSHA: Only after you asked me [to go only once a week].

RAHEEM: Okay. From what I've seen, I think she's a lot influenced by her mother. I do.

THERAPIST: So you feel like her mother interferes in your marriage?

RAHEEM: Yeah.

THERAPIST: Okay. How do you see Mom doing that?

RAHEEM: I don't know. From what I have been hearing about all of this that's been going on, I haven't had a first chance to talk with anybody. Nobody's ever talked to me, but what I have been hearing through Marsha's friend that was down here from back east and her mother talking to my friends, there have been some very upsetting things she said.

THERAPIST: Who said?

RAHEEM: Her mother. Which I really don't respect and I don't have any respect for her. And I'm being very open.

THERAPIST: Respect for?

RAHEEM: For her mother. I mean, after these things that have been said and these things which should be done . . .

THERAPIST: So you're pretty angry at her mother, it sounds like.

RAHEEM: I'm upset. Yes.

THERAPIST: [to Marsha] And you're pretty angry at his parents.

RAHEEM: But, I mean, her mother went and told one of my friends that "if Raheem doesn't straighten his act with Marsha, I'll get his little ass back to India." I don't think [a professional person] should be talking that way. I really don't care a damn right now. I mean, if I have to stay here, I will stay here. I mean, I really don't care about it and if I have to go back, I'm happy for that. I'm prepared. It won't make a difference to me. I mean, it will make a difference, of course, but it does—I cannot work like that. I mean, I cannot work if you put a gun to my head and say "change."

THERAPIST: I was just wondering how you see her mother interfering with your relationship . . . what did she do that interferes?

RAHEEM: I mean, just these little things. Marsha smokes and her mother doesn't know about it. I think it's about time. Because her mother would make these comments—"I don't want my daughter going around a smoker" [or when her mother says] "I don't want my daughter with a depressant."

THERAPIST: Going around what?

RAHEEM: A person who is depressed. "I don't want her to be around a person who is depressed." I mean, it seems people are looking for a danger. They are looking for a relationship with a lot of conditions.

THERAPIST: Conditions?

RAHEEM: You know, not be depressed. Don't smoke. Exercise. Don't get fat. She does not want a fat husband. It seems like we are trying to show off to somebody here.

THERAPIST: So you're feeling like you're getting some pressure put on you to behave in certain ways?

RAHEEM: Yes.

THERAPIST: [to Marsha] How about you? Does your mom put demands on you? Or requests on you to behave in certain ways?

MARSHA: I don't think so. I mean . . .

THERAPIST: What would your mom say about your marriage?

MARSHA: She really likes Raheem. It's just the way he's been acting a lot.

THERAPIST: And how has that been problematic for your mom?

MARSHA: I can't tell my mom anything about it. Cause one time when his parents were here, I went over there and I was doing the laundry and we were inside and I just started crying. I don't remember what it was—something about his parents and then she got mad. She called him up, and she said, "You know Raheem, either you get over here or I'm gonna yell at you over the phone!"

RAHEEM: Well, everybody heard. My parents did. My friends did. And everybody did. Because the guy we were staying with had speaker phones and I didn't know it was on. It was no big deal, everybody heard us yelling and saying all these things.

A little later on:

RAHEEM: I think we portray her [mom] differently. One is Marsha in front of her mother—I mean the good ol' daughter. And then the other with me. But I feel her mother's being overprotective. That's what I can get—and very possessive.

THERAPIST: So let me put it in my words and see if it fits. [to Raheem] You see mom as not letting go of daughter?

RAHEEM: Yeah.

THERAPIST: [to Marsha] How do you see it?

MARSHA: I don't see that.

THERAPIST: What do you see? Obviously there are some very disparate views here.

MARSHA: How do I see my mom? I know she's really overprotective, but I don't think she really ever *does* anything to me.

Raheem's Pride About Survival

Another theme that was clear from Raheem's point of view was that he was a survivor . . . he could handle whatever came his way. His independence at an early age seemed important in contextualizing his relationship with Marsha. He took so much pride in being mature, self-sufficient, and responsible that he thought he could incorporate the additional load of a marriage into his life.

RAHEEM: I left home when I was 16. I graduated from high school when I was 16. I've seen the world. I've come across continents. I was in London. I've been here, and I've made it on my own. I've never taken a penny from anyone. Yes, I have a very big ego. I know. I mean I have a big ego and I agree to it. I do. I don't compromise on that. But I'm mature in my actions the way I'm going about life, but I don't usually go and talk about it. It was a very stressful period. I think it was a very bad period, because I didn't know where to give how much attention.

And later on:

RAHEEM: I was 16 and my mom didn't want me to leave home. I mean America [is, to my folks] sex, drugs, and rock-and-roll and nobody really wanted that for me. It's just like if you had a 15-year-old son, you would want him to go to Australia or Europe and study. That's what they said . . . I knew my family could not afford it . . . So that's why I made a decision I'm not going to take anything for my further education [from them] . . . even though they have the money.

How Things Have Changed

In this segment, we attempted to extend and expand the story by expressing curiosity about their initial attraction to one another and how that had been sustained or changed. Early in the session, we asked about what brought them together: "What was the chemistry?" "How have things changed?" Here are their responses.

THERAPIST: What was the chemistry that brought the two of you together?

MARSHA: He was unlike any other guy I ever dated. He was intelligent, he was open, and he was lots of fun. When I'd meet him for the day, we'd spend all day together and talk all night on the phone. And when we'd go over to see each other, it was just like the day was so spontaneous. We could just be sitting around doing nothing and it was fun, but we had a great time together.

THERAPIST: [to Raheem] What would you add to that?

RAHEEM: We had a wonderful time.

THERAPIST: What was the chemistry for you?

RAHEEM: I was going through a really rough time because the semester was just ending in May and the INS was pressing these charges. It was just a very stressful year. Then I met Marsha and she was so laid back.

THERAPIST: That's what attracted you to her? She was laid back?

RAHEEM: She was not exactly laid back. She was more easygoing than I was. Definitely.

THERAPIST: How has that worked out for the two of you since those initial attractions?

MARSHA: We have to plan everything now. Before we had planned little things. Now we have to plan everything, everything, everything. I mean, after we started having arguments, I found out he'd have a plan before I went and picked him up after work. I get out of school earlier than he does, so I go and pick him up. So he had a plan before I picked him up, and when I get there, I have plans, he gets upset when I didn't even know he had a plan. But we have to plan everything now.

Raheem's Depression

Marsha described Raheem as appearing depressed, particularly after his parents returned to India. Raheem did not see himself as being depressed, but described himself as attempting to take responsibility for his life. This was another part of the story that was important to inquire about, and puzzle with them about, to explore new understandings. We introduced the metaphor of a "rudderless ship," which seemed to be something he could use in expanding his understanding in a positive way.

RAHEEM: I'm not depressed. I just have a lot of things to do. It's just that somebody has to take the responsibility here. I cannot go on living like this.

THERAPIST: Living like . . . ?

RAHEEM: Living like, without a direction. Never finding out anything . . .

THERAPIST: It sounds like you sort of feel like a rudderless ship.

RAHEEM: Yes. Definitely.

THERAPIST: Have you gotten a hold of the rudder yet?

RAHEEM: Yeah. I'm getting hold of it. I am and I will.

They Demand Too Much of Each Other

Just before the break for the reflecting team, there was another understanding or explanation about their problems. This was the result of an inquiry by the therapists that suggested that each of them probably had some very different views of how they came to have problems.

THERAPIST: My guess is that the two of you may have very different ideas about how come you are having problems. And if so, how do you each explain how you're having problems? What's your explanation for it? I'm sure you must have mulled this over a million times.

RAHEEM: I think so.

MARSHA: I feel like he demands too much from me. I can't give up too much of myself and I can't give everything.

THERAPIST: So you sense that he's making lots of demands on you. You can't meet all of those demands and so what happens?

MARSHA: I mean, eventually I get to a point where, well "Okay, I'll do that." And then I finally get to the point to where I don't want to do that or I can't do that.

THERAPIST: So you sort of resent it after a while?

MARSHA: Yeah.

Marsha has given another understanding for the couple's problems, and Raheem responds with a similar explanation except that he asserts that she asks too much of him.

RAHEEM: It's the same thing with me—things she wants to do. Last time she wanted to go for a movie, and I did not. I was tired. And she got all up- set over it. "What do you want to do? Sit around?" "Well, yes." I had gone to bed at 12 A.M. and gotten up at four in the morning, and I've been driving and going to the court this weekend. And I was tired that night. There are some things we cannot do right now because we are financially constrained, I think.

THERAPIST: So what I'm hearing from you is that she's making demands that you don't feel like you can do. Is that your explanation?

Raheem adds still another explanation.

RAHEEM: I think back on it. I think we compromised a lot on situations, and now we are taking stands.

The first part of the consultation concluded with the therapists joining with the couple, and complimenting them on their individual strengths. Still another frame was added concerning "tremendous pressures" and "tremendous changes in a very short period of time."

THERAPIST: Well, I think probably it is time to take a break and hear what the team has to say. The other thing I would like to say is that you two . . . I don't know if you have realized it or not . . . have been under tremendous, tremendous pressures. Even if the two of you were not going through a difficult relationship, the two of you would both be under tremendous pressures individually. That's got to really play on your minds. That, plus getting married, and having your family in town, and having mom in the same town, and so on. You two have done amazingly well considering you have gone through some tremendous changes in a very short period of time.

The Reflecting Team

A rich variety of ideas emerged from the reflecting team, which concentrated on developing meanings focused on the more positive understandings inherent in the couple's presentation of their dilemmas. The reflecting team found many strengths and skills and complimented them as individuals and as a couple. They introduced ideas that were not "too different" so as to be immediately rejected, so that the conversation with the couple could be expanded to include slightly new possibil- ities. The following is an abridged version of the reflecting team's comments:

JIM: A lot of information was generated in a short period of time. I just wanted to start by echoing what (the therapist) was saying toward the end. This couple certainly weathered a lot that most newlyweds don't usually do. Somehow they still came through it. So they must have some interest in maintaining this relationship.

BONNIE: And they are getting so much help from so many people.

JIM: There are a lot of people invested in this relationship . . . trying to help. You are right about that.

JEAN: In spite of the pain they're going through, they're still motivated.

BONNIE: Sometimes it's hard [for the couple] to know who to listen to.

JIM: Sometimes that could be a valuable resource—his family and her family and all their friends.

CAROL: I was rather amazed too by both their senses of independence. That's such a plus for an individual in terms of growth and . . .

BONNIE: What I was thinking too was that they started [their relationship] by facing large challenges with all this stress and change . . . and all of a sudden it's gone. They seemed to be doing a lot better when they had a lot to deal with. Maybe they need to learn to be together when things aren't so challenging.

JEAN: It seems like everything in the relationship has been at a much higher level of intensity than in a lot of other relationships. Just like last summer, they were together 24 hours a day. It was an intense courtship and their marriage happened so quickly with Mom kinda suggesting it. Then having to learn about one another's families and cultures. It was like someone pushed the fast-forward button. His family comes over and they're here for two months and [his] mom is trying to give Marsha a crash course in what their culture is about—daily involvement. It's like, when have they had a moment to get to know each other? It's been a crash course.

JIM: For most couples who grow up in the same culture and same kinds of backgrounds, there is this adjustment period—meeting each other's families—different ways of doing things. But it's been kind of a crash course for them, two different cultures coming together, trying to learn one another. It's like it just picked up the level of intensity for them. They're really kind of pioneers.

CAROL: I'm still thinking about his reference to forgetting [their awful beginning]. This could be one of those things a couple would not want to forget—that they would look back on years from now and think "If we could get through that we can get through anything. Wow! What a time that was!" After that, anything might seem little . . .

JIM: It took a lot of courage for them to get married—Like Raheem's parents (his parents were from different parts of India and from different castes), it took a lot of courage for people from such different backgrounds to decide to get married. . . . I was also struck by how easily [one of the therapists] was thinking that Raheem was 24 years old and he is 20. His life is a lot older than a lot of 20-year-olds. It would be real easy to think he is older. When he was 16, he was graduated from high school, traveling around the world, doing a whole lot of things most 20-year-olds haven't done. And all on his own. So it's easy to see how you can mistake him for being a man much older—and her, too.

JEAN: But it's almost as if maybe Marsha has a few things she could teach him—and that he can teach her.

DOROTHY: With two people so independent and strong, it is very difficult to be helpful for each other.

JIM: Raheem said he had a big ego, but I think he has a lot of self-confidence. He is self-reliant and Marsha is the same way, too.

JEAN: It's difficult for them to stand in the shadow of one another. [The analogy had earlier been given of two trees that do not want to be in the shadow of one another.]

BONNIE: Maybe they are both learning how to negotiate—to compromise. Marriage is a lot of negotiations and compromises.

JIM: I was just thinking about how protective each one was over the other one's independence. Raheem talked about whether Marsha's mother was interfering with Marsha, and Marsha was talking about how Raheem's parents were providing him with guidance and advice and support. . . . They are also very protective of anyone else's shade falling on their partner. They don't want any other trees getting around and getting in the way.

JEAN: Not overshadowing.

JIM: Somehow when the ceremony occurred, people figured they needed more help now that they were a couple. So lots of people were giving them advice.

CAROL: They [the friends] were trying to adjust to the change—no longer is this my friend but this is my *married* friend. I was also thinking about the question [the therapists] asked them about why they think they are having problems. I was speculating on that myself—kind of thinking about that, as they began their relationship, and they are going through this stressful time and [going through] change. Stress, change, stress. It's almost as though they had said, "Please no more change. Please no more stress." But the tension just tightened.

Post-Reflecting Team

After listening to the reflecting team, the therapists continued their session with the couple. It is common to ask the clients to give their reactions to the reflecting team. It is interesting to note that this couple seemed much more relaxed and upbeat after the reflecting team. Raheem told several funny stories about his first experiences with different meanings of certain English words in India and the United States. The focus then returned to their thoughts about the reflecting team. Both Marsha and Raheem indicated that they were favorably impressed with what they heard.

THERAPIST: Anything surprising?

RAHEEM: I think they brought some good points. This is the first time I've at least noticed somebody realizing the feeling of stress that we've been through, and there is still a lot to go; it's not over. I mean, both of us are in the wrong. I saw the respect and all that.

THERAPIST: How about you, Marsha?

MARSHA: They were a little more positive than some of the people.

RAHEEM: Yeah. That's right. They were more optimistic.

MARSHA: I was like, Wow!

THERAPIST: How was that? Did you think that what they said made sense?

MARSHA: Yes.

RAHEEM: Yes. They made sense.

THERAPIST: Is there something that struck you? One thing that really struck you?

RAHEEM: I think both of us are independent.

THERAPIST: I hadn't even thought about that.

RAHEEM: That we need to really think on how we can come about keeping those views intact and be together at the same time.

THERAPIST: Yes. And it's even more of a challenge for the two of you with the cultural differences that you bring to the relationship. While that is an enriching experience, it is also something to wrestle with—those differences. Not all are wonderful—at first, at least. I was thinking about something that you said and they commented on to you. You said that "Now we're taking a stand." And the way they looked at it, maybe you're just kind of stuck?

RAHEEM: What I was thinking, or why I said that was because last summer when we were together, it seemed like that I went with the flow that Marsha wanted to go with and she did the same for me, and I realized it. It just seems now as if we're just not willing to go with each other's flows any more.

THERAPIST: You know what came to my mind when I heard that as we were listening. It was almost like the two of you were trying to put some kind of structure on the relationship to stop some of the change. It was like "Damn, let's put on the brakes here, gee, somehow let's find a way to deal with all of this." It's a big package.

RAHEEM: We are trying to mold, trying to give it shape—structure it. That's true.

THERAPIST: You said a minute ago that you were willing to do what she wanted to do and she was willing to do some of the things you wanted to do last summer, and that was working for you. So, I just wondered if that was something you want to look at?

RAHEEM: I think that I have to . . . I'm sure we can see a compromise and give it a good effort. I think a lot had to do with the fact that we held things within ourselves. The resentment of the things that have gone on. I think that's really restricting.

THERAPIST: So. What would you do about that?

RAHEEM: I don't believe in divorce or annulment as a solution or an option. I'm sure we can work things out. I'm sure both of us can compromise to the same way . . . be a little more organized about the whole thing. I know I cannot function without a plan. I'm totally responsible for what happens in this country. There is nobody else. Nobody is going to be on the lookout. I'm responsible for the shape right now for me and Marsha.

THERAPIST: That must be a tremendous weight for you.

RAHEEM: Yes.

Raheem told a story about how strong Marsha was, and about how he felt a strong sense of responsibility. He compared himself to other students and workers he had encountered, and his belief that many people just put in time to pick up a paycheck. Other aspects of their relationship were amplified, such as his tendency toward planning for both of them and how, in his culture, that is expected of the man. These were seen as examples of new stories being developed. Marsha pointed out that Raheem makes plans for everyone and manages his older friends' finances. She suggested that he was accustomed to planning for everyone. She also highlighted the fact that she knew both of them were very independent, and that trying to be a couple and independent is difficult to do.

They both reported that the session had been helpful to them. Raheem said that it was the first time that both of them had sat down together and got the same feedback, at the same time, instead of getting different feedback from different people individually. The consultation ended soon thereafter, with plans for the couple to follow up with their original therapists.

Summary

In this chapter we have presented an overview of postmodern approaches to family practice. The term *postmodern* has become attached to a number of intellectual, theoretical, and pragmatic movements in the latter half of this century, all of which may be seen as attempts to account for the increasing diversity and complexity we are faced with in our daily professional lives. Postmodernism is expressed in many different ways in the practice of psychotherapy, preferring the adoption of language, metaphors, and stories to fit particular clients, communities, and cultures. The postmodern movement is frequently oversimplified and described as a form of nihilism. The postmodern mind does not deny the existence of a reality external to our experience of it; rather, it questions whether our perceptual and cognitive abilities can apprehend such a reality in an objective manner. Both the theory and therapeutic techniques used in postmodern practice were presented. Consistency of postmodern practice with social work was further highlighted. Research that is used to explore and explain social constructionism was discussed, as well as the body of experimentally based, theoretical research that undergirds its constructs and methods. Critiques of the model were further summarized. Finally, the influence of social constructionism, a postmodern epistemological position, on practice in working with families was presented and illustrated with a case study. The case illustrated one of several applications of a postmodern approach—working with culturally diverse couples and families.

Process Questions

1. Narrative/social constructionist practitioners work from a collaborative, not-knowing stance. They rely on processes such as reflecting in generating solutions to client problems. How does the work of the therapist with Raheem and Marsha illustrate these methods, and what effect do these methods have on the client system?

2. What are some examples of the cultural orientation and postmodern perspective in this case?

3. How does the therapist work to restructure the language, stories, and meanings that the client system is making about their problems?

4. Narrative and social constructionist therapists use a technique called "externalizing the problem." What examples are present in the case?

References

ADAMS-WESTCOTT, J., DAFFORN, T. A., & STERNE, P. (1993). Escaping victim life stories and co-constructing personal agency. In S. Gilligan & R. Price (Eds.), *Therapeutic conversations* (pp. 258–271). New York: Norton.

ANDERSEN, T. (1987). The reflecting team: Dialogue and meta-dialogue in clinical work. *Family Process, 26,* 415–428.

ANDERSEN, T. (1991). *The reflecting team: Dialogues and dialogues about the dialogues.* New York: Norton.

ANDERSEN, T. (1992). Reflections on reflecting with families. In S. McNamee & K. J. Gergen (Eds.), *Therapy as social construction* (pp. 54–68). Newbury Park, CA: Sage.

ANDERSEN, T. (1995). Reflecting processes: Acts of informing and forming. In S. Friedman (Eds.), *The reflecting team in action: Collaborative practice in family therapy* (pp. 11–37). New York: Guilford Press.

ANDERSON, H. (1986). *Therapeutic impasses: A breakdown in conversation.* Unpublished manuscript, Houston Galveston Institute.

ANDERSON, H. (1995). Collaborative language systems: Toward a postmodern therapy. In R. Mikesell, D. D. Lusterman, & S. McDaniel (Eds.), *Integrating family therapy: Handbook of family psychology and systems theory* (pp. 27–43). Washington, DC: American Psychological Association Press.

ANDERSON, H., & GOOLISHIAN, H. (1988). Human systems as linguistic systems: Preliminary and evolving ideas about the implications for clinical theory. *Family Process, 27,* 3–12.

ANDERSON, H., & GOOLISHIAN, H. (1992). The client is the expert: A not-knowing approach to therapy. In S. McNamee & K. J. Gergen (Eds.), *Therapy as so-cial construction* (pp. 25–39). Newbury Park, CA: Sage.

ANDERSON, H., & SWIM, S. (1993). Learning as collaborative conversation: Combining the student's and teacher's expertise. *Human Systems: The Journal of Systemic Consultation & Management, 4,* 145–160.

BERGER, P., & LUCKMAN, T. (1966). *Social construction of reality.* New York: Doubleday.

BESA, D. (1994). Evaluating narrative family therapy using single-system research designs. *Research on Social Work Practice, 4*(3), 309–325.

BIEVER, J. L., & FRANKLIN, C. (1997). Social constructionism in action: Using reflecting teams in family practice. In C. Franklin & P. Nurius (Eds.), *Practicing constructivism: Methods, evidence, and future challenges.* Milwaukee: Families International.

BIEVER, J. L., & GARDNER, G. T. (1995). The use of reflecting teams in social constructionist training. *Journal of Systemic Therapies, 14*(3), 47–56.

BOBELE, R. M., GARDNER, G. T., & BIEVER, J. L. (1995). Supervision as social construction. *Journal of Systemic Therapies, 14*(2), 14–25.

BOGRAD, M. (1984). Family systems approaches to wife battering: A feminist critique. *American Journal of Orthopsychiatry, 54,* 559–567.

BOGRAD, M. (1992). Values in conflict: Challenges to family therapists' thinking. *Journal of Marital and Family Therapy, 18,* 245–256.

CECCHIN, G. (1987). Hypothesizing, circularity, and neutrality revisited: An invitation to curiosity. *Family Process, 27,* 405–414.

CLIFFORD, J., & MARCUS, G. (Eds.). (1986). *Writing culture: The poetics and politics of ethnography.* Berkeley: University of California Press.

COMPTON B. R., & GALAWAY, B. (1989). *Social work processes* (4th ed.). Belmont, CA: Wadsworth.

DEAN, R. (1993). Constructivism: An approach to clinical practice. *Smith College Studies in Social Work, 63,* 127–146.

DE SHAZER, S. (1993). De Shazer and White: Vive la différence. In S. Gilligan & R. Price (Eds.), *Therapeutic conversations* (pp. 112–120). New York: Norton.

DURRANT, M., & KOWALSKI, K. (1990). Overcoming the effects of sexual abuse: Developing a self-perception of competence. In M. Durrant & C. White (Eds.), *Ideas for therapy with sexual abuse* (pp. 65–110). Adelaide, Australia: Dulwich Centre Publications.

EPSTON, D. (1993). Commentary. In S. Gilligan & R. Price (Eds.), *Therapeutic conversations* (pp. 231–234). New York: Norton.

FRANKLIN, C. (1995). Expanding the vision of the social constructionist debates: Creating relevance for practitioners. *Families in Society, 76*(7), 395–407.

FRANKLIN, C. (1998). Distinctions between social constructionism and cognitive constructivism: Practice applications. In C. Franklin & P. Nurius (Eds.). *Constructivism in practice: Methods and challenges.* Milwaukee: Families International.

FRANKLIN, C., BIEVER, J. L., & SCAMARDO, M. (1997). *Client perceptions of the process and outcomes of reflecting team therapy.* Unpublished manuscript.

FRANKLIN, C., & JORDAN, C. (1995). Qualitative assessment: A methodological review. *Families in Society, 76*(5), 281–295.

FRANKLIN, C., & NURIUS, P. (1996). Constructivist therapy: New directions in social work practice. *Families in Society, 77*(6), 323–325.

FREEDMAN, J., & COMBS, G. (1993). Invitations to new stories: Using questions to explore alternative possibilities. In S. Gilligan & R. Price (Eds.), *Therapeutic conversations* (pp. 291–303). New York: Norton.

FURMAN, B., & AHOLA, T. (1988). Return to the question "why": Advantages of exploring pre-existing explanations. *Family Process, 27,* 395–409.

FURMAN, B., & AHOLA, T. (1992). *Solution talk: Hosting therapeutic conversations.* New York: Norton.

GALE, J., & NEWFIELD, N. (1992). A conversation analysis of a solution-focused marital therapy session. *Journal of Marital and Family Therapy, 18,* 153–165.

GARDNER, R. A. (1971). *Therapeutic communication with children: The mutual storytelling technique.* New York: Jason Aronson.

GERGEN, K. J. (1985). The social constructionist movement in modern psychology. *American Psychologist, 40,* 266–275.

GERGEN, K. J., & KAYE, J. (1992). Beyond narrative in the negotiation of meaning. In S. McNamee & K. J. Gergen (Eds.), *Therapy as social construction* (pp. 25–39). Newbury Park, CA: Sage.

GONZÁLEZ, R. C., BIEVER, J. L., & GARDNER, G. T. (1994). The multicultural perspective in therapy: A social constructionist approach. *Psychotherapy, 31,* 515–524.

GREENWOOD, J. D. (1992a). Realism, empiricism and social constructionism: Psychological theory and the social dimensions of mind and action. *Theory and Psychology, 2,* 131–151.

GREENWOOD, J. D. (1992b). Realism, relativism and rhetoric: A response to comments on realism, empiricism and social constructionism. *Theory and Psychology, 2,* 183–192.

GRIFFITH, J. L., & GRIFFITH, M. E. (1994). *The body speaks: Therapeutic dialogues for mind-body problems.* New York: Basic Books.

GRIFFITH, J. L., GRIFFITH, M. E., KREJAMAS, N., MCLAIN, M., MITTAL, D., RAINS, J., & TINGLE, C. (1992). Reflecting team consultants and their impact upon family therapy for somatic symptoms as coded by Structural Analysis of Social Behavior (SASB). *Family Systems Medicine, 10,* 53–58.

HARRIS, J. F. (1992). *Against relativism: A philosophical defense of method.* LaSalle, IL: Open Court.

HEPWORTH, D. H., & LARSEN, J. A. (1993). *Direct social work practice: Theory and skills* (4th ed.). Belmont, CA: Brooks/Cole.

HOFFMAN, L. (1990). Constructing realities: An art of lenses. *Family Process, 29,* 1–12.

HOFFMAN, L. (1992). A reflexive stance for family therapy. In S. McNamee & K. J. Gergen (Eds.), *Therapy as social construction* (pp. 7–24). Newbury Park, CA: Sage.

HOLLINGER, R. (1994). *Postmodernism and the social sciences.* Thousand Oaks, CA.: Sage.

HOWARD, G. S. (1991). Cultural tales: A narrative approach to thinking, cross-cultural psychology, and psychotherapy. *American Psychologist, 46,* 187–197.

HUNSLEY, J. (1993). Research and family therapy: Exploring some hidden assumptions. *Journal of Systemic Therapies, 12,* 63–70.

HUNT, DAVID. (1987). *Beginning with ourselves: In practice, theory, and human affairs.* Cambridge, MS: Brookline Books.

JENKINS, A. (1990). *Invitations to responsibility.* Adelaide, Australia: Dulwich Centre Publications.

KASSIS, J. P., & MATHEWS, W. J. (1987). When families and helpers do not want the mirror: A brief report of one team's experience. *Journal of Strategic and Systemic Therapies, 6,* 33–43.

LAIRD, J. (1995). Family-centered practice in the postmodern era. *Families in Society, 76,* 150–162.

LEWIN, K. (1951). *Field theory in social sciences.* New York: Harper Torchbooks.

MADIGAN, S. P. (1993). Questions about questions: Situating the therapist's curiosity in front of the family. In S. Gilligan & R. Price (Eds.), *Therapeutic conversations* (pp. 219–230). New York: Norton.

MCNAMEE, S., & GERGEN, K. J. (1992). *Therapy as social construction: Inquiries in social construction.* London: Sage.

MORRIS, G. H., & CHENAIL, R. J. (Eds.). (1995). *The talk of the clinic.* Hillsdale, NJ: Lawrence Erlbaum.

O'HANLON, W. H. (1993). Possibility therapy: From iatrogenic injury to iatrogenic healing. In S. Gilligan & R. Price (Eds.), *Therapeutic conversations* (pp. 3–17). New York: Norton.

PARDECK, J. T., MURPHY, J. W., & JUNG, M. C. (1994). Some implications of postmodernism for social work practice. *Social Work, 39,* 343–345.

PARROTT, W. G. (1992). Rhetoric for realism in psychology. *Theory and Psychology, 2,* 159–165.

PARRY, A., & DOAN, R. E. (1994). *Story re-visions: Narrative therapy in the postmodern world.* New York: Guilford.

PINCUS, A., & MINAHAN, A. (1973). *Social work practice: Model and method.* Itasca, IL: Peacock.

POLKINGHORNE, D. E. (1992). Postmodern epistemology of practice. In S. Kvale (Ed.), *Psychology and postmodernism: Inquiries in social constructionism* (pp. 146–165). London: Sage.

POTTER, J. (1992). Constructing realism: Seven moves (plus or minus a couple). *Theory and Psychology, 2,* 167–173.

RICHARDSON, F., & FRANKLIN, C. (1998). Phenomenology, social constructionism, and hermeneutics. In S. P. Robinson, P. Chatterjee, and E. R. Canda (Eds.), *Contemporary human behavior theory: A critical perspective for social work.* Boston: Allyn & Bacon.

ROBERTS, J. (1994). *Tales and transformations: Stories in families and family therapy.* New York: Norton.

SALEEBY, D. (1994). Culture, theory, and narrative: The intersection of meanings in practice. *Social Work, 39,* 351–356.

SELLS, S. P., SMITH, T. E., YOSHIOKA, M., & ROBBIN, J. (1994). An ethnography of couple and therapist experiences in reflecting team practice. *Journal of Marital and Family Therapy, 20,* 247–266.

SELVINI-PALAZZOLI, M. S., BOSCOLO, L., CECCHIN, G., & PRATA, G. (1980). Hypothesizing–circularity–neutrality: Three guidelines for the conductor of the session. *Family Process, 19,* 3–12.

SHOTTER, J. (1992a). Getting in touch: The meta-methodology of a postmodern science of mental life. In S. Kvale (Ed.), *Psychology and postmodernism: Inquiries in social constructionism* (pp. 58–73). London: Sage.

SHOTTER, J. (1992b). Social constructionism and realism: Adequacy or accuracy? *Theory and Psychology, 2,* 175–182.

SIMON, R. (1993). Like a friendly editor: An interview with Lynn Hoffman. In L. Hoffman (Ed.), *Exchanging voices: A collaborative to family therapy* (pp. 69–79). London: Karnac Books.

SLUZKI, C. E. (1992). Transformations: A blueprint for narrative changes in therapy. *Family Process, 31,* 217–230.

SMALLEY, R. (1967). *Theory for social work practice.* New York: Columbia Press.

SMITH, H. (1989). *Beyond the postmodern mind.* New York: Quest Books.

SMITH, T. E., WINTON, M., & YOSHIOKA, M. (1992). A qualitative understanding of reflecting teams II: Therapist's perspectives. *Contemporary Family Therapy, 14,* 419–432.

SMITH, T. E., WINTON, M., & YOSHIOKA, M. (1993). A qualitative understanding of reflecting teams I: Client perspectives. *Journal of Systemic Therapies, 12*(3), 28–43.

SPEED, B. (1991). Reality exists O.K.? An argument against constructivism and social constructionism. *Journal of Family Therapy, 13,* 395–409.

TODTMAN, D. (1990). Therapeutic discourse: An analysis of therapists at work on a case. Unpublished doctoral dissertation, Texas Tech University.

WALDEGRAVE, C. (1990). Just therapy. *Dulwich Centre Newsletter, 1,* 6–46.

WANGBERG, F. (1991). Self-reflection: Turning the mirror inward. *Journal of Strategic and Systemic Therapies, 10*(4), 18–29.

WHITE, M. (1989). The conjoint therapy of men who are violent and the women with whom they live. In M. White (Ed.), *Selected papers* (pp. 101–105). Adelaide, Australia: Dulwich Centre Publications.

WHITE, M. (1993). Deconstruction and therapy. In S. Gilligan & R. Price (Eds.), *Therapeutic conversations* (pp. 22–61). New York: Norton.

WHITE, M., & EPSTON, D. (1990). *Narrative means to therapeutic ends.* New York: Norton.

CHAPTER SEVEN

Catheleen Jordan, Ph.D.
University of Texas at Arlington

Marjie Barrett, Ph.D.
University of Texas at Arlington

Vicki Vandiver, Ph.D.
Portland State University

Ara Lewellen, Ph.D.
Texas A&M University—Commerce

Psychoeducational Family Practice

amilies have known for years what mental health professionals are now coming to appreciate: There is strength and healing in numbers. Increasingly, families, patients/consumers, and mental health professionals are turning to formalized support groups as a means to gain knowledge, receive emotional support, and incorporate advice on how to cope with mental illness in the family. Commonly referred to as family psychoeducation, these groups provide additional knowledge beyond the traditional family therapy and biomedical interventions commonly available in mental health settings. Though rarely defined, the term *psychoeducational* refers to approaches that focus on giving information and developing skills in work with families (Hatfield, 1987).

Family psychoeducation is a brief and effective therapy approach that combines didactic presentations on the nature of mental illness with other techniques, including social skills training, cognitive-behavioral techniques, and family therapy. Applications of psychoeducation to ethnic families have been suggested. (For additional techniques that may be incorporated into a psychoeducational approach, see especially Chapters 4 and 10.)

Psychoeducation for families, with its focus on brief therapeutic techniques, is a useful approach in today's managed care environment. This chapter describes family psychoeducational practice in terms of its history, theory, and methods. Consistency of the approach with social work practice as well as research support and managed care applicability are addressed. A case example illustrates the practice of family psychoeducation.

History

The popularity of family psychoeducation has been fueled by several factors: (1) changes in health care economics (which promote the more cost-efficient method of group treatment over individual treatment), (2) studies showing the increased psychological and social benefits of "like members" (other families who have a mentally ill relative) getting together to provide support, and (3) new theories of mental illness that illuminate the social, environmental, and biological influences (e.g., biopsychosocial models) while reducing "family blaming" theories (e.g., psychoanalytic and family systems theories) (Corcoran & Vandiver, 1996; Johnson, 1987; McFarlane, 1991).

Family psychoeducation is best defined as an approach to dealing with mental illness rather than a "true" family therapy model (McFarlane, 1991). As an intervention approach, it is designed as an education and management strategy to lower the emotional climate (also known as "expressed emotion") in the home (Anderson, Reiss, & Hogarty, 1986), to provide client support in the community, and to empower families with new knowledge to cope with their mentally ill family members (Sands, 1991). Psychoeducation efforts have concentrated on educating the family and client about possible biological, interpersonal, and environmental contributors related to their experience with mental illness. As Johnson (1987) notes, education conveys to families that they are competent to learn and benefit from information and guidance. Through this process, family members, clients, and mental health professionals become allies in the treatment process.

As practical and healthy as this model seems, collaborative relationships between families and mental health professionals have not always been the case. Historically, families felt blamed by professionals for their relative's mental illness (Jordan, Lewellen, & Vandiver, 1995). Lefley (1989) notes that at one point, families were viewed as "primary toxic agents" in the relationship with their schizophrenic family member. Terkelsen (1983) has suggested that some types of family theories have inflicted iatrogenic damage.

In a review of the various theoretical models that have been used to understand schizophrenia, Johnson (1987) notes that psychoanalytic and family systems theories have been especially objectionable to families—due, in part, to their belief that mental illness is caused by families. When psychoanalytic theory was expanded to include weakened egos and interpersonal relationships, especially family relationships and the "schizophrenogenic mother" (Fromm-Reichman, 1948; Mahler, 1951), a parent-blaming approach to schizophrenia treatment was an unintentional result (Goldstein, 1986; Goldstein & Strachan, 1987; Simon, McNeil, Franklin, & Cooperman, 1991; Torrey, 1988). Gradually several other theories were developed that implicitly or explicitly blamed the family for the development of schizophrenia (Barter, 1984).

The work of Bateson (1956), Bowen (1961), Laing (1964), and Lidz, Cornelison, Fleck, and Terry (1987) was among the most influential of the new theories. Lidz's theory of development placed the schizophrenic person in a family that was either schismatic or skewed (Lidz, 1973; Lidz et al., 1987). A schismatic family is forced by hostility between parental figures to divide into two opposing groups. The skewed family, although appearing calmer, is dominated by one parent, usually the mother. Lidz's conclusion was that schizophrenic people come from families with severe parental discord and emotional strife (Falloon, Boyd, & McGill, 1984).

Bowen and the family systems theorists (1961), agreeing that the schizophrenic child was affected by the severe parental discord, hypothesized that the child manifested a process involving the entire family. Thus, the schizophrenic person is simply the person who displays a family psychosis. Meanwhile, Bateson and the Palo Alto group, while studying schizophrenia's socioanthropological aspects, developed the double-bind hypothesis of schizophrenia (Hatfield, 1987; Janzen & Harris, 1986). This theory places the schizophrenic person in an intense relationship with another person, usually the mother, who gives conflicting messages.

Extensive research has produced a body of literature suggesting that families high in expressed emotion (EE) (characterized by criticism, hostility, and over involvement) contributed to the client's relapse. Later research on the biological correlates of mental illness tempered this family-focused approach by finding that people with schizophrenia had information-processing deficits complicated by high arousal levels. These "learning" deficits led to difficulties in following sequential information, like understanding directions, and cognitive tracking, like staying with a conversation. Psychoeducation emerged as a practical approach to teach family members how to talk to their relative as well as to teach clients to recognize their own threshold levels of stimulation.

In summary, mental health professionals have moved from the notion of attributing mental illness to the schizophrenogenic relationship of the client with the mother to aberrant communication styles like expressed emotion, to examination of the catastrophic impact of mental illness in the family system (Lefley, 1989). From this evolution has emerged a new way of looking at family and client needs with family psychoeducation, a model that embraces the notions of education, empowerment, and encouragement.

Theoretical Basis for the Practice Model

Major Assumptions

Family psychoeducational therapy focuses on intervention with families who have a mentally ill member. The intervention combines education, support, and other therapeutic techniques. Psychoeducational family therapy assumes that families with a mentally ill member are healthy and operate at a functional level in terms of psychosocial functioning and coping. Family members are no longer presumed to be the cause of their ill member's sickness. The model assumes that family function can be optimized by reducing family members' expressed emotions and guilt, and by increasing the medication compliance of the ill family member. The approach is focused more on education than therapy, as members are believed to be healthy. Therapy is assumed necessary, not to delve into family members' pathology but to improve members' interpersonal interactions. Family psychoeducational therapy is focused on a strengths perspective. Assessment aims to strengthen families' functioning and coping and to develop necessary resources and social supports. The approach is brief and time limited, and it is effective with families such as those that have a member diagnosed with substance abuse, schizophrenia, and certain physical illnesses.

Key Constructs

Family psychoeducational treatment is most often administered in a group setting with multiple families over a specified time. Treatment components are education, social and community support, social skills, and family therapy. Education and information is given from the empirical literature on the specific illness experienced by the diagnosed family member. For instance, if the member has been diagnosed with schizophrenia, information on that illness is provided to the ill member and his or her family. This information may include a description of the symptoms and course of the illness, possible medications, and other strategies for coping. It is believed that educated family members will be able to prevent or reduce patient relapse.

Developing social and community support for the patient and his or her family is another focus of psychoeducational family therapy. Social supports may include other families who participate in the psychoeducational family therapy group intervention or other extended family, peers, or friends who are able to play a supportive role for the patient and family. Community supports may be developed from sheltered workshops that provide work opportunities for the patient, or church groups that support the family. Social skills training is provided as needed. For example, some patients may need training in how to interview for a job or how to develop friendships. Social skills training relies on instruction and modeling from the social worker and practice or rehearsals by the patient, followed by feedback from the social worker and further patient practice as needed.

Family therapy techniques are used by the social worker to help families improve communication and resolve any conflicts between the patient and the family members. For instance, the family therapy may be focused on reducing family members' expressed emotion, as this has been shown to reduce patient relapse rates. Other helpful family therapy goals may include improved family communication and problem solving, improved conflict resolution, or equitable division of household tasks among family members.

Therapeutic Methods

Family psychoeducation is designed to educate families and their mentally ill member about the illness and to help them develop strategies to lower the emotional climate in the home (Anderson, Reiss, & Hogarty, 1986). The program provides client support in the community and seeks to empower families with new knowledge to cope with their mentally ill family member (Sands, 1991). Family and client are educated about the biological, interpersonal, and environmental contributors related to mental illness. Conveying this information suggests that families are competent to learn, benefit from information, and participate fully in the client's treatment. Thus, families, clients, and mental health professionals become allies in the treatment process.

Assessment Techniques

Families are referred to the social worker for family psychoeducation after the ill member has been diagnosed by a physician or a psychiatrist. The social worker using a family psychoeducational model must have skills to assess the family's psychosocial functioning and coping. Important areas for assessment are family and community social supports as well as family communication and conflict resolution skills. A lack of medication compliance and participation in household activities are early warning signs of relapse and therefore should be a focus of the assessment so that they may be monitored during and after treatment.

A variety of assessment techniques may be useful in this phase of family psychoeducation (see Chapter 9). Ecomaps may be used to assess the family's social network. Role playing and sculpting to assess the family's communication and problem-solving strategies may be helpful, as are standardized measures that can be used for continued assessment and monitoring during the treatment phase. Jordan and Franklin (1995) and Fischer and Corcoran (1995) present measures and techniques useful in assessing families with a mentally ill member. Additionally, ethnically sensitive social work practice dictates that families be assessed on the unique ethnic and cultural characteristics of the family.

Therapeutic Models

Several models for family psychoeducation have been effective in preventing relapse. Psychoeducational family therapists emphasize education about schizophrenia to reduce the family's stress, which helps the family become more effective caregivers and helps the client avoid overwhelming stress. Five psychoeducation treatment models are identified in the literature.

Goldstein and colleagues (Goldstein & Kopeikin, 1981; Kopeikin, Marshall, & Goldstein, 1983) developed a crisis-oriented program specifically to help clients and families during the first six weeks after discharge from the hospital. The program features six structured weekly sessions, during which the therapist guides the family in identifying and solving problems associated with post-hospitalization stress. This model requires a concrete, problem-focused approach in which two or three stressors are identified, along with specific strategies the client and family can use to cope with the current stressors and possible future stressors. In conjunction with this therapy, injectable phenothiazine is prescribed.

A second program, developed by Leff and associates (Berkowitz, 1984; Berkowitz, Eberlein-Fries, Kuipers, & Leff, 1984; Berkowitz, Kuipers, Eberlein-Fries, & Leff, 1981), focuses on mental health education for the client and his or her immediate and extended families. Before the client is discharged from the hospital, the therapist meets with the family four times for educational talks. After discharge, the therapist conducts a joint interview in the family's home with the client and the relatives, with the goal of finding ways to reduce client-family conflict. The joint interviews can be repeated as often as needed for nine months. The relatives also meet every two weeks without the client to discuss ways of handling difficult situations.

Falloon and colleagues (Falloon, Boyd, McGill, Strang, & Moss, 1981; Falloon, Boyd, & McGill, 1984; Falloon & Liberman, 1983a, 1983b) developed a behavioral program to facilitate stress management and social rehabilitation. The family is considered the key resource for helping the client learn social-role behavior and independent functioning. Treatment lasts at least nine months, with three months of weekly sessions in the family home, followed by six months of biweekly sessions. This treatment can be followed by monthly sessions for up to two years. As with other models mentioned, treatment focuses on education, assessments of family strengths and weaknesses, and specific strategies for coping with stressors or behavioral disturbances. In conjunction with this treatment, oral medication is prescribed in the lowest optimal dose, with depot neuroleptics used if clients refuse or have difficulty taking the medication.

A very extensive model created by social workers (Anderson, 1983; Anderson, Hogarty, & Reiss, 1980, 1981) has two main goals: reducing clients' vulnerability to environmental stressors with maintenance medication and increasing family stability by educating family members. Treatment unfolds in four phases: connection, survival skills workshop, reentry and application, and continued treatment or disengagement. Phase I, connection, begins during the client's hospital stay and is focused on developing a working alliance with the family to decrease guilt and lower stress. The clinician assumes a nonjudgmental and empathic attitude by eliciting and acknowledging the family's feelings and experiences. The clinician acts as an advocate for the family and client, keeping the family informed on client's care and representing the family to the hospital treatment team. During this time the family's involvement is reframed as concern. Helplessness is channeled into commitment to perform tasks that will promote rehabilitation. Phase I concludes with a treatment contract, including specific, realistic, and attainable short-term goals.

Phase II is a structured multisession workshop for several families and the client. The major goal is to present current factual information about the disease, to share family experiences, and to develop supportive networks. The family is encouraged to recognize their own needs as well as those of the client. Phase III, reentry and application, begins when the client leaves the hospital; the goal is to facilitate a smooth move into the community. During regularly scheduled sessions every two or three weeks, the family develops and articulates rules and sets limits and boundaries. As the client becomes integrated into the family and community, tasks and expectations for the client may be slowly increased. Recurring issues in this phase are compliance with medical and social service plans and early warning signs of relapse.

Phase IV offers two options: Families may elect to gradually disengage from treatment or to change to a more traditional type of therapy. If families decide to disengage from treatment, they should be assured that they can return. Most families require about two years of periodic sessions to support them in their maintenance of the client, which seems like a long time, given the restraints of managed care; however, this is a short treatment time for a major mental illness.

Bernheim's model of supportive family counseling focuses on the family's adaptive capabilities rather than its pathologies (Bernheim, 1982; Bernheim & Lehman, 1985). In addition to educating the family about the disease and introducing coping strategies, the therapist should also try to adapt his or her counseling style to fit the family's needs and communicate acceptance of the family. The goal is to provide emotional support and recognition of the family's needs.

Variations of these models are possible as long as the essential goals exist—to promote psychosocial functioning and coping for the client and the client's family. However, multifamily sessions seem to have the best outcomes (McFarlane, Lukens, Link, & Dushay, 1995; McFarlane, Dushay, Stastny, & Deakins, 1996).

FAMILY PSYCHOEDUCATION WITH ETHNICALLY DIVERSE FAMILIES

The validation of family psychoeducation has been widespread; however, use of the model in its entirety is the exception rather than the rule (Francell, Conn, & Gray, 1988; Solomon, 1994). Many families, especially ethnically diverse families, report dissatisfaction with mental health professionals (Biegel, Li-yu, & Milligan, 1995). The family psychoeducation model can be adapted to address the specific concerns of minority families and to serve these families more effectively.

It is critical in providing care to all families that culture of origin be considered in framing family psychoeducation. Miller (1994), who has explored differences between individualistic and sociocentric (group and family oriented) culture, notes that the dominant culture in the United States is an individualist one, whereas most minority groups are more sociocentric. Individualistic societies stress personal responsibility and freedom of choice; sociocentric cultures emphasize one's duty to care for others. These positions affect family attitudes toward care as well as the ill member's attitude toward dependency and the need to be cared for.

Lefley (1996b), in an exhaustive review, reports that ethnically diverse families in the United States provide greater support to their mentally ill family members than do families in the larger population. Guarnaccia and colleagues (cited in Lefley, 1996a) have found that African-American and Hispanic families are deeply frustrated with inpatient services and inadequate family education. These families complain that their ill members are discharged with little or no information provided to the family about the illness. To even begin to address these concerns, clinicians must develop ethnically sensitive practice (Jordan, Lewellen, & Vandiver, 1995).

Ethnically sensitive practice requires an understanding of the unique characteristics of each population group, the differences between dominant and minority cultures, and the differences within cultures. The therapist must be able to balance consideration of universal norms, group-specific norms, and individual norms in assessment and treatment (Dana, 1993). Clinicians must understand these norms to differentiate between normal and abnormal behavior and to implement a treatment plan that includes the family. Two models that have been shown to help clinicians assess minority families are ethnic reality and bicultural continuum.

Devore and Schlesinger (1996) first proposed the concept of ethnic reality in 1981 and continue to affirm that the concept is broad enough to capture the diverse features of many ethnically diverse groups in the United States. The authors postulate that ethnic reality generates identifiable dispositions that rise out of a group's cultural values, history, rituals, religion, migration experiences, and organization of the family system. Social-class values and norms, especially perspectives on family, child rearing, sexuality, gender roles, and illness, join with ethnic experiences to shape the way people respond to psychosocial problems. Such beliefs and attitudes shape help-seeking behavior as well as expectations of and ways of relating to the professional helpers.

Souflee (1980) developed a bicultural continuum on which a person's or family's level of assimilation can be depicted. Defining biculturalism as the process by which one "maintain(s) cultural integrity and authenticity while at the same time developing the capacity to interface constructively with the dominant group" (p. 21), Souflee labeled opposite ends of the continuum *traditional* and *Anglicized*.

Eight factors are used to determine where an individual or family member may be on the continuum: language, religion, family lifestyle, parental expectation, attitude toward medicine, philosophy of life, size of ethnic community, and distance from country of origin. Therapists can use the continuum to discover the family's level of biculturalism and, equally important, the biculturalism of individual family members. Such an exercise may help therapists approach family psychoeducation with ethnically diverse families in more effective ways.

How to Conduct a Session of Family Psychoeducation

A session of family psychoeducational practice may include elements of didactic presentation about mental illness, a skills presentation, group support for family members, and homework assignments. Sessions may be with the family or with groups of families. The social worker's task is to be respectful, avoid blaming the family, and decrease family guilt. The social worker also keeps the family informed about the patient's progress in treatment, serving as a link between the family and the hospital treatment team.

The family's role is to mobilize the members to support their ill member. This will involve motivation and commitment to perform tasks, complete homework assignments, and participate in this educational model to learn new information about their ill member's disease. Sessions may last from six weeks to several months and are scheduled one or two times a week for one to two hours. An outline of a typical family psychoeducational session follows.

EXPRESSED EMOTION AND BEGINNING COMMUNICATION OF FACTUAL INFORMATION

Goal I.

Communication of factual information about the role of expressed emotion with schizophrenic patients and their families. *Social worker's task:* Thirty-minute presentation from Harriett Lefley's (1992) article "Expressed Emotion: Conceptual, Chemical, and Social Policy Issues." *Family members' task:* To listen to presentation, give feedback, ask questions.

Goal II.

Training in the first phase of communication skills training, specifically the use of active listening. *Social worker's task:* Thirty-minute presentation on components of active listening; next, the social worker models the techniques, family members rehearse the techniques, and the social worker offers feedback to members and assigns homework. *Family members' task:* Rehearsal and role play of the communication skill. Complete the homework assignment before the next session.

Goal III.

Sharing and development of a social support network among family members. *Social worker's task:* Thirty minutes of social worker-guided discussion of family's experiences related to the evening's topic of expressed emotion and communication. *Family members' task:* To share their own experiences and support and problem solve with other members as they share experiences. The session may be ended with a social time with refreshments and informal visiting among group members.

Consistency with Social Work Practice

Family psychoeducational practice qualifies as an ethical practice model for social work because of the value it places on increasing the individual's feelings of empowerment and strengths as well as its emphasis on reducing stigma, guilt, and isolation. Additionally, Jordan and colleagues (1995) have suggested modifications of the psychoeducational model to increase its applicability and usefulness to ethnic minority families. The reliance on education versus therapy and on family strengths versus pathology are consistent with a social work strengths perspective. Also, the model's focus on family communication and conflict resolution as well as on increasing social supports is consistent with social work's contextual view of human behavior and the importance of the person/family in the environment.

Research Support for the Model

When attempting to describe psychoeducation, researchers can readily outline its structured, educational format. Clinicians may, however, add that psychoeducation is best characterized through three key concepts: (1) enhanced personal empowerment through family, patient, and professional collaboration; (2) building on family and personal strengths through education and opportunities for personal growth and sharing; and (3) reducing the stigma and isolation for families and clients experiencing mental illness. Several studies illustrate how these concepts are used in psychoeducational approaches with differing populations and diagnostic-specific groups. Despite small sample sizes and restricted generalizability, these studies provide a broad overview of the many ways that psychoeducational approaches are integrated into treatment approaches.

Outcome Evaluation: Psychoeducation with Different Population Groups

Investigators have found psychoeducational interventions to have a positive impact on family burden and adaptation (Mannion, Mueser, & Solomon, 1994), but the true hallmark of the psychoeducational approach has been its emphasis on providing individuals with information about how to deal with mental illness and its treatment, advice on how to deal with symptoms, and resources to families (Milstein & Argiles, 1992). Additionally, cross-cultural research has long established that the family is a vital natural support system and should be integrated into treatment (Lefley, 1987) and involved in research and evaluation efforts.

Milstein and Argiles (1992) provide information on how psychoeducation approaches could be used with different cultural populations. Using qualitative methods, the authors interviewed families of patients involved in services through the local community mental health center system or state hospital system. Of the 90 families interviewed, 45 were of Hispanic heritage (67% Puerto Rican, 13% Cuban, and 20% Central or South American). The study variables consisted of examining families' perspectives on their relatives' mental illness, social response to mental illness, and coping skills. The researchers also considered gender, religion, and home environment. This study revealed that members of Hispanic families developed enhanced coping skills when the psychoeducational model incorporated a continuum model of health and illness and when extended family and community individuals were included in treatment.

Lefley (1987) examined the experiences of mental health professionals who also have a mentally ill relative. This study compared the psychological burden of 84 experienced mental health professionals who also had a chronic mentally ill relative with lay (nonprofessional) family members. Family/psychological burden was the central study variable. The study revealed no difference between mental health professionals and lay family members in their assessments of the psychological burden of patients' behaviors. This finding suggests that family burden generalizes across populations regardless of level of sophistication of the family members (Lefley, 1987). The study implies that psychoeducation may prove beneficial for all types of family groups—regardless of background and professional training.

Franklin and Streeter (1992) explored the benefits of incorporating a psychoeducational approach in a school setting designed to serve dropout youth. For the study, 102 middle-class dropout youths were enrolled in an experimental, private, alternative school program. Using a quasi-experimental pretest-posttest evaluation design, data were gathered using questionnaires and a family assessment instrument. The most critical variable was student completion of their education; additional variables consisted of psychoeducation skills training, parent training, and mutual aid support groups. The psychoeducation groups involved problem solving, communication skills training, independent living skills, relapse training, and anger management. The study revealed that by facilitating cognitive and behavioral changes within the youths and their parents, youths were able to complete their education. This study has implications for addressing the multiple needs of parents and their adolescent children who have dropped out of the formal educational system. In particular, the authors note that the middle-class families in the study revealed severe family dysfunction, suggesting that social class is not a defining characteristic of at-risk families and youth.

Finally, Mannion and colleagues (1994) describe an alternative psychoeducational group created through the collaboration efforts of mental health professionals and spouses of persons with severe mental illness. Previous literature reported that in one family coping skills workshop, well spouses represented the highest attrition rate (94%). Using a questionnaire developed by the spouses and mental health professionals, 19 participants completed the pretest-posttest questionnaires, which addressed attendance, knowledge about mental illness, coping, personal distress, and attitudes. Related questions explored spousal issues (e.g., unreliability, self-absorption, lethargy, raising children, maintaining a social life, sexuality). After these spouses participated in family psychoeducation, posttest scores and one-year follow up revealed differences in attendance, knowledge, coping, personal distress, and negative attitudes. The dropout rate was 32%, much lower than the dropout rate cited in previous literature. Participants reported an increase in knowledge about mental illness and ability to cope, and a decrease in personal distress and negative attitudes.

This study has implications for psychoeducation group facilitators who are planning to organize new groups. Consideration should be given to the relationship that the family member has with the mentally ill patient or client, spouse, or partner.

Outcome Evaluation: Psychoeducation with Diagnostic-Specific Groups

Psychoeducational treatment has been developed in the context of controlled outcome research, and several studies indicate its effectiveness (Falloon & Liberman, 1983a, 1983b; Simon et al., 1991). Brennan (1995) describes a step-by-step program guide on how to conduct a short-term psychoeducational multiple-family group for bipolar patients and their families. Using a closed group format, the author conducted 14 psychoeducational sessions with approximately 15 to 30 patients and family members (e.g., children, siblings, spouses, and parents). The patient sample was drawn from outpatient clinic populations at a psychiatric center in New York; a second sample was drawn from the general population who had bipolar illness but no special training in psychiatric matters. The inclusion criterion was a diagnosis of bipolar illness; priority was given to patients who lived with their families. The study variables consisted of increasing symptom control and effectiveness as a treatment team member using educational strategies.

At the end of each session, facilitators and participants evaluated each meeting using questions relevant to the group's theme for that day. Using qualitative procedures, participants and facilitators assessed the program on criteria related to program content, similarity of issues, and self-reports of personal experiences with mental illness. At the end of the sessions, participants assessed the psycho-educational format as positive on three main areas: program content that was focused on bipolar illness, similarity of issues shared by like members, and group sharing of personal experiences related to the illness. An interesting component of this program is the author's frequent use of small group exercises to bring together program content and increase participant interaction. The implications of this study are that psychoeducation programs can be beneficial when group composition is homogeneous, topics are illness-specific, and ample process time is incorporated into discussion period.

Anderson and colleagues (1986) reported the benefits of an integrated treatment program that included family treatment, medication, and social skills training. Following hospital admission, 103 schizophrenic or schizoaffective patients residing in high expressed emotion households were randomly assigned to a two-year aftercare study. The goal of the study was an examination of relapse rates for patients involved in different treatment groups: (1) family treatment plus medication; (2) social skills plus medication; (3) family treatment, social skills, and medication; and (4) medication only. Family treatment was defined as an approach that emphasized patient management techniques, diagnostic information, and coping information.

The study revealed that patients who had received the combination of family treatment, social skills training, and medication had 0% relapse rates at 12 months. Family treatment and medication alone revealed a relapse rate of 19%, whereas social skills with medication resulted in a 20% relapse rate. At 24 months, relapse rates began to increase. The study implies that an integrated treatment that includes all three components of treatment is effective in reducing relapse rates for people with schizophrenia. Follow-up studies at 24 months revealed that family intervention forestalled relapse, but the effect of social skills training was lost in the second year. Thus, treatment effect may be lost when intervention is discontinued. Hogarty and colleagues (1991) found that treatment effects generally favored the social skills alone condition at one year and the family condition or combined family/social skills condition at two years. This result suggests that psychoeducational programs may need to be ongoing for families and patients with a chronic course of mental illness.

Additionally, psychoeducation has been found useful in working with people with bipolar disorder (Brennan, 1995), affective disorders and neurological impairments (Johnson, 1988), and depression (Docherty, 1989). Docherty found that psychoeducational treatment is equivalent to individual cognitive therapy, individual psychodynamic treatment, and individual behavioral treatment. He noted four variables that suggest the likelihood of a positive response when used with depressed clients and their families: (1) expectation that treatment will help; (2) perceived social support from family members; (3) no physical handicap or disabling disease; and (4) perception control over what happens in the patient's life.

Goldstein and colleagues (Goldstein & Kopeikin, 1981; Kopeikin et al., 1983) conducted a study to evaluate their crisis-oriented model, randomly assigning 104 acute schizophrenic clients to one of four treatment programs: family therapy and low dosage of injectable phenothiazine; family therapy and moderate dosage of neuroleptic; low dosage of neuroleptic without therapy; and moderate dosage of neuroleptic without therapy. During the six-month follow-up period, no clients receiving therapy with a moderate dose of neuroleptic relapsed. Groups receiving a low dose and therapy or a moderate dose and no therapy relapsed at the rate of 20% whereas the low dose-no therapy group had a 48% relapse rate. The conclusion was that the crisis-oriented therapy and the higher medication dosage were effective, and they were most effective when used together. Long-term follow-ups indicated that the effects of treatment lasted only three to six years, emphasizing the program's original purpose—to help clients through the stressful period immediately after hospitalization.

In an evaluation of their model, Leff and colleagues (Berkowitz et al., 1984) randomly assigned 30 family groups with a parent or spouse with high expressed emotion to experimental and control groups. The control group received "routine clinical care" whereas the experimental group received treatment according to Leff's model, including education and joint family interviews. After nine months, relapse rates for the control group were 50%; relapse rates for the experimental groups were 9%.

Falloon and associates (Falloon et al., 1985; Falloon & Pederson, 1985) conducted a randomized controlled study in which their at-home family therapy was compared with clinic-based individual supportive care. After nine months, the family treatment approach appeared more effective in preventing major symptomatic exacerbations and in promoting remission of schizophrenia. The families also benefited from the treatment, learning how to obtain information about schizophrenia, reduce disruptive behavior, and limit environmental stress and the sense of burden (Falloon & Pederson, 1985; Doane, Goldstein, Milkowitz, & Falloon, 1986).

These studies reflect the broad utility of the family psychoeducation approach; however, the second generation of studies on psychoeducation are not as overwhelmingly positive as the first-generation studies. The second generation of research employed more sophisticated research designs and indicated that the effectiveness of psychoeducation models is limited by mediating variables, such as type of program and treatment setting. Research indicates that there are no advantages to adding intensive family psychoeducation programs to systems of care that have effective case management, support systems, and continuity of care (Goldstein & Miklowitz, 1995). These types of routine care get results equivalent to the more intensive family programs like Falloon's in-home psychoeducation treatment model. More research is needed on different populations and treatment settings to clarify further the benefits and cost effectiveness of intensive psychoeducation models.

Family Psychoeducation and Managed Behavioral Health Care

Family psychoeducation is compatible with the current managed care environment because of its brief focus, structured techniques, and action-oriented perspective. Its documented effectiveness increases its appeal to managed care systems.

Critiques of the Model

Because family psychoeducation focuses on reinforcing family and patient strengths and has empirical support for a wide range of problems, this model has not been widely criticized. However, Jordan and colleagues (1995) note the lack of research on use of the model with ethnically diverse families, proposing modifications in the treatment that require further testing. Simon and colleagues (1991) also make the point that the psychoeducation model has not completely freed itself from "family blaming," in that family processes such as high expressed emotion are associated with the relapse of a mentally ill member. These authors also discuss the fact that more attention needs to be given to how psychoeducation positively influences family processes rather than the exclusive focus that has been given to the relapse of a mentally ill member.

Case Example[1]

THERAPIST: Hi! It's good to see you again. Now that we have been apart for a couple of days have you had a chance to process what we talked about last time?

FAMILY: Yes.

THERAPIST: Do you have any comments or questions?

FAMILY: We can't think of any right now.
(OVERHEAD—"LEARNING ABOUT DEPRESSION")

THERAPIST: Today, we are going to move into the educational part of the therapy process. We are going to talk about and provide information about what depression is, its treatment and side effects, the effects that depression has on the family, and what each individual family member can do to help.

Let's now begin by looking at exactly what depression is. Clinical depression is a serious illness affecting millions of Americans. Each year, more than 11 million people suffer from this illness, which is as common as it is misunderstood. Many people go through life suffering from clinical depression, never understanding that it is a medical illness or that effective treatments are available. Too often the illness has carried with it fear and shame that prevented people from asking basic questions about its causes and treatments. Please feel free to ask questions at any time during the educational process.
(OVERHEAD—"DEPRESSION CAN AFFECT ANYONE")

THERAPIST: Most people who suffer from clinical depression feel a sense of relief when they learn the facts about this medical illness. They re-

---

[1]This case example was written by Jennifer Berry, Denise Edmiston, Allyn Lovins, Stacy Metrik, and Kenna Richmond.

alize that depression is not a personal weakness and that they are not alone—men and women from every walk of life, young and old, suffer from depression. They are also relieved to know that medical research has produced a variety of effective new medications to treat the illness. The National Institute of Mental Health estimates that 80% of people with clinical depression can now be successfully treated, usually with medication, psychotherapy, or a combination of both.

MRS. CARTER: Exactly what is clinical depression?
(OVERHEAD—"SYMPTOMS OF DEPRESSION")

THERAPIST: Clinical depression is much more than just a sad feeling or the "blues"; it is a serious medical illness that causes persistent changes in a person's mood, behavior, and feelings. If not treated, the episode can last nine months to a year and will probably happen again during a person's lifetime. This illness can interfere with and disrupt a person's job and family life. No amount of "cheering up" can make it go away, and vitamins or vacations cannot make clinical depression disappear. People with clinical depression need to get proper treatment.

MR. CARTER: I am always trying to get Holly to exercise because I always heard that exercise was supposed to relieve depression. I never realized that she needed medication or something in order to feel better. What actually causes the depression?
(OVERHEAD—"CAUSES OF DEPRESSION")

THERAPIST: We do not yet know all the causes of depression, but there seem to be biological and emotional factors that may increase the likelihood that an individual will develop a depressive disorder. Research over the past decade strongly suggests a genetic link to depressive disorder; thus, depression can run in families. This appears evident in your family history, as you can see by the genogram that I have developed of your family based on the information you provided. Bad life experiences and certain personality patterns, such as difficulty handling stress, low self-esteem, or extreme pessimism about the future can increase the chances of becoming depressed. It is important to remember the history of mental illness with Holly's biological mother.

MRS. CARTER: Exactly how common is depression? Will people think that Holly is "different"?
(OVERHEAD—"DEPRESSION IS A COMMON PROBLEM")

THERAPIST: As we discussed earlier, clinical depression is a lot more common than people think and affects people of all ages. Approximately 3% to 5% of the teen population experiences clinical depression every year. That means that among 100 friends, four could be clinically depressed. Sure, Holly is different, but aren't we all? Some people have blonde hair and some have brown—but if we don't feel good about our hair color, we can change it. The same is true

	with depression. Because Holly does not like feeling depressed, her condition can be treated with medication and therapy.
KRISTEN:	Everyone is making such a big deal out of this depression. Is it even serious?
THERAPIST:	Kristen, depression can be very serious. It has been linked to poor school performance, truancy, alcohol and drug abuse, running away, and feelings of worthlessness and hopelessness. In the last 25 years, the rate of suicide among teenagers and young adults has increased dramatically. Suicide is often linked to depression.
KRISTEN:	So, do you think that's why Holly tried to kill herself by taking too many pills?
THERAPIST:	Overdosing or taking too many pills is a warning sign that somebody is contemplating suicide. Unfortunately, research shows that 15% of people with severe clinical depression, like Holly, will die as a result of suicide. The hopelessness, helplessness, and acute pain experienced by these people often lead them to despair and thoughts of suicide.
	With your sister, she was so depressed that she said she was hearing voices or having what we call auditory hallucinations. That is when you hear things that no one else does. Holly let us know that the voices were repeatedly telling her to kill herself. Is that correct, Holly?
HOLLY:	Yes.
KRISTEN:	Hum, I just thought she was trying to get all of Mom and Dad's attention.
MR. CARTER:	How does a person with clinical depression get well? (OVERHEAD—"TREATMENT OF DEPRESSION")
THERAPIST:	Recovery from clinical depression involves proper treatment, support, and education. The most important steps to a person's recovery from clinical depression are to see a doctor and stick to a treatment plan of medication and therapy. That means taking the medication as prescribed and keeping all appointments with the doctor and therapist. Participating in a patient support group is also very helpful during the recovery process, as is educating oneself about depression and its treatments.
MRS. CARTER:	How can support groups help people with depression?
THERAPIST:	Many people with depression have found a wellspring of emotional support, acceptance, encouragement, and friendship by joining patient support groups. Support group members can share their experiences with the illness, learn coping skills, distribute information about new treatments, and refer people to doctors and therapists in their communities.
	This is similar to the multifamily therapy session you all attended the other night. Although many of the problems were different, the format is basically the same.

HOLLY: Can I be cured?

THERAPIST: Well, Holly, depression sometimes is not curable, but it can be treated. As I mentioned before, treatment usually includes medications and psychotherapy or a combination of the two. We usually describe depression being somewhat similar to diabetes. When people with diabetes consistently take insulin, they are able to have relatively normal lives. The same goes for depression and taking antidepressant medication. As we've already discussed the causes and symptoms of depression, I think it's important to talk about the treatment in more detail.

MRS. CARTER: You mentioned earlier that doctors use medication and therapy. How does this relate to Holly's current situation?

THERAPIST: First, depression is one of the most responsive illnesses to treatment. Many types of treatment are available, and the type chosen depends on the individual situation. However, for more severely depressed individuals, like Holly, medication is generally required. Thus, her treatment plan will involve a combination of therapy and medicine.

MRS. CARTER: What part of the body does this medication affect?

THERAPIST: Let me start by giving you some history about antidepressants, and that will lead me into answering your specific question.

MRS. CARTER: Okay.

THERAPIST: Antidepressant medications were discovered in the 1950s and have been used successfully ever since to treat clinical depression. Research has shown that imbalances of specific neurotransmitters—especially serotonin, norepinephrine, and dopamine—can be corrected with antidepressants, so these medications are prescribed to correct chemical imbalances in the brain. There are three principal categories of antidepressants, each working slightly differently. They are tricyclics, monoamine oxidase inhibitors, and serotonin reuptake inhibitors. The doctor has told Holly to continue taking Prozac, and this medication falls under the serotonin reuptake inhibitor category, so this will be our focus. However, information on the other types can be found in the literature that I will give you. The more common side effects of Prozac are anxiety and nervousness, diarrhea, drowsiness, headaches, increased sweating, nausea, and trouble sleeping.

                Holly, please remember how important it is that you let your doctor or one of the nurses know if you have any problems with your medication.

KRISTEN: Why does my sister still look so funny—like she's really sad or something?

THERAPIST: Kristen, that's a very good question. These pills do not work instantly. It takes anywhere from two to six weeks for them to take effect. Holly saw her doctor before coming to the hospital and he prescribed the pills then, so we feel that Holly's medication should be showing an effect soon.

	Holly, what other medication has the doctor prescribed for you and why?
HOLLY:	I'm taking resperidone because I am hearing voices that are telling me to hurt myself.
THERAPIST:	I'm glad you were able to share that with your family.
MRS. CARTER:	We are really concerned about the voices.
THERAPIST:	I definitely hear your concern, but let me tell you that this is quite common when someone is as severely depressed as Holly. Like she said, Dr. Mitchell has put her on resperidone to help control the hallucinations. This will help Holly be less upset and agitated. It will also help her to think more clearly. Some common side effects of this medication are dry mouth (which Holly has complained about), sleepiness, blurred vision, and weight gain.
MRS. CARTER:	How long will Holly have to be on these medications?
THERAPIST:	Well, I'm not Holly's doctor, but I can tell you that the resperidone will gradually be decreased over the next few months or so; most likely, Holly will need to continue with her Prozac for an extended period of time. Let me add that it is very important for you to keep your appointments with Dr. Mitchell after discharge and continue taking the medications as prescribed. Too often patients stop taking their medicine soon after they start feeling better, but symptoms just reappear.
	Please also feel free to contact Dr. Mitchell or any of the nurses on the unit with your questions regarding Holly's medications.
FAMILY:	All that information was really helpful.
THERAPIST:	As I previously said, Holly and you all as a family will also benefit from psychotherapy. I'm glad to see that you are already seeing a psychologist and that you have found him helpful. Continuing to visit with Dr. Jones will be important for the entire family.
HOLLY:	I feel so exhausted and helpless at times and feel no one really understands. Sometimes people say things that hurt me, but I know they don't really mean to hurt me. I just wish they could understand what it's like to feel like this. I know my family is frustrated with me and wishes I would just "snap out of it."
THERAPIST:	I want to commend you for opening up and sharing your feeling with us. This is often a difficult thing to do, but is so important in helping you and your family deal with your depression. You and your family need to know that your feelings of exhaustion, helplessness, and feeling misunderstood are normal feelings for someone who is experiencing depression. These feelings will begin to lessen as you progress through your treatment. Part of the reason we are here today is to educate your family about what you are experiencing and to involve them in your treatment and recovery. They are your best support.
	I would like to show you part of a video done by Dr. Sam Goldstein, a child psychologist, on childhood depression. It is titled "Why Isn't My Child Happy? A Video Guide About Childhood De-

pression." This segment shows a young girl discussing her feelings when she is depressed, and this may give you a better understanding of how Holly is feeling as well.

(VIDEO)

FAMILY: Very interesting. I enjoyed that.

MRS. CARTER: We just want her to be happy and well again. We will do anything it takes to make that happen.

(OVERHEAD—"THE FAMILY PLAYS AN IMPORTANT PART IN THE TREATMENT")

THERAPIST: You have done a great job in beginning that process. You have gotten Holly into treatment both inpatient and outpatient, you are learning about depression and how to deal with it, you have accepted the fact that Holly has a mental illness, and you are reacting with sympathy and support. These are all things that have helped and will continue to help Holly in her treatment and recovery.

MR. CARTER: I'm concerned about when Holly gets discharged from the hospital. Our family used to be very involved in our community and church, but once we began to experience problems, we stopped doing these activities. Should we try to start doing the things we did before?

(OVERHEAD—"MENTAL ILLNESS AFFECTS THE FAMILY")

THERAPIST: It is not uncommon for families to experience emotional and social strains and pressures as a result of having a depressed family member. Often, families feel confused and ashamed about what to tell other people about their relative's depression, fearing what they might think. This can lead to withdrawal from friends and activities. When Holly comes home, it will be important for you to involve her in outings, possibly going to a movie or for a walk. You will want to encourage her to participate in activities that once gave her pleasure, such as hobbies, sports, or religious activities. But don't push her to undertake too much too soon. We need to go slowly. She needs diversion and company, but too many demands can increase her feelings of failure.

MRS. CARTER: Holly played on her school basketball team and was also involved in her youth group at church.

THERAPIST: Those would be great activities for her to get back into. Does that sound like something you would be interested in Holly?

HOLLY: Yeah, that would be fine.

THERAPIST: With our time winding down. I just want to discuss some things that are specifically directed toward Holly. Some of the information may sound similar to some previous stuff, but it can't be stressed enough.

Holly, I know that sometimes being depressed makes you feel helpless and exhausted, right? Sometimes it even makes a person feel like giving up. I want you to realize that these negative views are part of the depression and usually do not accurately reflect your situation. Negative thinking fades as treatment begins to take effect, but in the meantime, Holly, I want you to remember a few simple guidelines.

- Do not set yourself difficult goals or take on a great deal of responsibility.
- Break large tasks into small ones, set some priorities, and do as much as you can.
- Do not expect too much from yourself.
- Participate in activities that may make you feel better, like basketball. But don't overdo it or get upset if your mood is not greatly improved right away.
- Do not make major life decisions.
- Do not expect to "snap out" of your depression. Help yourself as much as you can and don't blame yourself for not being up to par.
- Remember, do not accept your negative thinking. It is part of the depression and will disappear as you respond to treatment.

It is also very important that the family understand these guidelines as well in order to help Holly through this time.

KRISTEN: Does this mean that she doesn't have to do her chores?

THERAPIST: Well, I think that Holly will be able to do some of her chores. I just don't want her to do too much too soon. Do you understand that?

KRISTEN: Yes, I understand.

THERAPIST: Our time is up for today. I want to commend you on asking some great questions and being very patient while I provided a lot of information . We will continue with the second phase of what we call the psychoeducational process next time. Our focus will be on stress reduction and basic communication skills. If you don't have any more questions for me, you are free to go, and Holly and I are going to return to the unit. See you next time! Thanks again.

Summary

This chapter has described the history of family psychoeducational therapy as well as the theory and methods. Research showing this method to be highly effective with some families was reviewed. Proposed models recommending adaptations for ethnic minority families were presented. The applicability of the model for managed care was discussed, along with critiques of the model. Finally a case example was presented.

Process Questions

1. Identify the psychoeducational treatment components in the case example transcript.
2. Explain the role of the family in family psychoeducational treatment.

3. List some of the benefits of a support group that you might share with the Carter family.

4. What are issues that the social worker may address with the family when the patient is ready to be dismissed from the hospital?

References

ANDERSON, C. M. (1983). A psychoeducational program for families of clients with schizophrenia. In W. R. McFarlane (Ed.), *Family therapy in schizophrenia* (pp. 99–115). New York: Guilford.

ANDERSON, C., HOGARTY, G., & REISS, D. J. (1980). Family treatment of adult schizophrenic clients: A psychoeducational approach. *Schizophrenia Bulletin, 6,* 490–505.

ANDERSON, C., HOGARTY, G., & REISS, D. J. (1981). The psychoeducational treatment of schizophrenia. In M. J. Goldstein (Ed.), *New directions for mental health services: New developments in interventions with families of schizophrenics* (pp. 79–94). San Francisco: Jossey-Bass.

ANDERSON, C., REISS, D. J., & HOGARTY, G., (1986). *Schizophrenia and the family.* New York: Guilford.

BARTER, J. T. (1984). Psychoeducation. In J. A. Talbot (Ed.), *The chronic mental client: Five years later* (pp. 183–191). Orlando, FL: Grune & Stratton.

BATESON, G. (1956). Toward a theory of schizophrenia. *Behavioral Science, 1,* 251–264.

BERKOWITZ, R. (1984). Therapeutic intervention with schizophrenic clients and their families: A description of a clinical research project. *Journal of Family Therapy, 6,* 211–233.

BERKOWITZ, R., EBERLEIN-FRIES, R., KUIPERS, L., & LEFF, J. (1984). Educating relatives about schizophrenia. *Schizophrenia Bulletin, 10,* 418–429.

BERKOWITZ, R., KUIPERS, L., EBERLEIN-FRIES, R., & LEFF, J. (1981). Lowering expressed emotion in relatives of schizophrenics. In M. J. Goldstein (Ed.), *New directions for mental health services: New developments in interventions with families of schizophrenics* (pp. 27–48). San Francisco: Jossey-Bass.

BERNHEIM, K. F. (1982). Supportive family counseling. *Schizophrenia Bulletin, 8,* 634–640.

BERNHEIM, K. F., & LEHMAN, A. F. (1985). *Working with families of the mentally ill.* New York: Norton.

BIEGEL, D. E., LI-YU, S., & MILLIGAN, S. E. (1995). A comparative analysis of family caregivers' perceived relationship with mental health professionals. *Psychiatric Services, 46,* 477–482.

BOWEN, M. (1961). Family psychotherapy. *American Journal of Orthopsychiatry, 31,* 40–60.

BRENNAN, J. (1995). A short-term psychoeducational multiple-family group for bipolar patients and their families. *Social Work, 40(6),* 737–743.

CORCORAN, K., & VANDIVER, V. (1996). *Maneuvering the maze of managed care.* New York: Free Press.

DANA, R. (1993). *Multicultural assessment perspectives for professional psychology.* Boston: Allyn & Bacon.

DEVORE, W., & SCHLESINGER, E. G. (1996). *Ethnic-sensitive social work practice* (4th ed.). Boston: Allyn & Bacon.

DOANE, J. A., GOLDSTEIN, M. J., MILKOWITZ, D. J., & FALLOON, I. R. H. (1986). The impact of individual and family treatment on the affective climate of families of schizophrenics. *British Journal of Psychiatry, 148,* 241–258.

DOCHERTY, J. P. (1989). Group psychotherapy of depression. In H. I. Kaplan & B. J. Sadock (Eds.), *Comprehensive textbook of psychiatry* (Vol. 1, 5th ed., pp. 945–951). Baltimore: Williams & Wilkins.

FALLOON, I. R. H., BOYD, J. L., & MCGILL, C. W. (1984). *Family care of schizophrenia.* New York: Guilford.

FALLOON, I. R. H., BOYD, J. L., MCGILL, C. W., STRANG, J. S., & MOSS, M. B. (1981). Family management training in the community care of schizophrenia. In M. J. Goldstein (Ed.), *New directions for mental health services: New developments in interventions with families of schizophrenics* (pp. 49–62). San Francisco: Jossey-Bass.

FALLOON, I. R. H., BOYD, J. L., MCGILL, C. W., WILLIAMSON, M., RAZANI, J., MOSS, H. B., GILDREMAN, A. M., & SIMPSON, G. M. (1985). Family management in the prevention of morbidity of schizophrenia. *Archives of General Psychiatry, 42,* 887–896.

FALLOON, I. R. H., & LIBERMAN, R. P. (1983a). Interactions between drug and psychosocial therapy in schizophrenia. *Schizophrenia Bulletin, 3,* 544–554.

FALLOON, I. R. H., & LIBERMAN, R. P. (1983b). Behavioral family interventions in the management of chronic schizophrenia. In W. R. McFarlane (Ed.), *Family therapy in schizophrenia* (pp. 117–137). New York: Guilford.

FALLOON, I. R. H., & PEDERSON, J. (1985). Family management in the prevention of morbidity of schizophrenia: The adjustment of the family unit. *British Journal of Psychiatry, 147,* 156-163.

FISCHER, J., & CORCORAN, K. (1995). *Measures for clinical practice* (2nd ed.). New York: Free Press.

FRANCELL, C., CONN, V. S., & GRAY, D. P. (1988). Families' perceptions of burden of care for chronically mentally ill relatives. *Hospital and Community Psychiatry, 39,* 1296-1300.

FRANKLIN, C., & STREETER, C. L. (1992). Social support and psychoeducation interventions with middle class drop-out youth. *Child and Adolescent Social Work, 9*(2), 131-153.

FROMM-REICHMAN, F. (1948). Notes on the development of treatment of schizophrenics by psychoanalytic psychotherapy. *Psychiatry, 11,* 263-273.

GOLDSTEIN, M. J. (1986). Families of schizophrenic clients: A historical perspective. In M. J. Goldstein (Ed.), *Family involvement in the treatment of schizophrenia* (pp. 2-18). Washington, DC: American Psychiatric Association.

GOLDSTEIN, M. J., & KOPEIKIN, H. S. (1981). Short- and long-term effects of combining drug and family therapy. In M. J. Goldstein (Ed.), *New directions for mental health services: New developments in interventions with families of schizophrenics* (pp. 5-26). San Francisco: Jossey-Bass.

GOLDSTEIN, M. J., & MILKOWITZ, D. J. (1995). The effectiveness of psychoeducational family therapy in the treatment of schizophrenic disorders. *Journal of Marital and Family Therapy, 21,* 361-376.

GOLDSTEIN, M. J., & STRACHAN, A. M. (1987). The family and schizophrenia. In T. Jacobs (Ed.), *Family interaction and psychopathology* (pp. 481-508). New York: Plenum Press.

HATFIELD, A. B. (1987). Families as caregivers: A historical perspective. In A. B. Hatfield & H. P. Lefley (Eds.), *Families of the mentally ill* (pp. 3-29). New York: Guilford.

HOGARTY, G., ANDERSON, C., REISS, D., KORNBLITH, J., GREENWALD, D., ULRICH, R., & CARTER, M. (1991). Family psychoeducation, social skills training, and maintenance chemotherapy in the aftercare treatment of schizophrenia. *Archives of General Psychiatry, 48,* 340-347.

JANZEN, C., & HARRIS, O. (1986). *Family treatment in social work practice.* Chicago: F. E. Peacock.

JOHNSON, D. (1987). Professional-family collaboration. *New Directions for Mental Health Services, 34,* 73-79.

JOHNSON, H. C. (1988). Where is the border? Current issues in the treatment of the borderline. *Clinical Social Work Journal, 16*(3), 243-260.

JORDAN, C., & FRANKLIN, C. (1995). *Clinical assessment for social worker: Qualitative and quantitative methods.* Chicago: Lyceum.

JORDAN, C., LEWELLEN, A., & VANDIVER, V. (1995). Psychoeducation for minority families: A social work perspective. *International Journal of Mental Health, 23*(4), 27-43.

KOPEIKIN, H. S., MARSHALL, V., & GOLDSTEIN, M. J. (1983). Stages and impact of crisis-oriented family therapy in the aftercare of acute schizophrenia. In W. R. McFarlane (Ed.), *Family therapy in schizophrenia* (pp. 69-97). New York: Guilford.

LAING, R. D. (1964). Is schizophrenia a disease? *International Journal of Social Psychiatry, 10,* 184-193.

LEFLEY, H. (1992). Expressed emotion: Conceptual, clinical, and social policy issues. *Hospital and Community Psychiatry, 43,* 591-598.

LEFLEY, H. (1996a). *Family caregiving in mental illness.* Thousand Oaks, CA: Sage.

LEFLEY, H. (1996b, Spring). *The family's experience of schizophrenia in transcultural perspective.* Paper presented at schizophrenia conference, Portland, OR.

LEFLEY, H. P. (1987). Impact of mental illness in families of mental health professionals. *Journal of Nervous and Mental Disease, 175,* 613-619.

LEFLEY, H. P. (1989). Family burden and family stigma in major mental illness. *American Psychologist, 44*(3), 556-560.

LIDZ, T. (1973). *The origin and treatment of schizophrenic disorders.* New York: Basic Books.

LIDZ, T., CORNELISON, A., FLECK, S., & TERRY, D. (1987). The intrafamilial environment of schizophrenic clients: 2. Marital schism and marital skew. *American Journal of Psychiatry, 114,* 241-248.

MAHLER, M. S. (1951). On child psychosis and schizophrenia: Autistic and symbiotic infantile psychosis. In *The psychoanalytic study of the child* (Vol. 7, pp. 286-305). New York: International Universities Press.

MANNION, E., MUESER, K., & SOLOMON, P. (1994). Designing psychoeducational services for spouses of persons with serious mental illness. *Community Mental Health Journal, 30*(2), 177-190.

MCFARLANE, W. R. (1991). Family psychoeducational treatment. In A. S. Gurman & D. P. Kniskern (Eds.), *Handbook of family therapy* (Vol. 2, pp. 363-395). New York: Brunner-Mazel.

MCFARLANE, W. R., DUSHAY, R. A., STASTNY, P., & DEAKINS, S. M. (1996). A comparison of two levels of family-aided assertive community treatment. *Psychiatric Services, 47*(7), 744-750.

MCFARLANE, W. R., LUKENS, E., LINK, B., & DUSHAY, R. (1995). Multiple-family groups and psychoeducation in the treatment of schizophrenia. *Archives of General Psychiatry, 52*(8), 679-687.

MILLER, J. G. (1994). Cultural diversity in the morality of caring: Individually oriented vs. duty-based interpersonal moral codes. *Cross-Cultural Research, 28*(1), 3–39.

MILSTEIN, G., & ARGILES, N. (1992). Si dios quiere: Hispanic families' experience of caring for a seriously mentally ill family member. *Culture, Medicine, Psychiatry, 16,* 187–215.

SANDS, R. (1991). *Clinical social work practice in community mental health.* New York: Merrill.

SIMON, C. E., MCNEIL, J. S., FRANKLIN, C., & COOPERMAN, A. (1991). The family and schizophrenia: Toward a psychoeducational approach. *Families in Society, 72*(6), 323–334.

SOLOMON, P. (1994). Families' views of service delivery: An empirical assessment. In H. P. Lefley &

M. Wasow (Eds.), *Helping families cope with mental illness* (pp. 259–274) Newark, NJ: Harwood Academic.

SOUFLEE, F. (1980). Biculturalism: An existential phenomenon. In R. Wright (Ed.), *Black/Chicano elderly: Service delivery within a cultural context.* Arlington: University of Texas at Arlington.

TERKELSEN, K. G. (1983). Schizophrenia and the family: Adverse effects of family therapy. *Family Process, 22,* 191–200.

TORREY, E. F. (1988). *Surviving schizophrenia: A family manual* (rev. ed.). New York: Harper & Row.

CHAPTER EIGHT

Marianne Berry, Ph.D.
University of Texas at Arlington

Family Preservation Practice

State child welfare agencies are mandated to report and investigate child abuse, and in those families so identified, to provide reasonable efforts to keep the family together and prevent further harm to the children. Mental health and juvenile justice programs are also charged with preventing out-of-home placement of children in residential treatment facilities and/or juvenile detention or treatment sites. Family preservation programs are an emerging form of home-based family treatment targeted at families in crisis, based on the belief that families are more amenable to assistance and change when they are in crisis. Chapter 1 discusses the importance of home-based family treatments in today's practice contexts. Time-limited and cost-effective treatments are important to these contexts. Family preservation offers one such treatment alternative for helping families in crisis.

Family preservation practice is an intensive, home-based, family-centered model of family treatment aimed at doing "whatever it takes" to strengthen the family and prevent the unnecessary placement of children into substitute care. Thus, family preservation programs are suited to a variety of presenting problems, whether of a child welfare, mental health, or juvenile corrections origin. For family preservation workers, this commitment to maintain families with a number of presenting problems requires a wide range of skills and resources, the ability to work within the family's ecological system, including the community, and the commitment to be available to families whenever needed, day or night, weekday or weekend, as crises occur. The family preservationist seeks to mobilize the family in crisis to learn new skills and acquire needed resources through on-site, hands-on assessment, counseling, and teaching.

The practice model is intensive and time limited; services are provided to the family over large periods of time by the family preservationist and are often limited to four to six weeks of treatment. Duration of time-limited treatment varies greatly from program to program across the country, ranging from four weeks to one year, but the general agreement across programs is that treatment is brief and not open-ended. Brevity of treatment has strong implications for the types of treatment goals set by practitioners, in that goals are targeted, aimed at reducing the most serious risks facing the child and family. The practice model is also home based and family centered. The majority of service time is provided in the home, with as many family members involved as is possible or constructive.

This chapter describes intensive family preservation practice techniques based on an ecological model of family functioning. A history of home-based services that serve as progenitors of today's family preservation programs are discussed. The theoretical basis of family preservation and its major assumptions are summarized. Techniques used by family therapists working in family preservation programs are highlighted, and research studies supporting the effectiveness of family preservation programs and important critiques of the model are reviewed. Family preservation's unique compatibility with social work is also highlighted. The importance of such time-limited practice approaches as family preservation is discussed from the perspective of today's practice contexts. Finally, a case example is presented.

History

Home-based services have existed since the beginning of the social work profession and the use of home visitors. Indeed, home-based programs enjoyed a resurgence in the late 1960s and early 1970s when practitioners realized that many of their clients simply did not always have the resources to come to agencies for treatment and that services provided in the home afford many benefits to assessment and networking that surpass those in the office (Bell, 1978; Friedman, 1962; Speck, 1964; Sperekas, 1974). This type of service focuses on serving the client(s) in the home and is applied in programs such as Home Start (Collins, 1980; Halpern, 1984, 1986; O'Keefe, 1973), some parent training programs (Hirsch, Gailey, & Schmerl, 1976), and other social service provision models (Bloom, 1973; Montgomery, Shulman, & Pfenninger, 1972). Serving the child and family in the home is emphasized because clients are believed to be better served in the environment in which their problems are occurring.

Although home-based services are as old as the social work profession, only in the past 30 years or so have they begun to be systematically structured and evaluated. The St. Paul project (Birt, 1956; Horejsi, 1981) was one of the earliest such demonstrations of the utility of home-based family-centered services and garnered positive, if limited, support for the efficacy of such a model. This program was a response to a proposal that the city of St. Paul make an accounting of all families served by governmental and voluntary agencies in Ramsey County,

Minnesota. The resulting account found that a small percentage of families received a disproportionately large share of social welfare services, with some families receiving multiple services from numerous agencies, and in a piecemeal fashion. A pilot project grew out of this study, aimed at identifying these " 'hard-core' families in the making" (Birt, 1956, p. 42) through family-centered treatment by a coordination of public and voluntary casework agencies.

The St. Paul project had many problems. Because caseworkers worked for a variety of organizations, there was confusion over responsibility for treatment. Maintenance of cohesion between workers and supervisors and among various agencies was a continual struggle. Much work had to be done regarding coordination between agencies and definitions of responsibilities in a common treatment plan. This program is regarded as an ambitious first attempt, however, that has informed current practice about the importance of linkages between community agencies in any home-based program (Horejsi, 1981).

Homebuilders is the name of a private organization founded in the 1970s in Washington state. It was one of the first home-based, time-limited family preservation programs limited to families at imminent risk of child removal because of child abuse or neglect (Kinney, Madsen, Fleming, & Haapala, 1977). For the past 20 years this program has practiced and documented effective family preservation practice techniques based on a social learning theory model of family therapy and bolstered with other concrete methods of strengthening the family environment both physically and emotionally. Although there are other models, current practice in many family preservation programs nationwide is based on this Homebuilders model.

The federal Adoption Assistance and Child Welfare Act of 1980 mandates that "reasonable efforts" be made to keep the family together and prevent the placement of children into substitute care. This mandate provides an increased demand for concrete and proven practice methods to be used in a time-limited form with high-risk families. Further legislation, the Family Preservation and Family Support Act of 1993, strengthened this emphasis and demand for service. Thus, family preservation techniques such as those developed by the Homebuilders program are in increased demand across the United States, and programs in almost every state have instituted training in these techniques, either in pure or modified form. This chapter presents service elements common to most intensive family preservation programs and should not be viewed as a description of the Homebuilders program only.[1]

Theoretical Basis for the Practice Model

Ecological Paradigm

Family preservation programs do whatever it takes to strengthen the family and the family environment. This rather expansive and vague goal, accompanied by a time-limited period of treatment, necessitates an ecological focus of treatment,

[1]More detailed descriptions of the Homebuilders program can be found in J. K. Whittaker, J. Kinney, E. M. Tracy, and C. Booth, (Eds.), *Reaching High-Risk Families: Intensive Family Preservation in Human Services*. Hawthorne, NY: Aldine de Gruyter.

incorporating and strengthening the family's social network and its skills to operate within that system. (See Chapter 14 for a more detailed discussion of the ecological systems theory.) Social learning theory and cognitive-behavioral theories also undergird several family preservation interventions and programs. (See Chapter 4 for a more detailed discussion of the cognitive-behavioral methods.)

Kinney and colleagues (Kinney, Haapala, Booth, & Leavitt, 1990) at Homebuilders caution that because of the time-limited nature of treatment, goals must be realistic. Using social supports and building family social skills during treatment assumes that these supports and skills can and will continue to bolster family functioning after formal family preservation services have ended. Thus, family functioning is viewed in an ecological or systems framework.

Families who are isolated with few social supports are at greater risk of child abuse and neglect than are families more in the mainstream (Cochran & Brassard, 1979; Saulnier & Rowland, 1985); they are also less likely to have their children returned if placed in foster care (Maluccio & Whittaker, 1988). Research in child abuse and neglect indicates that abusive parents are likely to have few or impotent resources to help them cope (Gaudin & Pollane, 1983; McClelland, 1973; Salzinger, Kaplan, & Artemyeff, 1983). The parents are isolated from social networks and other sources of modeling and support (Polansky & Gaudin, 1983) and have histories of deprivation, mental illness, and low self-esteem (Gaines, Sandgrund, Green, & Power, 1978; Garbarino, 1976; Paulson, Afifi, Chaleff, Liu, & Thomason, 1975; Shapiro, 1980). These families are often, but not always, from a lower socioeconomic group (Garbarino, 1976; Shapiro, 1980). Their resource deficits and stressors contribute to family tension and a way of life that promotes antisocial and aggressive behavior. In addition to these resource deficits, individuals in abusive families also have fewer than average positive exchanges within the family to reinforce pro-social behavior and greater than average negative and coercive exchanges (Patterson, 1982). Such patterns over time create a stressful and demanding family environment and decrease the number of reinforcers and resources for individuals, especially mothers (Patterson, 1980).

Wahler and Dumas (1984) have identified abuse in families with insular mothers. Insularity is defined as

> a specific pattern of social contacts within the community that are characterized by a high level of negatively perceived coercive interchanges with relatives and/or helping agency representatives and by a low level of positively perceived supportive interchanges with friends. (Wahler & Dumas, 1984, p. 387)

Children with insular mothers are at risk of abuse because their mothers have limited opportunities to defuse stress and few models of positive interaction. Increasing and developing support networks for these mothers can help them reduce their stress and manage day-to-day stress without abusing their children.

Crises like child abuse, emotional or behavioral disorders, and juvenile delinquency occur when stressors outweigh resources. Stressors correlated with child abuse and family stress include "different" child characteristics (such as prematurity or mental retardation), marital difficulties, unemployment, unwanted pregnancy, and crowded living conditions (Parke & Collmer, 1975). These stressors, if not adequately resolved or managed, can pile up over time to produce great social stress, often a precursor of abuse. "It is the unmanageability of the stress which is the most important factor and unmanageability is a product of a mismatch between the level of stress and the availability and potency of support systems" (Garbarino, 1977, p. 727).

Changes in economic and family structures in the recent past have increased social isolation and amplified the importance of support for families. The increase in the mobility of the American family has resulted in a decline of support from extended family. Many families no longer live in the same neighborhood or city with other relatives, reducing the availability of relatives for baby-sitting and child care as well as for social and recreational opportunities. When child abuse and neglect are defined as a result of social isolation and overwhelming stress, the solution is identified as eliminating or reducing that isolation and stress. Intensive family preservation services are aimed at linking families with resources in their family and community that they have not utilized and of which they may not be aware. The resources these programs provide include money, help with housing and food, education about child rearing and job skills, modeling of house cleaning and shopping skills, transportation, and improvement of family communication patterns. Thus, family preservation programs are viewed as a mediating influence between family stress and family breakdown (as evidenced by child placement in foster care, residential treatment, or juvenile detention). Ecological family preservation programs assess family stressors and resources and help to bolster and increase the family's resources to the point that the stressors associated with risk of placement can be ameliorated.

Major Assumptions

Whittaker, Schinke, and Gilchrist (1986) propose the two essential elements of an ecologically oriented intervention:

> building more supportive, nurturant environments for clients through various forms of environmental helping that are designed to increase social support, and improving clients' competence in dealing with both proximate and distal environments through the teaching of specific life skills. (p. 492)

These two elements, supportive environments and life skills, are crucial to the development of resources for impoverished families, who may lack monetary, informational, social, and emotional resources.

Because many insular mothers may indeed be stressed more than helped by interchanges with relatives and friends (Tracy, 1990; Van Meter, Haynes, & Kropp, 1987; Wahler & Dumas, 1984), social support in a more formal sense may be needed. Sustaining informal networks may be more stressful than productive to isolated parents (Belle, 1982; Tracy, 1990), and linking families with more formal services and supports, if sensitive and meaningful, may be appropriate. Formal services do not necessarily entail involving a family in a long-term and complicated system of intrusive family services, such as child protective services. Formal social support can be any agency or service of help to the family, such as the housing bureau, food stamps, day care centers and schools, and hospitals. Through ecologically oriented family preservation services, families can be helped to negotiate the maze of applying for the supportive services these agencies offer and need not be permanently enrolled in any particular course of action provided by these agencies. Often, simply making families aware of these resources for their future use is enough. Other families may need to be guided through initial use of services to ensure that the family understands and can repeat the process.

An equally important form of social support identified by Whittaker and colleagues (1986) is the teaching of specific life skills. This concrete form of social support is especially applicable in short-term interventions when the emotional support from agency workers is available for a finite period, usually two to three months. By learning these skills, family members will be able to support and reinforce their own positive family interactions after formal services have ended.

Treatment based on a social learning model focuses on modeling of these life skills, such as parenting skills, and teaching and practicing with family members the positive and constructive communication and negotiation skills that will contribute to a more positive and less abusive family environment. Workers assess parenting and communication skills, help parents and children identify nonpunitive methods of interacting, and model and practice positive interaction. These skills not only apply to parent and child interactions, but also help families interact more productively with landlords, doctors, teachers, social workers, neighbors, relatives, and other members who contribute to the support or stress in the family's social environment.

Family preservation programs are being delivered to families by a variety of service agencies, including child protective services, juvenile justice services, and mental health services. Although the populations served by these three types of agencies may be somewhat different, the goal is the same: to reduce the risk of removal of the child from the family, whether that removal is to foster care, detention or incarceration, or institutionalization in residential care. This chapter focuses on services delivered by child protective service agencies, but the nature and philosophy of services are fairly consistent across programs.

Therapeutic Methods

Assessment Techniques

Treatment consists of both "hard" and "soft" services to all family members. Family preservation programs differ somewhat in their concentration of intervention efforts on the more concrete or abstract elements of the family and family environment. However, most assessment skills focus on the concrete elements of the family environment. For the most part, family preservationists must be able to assess effectively the degree of risk of placement; the strengths, resources, and supports of the family; and indicators of the safety and stability of the family environment.

IMMINENT RISK OF PLACEMENT

Family preservation programs emphasize working with families at imminent risk of removal of the child. Degree of risk is often determined by the state's department of social services, if this agency is the referral source. If the referral is from another source, the intake worker determines the degree of risk after discussion with the referral source and based on the prior placement history of the family as well as other risk factors.

Removal of a child and placement into foster care is intended to prevent continued harm to the child or to reduce the potential for danger to the child in the home. Parental and child factors associated with child abuse and neglect abound in the research literature, and these factors are included in the many risk assessment tools being developed and used in many states (Johnson & L'Esperance, 1984; Magura & Moses, 1986; Pecora, 1988). Jordan and Franklin (1995) discuss and illustrate a number of risk assessment tools and the factors that are used to determine risk. Such factors include social isolation, a parent's history of being abused in childhood, social and economic stress, and substance abuse. An assessment of these factors within any one family can be a good predictive tool for risk of abuse. Reducing or eliminating such factors may also serve as an important outcome measure for family preservation services. As is discussed in Chapter 9, having assessment measures that can also serve as outcome measures is important to today's outcome-driven social services field. Standardized measures may be used to assess changes in risk factors and the increases in family well-being, providing helpful tools for outcome measurement in family preservation programs. Assessment is discussed in more detail later in the chapter.

A variety of factors may predict whether a child is in danger of abuse, but there are additional factors that determine whether a child is to be removed from the home. Some of these are intrafamilial characteristics and problems; other, more external, factors are the availability of foster homes, reporting mechanisms, and so on. Thus, there can be a wide disparity between the children identified as being at risk of abuse and those who would actually become placement statistics without intervention (AuClaire & Schwartz, 1986; Tracy, 1991; Yuan & Struckman-Johnson, 1991). The factors that predict placement are not always included in risk assessment tools, which may focus on parent-child interaction and disregard other environmental factors or systems decision-making factors. Many studies have shown that despite the reluctance of workers to place children out of the home for reasons of poverty (Pelton, 1989), the income level of the family is often a key predictor of whether a child is removed, over and above the severity of abuse or neglect (Lindsey, 1991; Katz, Hampton, Newberger, Bowles, & Snyder, 1986).

Many programs like Homebuilders agree that placement is imminent if the child protective service's worker details a plan to place the child within 24 to 48 hours (Kinney et al., 1990). Other family preservation programs broaden imminent risk to include families with many risk factors, such as prior placement, a history of abuse, or an out-of-control adolescent (Pecora, Fraser, Haapala, & Bartlomae, 1987; Showell, Hartley, & Allen, 1987). These programs may limit their population to child protective service cases or they can use these risk factors to define other families as soon-to-be child protective service cases. Determination of risk level can vary greatly from program to program and should follow very specific and reliable guidelines (Tracy, 1991). Tracy posits that such guidelines cannot be developed without further research on the differential effectiveness of family preservation services with families that have varying characteristics and presenting problems.

In most programs, referring agencies must document that the child will be removed if services are not provided (Kinney, Haapala, Booth, & Leavitt, 1990). This is often the sole determination of imminent risk of placement. Other programs do not require such documentation but calculate their own determination of risk. For example, one family preservation program in northern California first defined families at risk (in 1983) as those families in which the following were true: the referral came from the Department of Social Services, the family had more than one child, and the family was of minority ethnicity (Remy & Hanson, 1983). Based on more rigorous family risk assessment research findings since 1983, risk was then further specified as pertaining to families with a child currently in placement, a child with a prior history of placement, a family history of abuse or neglect, or any of the following characteristics: a multiproblem family, a multiracial family, possible abuse, an absent parent, parental substance abuse, psychiatric history, developmental disability, or severe physical illness.

In any determination of appropriateness of services for families, programs should also determine the families for which services are inappropriate. In the northern California program, for example, families may be deemed ineligible if there is too much danger to the worker, other help is available, no children are at risk, parents are unavailable, parents decline service, or all children are older than 14 years (Berry, 1991). Families are not excluded because of mental retardation or substance abuse, as they are in other family preservation programs (AuClaire & Schwartz, 1986; Landsman, 1985). Referrals to this program come from a variety of sources, including hospitals, the Department of Social Services, private social services, public health agencies, and self-referrals.

FAMILY RESOURCES, STRENGTHS, AND SUPPORTS

Families in family preservation programs are highly stressed families facing multiple problems or crises. Even so, these families may possess many strengths as well. Family preservation practice has the stated philosophical advantage of a strengths perspective. Practice aims to assess and build on the strengths families do have and to help families to acquire new strengths as well.

This model seeks to improve the physical and social family environment, with resulting impacts on child health, behavior, safety, and development; it teaches family care skills to parents, with resulting impacts on parenting skills, environmental conditions, and acquisition of resources. Changes in these conditions and skills should be assessed through standardized instruments completed by the family preservationist at case opening, case closing, and at suggested one-month, six-month, and one-year follow-up visits. Use of standardized forms allows for the tracking of items with empirical support for their contribution to family well-being, and follow-up assessments provide information on the longevity of effects, a component of assessment too often missing from practice evaluation (Rzepnicki, 1991).

The Family Risk Scales (Magura, Moses, & Jones, 1987) and the Child Well-Being Scales (Magura & Moses, 1986) are good assessment tools for identifying resources for and deficits in the family. The Family Risk Scales gather information about the financial problems, social support, physical and mental health, parenting practices, and behavior of family members. These scales are extremely practical and fairly reliable (reliability coefficient = .80) indicators of family risk, are very helpful assessment tools, and are achieving popular usage in family preservation research (Nelson, 1991b). Fraser, Pecora, and Haapala (1991) find that "while some of the scales need to be revised to be more unidimensional or more sensitive to change . . . , these scales represented a good balance of clarity, breadth, and practicality for evaluation of IFPS [intensive family preservation services] programs" (p. 132).

Therapist's Role

Compher (1983) reviewed the various roles of social workers in home-based services to children, and classifies them as general case manager, the comprehensive social worker, the in-home team, and the interagency team. These are listed in ascending order of family needs. General case management in the home setting focuses on the client's contextual needs in order to strengthen family resources and prevent the need for placement of the children. The comprehensive social worker emphasizes strengthening family functioning through family counseling and secondarily facilitates resource development. This approach is thus the most family-centered of the four types. The in-house team consists of two or three social workers who can develop resources and provide intensive counseling simultaneously. The interagency team has three roles: case manager, clinical family therapist, and family aide. Family preservationists typically find themselves in the most intensive of these roles.

Case management and service coordination are two related methods child welfare agencies use to help provide services to families. These methods are useful for the child protective services caseworker and they also contribute to the efficacy of home-based placement prevention efforts. In family preservation programs, case management and service coordination are important components of an ecological approach with an emphasis on client empowerment (Allen, 1990). One of the basic tenets of family-centered practice and short-term treatment is that for services to be effective and for progress to continue after services have concluded, resources and supports in the family's social environment must be mobilized and strengthened (Stehno, 1986; Polansky & Gaudin, 1983; Lovell & Hawkins, 1988). Thus, formal and informal social resources have become an important component of permanency planning practice and family preservation services, and the effective case manager helps to assess the need for supports and to coordinate the acquisition of these supports for the family.

The family preservationist is not only a case manager but also a teacher. These caseworkers teach and model such skills as positive (nonpunitive) parenting and household care. Caseworkers are constantly interacting with the children in a firm but nurturing manner, modeling these skills to parents. Such teaching is not done by a merely didactic method (through handouts and "lecturing") but in hands-on modeling and practicing of the skills. Parents can see and practice the skills with the caseworker.

Change Techniques

TASK-CENTERED TECHNIQUES

The primary goal of services is to prevent the need for out-of-home placement of the children. This goal usually entails resolving immediate crises and teaching the family skills necessary to maintain family integrity independently. To accomplish this, the workers must have some level of proficiency at problem-solving and communication skills, but they also provide such concrete services as house cleaning and transportation. A worker models how to do these skills and demonstrates his or her commitment to the family (Kinney et al., 1990). During the provision of such "hard" services, therapists can also observe clients' skills and talk about other problems the family is experiencing. Following the framework developed by Whittaker and colleagues (1986), the ecologically based family preservation program seeks both to increase social support and to teach specific life skills. Depending on the family's presenting problems, workers may help parents learn positive child-rearing skills instead of punitive and abusive patterns. They may help families acquire adequate housing and apply for appropriate financial aid as well as learn how to budget the income they do have. Family care workers address any problems in the condition of the family's building or living unit and help parents fix broken windows and plumbing; they also help convince landlords to fix the heating system, which is often permanently on or permanently off. Families are taught health care and nutrition practices and directed to legal assistance, if needed. Families are thus assessed for their resource deficits, and these deficits are diminished by skill building and resource mobilization, including support networks.

EMPOWERMENT

The family preservation model is based on the collegial model in which the family preservation worker and the family work together toward the common goal of family strengthening. Workers do not impose the treatment goals on the family; rather, the family and worker together explore and choose the goals, objectives, and tasks that will lead to family stability and prevent the removal of the child. The home-based focus of the model supports the notion that the worker is the guest in the family's home; the worker is there to help the family meet its goals, not tell the family what to do. Typically, families at the crisis level of imminent child removal have been recipients of child protective services before and may perhaps have built resentment and resistance to system intervention. By working with the family's goals, family preservation works toward empowering families to interact with and change their own environment to meet their needs or "to handle their own problems rather than continually relying on the state to rescue them when things get rough" (Kinney et al., 1990, p. 32).

How to Conduct a Session of Family Preservation Therapy

When a case is opened for intensive family preservation services, the worker and the family members often make service agreements involving tasks that the worker and the family members agree to perform. Agreements are written that specify the task, who will perform it, and where, when, and how often it will be performed. Objectives of service are specified in behavioral terms. For example, one such agreement may stipulate that the son will control his aggressive behavior, the mother will keep track of good behavior of the son and praise him, and the worker will supply ice cream cones to both mother and son at the end of the week for some agreed-on level of task accomplishment. Everyone signs the agreement when it is acceptable, and workers track progress on tasks. New tasks are typically set at every meeting of family and worker.

Family preservation programs typically have weekly staff meetings in which workers can brainstorm with each other about case strategies and community resources. During team meetings, social workers model how to teach skills to families by teaching skills to each other. Caseworkers often share expertise in window replacement techniques, constructive negotiation skills with landlords, and baby care. In this way, the collegial relationship is extended to the supervisory situation with fellow caseworkers.

Consistency with Social Work Practice

Family preservation programs have a unique compatibility with the social work practice philosophy and vision. In addition, the theoretical and values base of the model is consistent with traditional social work practice. First, therapists working in family preservation programs serve clients in their natural environments. Assessments and treatments are offered in the home setting. This approach is consonant with social work's historic environmental perspective, which concluded that it is important to intervene in the social environment. As mentioned in the history section above, the idea of home visiting goes back to the early friendly visitors and case workers who believed in the importance of intervening with people in their natural contexts. Second, family preservation programs evolved out of policy changes in child welfare and other social services programs when regulations began to require that practitioners work to keep families in crisis together. The development of family-centered child welfare policies that provide a safety net for poor families has been a long-standing mission of the social work profession. In this regard, family preservation has the unique history of being associated with reforms in social welfare programs aimed at improving the lives of children and families. Current reforms such as the integrated services delivery models discussed in Chapter 1 are a continuation of this philosophy. In fact, family preservation services offered in mental health programs are often associated with "wrap-around" services and other programs aimed at improving the delivery of human services to children and families.

Third, family preservation programs use an empowerment and a strengths perspective of families in crisis. This philosophy is also consistent with social work practice. In particular, the programs promote the welfare of families by emphasizing respect and self-determination for all families. These values are also an integral part of the social work profession. Finally, family preservation programs use the ecological systems theory, an open systems perspective that has been a guiding paradigm of the social work profession for the past 20 to 30 years.

Research Support for the Model

Empirical Support

A large body of empirical support for practice models is based on a social learning foundation (Bandura, 1977). Barth's (1990) review of the theoretical bases of family preservation services notes that "no other intervention [social learning] for families with antisocial children has been investigated so carefully and shown such favorable results" (p. 99). The ecological paradigm is also based on empirically validated methods (Whittaker et al., 1986). Whittaker and colleagues' extensive review of the supportive empirical evidence for the ecological paradigm (Whittaker et al., 1986) cites the work of Achenbach and Edelbrock (1981) and Patterson (1982), among others, in establishing the connection between life stresses and social incompetencies and the presence of child behavior problems and the use of clinical mental health services.

Outcome Evaluations

PLACEMENT PREVENTION

The primary goal of intensive family preservation services is to prevent unnecessary out-of-home child placement. A variety of intensive family preservation programs have been evaluated, and most report their placement prevention rate as the primary criterion of success. These programs report success rates ranging from 71% (Pecora et al., 1987) to 93% (Reid, Kagan, & Schlosberg, 1988) to 96% (Berry, 1991), with Homebuilders averaging 90% of families intact at the end of treatment (Kinney et al., 1990). At the one-year follow-up point, Homebuilders reports that 88% of families are still intact (Behavioral Sciences Institute, 1987). Berry (1992) also reports an 88% success rate for the In-Home Family Care Program (a program of the private Children's Home Society of California), and Oregon's Intensive Family Services has a 73% success rate (Showell, 1985). Placement prevention rates for many family preservation programs across the United States are shown in Table 8.1. Most of the evaluations of these programs have not included control groups (which would provide information on the placement outcomes for children not receiving services). Most studies have been focused on imminent risk cases, but the determination of imminence is, again, diverse.

Success rates are comparable when placements are counted by child, instead of by family. A total of 896 children were served in the three-year period in the In-Home Family Care program (Berry, 1991); of those children, 96, or 11%, were later placed in out-of-home care. The average length of time from case closing to child removal was 150 days, or about five months. Eight families experienced a child placement prior to the closing of the case, but services were continued to other children in the family.

REDUCTION OF RISK AND INCREASES IN SKILLS

These services are meant to reduce a variety of risks, with prevention of placement being the primary goal. Of course, provision of these services should also reduce the risk of poor developmental outcomes for the child and continued abuse or neglect. Only a few evaluations of preservation programs have addressed ef-

TABLE 8.1   Outcomes among family preservation programs

Program	Number of families N	At termination of services	Families remaining intact At follow up 3 months	12 months
In-Home Family Care–Alameda (Berry, 1990a)	40	90%	85%	75%
In-Home Family Care–San Francisco (Berry, 1990b)	327	97	93	90
Family Program Northern Virginia Family Service (Bribitzer & Verdieck, 1988)	42	55	—	—
Hennepin County, Minnesota Family Study Project (AuClaire & Schwartz, 1986)	55	55	—	—
Homebuilders 1989 (Pecora, Fraser, & Haapala, 1990)	409	94	—	—
Homebuilders 1986–1987 (BSI, 1987)	444	97	—	—
Homebuilders 1975–1976 (Kinney et al., 1977)	80	97	—	—
Nebraska Intensive Services (Stein, 1985)	73	89	—	—
Oregon Intensive Family Support (Showell, 1985)	261	88	—	73
Parsons Child and Family Center (Reid, Kagan, & Schlosberg, 1988)	431	93	—	—
Ramsey County, Minnesota (Lyle & Nelson, 1983)	34	76	—	—
Utah Family Preservation (Callister et al., 1986)	168	85	—	—
Utah Family Preservation (Pecora et al., 1987)	120	71	—	—
Utah Family Preservation (Pecora, Fraser, & Haapala, 1990)	172	91	—	—

fects on the reduction of maltreatment factors, such as child behavior problems or family functioning (Kinney et al., 1990; Pecora et al., 1987). In the evaluation by Nelson (1991a) of 11 family-based placement prevention programs in six states, family preservation was associated with the following changes during services: improvements in behavior, material resources, family structure, family dynamics, emotional climate, perceptions of problems, community perceptions of the family, informal support network, and community involvement. Even families from which children were removed showed significant declines in inappropriate behavior, dysfunctional family dynamics, tense emotional climate, negative community perception of the family, and low community involvement. Given the short-term nature of these preventive programs, a compelling question is whether they have long-term effects. This study does not assess the longevity of families' gains. Especially problematic is the absence of documentation showing whether abuse and neglect recur over time.

One evaluation of the Homebuilders program (Kinney et al., 1990) reports that in the majority of families, the child's school attendance improved and the child showed declines in hyperactivity, delinquent acts, and peer problems as judged by the parent or a therapist at the end of treatment. However, all families were judged to have remained the same in their handling of medical problems or physical handicaps, and the majority of families remained the same regarding alcohol abuse or learning disabilities. Another evaluation of the Homebuilders program looked at school adjustment, delinquent behavior, home-related behavior, and cooperation with the agency (Pecora et al., 1987). Except for cooperation, children in the program made significant positive improvements during service. Parents also made significant improvements in supervision of younger children, parenting of older children, attitudes toward preventing placement, and their knowledge of child care. In the Utah Family Preservation program (Pecora et al., 1987), children made significant gains in school adjustment and behavior, and parents improved in parenting behavior, attitudes, and knowledge.

The In-Home Family Care program (Berry, 1992) looked very specifically at skill gains of parents in the program and found that parents made modest gains from the opening to the closing of a case, on average, in discipline, general child care, and encouragement of child development. Those families who remained intact had made significant improvements over the course of treatment (as judged by workers) in all areas except for household safety, and these gains remained relatively high across treatment. In comparison, families who subsequently had a child removed showed significant deterioration during treatment in the cleanliness of the home; also, in most other skills, they declined or did not improve. After a case was closed, some of the gains deteriorated, as in the areas of safety and health care (judged at one-month, six-month, and one-year follow-up visits). The areas that showed continued improvements, on average, were in general child care skills, discipline, and encouragement of child development as well as orderliness and cleanliness of the household. Families who made substantial gains from closing to the six-month follow-up point in the areas of household cleanliness and the physical condition of the home were less likely to have children removed.

Fraser and colleagues (Fraser, Pecora, & Haapala, 1991) evaluated the Homebuilders programs in Utah and Washington and reported statistically significant gains in family environment and parenting skills, as rated by the Family Risk Scales (Magura, Moses, & Jones, 1987). The assessment included the physical environment, financial problems, parenting skills, and child behavior. The program goals most associated with service success were decreasing depression, increasing social support, increasing use of community services, decreasing running away, and increasing parental skills.

SERVICE COMPONENTS ASSOCIATED WITH TREATMENT SUCCESS

Several service components do seem to make a difference for families. Berry (1992) looked at actual service time spent with families. She found that the average family received 67 hours of service over about 77 days (about 9 hours a week), and over a third of service time was spent in the home. Of course, the typical family received service intermittently, with some days of several hours of service and some days of little or no service. Length of service varied with the presenting problems of the family. Cases of families who were treated for child neglect, child emotional disturbance, child abuse, or family interaction problems were open a significantly longer time than those for families without these problems.

Berry's analysis indicates that while the total length of time the family is served is not related to outcome, the proportion of time that is spent *in the home* is highly related to success. No families experienced child placement when more than half the service time had been spent in the home. Conversely, the placement rate skyrocketed to 28% (twice that of the entire sample) when over half the service time had been spent in the agency. Families that received larger proportions of their service time in the home were more likely to stay together. In addition to a home focus, the type of service provided made a difference in outcome. Families were best served and more likely to remain intact when services were particularly concrete, such as the teaching of family care, supplemental parenting, medical care, help in the securing of food, and financial services. Families that experienced later placements had received somewhat (but not significantly) larger amounts of assessment, crisis intervention, and help with housing and legal matters, and somewhat smaller amounts of respite care, help in securing food, and parent education. These services were associated with parents making the greatest gains in skills and in families remaining intact after leaving the program. Also, when services had involved formal social supports, such as talklines, day care, respite care, and health care, families were more likely to stay together.

Fraser, Pecora, and Haapala (1991) found that concrete and life skills building services were associated with prevention of placement as well as goal achievement in terms of parenting skills, anger management, children's school performance, self-esteem, depression, and oppositional behavior. These findings demonstrate that short-term services can be effective when they include concrete services and the mobilization of resources. Families who receive training in parenting and family care can be quite successful in remaining a family.

The skill gains associated with placement prevention are more concrete than usually assumed. In Berry's (1992) evaluation, improvements in the cleanliness and overall condition of the living unit and in health care and encouragement of child development were significantly correlated with placement prevention. Also, when clients continued to make gains in the cleanliness and condition of the living unit after the case was closed, families were much more likely to keep their children. These physical conditions are visible and tangible indicators of the family environment and influence placement decisions.

Family care workers utilize a variety of social supports in providing service to clients. Most of these collateral supports involve formal agencies, particularly the Department of Social Services and private social service agencies. Other formal agencies commonly used in service are hospitals and public health agencies. Berry's (1992) study found that agencies with specific contact with the children were an important collateral contact, with 27% of cases involving respite care, 26% involving the schools, and 21% involving nursery schools or day care. Friends (11%), relatives (10%), churches (10%), and talk lines (23%) were the types of collateral contacts that involved more informal social support. Whether a particular social resource was utilized did not make a difference in treatment outcome, but the amount of time spent with a collateral resource did make a difference: families remaining intact had workers who had spent somewhat more case time, on average, arranging help with talk lines, private health care, day care providers, and respite care.

ECONOMIC SUPPORTS

Because family preservation programs are aimed at preventing out-of-home child placement and the decision to remove a child is often associated with economic indicators rather than severity of maltreatment (Pelton, 1989; Lindsey, 1991), the outcome of placement may or may not be directly affected by changing parenting practices or improving family relations. It may be that improving economic conditions and environmental indicators of safety and orderliness will have the greatest impact on reducing the risk of placement because these physical, visual indicators of family functioning are the most dramatic indicators of maltreatment.

Some family preservation programs recognize the importance of these physical and economic factors by providing flexible funds of $100 to $500 per case, with which in-home workers can improve economic or environmental conditions like installing a phone, repairing the car, or buying a child's bed without making such an expenditure fit into some billable category of service. This practice illustrates a recognition of the contribution of the physical environment to family functioning and the decision to remove children.

Critiques of the Model

Practice Critiques

In the California program (Berry, 1992), families suffering a child placement following services had been rated as more physically capable but less mentally capable of participating in service. A total of 38 families (10%) had a member with a developmental disability, either a parent (4%), a child (5%), or both (1%). When all indicators are collapsed to any developmental disability or mental incapacity in the family (n = 50), this was a significant contributor to child placement (a 24% placement rate versus a 13% placement rate for all others).

The environment of neglectful families has been well researched (American Humane Association, 1988; Polansky, Gaudin, Ammons, & Davis, 1985), and many studies of family preservation programs have found lessened success rates among this population (Berry, 1992; Yuan & Struckman-Johnson, 1991). In the Berry (1992) evaluation, the neglectful families were judged by workers to have significantly poorer family functioning than others and to display poorer child care skills, health care skills, and encouragement of child development. The level of household resources available to the family was rated much worse for neglect cases. More than a third of neglect cases had been referred by the department of social services (compared to only 7% of other cases). These cases were also much more likely to have had previous child removals (68% versus 22%, p < .001). The problem of child neglect was not an isolated problem but was often associated with other presenting problems, especially child abuse, child developmental disability, child handicaps or illness, and parental substance abuse.

All these stressors combine to result in an environment in great need of strengthening through the provision of resources and the building of family care and home care skills. Neglect is less a crisis-producing incident than it is a chronic state of family disrepair. Neglectful families thus need service at least as intensive if not more so than that provided to most families if they are to mobilize needed resources and skills. This service should teach skills in the home and link families with more formal helping agencies in the neighborhood who can continue to help on a more long-term basis.

Research Critiques

The field of family preservation is relatively young (about 15 years old), and the research reflects this. Many program evaluations have not utilized control groups, and those that have often found no difference in child removal rates between families served by the program and those receiving conventional services (Yuan & Struckman-Johnson, 1991). Much more research is needed regarding multiple outcomes for families in these programs, over and above the prevention of placement. Research must build on the burgeoning research by Fraser, Pecora, and Haapala (1991), Tracy (1990), Yuan and Struckman-Johnson (1991), and Berry (1992) by looking at the impact of family preservation on prevention of placement, increases in safety levels for the children, and increases in family skills. Only when the impact of the program on these larger goals is known can child protective service agencies be assured that family preservation programs attain real changes in family functioning that will keep families out of the revolving door of short-term services.

Family Preservation and Managed Behavioral Health Care

As we move into the era of managed behavioral health care and public child welfare services are folded into a system of managed care, family preservation becomes important to a mix of services that are likely to be offered. First, family preservation is an intensive, time-limited approach usually lasting only four to six weeks. This type of approach gained some funding and support in the 1980s because proponents believed that with services, troubled families could be kept together, and that if families stayed together, the costs of foster care, residential treatment, and other substitute care options could be reduced. The goal of family preservation is to keep children out of substitute care. Managed behavioral health care organizations prefer to fund shorter term and community-based practices. Within those service delivery systems, it is desirable to keep children out of long-term, expensive substitute care. Family preservation and other crisis intervention alternatives, therefore, may be viewed as a first line of defense that will be preferred by funders.

Case Example[2]

Identifying Information

Family members living at home: Ray Smith, 33, father, unemployed; Melissa Smith, 27, mother, unemployed; Amy Smith, 5; Amber Smith, 4; Bobby Smith, 3.
Income: Food stamps only

Referral source: Child Protective Services

Presenting problem: The Smith family is being referred from Child Protective Services for the suspected abuse of their son, Bobby Smith. Bobby received burns on the inside of both arms. The burns were reported to be from hot soup. The parents, Ray and Melissa, state that Amber stepped on the door of the oven causing the oven to tilt and the soup to fall on Bobby. The doctors treating the burns determined that the burns could not have occurred the way the parents reported. The Smiths have been referred to Child Protective Services on three prior occasions for neglect of their three children.

The history of the Smith family revealed that Bobby has suffered two other serious injuries. He has had a previous burn to the eye and a skull fracture. Melissa Smith has been the primary caretaker of the children during the times most of these injuries have occurred. Melissa and Ray deny any abuse in the family home. Melissa does state that she gets upset and uses physical punishment with the children when they do not mind her. Melissa also states that these occurrences usually happen when Ray is not in the home and that he interacts very little with the children.

Goals: With the help of the caseworker, Melissa and Ray say that they define their family's strengths as Melissa's willingness to take care of the children while Ray looks for work, Ray's willingness to look for work, the fact that the family is still together, and the ability to call on extended family for help. Ray, Melissa, and the caseworker will pursue the following goals:

1. To avoid out-of-home placement of the children.
2. To assist the parents in obtaining employment.

---

[2]The author thanks Melynn Conway, Lisa Greene, and David Tatum, MSSW students in the School of Social Work at the University of Texas, for their case example.

3. To improve parenting skills and learn effective means of discipline to prevent injury to the children.
4. To arrange for developmental testing for the children and any other needed services.
5. To assist the parents in improving their problem-solving skills.

Session 1

The first session is very important as the interventions for this program are so intensive and quick. Therefore, the worker meets with all family members available to identify with them their perceptions of the problems and strengths in the family. Going through the Family Risk Scales with the family is a good way to identify with the parents their strengths in parenting and the risk factors that may compromise child safety. Incorporating the parents' assessments into the development of the family assessment and goal development helps to assure parent motivation and cooperation in treatment.

The worker uses active listening techniques. The worker elicits information through such activities as remaining silent, reflecting feelings, reflecting content, and paraphrasing the talker's comments (Kinney, Haapala, & Booth, 1991). Empathy is also a strong tool used in developing rapport with families. With an empathetic caseworker, the parents will agree on goals with the worker and help to prioritize areas in which to begin. Once goals are outlined, the worker and family will make a task contract to help make tasks clear and to help the parents maintain the desire to reach their goals from session to session.

The parents and worker discuss the parents' becoming frustrated with the children, and the worker assures them that this is normal. The worker asks the parents to discuss ways rather than physical punishment to deal with this frustration. The parents use brainstorming to decide how to handle the times when they become angry enough to hit the children. The worker assists this process to help facilitate an alternate plan. The worker explains a procedure of time-out (Kinney, Haapala, & Booth, 1991). The worker explains that time-out is used to get away from children for a short while to help the parents gather their thoughts and cool down to the point that they will be able to control the situation without injuring the child. The parents are asked to discuss situations when they feel time-out may have worked in the past. The worker informs the parents that at any time the situation could get out of control, they should call her for assistance immediately. The worker gives her home phone number and beeper number to the parents. The parents are also given examples of appropriate times to call the worker. The worker and parents conclude the session by agreeing on the next time the worker should visit the home.

Session 2

The worker sits down with the family and summarizes the last session and discusses occurrences since the last visit. The goals are again discussed along with resources to help the family attain these goals. The worker and parent sit down and discuss the contract they had made on using no physical punishment toward the children. The parents discuss their difficulty with maintaining the contract. They discuss how time-out worked in times of stress. The worker asks Melissa to identify what she feels when she wants to hit one of the children; they develop a "crisis card" to help Melissa identify and divert her escalating feelings. Use of the crisis card comes from the Homebuilders model (Kinney, Haapala, & Booth, 1991). Melissa describes the feelings at the point when she feels like hitting the children. The worker asks her to place a number from 1 to 6 on these feelings. This scale is to chart the danger point of her feelings as it is associated with the time she usually decides to use physical punishment. The worker asks Melissa to discuss her feelings that lead up to the danger point and place numbers for these feelings between 0 and 6.

The worker makes a visual chart and displays Melissa's feelings and the number she has given to each one. The chart builds from minor feelings like no anger (0) to hitting the children (6). The worker then assists both parents in brainstorming ways for decreasing Melissa's feelings that would lead to hitting the children. They problem solve together on the pros and cons of various solutions. The parents then decide the point on the scale at which it might be best for Ray to take the children to the park to give Melissa a time-out. Ray is thus brought into the solution and Melissa's need for help is validated.

The worker and Melissa discuss times when Ray will not be home to help Melissa. They discuss how to use the time-out procedure effectively when Ray is not at home. The worker also tells Melissa that if the situation gets to a "5" on the crisis card, Melissa should call her immediately.

Transcript

The family preservationist has already had one session with the family to determine whether they are appropriate for services and to establish goals with the family. The social worker listens to each parent for their perspectives on the problem. The parents state that they have difficulty controlling the behavior of the children and report that this frustration sometimes leads to physical punishment. Both parents deny causing any injuries to the 3-year-old child. The family is willing to cooperate with the program.

The Child Protective Services agency and the family preservationist have decided to use a social learning family preservation model with this family to prevent the out-of-home placement of the children. The parents contracted with the family preservationist to participate in the program for at least four weeks and to refrain from using physical discipline with their children until the next meeting. They will call the family preservationist if needed.

During this session, early in treatment, the family preservationist (Maya) is in the home of the family: Melissa (mother), Ray (father), and the three children, Amy, Bobby, and Amber. The family preservationist enters the home and sits down with the parents at the kitchen table.

MAYA:	I brought some glass and putty to fix those broken windows in Amber's and your rooms. I'll show you how to fix Amber's, and then you'll know how to fix the other one. That should help cut down on Amber's colds. How have things been going since we last talked?
RAY:	Things have gone pretty good. I have been looking around and may have a job lined up. I have an interview coming up, but I don't have anything to wear.
MAYA:	I know some agencies in town that might be able to help us out. Let's try some of them to get something for you to wear. How have the kids been doing?
RAY:	I haven't had any problems with them.
MAYA:	Melissa, how have things been going for you?
MELISSA:	Well, Amber is into everything and won't listen to me. Ray is never home to help with the kids.
RAY:	I've been out looking for a job!
MAYA:	It sounds like it is very frustrating to have to deal with kids all day long, Melissa. One of the things I'd like to talk about today is how we can work toward helping you to deal with that frustration. Has either of you been frustrated enough with the children to use physical discipline since our last talk?
RAY:	I haven't had any problem.
MELISSA:	That's because you are never here. I've come pretty close, but I've followed the rules.
MAYA:	Melissa, it sounds like you are working really hard to avoid physically disciplining the children. That's great. How did you do that?
MELISSA:	I did what you told me to and went to another room until I calmed down.
MAYA:	That sounds good. Very good. Let's talk about some ways to avoid becoming angry to the point of wanting to hit the children.
RAY:	Okay.
MELISSA:	Okay.
MAYA:	I'd like for us to make a crisis card. This will help you notice your feelings before you get to the point of losing control. If we were to rate your feelings on a scale of 0 to 6, 0 would be feeling no anger and 6 would be feeling angry enough to hit your child. What's happening when you are feeling a level 6?
MELISSA:	Amy is crying, Bobby is getting into things, and Amber is pulling on me because she wants me to do something for her.
MAYA:	Where is Ray?
MELISSA:	Out.
MAYA:	So, that is a number 6. Melissa, where is it on this scale that you start losing control?
MELISSA:	Well, whenever I try to get the kids to mind and settle down and they won't. I try again and they still won't. Then I start to feel like hitting them. That's probably about a 4.

MAYA: So, level 6 is hitting your children, and level 4 is beginning to lose control. What would level 5 be?

MELISSA: I start to yell at the kids.

MAYA: That's a good description. Let's go back to level 1 now. How would that feel?

MELISSA: Maybe I'd be just a little upset.

MAYA: Okay. How about level 2?

MELISSA: I start feeling frustrated with Ray because he's either not there or he is not paying attention to what's going on.

RAY: I help with the kids when I'm not out looking for a job!

MAYA: So level 2 is being more frustrated. What about level 3?

MELISSA: I get more and more frustrated with Ray and with the children.

RAY: She is always yelling at me when I'm home.

MAYA: Melissa, now we have determined when you start losing control. Now, I'd like for you and Ray to think of some ways to keep from getting to that point.

MELISSA: If I had more time to myself, if Ray would help take care of the kids, if the kids would mind me, or maybe I could just leave the room, as I have been.

RAY: Yeah, that worked last time. Maybe, I could take the kids to the park.

MAYA: That's a good idea, Ray. You both have some good ideas. Another thing that could help is for both of you to have time together without the children. How about if I take care of the kids tomorrow for three hours to give you some time together?

RAY: Okay.

MELISSA: Okay.

MAYA: Melissa, I would like you to call me when you reach a level 5. Ray, if you are home, when Melissa reaches a level 4, could you take the kids to the park?

RAY: Yeah, I could do that.

MELISSA: Well, what if he's not at home.

MAYA: Then call me.

MELISSA: Okay.

MAYA: We have done some good work today. We've determined some levels of anger for you, Melissa, and both of you have come up with some good ways to decrease your anger. So, do both of you agree to try these things?

RAY: Yeah.

MELISSA: Yeah.

MAYA: I'm going to leave this chart with you to help you identify what level you are at. Remember, you can call me anytime. I'll also come over tomorrow to watch the kids. When shall I come?

MELISSA: How about 2:00. Then we can go to a movie.

RAY: Yeah, 2:00 would be good.

MAYA: Sounds good to me. Now, let's go fix that window.

Summary

This chapter reviewed intensive family preservation practice techniques based on an ecological model of family functioning. A history of home-based services that have served as progenitors to today's family preservation programs was highlighted. The theoretical basis of family preservation and its major assumptions were summarized, and techniques used by family therapists working in family preservation programs were defined. Research studies supporting the effectiveness of family preservation programs were reviewed, along with important critiques of the model. Family preservation's unique compatibilities with social work were also highlighted. The importance of such time-limited practice approaches as family preservation was also discussed from the perspective of today's practice contexts. Finally, a case example illustrating how to work in a family preservation program was presented.

Process Questions

1. What is meant by intensive treatment? List some examples of intensive work with the Smith family.

2. What are the main risk factors in this case, and how do these relate to the family preservation approach?

3. Family preservation emphasizes the strengths of the family. What are some examples of strengths of the Smith family?

4. Family preservationists do whatever it takes to strengthen families and help them solve their immediate crisis. What are some examples of interventions that the practitioner uses and how do they affect the family?

References

ACHENBACH, T. M., & EDELBROCK, C. S. (1981). Behavioral problems and competencies reported by parents of normal and disturbed children aged four through sixteen. *Monograph of the Society for Research in Child Development, 46*(1), serial no.188. Chicago: University of Chicago Press.

ALLEN, M. (1990, Spring). Why are we talking about case management again? *The Prevention Report,* 1–2.

AMERICAN HUMANE ASSOCIATION. (1988). *Highlights of official child neglect and abuse reporting, 1986.* Denver, CO: Author.

AUCLAIRE, P., & SCHWARTZ, I. M. (1986). *An evaluation of the effectiveness of intensive home-based services as an alternative to placement for adolescents and their families.* Minneapolis: University of Minnesota, Hubert H. Humphrey Institute of Public Affairs.

BANDURA, A. (1977). *Social learning theory.* Englewood Cliffs, NJ: Prentice-Hall.

BARTH, R. P. (1990). Theories guiding home-based intensive family preservation services. In J. K. Whittaker, J. Kinney, E. M. Tracy, & C. Booth (Eds.), *Reaching high-risk families: Intensive family preservation in human services.* Hawthorne, NY: Aldine de Gruyter.

BEHAVIORAL SCIENCES INSTITUTE. (1987). *Summary of King, Pierce, Snohomish, and Spokane county Homebuilders service, September 1, 1986–August 31, 1987.* Federal Way, WA: Author.

BELL, J. E. (1978). Family context therapy: A model for family change. *Journal of Marriage and Family Counseling, 4,* 111–126.

BELLE, D. (1982). Social ties and social support. In D. Belle (Ed.), *Lives in stress: Women and depression.* Beverly Hills, CA: Sage.

BERRY, M. (1991). The assessment of imminence of risk of placement: Lessons from a family preservation program. *Children and Youth Services Review, 13,* 239–256.

BERRY, M. (1992). An evaluation of family preservation services: Fitting agency services to family needs. *Social Work, 37,* 314–321.

BIRT, C. J. (1956). Family centered project of St. Paul. *Social Work, 1,* 41–47.

BLOOM, M. L. (1973). Usefulness of the home visit for diagnosis and treatment. *Social Welfare, 54,* 67–75.

BRIBITZER, M. P., & VERDIECK, M. J. (1988). Home-based, family-centered intervention: Evaluation of a foster care prevention program. *Child Welfare, 67,* 255–266.

CALLISTER, J. P., MITCHELL, L., & TOLLEY, G. (1986). Profiling family preservation efforts in Utah. *Children Today, 15*(6), 23–25.

COCHRAN, M. M., & BRASSARD, J. A. (1979). Child development and personal social networks. *Child Development, 50,* 601–616.

COLLINS, R. C. (1980). Home Start and its implications for family policy. *Children Today, 9*(3), 12–16.

COMPHER, J. V. (1983). Home services to families to prevent child placement. *Social Work, 28,* 360–364.

FRASER, M. W., PECORA, P. J., & HAAPALA, D. A. (1991). *Families in crisis: The impact of intensive family preservation services.* Hawthorne, NY: Aldine de Gruyter.

FRIEDMAN, A. S. (1962). Family therapy as conducted in the home. *Family Process, 1,* 132–140.

GAINES, R., SANDGRUND, A., GREEN, A. H., & POWER, E. (1978). Etiological factors in child maltreatment: A multivariate study of abusing, neglecting and normal mothers. *Journal of Abnormal Psychology, 87,* 531–540.

GARBARINO, J. (1976). A preliminary study of some ecological correlates of child abuse: The impact of socioeconomic stress on mothers. *Child Development, 47,* 178–185.

GARBARINO, J. (1977). The human ecology of child maltreatment: A conceptual model for research. *Journal of Marriage and the Family, 39,* 721–735.

GAUDIN, J., & POLLANE, L. (1983). Social networks, stress and child abuse. *Children and Youth Services Review, 5,* 91–102.

HALPERN, R. (1984). Lack of effects for home-based early intervention? Some possible explanations. *American Journal of Orthopsychiatry, 54,* 33–42.

HALPERN, R. (1986). Home-based early intervention: Dimensions of current practice. *Child Welfare, 65,* 387–397.

HIRSCH, J. S., GAILEY, J., & SCHMERL, E. (1976). A child welfare agency's program of service to children in their own homes. *Child Welfare, 55*(3), 193–205.

HOREJSI, C. R. (1981). The St. Paul Family Centered Project revisited: Exploring an old gold mine. In M. Bryce & J. Lloyd (Eds.), *Treatment of families in the home.* Springfield, IL: Charles C. Thomas.

JOHNSON, W., & L'ESPERANCE, J. (1984). Predicting the recurrence of child abuse. *Social Work Research and Abstracts, 20,* 21–31.

JORDAN, C., & FRANKLIN, C. (1995). *Clinical assessment for social workers: Quantitative and qualitative methods.* Chicago: Lyceum/Nelson Hall.

KATZ, M. H., HAMPTON, R. L., NEWBERGER, E. H., BOWLES, R. T., & SNYDER, J. C. (1986). Returning children home: Clinical decision making in cases of child abuse and neglect. *American Journal of Orthopsychiatry, 56,* 253–263.

KINNEY, J., HAAPALA, D., & BOOTH, C. (1991). *Keeping families together: The Homebuilders model.* Hawthorne, NY: Aldine de Gruyter.

KINNEY, J., HAAPALA, D., BOOTH, C., & LEAVITT, S. (1990). The Homebuilders model. In J. K. Whittaker, J. Kinney, E. M. Tracy, & C. Booth (Eds.), *Reaching high-risk families: Intensive family preservation in human services.* Hawthorne, NY: Aldine de Gruyter.

KINNEY, J. MADSEN, B., FLEMING, T., & HAAPALA, D. A. (1977). Homebuilders: Keeping families together. *Journal of Consulting and Clinical Psychology, 45,* 667–673.

LANDSMAN, M. J. (1985). *Evaluation of fourteen child placement prevention projects in Wisconsin, 1983–1985.* Iowa City, IA: National Resource Center on Family Based Services.

LINDSEY, D. (1991). Factors affecting the foster care placement decision: An analysis of national survey data. *American Journal of Orthopsychiatry, 61*(2), 272–281.

LOVELL, M. L., & HAWKINS, J. D. (1988). An evaluation of a group intervention to increase the personal social networks of abusive mothers. *Children and Youth Services Review, 10,* 175–188.

LYLE, C. G., & NELSON, J. (1983). *Home-based vs. traditional child protection services: A study of the home based services demonstration project in the Ramsey County community human services department.* Oakdale, IA: National Resource Center on Family Based Services.

MAGURA, S., & MOSES, B. S. (1986). *Outcome measures for child welfare services: Theory and applications.* Washington, DC: Child Welfare League of America.

MAGURA, S., MOSES, B. S., & JONES, M. A. (1987). *Assessing risk and measuring change in families: The Family Risk Scales.* Washington, DC: Child Welfare League of America.

MALUCCIO, A. N., & WHITTAKER, J. K. (1988). Helping the biological families of children in out-of-home placement. In E. W. Nunnally, C. S. Chilman, & F. M. Cox (Eds.), *Families in trouble: Troubled relationships.* Beverly Hills, CA: Sage.

MCCLELLAND, D. (1973). Testing for competence rather than intelligence. *American Psychologist, 28,* 1–14.

MONTGOMERY, D. G., SHULMAN, D. A., & PFENNINGER, G. (1972). Use of social work teams to provide services to children in their own homes. *Child Welfare, 51,* 587–597.

NELSON, K. E. (1991a). Populations and outcomes in five family preservation programs. In K. Wells & D. E. Biegel (Eds.), *Family preservation services: Research and evaluation.* Newbury Park, CA: Sage.

NELSON, K. E. (1991b, December). Comparing measures of family well-being. Presentation to the National Conference on Family-Based Services, St. Louis, Missouri.

O'KEEFE, R. A. (1973). Home Start: Partnership with parents. *Children Today, 2*(1), 12–16.

PARKE, R., & COLLMER, C. W. (1975). Child abuse: An interdisciplinary analysis. In E. M. Hetherington (Ed.), *Review of child developmental research* (Vol. 5). Chicago: University of Chicago Press.

PATTERSON, G. R. (1980). Mothers: The unacknowledged victims. *Monographs of the Society for Research in Child Development, 45*(5), 1–64.

PATTERSON, G. R. (1982). *Coercive family process.* Eugene, OR: Castalia.

PAULSON, M. J., AFIFI, A. A., CHALEFF, A., LIU, V. Y., & THOMASON, M. L. (1975). A discriminant function procedure for identifying abusive parents. *Suicide, 5,* 104–114.

PECORA, P. (1988). Evaluating risk assessment systems: Methodological issues and selected research findings. In P. Schene & K. Bond (Ed.), *Research issues in risk assessment for child protection.* Denver, CO: American Association for Protecting Children.

PECORA, P. J., FRASER, M. W., & HAAPALA, D. (1990). Intensive home-based family preservation services: Client outcomes and issues for program design. In D. E. Biegel & K. Wells (Ed.), *Family preservation services: Research and evaluation.* Newbury Park, CA: Sage.

PECORA, P. J., FRASER, M. W., HAAPALA, D., & BARTLOMAE, J. A. (1987). *Defining family preservation services: Three intensive home-based treatment programs.* Salt Lake City, UT: University of Utah Social Research Institute.

PELTON, L. (1989). *For reasons of poverty: An evaluation of child welfare policy.* New York: Praeger.

POLANSKY, N. A., & GAUDIN, J. M. (1983). Social distancing of the neglectful family. *Social Service Review, 57,* 196–208.

POLANSKY, N. A., GAUDIN, J. M., AMMONS, P. W., & DAVIS, K. B. (1985). The psychological ecology of the neglectful mother. *Child Abuse and Neglect, 9,* 263–275.

REID, W. J., KAGAN, R. M., & SCHLOSBERG, S. B. (1988). Prevention of placement: Critical factors in program success. *Child Welfare, 67,* 25–36.

REMY, L. L., & HANSON, S. P. (1983). *Evaluation of the emergency family care program, San Francisco home health service: Final report.* San Francisco: San Francisco Home Health Service.

RZEPNICKI, T. L. (1991). Enhancing the durability of intervention gains: A challenge for the 1990s. *Social Service Review, 65,* 92–111.

SALZINGER, S., KAPLAN, S., & ARTEMYEFF, C. (1983). Mothers' personal social networks and child maltreatment. *Journal of Abnormal Psychology, 92,* 68–76.

SAULNIER, K. M., & ROWLAND, C. (1985). Missing links: An empirical investigation of network variables in high risk families. *Family Relations, 34,* 557–560.

SHAPIRO, D. (1980). A CWLA study of factors involved in child abuse. *Child Welfare, 59,* 242–243.

SHOWELL, W. H. (1985). *1983–1985 biennial report of CSD's intensive family services.* Salem: State of Oregon Children's Services Division.

SHOWELL, W., HARTLEY, R., & ALLEN, M. (1987). *Outcomes of Oregon's family therapy programs: A descriptive study of 999 families.* Salem: State of Oregon Children's Services Division.

SPECK, R. V. (1964). Family therapy in the home. *Journal of Marriage and the Family, 26,* 72–76.

SPEREKAS, N. B. (1974). Home visiting in family therapy. *Family Therapy, 1,* 171–178.

STEHNO, S. (1986). Family-centered child welfare services: New life for a historic idea. *Child Welfare, 65,* 231–240.

STEIN, T. J. (1985). Projects to prevent out-of-home placement. *Children and Youth Services Review, 7,* 109–121.

TRACY, E. M. (1990). Identifying social support resources of at-risk families. *Social Work, 35,* 252–258.

TRACY, E. M. (1991). Defining the target population for family preservation services. In K. Wells & D. E. Biegel (Eds.), *Family preservation services: Research and evaluation.* Newbury Park, CA: Sage.

VAN METER, M. J. S., HAYNES, O. M., & KROPP, J. P. (1987). The negative social work network: When friends are foes. *Child Welfare, 66,* 69–75.

WAHLER, R. G., & DUMAS, J. E. (1984). Changing the observational coding styles of insular and noninsular mothers: A step toward maintenance of parent training effects. In R. F. Dangel & R. A. Polster (Eds.), *Parent training: Foundations of research and practice.* New York: Guilford.

WHITTAKER, J. K., KINNEY, J., TRACY, E. M., & BOOTH, C. (Eds.). (1990). Reaching high-risk families: Intensive family preservation in human services. Hawthorne, NY: Aldine de Gruyter.

WHITTAKER, J. K., SCHINKE, S. P., & GILCHRIST, L. D. (1986). The ecological paradigm in child, youth, and family services: Implications for policy and practice. *Social Service Review, 60,* 483–503.

YUAN, Y-Y. T., & STRUCKMAN-JOHNSON, D. L. (1991). Placement outcomes for neglected children with prior placements in family preservation programs. In K. Wells & D. E. Biegel (Eds.), *Family preservation services: Research and evaluation.* Newbury Park, CA: Sage.

CHAPTER NINE

Cynthia Franklin, Ph.D.
University of Texas at Austin
Catheleen Jordan, Ph.D.
University of Texas at Arlington

Rapid Assessment in Family Practice

Every practitioner needs a large repertoire of skills for assessing families. The term *assessment* can be used to refer to four different but related processes in family practice. The first process is defining a problem area for the purposes of determining what interventions and resources are needed to help a client solve problems. Second, assessment also refers to an evaluation leading to the formulation of a clinical diagnosis from recognized nosological systems such as the *Diagnostic and Statistical Manual for Mental Disorders (DSM-IV)* (American Psychiatric Association, 1994). Third, assessment may be used as a set of interventions that simultaneously reveal relevant information about the family system and introduce information that produces change. Finally, assessment is used to denote an ongoing evaluation of a family's progress toward treatment goals.

This chapter focuses on assessment as intervention, as a way to define family problems, and as approaches that may be used in the ongoing evaluation of the progress of families in treatment. These methods hold particular relevance for the current practice contexts of brief therapy and managed behavioral health care because they provide rapid assessment approaches. Techniques developed for assessing "whole system" functioning of families are reviewed. Several types of family systems assessment methods are discussed, including interviewing and questioning methods, the scaling technique, family task observations, and empirically derived measurement approaches. This chapter further discusses the clinical utility of family assessment methods for today's brief practice environments and draws comparisons between the different methods reviewed.

History

Assessment as Intervention

Historically, assessment within social work practice was conceptualized as serving its own important functions, distinct from change interventions, and sometimes being thought of as a first phase of practice, before the initiation of an intervention plan (Hepworth & Larsen, 1991). In contrast, family systems assessment views assessment as serving dual functions: discovering how a family system is functioning and intervening in the patterns of a family system. The processes of assessment and change interventions are not distinct but interactive and circular, allowing assessment methods to serve this dual function (Tomm, 1987). This view of assessment is sometimes called assessment as intervention (Franklin & Jordan, 1995; Jordan & Franklin, 1995; O'Hanlon & Weiner-Davis, 1989).

In contrast to assessment as intervention, assessment within social work practice has recently been described as an ongoing process of collecting information from clients (Jordan & Franklin, 1995). Compton and Galaway (1989) state that assessment serves the purpose of "reaching an understanding of the problem, client, and situation so that one can construct a plan to solve and alleviate the problem" (p. 443). These authors also emphasize the structure of the assessment process: It is not linear, but spiral, and it continues throughout the problem-solving process. Clinical researchers have also expanded the scope and functions of assessment to serve multiple functions within practice agencies. Assessment provides viable tools for assessing client characteristics, tracking client progress in treatment, and providing data for agency reports and program evaluation (Franklin, Nowicki, Trapp, Schwab, & Petersen, 1993).

Viewing assessment as intervention focuses totally on the processes involved in a change effort, whereas viewing assessment as a first stage in a treatment effort focuses on a stage model or set of sequences that must be followed in a problem-solving endeavor. These two approaches are not necessarily incompatible. Both can be used together in practice to bring forth change in clients. For example, even if the practitioner uses assessment as intervention, a problem has to be defined and a viable treatment plan has to be constructed during the process of the assessment and intervention.

Viewing assessment as intervention as it is described in this chapter, however, blurs the boundaries between the methods used for assessment and the methods used for change. Assessment as intervention means that there is no delay between the collection of information and the introduction of change processes. Family systems assessment methods are designed to serve both functions. Change happens simultaneously or back and forth as the system is being assessed by the clinician. Therefore, assessment and change become a part of the same process as patterns are identified, changed and identified, and changed reciprocally. Family systems assessment methods covered in this chapter are based on the assessment as intervention approach, with the exception of the empirically derived measurement models that help practitioners identify problems and may be used to measure progress in treatment. The authors believe, however, that family systems assessment with standardized measures may also be used to encourage change, and are in fact used to intervene by family therapists.

Theoretical Basis for the Practice Model

Assessing Family Systems

Over the past 15 years, the family therapy field has developed multiple methodologies for assessing families as systems. These new methods focus on "whole systems" functioning and assess the interactional, interpersonal, and systems functioning of family groups (Grotevant & Carlson, 1989; Jordan & Franklin, 1995). Systems functioning specifically refers to the circular, patterned way in which family groups are believed to behave. Assessment of "whole systems" (family groups) functioning is based on systems theory and assumes that the interactions of a family group take on measurable and/or observable behavior patterns and characteristics that extend beyond the individual behaviors of each of its family members (Goldenberg & Goldenberg, 1991).

The interactional patterns of the family group or system become the focus of the family systems assessment and extend to the systems or relational network characteristics of family functioning and associated presenting problems. Behavior patterns in family systems are nonlinear and recursive and operate in a repetitive, circular, and reflexive manner (Becvar & Becvar, 1988; de Shazer, 1982; Hoffman, 1981; O'Hanlon & Wilk, 1987; Palazzoli, Boscolo, Cecchin, & Prata, 1980; Tomm, 1987). Systems behavior patterns are contextual and are established as families respond to situational difficulties, developmental transitions, and the problems of everyday living. Once such a pattern is established, however, it may become a repetitive interpersonal process that may recur in multiple contexts. In other words, the pattern comes to resemble automatic behavior or a ritual, and it may happen in multiple situations regardless of the specific content being discussed or set of behaviors being transacted.

Some family clinicians believe that systemic family patterns have meaning or serve a function for the family system, such as helping the family to stay intact or to avoid marital conflict (Haley, 1990; Madanes, 1984; Palazzoli, Cirillo, Selvini, & Sorrentino, 1989). Other clinicians focus more on the behavioral aspects of the systemic functioning or the self-reinforcing nature of the pattern and make few interpretations about its meaning or function (Cade & O'Hanlon, 1993; Fisch, Weakland, & Segal, 1982; Watzlawick, Weakland, & Fisch, 1974). Regardless of theoretical orientation, to assess family systems effectively, clinicians must use assessment methods that can focus on the interactive sequences and relational network patterns of the entire family.

Therapeutic Methods

Interviewing and questioning methods are verbal techniques used to join, assess, and change the systemic processes within a family. They are used simultaneously to gather information and introduce information into a family system. Six methods are briefly described and illustrated: (1) circular questions; (2) conversational/ therapeutic questions; (3) hypothesizing, circularity, and neutrality; (4) tracking problems, solutions, and/or exceptions to problems; (5) pretherapy change assessment; and (6) the scaling technique.

Circular Questions

Circular questions provide a structure for eliciting information from various family members about the transactions and operations embedded in a family system (Fleuridas, Nelson, & Rosenthal, 1986; O'Brien & Bruggen, 1985). This method originated with the Milan family research team (Palazzoli et al., 1980). (See Chapter 3 for a description of the Milan approach.) The structure of circular questions is nonthreatening to the family because the questions generally ask family members to comment on the family structure and process from the view of an outside observer. Thus, a father might be asked to comment on how he believes his wife is feeling about their son's behavior, or a daughter might be asked about what her mother does in response to her brother's behavior. O'Brien and Bruggen (1985) provide a schema for categorizing different types of circular questions:

1. *Relationship to others.* These questions refer to the relationship between two people in a family. For example, "How do your mom and dad solve disagreements between them?"
2. *Family members' relationship to events in family life.* "When mom comes home late from work, what does dad do?"
3. *Ranking behavior within the family.* Actual or hypothetical situations can be used. "Who is most strict, your mother or your father?" "Pretend for a moment that I am a magic fairy with the powers to send you on a vacation to an adventurous island. Who in your family would you take with you?"
4. *Relationships to time.* Both events in time and specific points in time may be used. "How was your husband different before you moved to this city?" "How were things different between you a year ago?"
5. *Eliciting information from the perspective of the silent member.* This may include members not present at family sessions or those who will not talk. "If your father were here in the session, what do you think he might say about your family?" "If your brother were to answer my question, what do you think he might say?"

Fleuridas, Nelson, and Rosenthal (1986) offer a more detailed categorization for understanding different types of circular questions. Circular questions help the clinician assess the relationship processes and network within a family by tracking the systemic pattern associated with complaints or a presenting problem. As the clinician uncovers the pattern through the use of circular questions, the family also sees the pattern. The clinician modifies the pattern by opening it up to family awareness but also by using the questions to suggest a new view or set of behaviors that may be associated with the pattern. The short transcript below gives an example of circular questions used by a clinician to assess and intervene in family systems. Notice that the transcript illustrates how circular questions make it possible for the clinician both to gather information about the systemic pattern and to insert information about the pattern.

A DIALOGUE USING CIRCULAR QUESTIONS

Family in session: Mrs. Jones, mother; Betsy, 11, identified patient; Mrs. Rutgers, grandmother (lives across the street); Mr. Jones, stepfather; Veronica, 17, sister.

Presenting problem: Child's school refusal.

THERAPIST:	What brings you in today?
MRS. JONES:	It's Betsy. I don't know what is wrong with Betsy. She doesn't want to go to school. She complains of a stomachache and starts crying every morning before school. I know she has to go to school. They've even been calling, but her crying really unnerves me.
THERAPIST:	How long has this been going on, the crying?
MRS. JONES:	Oh, for about five or six weeks. Maybe a little longer.
THERAPIST:	This may sound like a strange question, but what did she do before the crying?
MRS. JONES:	What?
THERAPIST:	Yes, before the crying, what did she do in the mornings before school?
MRS. JONES:	Well, she didn't cry, uh, I guess she used to be hard to get up and I always had to do a lot of things for her, like help her pick out her clothes, and make sure I checked on her a lot to see if she was coming along. Yes, that's it, she needed a lot of attention from me. But nothing like now. She doesn't want me to leave her sight.
THERAPIST:	So, Betsy is close to you and likes for you to do things with her, but the crying and not wanting to go to school, this is different from before.
MRS. JONES:	Yes, that's right.
THERAPIST:	A child crying, well that can be very unnerving. Betsy, what does your mother do when you start crying in the morning?
BETSY:	She talks to me. She tries to find out what is wrong and where it hurts. Sometimes she gives me medicine.
THERAPIST:	What kinds of things does she say to you?
BETSY:	She says did I eat something bad? She tells me not to worry, because that can cause stomachaches sometimes.
THERAPIST:	Who else would agree with your mom that stomachaches might be caused by worrying?
BETSY:	Uh, Bill [stepfather] does.

THERAPIST:	Mr. Jones [stepfather], when Betsy cries in the morning, where are you?
MR. JONES [STEPFATHER]:	Well, usually in bed, you know, I work at night. I hear her howling and I hear Amanda [mother] talking to her, really more like pleading with her to at least try and go to school. It usually wakes me up.
THERAPIST:	Who else does it wake up?
MR. JONES:	Just me, because Veronica [sister] is usually awake. But I guess sometimes it may wake Delores [grandmother] because Amanda will call her for advice or help with Betsy.
MRS. RUTGERS:	Oh, I've been awake for hours.
THERAPIST:	Mr. Jones, what kind of advice does she get from Mrs. Rutgers?
MR. JONES:	I am not really sure, but I don't know if it helps since she keeps encouraging her to take off work and go to different doctors. Sometimes she does come over and stay with Betsy or help Amanda take her to the doctor.
THERAPIST:	You mean they go to the doctor together?
MR. JONES:	Yes, and sometimes we will all take her, or since I do not work in the daytime, I will take her with Mrs. Rutgers, so Amanda can go to work.
THERAPIST:	How do you think your wife may be feeling about the crying?
MR. JONES:	She is worried. She worries too much and feels a little helpless because she can't get her to stop crying. The whole family are worrywarts. That is where Betsy gets it from, if you ask me.
THERAPIST:	Veronica, you are awake when Betsy starts crying; what do you notice Mr. Jones and Mrs. Rutgers doing to help your mother?
VERONICA:	He comes in and tells Mom that it will be okay and not to worry because Betsy isn't really that sick. He usually tries to talk to Betsy about school, and Mom and he talk about what to do. Grandma, she usually comes over and stays with Betsy and tries to cheer her up. She can usually get her to stop crying.
THERAPIST:	How is Mr. Jones's opinion about what to do about the crying the same or different from your mother's?
VERONICA:	That is a weird question.
THERAPIST:	Yes I know, but would you please answer it anyway?
VERONICA:	Well, I guess they both think Betsy is having a head problem, maybe scared about something at school. That's why we are here. But Mom still worries that she may really be sick and the doctors haven't found out yet.
THERAPIST:	And who in your family would disagree with Betsy's problem being a head problem?
VERONICA:	Grandma and I guess me too. I think she must really be sick since she cries so much and even vomits sometimes. Maybe it is one of those strange new diseases or something else. Anyway she doesn't just act scared that way in the morning before school but at other times too. I think Bill doesn't take her seri-

ously enough. He just tries to get Mom to ignore her and us by telling her we all jump to conclusions and worry too much. Anyway, nothing bad happened at school.

THERAPIST: Mrs. Rutgers, you seem to be an expert on this crying since you can get it to stop for awhile. How do you explain the crying?

MRS. RUTGERS: Well, I don't know, but it's not being scared about school. She must really be sick. Anyway, I think she really needs her mother. She gets real scared about Amanda leaving her and going to work. I can get her to stop crying by reassuring her about her mother not leaving her and telling her she does not have to go to school because we are going to stay with her and take her to the doctor.

MR. JONES: Delores, that does not help us to get her to go to school. That's the big worry, her not going to school.

MRS. JONES: Now, Bill, you know she is trying to help. She is the only one that gets her to stop crying. What would we do without her help? We haven't found out what is wrong with Betsy yet. We are all puzzled and worried about what might be wrong.

THERAPIST: It is interesting that you are all worried, but not all of you are worried for the same reasons. You seem to agree that there is something wrong in this family and that it is somehow related to what is happening to Betsy. Tell me, Mrs. Jones, who else is worried about you leaving them or going to work besides Betsy?

MRS. JONES: I do not know what you mean.

THERAPIST: Sure you do; who else has let you know that they worry about you leaving them?

MRS. JONES: Well, mother has some, and of course Veronica usually agrees with mother [sarcastically]. I haven't always worked or been so active outside the home. And I guess even I was a little worried about the effect on the children, at first.

THERAPIST: So, everyone but Mr. Jones has worried about you leaving them.

MRS. JONES: Yes, he really liked the extra money and he thought the children were old enough. Of course, I may lose my job if Betsy does not get better soon.

THERAPIST: When did you start working?

MRS. JONES: Oh, about six months ago.

THERAPIST: Mrs. Rutgers, how did your daughter feel about going to work?

MRS. RUTGERS: She was reluctant at first to leave the children and me alone but Bill really encouraged her to do it. You know, I have serious asthma and bronchitis and need medical attention myself sometimes. I can't always watch after the children when I have attacks. Bill, he isn't much help because of his work schedule either.

THERAPIST: Mrs. Jones, who takes care of your mother when she has attacks since you went to work?

MRS. JONES: Well, she is alone most of the time but when Veronica comes home from school she looks in on her. Although Bill is sleeping, he is around if something bad happened during the day. Of course, recently she has been giving me extra help with Betsy and we spend a lot of time at the doctor anyway. In fact, the other day she had an attack on the way to taking Betsy to the doctor's office. That was a double ordeal.

MRS. RUTGERS: Poor Betsy, I was wheezing and she was so sick too. It was a good thing you were there, Amanda.

Conversational/Therapeutic Questions

Conversational/therapeutic questions help clinicians understand family processes and private meanings. This questioning method is used by clinicians who work from a collaborative language systems and/or narrative perspective (Goolishian & Anderson, 1987; Anderson & Goolishian, 1992); it helps clinicians become like anthropologists, seeking more and more understanding about the family from the insider's views. (See Chapter 6 for a description of the narrative approach.) By definition, family systems are private and difficult to understand; therefore, gaining access to and understanding private information about systems functioning and its personal meanings is difficult at best. Conversational questions take clinicians out of the "expert role" and help them assume a collaborative, "not-knowing" stance so they can be nonthreatening to the family and gain an understanding of the family system at the same time (Goolishian & Anderson, 1987; Anderson & Goolishian, 1992).

A mutual understanding of family processes is negotiated as the clinician interviews or engages in dialogues with the family. Clinicians learn about the family by *not* testing their clinical hypothesis or imposing their preplanned diagnostic questions and theories. Instead, family systems are understood by listening intently and joining the conversation. The goal of the assessment is to gain more and more understanding from the real experts about the problems and the family—the family themselves. At the same time this dialogue between clinician and family emerges and the clinician negotiates a mutual understanding of the family, it becomes possible to expand the dialogue to possibilities for change in the system.

This form of questioning and interviewing is similar to ethnographic interviewing and other methods that developed from the qualitative/naturalistic research paradigm (Franklin & Jordan, 1995). Conversational questions are similar to Socratic questions. The "not-knowing" nature of these questions brings into light processes and patterns that could not be seen previously (Anderson & Goolishian, 1992). In fact, the therapist's understanding of these patterns might be blocked if he or she used a more traditional interviewing format, because therapists generally ask explanatory questions aimed at confirming clinical hypotheses. The following transcript shows a sample conversational dialogue between a clinician and family.

A DIALOGUE USING CONVERSATIONAL QUESTIONS

Family in session: Peter, father; Robert, 15, identified patient; Gretchen, stepmother

CLINICIAN:	Hello. I am the social worker, Janet Reeves. I like to be called Jan, but you may also call me Dr. Reeves, if you wish. What would each of you like for me to call you?
FATHER:	Pete.
STEPMOTHER:	Gretch.
ROBERT:	[silence]
GRETCH:	He likes to be called Bobby.
CLINICIAN:	Bobby, is that what you would like to be called?
BOBBY:	Yeah.
CLINICIAN:	I do not know anything about you and hope that today through our talk you will help me begin to understand you and your situation. Will you help me?
PETE:	Sure.
CLINICIAN:	Thank you, Pete. What about you, Gretch and Bobby? Will you also help me?
GRETCH:	Yes.
BOBBY:	[Nods and shrugs.]
CLINICIAN:	Good, I find that the families I work with are real experts concerning their situation, and with your help we can find solutions. To begin, out of curiosity, I am wondering, what do you call this place where you have come today?
PETE:	Huh? Uh, counselor. You're a counselor.
BOBBY:	Shrink.
GRETCH:	Counselor.
CLINICIAN:	So, how did you decide to come to a counselor/shrink?
PETE:	The school told us to come or Bobby couldn't get back in his classes. He got kicked out for getting in a "ruckus" with another kid.
CLINICIAN:	You got sent here by the school because of Bobby's ruckus? So you're here to get him back in school?
PETE:	That's it. Don't know much else because I wasn't there. Bobby, tell her what happened.
BOBBY:	Not much to tell. This kid smarted off to me and I kicked his ass [bragging]. Mr. Johnson came and took me down to Mr. Douglas, the vice-principal, and he wouldn't listen to what happened. He doesn't like me, so the other kid got off and I got expelled.
CLINICIAN:	So, you enjoyed kicking his ass?
BOBBY:	Yeah, well, he deserved it. If you had heard what he called me. . .
GRETCH:	Bobby, you can't just punch everyone that gives you lip. You are getting in a lot of trouble lately for fighting, like being kicked out of school.
CLINICIAN:	Gretch, you are sounding very concerned about Bobby punching others.
GRETCH:	Yes, he has a bad temper and a mouth of his own. I've been the victim of it myself. [Bobby rolls his eyes.]

CLINICIAN: Bobby, I noticed you rolled your eyes when Gretch was talking about your bad temper. What did that mean?

BOBBY: I don't know. I guess I'm not the only one with lip. [frowns]

CLINICIAN: Ah! You're saying Gretch gives you lip, too?

BOBBY: Yeah, and she is always bitching at me about school and to dad. He gets mad at me because of her.

GRETCH: I am the one who has to go to the school and face those people when you're in trouble. If you didn't punch every kid that has a mouth, I wouldn't have to be bitching about you always. That's why I say you have a bad temper.

BOBBY: Don't go; I don't want you to go.

CLINICIAN: Who would you like to go?

BOBBY: Nobody; I can take care of it myself.

CLINICIAN: I am sure you can Bobby. You sound like a pretty independent young man who can take care of yourself.

BOBBY: Yeah! That's right; I don't take anything off nobody.

CLINICIAN: Yes, you kick ass. Would you agree with Gretch that you have a bad temper?

BOBBY: Well, I don't know about a bad temper [smiles], but like you say I take care of myself and don't let people push me around.

GRETCH: With that attitude you are never going to be able to hold a job.

CLINICIAN: So, Gretch you want Bobby to be able to hold a job and you are concerned that his temper may get in his way?

GRETCH: Yes, that's right! It is keeping him from getting his education right now.

CLINICIAN: And you're the one who goes to the school to talk when Bobby's temper gets in the way of his education?

GRETCH: Uh, well, yes, it is easier for me to get off my job than Pete.

CLINICIAN: So, that means, Gretch, if I understand what you are saying, that you are the one who handles the school and Bobby.

GRETCH: Yeah, I am the one who goes down there and tries to work things out between them so that Bobby can stay in school.

CLINICIAN: Wow, that's a big job! You really have two jobs, it seems?

GRETCH: Yeah, I never have thought about it quite like that, but it's a big hassle and it ain't easy for me to get off work.

CLINICIAN: Now, let me check to see if I have this right. You take off your work and work things out with the school? And I am only guessing then that you are also the one who tries to get Bobby to stop punching others?

GRETCH: Yeah, I ground him and he loses his temper at me and stomps out. He ain't ever hit me yet, but he has raised his hand a few times. Of course, I tell Pete and he talks to Bobby. Chews him out real good. But the next time it happens they call me again. I just want him to keep his temper. I keep telling him he doesn't have to punch those boys to stick up for himself.

Hypothesizing, Circularity, and Neutrality

Hypothesizing, circularity, and neutrality are methods used conjointly to discover systemic patterns and introduce change into the system. These methods evolved from the work of the Milan family research team (Tomm, 1984). The Milan team assessed families and delivered a five-part intervention process: (1) presession—discussing the family situation and developing a hypothesis for what systemic processes were associated with the presenting problem; (2) interview—one therapist of the team interviews the family while the others watch from behind a one-way mirror; (3) the intersession break—the team meets to discuss the emergent information from the interview and to develop further hypotheses and/or interventions; (4) interviewer rejoins the family and discusses the hypotheses and/or delivers an intervention; (5) the team meets to debrief and discuss the family's reaction to the intervention (Tomm, 1984). (See Chapter 3 for a discussion of the Milan approach to family therapy.) One weakness of the traditional Milan model for current practice contexts is that the therapists work as a team—cost prohibitive in most situations, though it is generally a good approach for training and live supervision. One way to think about the Milan approach, however, is that it is an intermittent, long, brief therapy model. Even though the therapists work as a team, they see the families only once a month or so instead of every week. In some situations, this might justify the cost of using more than one therapist at a time, especially if you could obtain quick resolution of presenting problems. The hypothesizing approach used by the team, however, can be used by one therapist as well as a team of therapists.

Hypothesizing is a systemic assessment method that introduces an exploratory narrative or research process into assessment. Before the first session with the family, the therapy team compiles available information about the family and meets and develops a preliminary assessment or hypothesis about the family functioning. This hypothesis is treated as a beginning assessment or tentative hypothesis for how the family processes may be operating to maintain the presenting problem. Although the team may spend 30 minutes developing the hypothesis, they quickly discard it if it doesn't match the patterns observed in the family session (Cecchin, 1987).

In the first session, the clinician interviewing the family systematically directs questioning in a manner that will yield information about the hypothesis. To test the hypothesis, the clinician asks questions that uncover the circularity or systemic family patterns associated with the presenting problem. Circular questions intermixed with other types of questions provide information to assess the systemic pattern. Questioning allows information to emerge from the family regarding differences and relationship patterns, and this relational information subsequently guides the clinician toward the information that should be put back into the family through further use of the questioning method.

The goal of hypothesizing is to explore the relational network and interactional patterns associated with the problem. For example, the presenting problem is the acting out behavior of a child, but the available information also indicates that the parents may be having marital difficulties associated with numerous psychosocial problems. Then the team may hypothesize that the child's symptomatic behavior serves a homeostatic function for the family system and that the symptomatic child is triangulated between his parents. Based on the formulation of this hypothesis, the clinician asks direct questions such as, "Who notices that the child is acting up?" "Whose idea was it to come to therapy?" "How do the different family members explain the acting-out behavior?" "Who in the family agrees with the different explanations?" "How would family members be acting differently if the child weren't acting up?" "Who does what and when in relation to the acting up, and then who does what?" The clinician is satisfied that she has assessed the circularity of the family relational pattern when the family responses come full circle, back to the child's behavior problem.

As family members respond to the questions in the session, the hypothesis may or may not be accepted, or other hypotheses based on the information coming from the family may emerge. The clinician may explore several different hypotheses in the interview in a similar manner as described above. Questions are purposeful and guided by the hypothesized patterns. This method is believed to help the family and clinician quickly uncover the covert family processes and systemic patterns that are connected to problems.

To test hypotheses and assess systemic patterns, clinicians must maintain neutrality in the interviewing process. Being neutral means that the clinician must maintain a curiosity, respect, and admiration for the family system. Respect must be maintained in relationship to the family's structure, values, beliefs, and behaviors (Cecchin, 1987). Neutrality is an active process that requires the clinician to give equal amounts of empathy, warmth, and attention to each family member. The clinician is careful not to side with different family members in the interview. Family members should leave the session feeling as if the clinician was on his or her side and was aligned with each one individually. When a hypothesis is confirmed, the clinician immediately affirms or positively connotes the systemic pattern by reframing symptomatic or problem behavior as being helpful or functional within the context of the family relational pattern. Thus, we see how assessing a pattern initiates new information or a change procedure. For example, if the triangulation pattern mentioned above were to be confirmed, the clinician might follow up the confirmed hypothesis with the following positive connotation:

> It seems Carlos is a type of spokesman, and we think he is helping out the family by acting up in school. Family members seem to have been suffering in silence for the past two years, and Carlos is bringing a lot of attention to your silent pain. In fact, we think there is a lot of suffering going on in your family. Mr. J., your job loss has caused you and your family suffering. You, Mrs. J., are in pain also because of your mother's illness, and I am not sure you have felt as much support from Mr. J. as you would like. You have suffered in silence away from home, caretaking for your mother. You have felt lonely and guilty for leaving your husband alone to take care of Carlos, and Carlos has felt lonely too. And you, Mr. J., have suffered in silence too, because your wife has been gone so much and preoccupied with her mother. You have been lonely and weren't able to get as much support as you would have liked during this career crisis. We think your marriage has suffered a great deal. However, since Carlos has been acting up in school, Mrs. J., you have had to call in your brother to help with your mother, and you have spent a lot more time at home with your husband and Carlos. You and Mr. J. have been talking again and supporting one another. Of course, you have been

talking about how to help Carlos. Maybe this talking will help your marriage and you won't get a divorce. So, you see, we think Carlos's acting up has been very important to this family.

Tracking Problems, Attempted Solutions, and/or Exceptions to the Problem

The next series of techniques to be discussed come from the Mental Research Institute (MRI) of Palo Alto, California (Fisch, Weakland, & Segal, 1982; Watzlawick, Weakland, & Fisch, 1974). Tracking is one of the best known of the family systems interviewing methods. It has been referred to in different ways, including assessing interactional patterns, specifying the problem sequences, defining the problem, and assessing the relational context. Variations of this interviewing method have been detailed by several authors (Cade & O'Hanlon, 1993; Haley, 1990).

Using tracking, the clinician assesses the family context and interactions associated with a problem that has been behaviorally defined. According to Weakland and Fisch (1992), assessment begins with who is doing what that is seen as a problem, who sees it as a problem, and how the behavior is seen as a problem: "Our aim is to get as clear and specific a description as possible—who is observably doing and saying what" (p. 308). Clinicians ask questions such as "When does the problem occur?" "How often?" "Where does the problem occur?" "What would I see and hear if I were an invisible observer?" (Cade & O'Hanlon, 1993). Hudson and O'Hanlon (1991) use the term *videotalk* to describe this process. Videotalk is a way to focus families on describing the problem as it would be seen on a videotape. This is an alternative to vague words, interpretations, or generalizations describing the problem, and instead focuses on the facts or what the situation looks or sounds like.

Similarly, the clinician tracks the ways the family has tried to solve the problem. Attempted solutions are often observed to be the vicious interactional cycles that actually maintain the problem. The clinician asks questions such as "How have you tried to solve the problem?" "What does each family member do before and after the problem to try to keep it from happening?" "Who does what to make it better?" "Does it work?" In addition, the exceptions to the problem may also be tracked, so that the clinician has a clear picture of when the problem does not occur and what types of family interactions are associated with those times. The clinician may ask questions such as "Tell me when the problem does not happen." "What did you do differently?" "What activities prevent the problem?" "What activities are prevented because of the problem?" (Cade & O'Hanlon, 1993).

One interviewing technique used to help clinicians systematically track family interactions and context associated with a presenting problem is the Film Strip. In this method, the sequences of behavior are defined and the persons involved before and after the problem behavior are specified. In the first session, the family is told that the clinician would like to see the film of their problem. The clinician may draw a Film Strip on a piece of paper, a chalkboard, or a flip chart; usually the clinician will draw two vertical lines with several horizontal lines, making up blocks, or "frames," up and down the vertical lines so that when the drawing is complete, it looks like a ladder. Then the clinician may write the problem in one of the blocks (usually near the middle) and proceed to find out more about the interactional context of the problem. For example, the clinician may ask "Who was there when the problem occurred?" "What were they doing?" "Where in the house did it happen?" and so on.

After the clinician has fully identified the context of the problem and has a clear picture of what was happening at the time it occurred, he or she may proceed to ask the family about the "frames" that occurred just before the problem happened. Usually, the "frames" are broken into blocks of five or 10 minutes to track the antecedents and context of a problem. For example, the clinician will ask "What were you doing just five minutes before the problem happened?" "Who was doing what?" "Where were you in the house?" "Who was gone and who was present?" In this manner, the clinician develops a clear and descriptive assessment of the behavior of the family just prior to the occurrence of the problem and records it on the Film Strip drawing. Together, they proceed in the same way to track what happened after the problem occurred. This continues until some type of resolution to the problem is reached or a stand-off occurs in which nothing else seems to be happening; for example, family members may elect just to go away from each other or forget it. However, the social worker always seeks to know how the Film Strip ended.

Tracking the problem, attempted solutions, and exceptions to the problem unveil the systemic pattern that maintains the problem. As the pattern emerges, clinicians may introduce small changes into the family pattern even as they continue to assess it. These small changes, called pattern interventions, may be introduced very quickly and may make a big difference in the presenting problem (O'Hanlon, 1982).

Pretherapy Change Assessment

Pretherapy change assessment is an interviewing or questioning method that helps clinicians assess family strengths and patterns associated with their problem-solving resources. This method developed within the brief, solution-focused family therapies (de Shazer, 1982, 1985; Lipchick, 1986; Weiner-Davis, de Shazer, & Gingerich, 1987). (See Chapter 5 for a review of solution-focused therapy.) Although pretherapy change assessment may be employed in different ways, basically its purpose is to find out how the family is managing the problem and changing before the first session. The assumption is that people often improve even before they come to the first session, and there are times when the problem is not occurring and the family is coping well. Information about presession change may be collected by a clinician in a telephone interview and is used immediately to begin constructing the therapeutic solution within the first session.

Pretherapy assessment questions are similar to the ones used in the tracking method described above. Clinicians are especially interested in those situations when the problem does not occur and in any improvements that may happen before the first session. In addition, the clinician wants to know how families will know the problem is solved and what would have to happen for the family to notice the first signs of improvement. The questions are shaped to get families to describe the presenting problem specifically, how often it occurs, and the times and patterns present when the presenting problem does not occur. These types of questions make it possible for clinicians to assess the family patterns associated with problem resolution and to amplify changes in those patterns. The following marital case is an example of a pretherapy assessment.

Carly, an Anglo woman in her late 20s, entered therapy to deal with the issue of her inability to achieve orgasm. She has no physical problems that would cause her not to achieve orgasm, and she has been able to achieve orgasm with her husband (Ethan) of six years on nine or ten occasions. However, it has been two years since she was last able to do so.

According to Carly, Ethan becomes frustrated with Carly's problem. He can't understand why her obtaining an orgasm is so difficult. She states that Ethan tries everything to help her, every position and technique he knows. He tells her that he has never had this problem with other partners. Carly claims that she had never experienced difficulty achieving orgasm until her marriage to Ethan. She states that it doesn't bother her much that she doesn't have orgasms, but she feels she is disappointing her husband, and he has become very frustrated and angry with her. Her sex drive, she says, is generally much lower than Ethan's, and they often fight about her unwillingness to engage in sexual activity. Although she is attracted to Ethan, Carly would like more nonsexual contact with him. She says she has told Ethan she likes to be held and cuddled, but he rarely pleases her in this way. He almost never kisses her (Biever & Gardner, 1993).

PRETHERAPY ASSESSMENT[1]

Ethan

CLINICIAN: What makes you think your family needs our services?

ETHAN: Carly cannot have orgasms. I want more sex, but she doesn't like to have sex.

CLINICIAN: What do you expect to happen here that will be helpful to your family?

ETHAN: Learn how to have better sex. Find out why Carly isn't having orgasms.

CLINICIAN: What will convince you that your family does not need to come here?

ETHAN: When we are having good sex again and Carly is having orgasms.

CLINICIAN: How many days per week does the problem occur? [please circle]

ETHAN: 1   2   3   4   5   6   ⑦

CLINICIAN: How many hours per day is the problem present?

ETHAN: All the time.

CLINICIAN: Please place an X indicating the severity of the problem.

ETHAN: 1<——————————-5——————————X>10
very mild   very severe

CLINICIAN: Who will be the first person to notice an improvement in the problem?

ETHAN: I will because I will notice that we are having more sex and she is enjoying it.

CLINICIAN: What is one of the first things your family will be doing differently when they notice improvement?
ETHAN: Having more sex.
CLINICIAN: What are you doing to keep things from getting worse?
ETHAN: I don't know; I guess, coming to see a therapist.

Carly

CLINICIAN: What makes you think your family needs our services?
CARLY: We are fighting about sex. I don't have orgasms and my husband is very upset with me. We need to improve our relationship. I would like more nonsexual contact with him.
CLINICIAN: What do you expect to happen here that will be helpful to your family?
CARLY: I am not sure, but I hope we will improve our relationship and that we both will be happy with our sex life.
CLINICIAN: What will convince you that your family does not need to come here?
CARLY: If we got along better, stopped fighting about sex. I think Ethan would be happier with me and stop pressuring me to have orgasms. We would have more nonsexual contact.
CLINICIAN: How many days per week does the problem occur? [please circle]
CARLY: 1   2   3   4   5   6   ⑦(Every day we try to have sex.)
CLINICIAN: How many hours per day is the problem present?
CARLY: Only when we try to have sex.
CLINICIAN: Please place an X indicating the severity of the problem.
CARLY: 1<————————————-5—————————-X————>10
              very mild   very severe
CLINICIAN: Who will be the first person to notice an improvement in the problem?
CARLY: I am not sure who would be first. I will notice that Ethan isn't angry with me and isn't pressuring me to have sex.
CLINICIAN: What is one of the first things your family will be doing differently when they notice improvement?
CARLY: I think we will be spending more time together and not fighting about sex. Ethan will give me more affection.
CLINICIAN: When does your family *not* have the problem?
CARLY: The problem has been getting worse lately. It has been about two years since we didn't have the problem. It is better when we don't try and have sex because we fight about me not having orgasms and Ethan gets very upset.
CLINICIAN: How do you explain when the problem does not happen?
CARLY: It doesn't happen mostly when I stay away from Ethan or we spend time together without having sex or bringing up our other problems we disagree about.
CLINICIAN: How will you know when the problem is really solved?

CARLY: When I can spend time with Ethan and enjoy it, without feeling pressured. When he gives me a lot of affection and isn't angry with me about sex.

CLINICIAN: What are you doing to keep things from getting worse?

CARLY: I try not to get in arguments with Ethan by saying "let's do something else besides having sex." Sometimes this works and we may even end up having sex later but the pressure is off.

CLINICIAN: What would tell you that things are getting a little better?

CARLY: If Ethan and I had some really good times together like we used to have about two years ago without all the fighting and pressure.

Scaling Technique

The scaling technique, developed by de Shazer, Berg, and colleagues at the Brief Family Therapy Center in Milwaukee (see Chapter 5 this volume), is used by the therapist to depict the client's problems along a 10-point continuum or another ordinal scale (e.g., "On a scale of 1 to 10, with 1 showing that you are getting in trouble every day in the class, picking on Johnny and Susi, getting out of your seat and being scolded by your teacher, and 10 showing that instead of fighting with Johnny and Susi you are doing your work, and that you ask permission to get out of your seat, and your teacher says something nice to you, where would you be on that scale now?"). With children, often smiley and sad faces are also used to anchor the two ends of the scale (Franklin & Biever, 1996).

Similar to the scaling technique, Bloom, Fischer, and Orme (1995) describe a "do-it-yourself" measurement technique, referred to here as a "self-anchored scale." Self-anchored scales have also been referred to in the literature as "target complaint scales," "individual problem rating scales," and more recently, "individualized rating scales" (p. 160). As measurement instruments, these serve as ordinal scales.

A wide variety of individualized behaviors, emotions, thoughts, or other experiences may be rated on different metrics on the self-anchored scales. For example, seriousness, intensity, frequency, or importance may be used for the rating dimensions of scales (Bloom et al., 1995). Ratings represent the quantitative dimensions of the scales, but anchors represent the qualitative definitions that give the scale meaning. According to Bloom and colleagues (1995), anchors are important because they define the meaning of the numbers on a rating scale. For this reason, anchors must be collaboratively constructed with the client, using the client's own words and experience. Studies on the psychometric properties of self-anchored scales demonstrate that these scales usually have acceptable validity and reliability. They are a clinically sensitive outcome method compatible with single-case designs. A review of the literature on the validity and reliability of self-anchored scales is provided by Nugent (1992).

Consistent with the previous assessment approaches described, the scaling technique as used in solution-focused therapy is also an intervention method and provides a technique with which practitioners can help clients develop rapid

[1]Unpublished Assessment. (n.d.). The Brief Therapy Institute of Denver, 8120 Sheridan Blvd., Ste. C-112. Westminster, CO, 80030.

solutions to presenting problems. Uses of the scaling technique in the therapy process include the following: asking questions about where the client is on the scale in relation to solving the problem, using the scaling experience to find exceptions to the problems, and employing scales to construct "miracles" or to identify solution behaviors. For example, the therapist asks where on the scale (with 1 representing low and 10 representing high) the client is, and proceeds to ask how the client will get from 1 to 3. The therapist also ask how clients managed to move from a 4 rating to a 5 rating. How did they get that to happen? What new behaviors did they implement or what was different in their lives that made the changes?

Solution-focused therapists may also express surprise that the problem is not worse on the scale as a way of complimenting the client's coping behavior. This may also help change the client's perception of the intractable nature of the problem. The therapist may use the scale along with the "miracle question" by asking the client, "If there were an overnight miracle and you could get to a 9 or 10 on the scale, what would be the first thing you would notice different?" (See Chapter 5 for a description of the miracle question and other methods used in solution-focused therapy.) Solution behaviors described through the use of the scaling technique are often used as specific tasks or homework assignments, prescribed and discussed in future sessions (Franklin, Corcoran, Streeter, & Nowicki, 1997).

Because the scaling technique is a well-known method used in solution-focused therapy, it seems to be a natural approach for monitoring the outcomes of practice. In this way, the scaling technique can be used as an outcome measure in a manner similar to that described by Bloom et al. (1995). Practitioners have recently illustrated its uses for this purpose (e.g., Berg & DeJong, 1996; Franklin et al., 1993, 1997). Franklin and colleagues (1993), for example, illustrate how clinicians working in an agency for homeless and runaway youth used the scaling technique to assess outcomes in their practice.

The scaling technique is demonstrated below with a 15-year-old Hispanic male taken to treatment by his mother for fighting with her and for an active juvenile court case for burglary and criminal trespassing. The solution-oriented goal set by the family was "to get along better with mom." Behaviors anchored at the negative end of the scale included "when asked to do something, talks back," "doesn't do what is asked," and "mom screams and yells." The therapist built on exceptions to the problem to formulate an intervention with the family. Ratings on the client self-anchored scale indicated that the son maintained pretreatment changes, scoring 7 and 8 for the brief duration of the therapy. Statistical analysis indicated significant changes from baseline to intervention. At a three-month follow-up, his mother reported by phone that he was still doing better than he had been before coming to the therapy (Franklin et al., 1997).

Family Task Observations

Observations of family members undertaking structured tasks and role plays are important for assessing family systems functioning. Such tasks as playing a game, planning a vacation, solving a problem, and making a decision have been used to observe the structure and processes in a family. For example, families may be

PROBLEM: Fighting with Mom   GOAL: To get along better with Mom

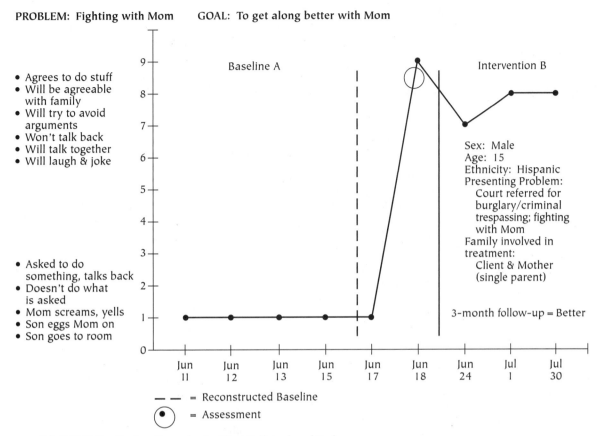

- Agrees to do stuff
- Will be agreeable with family
- Will try to avoid arguments
- Won't talk back
- Will talk together
- Will laugh & joke

- Asked to do something, talks back
- Doesn't do what is asked
- Mom screams, yells
- Son eggs Mom on
- Son goes to room

Baseline A

Intervention B

Sex: Male
Age: 15
Ethnicity: Hispanic
Presenting Problem:
   Court referred for burglary/criminal trespassing; fighting with Mom
Family involved in treatment:
   Client & Mother (single parent)

3-month follow-up = Better

Jun 11   Jun 12   Jun 13   Jun 15   Jun 17   Jun 18   Jun 24   Jul 1   Jul 30

— — = Reconstructed Baseline
⊙ = Assessment

FIGURE 9.1   *Example of a Client Self-Anchored Scale*

asked to decide together what their main issue in therapy is or to plan a vacation together while being observed by the clinician from the corner of the room or through a one-way mirror. Observing families in such a task allows the clinician to view many aspects of family systems functioning, such as roles, power, communication, and decision-making processes. These observations of family processes create a basis for the clinician to begin intervening in the first session by interpreting the information and introducing it back into the family system.

Enactment is another type of structured family task often used in the structural family model. (See Chapter 2 for a discussion of structural family therapy.) Using this method, the practitioner instructs the family to role play or act out a previous situation (Minuchin, 1974). For example, a couple who complains that they argue about how to spend their free time on weekends is asked to reenact the argument in the office while the practitioner observes. In another example, a wife who complains that she is depressed because she cannot talk to her husband might be instructed to tell her husband those feelings now in the session and to talk to him about her feelings. The clinician observes the enactment and begins intervening immediately, even as the role play is going on, to change the family structure and processes. For example, if the therapist observes that the couple avoids conflict and "detours" it onto a child, they may be instructed to solve their own problems and leave the child out of their conversation.

Empirically Derived Assessment Models

Empirical assessment models are derived from research on the classification and assessment of family systems functioning. Empirically derived models to be reviewed include the Olson circumplex family model (Olson, Sprenkle, & Russel, 1979; Olson et al., 1985; Olson, 1986), Beavers's levels of family functioning and competence model (Beavers, 1981; Beavers & Hampson, 1990; Beavers & Voeller, 1983), the McMaster family model (Epstein, Baldwin, & Bishop, 1982, 1983), the Walmyr Family Assessment scales, and the Family Environment Scale. A full exploration of family measurement instruments is beyond the scope of this chapter. Practitioners may wish to consult Jordan and Franklin (1995), Grotevant and Carlson (1989), Corcoran and Fischer (1994), and Toulitas, Perlmutter, and Strauss (1990) for more comprehensive reviews of measurement instruments for family practice.

Olson Circumplex Model

The Olson circumplex model is derived from systems theory and provides a classification schema for understanding marital and family functioning. The classification schema provides a typology of family functioning along three important dimensions: cohesion (emotional bonding), adaptability/flexibility (degree of change in family rules and structure), and communication (facilitative dimension). The communication dimension is considered important for establishing appropriate levels of the other two dimensions. Through research on over 1,000 families over 10 years, Olson and colleagues (1985) have developed a number of empirically derived family inventories that measure these three dimensions of family life, including the Family Satisfaction Inventory and the Family Crisis Oriented Personal Evaluation Scales (F-Copes).

The most famous of the assessment measures is the Family Adaptability and Cohesion Scale (FACES III), which measures the first two dimensions of the circumplex model: cohesion and adaptability/flexibility. The third dimension, communication, may also be assessed using other inventories developed by the authors (e.g., Parent and Adolescent Communication Form). The FACES III is a 20-item, normative-based, paper-and-pencil self-report inventory. It is a brief assessment instrument, taking only about 10 to 15 minutes to complete. The original circumplex model posits a curvilinear understanding of family systems functioning that emphasizes the need for balance in family relationships. Families falling along extreme dimensions of family functioning in cohesion, adaptability, or communication styles are believed to be at risk for dysfunction, whereas those falling into balanced or midrange dimensions are believed to be better adjusted. FACES III categorizes families into 16 types, from lowest to highest, on four categories of the cohesion and adaptability dimensions.

Family systems dimensions of the circumplex model	
Cohesion dimesion	*Adaptability dimension*
a. Disengaged	a. Rigid
b. Separated	b. Structured
c. Connected	c. Flexible
d. Enmeshed	d. Chaotic

Considerable research supports the curvilinear circumplex model using the Clinical Rating Scale (CRS) (Thomas & Olson, 1993), but less support has been found for the self-report measure FACES III (Green, Harris, Forte, & Robinson, 1991). Recently, in response to criticisms concerning the lack of validity of the FACES III to measure the curvilinear circumplex model, Olson and colleagues have reconceptualized the circumplex model as a three-dimensional (3-D) circumplex model. The 3-D model is linear, and the FACES III, when used in conjunction with this model, is believed to provide a valid assessment of family functioning (Olson, 1991). Family practitioners are instructed to use the full 3-D model for their clinical assessments when using the FACES III instrument (Franklin & Streeter, 1993). However, Olson and his colleagues have just completed the new FACES IV, which may allow for a better measurement of the circumplex model using a self-report measure. The FACES II, III, and IV are suitable as screening tools and outcome measures. Practitioners have found it useful to administer both the FACES III and the Family Satisfaction Inventory in a brief therapy setting (Franklin, Nowicki, Trapp, Schwab, & Peterson, 1993).

Beavers Systems Model

The Beavers Systems Model developed over a 25-year period from clinical observations of healthy/competent versus dysfunctional families in treatment and research settings. From this work, three assessment instruments were developed: Beavers Interactional Scales, Family Competence and Style, and the Self-Report Family Inventory. The first two scales are observational clinical rating scales, and the third is a self-report instrument completed by family members (Beavers & Hampson, 1990). The Self-Report Family Inventory is a 36-item, normative-based brief measure. It has acceptable validity and reliability and appears to be suitable as a screening tool and outcome measure.

The Beavers Systems Model (Beavers, 1981; Beavers & Hampson, 1990; Beavers & Voeller, 1983) integrates family systems theory with developmental theory. It seeks to understand the health and competence of families in relation to their ability to produce healthy and competent children. This model classifies families on two axes related to family competence and style. The competence axis classifies families into types along a continuum according to their level of functioning: optimal, adequate, midrange, borderline, and severely disturbed. The stylistic axis classifies families according to their quality of interaction: centripetal and centrifugal. Centrifugal families turn inward and seek pleasure and gratification from within the family, whereas centripetal families turn outward and seek fulfillment in relationships outside the family. Family competence and style converge to produce levels of family functioning that are believed to have implications for the types of difficulties children may have in relation to psychiatric categories.

The McMaster Model of Family Functioning

The McMaster family functioning model (Epstein, Baldwin, & Bishop, 1982) was developed over the past 15 years from clinical work with families at the Brown University and Butler Hospital Family Research Program. This model assesses whole systems functioning and evaluates family structure, organization, and transactional patterns that distinguish healthy from unhealthy families. Two assessment instruments have emerged from this work: the McMaster Clinical Rating Scale, and a self-report family measure, the McMaster Family Assessment Device (FAD), version three. These scales assess seven dimensions of family functioning: problem solving, communication, roles, affective responses, affective involvement, behavior control, and overall family functioning. Each dimension is summarized below.

FAMILY PROBLEM SOLVING

How families solve both instrumental and affective problems. Families are assessed to be most effective when they follow seven steps in their problem-solving efforts:

1. Problem identification
2. Communication of the problem to the appropriate family members
3. Development of a plan and subsequent alternatives (brainstorming)
4. Commitment to a plan
5. Action on the plan
6. Accountability and monitoring of the action
7. Outcome evaluation

Families are assessed as least effective in their problem solving if they cannot accomplish step one.

COMMUNICATION

Clear and direct to masked and indirect. Families with effective communication use a clear and direct style. Those with the least effective style use a masked and indirect style.

ROLES

Instrumental (e.g., financial support), affective (e.g., nurturance and emotional support), and mixed dimensions (e.g., systems maintenance, teaching independent living skills). Assessment of role functioning examines how the family assigns role functions and handles accountability for those functions. Families are assessed to have effective role assignments when all the necessary family functions have been clearly allocated to appropriate family members and some form of monitoring and accountability takes place. Least effective role functioning occurs when the necessary family functions are not addressed or accountability for those functions is not maintained.

AFFECTIVE RESPONSIVENESS

Emotional responses aimed at the well-being of family members and responses to crisis. Families are assessed to have appropriate affective responses when they can demonstrate a full range of emotional responses consistent in degree and congruent with context. Families are least effective when the type and severity of emotional responsiveness is incongruent with context.

AFFECTIVE INVOLVEMENT

A range of emotional involvement, from absence of involvement to symbiotic involvement. Families are assessed to be most effective when they express empathic involvement and least effective with an absence of involvement.

BEHAVIOR CONTROL

Behavioral style assessed from rigid to chaotic. Control of behavior assessed in three areas: dangerous or threatening situations, meeting and expressing family members' needs and drives such as eating, sleeping, or sex, and monitoring interpersonal socializing both within and outside the family. Flexible behavior control is assessed to be most effective and chaotic least effective (Jordan & Franklin, 1995).

The FAD is a 53-item, normative-based measure that can be completed in 15 to 20 minutes, making it a fairly brief comprehensive measure but not a rapid assessment instrument. It does provide a thorough evaluation of families and may be used as an outcome measure.

The Walmyr Assessment Scales

Over the past 20 years, Walter Hudson has developed a set of normative-based, rapid assessment, paper-and-pencil measures for use with families, adolescents, and adult clients (Hudson, Acklin, & Bartosh, 1980; Hudson, 1982; Hudson & Mc-Murtry, 1997). The set of scales was originally called the Clinical Measurement Package. Over the years, Hudson has added to the scales, and they are now referred to as the Walmyr Assessment Scales. A wide variety of clinical measures, they comprise approximately 30 different measurement instruments. Most of the scales were found to have acceptable validity and reliability, and their psychometric characteristics continue to be studied. Most Walmyr Assessment Scales are self-report inventories with 25 items and are scaled on a Likert-type scale from 1 to 7. Clients rate themselves on the following scale:

1 = None of the time
2 = Very rarely
3 = A little of the time
4 = Some of the time
5 = A good part of the time
6 = Most of the time
7 = All of the time

The scales were developed for brief assessment and can be filled out in 10 to 15 minutes. The Walmyr Assessment Scales were developed with the social work practitioner in mind, to provide handy tools for measuring outcomes and monitoring the effectiveness of practice. The goal was to provide social workers with standardized measures that were quick, efficient, easy to use, and applicable to a diversity of problem areas that social workers assess and treat. Among these measures are several instruments that assess marital and family problems and relationships:

1. Index of Marital Satisfaction. Measures degree of satisfaction a client has with his or her present marriage.
2. Index of Family Relations. Measures how clients feel about their family as a whole.
3. Partner Abuse Scale: Nonphysical. Measures the nonphysical abuse a client has experienced in the relationship.
4. Nonphysical Abuse of Partner Scale. Measures the nonphysical abuse a client has inflicted on his or her partner.
5. Partner Abuse Scale: Physical. Measures the physical abuse a client has experienced in the relationship.
6. Physical Abuse of Partner Scale. Measures the physical abuse a client has inflicted on his or her partner.
7. Index of Sexual Satisfaction. Measures the degree of sexual satisfaction a client has in the relationship.
8. Index of Parental Attitudes. Measures the degree of contentment clients have in relationships with their children.
9. Child's Attitude Toward Mother. Measures the magnitude of a child's problem with his or her mother.
10. Child's Attitude Toward Father. Measures the magnitude of a child's problem with his or her father.

Recently, Hudson has also shortened and combined 27 of the Walmyr scales into a comprehensive screening tool known as the Multi-Problem Screening Inventory (Hudson & McMurtry, 1997). The scales on the Multi-Problem Screening Inventory have 9 to 20 items, though most of the scales are very brief, with only 9 to 13 items. The Multi-Problem Screening Inventory gathers information on a wide variety of personal and social problems, including the marital and family areas mentioned above. The measure can be used for problem screening and outcome measurement, which adds to its clinical utility for managed behavioral health care.

The Moos Family Environment Scales

The Moos Family Environment Scales (FES) (Moos & Moos, 1986; Moos & Spinrad, 1984) evolved from research on social climates—that is, the unique personality or attributes of social environments. The FES is a 90-item, normative-based self-report measure that assesses whole family functioning and is compatible with social and ecological systems theory. It serves as a comprehensive measure and not as a rapid assessment tool. Widely used in both clinical research and practice, the FES has been demonstrated to be an effective outcome measure. The FES is made up of 10 subscales and evaluates families' perceptions of their social or interpersonal climate along three dimensions: interpersonal relationships, personal growth, and systems maintenance. Each of these dimensions is made up of subscales that evaluate diverse areas of family functioning.

RELATIONSHIP DIMENSIONS

The first three dimensions measured by the FES are the Relationship Dimensions—cohesion, expressiveness, and conflict—which assess how involved people are in their family and how openly they express both positive and negative feelings. The Cohesion subscale measures the degree of commitment, help, and support family members provide for one another. The Expressiveness subscale taps the extent to which family members are encouraged to act openly and express their feelings directly. The Conflict subscale measures the amount of openly expressed anger, aggression, and conflict among family members.

PERSONAL GROWTH DIMENSIONS

The Personal Growth, or Goal Orientation, subscales focus on the family's goals by tapping the major ways in which a family encourages or inhibits personal growth. The Personal Growth Dimensions include the Independence, Achievement Orientation, Intellectual-Cultural Orientation, Active-Recreational Orientation, and Moral-Religious Emphasis subscales.

The Independence subscale measures the extent to which family members are assertive, are self-sufficient, and make their own decisions. The Achievement Orientation (AO) subscale discovers the extent to which activities, such as school and work, are cast into an achievement-oriented or competitive framework. Degree of interest in political, social, intellectual, and cultural activities is measured by the Intellectual-Cultural Orientation (ICO) subscale. The Active-Recreational Orientation (ARO) subscale taps the extent of participation of social and recreational activities. The Moral-Religious (MR) subscale measures the degree of emphasis on ethical and religious issues and values.

SYSTEM MAINTENANCE DIMENSIONS

The System Maintenance Dimensions, the last set of dimensions measured by the FES, assess the family's emphasis on clear organization, structure, rules, and procedures in running family life. The two subscales in this set are Organization and Control. The Organization subscale measures the importance of clear organization and structure in planning family activities and responsibilities. The Control subscale assesses the extent to which set rules and procedures are used to run family life.

Using Measures as Methods for Change

Throughout this chapter we have been discussing how the family systems assessment methods conceptualize assessment as intervention. The empirically derived assessment measures were developed to provide valid and reliable assessments of specific characteristics and functioning of families; however, these assessment measures may be used to begin facilitating change within the family system and are, indeed, used this way by family therapists (Bagarozzi, 1989). The results of measures are often shared with the family, and this sharing is used to discuss how the family is functioning and the related system's processes and goals for change. For example, if parents of an acting-out adolescent scored as chaotically enmeshed on the FACES III measure, the family therapist might share with the family that the measure seemed to indicate that they were an extremely close family who liked to be very flexible in the way they did things. The clinician may also explain that such closeness and flexibility may become a problem for families during a child's adolescence. Adolescents generally try to become more independent from the family, and they usually need consistent rules and structure to counter their tendencies toward rebellion. In addition, the adolescent may feel a need to assert himself or herself and may be rebelling against the closeness. The clinician may relate the results of the measure back to the family's presenting problem, identify specific patterns, and negotiate goals for change.

Franklin (1996) further demonstrated how standardized measures like the Family Environment Scale described above could be used like the scaling technique to shift cognitive meanings clients develop about the hopelessness of their presenting problems and to move them toward change. For example, with one couple, Rita and John, the FES was used to indicate that in contrast to their presenting complaint, more communication and expressiveness of feelings was happening in their family than they believed. John saw them as expressing themselves less than other families, but at the same time, their situation was not so bad compared to other families. Although Rita wanted John to share more of his feelings, the measure indicated that the amount of sharing was about the same as it was in other families.

Using this favorable comparison, the therapist said, "I would have thought these measures would have been much worse because of all the conflicts reported." The therapist discussed with the couple what they could do to get the measures to change even more into the type of family they wanted. This particular intervention using measurement instruments is logically consistent with the scaling technique and could be considered a modified version of that strategy.

Family Assessment Models in Current Practice Environments

Because family assessment methods focus on introducing rapid change, they seem especially suited for brief therapy settings. In general, family therapy has always been a shorter term practice method, and the brevity of this approach adds to its utility for managed behavioral health care. One of the caveats to this approach for managed care, however, is that all the interventions are based on systems theory, which states that if we alter the functioning of the whole system, the presenting problem will also resolve. The majority of family approaches covered in this book, such as the MRI, solution-focused, and cognitive-behavioral therapies, set as goals the resolution of the presenting problem and alteration of the relationship patterns in the family system. This adds to their utility for brief therapy settings because the focus of the therapy includes behaviorally specific goals, and practitioners and families work toward resolving specific problems as a part of the therapy.

The emphasis on resolution of the presenting problem is important to practitioners because this is what payers and clients are often interested in seeing happen. It may be easy, for example, to sell managed care companies, or clients for that matter, on the idea that family relationships are an important target of intervention when the client's difficulties are primarily interpersonal in nature (e.g., marital conflict, battering), but harder when the problem is more individually focused on mental health issues (e.g., depression, psychosis). Fortunately, a body of empirical literature points to the importance of relationship problems in such areas as depression (Jacobson & Christensen, 1997; O'Leary & Beach, 1990). There is also considerable empirical support for the effectiveness of family therapy with a variety of mental health disorders (Pinsof & Wynne, 1995). The psychoeducational family approach covered in Chapter 7, for example, has been more effective than medication alone and standard care in reducing the relapse rates of clients with schizophrenia (Simon, McNeil, Franklin, & Cooperman, 1991; Goldstein & Milkowitz, 1995).

The pragmatic goal of family practice is to change the problems that brought the person to therapy. Theoretical notions about whether changing family patterns will eliminate presenting problems of clients remain empirical questions. Another caveat for managed care is that because of the process-driven nature of the family assessments and interventions, it may be somewhat difficult to understand the processes employed in using "assessments as interventions." It is difficult, for example, to tell when the assessment ends and the intervention begins. In this manner, assessment has to be treated as just another intervention in change efforts. This characteristic is positive in that there are no delays in treatment, but negative in that it is difficult in systems models to specify what assessment means. For example, how does assessment help us determine which interventions to choose, or how is it used to monitor the progress in treatment? Fortunately, the development of standardized family assessment measures may help by suggesting methods for defining problems and monitoring outcomes in treatment. Combining interviewing and questioning methods with standardized measures may provide popular approaches for use in today's practice contexts.

Commonalities of Family Assessment Methods

This chapter reviewed methods for assessing family systems. Samples and illustrations of interviewing and questioning methods, family task observations, the scaling technique, and empirical assessment models provide a diversity of assessment methods, but they all have important commonalities. First, an essential characteristic emphasized throughout this chapter is that family systems assessment methods serve a dual function and facilitate both assessment and change in family systems. Assessment as intervention is the rule and not the exception in work with families.

Second, family systems assessment methods are based on general systems theory, first-order and second-order cybernetics, and the more recent addition of narrative models (McNamee & Gergen, 1992). Among the underlying assumptions of these theories is the belief that the interactional patterns of family systems exist contextually and that these systemic patterns can be observed and measured, or at least understood.

Third, consistent with their theoretical base in the systems theories, these assessment methods focus on eliciting understanding of the presenting problems of families. The assumption is that presenting problems are relational or interactional and are intricately intertwined with the embedded systemic patterns of the family. It is the job of the family clinician to assess those interactional patterns and intervene in the emergent patterns to resolve the presenting problem. At the same time, however, family therapists usually focus on the resolution of the presenting problems as a first priority for treatment.

Fourth, family systems assessment methods go beyond gaining an understanding of family processes. These methods purposefully assess and intervene in systems patterns in order to get a desired effect. Assessment methods are systematic and are designed to engage or join with the family, or specifically to track systems patterns. Family systems assessment methods generally have been directive and interventive. Even less directive assessment methods, such as circular questions and conversational questions, appear to be indirectly interventive because they purposefully discover and influence the systems patterns of families. In these later methods, however, assessment information and change is viewed as coming from the families and not from the interpretations and manipulations of the clinician.

Finally, systems assessment methods are mostly based on practice wisdom and clinical experience with families. With the exception of the empirically derived assessment measures, no specific studies have examined the effectiveness of these methods or questioned their ability to assess the family systems patterns they claim to assess. However, many clinical case studies point to the creativity, clinical utility, and effectiveness of the family systems assessment methods. These assessment methods are applied with a wide range of family problems and situations and have been judged by clinicians to be useful and effective. Combining methods seems especially useful in today's practice contexts. Family practitioners and researchers will want to experiment further with these methods in their practices and to perform research on the methods' effectiveness.

Summary

This chapter reviewed several techniques for assessing the "whole systems" functioning or systems functioning of family systems. Assessment of systems family functioning is based on systems theory and assumes that the interactions of a family group take on measurable or observable systems behavior patterns that extend beyond the behavior of each family member. Types of family assessment methods reviewed include interviewing and questioning methods, family task observations, the scaling technique, and empirically derived measurement instruments. Assessment as intervention is a unique feature of family assessment methods. Techniques were illustrated using clinical transcripts, examples of specific questions used to assess family interactional patterns, and clinical case materials. The clinical utility of family assessment methods for managed behavioral health care was also discussed. Finally, several similarities between the different family assessment techniques were summarized.

Process Questions

1. What is meant by the phrase "assessment as intervention," and what does this idea mean for practice?

2. What are some examples of questioning techniques used in assessment, and what do these techniques have in common?

3. What is pretherapy change assessment, and how is it important to family practice?

4. What strengths do empirically derived assessment measures such as the FACES III and Hudson scales provide practitioners?

References

ANDERSON, H., & GOOLISHIAN, H. (1992). The client is the expert: A not-knowing approach to therapy. In S. McNamee & K. J. Gergen (Eds.), *Therapy as social construction* (pp. 25–39). Newbury Park, CA: Sage.

AMERICAN PSYCHIATRIC ASSOCIATION. (1994). *Diagnostic and statistical manual of mental disorders* (4th edition). Washington, DC: Author.

BAGAROZZI, D. A. (1989). Family diagnostic testing: A neglected area of expertise for the family psychologist. *The American Journal of Family Therapy, 17*(3), 257–273.

BEAVERS, W. R. (1981). A systems model of family for family therapists. *Journal of Marital and Family Therapy, 7*, 229–307.

BEAVERS, W. R., & HAMPSON, R. B. (1990). *Successful families: Assessment and intervention.* New York: Norton.

BEAVERS, W. R., & VOELLER, M. N. (1983). Family models: Comparing the Olson circumplex model with the Beavers systems model. *Family Process, 22*, 85–98.

BECVAR, D. S., & BECVAR, R. J. (1988). *Family therapy: A systemic integration.* Needleham, MA: Allyn & Bacon.

BERG, I. K., & DEJONG, P. (1996). Solution-building conversations: Co-constructing a sense of competence with clients. *Families in Society, 77*(6), 376–390.

BIEVER, J., & GARDNER, G. (1993). Unpublished Case. San Antonio, TX: Our Lady of the Lake University, Department of Psychology.

BLOOM, M., FISCHER, J., & ORME, J. (1995). *Evaluating practice: Guidelines for the accountable professional.* Englewood Cliffs, NJ: Prentice-Hall.

CADE, B., & O'HANLON, W. H. (1993). *A brief guide to brief therapy.* New York: Norton.

CECCHIN, G. (1987). Hypothesizing, circularity and neutrality revisited: An invitation to curiosity. *Family Process, 26*(4), 405–414.

COMPTON, B., & GALAWAY, B. (1989). *Social work process* (4th ed.). Belmont, CA: Wadsworth.

CORCORAN, K., & FISCHER, J. (1994). *Measures for clinical practice* (2nd ed., Vols. 1–2). New York: Free Press.

DE SHAZER, S. (1982). *Patterns of brief family therapy: An ecosystemic approach.* New York: Guilford.

DE SHAZER, S. (1985). *Keys to solution in brief therapy.* New York: Norton.

EPSTEIN, N. B., BALDWIN, L. M., & BISHOP, D. S. (1982). *McMaster family assessment device (FAD) version 3, manual.* Providence, RI: The Brown University/Butler Hospital Family Research Program.

EPSTEIN, N. B., BALDWIN, L. M., & BISHOP, D. S. (1983). The McMaster family assessment device. *Journal of Marital and Family Therapy, 9*(2), 171–180.

FISCH, R., WEAKLAND, J. H., & SEGAL, L. (1982). *Tactics of change: Doing therapy briefly.* San Francisco: Jossey-Bass.

FLEURIDAS, C., NELSON, T. S., & ROSENTHAL, D. M. (1986). The evolution of circular questions: Training family therapists. *Journal of Marital and Family Therapy, 12*(2), 113–127.

FRANKLIN, C. (1996). Solution-focused therapy: A marital case study using recursive dialectic analysis. *Journal of Family Psychotherapy, 7*(1), 31–51.

FRANKLIN, C., & BIEVER, J. (1996). *Evaluating the effectiveness of solution-focused therapy with learning challenged students using single case designs.* Unpublished manuscript: University of Texas at Austin.

FRANKLIN, C., CORCORAN, J., STREETER, C. L., & NOWICKI, J. (1997). Using client self-anchored scales to measure outcomes in solution-focused therapy. *The Journal of Systemic Therapies, 16*(3), 246–265.

FRANKLIN C., & JORDAN C. (1995). Qualitative assessment: A methodological review. *Families in Society, 76*(5), 281–295.

FRANKLIN, C., NOWICKI, J., TRAPP, J., SCHWAB, A. J., & PETERSEN, J. (1993). A computerized assessment system for brief, crisis oriented youth services. In J. B. Rauch (Ed.), *Assessment: A sourcebook for social work practitioners.* Milwaukee: Families International.

FRANKLIN, C., & STREETER, C. L. (1993). Validity of the 3-D circumplex model for family assessment. *Research on Social Work Practice, 3*(3), 258–275.

GOLDENBERG, I., & GOLDENBERG, H. (1991). *Family therapy: An overview.* Pacific Grove, CA: Brooks/Cole.

GOLDSTEIN, M. J., & MILKOWITZ, D. J. (1995). The effectiveness of psychoeducational family therapy in the treatment of schizophrenic disorders. *Journal of Marital and Family Therapy, 21*, 361–376.

GOOLISHIAN, H., & ANDERSON, H. (1987). Language systems and therapy: An evolving idea. *Psychotherapy, 24*(3S), 529–538.

GREEN, R. G., HARRIS, R. N., FORTE, J. A., & ROBINSON, M. (1991). Evaluating FACES III and the circumplex model: 2,440 families. *Family Process, 30*, 55–73.

GROTEVANT, H. D., & CARLSON, C. I. (1989). *Family assessment: A guide to methods and measures.* New York: Guilford.

HALEY, J. (1990). *Problem solving therapy.* San Francisco: Jossey-Bass.

HEPWORTH, D. H., & LARSEN, J. A. (1991). *Direct social work practice* (4th ed.). Belmont, CA: Wadsworth.

HOFFMAN, L. (1981). *Foundations of family therapy.* New York: Basic Books.

HUDSON, P. O., & O'HANLON, W. H. (1991). *Rewriting love stories: Brief marital therapy.* New York: Norton.

HUDSON, W. W. (1982). *The clinical measurement package.* Homewood, IL: Dorsey Press.

HUDSON, W. W., ACKLIN, J. D., & BARTOSH, J. C. (1980). Assessing discord in family relationships. *Social Work Research and Abstracts, 16*, 21–29.

HUDSON, W. W., & MCMURTRY, S. (1997). Comprehensive assessment in social work practice: The multi-problem screening inventory. *Research on Social Work Practice, 7*, 79–98.

JACOBSON, N. S., & CHRISTENSEN, A. (1997). *Integrative couple therapy.* New York: Norton.

JORDAN, C., & FRANKLIN, C. (1995). *Clinical assessment for social workers: Quantitative and qualitative methods.* Chicago: Lyceum Press.

LIPCHICK, E. (1986). The purposeful interview. *The Journal of Strategic and Systemic Therapies, 5*(1/2), 88–99.

MADANES, C. (1984). *Behind the one-way mirror: Advances in the practice of strategic therapy.* San Francisco: Jossey Bass.

MCNAMEE, S. A., & GERGEN, K. J. (1992). *Therapy as social construction.* Newbury Park, CA: Sage.

MINUCHIN, S. (1974). *Families and family therapy.* Cambridge, MA: Harvard University Press.

MOOS, R. H., & MOOS, B. S. (1986). *Family environment scale.* Palo Alto, CA: Consulting Psychologists Press.

MOOS, R. H., & SPINRAD, S. (1984). *The social climate scales: An annotated bibliography.* Palo Alto, CA: Consulting Psychologists Press.

NUGENT, W. R. (1992). Psychometric characteristics of self-anchored scales in clinical application. *Journal of Social Service Research, 15*, 137–152.

O'BRIEN, C., & BRUGGEN, P. (1985). Our personal and professional lives: Learning positive connotation and circular questioning. *Family Process, 24*, 311–322.

O'HANLON, W. H. (1982). Strategic pattern intervention. *Journal of Strategic and Systemic Therapies, 1*, 26–33.

O'HANLON, W. H., & WEINER-DAVIS M. (1989). *In search of solutions: A new direction in psychotherapy.* New York: Norton.

O'HANLON, W. H., & WILK, J. (1987). *Shifting contexts: A generation of effective psychotherapies.* New York: Guilford.

O'LEARY, K. D., & BEACH, S. R. H. (1990). Marital therapy: A viable treatment for depression and marital discord. *American Journal of Psychiatry, 147*(2), 183–186.

OLSON, D. H. (1986). Circumplex model VII: Validation studies and FACES III. *Family Process, 26*, 337–351.

OLSON, D. H. (1991). Commentary: Three-dimensional (3-D) circumplex model and revised scoring of FACES III. *Family Process, 30*, 74–79.

OLSON, D. H., MCCUBBIN, H. I., BARNES, H., LARSEN, A., MUXEN, M., & WILSON, M. (1985). *Family inventories: Inventories in a national survey of families across the family life cycle* (revised ed.). (Available from Family Social Science, 290 McNeal Hall, University of Minnesota, St. Paul, MN 55108).

OLSON, D. H., SPRENKLE, D. H., & RUSSEL, C. S. (1979). Circumplex model of marital and family systems: Cohesion and adaptability dimensions, family types and clinical applications. *Family Process, 18*, 3–28.

PALAZZOLI, M. S., BOSCOLO, L., CECCHIN, G., & PRATA, G. (1980). Hypothesizing-circularity-neutrality: Three guidelines for the conduct of the session. *Family Process, 19*, 3–12.

PALAZZOLI, M. S., CIRILLO, S., SELVINI, M., & SORRENTINO, A. M. (1989). *Family games: General model of psychotic processes in the family.* New York: Norton.

PINSOF, W. M., & WYNNE, L. C. (1995). The efficacy of marital and family therapy: An empirical overview, conclusions, and recommendations. *Journal of Marital and Family Therapy, 21*, 585–613.

SIMON, C., MCNEIL, J. S., FRANKLIN, C., & COOPERMAN, A. (1991). The family and schizophrenia: Toward a psychoeducational approach. *Families in Society, 72*(6), 323–334.

THOMAS, V., & OLSON, D. H. (1993). Problem families and the Circumplex Model: Observational assessment using the clinical rating scale (CRS). *Journal of Marital and Family Therapy, 19*(2), 159–175.

TOMM, K. (1984). One perspective in the Milan systemic approach: Part II. Description of session format, interviewing style and interventions. *Journal of Marital and Family Therapy, 10*(3), 253–271.

TOMM, K. (1987). Interventive interviewing. *Family Process, 26*(2), 167–183.

TOULITAS, J., PERLMUTTER, B. F., & STRAUS, M. A. (1990). *Handbook of family measurement techniques.* Newbury Park, CA: Sage.

UNPUBLISHED ASSESSMENT. (n.d.). The Brief Therapy Institute of Denver, 8120 Sheridan Blvd., Ste. C-112. Westminster, CO, 80030.

WATZLAWICK, P., WEAKLAND, J. H., & FISCH, R. (1974). *Change: Principles of problem formulation and problem resolution.* New York: Norton.

WEAKLAND, J. H., & FISCH, R. (1992). Brief therapy-MRI style. In S. H. Budman, M. F. Hoyt, & S. Friedman (Eds.), *The first session in brief therapy* (pp. 306–323). New York: Guilford.

WEINER-DAVIS, M., DE SHAZER, S., & GINGERICH, W. (1987). Building on pre-treatment change to construct the therapeutic solution: An exploratory study. *Journal of Marital and Family Therapy, 13*(4), 359–363.

PART THREE

Intervening in Larger Systems and the Sociopolitical Context of Family Practice

hapters 10 through 13 address some of the larger systemic and sociopolitical issues that affect family practice. From a systems viewpoint, family therapy is constrained by the cultural and societal context in which it is practiced. Implementing effective brief therapies without also addressing these larger systems issues is
impossible. Issues such as poverty, oppression, and a history of institutional discrimination affect many families seen by practitioners. In today's practice contexts, therapists work in a multicultural world, and their practices bring them into
contact with people of different socioeconomic status, ethnicity, gender roles, and
sexual orientations. Effective practitioners must be prepared to work with a diversity of lifestyles and beliefs. In addition, they must have a thorough understanding
of the societal and political contexts that affect different family groups within society and be prepared to make interventions in the social policies and larger systems that influence the oppression of families.

Chapter 10 discusses ethnic families of color who have been marginalized by
society and have experienced institutional discrimination. This chapter explores
common problems experienced by African American, Latino, and Native American families and suggests effective family interventions. Case studies are further
presented to help illustrate the interventions. Chapter 11 offers an overview of issues faced by gay and lesbian couples and their families. Effective interventions
for commonly experienced problems are suggested, as well as ways for therapists
to overcome their own heterosexist biases. A case study is presented illustrating
the practical application of these ideas. Chapter 12 addresses gender issues, the

historic oppression of women, and the need for family therapists to become more gender sensitive in their application of family therapy models. A case study is presented showing how a therapist can be gender sensitive in practice. Finally, Chapter 13 examines family policy from the viewpoint of the social policies that influence the oppression of families. The importance of policy interventions to family practice is illustrated by the lack of family-sensitive policy in the United States. In particular, the unfortunate plight of poor families is examined. A case study addresses how these types of issues affect families encountered in clinical practice settings and illustrates what practitioners can do to help families affected by poverty.

Darlene Grant, Ph.D.
University of Texas at Austin

Effective Therapeutic Approaches with Ethnic Families

The primary goal of this chapter is to provide information and insights necessary to inform and enhance treatment with Native American, Latino, and African American families in light of the changing world and growing choice of approaches in family therapy. Numerous authors suggest that knowledge of diversity and its impact on families is of primary importance in achieving effectiveness in today's practice contexts. Ethnic diversity contributes to the ways different groups have come to define problems encountered, the establishment of therapist credibility and rapport, relationship building, and therapeutic efficacy (Atkinson, Morten, & Sue, 1993; Ho, 1987; Lum, 1992; McNeece & DiNitto, 1994; Newfield, 1995; Paniagua, 1994; Sotomayor, 1991; Sue & Zane, 1987). Review of the research literature indicates, however, that knowledge of the clients' cultures is only a beginning: "The knowledge must be transformed into concrete operations and strategies" (Sue & Zane, 1987, p. 39). Effective change strategies are especially important for today's practice contexts of managed behavioral health care.

Consistent with the need to move from knowledge building to application, this chapter presents an overview of concrete, culture-specific techniques responsive to the changing dynamics of the individual, family, and communities—techniques that will remain viable as perspectives on culturally competent practices change over time. Key to these ideals is the growing sense that clients have an ownership role in the change process; equally important is increased attention to reducing potential sources of therapist bias related to racial and ethnic stereotypes that might result in therapeutic ineffectiveness. This chapter also provides a summarized version of the "state of the art" on effective family practice with Native American, Latino, and African-American groups. In attempting to focus on salient group characteristics and concerns that affect family therapy with these groups, the discussion is necessarily cursory and broad at times. The emphasis here is on showing therapists how different ethnic minority groups have coped with oppression and injustice and how therapists can use that knowledge. In other words, to help therapists see how oppression and injustice play a role in problem development and perpetuation. Emphasis is placed on acquiring knowledge of cultures; heterogeneity among groups; susceptibility to numerous problems, strengths, and resiliencies; and the therapeutic skills of listening, developing rapport, expressing honesty, and using flexible thinking approaches and techniques.

These emphases are intended to begin construction of a framework within which to conceptualize client strengths, individual and family roles, relationships and support systems, beliefs, problems and behaviors, anticipated therapeutic outcome, assessments, and specific family therapy modalities and techniques. Using knowledge of salient ethnic issues including race, social class, and use of language, the therapist can build a foundation for choosing appropriate family therapy techniques (Preli & Bernard, 1993). It is important for family therapists to be able to distinguish between behaviors and beliefs representative of the family's ethnicity and related functioning, and their behaviors and beliefs indicative of particular family idiosyncrasies. Therapists must be able to tell when this family functioning is not indicative of pathology but of strength and resourcefulness; examples might be the positive authority of the father, the church as a resource, higher education as a goal, and spirituality. For the purposes of this chapter, ethnicity refers to "shared culture and lifestyles," and race is defined as "a category of persons who are related by a common heredity or ancestry and who are perceived and responded to in terms of external features or traits" (Wilkinson, 1993, p. 19).

This chapter is organized to provide a brief history of the treatment of Native American, Latino, and African Americans in the United States, followed by an examination of family types, customs, major problems or issues, and special considerations for working with families from each group. It would have been desirable to have included other ethnic groups (like Asian-Americans) in addition to those discussed, but the space limitations do not permit a comprehensive examination of family types. Readers are referred to McGoldrick (1996) for a more comprehensive examination of ethnic families. Although other ethnic groups are of critical importance in our practice and political and research dialogue, the ones covered here represent a large number of clients therapists will encounter. Many of the issues of groups that do not appear here—such as their vulnerability to racist, oppressive, discriminatory, and inequitable therapeutic approaches—are similar to those of the groups in this discussion. Note that there is considerable diversity within each group discussed. African Americans, for example, a homogeneous group, exhibit great diversity among families—how and where they live, their language, beliefs about parentage, and so on. In sum, the chapter encourages practitioners to move beyond assimilationist-grounded traditional therapy to approaches that challenge traditional hierarchical relationships between client and therapist, and to move toward true collaboration and client empowerment in the process.

This chapter also offers suggestions regarding effective family treatment models with each group and a number of practical approaches to dealing with problems or issues amenable to family treatment. Some specific problems discussed are alcoholism and other substance abuse, divorce, family violence, juvenile delinquency, and suicide. African American, Latino, and Native American individuals and families have historically been scapegoated in the literature as illustrations of a variety of social problems. In discussions of people of color, readers frequently encounter the pathological perspective, which highlights such issues as poverty and ethnicity, acculturation and assimilation, substance abuse, juvenile delinquency, suicide, family violence, teen pregnancy, spousal abuse, divorce, and HIV (human immunodeficiency virus) and AIDS (acquired immunodeficiency syndrome). Arguments can be made for and against the use of such examples in our discussions of family practice with ethnic families.

In this chapter, reference to such issues is not for the purpose of creating stereotypes but to use cultural context and current therapeutic approaches to explode stereotypes. The greatest contribution of current systemic therapeutic approaches in work with ethnic families is to accomplish more effective and sensitive practice, policy, and research; develop a more informed picture of family structure and functioning; and avoid misinformation and stereotyping. One goal of this discussion is to provide a framework of practice for students and therapists in which they anticipate the positive aspects of ethnic clients and operate from a strengths perspective—behavior that should undergird all of social work practice (Billingsley, 1992; Dickerson, 1995).

Because of practical limitations, *all* the problems resulting from living with cultural stigma, stereotyping, social and institutional disadvantage, discrimination, and prejudice are not presented in this chapter. The omission does not imply irrelevance, nor does it suggest that one problem exists in one group and not the others, or that one type of problem is more widespread or more serious. The reader is referred to the references for this chapter for further resources on problem manifestation and recommended family therapy interventions. Finally, some attempt is made to integrate information about the strengths of each ethnic group that, in the context of family therapy, help to ameliorate problems. Specific therapies explored are network therapy, narrative therapy, structural family therapy, functional family therapy, strategic family therapy, and solution-focused therapy. More specifically, the body of literature related to family empowerment therapy with African Americans, existential therapy with Native Americans, and structural family therapy with Latino-Americans is explored. All these approaches, with the exception of network therapy, are covered in more detail in Chapters 2 through 9. However, many aspects of network therapy, including its emphasis on community-based interventions, are also used in the family preservation approach, which is covered in Chapter 8. In addition, case material is presented illustrating effective intervention with families from each group.

The Impact of Sociocultural Context on Effective Therapy Approaches with Ethnic Families

Our knowledge about ethnic and racial groups is not static. An evolution of knowledge and subsequent practice considerations is particularly evident within the sociopolitical climate of today, in which professional education and training goals focus on building therapists' cultural competence and proficiency. A review of the literature shows that relationship variables, including empathy, respect, validation, and genuineness, rather than specific techniques, are commonly related to positive outcomes (Duncan, 1992). Each of these qualities remains important as therapists evaluate and implement the family therapy approaches discussed in this chapter. Efforts to keep up with trends in practice and the literature will help us understand—within the context of the therapeutic relationship—the circumstances that strengthen or threaten the cultures, and that place groups of people at risk for victimization through the very medium that purports to help (Ruiz & Langrod, 1992).

Some arguments appear in the literature against the proliferation of practice-based paradigms focused on multiculturalism or cultural competency. Satel and Forster (1996) describe multicultural mental health as a

> racial inquisition . . . a disturbing new movement in the mental health field . . . [that] threatens to discredit traditional therapy and replace it with identity politics . . . ranges from gratuitous (advising clinicians to "respect" a patient's cultural heritage) to the misguided (believing that human identity and behavior are primarily culture-dependent) to the near-paranoid (presuming that therapists and patients of different racial groups will experience so much miscommunication and mistrust that the therapist must learn a different set of rules for treating patients of a different race . . . psychobabble . . . particularly mindnumbing . . . [concerned with] discrediting traditional therapy as an oppressive manifestation of a white-dominated culture). (p. 1)

The intent of this chapter is clear: to acknowledge evidence in the literature suggesting that using traditional therapeutic approaches without implicit integration of the cultural specifics of ethnic people may not be as effective as using approaches that do take these issues into consideration. The purpose here is not to disenfranchise therapists but to provide information on therapeutic tools designed to enhance their practice with ethnic families.

Poverty and Ethnicity

Cumulative stress can have many causes for members of ethnic groups: language barriers, poverty, being caught between cultures, loss of identity, marginalization, or changes in cultural values. These can both precipitate and perpetuate problems experienced by Native Americans, Latinos, and African Americans (Ruiz & Langrod, 1992). Specifically highlighting the impact of poverty on Native American, Latino, and African-American family functioning and subsequent efforts in family therapy is important because the stereotype of the poor person in the United States continues to be African American. This perception persists although census figures indicate that about two-thirds of the poor in the United States are white; "however, the percentage of whites below the poverty line is considerably lower than the percentage of minorities below that line" (Coleman & Cressey, 1990, p. 166).

A review of the literature indicates that median incomes in the United States "are differentiated by race, ethnicity, and gender. Blacks receive lower incomes than whites and Hispanics. Females receive lower incomes than males among all racial and ethnic groups" (Tuma & Haworth, 1993, pp. 53–55). (See Chapter 12 for a more detailed discussion of gender issues.) Other correlations are also relevant, such as those among race, poverty, and the occurrence of under-education, higher divorce rates, out-of-marriage childbirth, unemployment, alcoholism, and family violence.

Clearly, ethnic minority groups are differentially treated, have different access to, and differentially utilize goods and services that offer the possibility of problem resolution. All these indicators suggest that a careful therapist will examine different approaches when considering ethnic-sensitive family practice. To work effectively within the context of ethnic diversity, therapists must be aware of clients' cultural backgrounds and be constantly vigilant of any stereotypes they may unconsciously or consciously apply to clients or client situations.

Client-Therapist Matching

Family therapy is typically recommended when an individual's problem is closely related to or negatively impacts family functioning. A primary issue encountered in most discussions of effective intervention with ethnic families is that of the ethnic or racial match or mismatch between client and therapist. Opinions vary on whether matching makes a difference in the establishment and outcome of therapy (Sue, 1988).

The matching issue is a complex one, considering the heterogeneous makeup of ethnic groups, as well as heterogeneity among therapists. The assumption in this discussion is that ethnicity and race do make a difference, but that mismatches are not necessarily detrimental when the cultural competence of the therapist is an implicit requirement of professional education, training, and licensure. This stance suggests, then, that ethnicity and race are critical variables that, when ignored, serve to invalidate important aspects of clients and their families—an invalidation that threatens accessibility to effective therapeutic practices with ethnic families. It is suggested, then, that the white therapist as well as the Native American, Latino, and African American therapist develop a sensitivity to the unique ways client-therapist race and ethnicity affect prognosis, diagnosis, and course of treatment.

Level of Client Acculturation

Variously defined in the literature, *acculturation* used in this discussion is an internal and/or external process involving "the degree of integration of new cultural patterns into the original cultural patterns" (Paniagua, 1994, p. 8). Internal acculturation is exemplified in the movement of African Americans from southern states to northern states during the 1920s and 1940s, or the migration of Mexican-Americans from New York to Florida, or the move of a Native American family from one reservation to another reservation in the United States (Paniagua, 1994). Conversely, external acculturation is exemplified in the migration of residents to other countries, where the values and lifestyles may be dramatically different and the impact of the acculturation processes is more dramatic. Each historical group did encounter new values and lifestyles following their moves that, although new to them, were nevertheless still part of the broader context of American social patterns.

The literature suggests that the more different the new culture is, from what a family is accustomed to, the more dramatic the process of acculturation will be for an individual and family. For example, the impact of acculturation as an internal process would have significant impact on a Native American family's move from a reservation in the Midwest or to New York City. Further, the younger a person is, the easier will be the acculturation process; for older people, it is more difficult. Also, the longer a person is involved in the process of acculturation, the more acculturated he or she becomes (Paniagua, 1994). Inattention to the level of acculturation of a client family may cause difficulty in therapy. The assumption has been that the more unacculturated the client is to American society, the less willing the client or the family will be to yield to the techniques and methods of a therapist who may not be sensitive to cultural rules and taboos.

Native Americans

Historical Context and Characteristics of Native Americans

Native American people have been exploited, oppressed, and nearly decimated since the arrival of white settlers in the Americas. The U.S. government demonstrated disrespect for Native American culture and survival by the forcible removal of Native Americans from their land in the southern United States to land west of the Mississippi River with the Indian Removal Act of 1830 (the Trail of Tears), the systematic killing of Native Americans during the 1849 California Gold Rush, and the 1871 "decree that no American Indian tribe would be recognized as an independent power and that all Native Americans were wards of the federal government" (Lum, 1992, p. 9). Catastrophes like the smallpox epidemics that occurred intermittently from 1520 through 1899, influenza epidemics from 1559 through 1918, and the scarlet fever epidemics from 1637 through 1865 resulted largely from organisms introduced to the population by early explorers and contributed to the death of thousands upon thousands of Native Americans (Stiffarm & Lane, 1992). The medicine man was looked to for healing during these times. The absence of effective "medicine" against the new diseases resulted in the undermining of the medicine man's value to the tribe. This process may have set up an interesting and adversarial precedent for members of the Native American groups who view therapists as medicine people (Paniagua, 1994).

Euroamericans of the time practiced genocidal activities in the form of Indian Wars and extermination campaigns from 1540 through the 1890 massacre at Wounded Knee, South Dakota (Stiffarm & Lane, 1992). When we look at the numbers of Native Americans today, we find a relatively young population whose median age is 18 years (Blount, Thyer, & Frye, 1992). There is an estimated 80% fertility rate for Native American women in urban areas—a statistic that is as much as 210% higher for women in rural areas (Blount et al., 1992).

During the early part of the 20th century, a U.S. policy of assimilation led to Native American children being shipped away to boarding schools as a part of a systematic destruction of Native American traditions, culture, language, and family life (Lum, 1992). The American Indian Education Act of 1972 and the reauthorizations of that act in 1975, 1988, and 1994 have brought improvements in education for Native Americans (Franklin, Waukechon, & Larney, 1995).

The issues of encroachment and dilution remain concerns for Native Americans today, as there is a steady stream of non-Native Americans moving onto reservation land under acts permitted by the 1980 Bureau of Indian Affairs leasing policies (Stiffarm & Lane, 1992). In 1980, as few as 12.1% of residents on some reservations were Native Americans (Stiffarm & Lane, 1992).

Poverty and unemployment are disproportionate problems in the lives of Native Americans. Lum (1992) states that Native Americans have the highest rates of arrest, drinking, and unemployment of any ethnic group. The unemployment rate for Native Americans is reportedly four times that of the national average, and three of the five poorest counties in the nation include Indian reservations (Blount et al., 1992). Chronic poverty and extended periods of unemployment have resulted in substandard housing, poor nutrition, poor health care, and a shortened life expectancy (Blount et al., 1992). The average life expectancy for a Native American is only 44 years, and infant mortality rates are reportedly four times that of whites (Ho, 1987). Along with their effect on basic health, poverty and high unemployment have led many younger Native Americans to move to more urban areas, thereby weakening their ties to the reservation and Native American traditions (Sue & Sue, 1990).

Family Structure and Customs

Today, over half of Native Americans (about 63%) live in multiethnic urban areas instead of traditional communities (Westermeyer, 1992). An estimated 173 (Lum, 1992) to 530 (Sue & Sue, 1990) Native American tribes exist today, each with its own culture, beliefs, and values, and these tribes represent more than 200 different spoken languages (Franklin et al., 1995). Family structure varies from tribe to tribe; however, scholars have attempted to offer some general observations about the family and social structure of Native Americans.

A common division of Native American values yields four spheres of influence: God, the self, relationship with others, and relationship with the world (Axelson, 1993). Several related themes appear, including general cultural rules that apply across tribes; these include taboos against violent behavior, casual sexuality, or putting individual needs above the needs of the tribe or community (Westermeyer, 1992).

The first of these values, religion, plays a major role in the development and lives of Native Americans. Ho (1987) writes:

> Religion is incorporated into their being from the time of conception, when many tribes perform rites and rituals to ensure the delivery of a healthy baby, to the death ceremonies, where great care is taken to promote the return of the person's spirit to the life after this one. (p. 73)

The types of ceremonies and religions practiced may vary, but the importance of spirituality is fairly universal among Native American tribes. The "God" of the Native American is viewed as positive, benevolent, and part of daily living (Axelson, 1993). Whereas religion is more formalized in mainstream culture, it is an integral part of Native American culture, with praying and observances of spirituality being common, daily experiences.

The other three major values—the self, the relationship with others, and the relationship with the world—are often so enmeshed that they can be discussed together. Traditionally, the model of family structure assigned by scholars to Native Americans was that of the extended family. Sue and Sue (1990) refer to the extended family as "the basic unit" for most tribes. Despite the popularity of this idea, the traditional extended family model of family structure is not universally found among Native Americans (Devore & Schlesinger, 1991). This often-asserted misconception has its basis in early anthropological studies of Native American family life. The literature on the family and culture of Native Americans is changing, with new concepts replacing outdated reports.

The most recent research details a more flexible model based on interdependence rather than the traditional extended family network. Devore and Schlesinger (1991) maintain that while some family structures may include aspects of the nuclear and extended family models, Native American families are not limited to these traditional boundaries:

> An American Indian family may be a network that includes several households who may live in close proximity, assuming village-type community characteristics, or it may consist of several households in each of several states, forming an interstate family structure. These families, villages or interstate structures, are active kinship networks that include parents, children, aunts, uncles, cousins, and grandparents. . . . The openness of the structure allows for the incorporation of significant nonkin as family members with responsibilities equal to those of all other family members. (p. 272)

Closeness, collective problem solving, equal responsibility for young children, and sharing of resources are indicative of interdependence (Blount et al., 1992). The interdependence observed in Native American families reflects a connection and tie between family members that influences many decisions and actions. For example, family members may limit the geographical areas in which they are willing to accept a job in order to remain close to their families (Devore & Schlesinger, 1991).

Interdependence is also revealed in the responsibility family members take for each other and for the raising and disciplining of children. "Among all tribes, children are of utmost importance for they represent the renewal of life" (Ho, 1987). Frequently, children are raised by aunts, uncles, and grandparents, who, while living in separate households, still strive to play a vital, traditional role in the upbringing of the family's children. In fact, grandparents "retain official and symbolic leadership in family communities" (Lum, 1992, p. 42). This leadership is exhibited by the daily contact and communication between grandparents and grandchildren. Grandparents have the right and obligation to help rear their children's children. In this light, Native American parents "seldom overrule corrective measures from their elders" (Lum, 1992, p. 42).

Elders in Native American culture are viewed as the norm-setters, with their acceptance and approval being sought by younger members of the community. However, with more and more younger Native Americans living in the majority culture instead of in the traditional community, the position of elders is not as highly revered as in the past (Ho, 1987). For more traditional or bicultural Indians, however, elders are still considered the reservoirs for "the wisdom of life" and are given the task of acquainting children with traditions, customs, legends, and myths (Axelson, 1993). This respect for elders also allows unrelated community leaders to be incorporated into the family and assume caretaking and instructive roles (Lum, 1992).

The tribe is perceived as extended family and valued in that capacity. Axelson (1993) maintains that while tribal affiliations and relationships do not fall strictly under the umbrella of a family structure model, "the feeling of never being alone has dimensions similar to those of an extended family" (p. 290). Native Americans view themselves and their families as extensions of their tribe, and this perception provides a sense of belonging and security and promotes the interdependent relationship (Sue & Sue, 1990).

The individual's functioning in interpersonal relationships is of key importance to understanding and gaining competence in work with Native American families. According to many Native Americans, "the self" is a vital component of nature, "woven into life, the universe, and the total scheme of the world" (Axelson, 1993, p. 69). One's true self is reflected by what nature shows. In other words, the accurate measure of an individual will be shown through his or her actions in and reactions to life and its hardships. Whereas mainstream culture maintains that individual needs and rights often take precedence over the welfare of the group, Native American culture asserts the precedence of the individual only when it is in harmony with nature and functioning for the good of the tribe (Axelson, 1993).

Paniagua (1994) notes that Native Americans on reservations place little value on competition and individualism. However, these traits are necessary for anyone living outside a reservation. This dichotomy provides some insight into the internal dissonance and problems experienced by Native Americans who move from the reservation to large urban settings, where competition for limited resources is fierce and rugged individualism remains the main rule of survival. Even so, Paniagua (1994) and McNeece and DiNitto (1994) caution against the presumption that the move from the reservation to an urban area is automatically associated with impaired functioning and coping difficulties. Research is necessary to help us move away from broad generalities that result in the perpetuation of such presumptions.

Native Americans hold a strong belief in noninterference, a "respect of the rights of others to do as they will, and not to meddle in their affairs" (Ho, 1987, p. 73). Interference in someone's choices without invitation is a blatant insult and sign of disrespect. This does not, however, undermine the value placed on relationships with others, which foster sharing, cooperation, honor, and respect (Sue & Sue, 1990). Life's harshness necessitates cooperation and generosity. Ho (1987) states that this need for cooperation is demonstrated by the common occurrence of "long and arduous discussions generally held until a group decision can be reached" (p. 72). As family and group take precedence over the individual, decisions and actions must not only reflect the consensus of the group but also have the group's best interest in mind.

Major Problems or Issues Encountered by Native Americans Requiring Family Treatment

Native Americans have significant needs in the areas of income, education, health, and mental health (Lum, 1992). Despite these significant needs, Native Americans are the least likely ethnic group to seek or receive services. A variety of factors play into this low utilization of services; among these are the belief that seeking services for psychological problems is a weakness; the presence of institutional barriers such as cost, transportation, waiting time, and impersonal interaction; unwillingness to invite outsiders into the business of the family or tribe; and finally, the lack of Native American counselors (Blount et al., 1992; Ho, 1987; Lum, 1992; Sue & Sue, 1990). It is typical that only when all other resources—family, religious leaders, and tribal leaders—have failed to help resolve the problem will Native American families consider seeking help from the mainstream family health or mental health care system.

ALCOHOLISM AND OTHER SUBSTANCE ABUSE

Of the many problems experienced by the estimated 1.5 million Native Americans in the United States, alcoholism is perhaps the most noted and most virulent (Attneave, 1982; Winick, 1992). Although alcohol usage varies among tribes, it is generally viewed as the leading medical and social problem in Native American culture (Blount et al., 1992; McNeece & DiNitto, 1994). Other substance abuse is more prevalent among Native American youth. McNeece and DiNitto (1994) suggest a correlation between current prohibition of alcohol on 69% of reservations and increased use of inhalants, marijuana, and other drugs by Native American youths. They further suggest that the low cost and accessibility of gasoline, paint, and glue on and off reservations has contributed to this increased use. Blount, Thyer, and Frye (1992) report that inhalant use for Native American youths is twice as high as for white youths.

Devore and Schlesinger (1991) suggest that a disproportionate number of Native Americans become alcoholics and develop medical problems associated with chronic heavy drinking, such as accidents, liver cirrhosis, homicide, and suicide. Estimates suggest that as many as 75% of Native American deaths can be traced to alcohol use and abuse (Blount et al., 1992). Death from alcoholism is six-anda-half times greater in the Native American population than in the U.S. population at large (Sue & Sue, 1990). McNeece and DiNitto (1994) report that "American Indian men between the ages of 25 and 44 have the highest rates of alcohol consumption of any ethnic group" (p. 9). The rates of heavy drinking for Native American women are very high as well. The related prevalence of fetal alcohol syndrome is estimated at one out of every 100 births (Blount et al., 1992). The impact of alcoholism on the Native American culture has historically been and remains quite dramatic as suggested by Winick (1992):

> Tribes with low traditional social integration and undergoing acculturation stress are likely to have higher levels of drug dependence. Persons not well-established in socially integrated roles in either white or American Indian society are most likely to become drug dependent. (p. 23)

JUVENILE DELINQUENCY

Native American youths typically have role models who abuse alcohol and/or other drugs. Young (1988) reports that nonalcohol drug use by Native American youths begins at about 11.5 years, and first-time intoxication occurs at approximately 12.3 years. As drugs lower the inhibitions of these youths, involvement in crime and violence will steadily increase, and attention to the values and mores of the family and larger tribe will steadily decrease.

Further, suicide is on the increase among Native American youth, reaching proportions greater than those found among white youths. This suggests two issues: first, drug use has devastating effects, resulting in the deaths of many of young Native Americans; second, many youths are living unengaged on the peripheries of Native American culture and mainstream cultures. Many of these youths live in poverty, with high levels of welfare dependence, school dropout, and unemployment rates (McNeece & DiNitto, 1994). Lacking satisfactory ties to the tribe, societal support, and access to "the American Dream," many of these youths are losing hope, have no identity, and have been unable to find coping strategies that will keep them alive.

SUICIDE

Axelson (1993) asserts that the high suicide rate attributed to Native Americans is occurring only in specific age and sex groups. Males between the ages of 15 and 45 have a substantially higher rate of suicide than non-Native American males, but after the age of 45, Native American male suicide rates are much lower than the national average. Suicide rates among Native Americans peak during their 20s and 30s (Devore & Schlesinger, 1991). Blount, Thyer, and Frye (1992) similarly report that the incidence of suicide for Native Americans over 50 is very low. Nevertheless, Native Americans in general have a disproportionately high suicide rate. Population estimates suggest that 11.6 persons per 100,000 of the U.S. population commit suicide, where as 14.2 per 100,000 in the Native American population commit suicide (Blount et al., 1992). The rate for whites is 12.4 persons per 100,000. Devore and Schlesinger (1991) report that the suicide rates are increasing in some tribes. Although there is controversy as to the exact number and degree of suicides among Native Americans, most scholars and practitioners recognize that it is indeed a major problem in contemporary Native American culture.

Effective Family Treatment Models and Intervention

Many of the problems encountered in family therapy with Native Americans have their origins in cultural deprivation, generational loss of dignity, reservation status, poverty, poor health, lack of education, and loss of ethnic and personal identity (Blount et al., 1992; Tseng & Hsu, 1991). These origins function to shape client-therapist perception and response to the problems. Cultural and family dynamics further contribute to how the therapist assesses and proceeds in family therapy with Native Americans.

The literature suggests three family therapy approaches that give consideration to the interplay of influences of these cultural, familial, and societal dynamics, offering therapists approaches that have yet to produce research of sufficient quantity and quality to be proven effective with Native American families. However, each approach has shown promise as a viable clinical method. These family therapy approaches are network therapy, social construction's narrative therapy, and existential family therapy. (See Chapters 2 through 9 for more detailed illustrations of specific therapy models.) Keeping in mind Shields's (1986) call for a family theory that can be tested, one can see the number of testable concepts in each of these approaches. As noted in Chapter 1, family therapy methods must be researchable, and each method discussed here is backed by research supporting its effectiveness. Measurement capabilities provide the basis for a scientific method for continued theory building and testing of the degree of effectiveness of these approaches with Native Americans and other ethnic groups.

NETWORK THERAPY

Attneave (1982) and Speck and Attneave (1973) developed network therapy while focusing on problems with alcoholism in the Native American family and community. Network therapy allows the therapist to engage the family in "keeping alive their own native language, folkways, crafts, and values associated with their tribal identities" (Tseng & Hsu, 1991, p. 202). Interdependence of members is stressed, as the natural support system is convened to develop individual and group understanding and creative problem solving (La Fromboise & Low, 1989). The system is used to develop plans for the coordination and effective utilization of resources. The purpose of coordination is to position the system so that "benefits will be experienced by more than just the identified client" (Ivey, Ivey, & Simek-Morgan, 1993, p. 341).

Individuals are able to gain a better sense of how they are part of the broader system and how that system functions at full or diminished capacity according to how individuals function. This approach highlights the concept of group renewal through the use of group consensus techniques, assessment of conflicting positions within the system, mobilization of individuals, working through resistance, and change at the larger community level (Ivey et al., 1993).

Clarification of individual accountability to the group is a challenge for the therapist using network therapy. Perceptions of each individual should be explored and a plan developed that encourages connections with others in the system. The focus on the system in network therapy is a natural fit with the Native American emphasis on building strong interrelationships while maintaining a sense of independence among members. The role of the therapist is not to tell members directly what to do but to facilitate the process of group consensus—a process that may take a long time but is natural to the Native American family (Paniagua, 1994).

The flexibility offered the therapist and the client is characteristic of the need for minimal rule structure, as is the ability to invite new participants such as tribal leaders into the therapeutic process. The goals and purposes of network therapy are congruent with Paniagua's (1994) suggestions of what therapists working with Native Americans should do during the first session, these suggestions include recognizing one's own limited understanding of Native American culture; accepting relatives, friends, medicine people, and tribal leaders; and respecting the family's refusal to answer personal questions.

The challenge for the family therapist using network therapy is the measurement and testability of therapeutic concepts/components. A diagram of individual and family networks and component interrelationships may provide an indication of the system's capacities and areas of weakness or stress. The therapist might also record the areas and number of times the group reaches consensus. The family should gain particular insights into topical areas causing stress and conflict and focus their problem-solving efforts accordingly. Once the family understands the nature of the problem and relates it to the family's ability to mobilize and utilize themselves and their resources, their attempts to solve problems should improve.

NARRATIVE THERAPY

Kilpatrick and Holland (1995) define social constructionism as "a metatheory where behaviors and relationships are seen in terms of organized efforts to create meaning out of personal experiences" (p. 242). In this context, reality is seen as constructed by the client or family; the therapist helps the family author this living story for themselves. The narrative therapy of social constructionism permits the therapeutic "utilization of the power of myth, magic, and ritual" (Tseng & Hsu, 1991, p. 202), which play a significant traditional role in Native American culture. In this approach, the family therapist uses analogies or stories created by clients to illustrate their perspective on everyday life, the meaning events hold for them, and how the whole is organized for them (Holland & Kilpatrick, 1995; Kurtz & Tandy, 1995; Monk, 1996; Walsh & McGraw, 1996). Reality is constructed and reconstructed by the client through the story, which can offer a range of family structures and outcomes, including progress toward a goal, no change in progress, or movement away from a goal (Borden, 1992).

The family therapist attends to various elements in family member narrative accounts to understand what has stressed and what has strengthened each member. As the client tells and retells the story of significant life events, he or she describes philosophies, beliefs, plans, resources, and barriers (Borden, 1992). Intervention, then, focuses on narrative content retold to reframe appraisals of experiences that block efforts toward healing and health. The evolution of narratives that tap into hope, courage, and a higher sense of self and identity is a major goal in the therapeutic approach.

Using the technique "externalization of the problem," the narrative therapist helps the client reframe the problem so that the client no longer sees himself or herself as the problem (O'Hanlon, 1994; Wylie, 1994). "Externalization offers a way of viewing clients as having parts of them that are uncontaminated by the symptom" (O'Hanlon, 1994, p. 24). The therapist attends to each member's construction of the "narrative" truth (Cleveland & Lindsey, 1995), acknowledging the clients' expertise in their own lives. No narrative is right or wrong in comparison to the others. It is the therapist's job to find the alternative themes, values, and plots among stories and interpretations in a family network; these themes will indicate the degree and kind of patterns of meaning all the family members share as well as those that conflict (Holland & Kilpatrick, 1995). The therapist then reflects alternative themes, values, and plots back to the clients.

Holland and Kilpatrick (1995) note that the focus of narrative therapy is not on the problem but on bringing the family's themes and values to awareness. The therapist, while not offering "technical" fixes, must attend to any denials or destructive interpretations the family may construct. In this capacity, the therapist searches for barriers to a family's healthy construction of themes and values; these barriers, particularly with ethnic families, will often be issues of prejudice, discrimination, and social injustice, such as being denied basic resources and opportunities. Korin (1994) cautions the family therapist that the "narrative approaches for culturally and socially disempowered clients are ineffective if they do not also incorporate the impact of cultural context and social status on the problems at hand" (p. 138). Korin suggests incorporating the development of personal and social consciousness into narrative approaches. The enhanced narrative approach would promote the critical thinking necessary to examine the dynamics and role of oppression in problem manifestation and change—in sum, to promote client empowerment.

With an emphasis on inner experience, narrative family therapy offers numerous ways a therapist can measure and test concepts and therapeutic components. Using a qualitative approach, the therapist might track and assess the various ways the client constructs and reconstructs (1) the problem, (2) events, (3) dialogue, (4) self, and/or (5) family structure. The therapist then focuses on coherence, continuity, and meaning in the telling and retelling to assist clients in learning about and changing their event appraisal and coping skills. This evaluative approach is characteristic of "progressive narrative" and its focus on "movement toward a goal condition" (Borden, 1992, p. 136). (See Chapter 6 for a more detailed discussion of qualitative process outcome studies on narrative approaches.)

EXISTENTIAL FAMILY THERAPY

The therapist using an existential approach is primarily focused on the present—interested in the clients' awareness and sense of "meaning in the world," including an understanding of family and family potentials. The more the family understands meaning and potentials, the greater will be its opportunity to make gains in therapy. This approach is particularly valuable in addressing the needs of Native American families as it may take the form of brief therapy or longer term therapy, and it avoids categorization and "paternalistic efforts by therapists to adjust the values of clients to those of their therapist or those of the established society" (Krill, 1979, p. 147). Further, existentialists' own self-awareness and appreciation for people's complexity plays a critical role in working with the family. In therapeutic interaction, the therapist focuses on understanding the subjective reality of the family. Family members offer insights into the meaning of the situations and relational connections related to the problem and anxieties they are experiencing.

Existential therapy has its roots in the third force or humanistic psychology movement and the work and writings of Viktor Frankl (1965) and Rollo May (1961). Existential and gestalt therapy, as developed by Frederick Perls (1969), are frequently considered related therapies. Existential therapy operates on six assumptions: (1) We have the capacity for self-awareness, (2) we are free agents and therefore must accept responsibility for our choices, (3) we struggle to have a unique identity in relation to knowing and interacting with others, (4) our capacities to recreate ourselves are unlimited, (5) suffering and anxiety are a part of being human, and (6) death is inevitable (Downing, 1975; Krill, 1979). Families may experience anxiety related to existential conflicts, such as making key choices about an individual member, accepting the responsibility of freedom of choice, and facing the eventual death of a family member.

Few "existential techniques" flow from an examination of existential family therapy, making a precise description and measurement of this highly philosophical approach somewhat intangible. However, consistency with these basic philosophical assumptions suggests that the existential therapist's overall technique involves reflection of feelings and information in a warm, understanding, accepting, and permissive relational environment. Measurement and testability of concepts in existential family therapy might, for example, involve the tracking of therapist reflection, task assignments, and client response in a qualitative manner. The family therapist using an existential approach encourages the client to (1) go beyond the surface or obvious to achieve greater understanding of self, (2) be aware of responsibility for behavior, and face the reality of existing unchangeable conditions, and (3) transcend the present, and transcend control by contemplating and pursuing what can be (Downing, 1975).

Case Example

Peggy was a 28-year-old Native American registered nurse with no children. She lived with two older brothers, one younger brother, and her 65-year-old mother who was in failing health due to cirrhosis of the liver. Peggy had been her mother's primary caretaker since her father's death two years prior to initiating therapy. She paid the bills and frequently bailed her older brothers out of jail for drunk driving and public intoxication. She worked hard to isolate her younger brother from the family problems and keep him in school, hoping that he would be the one to escape the curse of alcoholism and death that seemed to plague their family.

Peggy had hurt her back on the job while lifting a noncooperative patient and had experienced severe back pain, which had made working on her feet difficult for several months. She had tried exercise and physical therapy and later muscle relaxants to relieve the discomfort. These administrations did not seem to work. Life at home was increasingly stressful as her mother and older brothers continued to drink and have drinking-related problems; as a result, she had to work late into the night, cleaning and keeping the peace. When intoxicated, her older brothers frequently accused her of turning her back on family traditions since she had become a registered nurse earning what they considered a lot of money.

Still experiencing severe back pain, she turned to drinking vodka with and without the muscle relaxants after work to numb herself to the discomfort. Referred by her nurse supervisor, Peggy sought the help of a therapist after reading a school essay written by her younger brother; it spoke of a mythical woman who carried a house on her back for so long that her back broke and she disappeared from her family forever.

During the first therapy session, Peggy reported having been only minimally involved in tribal activities since early adolescence, that she did not sleep well, and that she had a recurring dream about her father and grandfather (both deceased) in which they did chores together around her grandfather's cabin. She described awakening from the dream with a strong feeling that the two men were guiding her toward a way to resolve some of the problems in her life, but she didn't know how to interpret the dream.

Peggy's case provides an example of a Native American family system struggling to survive in a mainstream community. The family is currently unable to provide the structure needed to maximize the potential growth of its members because of extreme stress, sibling alcoholism, and a critically ill parent. The case exhibits numerous culturally related issues, including the brothers' accusations and Peggy's own anxiety about family traditions and the current family situation.

APPLICATION OF EXISTENTIAL FAMILY THERAPY

During evaluation, the therapist's focus was on understanding the family's current experience without focusing on "techniques" other than listening and assessment skills. Peggy, her younger brother, and her mother, it was discovered, were each sensitive to the connection of Peggy's symptoms to the family's dependence on her to keep the family together, just as they had depended on the deceased father and grandfather to do so. Both had died within the past three years. Their desires for change focused on Peggy's ability to maintain control over the two older brothers, keep the mother healthy, and work with the younger brother to succeed. Peggy's little brother was afraid that his mother would die soon and that Peggy would either choose to leave the family because all the work was always left to her, or that she would die also. Peggy's mother had given up on living, and she had anxieties similar to those of her youngest son. Peggy, on the other hand, wanted to be pain-, alcohol-, and pill-free and able to handle family responsibilities while pursuing a life for herself.

The existentialist might assess that this family was living in an *existential vacuum*, "a condition of emptiness and hollowness that results from meaninglessness in life" (Corey, 1996, p. 115), and that each family member suffered from *existential guilt*, "evading the commitment to choosing for themselves" (Corey, 1996, p. 115). In this case, existential therapy dealt primarily with the goals of helping these family members challenge themselves to make choices that would open up their growth possibilities. They were challenged that life wasn't just "happening to them" but that their choices and actions either blocked or enhanced their freedom and growth potential.

Dealing with the symptoms of pain, loss, and helplessness that the therapist had sensed was inhibiting the growth potential of these family members. The therapist actively focused on information from each member's narrative about the family to assign outside tasks or projects. The goal of the tasks was to provide opportunities to raise each family member's self-awareness and enlighten each to his or her own possibilities. Peggy was challenged to join a pain- and stress-management group run by the tribe; here she could also extend her friendship network and immerse herself in cultural awareness. Peggy's younger brother was given the task of attending a 15-week storyteller's workshop run by a tribal chieftain who had a weekly storytelling show on access television. The workshop dealt with building stories about inner strength and spirituality, focusing on self in relation with others past and present, and self in relation to the world. Peggy's mother was encouraged to sit down with her best friend over tea and develop a list of the ways that memories of her husband and father helped her have hope in life and ways they made her sad and want to give up on life. Each of these assignments provided opportunities to move outside the existential vacuum that had evolved following the two significant deaths in the family and allowed each member to choose for himself or herself to what degree their loss, fear, and loneliness would control each one's life.

Section Summary

Considering common treatment issues with Native American families and the case example of Peggy, several recommendations from the empirical and practice literatures for culturally competent family treatment and techniques can be highlighted. This case presents several dilemmas for the therapist, such as a need for consideration of the therapist's own views on alcoholism and how those views affected the interventions chosen. A comprehensive look at the approaches discussed here will emphasize that, in dealing with Native American families, the therapist should learn through observation and participation, invite extended family or other supportive community members, work toward consensus in problem solving, give advice not as a therapist but as a group member, and try to reframe problems to remove blame from group members.

Latino-Americans

Historical Context and Characteristics of Latino-Americans

Latino-Americans comprise the second largest ethnic group in the United States, totaling approximately 21.4 to 22.3 million members in 1990 and 1991 (Axelson, 1993; Paniagua, 1994). Growth of this group is estimated to reach over 39 million by the year 2025 (Axelson, 1993). One reason for this projected growth is the high proportion of women near or at childbearing age in this population. The median age for Latinos was 26.0 in 1990, while it was 33.5 for non-Latinos (Castex, 1994). The U.S. Census Bureau categorizes Latino people as those with ethnic roots in Latin, Central, or South America, including Mexican-Americans, Puerto Ricans, and Cubans, who comprise the majority and largest growing group of Hispanics/Latinos in the United States. The term *Latino* also designates other island dwellers such as Dominicans and Panamanians (Ho, 1987; McNeece, & DiNitto, 1994; Paniagua, 1994).

Latino-Americans are a culturally and ethnically diverse heterogeneous group. Though they have common cultural identities rooted in language, religion, customs, and attitudes toward self, family, and community, these identities are affected by the degree of assimilation into mainstream U.S. society (Axelson, 1993). The incorporation of other European, Indian, and African influences with the Latino culture through intermarriage and cultural fusion has resulted in a balancing of dual cultural values and traditions for many families. Understanding the structure and content of the balance reached is important when intervening with Latino families.

This discussion focuses on the three largest groups of Latinos in the United States: Mexican-Americans, Puerto Rican-Americans, and Cuban-Americans. An estimated 14 million Mexican-Americans live in the United States today (Axelson, 1993). Most Mexicans are of mixed Spanish and Indian ancestry. From the 17th through the 19th centuries, Spain ruled the lands most Indians inhabited, and subsequent domestic unions resulted in a mixture of Spanish and Indian child rearing, Spanish Catholicism, rituals, art, values, and beliefs (Falicov, 1982). Large numbers of Mexicans became American citizens following the American revolt against Mexicans in 1835, after which Arizona, California, Colorado, Nevada, New Mexico, Utah, and Wyoming became part of the United States (Falicov, 1982). Mexico and the United States have had a conflictual relationship. After the Texas War for Independence, 1821 to 1848, Texas was annexed to the United States (1845), and Mexican-Americans lost their lands, attended separate schools, lived in separate neighborhoods, shopped at separate stores, were readily exploited, and migrated en masse from Mexico to the land of opportunity in the Southwestern United States (Falicov, 1982). In California during the 1920s, for example, Mexican-American families, viewed as "expendable and undesirable labor" (Lum, 1992, p. 21), had limited access to social services, were denied relief payments, and were included in mass deportation to Mexico.

The history of Mexican-Americans in this country is one of depressed wages, institutionally imposed poverty, migrant farm work, and child labor (Lum, 1992).

Since the 1960s, lack of employment opportunities in their home countries and poor wages have contributed to an increase in Mexican immigration to the United States; at the same time, U.S. policies prohibiting immigration without sufficient cause has resulted in a large number of Mexicans immigrating illegally (Falicov, 1982; Lum, 1992). Both legal and illegal Mexicans and Mexican-Americans

> suffer discrimination in housing, education and jobs. They work hard at low-paying and low-prestige jobs, are often exploited by employers, have very high unemployment and school dropout rates. The school dropout rate is probably caused by a combination of language difficulties, racial prejudice, and cultural dissonance. (Falicov, 1982, p. 136)

Puerto Ricans experience the same difficulties. Though Puerto Ricans were made citizens of the United States at the beginning of World War I and Puerto Rico has been a commonwealth territory of this country since 1952, the historical relationship of Puerto Rican families as U.S. citizens is framed within a socioeconomic/political context of inequities, classism, and racism.

Facundo (1991) offers one example of how historical practices have contributed to the context within which primarily low-income Puerto Rican families negotiate life. Prior to 1940, Puerto Rico's economy depended on its single major crop, sugar. The U.S. and Puerto Rican governments collaborated to foster Puerto Rico's economic growth. This collaboration, however, did not seem to benefit most Puerto Ricans, as the Puerto Rican government offered U.S. industrialists tax exemptions and cheap labor. Fearing that a larger Puerto Rican population in Puerto Rico would hinder the economy, the governments promoted Puerto Rican immigration to the United States and recommended (sometimes even forced) sterilization for poor women (Facundo, 1991).

Values, beliefs, and ideologies of Puerto Ricans are traditionally linked to social position and class. An estimated 38% of Puerto Rican families in the United States live below the poverty level, with a median family income of $15,185, compared with the mean U.S. family income of $30,853 (Castex, 1994; Facundo, 1991).

Similarly, Cuba has suffered exploitive treatment at U.S. and European hands. Cuba's native Indians were decimated by ill treatment and disease following the landing of Spanish explorers in the late 1400s. West African blacks were imported in the 18th century as slave labor on sugar plantations (Castex, 1994; Facundo, 1991). A nationalist uprising in the 19th century led to Cuba's independence, although the island nation was under U.S. military occupation from 1899 to 1902 and 1906 to 1909, during which time the United States invested heavily in its economy. Fidel Castro took power in 1959 and established a socialist state with sweeping industrial and educational reform, prompting wealthy, predominantly white Cubans to flee the island. A second major wave of immigrants, primarily middle- and upper-class professionals, arrived in the United States from Cuba in the years following the Bay of Pigs invasion in 1961. The refugees in these earlier migrations experienced minimal racial barriers once in the United States, having the educational and financial backing that aided in quick integration into U.S. society (Bernal, 1982).

In 1980, Castro allowed Cubans eager for immigration to the United States to leave Cuba in boats from Mariel, a coastal town on the north side of the island, and they floated to Key West, Florida. Overall, this group of immigrants, predominantly uneducated, nonwhite male laborers, were not as easily accepted into U.S. society and continue to face race and class barriers to their assimilation (Bernal, 1982).

Family Structure and Customs

The wide variations in regional, generational, and socioeconomic features of the three Latino groups described here necessitate rather broad generalizations in this limited space. These generalizations can introduce the reader to common tendencies among Latino populations, but intervention with families in any Latino-American group should be modified to suit the specific needs of that group and that family.

The poverty rate for Latino-Americans is higher than that of whites and the general population (McNeece & DiNitto, 1994). A review of the literature suggests that the stress of poverty and dual cultural expectations contributes to higher rates of single-parent female Latino households than are found in the general U.S. population (Castex, 1994; Devore & Schlesinger, 1991; McNeece & DiNitto, 1994). This difficult socioeconomic situation is alleviated somewhat by the traditional Latino emphasis on extended family relationships (Ho, 1987; Paniagua, 1994). The family relationship is paramount, particularly for more traditional families. When possible, aunts, uncles, grandparents, and cousins will often live as close to each other as possible. Godparents also play an important role as additional parents, accepting the responsibility of acting as guardians throughout the child's life. However, the cohesion that accompanies this tradition of extended kinship ties, or *familismo*, often diminishes in the second and third generations of immigrants or migrants (Ho, 1987). Younger Latinos often see the traditional family values, customs, and language as restrictive (Devore & Schlesinger, 1991). In spite of generational differentiation, members of the younger generation continue to adhere to the traditional launching of young adults through marriage, frequently establishing residence with the husband's parents because of economic constraints on establishing their own households (Falicov, 1982).

Although the family is of great importance in the traditional Latino culture, the individual is also important for what he or she has to offer the community (Paniagua, 1994; Romo & Falbo, 1996). The collective is important, and affiliation and cooperation among kin often contribute to successful problem resolution. This emphasis on *familismo* lends itself to family therapy approaches that emphasize structure and generational boundaries. Falicov (1982) recommends culturally sensitive modifications to structural and strategic family therapy approaches in work with Latino families.

Traditionally, Latino cultures value linearity demonstrated in hierarchical role-structured relationships, determined by age, sex, generation, and birth order, with little or no role flexibility (Falicov, 1982; Ho, 1987; Ordaz & de Anda, 1996; Sue & Zane, 1987). In the traditional family system, the father is the head of the family—aggressive, courageous, and protective of women and children; and women are expected to be humble, submissive, and virtuous—to take care of the children, to be Madonna-like, and to be spiritually superior to men, though not as autonomous (Falicov, 1982; Paniagua, 1994). The therapist should not begin intervention by focusing on changing these beliefs but should instead focus on enhancing the family's understanding of how their beliefs, acculturation, and other issues contribute to conflicts among members and exploring ways to function biculturally.

Major Problems or Issues Encountered by Hispanics Requiring Family Treatment

ALCOHOLISM AND DRUG ADDICTION

Results of the 1988 National Household Survey on Drug Abuse (NHSDA) show that Latino-Americans have lower rates of alcohol problems than the general U.S. population. The results also suggest, however, that Latino-Americans use cocaine, crack, inhalants, and heroin at a rate slightly higher than that of the general population (Ruiz & Langrod, 1992). Negative consequences of alcoholism and drug addiction include overdoses, accidents, adverse birth outcomes, suicides, psychiatric problems, and failure in school or employment (De la Rosa, 1991, p. 46). When language complicates the acculturation process, Latino Americans have increased vulnerability to alcoholism and drug addiction. However, despite these common problems, several Latino cultural variables contribute to decreased risk from and increased resilience to addiction, including strong ties to Latino family and culture.

FAMILY VIOLENCE

Traditional Latino cultural norms sanction the absolute authority of men in the family. Espin (1995) suggested that many Latino women will put up with a man's abuses because "having a man around is an important source of a woman's sense of self-worth" (p. 424). This situation, coupled with psychological distress, alcoholism, and low income, contributes to frequent reports of domestic violence, particularly in low-income Latino families (Facundo, 1991). Facundo (1991) warns that therapeutic approaches that fail to consider these issues may be ineffective.

JUVENILE DELINQUENCY

The occurrence among adolescents of problems of school failure, juvenile drug abuse, and juvenile delinquency tend to coexist and reinforce each other in Native American, Latino-American, and African-American groups (De la Rosa, 1991; Rio, Santisteban, & Szapocznik, 1991). Of Americans with Hispanic/Latino heritage, for example, Puerto Rican students have the highest school dropout rate and high levels of adult male alcoholism and drug addiction (Facundo, 1991; McNeece & DiNitto, 1994). Rio, Santisteban, and Szapocznik (1991) emphasize the impact of acculturation, which happens relatively quickly in Latino youth and much slower in adults. A perceived need to acculturate quickly commonly results in the rejection of Latino culture by the young Latinos, and discomfort within the new culture often results in a rejection of it by their parents. This new difference in cultural perceptions often exacerbates existing rifts between parents and adolescents, and this strained relationship is sometimes made even more so by adolescent alcohol and drug use. Family dynamics and interactions that develop will reinforce and maintain the rift and problem behavior. Intercultural and intergenerational conflict escalate and are believed "to give rise to high rates of behavioral-problem syndromes in adolescents" (Rio et al., 1991, p. 202).

TEEN PREGNANCY

Teen pregnancy is a problem confronting adolescents from all groups in the United States. Alan Guttmacher Institute statistics from 1994 show that one million teens—12% of all women aged 15 to 19—become pregnant each year in the United States. Eighty-three percent of these teen mothers are from poor or low-income families, and a disproportionate number of them are Latino or African American. Latino-Americans currently have the second highest birth rate of all ethnic minority groups. Puerto Ricans and Mexican-Americans have higher fertility rates than Cuban-Americans (Aponte & Crouch, 1995). Many Latino-American children under age six (44%) live with only one parent (Chavez & Roney, 1990).

Effective Family Treatment Models and Intervention

The previous discussion implies evidence of cultural characteristics and dynamics of *familismo* that when given attention can result in a match, or fit, with several family therapy approaches and may result in more effective service delivery. Ho (1987), for example, suggested that the traditional hierarchical structure of communication in the family results in a view of therapists as authority figures, who, although high on the vertical and hierarchical role structure, can loose credibility if the authoritarian parental position is not respected or if the power of the therapist is used in a threatening or culturally insensitive manner. Further, the service provider must consider tapping into the mental health services tradition that is characteristic of the culture. *Curanderas, espiritistas,* or *santeras,* for example, are Latino women who unofficially provide these services to those who believe in alternative approaches to health care (Espin, 1995).

Sue and Zane (1987) suggest that Latino-Americans value "a present-time orientation in therapy" (p. 38), and failure to recognize this will impede effective therapy. Network therapy and narrative therapy as discussed above, are each recommended in work with Latino families. Rio, Santisteban, and Szapocznik (1991) suggest that the strategic/structural systems approach is also effective, with its emphasis on antecedent conditions that give rise to and reinforce maladaptive patterns of family behavior and its focus on family and problem structure. Using this approach, the therapist focuses on "minimizing intergenerational culture conflict by teaching the family bicultural skills and a transcultural perspective that could be applied to all areas of family functioning" (Rio et al., 1991, p. 205).

Functional family therapy is also a recommended approach for use with Latino families. Its relabeling component is consistent with Haley's (1963, 1976) techniques of reframing and consistent with Latino families' willingness and ability to shift from a divisive problem focus to an interpersonal, cooperative, *familismo* focus (Ho, 1987). (See Chapter 4, on cognitive-behavioral therapies, for a review of the functional model.) Like the therapies already discussed, the functional family therapy approach contains a number of observable, measurable, and testable concepts, including attitudes, decision-making patterns, relabeling, communication skills, expression of feelings, feedback, and active listening. In fact, it is one of the best researched of family therapy models. Measurement capabilities provide the basis for a scientific method for continued theory building and testing of the degree of effectiveness of functional family therapy with Latino-American and other ethnic minority groups. The use of functional family therapy and structural family therapy with Latino-American families are discussed in more detail next, and the reader should refer to the preceding discussion of the network and narrative therapies as well. Strategic family therapy and solution-focused therapy, discussed in the African-American section of this chapter, are also useful for work with Latino-American families.

FUNCTIONAL FAMILY THERAPY

The functional family therapy model is made up of components from ecological, learning, and cognitive theories (Alexander & Parsons, 1982). Alexander and Parsons (1982) define function as "a person's pattern of behaviors, feelings, and thoughts that mediate the amount of psychological relatedness in a relationship with another person" (p. 121). In functional family therapy, the system in which problems and subsequent problem behaviors occur is important. Stimuli-response contingencies are also important when considering the process of behavioral change and information processing for cognitive and behavioral change. (See Chapter 7 for a more detailed discussion of the functional approach.)

In the first phase of functional family therapy, the therapist focuses on client attitude change. After considering the assumptions and expectations family members have of the problem, each other, and the therapy process, in addition to labels family members give the problem and each other, the therapist attempts to initiate more positive perceptions of these concepts. For example, the therapist may reframe the problem to understand and to help the client understand its impact. The therapist may also point out family themes that clarify similarities and differences (Alexander & Parsons, 1982; Barton & Alexander, 1981). The second phase of functional family therapy is an educational phase that focuses on behavioral change through the use of technical aids such as token economies, behavior change charts, and contracting (Alexander & Parsons, 1982). The therapist's goal is to enhance the client's communication and negotiation skills in the family and society. The therapist is also concerned with improving the client's ability to express feelings, be direct, listen, and give feedback (Alexander & Parsons, 1982).

STRUCTURAL FAMILY THERAPY

Napoliello and Sweet (1992) suggest Minuchin's (1974) structural family therapy as an effective modality of choice with Latino families. Structural family therapy has also been suggested as effective in work with African Americans (Sykes, 1987). The structural approach emphasizes the individual in relation to his or her familial and social context as comprising "a whole"; in other words, the individual's interrelationships define who the individual is. Family history is not as important to this approach as present family structure, although the fact that current family structure evolved out of family history is acknowledged (Cleveland & Lindsey, 1995). The therapist looks for historical and current themes, beliefs, and views that reinforce the structure of the family, coalitions, balances and imbalances, number of members, flexibility and capacity to change, subsystems, and interesting dynamics (Cleveland & Lindsey, 1995; Figley & Nelson, 1990).

There is a natural complementarity in Latinos' beliefs and practices, in structural family therapy's mutuality, support, and reciprocity, and in the view of the family as both dynamic and powerful. Free to act spontaneously as an active member and leader of the family (Cleveland & Lindsey, 1995), the structural family therapist should have as a goal joining the family, experiencing their reality, and "assuming a leadership role in order to dissolve dysfunctional family transactions" (Napoliello & Sweet, 1992, p. 157). It is important that this leadership role not usurp the power of father, mother, or grandparents; at the same time, the therapist should use his or her credibility as an empathic, knowledgeable advocate for the family's health and success. Joining the family also means the therapist must be accommodating and make adjustments in therapeutic style while working to change the behavior of family members. In this effort, it is recommended that the therapist attend ceremonies, be spontaneous and honest in therapy, have a sense of humor, and demonstrate the ability to function in the present context instead of the linear strictures of Western time consciousness (Napoliello & Sweet, 1992).

Cleveland and Lindsey (1995) summarize the techniques for structured family interventions to include actualizing family transactional patterns through interpretations and the family's descriptions about themselves; enacting transactional patterns through telling and talking; manipulating space through relocating family during sessions based on the use of metaphor; marking boundaries, delineating individual and subsystem boundaries; and redirecting stress. Figley and Nelson (1990) incorporate concepts and direct techniques, recommending that the therapist engage in some of the following: altering conversational sequences, blocking communication, challenging individuals to speak for themselves, raising intensity to threshold levels so that the family must reorganize, challenging family myths, and coaching new communication patterns. Some indirect techniques include challenging the family's belief system, reframing, and offering metaphors. The therapist is cautioned to consider ways to temper use of direct techniques such as "blocking communication" when working with ethnic families.

Structural family therapy has a large history of empirical examination with roots in the child guidance movement (Figley & Nelson, 1990; Lappin, 1988). Figley and Nelson (1990), for example, developed a list of empirically derived structural family therapy skills that can be linked to therapeutic effectiveness, the top 20 (out of 100) including "read a family structurally, support family strengths, define the problem, assess how structure is dysfunctional, recognize coalition problems, strengthen boundaries appropriately, conceptualize family interaction, track, intervene in cycle of interaction, keep family connected with therapy process, restructure, join with everyone, demonstrate respect for system's boundaries, loosen boundaries appropriately, establish goals for change, and focus" (p. 230). Each of these components of structural family therapy are measurable using videotaped sessions in which the occurrence of specific techniques during therapy sessions are tracked and counted.

Case Example

Angela, a 17-year-old Mexican-American woman, graduated from high school, got married, and had a son three months later. She and her 18-year-old husband live in subsidized housing several miles from her parents' and sisters' apartments. Angela came to the attention of the hospital social worker early in the pregnancy as a 16-year-old teen mother and was recruited into a teen parenting project at the hospital. Angela was not able to convince the baby's father to attend the program, frequently telling program personnel that he wanted to but could not because his boss depended on him.

When the social worker volunteered to contact his employer to explain the importance of at least monthly participation, Angela became agitated and cried. She eventually admitted that he could not be convinced to attend because he considered raising the child to be her responsibility, not a man's. It was true that he worked a lot, however. Angela thought that he also used work to avoid dealing with their parents, who were upset at the pregnancy before marriage. Angela's father yelled when she visited and called her a whore. Her mother only cried, shaking her head during these episodes. Her husband's mother seemed to be more sympathetic to Angela's situation and offered them a place to live six months before they moved into their apartment after Angela was kicked out of her parent's home.

Six months into the pregnancy, Angela's teen parenting project therapist asked her to develop a list of family, friends, human service providers, and others that she wanted to be involved in raising her son and how she thought they might be involved. Angela was pleasantly surprised to find that her extended family was quite large, including her confirmation teacher and high school counselor; this support group would provide much-needed child care to enable her to hold a job and save money for a better housing situation. Once the list was completed, Angela and the therapist began developing a plan for bringing the extended family together to develop a plan for raising the new baby and improving feelings toward the baby's parents.

This case illustration provides an example of culturally sensitive relationship building and therapeutic techniques indicative of effective individual and family treatment and intervention. The therapist working with Angela used network therapy to help her discover a support system she already had. In accordance with recommended culturally sensitive approaches, the therapist did not rush to her parents' home in an effort to get the parents to change their beliefs, values, and behaviors. However, the therapist was aware of the power of *familismo* in developing an extended family network that would help the young couple with child rearing. In the absence of support from Angela's parents, it was necessary and helpful to reach out to other members of Angela's community, even those who would not typically be considered "family."

APPLICATION OF STRUCTURAL FAMILY THERAPY

Difficulties experienced by the Latino family described in the example can be examined as they relate to family structure. Haley (1976) notes that insight for the therapist and family occurs during and after structural change. The problems experienced by Angela and her husband occurred within a system of individuals committed to traditional role, religious, and economic patterns of transacting. Traditional family roles are seen as necessary for raising a child "properly." The rules in the family were both explicit and implicit, as illustrated by Angela's tearful report that working was her husband's duty and caring for the child was hers. Angela's premarital pregnancy disrupted the homeostasis in both her and her boyfriend's families, a disruption that resulted in marriage and a firm adherence to traditional roles and rules of family transaction. Angela's efforts to work with her teen parenting project social worker were blocked in numerous ways by family pressures for her to take care of the child and her husband, not to worry her husband, and not to depend on a "stranger's" (the social worker's) advice.

During an individual session with Angela, the social worker focused on the fact that all family members were invested in the health and welfare of the unborn child. Using Angela's next "Healthy Baby" examination as the backdrop, the entire family, including Angela's husband and the child's maternal and fraternal grandparents, was invited to participate in gathering family medical and social history information. During the session, which all invited family members attended, the family therapist attended to how members were seated, who was aligned with whom, who was in charge, who interrupted whom, how often, during what content, and how Angela and her husband handled all the interaction. It was clear that Angela and her husband were both overwhelmed during the interaction. He deferred to his mother, who controlled most of the conversation. Angela seemed to be angry with his refusal to challenge his mother; at the same time she emphasized that she wanted to do what her own mother and father thought best.

Lappin (1988) emphasizes that "the therapist's job is to organize the family so that its members can begin to restructure their relationship in the here and now" (p. 235). The therapist in this situation was able to schedule a second family interview to collect further medical and social information. Once they arrived and following a period of information gathering, the therapist confirmed that the pending birth was important to everyone and discussed their strengths in contributing to a strong family system for the child. The therapist then presented a map of the family structure, involving the family in a discussion about which areas of tension contributed to concerns they had about the baby's well-being. Once all family members joined in an examination of how interesting their family structure was, subsequent work focused on new family structure, boundary making, and reframing in light of the marriage of Angela and her husband. New rules and relationships were explored; those that served the purpose of raising the child in a family environment that was as stress free as possible were applauded and celebrated. During a subsequent family session, the therapist developed a new map of the family structure and asked members to comment on the apparent and not-so-apparent changes they had made, including where they sat, who faced whom, and who talked following whom. Angela's husband recounted a recent family cookout when the family had talked about how different they felt toward each other since paying attention to those same structural characteristics of the family. He summarized his discussion with a comment that he finally knew why he worked so much: to avoid all the advice giving and challenges from both families that he felt was strangling him because he was anxious about whether he could even be a good father.

Section Summary

Considering common treatment issues with Latino-American families and the case example of Angela, several recommendations from the empirical and practice literatures for culturally competent family treatment and techniques can be highlighted. This case presents dilemmas for the therapist, such as how to address cross-cultural issues with Angela and her family. A comprehensive look at the approaches discussed here will emphasize that in dealing with Latino-American families, the therapist should learn through observation and participation; he or she should invite extended family or other supportive community members, always being careful not to interfere with or criticize cultural traditions. Reframing problems is an important part of therapy, and clients should be urged to think of a problem as an impetus for a positive change.

African Americans

Historical Context and Characteristics of African Americans

African Americans have been a disenfranchised people in America even before the 1787 legislation that considered an African American property—only three-fifths of a person. Their status in American society barely improved for centuries, often worsening—from indentured servitude to slavery, to the post–Civil War domination of Jim Crow laws and the power of the Ku Klux Klan in the South through the early 1950s. Symbolic of the general sentiment of the day, the 1863 emancipation of the slaves was less a response to the human rights of African Americans than a political strategy to unify the country (Lum, 1992). The brief period of Reconstruction notwithstanding, citizenship was not extended to the free African American, nor were African Americans granted political power or the right to vote. Even today, some Americans view African Americans as uncivilized and inferior (Lum, 1992).

Long-lasting exclusion of African Americans from public services such as orphanages, schools, hospitals, and other state facilities resulted in the development of a familial and community self-help network that addressed the needs of African Americans of all ages, from long before the Civil War and continuing today (Lum, 1992). An example of the impact of informal self-help systems in the African-American community is provided by Link and McCormick (1983):

By 1915, South Carolina (an extreme example) was spending twelve times as much per capita for the education of white children as it did for black children. As a result of these efforts, the illiteracy rate among southern whites was cut in half between 1900 and 1920. Despite all their obstacles, southern blacks made heroic progress, often through educational self-improvement. Black illiteracy declined from 45.5 per cent in 1900 to 23 per cent in 1920. (p. 91)

The psychoanalytic/intrapsychic focus of most therapies during the 1920s, viewing African Americans as rarely amenable to intrapsychic treatment, resulted in even less attention to the social situation that negatively impacted African-American functioning (Lum, 1992). Development and use of culturally biased intelligence tests during this period provided "scientific" evidence of the feeble-mindedness of African Americans. This belief in the inferior mental capacity of African Americans was used to justify the continued exclusion of them from American public life (Link & McCormick, 1983). Further, the focus on cultural pluralism during this time in the United States—the result of mass immigration of people from European countries—perpetuated negative perceptions of African Americans as difficult if not impossible to assimilate (Lum, 1992).

The mid-20th century saw the beginning of real (if slow) changes in African-American social status, with Supreme Court decisions against restrictive housing, segregated interstate busing, and segregated public schooling in 1954 (Lum, 1992). The 1970s and 1980s were a period of recession in the United States, however, and social and political progress for African Americans slowed. Despite this, 25 African Americans were serving in the United States Congress in 1986–1987, and over 100 African Americans were mayors of U.S. cities during that same period.

The situation of African Americans in the United States in the 1990s remains unequal, however. An estimated 40% of young African Americans are unemployed or underemployed (Devore & Schlesinger, 1991). Median income for African Americans in 1991 was $21,423, considerably below the national average of $35,262 and the median income of whites, which was $36,915 (Paniagua, 1994).

Family Structure and Customs

In the face of pervasive institutional and social devaluation in the United States, the African-American community has traditionally functioned as a strong communal interpersonal network of extended families (Billingsley, 1992; Crosbie-Burnett & Lewis, 1993). African-American familism, a critical cultural survival strategy, is similar to that of Native American and Latino families, in which the family's needs take priority over those of the individual (Paniagua, 1994). Various adults contribute to raising African-American children, a practice that extends back to slavery when the child's survival depended on extra-parental caretakers and has continued to the present, when both parents often work outside the home and need extended family child care (Crosbie-Burnett & Lewis, 1994).

A review of the literature suggests that the traditional African-American family centers on children. Informal adoption, for example, is an African-American family tradition. The 1990 U.S. Bureau of the Census, for example, showed that two-thirds of African-American children under 18 live with their grandparents, whose strong kinship ties provide a positive source of nurturance and support. Another reason for the development of the kinship network lies in statistics related to the loss of African-American men through the stresses and impact of stigmatization, discrimination, violence, imprisonment, substance abuse problems, high crime, high school dropout rates, death, and the subsequent prevalence of mother-only households (Griffith & Baker, 1993).

The development of flexible/fluid family roles is a strategy to cope with living as an oppressed people in American society (Crosbie-Burnett & Lewis, 1994; Paniagua, 1994). This flexibility has not always been the case, as patriarchal family structures predate slavery in America (Crosbie-Burnett & Lewis, 1994). This fluidity of roles was a functional adaptation to adverse external conditions (Freeman, 1990). Now, with flexible family/sex roles and household boundaries, both men and women perform traditional housekeeping and child-rearing functions; and when parents are not available, this flexibility allows other members of the family to help bring up the children.

Another adaptation characteristic of African-American families is the value placed on education, which has been traditionally linked to moving the family out of impoverished economic circumstances (Freeman, 1990; Taylor, Chatters, Tucker, & Lewis, 1990). Familism dictates that the family member who is able to obtain a college education, for example, helps parents and siblings lead a more comfortable life.

Major Problems or Issues Encountered by African Americans Requiring Family Treatment

As a minority group in the United States, African-American families face a number of difficulties, including poverty, high rates of HIV and AIDS, high rates of alcohol and drug abuse, violent crime, imprisonment, high birth rates among teens and single women, early school dropout, predominance of mother-only households, high unemployment and underemployment rates, and high rates of marital dissolution (Aponte & Crouch, 1995; Wilson, Phillip, Kohn, & Curry-El, 1995).

ALCOHOLISM AND OTHER SUBSTANCE ABUSE

Though historically African Americans have been temperate, today, cirrhosis due to alcoholism is one of the top 10 causes of mortality in African Americans (Griffith & Baker, 1993; Winick, 1992). Alcoholism became a public health problem for African Americans during Prohibition and the Great Depression (Griffith & Baker 1993; McNeece & DiNitto, 1994). Reasons for the heavy drinking and drug use evident primarily in African-American males include expectations of temporary escape from oppression, high unemployment, and economic depression as well as the disproportionate number of liquor stores and bars operating in African-American residential neighborhoods (McNeece & DiNitto, 1994). With African Americans' high dropout rates from school, marginality, limited access to resources, and impoverished and discriminatory environments, it is not surprising that they are the ethnic group in the United States most vulnerable to drug use and abuse (Brown & Alterman, 1992, p. 863). Research literature suggests that over 3.2 million African Americans use illicit drugs (Brown & Alterman, 1992). There is evidence of lower rates of alcohol use and abuse among African-American teens when compared to white teens; but beyond the age of 20, drinking for whites levels off whereas the number of African Americans who drink heavily increases (Winick, 1992).

DIVORCE

Divorce rates for all Americans have increased since the 1960s (Aponte & Crouch, 1995). At the same time, the percentage of ethnic women who have never married is also increasing. Ahlburg and De Vita (1992) reported that in 1988, nearly half of all African-American women ages 15 to 44 had experienced the dissolution of their first marriage by divorce. The literature suggests that primary reasons for this trend are not related to family stability but to the socioeconomic conditions that have a destructive impact on the African-American family and its support systems (Delaney, 1981; Ho, 1987). It is well documented throughout the literature that more African-American women than men receive college educations (Delaney, 1981; Griffith & Baker, 1993). Because there are more African-American women than men, many women either remain single or marry men with less education—marriages that are at high risk for dissolution (Delaney, 1981)—or marry outside the race—marriages that are even less likely than other African-American marriages to remain intact (Ho, 1987). The rapid increase in divorce rates for African-American couples is illustrated by startling statistics: Since the early 1940s, the percentage of African-American women who divorce has risen from 18% to 67% compared to the steady 50% divorce rate among white Americans (Ahlburg & De Vita, 1992; McKenry & Price, 1995).

Numerous authors discuss the egalitarian structure of African-American marital relationships and suggest power management and conflict resolution as two of the primary problems encountered in marriages established and functioning in the context of societal hostility, discrimination, and racism (Ahlburg & De Vita 1992; McKenry & Price, 1995; Pinderhughes, 1982, 1995). Therapists should recognize this vulnerability of African-American families to power conflicts.

HIV AND AIDS

African Americans and members of other ethnic groups who are diagnosed HIV-positive face homophobia, racism, limited financial resources, alienation, and a lack of ethnic educators (Chavez, 1995). African Americans represent approximately 12% of the U.S. population and 31% of reported AIDS cases (Centers for Disease Control, 1993; Chavez, 1995). Similarly over-represented in the HIV/AIDS population, Latinos represent 6% of the U.S. population and 17% of reported AIDS cases (Centers for Disease Control, 1993; Chavez, 1995). Native Americans make up an estimated 1% of reported AIDS cases (Cummings & Dehart, 1995).

Health beliefs, religious ideals, social mores, family stigma, and limited accessibility of education and services all play a role in HIV/AIDS risk behavior of African Americans (Chavez, 1995; Cummings & Dehart, 1995). Concerns about maintaining relationships are reported most frequently as reasons that about one-third of African-American women take no measures to reduce their risk of HIV infection (Centers for Disease Control, 1993; Cummings & Dehart, 1995, p. 237). Cummings and Dehart (1995) suggest that the sex-ratio imbalances and low marriage success rates may cause females in these African-American and Latino communities to feel pressured into sexual compliance to stay in a relationship. Any adherence to the concept of machismo in both the African-American and Latino communities places both men and women at risk for contracting HIV, as promiscuity continues to be related to virility, and assertive sexual communication by a woman threatens the relationship or results in some form of abuse (Cummings & Dehart, 1995).

Complicating this tendency to ignore safety precautions is the absence of good HIV/AIDS education for African-American communities. A Johns Hopkins School of Medicine study "shows that African Americans do not seek care, do not receive it, and often fail to have the risks of HIV adequately explained" (Chavez, 1995, p. 17). Culturally sensitive family therapy in the context of HIV/AIDS centers around providing education about the disease, mobilizing family and community support systems; providing advocacy with health care, insurance, and housing systems; and engaging clients in focusing on their roles as responsible members of a larger collective. The family therapist should also be aware of the roots of African Americans' distrust of the health care system, which results from repeated negative experiences. In the advocacy role, the therapist may encourage health care providers to take time to explain the risks and consequences of HIV/AIDS to African-American clients. These clients may miss opportunities for involvement in HIV-related clinical trials. The family therapist can ensure that a member of the individual's or family's support network includes someone who can access AIDS research resources to keep abreast of advances in this area.

Effective Family Treatment Models and Intervention

Pinderhughes (1982) states the importance of addressing race in therapy with ethnic families: "As long as racism and oppression maintain the victim system, the goal of family treatment must be to enable the family to cope constructively with those stresses and to counteract their pervasive influence" (pp. 114–115). As racism is multileveled, its impact must be addressed in family therapy at the levels of family, friendship, community, and the larger social system. Cultural sensitivity and competency is conveyed when the therapist expresses interest in family strengths, raises issues of race early in the therapeutic relationship (especially when the therapist is of a different race), and facilitates open discussion of these areas when working with African-American families (Rivers & Morrow, 1995).

Ivey, Ivey, and Simek-Morgan (1993) suggest that in work with African-American families, therapists should use approaches that are active, are intervention oriented, and emphasize social functioning. Family intervention should also address the role and influence of the extended family and social institutions, such as the church, in the lives of African Americans (Cheatham & Stewart, 1990;

Ivey et al., 1993). Community-level work to combat racism aids in the development of rapport with African-American families. The therapist should acknowledge the ability of the individual and family to survive in often hostile and racist social and institutional environments and should always be aware that he or she is conducting the assessment of individual and family functioning in the context of sustained suffering.

Several family therapy approaches can be effective with African-American families, including structural family therapy, strategic family therapy, and solution-focused therapy. Because structural therapy is discussed at some length in the Native American section of this chapter, only strategic family therapy and solution-focused therapy are explored here; however, therapists should not forget the usefulness of structural family therapy with African-American families. (Chapters 2, 3, and 5 discuss these approaches in more detail.)

STRATEGIC FAMILY THERAPY

The focus of strategic family therapy is on changing recurring behaviors that seem to be maintaining the presenting problem (Kilpatrick & Holland, 1995). Therapist interventions require members of the family system to modify their interactions that contribute to the problem, and interventions can be used at any stage of problem development (Kilpatrick & Holland, 1995; Rio et al., 1991). For example, the African-American family's tendency to seek help from family and traditional resources—the church, family and friends—before seeking help from mental health professions frequently results in therapists seeing families who have become fairly entrenched in problem functioning (Paniagua, 1994; Rio et al., 1991). An approach that holds promise for effectiveness regardless of the stage of problem development is important for the repertoire of the culturally competent therapist.

Cheatham and Stewart (1990) devised a five-stage model of family therapy with African-American families, including a strategic stage, during which the therapist assists the family in enacting and owning the plan for change and problem resolution. Guided practice and constructive feedback are used in strategy development (Ivey et al., 1993).

SOLUTION-FOCUSED FAMILY THERAPY

Solution-focused treatment offers African-American clients the opportunity for therapeutic involvement in a brief, nonpathological therapy that uses clients' strengths and resources to develop new ways of viewing their problems and behaving differently (Kilpatrick & Holland, 1995; Kiser & Piercy, 1993). The practice collaboration between therapist and client provides the foundation on which change occurs and clients are supported in change efforts (Kiser & Piercy, 1993). During this collaboration, the African-American client is encouraged to discuss what he or she is doing that is useful toward enhancing the situation. The focus on collaboration, client strengths, and client action is intended to diffuse any threat the client might feel regarding involvement in therapy. This approach holds particular promise in work with African-American families and families from other ethnic groups, because it highlights the importance of "the context in which behaviors occur, the meanings attached to behaviors or contexts, and/or the more general world view of the client" (Kiser & Piercy, 1993, p. 235). In addition, it focuses more on solving the problem than on exploring clients' backgrounds, and this may make ethnic families who are distrustful of therapy more comfortable, as they do not have to provide lengthy personal histories.

As often as possible, the therapist should use compliments to reinforce strengths evident in the client and the client's family. The therapist's interpersonal skills are important in the use of compliments, as overuse would make families suspicious. Kilpatrick and Holland (1995) suggest the use of four formula interventions: (1) asking the client and the family to observe and track family interaction between the current session and the next; (2) asking the client and family to do something different; (3) asking the family to exert some influence over the problem; and (4) suggesting alternative solutions. Finally, the therapist can devise scales and descriptive graphs to quantify the problem and progress on a session-by-session basis.

The solution-focused client-therapist relationship is a partnership that emphasizes client resources and the construction of solutions. Solutions are often developed based on the client's strengths and the client's view of a problem-free life in the future (Kok & Leskela, 1996). With this emphasis, measurement opportunities and concept/therapeutic component testability in solution-focused therapy are quickly available to the therapist; these include the identification and tracking of exceptions (such as times when the family has successfully confronted the problem or escaped it altogether [Kuehl, 1995]), the identification and tracking of therapist compliments and client response, and homework assignments.

Case Example

Joan was a 27-year-old African-American mother of a 6-year-old daughter and a 10-year-old son. All were living with Joan's mother in a two-bedroom apartment in a large northeastern city for three weeks following the breakup of a two-year live-in relationship with Milton. Joan was unemployed and receiving Aid to Families with Dependent Children. Her mother was working full-time at night cleaning offices downtown and had been receiving a small Social Security check since the death of her husband two years before. Child Protective Services (CPS) became involved with this family after Joan voluntarily entered a shelter for battered women following a battering incident and reported that her son had also been physically abused by Milton.

Joan was referred by the CPS worker who was white to a therapist at the Child Guidance Center (CGC) who was also white. During the first session, following an introduction to each other, the therapist asked, "How do you feel about working with a white therapist?" Joan responded that she felt okay about it, and the CGC therapist suggested that Joan feel free to bring racial issues to her attention if they should come up.

Joan reported that her mother nagged her about getting into a cosmetology training program and getting a good job, and her children nagged her about going back home with Milton. Since Joan was then living in a safe environment, the therapist chose to focus on the presenting problems with Joan's mother and the children, proceeding in a way that validated Joan's experience and concerns. Joan revealed that her relationship with Milton had been constantly criticized by her mother; Joan felt ashamed and incompetent because she had to return to her mother for a place to live, and she was untrained and unemployed.

Joan's mother was invited to the third session and spent a large amount of time discussing her desire that Joan use her talents at "doing hair" to get training and a good job. Joan agreed to investigate getting into a cosmetology school. Little headway was made, however, on clarifying other issues that caused problems in their relationship. The therapist emphasized the need for both to minimize criticism of each other until they could work out a strategy for getting along better.

Neither Joan nor her mother went to the next three appointments. The therapist contacted the CPS worker. Joan later reestablished contact with the therapist, explaining that the CPS worker had told her that attendance in therapy had been mandated in her CPS case plan.

APPLICATION OF SOLUTION-FOCUSED THERAPY

This case illustration provides an example of numerous therapeutic challenges as well as challenges in building a culturally sensitive relationship in cross-cultural individual and family treatment and intervention. The therapist used the strategic therapy technique of problem prescription to find out that Joan's problems with her mother involved more than getting into cosmetology school and that these conflicts were affecting Joan's sense of self-worth. The therapist could have continued helping Joan by initiating solution-focused therapy, focusing on how Joan's family behaves in response to the problems, and specifically looking for family resources and strengths available to resolve the problem (Kiser & Piercy, 1993). Joan and her mother would, for example, be asked to list exceptions to how the problem is usually dealt with, which would help them use ways they already knew to deal with problems more effectively, more often.

During the previous relationship with Joan, the therapist had delved into family systems issues before understanding the potential volatility hidden in different problems as voiced by Joan and her mother. The therapist had begun intervention before either family member understood the therapeutic approach that was to be used. Neither Joan nor her mother gained an initial sense of "personal authority" in their efforts to resolve their problems and were quickly suspicious of the purpose and possible outcome of the process with a white therapist. Subsequently, they abandoned the therapeutic process.

A new, solution-focused family strategy was developed for work with Joan after therapy was mandated in her CPS case plan. Joan's mother was easily convinced to attend, as the children's custody was in jeopardy. The same therapist was assigned. This time, the therapist took pains during the initial session to build a relationship and describe the solution-focused/family empowerment approach that would be used in therapy. Boyd-Franklin (1987, 1990) speaks frequently to the need for therapists working with African-American families to organize their perceptions of the family, the problem, and the treatment around the concept/theory of family empowerment. Working with the strengths of African-American families is particularly important in a societal context, where the media and even educational focus is on "the demise of the black family," the high proportion of African-American male prison inmates, teen pregnancy, and addiction. Consequently, moving from a problem-focused framework to a solution-focused one invites the African-American family into the therapeutic alliance in a more positive and empowering way.

In continuing work with Joan and her mother, the therapist, following lengthy discussion with her supervisor and an African-American co-worker, purposefully avoided discussing race during the initial session, focusing instead on how the family, with resource assistance from the system, could solve problems. During the initial session, Joan and her mother recounted their problem-saturated lives, demonstrating a constant attention to the problems with the subsequent frustration and anger that accompanied a lack of change. Kuehl (1995) recommends the use of the solution-oriented genogram to "help clients stem vicious intergenerational cycles of interaction that have interfered in their lives and replace them with virtuous cycles" (p. 239). Considering a solution-oriented focus on self-determination and client empowerment, the therapist worked with Joan and her mother to recreate a family genogram that subsequently illustrated how women throughout their family's history had struggled and succeeded in raising children without the children's fathers.

As they spent time recounting how other women in their family tree had responded to difficult relational and parenting situations, both Joan and her mother were quickly caught up in storytelling about the strong women and men in their family history. The results of this and further solution-focused therapy helped them gain a clearer image of ways to access the extended family network and social service system to bolster Joan's parenting capabilities and educational opportunities. New alternatives to the previous "all you need to do is go to cosmetology school" were discussed and tested. Between sessions, Joan and her mother were given assignments to note the positive characteristics and processes they both possessed in their relationship with each other and Joan's children. The use of between-session investigations and focus on improving problem-solving characteristics of the family for the future are also indicative of solution-focused therapy (Kuehl, 1995).

Section Summary

Realizing that achievement of success occurs in the context of oppression for African Americans, the family therapist's role is to help reconnect the family with the African-American community. In doing so, the family therapist, using a strengths model, provides the African-American family a model of coping skills and networking that extends outside the therapeutic relationship. This case presents dilemmas that the therapist would need to consider carefully, such as how to address the client-therapist racial difference and what effect the family's battering relationships would have on the interventions chosen.

Summary

Examination of useful, culturally aware family therapies has just begun. The exploration here of common issues in African-American, Latino, and Native American families is a general one. Research is needed to discover specific causes and solutions to the problems dealt with daily by ethnic families in the United States. However, the approaches discussed in this chapter—network therapy, narrative therapy, structural family therapy, functional family therapy, strategic family therapy, and solution-focused therapy—are flexible enough to remain viable as perspectives on culturally competent practices change over time. Each approach allows the therapist to recognize and address the culture-specific needs of ethnic families.

Process Questions

1. What do you see as your major challenge in using existential family therapy in your own practice?

2. What do you see as your major challenge in using structural family therapy in your own practice?

3. Of the therapies discussed, what is one skill you would most like to acquire in your work with families from cultures other than your own?

4. Describe areas in which family empowerment theory might be used in each of the therapeutic approaches discussed in this chapter.

References

AHLBURG, D. A., & DE VITA, C. J. (1992). New realities of the American family. *Population Bulletin, 47*(2), 1–44.

ALEXANDER, J. F., & PARSONS, B. V. (1982). *Functional family therapy.* Monterey, CA: Brooks/Cole.

ALAN GUTTMACHER INSTITUTE. (1994). *Facts in brief: Teenage reproductive health in the United States.* New York: Author.

APONTE, J. F., & CROUCH, R. T. (1995). The changing ethnic profile of the United States. In J. F. Aponte, R. Y. Rivers, & J. Wohl, (Eds.), *Psychological interventions and cultural diversity* (pp. 1–18). Boston: Allyn & Bacon.

ATKINSON, D. R., MORTEN, G., & SUE, D. W. (1993). *Counseling American minorities: A cross-cultural perspective* (4th ed.). Dubuque, IA: WCB Brown & Benchmark.

ATTNEAVE, C. (1982). American Indians and Alaska Native families: Emigrants in their own homeland. In M. McGoldrick, J. K. Pearce, & J. Giordano (Eds.),

Ethnicity and family therapy (pp. 87–123). New York: Guilford.

AXELSON, J. A. (1993). *Counseling and development in a multicultural society* (2nd ed). Pacific Grove, CA: Brooks/Cole.

BARTON, C., & ALEXANDER, J. F. (1981). Functional family therapy. In A. S. Gurman & D. P. Kniskern (Eds.), *Handbook of family therapy* (pp. 403–443). New York: Brunner/Mazel.

BERNAL, G. (1982). Cuban families. In M. McGoldrick, J. K. Pearce, & J. Giordano (Eds.), *Ethnicity and family therapy* (pp. 187–207). New York: Guilford.

BILLINGSLEY, A. (1992). *Climbing Jacob's ladder: The enduring legacy of African-American families.* New York: Simon & Schuster.

BLOUNT, M., THYER, B. A., & FRYE, T. (1992). Social work practice with Native Americans. In D. F. Harrison, J. S. Wodarski, & B. A. Thyer (Eds.), *Cultural diversity and social work* (pp. 107–119). Springfield, IL: Charles C. Thomas.

BORDEN, W. (1992). Narrative perspectives in psychosocial intervention following adverse life events. *Social Work, 37*(2), 135–141.

BOYD-FRANKLIN, N. (1987). Group therapy for black women: A therapeutic support model. *American Journal of Orthopsychiatry, 57,* 394–402.

BOYD-FRANKLIN, N. (1990). A multisystems approach to the treatment of a black, inner-city family with a schizophrenic mother. *American Journal of Orthopsychiatry, 60,* 186–196.

BROWN, L. S., Jr., & ALTERMAN, A. I. (1992). Substance abuse in special populations: African Americans. In J. H. Lowinson, P. Ruiz, R. B. Millman, & J. G. Langrod (Eds.), *Substance abuse: A comprehensive textbook* (2nd ed., pp. 861–867). Baltimore: Williams & Wilkins.

CASTEX, G. M. (1994). Providing services to Hispanic/Latino populations: Profiles in diversity. *Social Work, 39*(3), 288–296.

CENTERS FOR DISEASE CONTROL. (1993). HIV/AIDS surveillance report, second quarter (July) edition (Vol. 5, no. 2). *United States AIDS cases reported through June 1993.* Atlanta: Department of Health and Human Services.

CHAVEZ, J. M., & RONEY, C. E. (1990). Psychocultural factors affecting the mental health status of Mexican American adolescents. In A. R. Stiffman & L. E. Davis (Eds.), *Ethnic issues in adolescent mental health* (pp. 73–91). Newbury Park, CA: Sage.

CHAVEZ, L. (1995, March/April). Pride, prejudice, and the plague: Is AIDS healthcare failing for people of color? *Positively Aware,* pp. 16–19.

CHEATHAM, H., & STEWART, J. (1990). *Black families: Interdisciplinary perspectives.* New Brunswick, NJ: Transactional Publishers.

CLEVELAND, P. H., & LINDSEY, E. W. (1995). Solution-focused family interventions. In A. C. Kilpatrick & T. P. Holland (Eds.), *Working with families: An integrative model by level of functioning* (pp. 145–160). Boston: Allyn & Bacon.

COLEMAN, J. W., & CRESSEY, D. R. (1990). *Social problems* (4th ed.). New York: Harper & Row.

COREY, G. (1996). *Theory and practice of counseling and psychotherapy* (5th ed.). Pacific Grove, CA: Brooks/Cole.

CROSBIE-BURNETT, M., & LEWIS, E. A. (1994). Use of African-American family structures and functioning to address the challenges of European-American postdivorce families. *Family Relations, 42*(3), 243–248.

CUMMINGS, C. M., & DEHART, D. D. (1995). Ethnic minority physical health: Issues and interventions. In J. F. Aponte, R. Y. Rivers, & J. Wohl (Eds.), *Psychological interventions and cultural diversity* (pp. 234–249). Boston: Allyn & Bacon.

DE LA ROSA, M. (1991). Patterns and consequences of illegal drug use among Hispanics. In M. Sotomayor (Ed.), *Empowering Hispanic families: A critical issue for the '90s* (pp. 39–57). Milwaukee: Family Service America.

DELANEY, A. J. (1981). The Black cultural process. In E. Mizio & A. J. Delaney (Eds.), *Training for service delivery to minority clients* (pp. 89–98). New York: Family Service Association of America.

DEVORE, W., & SCHLESINGER, E. G. (1991). *Ethnic-sensitive social work practice* (3rd. ed.). New York: Merrill.

DICKERSON, B. J. (1995). *African American single mothers: Understanding their lives and families.* Newbury Park, CA: Sage.

DOWNING, L. N. (1975). *Counseling theories and techniques.* Chicago: Nelson-Hall.

DUNCAN, B. L. (1992). Strategic therapy, eclecticism, and the therapeutic relationship. *Journal of Marital and Family Therapy, 18*(1), 17–24.

ESPIN, O. M. (1995). Cultural and historical influences on sexuality in Hispanic/Latin women: Implications for psychotherapy. In M. L. Andersen & P. H. Collins (Eds.), *Race, class, and gender: An anthology* (2nd ed., pp. 423–428). Needham Heights, MA: Allyn & Bacon.

FACUNDO, A. (1991). Sensitive mental health services for low-income Puerto Rican families. In M. Sotomayor (Ed.), *Empowering Hispanic families: A critical issue for the '90s* (pp. 121–139). Milwaukee: Family Service America.

FALICOV, C. J. (1982). Mexican families. In M. McGoldrick, J. K. Pearce, & J. Giordano (Eds.), *Ethnicity and family therapy* (pp. 134–163). New York: Guilford.

FIGLEY, C. R., & NELSON, T. S. (1990). Basic family therapy skills, II: Structural family therapy. *Journal of Marital Family Therapy, 16*(3), 225–239.

FRANKL, V. E. (1965). *The doctor and the soul. From psychotherapy to logotherapy.* New York: Simon & Schuster.

FRANKLIN, C., WAUKECHON, J., & LARNEY, P. S. (1995). Culturally relevant school programs for American Indian children and families. *Social Work in Education, 17*(3), 183–192.

FREEMAN, E. M. (1990). The Black family's life cycle: Operationalizing a strengths perspective. In S. M. L. Logan, E. M. Freeman, & R. G. McRoy (Eds.), *Social practice with Black families* (pp. 55–72). New York: Longman.

GRIFFITH, E. E. H., & BAKER, F. M. (1993). Psychiatric care of African Americans. In A. G. Gaw (Ed.), *Culture, ethnicity, and mental illness* (pp. 147–173). Washington, DC: American Psychiatric Press.

HALEY, J. (1963). *Strategies of psychotherapy.* New York: Grune and Stratton.

HALEY, J. (1976). *Problem-solving therapy: New strategies for effective family therapy.* San Francisco: Jossey-Bass.

HO, M. K. (1987). *Family therapy with ethnic minorities.* Newbury Park, CA: Sage.

HOLLAND, T. P., & KILPATRICK, A. C. (1995). An ecological systems social constructionism approach to family practice. In A. C. Kilpatrick & T. P. Holland (Eds.), *Working with families: An integrative model by level of functioning* (pp. 17–38). Boston: Allyn & Bacon.

IVEY, A. E., IVEY, M. B., & SIMEK-MORGAN, L. (1993). *Counseling and psychotherapy: A multicultural perspective* (3rd ed.). Boston: Allyn & Bacon.

KILPATRICK, A. C., & HOLLAND, T. P. (1995). *Working with families: An integrative model by level of functioning.* Boston: Allyn & Bacon.

KISER, D. J., & PIERCY, F. P. (1993). The integration of emotion in solution-focused therapy. *Journal of Marital and Family Therapy, 19*(3), 233–242.

KOK, C. J., & LESKELA, J. (1996). Solution-focused therapy in a psychiatric hospital. *Journal of Marital and Family Therapy, 22*(3), 397–406.

KORIN, E. (1994). Social inequalities and therapeutic relationships: Applying Freire's ideas to clinical practice. In R. Almeida (Ed.), *Expansions of feminist family therapy through diversity* (pp. 75–98). New York: Haworth.

KRILL, D. F. (1979). Existential social work. In F. J. Turner (Ed.), *Social work treatment: Interlocking theoretical approaches* (2nd ed., pp. 147–175). New York: Free Press.

KUEHL, B. P. (1995). The solution oriented genogram: A collaborative approach. *Journal of Marital and Family Therapy, 21*(3), 239–250.

KURTZ, D., & TANDY, C. C. (1995). Narrative family interventions. In A. C. Kilpatrick & T. P. Holland (Eds.), *Working with families: An integrative model by level of functioning* (pp. 177–197). Boston: Allyn & Bacon.

LA FROMBOISE, T., & LOW, K. (1989). American Indian adolescents. In J. Gibbs & L. Hwang (Eds.), *Children of color* (pp. 114–147). San Francisco: Jossey-Bass.

LAPPIN, J. (1988). Family therapy: A structural approach. In R. A. Dorfman (Ed.), *Paradigms of clinical social work* (pp. 220–252). New York: Brunner/Mazel.

LINK, A. S., & McCormick, R. L. (1983). *Progressivism.* Arlington Heights, IL: Harlan Davidson.

LUM, D. (1992). *Social work practice & people of color: A process-stage approach* (2nd ed.). Pacific Grove, CA: Brooks/Cole.

MAY, R. E. (Ed.). (1961). *Existential psychology.* New York: Random House.

MCGOLDRICK, M. (1996). *Ethnicity and family therapy.* New York: Guilford.

MCKENRY, P. C., & PRICE, S. J. (1995). Divorce: A comparative perspective. In B. B. Ingoldsby & S. Smith (Eds.), *Families in multicultural perspective* (pp. 187–212). New York: Guilford.

MCNEECE, C. A., & DINITTO, D. M. (1994). *Chemical dependency: A systems approach.* Englewood Cliffs, NJ: Prentice Hall.

MINUCHIN, S. (1974). *Families and family therapy.* Cambridge, MA: Harvard University Press.

MONK, G. (1996). Narrative approaches to therapy: The "Fourth Wave" in family therapy. *Guidance & Counselling, 11*(2), 41–47.

NAPOLIELLO, A. L., & SWEET, E. S. (1992). Salvador Minuchin's structural family therapy and its application to American Indians. *Family Therapy, 19*(2), 155–165.

NEWFIELD, N. (1995). Family social work/family therapy: A Tweedledum/Tweedledee distinction. *Journal of Family Social Work, 1*(1), 47–53.

O'HANLON, B. (1994). The third wave. *The Family Therapy Networker, 18*(6), 18–26.

ORDAZ, M., & DE ANDA, D. (1996). Cultural legacies: Operationalizing Chicano cultural values. *Multicultural Social Work, 4*(3), 57–67.

PANIAGUA, F. A. (1994). *Assessing and treating culturally diverse clients: A practical guide* (Multicultural aspects of counseling series, 4). Thousand Oaks, CA: Sage.

PERLS, F. S. (1969). *Gestalt therapy verbatim.* Lafayette, CA: Real People Press.

PINDERHUGHES, E. (1982). Afro-American families and the victim system. In M. McGoldrick, J. K. Pearce, & J. Giordano (Eds.), *Ethnicity and family therapy* (pp. 108–122). New York: Guilford.

PINDERHUGHES, E. (1995). Empowering diverse populations: Family practice in the 21st century. *Families in Society,* 131–140.

PRELI, R., & BERNARD, J. M. (1993). Making multiculturalism relevant for majority culture graduate students. *Journal of Marital and Family Therapy, 19*(1), 5–16.

RIO, A. T., SANTISTEBAN, D. A., & SZAPOCZNIK, J. (1991). Juvenile delinquency among Hispanics: The role of the family in prevention and treatment. In M. Sotomayor, (Ed.), *Empowering Hispanic families: A critical issue for the '90s* (pp. 191–214). Milwaukee: Family Service America.

RIVERS, R. Y., & MORROW, C. A. (1995). Understanding and treating ethnic minority youth. In J. F. Aponte, R. Y. Rivers, & J. Wohl, (Eds.), *Psychological interventions and cultural diversity* (pp. 164–180). Boston: Allyn & Bacon.

ROMO, H. D., & FALBO, T. (1996). *Latino high school graduation: Defying the odds.* Austin: University of Texas Press.

RUIZ, P., & LANGROD, J. G. (1992). In J. H. Lowinson, P. Ruiz, R. B. Millman, & J. G. Langrod (Eds.), *Substance abuse: A comprehensive textbook* (2nd ed., pp. 868–874). Baltimore: Williams & Wilkins.

SATEL, S., & FORSTER, G. (1996). *Multicultural mental health: Does your skin color matter more than your mind?* Center for Equal Opportunity. Address: www.ceousa.org/health.html.

SHIELDS, C. G. (1986). Critiquing the new epistemologies: Toward minimum requirements for a scientific theory of family therapy. *Journal of Marital and Family Therapy, 12*(4), 359–372.

SOTOMAYOR, M. (Ed.). (1991). *Empowering Hispanic families: A critical issue for the '90s.* Milwaukee: Family Service America.

SPECK, R., & ATTNEAVE, C. (1973). *Family process.* New York: Pantheon.

STIFFARM, L. A., & LANE, P., Jr. (1992). The demography of native North America: A question of American Indian survival. In M. A. Jaimes (Ed.), *The state of Native America* (pp. 23–53). Boston: South End Press.

SUE, D. W., & SUE, D. (1990). *Counseling the culturally different: Theory and practice* (2nd ed.). New York: John Wiley.

SUE, S. (1988). Psychotherapeutic services for ethnic minorities: Two decades of research findings. *American Psychologist, 43*(4), 301–308.

SUE, S., & ZANE, N. (1987). The role of culture and cultural techniques in psychotherapy: A critique and reformulation. *American Psychologist, 42*(1), 37–45.

SYKES, D. K., Jr. (1987). An approach to working with Black youth in cross cultural therapy. *Clinical Social Work Journal, 15,* 260–270.

TAYLOR, R., CHATTERS, L., TUCKER, M., & LEWIS, E. (1990). Developments in research on black families: A decade review. *Journal of Marriage and the Family, 52,* 993–1014.

TSENG, W. S., & HSU, J. (1991). *Culture and family: Problems and therapy.* New York: Haworth Press.

TUMA, E. H., & HAWORTH, B. (1993). *Cultural diversity and economic education.* Palo Alto, CA: Pacific Books.

WALSH, W. M., & MCGRAW, J. A. (1996). *Essentials of family therapy: A therapist's guide to eight approaches.* New York: McGraw-Hill.

WESTERMEYER, J. (1992). Cultural perspectives: American Indians, Asians, and new immigrants. In J. H. Lowinson, P. Ruiz, R. B. Millman, & J. G. Langrod (Eds.), *Substance abuse: A comprehensive textbook,* (2nd ed., pp. 890–896). Baltimore: Williams & Wilkins.

WILKINSON, D. (1993). Family ethnicity in America. In H. P. McAdoo (Ed.), *Family ethnicity: Strength in diversity* (pp. 15–59). Newbury Park, CA: Sage.

WILSON, M. N., PHILLIP, D. A., KOHN, L. P., & CURRY-EL, J. A. (1995). Cultural relativistic approach toward ethnic minorities in family therapy. In J. F. Aponte, R. Y. Rivers, & J. Wohl (Eds.), *Psychological interventions and cultural diversity* (pp. 92–108). Boston: Allyn & Bacon.

WINICK, C. (1992). Epidemiology of alcohol and drug abuse. In J. H. Lowinson, P. Ruiz, R. B. Millman, & J. G. Langrod (Eds.), *Substance abuse: A comprehensive textbook* (2nd ed., pp. 15–29). Baltimore: Williams & Wilkins.

WYLIE, M. S. (1994). Panning for gold. *The Family Therapy Networker, 18*(6), 40–47.

YOUNG, T. (1988). Substance use and abuse among Native Americans. *Clinical Psychology Review, 8,* 125–138.

CHAPTER ELEVEN

Donald K. Granvold, Ph.D.
University of Texas at Arlington

James I. Martin, Ph.D.
University of Texas at Arlington

Family Therapy with Gay and Lesbian Clients

Gay and lesbian families have many of the same problems as heterosexual families, including those involving finances, decision making, division of labor, and sex. However, they also experience unique problems that could result in referral for therapeutic intervention. In this chapter, we focus on the unique characteristics and experiences of gay and lesbian families so that family therapists might be more sensitive and effective in treating them.

We believe that including material on gay and lesbian families in a book on family therapy is highly relevant for the informed practitioner. It is imperative that family therapists be open and accepting of their gay or lesbian clients and knowledgeable about their lifestyles. To be effective in today's practice contexts, therapists must prepare themselves to work with a diversity of lifestyles and family types. Laird and Green (1996) noted that until the 1990s little was written about the gay and lesbian population within the family therapy field. Many family therapists are likely to have limited knowledge about gay or lesbian families, and much of what they do know may contain biases derived from a heterosexist paradigm that assumes such families to be inherently pathological, even if they show no signs of distress (Ussher, 1991). However, research indicates that gay and lesbian families are no more likely than heterosexual families to experience distress or dysfunction, and that the dysfunction they do experience may result from discrimination and other external stress sources (DePoy & Noble, 1992; Lott-Whitehead & Tully, 1993; Rohrbaugh, 1992; Savin-Williams, 1994; Swigonski, 1995). Social workers doing family therapy and those who are providing other forms of social work service to families are obligated to work toward the elimination of all forms of discrimination by virtue of their Code of Ethics (National Association of Social Workers, 1996). Furthermore, they are ethically bound to uphold their clients' right of self-determination. It is in the spirit of these principles that we examine gay and lesbian families. We hope that social workers and family therapists from all disciplines will use this information to build knowledge-based expertise and to maintain high ethical standards in working with this population.

A primary challenge for therapists seeking to understand lesbian and gay families lies in being able to define who they are. As noted by DiNitto and Gustavsson in Chapter 13, from a social work perspective, a family is any constellation of people who believe themselves to be a family. However, the traditional definition of families as consisting of two or more people "related by blood, marriage, or adoption" (Garbarino, 1982, p. 63) does not apply to most gay and lesbian families. According to Allen and Demo (1995), gay and lesbian families consist of two or more adults who are themselves gay or lesbian or at least one gay or lesbian adult with children. We will distinguish between childless families and families with children by calling the former "gay or lesbian couples" and the latter, following the suggestion of Casper, Schultz, and Wickens (1992), "gay- or lesbian-headed families." Gay- or lesbian-headed families may have a variety of structures including single-parent, blended, and parallel parenting by ex-mates. Children in these families might have come from previous heterosexual marriages, artificial insemination, or adoption (Rohrbaugh, 1992).

Lesbian and gay families are *similar* to heterosexual families in a great variety of ways. Like heterosexual families, relationships in functioning lesbian and gay families are likely to be based on "mutual commitment, property sharing, and emotional and physical intimacies" (Baptiste, 1987, p. 224). As with heterosexual families, common sources of conflict in lesbian and gay families include their finances and their families of origin (Berger, 1990). Flaks, Ficher, Masterpasqua, and Joseph (1995) found the relationship quality of lesbian couples with children and heterosexual couples with children to be equivalent. Bigner and Jacobson (1992) found divorced gay and heterosexual fathers to have similar attitudes toward parenting. Hare (1994) found lesbian mothers to be "strongly committed to their family and to successful child rearing" (p. 33).

Gay and lesbian families are also *dissimilar* to heterosexual families. They have many unique characteristics, the most basic of which is that they are outside the definition of "family" held by many people (Hare, 1994; Hunter, Shannon, Martin, & Knox, in press). As a result, these families often struggle against various barriers and efforts that deny their existence or violate their boundaries (Hartman, 1996; Swigonski, 1995). The current public debate over same-gender marriage illustrates this struggle. Although no state has ever sanctioned same-gender marriages, many states have recently passed legislation to make sure such sanctioning never occurs. Motivated by the possibility that the Supreme Court of Hawaii might require that state to issue marriage licenses to same-gender couples (Lambda Legal Defense and Education Fund, 1995), legislators in other states took action to protect a heterosexual definition of "marriage" and "family." These actions suggest an underlying belief that acknowledging gay and lesbian coupling through legal sanction would threaten this definition. Likewise, institutional discrimination in the absence of health benefits and legal protections for same-gender partners reflects a denial of their existence.

On a more personal level, members of same-gender couples may also encounter from their families of origin an unwillingness to accept them as a legitimate family. Treating a partnered gay or lesbian family member as single through acts such as arranging heterosexual dates for the individual, excluding his or her partner from family gatherings, or shunning a partner attending a family function are examples of this unwillingness (Slater & Mencher, 1991). Some children of lesbian or gay parents, especially younger children, may not know about their parents' sexual orientation. Older children who have this knowledge about their parents may keep it secret from peers, teachers, and other adults (Bigner & Bozett, 1990; Hare, 1994).

The following is a summary of other unique characteristics of lesbian and gay families that will be examined later in more depth.

1. Lesbian and gay families are likely to face discrimination, bias, or even violence (DePoy & Noble, 1992; Herek, 1989). Lesbian mothers, in particular, are vulnerable to having their children legally taken away from them by ex-husbands or family of origin members (Meyer, 1992). Even families who have not directly encountered hostility, violence, or discrimination might experience stress due to their expectancies of such treatment (Lott-Whitehead & Tully, 1993). They must develop strategies for coping with this stress, especially in the absence of legal protections against sexual orientation-related discrimination (Levy, 1992).

2. Lesbian and gay families have few culturally idealized models for appropriate functioning (Murphy, 1994). They must manage major transitions, such as formalizing and dissolving their couplehood, without the guidance of mutually recognized traditions. For instance, there is no event comparable to a heterosexual engagement to signify the beginning of a lesbian or gay relationship (Berger, 1990). No traditions are available to guide lesbian or gay parents in deciding how, or even whether, to come out to their children or to their children's teachers or peers.

3. Traditional gender roles that might be complementary in heterosexual relationships may provide little direction for couples in which both partners have had the same gender socialization. Although in some ways a liability, the lack of prescribed gender roles for these couples may also be a strength. Lesbian and gay couples tend to be flexible, egalitarian, and pragmatic in their assignment of roles. Tasks are likely to be assigned on the basis of which partner is "best suited" rather than according to gender (DePoy & Noble, 1992, p. 55). In comparison to heterosexual couples, task assignment may be more balanced in gay and lesbian couples (Kurdek, 1993). Power may be shared more equally, especially with respect to decision making (Reilly & Lynch, 1990).

4. Gay and lesbian families may lack extended family support, especially if they are not *out*—that is, they have not publicly acknowledged their gay or lesbian status—to extended family members or if their family of origin has rejected them (Brown, 1989; Leslie, 1995). However, many such families compensate by building a support system of friends that they consider their "chosen family" (Weston, 1991). Therapists must not minimize the importance of this support system in their

assessment of gay and lesbian families (Murphy, 1994). Some families may need help with developing a more responsive support system or with removing obstacles that prevent them from finding or accepting support.

5. Although monogamy appears be more common among gay men than it was in the 1970s (Berger, 1990), nonmonogamy may continue to be practiced by gay couples more frequently than by either lesbian or heterosexual couples (Johnson & Keren, 1996). Nevertheless, according to Deneen, Gijs, and van Naerssen (1994), gay men place high value on intimacy in their relationships. It may be that nonmonogamy has a unique meaning for many gay couples in which outside sexual relationships are not considered to be a threat to the couple's boundaries (Johnson & Keren, 1996). In comparison to heterosexual couples, gay couples may also engage in a greater variety of sexual activities (Blumstein & Schwartz, 1983), while lesbian couples may have sex less frequently (Loulan, 1987).

6. HIV (human immunodeficiency virus) has had a profound impact on many gay and lesbian families. Many lesbians and gay men, especially those living in the major cities, have lost important members of their support system to AIDS (acquired immune deficiency syndrome) during the past 15 years. Some of them have lost their entire support system. These losses may be devastating to a couple's ability to maintain a high level of functioning. Gay and lesbian families may experience added burdens from assuming caretaking responsibilities for someone living with HIV. Families in which an adult member has HIV face numerous possible challenges, such as bearing the financial burden of medical treatment, role changes or reversals, permanency planning for children, and managing difficult feelings such as guilt and loss (Shuster, 1996). Some gay couples may experience sexual dysfunction from fear of contracting HIV. Anxiety and guilt may interfere with the sexual relationships of HIV-serodiscordant couples (couples in which one partner is seropositive for HIV). Many gay couples engage in unprotected anal intercourse, the most likely way for HIV to be sexually transmitted from an infected partner (Berger, 1990; Buchanan, Poppen, & Reisen, 1996). Although partners might know that condoms are important for avoiding HIV transmission, using condoms could connote a lack of trust in each other's fidelity or present other barriers to intimacy (McLean et al., 1994; Remien, Carballo-Diéguez, & Wagner, 1995). Some couples may have sharp disagreements about limiting themselves to only "safer" sex activities.

In the following sections, several major issues confronting gay and lesbian couples will be discussed. These represent the concerns most likely to be encountered by family therapists in treating gay or lesbian couples and their families.

Heterosexism, Discrimination, and Violence

Family therapists must be cognizant of the numerous ways in which oppressive social forces impact their lesbian and gay clients. Without sufficient awareness of the dangers such clients face, therapists might inappropriately encourage some clients to come out prematurely (Hartman, 1996) or to take other actions that could have negative consequences for them. Oppressive social forces include heterosexist attitudes and prejudice, discriminatory policies, and hate-based physical violence. *Homophobia*, an irrational dread of gay and lesbian people (Weinberg, 1972), is sometimes included on this list. However, "homophobia" is a concept that inappropriately pathologizes people holding anti-gay or lesbian attitudes and has limited value for explaining the institutional oppression faced by lesbians and gay men (Plummer, 1981).

Heterosexism

Heterosexism is the belief that heterosexuality is normal and any other sexual orientation is abnormal. Thus heterosexual behaviors, attitudes, and feelings are the standards by which everything else must be measured (Morin, 1977). American society is pervasively heterosexist (Anderson, 1996). For example, Aguero, Bloch, and Byrne (1984) reported that "homosexuals" were rated the third most dangerous group of people in America on a 1960s public opinion survey. Some attitudes toward lesbians and gay men might be improving with time (Pratte, 1993), but these changes vary according to people's gender, religiosity, political ideology, and level of education. For instance, men are more likely than women to hold negative attitudes, and people who don't know any gay men are much more likely to have negative attitudes toward them (Herek & Glunt, 1993). In addition, Viss and Burn (1992) found that though some people might change their attitudes toward someone they know who reveals herself to be a lesbian, this change might not cause them to have more positive attitudes toward lesbians in general.

Discrimination

Heterosexist attitudes form the basis for numerous forms of discrimination against lesbians and gay men. Examples of discrimination in employment, health care, family law, and the social services are particularly common among gay and lesbian families, though discrimination exists in many other forms as well. In one study, 71% of gay and lesbian couples reported experiencing discrimination of some kind (Bryant & Demian, 1994).

During a 1995 Dallas City Council meeting in which passage of a sexual orientation nondiscrimination ordinance for city employees was debated, the city's attorney verified the absence of any existing legal redress for people who might lose their jobs because of being gay or lesbian. Other people maintained disbelief that sexual orientation discrimination actually occurred in employment or that gay men and lesbians had no legal protection against it. However, Levine and Leonard (1984) found that 13% of surveyed lesbians had experienced employment discrimination and 31% anticipated it. In addition, most employers do not allow typical benefits such as health insurance, bereavement and family leave, relocation assistance, use of recreation facilities, and employee assistance program eligibility to include the partners of their gay or lesbian employees (Spielman & Winfeld, 1996). The Family and Medical Leave Act of 1993 requires employers having at least 50 employees to allow extended leave for taking care of a spouse, child, or parent who is seriously ill, but it does not allow for employees to take leave in order to care for an unmarried partner (Chambers, 1996). In a recent study by Bryant and Demian (1994), 58% of lesbian couples and 40% of gay couples reported employment benefit discrimination.

Lesbians and gay men may be afraid to access health care services from fear of discrimination. In a study by Stevens and Hall (1988), some lesbians reported feeling that they were treated in a hostile manner by judgmental health care providers. In another study, 17% of lesbians were uncomfortable with obstetrical providers (Harvey, Carr, & Bernheine, 1989). According to Levy (1996), lesbians often seek alternative health care services because of expected negative experiences with mainstream services. Reamer (1993) reported that many health care providers have refused treatment to gay men with AIDS. In Wallach's (1989) study, 9% of nurses and physicians believed that AIDS was God's punishment for being gay.

When members of lesbian or gay couples need hospital treatment, their partners are sometimes excluded from consultation on decisions about treatment and may even be excluded from visitation because they are not considered part of the immediate family (Ettelbrick, 1996). In all states, either statutes or common law doctrines automatically give parents, offspring, or other blood relations the right to make emergency medical decisions for an incapacitated unmarried person (Chambers, 1996). Unlike married couples, members of lesbian and gay couples must have documentation such as a durable medical power of attorney or a general durable power of attorney to ensure that their partner will retain decision-making authority at such times (Ettelbrick, 1996). When illness and hospitalization are issues, the family therapist should discuss the objectives and rights over which they are concerned and make appropriate referrals for legal services.

Lesbians and gay men face considerable discrimination in the American family law system because the system is "resolutely heterosexual in its structure and its presumptions" (Ettelbrick, 1993, p. 514). Especially at risk are lesbian mothers, many of whom have lost custody of children they conceived within the context of a heterosexual marriage. In addition, family courts have sometimes used the HIV-positive status of some gay fathers as evidence to justify removing their children from them (Hartman, 1996). Although a lesbian's custody of her child is most often challenged by her ex-husband when he learns that she has established a live-in relationship with a female partner, families of origin might also challenge her suitability for parenthood. Many states allow challenges to child custody at any time, not just during a divorce. Even lesbian couples who conceive through artificial insemination are not necessarily immune to these risks, particularly if the sperm donor is known. Some donors might be able to sue for custody, even if they had previously agreed not to do so (Meyer, 1992).

Courts base their decisions about challenges to child custody on the "best interest of the child" standard, which they apply in many different ways (Stein, 1996). Using a purposive sample, Stein (1996) found that 33% of contested custody cases involving a lesbian or gay parent applied the *per se* approach to decision making. This standard considers a parent's sexual orientation sufficient reason for denying custody, although it may allow for visitation. Seventy percent of cases used the *nexus* approach in which lesbian or gay parents can be denied custody only if there is sufficient evidence that their sexual orientation or related behavior has been harmful to their child. Stein called the continued categorical use of the *per se* approach by some courts "state-sanctioned discrimination" (p. 445).

Same-gender partners of lesbian or gay parents (co-parents) have virtually no parental rights, according to family law. Attempts by co-parents to obtain legal definition or protection of their parental rights have usually been denied by the courts (Hartman, 1996). Most courts have refused to allow co-parents to adopt their partner's child, and in those cases where such adoption is possible it requires an extremely lengthy and intrusive process costing thousands of dollars (Chambers, 1996). Because of this lack of legal sanction, a nonbiological lesbian mother could lose all contact with a child conceived through artificial insemination if her partnership with the child's biological mother dissolves (Meyer, 1992), or if the biological mother dies and her family of origin decides to adopt the child (Hartman, 1996).

When lesbian and gay partnerships dissolve, there are no legal guidelines to govern even the division of their property because the relationship lacks public sanction. The resolution of disputes over these issues depends upon goodwill between the separating partners, which is rarely the case. Lesbian and gay couples who formalize a financial plan specifying how their property and resources should be divided if the relationship terminates are less likely on separation to become mired in acrimonious disputes. Couples who cannot resolve such disputes on their own might benefit from engaging in mediation (Hartman, 1996).

Lesbians and gay men also face discriminatory policies in the social services, particularly with adoptions. State laws in Florida and New Hampshire prohibit adoptions by lesbians and gay men. In most states, lesbian or gay couples may be able to adopt a child if they can locate a sympathetic caseworker, although Michigan and New Jersey also require that suitable heterosexual adoptive parents cannot be located (Pierce, 1995). According to Hartman (1996), in many cases in which a gay or lesbian couple is prohibited from adopting a child, one of the partners might be able to adopt as a single parent. However, this type of arrangement could lead to asymmetrical family relationships. In addition, single gay or lesbian parents might be able to adopt only the most difficult-to-place children, such as those who are older, with multiple handicaps, or with a history of multiple foster placements (Chambers, 1996).

Violence

Members of gay and lesbian families may be far more concerned about violence than are members of heterosexual families, and with good reason. Herek (1989) reported that in some surveys, as many as 92% of lesbians and gay men claimed to have experienced verbal abuse or threats due to their sexual orientation, and up to 24% said they were victims of physical assault. However, most acts of violence against lesbians and gay men are never reported to local authorities (Dean, Wu, & Martin, 1992; Von Schulthess, 1992) out of fear of further victimization (Murphy, 1994). According to Finn and McNeil (1987), lesbians and gay men are the most frequent victims of bias-related crimes in the United States. Gay men might be more likely than lesbians to be physically assaulted in gay/lesbian-identified locations and because of their sexual orientation. Lesbians are more likely than gay men to be assaulted in locations that are not gay/lesbian-identified and because of their gender (Berrill, 1992; Murphy, 1994). Some bias crimes involve rape or sexual assault, especially crimes against lesbians in which the perpetrator thinks the victim needs a "real man" in order to be heterosexual (Hanson, 1996).

Gender Role Flexibility

Gay and lesbian couples tend to function with role flexibility. Weisstub and Shoenfeld (1987) note that "issues of control and dependency in homosexual[1] couples are less influenced by social norms and more directly related to the psychological dynamics and needs of the partners involved" (p. 101). At times, same-sex couples have been viewed as assuming fixed masculine/feminine ("butch/femme") roles; however, research findings have established a strong trend toward equality and gender-role flexibility (Green, Bettinger, & Zacks, 1996; Kurdek, 1995; Peplau, 1991; Reilly & Lynch, 1990). A recent study of lesbian couples showed that despite the trend toward egalitarianism, power differences existed in the relationships and could not be explained by the social status variables observed in heterosexual relationships: age, income, education, and financial assets (Reilly & Lynch, 1990). Traditional gender-role division of labor structure does not exist for many same-sex couples, and this lack of structure has varied consequences. On one hand, it promotes flexibility, allowing aptitudes, interests, and sex-role unencumbered proclivities to prevail in the determination of who will be responsible for performing what tasks. On the other hand, the lack of traditional gender-role divisions may result in role ambiguity, uncertainty, confusion, and conflict. For some couples, less structure and greater flexibility may be preferable; for other couples, the lack of structure may contribute to their dysfunction.

In heterosexual couples, the therapist may seek family-of-origin information to help define, clarify, and explain an individual's expectations regarding the characteristics of a husband or wife and views about the way a couple relationship should be. Inasmuch as most gays and lesbians are heterosocialized, their "models" of social role fulfillment fail to provide a viable pattern for their same-sex relationships.

The family therapist is challenged to guide same-sex couples in clarifying their expectations regarding the "desirable" characteristics and traits of a mate and further, to help explicate their views of the ways a relationship should function (e.g., control, division of labor, decision making). Sager (1976) contends that couples function with implicit contracts by which the mate and the process of interacting are viewed and evaluated. Individual behavior, satisfaction with the union, commitment to remain coupled, and expectations for relationship change

---

[1] Most authors no longer use the word *homosexual* except when referring specifically to sexual behavior between members of the same gender. The preferred words *gay* and *lesbian* refer to people's identities, of which sexual attractions and behaviors are only one part. Family therapists should be aware that many gay and lesbian clients may consider *homosexual* to be a pejorative term.

derive from the contract. The individual contract may be expressed openly as an expectation or may go unexpressed. Furthermore, people function with both explicit and implicit levels of self-knowledge (Guidano, 1987); therefore, they may lack awareness of portions of the contract. Of particular significance is that the contract is reciprocal, encompassing both what the individual expects to give (obligations) and the benefits he or she expects to derive from the mate and the relationship in general (Sager, 1976).

Therapists may recommend that clients use journaling to determine their partnership role behavior expectations both in terms of what each mate believes he or she is obligated to provide and what each wants to receive from the partner. Journaling can uncover the sources of their expectations by identifying models, values, and beliefs, and contemporary narratives often effectively expose contentment and malcontentment in key aspects of partnership role taking. For many couples, relationship patterns characterized by power imbalances, unilateral decision making, inequitable distribution of labor, and role inflexibility are likely to result in conflict, hostile feelings, relationship dissatisfaction, and, in some cases, low self-esteem in the disadvantaged partner. These couples may benefit from training in conflict management, problem solving, and behavioral contracting (Granvold, in press; Granvold & Jordan, 1994; Metz, Rosser, & Strapko, 1994). These therapeutic approaches are found in the cognitive-behavioral and narrative models discussed in Chapters 4 and 6.

As noted earlier, same-sex couples have fewer role models for their relationships than do heterosexual couples. Sensual and sexual intimacy are predominantly portrayed heterosexually, a fact that has remarkable implications for lesbian women in particular. Men in heterosexual relationships are represented as being more likely to initiate and orchestrate sexual behavior. Murphy (1994) notes that "women are taught to deny or downplay their sexual needs, to be passive and non-initiating, to subjugate their pleasure to that of their partners" (p. 21). She states that the actual mechanics of sex may pose problems for lesbian women. "The most frequent form of heterosexual sex is vaginal intercourse. In this method of sex, the woman can, if she chooses, be passive and receptive while still providing stimulation to her partner. Lesbian sex requires more action. The most common form of genital sex for lesbian couples is oral-genital stimulation (Bell & Weinberg, 1978). Both require that women learn to feel more comfortable with the active involvement in the stimulation of their partners and take pleasure in the female body, its appearance, its feel, its smell, and its taste" (pp. 21–22).

Considering lesbian sexuality in the context of gender role flexibility suggests that while either partner can freely assume initiator and/or orchestrator roles, neither may readily exercise the initiative. By some reports, lesbian couples are less active sexually than either gay male or heterosexual couples (Blumstein & Schwartz, 1983; Kurdek, 1995). Socialization to be more passive than initiating, difficulty with mechanics, and a history of low to moderate subjective enjoyment with sexual behavior (conditioning) may largely account for this comparatively low frequency rate. The treatment implications are many. First, the therapist must become comfortable discussing lesbian sexual behavior in explicit detail. Second, the terms used should be free of ambiguity. Third, affection that is free of breast and genital touching should not be diminished in meaning. Fourth, the potential negative effects of the client's socialization as a sexual being should be explicated and evaluated. Discuss the concepts that (1) sex is "normal," (2) women are free to initiate and orchestrate sex with comfort and enjoyment, and (3) comfort and increased pleasure may require time to develop. Fifth, make in vivo homework assignments that provide the successive development of sexual skill and comfort. Sixth, consider assigning self-help books (recommended by Murphy, 1994) specifically written for lesbian women (Loulan, 1984, 1987; Sisley & Harris, 1977).

Extended Family and Family of Creation

Gay and lesbian clients are vulnerable to an array of problems associated with their families of origin. The coming out decision has major consequences, ranging from the family's experiencing a state of disequilibrium followed by some degree of accommodation to a rejection of the gay or lesbian member and loss of family support. Ussher (1991) notes that families' frame of reference is rarely one of gay/lesbian sexuality. Coming out is typically traumatic for both the disclosing person and his or her family members (Shernoff, 1984). It is not uncommon for a sibling, parent, grandparent, or other extended family member to attribute gay or lesbian sexuality to the parenting style of one or both parents or to social learning (e.g., failed heterosexual experiences) (VanWyk & Geist, 1984). Coming out may also lead other family members to question their own sexual orientation and to endure the discomfort (e.g., homophobia) and identity challenge associated with such contemplation. Self-denial of one's gay or lesbian identity is easier to sustain if the family system is closed to such degrees of individuation. Hence, a strong family bias may be operating against acceptance of the disclosure. Approval needs loom powerfully in relation to families' accommodating a gay or lesbian member. The stigma many consider to be associated with having a gay or lesbian child or sibling drive the family's disbelief, rejection, and pathologizing of the disclosing member. Furthermore, family members may fear not only the possibility of discrimination and threats to the physical safety of the disclosing member, but they may see themselves as vulnerable as well.

Many times, parents must give up their dreams of their son or daughter marrying and having children. The heterosexist view of family becomes a lost illusion, one that likely carries remarkable pain with it. The family therapist may engage the couple in modifying their definition of family to encompass same-sex relationships, a process requiring gradual reformation. Parents who consider procreation a critical ingredient in "normal" living view their offspring's coming out to represent a loss of generativity. Not only will they personally miss out on grandchildren from this offspring, but they see their son or daughter forgoing a highly meaningful part of life. The net effect is personal and empathic sadness and pain of the loss (and perhaps anger, resentment, and other negative feelings toward their son or daughter for taking away their anticipated joys and life rewards).

Ussher (1991) has suggested that a family goes through "a developmental series of systemic stages" following disclosure (p. 136). Disequilibrium is followed by adjustment, resolution, and integration. Family therapy is a viable format for facilitating movement through these stages. Individual or couple treatment may also be appropriate for family members whose needs are incompatible with an exclusive family therapy format.

Many families show an inability to accept and integrate a gay or lesbian family member into the family system. The consequence is that an individual is forced to choose between his or her identity as a lesbian or a gay man (and a partner if coupled) and his or her family (Krestan & Bepko, 1980). This is a tremendously difficult choice (one in which the therapist may participate), but as individuals age and mature, the power of their sexual orientation tends to become stronger relative to the influence of their family of origin. Some individuals have attempted to come out in the past by bringing a roommate or same-sex friend to family gatherings only to perceive the "test" to be a confirmation that family members hold intractable expectations of heterosexual coupling and procreation for *all* family members. These individuals may remain *closed* to their families—that is, their gay or lesbian status is not disclosed—or they may selectively come out to trusted family members. Over time, however, the burden of nondisclosure along with the wish to be accepted for one's true self may prompt explicit coming out. Some of these individuals will be blatantly rejected or experience little or no family support at times of crises. For example, the literature on physically and psychologically abused lesbians identifies the victims as characterized by alienation, isolation, and lack of a support system (Morrow & Hawxhurst, 1989; Renzetti, 1989; Schilit, Lie, Bush, Montagne, & Reyes, 1991). For many of these women, even though they have families, the family members do not offer them protection and support. They tend to go through crises and remarkable life events of both a positive and negative nature independent of family involvement. These events include such phenomena as life-mate relationship termination, job loss, physical illness and disability, and more positive experiences such as job promotions, college graduations, child adoption, and couple relationship rituals.

Loss of family support may evidence itself through acts that invalidate the couple relationship. A life-mate may be uninvited to holiday gatherings, family rituals, and other family social events. If invited, the mate may experience insensitive or abusive verbal behavior, or be ignored. In either case, the family is sending the message to the individual to "keep your sexual orientation invisible and your partner hidden." The result may be conflict between the mates as the issue of divided loyalties comes into play. For example, if a partner is excluded from a family event, should the gay or lesbian family member attend the occasion? The family therapist should guide the conflicted couple in a cost/benefit analysis of the decision to determine ways in which the "costs" to the couple can be minimized while preserving the family member's independent involvement with the family of origin if that is a preference. Alternative outcomes might be the preparation for and confrontation of the family to assert one's preference to be accepted (or tolerated with less offensiveness) *with* one's mate, or to initiate the process of withdrawal from the family of origin (emotional consequences, loss of physical contact, financial loss, etc.).

Many gays and lesbians turn to their community to build a support network, particularly when family relationships are limited or lost. This "chosen family" (Weston, 1991), or "family of creation" (Johnson & Keren, 1996), comprises close friends who provide support and validation in their lives. In these associations, gay and lesbian relationships are celebrated, rituals conducted, critical information shared, and advice offered. There is power in these informal affiliations and an important set of functions served not only for those who have maladaptive or nonexistent current relationships with their families of origin, but for those who remain actively connected with their bio-families as well. The family therapist should consider the family of choice to be a viable resource in addressing the needs of the gay or lesbian family.

Sexual Freedom

There appears to be greater sexual freedom among coupled gay men than is the case among their married heterosexual male counterparts. To generalize, sexual relationships with others appear to be less threatening to many gay unions than to heterosexual unions. Gay men in these unions function with resilience and a capacity to accommodate sexual openness, even if it isn't really their preference. The same openness to sexual freedom does not, however, characterize lesbian couples. To the contrary, Ussher (1991) notes that lesbian couples are "invariably monogamous." And further, as noted earlier, lesbians are reportedly less sexually active within their unions than either heterosexual or gay male couples (Blumstein & Schwartz, 1983).

Whereas sexual freedom tends to characterize many gay couples, this is not to say that significant problems do not arise from exercising this freedom. Sexual openness may be responsible for couple conflict, insecurity, distrust, jealousy, and fear of contracting AIDS through one's own or his mate's sexual behavior outside the relationship. Gay couples may present for treatment with one or more of these negative responses. Treatment goals will vary depending on the couple's individual views. If one or both partners continues to have sex outside their relationship, safer sex practices should be discussed, and a commitment to such practices established between the partners. This may actually take the form of a written agreement between the partners specifying safer sex practices with extra-relationship partners. Issues of insecurity, distrust, and jealousy may mark a need to discuss each partner's commitment to the relationship, satisfaction levels, and ways to communicate caring and long-term commitment while functioning nonmonogamously. If the couple is in disagreement regarding sexual openness, this issue should be explored in depth. For some, monogamy may be necessary for the individual to feel secure, confident in the relationship, and comfortably committed. Others may view sex outside the relationship as an enhancement to the couple relationship and an imperative for oneself. Strong stances in either direction require careful assessment. The family therapist is cautioned to keep in check his or her personal biases regarding sexual openness as the couple deliberates their dilemma. This issue could result in an impasse and lead to a decision to end the relationship. It is noteworthy that the very sanctions that operate to keep heterosexual couples together, even though they may be highly dissatisfied, work in the opposite direction with gay couples (Bancroft, 1983; Ussher, 1991). The "till death do us part" ethic and legal processes of divorce represent barriers to the married heterosexual contemplating divorce. The social, psychological, legal, and subcultural barriers to separation range from less formidable for some gay and lesbian couples to nearly nonexistent for others.

If your gay/lesbian client couple decide that they cannot resolve their differences regarding sexual freedom and elect to separate, this should not be a cue to terminate treatment. Rather, the focus should change from relationship maintenance to letting go, and the format should shift ultimately from couple to individual treatment. The transition to being "single" and developing a healthy postrelationship (postdivorce) adjustment poses very different challenges to the family therapist for which there is a body of clinical literature (Everett & Everett, 1994; Granvold, 1989, 1994; Kaslow & Schwartz, 1987; Rice & Rice, 1986; Textor, 1989).

For couples who choose to remain together despite functioning with opposing stances regarding sexual freedom, each partner may be experiencing a range of negative emotional responses, and the behavioral exchanges between them are likely to be punctuated negatively. Partners seeking greater freedom report feeling controlled, stifled, smothered, and unable to be themselves. Their views of the mate include weak, unenlightened, possessive, jealous, distrusting, and psychologically maladjusted. The emotions they experience include hostility, frustration, resentment, anger, disregard, and intolerance. The partner whose sexual attitudes more closely mirror majority norms and mores that promote sexual monogamy between committed couples will report feeling insecure, threatened, embarrassed, distrusting, and uncertain of his or her future in the relationship. Emotional responses include anger, anxiety, resentment, fear, jealousy and, for some, self-loathing and self-doubt. Behavioral responses include jealousy (accusations, anger, pouting, crying), retaliation by seeking others' attention, withdrawal and sexual withholding, fierce competitiveness with the "other man," and the initiation of various control sanctions. These couples typically present with high conflict, extreme emotional reactivity, and maladaptive behavioral interchanges.

Impact of HIV on Gay and Lesbian Families

The HIV epidemic has had a more significant impact on gay men, lesbians, and their families than perhaps any other segment of the American population. Therapists treating these families are likely to confront a variety of important issues related to the epidemic, including grief and loss, caregiver burden, sexual dysfunction, and decision making around the adoption or maintenance of safer sex habits. Many lesbians and gay men have experienced the deaths of multiple partners, friends, and family members from AIDS. According to Nord (1996), such bereavement overload has had grave implications for gays and lesbians beyond just the experience of grief for loved ones. These implications may include the loss of their support system, their community leaders and role models, their belief in the future, and their sexual spontaneity. Dworkin and Kaufer (1995) compared the effects of these experiences to situations involving natural disasters or war.

Some survivors might not find support or assistance in traditional sources such as clergy, employers, or families of origin because of anti-gay/lesbian bias and discrimination. Some grieving partners might be excluded from their loved one's funeral or have their loved one's possessions, and even possessions they held in common, taken away by families of origin who had never accepted what might have been a long-term relationship. In response to these losses, some individuals may retreat into social isolation, experience feelings of distrust and fear, and become reluctant to develop new relationships (Nord, 1996). Members of gay couples who have lost previous partners and friends to AIDS might present symptoms of bereavement overload. One or both partners might be socially isolated, anxious, or depressed. They might be abusing chemicals or experiencing dysfunction in their sexual relationship (Dworkin & Kaufer, 1995; Harowski, 1987; Nord, 1996).

Serodiscordant couples, or couples in which one partner is seropositive for HIV, can experience a variety of problems that might be amenable to family therapy intervention. Mattison and McWhirter (1994) describe three types of such couples. The first type consists of couples experiencing serious conflict leading toward breakup on learning that one partner is HIV positive. The second type consists of couples in which both partners experience troubling emotions, including guilt, anger, and sorrow when one partner seroconverts. The third type consists of couples who began their relationship knowing that one partner was HIV positive. Mattison and McWhirter (1994) reported that most serodiscordant couples they treated presented problems with communication or some other aspect of their relationship, and they avoided discussing their serodiscordance. In many cases they actively avoided talking about it. Some couples experienced sexual dysfunction due either to fear of infecting the seronegative partner or to the interference of unexpressed feelings such as guilt, anxiety, or depression. These couples benefited from encouragement to verbalize their feelings to one another or from coaching on how to communicate positively.

Serodiscordant couples might also need help facing existential issues such as knowledge that their relationship will not last forever (Mattison & McWhirter, 1994). According to Powell-Cope (1995), the partner living with HIV may fear his own impending death wheras his partner's fear may relate to losing his most important relationship. On a more concrete level, these couples may be dealing with stressors such as possible loss of the HIV-positive partner's job and income, or denial of insurance or public services. Family therapists can provide needed support in all these areas of concern (Mattison & McWhirter, 1994). In addition to conjoint therapy, these couples might also benefit from participation in multiple family therapy groups (Livingston, 1996) and family therapy involving extended family members.

Among couples in which one partner is ill, caregiver burden may be a significant problem, especially if the caregiver lacks sufficient support (Folkman, Chesney, & Christopher-Richards, 1994). Gay men who are the primary caregivers for their ill partner may experience stress, partly due to their lack of preparedness for this role; in most other circumstances, family caregivers tend to be women. In some couples, the caregiver may find it difficult to balance protection of his partner from physical and emotional harm with maintenance of his partner's strong desire to remain independent. This balancing becomes increasingly problematical as the illness progresses. Family therapists may be able to help such couples adjust to these new roles (Powell-Cope, 1995). Support groups for partners of persons living with AIDS may also be helpful (Land & Harangody, 1990).

The sexual relationships of serodiscordant couples may also be threatened by the disease. The seropositive partner might have decreased interest in sex, especially when his health status deteriorates, or he might be burdened by the fear of infecting his partner (Powell-Cope, 1995). The couple might decide to use condoms and avoid riskier sexual activities, often reducing sexual enjoyment (Bryant & Demian, 1994). However, many couples are able to preserve and even strengthen intimacy by focusing more on their relationship's nonsexual aspects (McLean & Roberts, 1995; Powell-Cope, 1995). Other couples may continue to engage in sexual activities that risk HIV transmission to the uninfected partner.

Some couples may be unclear regarding the risks inherent in certain sexual activities; others, however, clearly understand and proceed with a willingness to accept a certain level of risk. Some men report that using condoms interferes with their enjoyment of sex. Episodes of risky sex may be more likely when partners are emotionally distressed or intoxicated (Remien, Carballo-Diéguez, & Wagner, 1995). Unprotected sex may also have deeper meaning for some couples. According to McLean and colleagues (1994), "Having unprotected intercourse is confirmation that a partner is not a risk to one's life and may be a demonstration of mutual affection and trust" (p. 339). In these cases, the family therapist may engage the couple in a discussion of the risks, clarify the motives supporting their choices, and explicate the perceived consequences each partner holds regarding the options to engage in protected or alternatively unprotected sex. For example, the noninfected partner may consider the request to engage in protected sex to be a form of rejection of the mate or to interfere with their pleasure too much. The therapist should guide the couple in openly discussing the current choices being made and their risk potential. The thinking of the noninfected partner should be drawn out and clarified with the mate to expose any misconceptions. Obviously, it would be preferable for the couple to sustain an active, rewarding sexual relationship albeit safe for the noninfected partner. Expectations, meanings, viewpoints, and reactions on the part of either partner that interfere with the above objective are ripe targets for intervention.

In some cases, an HIV-infected gay man might also be a parent. Shuster (1996) recommends several tasks for therapists assessing and treating families such as these. First, therapists must assess how HIV has impacted the family system, including a consideration of the family's level of functioning prior to the disclosure of HIV serostatus. Although many families experience stress associated with a parent's HIV-related illness, the existence of long-standing family dysfunction can complicate their ability to cope with this stress. Second, therapists must determine the extent to which family members are comfortable with the parent's HIV status and sexual orientation. A diagnosis of AIDS may result in a resurgence of negative feelings among family members regarding the parent's gay sexual orientation.

The first treatment task is to join with the family system. Next, the therapist should reframe family members' emotional responses as normal and encourage their open expression. Hidden emotional issues should be identified, especially ones that children are acting out behaviorally. As treatment progresses, the therapist may need to address needs of family members that have been displaced by the focus on the parent's illness. Additional therapeutic objectives include guiding the family in broadening its support system and identifying and modifying dysfunctional coping strategies.

Clinical Judgment and Decision Making

The clinical judgment and treatment decision making of family therapists are highly subject to heterosexist biases. The American Psychiatric Association officially declassified homosexuality as a mental illness in 1973, and within the next few years the psychology and social work professions made similar moves to depathologize homosexual behavior. Nevertheless, not all professionals across disciplines have adopted views that correspond with this change (Martin, 1997). Many of those who have modified their views on a peripheral level may continue to experience the effects of heterosocialization. As family therapists, we are obligated to check our heterosexist biases as they subtly, and perhaps not-so-subtly, evidence themselves in such ways as our assessments of pathology, treatment goals, formats, procedures, and criteria for "success." For example, all things considered comparable, do you find yourself less disappointed when a gay or lesbian couple separates than you do when a heterosexual couple separates? If a bisexual member of a couple engages in heterosexual sex, do you find yourself hopeful, relieved, or "pulling" for the extra-couple relationship? When you are guiding an individual in his or her struggle with issues of coming out, are the cost/benefit factors skewed in a reflection of your bias and lacking in supportive rationale? It is in these types of circumstances that the power of therapeutic "authority" and expertise may be wielded unprofessionally and unethically. (See Brown, 1995, for an enumeration of several common manifestations of therapist bias.)

Our recommendation is that measures must be taken to self-assess, check, and modify heterosexist clinical bias. Reading literature devoted specifically to heterosexism and clinical judgment, retrospective review of treatment sessions with a focus on assessing for bias, and supervision and consultation represent viable approaches to reducing vulnerability to heterosexist practice.

Gay and lesbian family therapists are no less exempt from biases than their heterosexual counterparts, including the possibility of maintaining a heterosexist bias. Common circumstances and shared views may also promote overidentification with clients and the potential loss of objectivity. Similar measures to those noted above should be taken by these therapists to reduce their therapist bias.

Case Example

Randy (age 29) and Eric (age 30) presented for counseling in a state of couple distress following a gathering of Randy's family at which they were both in attendance. Although Randy's family members were aware that Randy is gay and in a committed relationship with Eric, the recent gathering was the first time Eric had met the family (aside from a brief interaction two months earlier with Randy's parents), and this was the first time Randy had brought a mate to a family event. Eric was greeted cordially but awkwardly by Randy's parents and his younger sister, Liz (age 25). Randy's brother, Bob (age 24), and Liz's husband, Troy (age 28), acted cold and distant toward him. Throughout the evening, Eric overheard Bob and Troy talking negatively about him and his relationship with Randy. Eric believed that both men used pejorative terminology in reference to him, Randy, and their relationship.

Following that family gathering, Eric told Randy that he wanted no more contact with the family, and that if Randy loved him, he would have no more contact with them either. Randy agreed with Eric that he had been treated badly by his family, and he expressed feeling disheartened about it. He went on to state, however, that he felt torn between his feelings for his family and his feelings for Eric. In the discussion, Randy got angry with Eric and stated his disappreciation toward him for being asked to choose between him and his family. He considered it an unreasonable request and believed it would be possible to develop relationships with some family members and perhaps all of them over time, if each of them put some positive effort into it. In short, he thought that Eric was extrasensitive, had unrealistically high expectations, and had overreacted to the family members who behaved inappropriately.

Eric accused Randy of "pathetic passivity" in relation to the behavior of both Bob and Troy. He thought Randy should have confronted them at the time. He challenged Randy that his failure to confront the impropriety was a sign of Randy's own heterosexism. Furthermore, he considered Randy to be aligned with his family and against him.

The discussion of the family gathering evolved into an argument in which both Randy and Eric lost anger control. While they avoided physical attacks, they both reported being verbally abusive: swearing; name calling; blaming; using sarcasm, put downs, and exaggerations; and shouting. The argument ended with Randy and Eric both feeling extremely hurt and frustrated, and sensing that they were at an impasse.

This information was disclosed in the first treatment session. It was collaboratively determined that the issue of involvement with Randy's family was of highest priority and that conflict management and anger control would be addressed subsequently. The therapist listened to each client's views and feelings regarding the family gathering, and each was asked a series of questions to further expose the meaning of events. The impasse was clarified as follows: Randy was completely unwilling to abandon his family and have no further contact with them. He actually preferred that Eric continued to accompany him, on occasion, when he went to see his family. Furthermore, he thought that Eric should see and credit the positive aspects of his family members' behavior toward them both. He acknowledged that his coming out had been difficult for his parents, siblings, and other family members to accommodate, but for the most part he was pleased with their developing acceptance and apparent greater comfort. He stated displeasure with the behavior of Bob and Troy and that he would be inclined to confront them in the future if they continued to behave offensively toward him or Eric. He did not, however, want "to create dissension in the family with a confrontation when things are progressing positively."

Eric felt highly offended by Randy's family and considered exposure to them to threaten his own sense of self-respect. He believed that Randy should maintain the same view. Further, he believed that Randy should cease involvement with them out of respect for their relationship. He believed that Randy was compromising himself by involving himself with them and that he wanted no part of it. All family should be openly accepting of them, he said, to merit devoting time to be with them, particularly as Eric and Randy had so many alternative options.

The intervention was focused on the development of a compromise in which the "costs" to each of them would be minimized. The therapist stated that it appeared most important to disallow the issue of family to create a schism in their relationship and that therapy should proceed with the objective of positively preserving the couple relationship. Both agreed. Through the use of Socratic questioning from the cognitive family therapy model, the therapist helped Eric reach the following conclusions: (1) It was unreasonable to expect Randy to terminate contact with his family; (2) he did not want to have family issues undermine their relationship; (3) it might be possible over time for both of them to be involved with some of Randy's family members; and (4) it would be appropriate for Randy to interact with his family without Eric on some occasions.

Randy was guided by the therapist in extending his strong appreciation to Eric for these conclusions, and he told Eric how meaningful it was to him that Eric was willing to compromise in such a manner. Recognizing that the compromising was primarily on Eric's part, the therapist solicited from Eric ways that Randy could compensate him for his concessions. Before Eric could respond, Randy challenged the need for compensation, saying that Eric was doing only what was right. The therapist, Randy, and Eric then discussed the unique meanings that individuals form regarding the same issues, that each of them may hold different yet respectively viable views of the same event or issue.

For Randy, based on the realization that Eric believed he was truly making sacrifices, Randy agreed to listen to Eric's thoughts. Eric first stated that he would like Randy to acknowledge and make positive comments to him in relation to future contacts with Randy's family members. Randy readily agreed. Eric then identified several social and recreational activities that he had suggested they do in the past, all of which Randy had been unwilling to do. Randy agreed to go with Eric to some outings of Eric's choosing and, further, to behave pleasantly. Randy and Eric agreed that a successful compromise had been reached. The session concluded with the targeting of several issues identified for consideration in future sessions.

Summary

In conclusion, this chapter has shown that although there are many similarities between heterosexual families and gay and lesbian families, there are remarkable differences. Several major dissimilarities have been identified and discussed. The family therapist working with gay and lesbian families should be aware of these and other factors that contribute to the experience of being gay or lesbian in society today. Therapists are challenged to expand their knowledge base to address the clinical needs of this population more effectively and to check their own clinical judgment for biases.

Process Questions

1. In what other ways might you have promoted compromise between Randy and Eric with regard to Randy's family?

2. What approaches would you use if Eric were to remain unyielding and refuse to interact with Randy's family ever again?

3. What would you do differently as a therapist if this were a heterosexual couple?

4. What would you do if you found yourself extremely uncomfortable working with this gay couple?

References

AGUERO, J. E., BLOCH, L., & BYRNE, D. (1984). The relationships among sexual beliefs, attitudes, experience, and homophobia. *Journal of Homosexuality, 10*(1/2), 95–107.

ALLEN, K., & DEMO, D. (1995). The families of lesbians and gay men: A new frontier in family research. *Journal of Marriage and the Family, 57,* 1–17.

ANDERSON, S. C. (1996). Addressing heterosexist bias in the treatment of lesbian couples with chemical dependency. In J. Laird & R. J. Green (Eds.), *Lesbians and gays in couples and families* (pp. 316–340). San Francisco: Jossey-Bass.

BANCROFT, J. (1983). *Human sexuality and its problems.* London: Churchill.

BAPTISTE, D. A. (1987). Psychotherapy with gay/lesbian couples and their children in "stepfamilies": A challenge for marriage and family therapists. *Journal of Homosexuality, 14*(1/2), 223–238.

BELL, A., & WEINBERG, M. (1978). *Homosexualities: A study of diversity among men and women.* New York: Simon & Schuster.

BERGER, R. M. (1990). Men together: Understanding the gay couple. *Journal of Homosexuality, 19*(3), 31–49.

BERRILL, K. T. (1992). Anti-gay violence and victimization in the United States: An overview. In G. M. Herek & K. T. Berrill (Eds.), *Hate crimes: Confronting violence against lesbians and gay men* (pp. 19–45). Newbury Park, CA: Sage.

BIGNER, J. J., & BOZETT, F. W. (1990). Parenting by gay fathers. In F. W. Bozett & M. B. Sussman (Eds.), *Homosexuality and family relations* (pp. 155–176). New York: Harrington Park Press.

BIGNER, J. J., & JACOBSON, R. B. (1992). Adult responses to child behavior and attitudes toward fathering: Gay and nongay fathers. *Journal of Homosexuality, 23*(3), 99–112.

BLUMSTEIN, P., & SCHWARTZ, P. (1983). *American couples: Money, work and sex.* New York: Pocket Books.

BROWN, L. (1989). Lesbians, gay men, and their families: Common clinical issues. *Journal of Gay and Lesbian Psychotherapy, 1*(1), 65–77.

BROWN, L. S. (1995). Therapy with same-sex couples: An introduction. In N. S. Jacobson & A. S. Gurman (Eds.), *Clinical handbook of couple therapy* (pp. 295–316). New York: Guilford Press.

BRYANT, A. S., & DEMIAN. (1994). Relationship characteristics of American gay and lesbian couples: Findings from a national survey. *Journal of Gay & Lesbian Social Services, 1*(2), 101–117.

BUCHANAN, D. R., POPPEN, P. J., & REISEN, C. A. (1996). The nature of partner relationship and AIDS sexual risk-taking in gay men. *Psychology and Health, 11*, 541–555.

CASPER, V., SCHULTZ, S., & WICKENS, E. (1992). Breaking the silences: Lesbian and gay parents and the schools. *Teachers College Record, 94*(1), 109–137.

CHAMBERS, D. L. (1996). What if? The legal consequences of marriage and the legal needs of lesbian and gay male couples. *Michigan Law Review, 95*, 447–491.

DEAN, L., WU, S., & MARTIN, J. (1992). Trends in violence and discrimination against gay men in New York City: 1984 to 1990. In G. M. Herek & K. T. Berrill (Eds.), *Hate crimes: Confronting violence against lesbians and gay men* (pp. 46–64). Newbury Park, CA: Sage.

DENEEN, A. A., GIJS, L., & VAN NAERSSEN, A. X. (1994). Intimacy and sexuality in gay male couples. *Journal of Sexual Behavior, 23*, 421–431.

DEPOY, E., & NOBLE, S. (1992). The structure of lesbian relationships in response to oppression. *Affilia, 7*, 49–64.

DWORKIN, J., & KAUFER, D. (1995). Social services and bereavement in the lesbian and gay community. *Journal of Gay & Lesbian Social Services, 2*(3/4), 41–60.

ETTLEBRICK, P. L. (1993). Who is a parent? The need for a lesbian conscious family law. *New York Law School Journal of Human Rights, 10*(2), 513–553.

ETTELBRICK, P. L. (1996). Legal issues in health care for lesbians and gay men. *Journal of Gay & Lesbian Social Services, 5*(1), 93–109.

EVERETT, C., & EVERETT, S. V. (1994). *Healthy divorce.* San Francisco, CA: Jossey-Bass.

FINN, P., & McNEIL, T. (1987). *The response of the criminal justice system to bias crime: An exploratory review.* Cambridge, MA: Abt Associates.

FLAKS, D. K., FICHER, I., MASTERPASQUA, F., & JOSEPH, G. (1995). Lesbians choosing motherhood: A comparative study of lesbian and heterosexual parents and their children. *Developmental Psychology, 31*, 105–114.

FOLKMAN, S., CHESNEY, M. A., & CHRISTOPHER-RICHARDS, A. (1994). Stress and coping in caregiving partners of men with AIDS. *Psychiatric Clinics of North America, 17*, 35–53.

GARBARINO, J. (1982). *Children and families in the social environment.* New York: Aldine de Gruyter.

GRANVOLD, D. K. (1989). Postdivorce treatment. In M. R. Textor (Ed.), *The divorce and divorce therapy handbook* (pp. 197–223). Northvale, NJ: Aronson.

GRANVOLD, D. K. (1994). Cognitive-behavioral divorce therapy. In D. K. Granvold (Ed.), *Cognitive and behavioral treatment: Methods and applications* (pp. 222–246). Pacific Grove, CA: Brooks/Cole.

GRANVOLD, D. K. (in press). Brief cognitive-behavioral couples therapy. *Crisis Intervention and Time-Limited Treatment, 4*(1).

GRANVOLD, D. K., & JORDAN, C. (1994). The cognitive-behavioral treatment of marital distress. In D. K. Granvold (Ed.), *Cognitive and behavioral treatment: Methods and applications* (pp. 174–201). Pacific Grove, CA: Brooks/Cole.

GREEN, R. J., BETTINGER, M., & ZACKS, E. (1996). Are lesbian couples fused and gay male couples disengaged? Questioning gender straightjackets. In J. Laird & R. J. Green (Eds.), *Lesbians and gays in couples and families* (pp. 185–230). San Francisco: Jossey-Bass.

GUIDANO, V. F. (1987). *Complexity of the self: A developmental approach to psychopathology and therapy.* New York: Guilford Press.

HANSON, B. (1996). The violence we face as lesbians and gay men: The landscape both outside and inside our communities. *Journal of Gay & Lesbian Social Services, 4*(2), 95–113.

HARE, J. (1994). Concerns and issues faced by families headed by a lesbian couple. *Families in Society, 75*, 27–35.

HAROWSKI, K. J. (1987). The worried well: Maximizing coping in the face of AIDS. *Journal of Homosexuality, 14*(1/2), 299–306.

HARTMAN, A. (1996). Social policy as a context for lesbian and gay families: The political is personal. In J. Laird & R. J. Green (Eds.), *Lesbians and gays in couples and families* (pp. 69–85). San Francisco: Jossey-Bass.

HARVEY, S. M., CARR, C., & BERNHEINE, S. (1989). Lesbian mothers: Health care experiences. *Journal of Nurse-Midwifery, 34*(3), 115–119.

HEREK, G. (1989). Hate crimes against lesbians and gay men. *American Psychologist, 44*, 948–955.

HEREK, G. M., & GLUNT, E. K. (1993). Interpersonal contact and heterosexuals' attitudes toward gay men: Results from a national survey. *The Journal of Sex Research, 30*, 239–244.

HUNTER, S., SHANNON, C., MARTIN, J. I., & KNOX, J. (in press). *Knowledge for human services practice with lesbian, gay, and bisexual people.* Thousand Oaks, CA: Sage.

JOHNSON, T. W., & KEREN, M. S. (1996). Creating and maintaining boundaries in male couples. In J. Laird & R. J. Green (Eds.), *Lesbians and gays in couples and families* (pp. 231–250). San Francisco: Jossey-Bass.

KASLOW, F. W., & SCHWARTZ, L. L. (1987). *The dynamics of divorce: A life cycle perspective.* New York: Brunner/Mazel.

KRESTAN, K., & BEPKO, C. (1980). The problem of fusion in the lesbian relationship. *Family Process, 19,* 277–289.

KURDEK, L. A. (1993). The allocation of household labor in gay, lesbian, and heterosexual married couples. *Journal of Social Issues, 49*(3), 127–139.

KURDEK, L. A. (1995). Lesbian and gay couples. In A. R. D'Augelli & C. J. Patterson (Eds.), *Lesbian, gay, and bisexual identities over the lifespan: Psychological perspectives* (pp. 243–261). New York: Oxford University Press.

LAIRD, J., & GREEN, R. J. (1996). Lesbians and gays in couples and families: Central issues. In J. Laird & R. J. Green (Eds.), *Lesbians and gays in couples and families* (pp. 1–12). San Francisco: Jossey-Bass.

Lambda Legal Defense and Education Fund, Inc. (1995). Marriage project: Background. (Available from Author, 120 Wall Street, New York NY 10005.)

LAND, H., & HARANGODY, G. (1990). A support group for partners of persons with AIDS. *Families in Society, 71,* 471–481.

LESLIE, L. A. (1995). The evolving treatment of gender, ethnicity, and sexual orientation in marital and family therapy. *Family Relations, 44,* 359–367.

LEVINE, M. P., & LEONARD, R. (1984). Discrimination against lesbians in the work force. *Signs: Journal of Women in Culture and Society, 9,* 700–710.

LEVY, E. (1996). Reproductive issues for lesbians. *Journal of Gay & Lesbian Social Services, 5*(1), 49–58.

LEVY, E. F. (1992). Strengthening the coping resources of lesbian families. *Families in Society, 73,* 23–31.

LIVINGSTON, D. (1996). A systems approach to AIDS counseling for gay couples. *Journal of Gay & Lesbian Social Services, 4*(2), 83–93.

LOTT-WHITEHEAD, L., & TULLY, C. T. (1993). The family lives of lesbian mothers. *Smith College Studies in Social Work, 63,* 266–280.

LOULAN, J. (1984). *Lesbian sex.* San Francisco: Spinsters, Inc.

LOULAN, J. (1987). *Lesbian passion.* San Francisco: Spinsters, Inc.

MARTIN, J. I., (1997). Political aspects of mental health treatment. In T. R. Watkins & J. W. Callicutt (Eds.), *Mental health policy and practice today* (pp. 32–48). Thousand Oaks, CA: Sage.

MATTISON, A. M., & MCWHIRTER, D. P. (1994). Serodiscordant male couples. *Journal of Gay & Lesbian Social Services, 1*(2), 83–99.

MCLEAN, C., & ROBERTS, R. (1995). Sex, intimacy, and AIDS: Lessons in relationships from thirteen Australian gay men. *AIDS Patient Care, 9,* 166–171.

MCLEAN, J., BOULTON, M., BROOKES, M., LAKHANI, D., FITZPATRICK, R., DAWSON, J., MCKECHNIE, R., & HART, G. (1994). Regular partners and risky behaviour: Why do gay men have unprotected intercourse? *AIDS Care, 6,* 331–341.

METZ, M. E., ROSSER, B. R. S., & STRAPKO, N. (1994). Differences in conflict-resolution styles among heterosexual, gay, and lesbian couples. *The Journal of Sex Research, 31*(4), 293–308.

MEYER, C. L. (1992). Legal, psychological, and medical considerations in lesbian parenting. *Law and Sexuality, 2,* 237–264.

MORIN, S. F. (1977). Heterosexist bias in psychological research on lesbianism and male homosexuality. *American Psychologist, 32,* 629–637.

MORROW, S., & HAWXHURST, D. (1989). Lesbian partner abuse: Implications for therapists. *Journal of Counseling and Development, 68,* 58–62.

MURPHY, B. C. (1994). Difference and diversity: Gay and lesbian couples. *Journal of Gay & Lesbian Social Services, 1*(2), 5–31.

National Association of Social Workers. (1996). The National Association of Social Workers code of ethics. *NASW News, 41*(10), A1–4.

NORD, D. (1996). Assessing the negative effects of multiple AIDS-related loss on the gay individual and community. *Journal of Gay & Lesbian Social Services, 4*(3), 1–34.

PEPLAU, L. A. (1991). Lesbian and gay relationships. In J. C. Gonsiorek & J. D. Weinrich (Eds.), *Homosexuality: Research implications for public policy* (pp. 177–196). Newbury Park, CA: Sage.

PIERCE, D. (1995, March). *Lesbian/gay adoption services in the United States: Policy and practice implications.* Paper presented at the 41st Annual Program Meeting of the Council on Social Work Education, San Diego, CA.

PLUMMER, K. (1981). Homosexual categories: Some research problems in the labeling perspective of homosexuality. In K. Plummer (Ed.), *The making of the modern homosexual* (pp. 53–75). Totowa, NJ: Barnes & Noble.

POWELL-COPE, G. M. (1995). The experiences of gay couples affected by HIV infection. *Qualitative Health Research, 5,* 36–62.

PRATTE, T. (1993). A comparative study of attitudes toward homosexuality: 1986 and 1991. *Journal of Homosexuality, 26*(1), 77–83.

REAMER, F. G. (1993). AIDS and social work: The ethics and civil liberties agenda. *Social Work, 38,* 412–419.

REILLY, M. E., & LYNCH, J. M. (1990). Power-sharing in lesbian partnerships. *Journal of Homosexuality, 19*(3), 1–30.

REMIEN, R. H., CARBALLO-DIÉGUEZ, A., & WAGNER, G. (1995). Intimacy and sexual risk behaviour in serodiscordant male couples. *AIDS Care, 7,* 429–438.

RENZETTI, C. (1989). Building a second closet: Third party responses to victims of lesbian partner abuse. *Family Relations, 38,* 157–163.

RICE, J. K., & RICE, D. G. (1986). *Living through divorce: A developmental approach to divorce therapy.* New York: Guilford Press.

ROHRBAUGH, J. B. (1992). Lesbian families: Clinical issues and theoretical implications. *Professional Psychology: Research and Practice, 23,* 467–473.

SAGER, C. J. (1976). *Marriage contracts and couple therapy: Hidden forces in intimate relationships.* New York: Brunner/Mazel.

SAVIN-WILLIAMS, R. C. (1994). Verbal and physical abuse as stressors in the lives of lesbian, gay male, and bisexual youths: Associations with school problems, running away, substance abuse, prostitution, and suicide. *Journal of Consulting and Clinical Psychology, 62,* 261–269.

SCHILIT, R., LIE, G., BUSH, J., MONTAGNE, M., & REYES, L. (1991). Intergenerational transmission of violence in lesbian relationships. *Affilia, 6*(1), 72–87.

SHERNOFF, M. (1984). Family therapy for lesbians and gay clients. *Social Work, 29,* 393–396.

SHUSTER, S. (1996). Families coping with HIV disease in gay fathers. In J. Laird & R. J. Green (Eds.), *Lesbians and gays in couples and families* (pp. 404–419). San Francisco: Jossey-Bass.

SISLEY, E., & HARRIS, B. (1977). *The joy of lesbian sex.* New York: Simon & Schuster.

SLATER, S., & MENCHER, J. (1991). The lesbian family life cycle: A contextual approach. *American Journal of Orthopsychiatry, 6,* 372–382.

SPIELMAN, S., & WINFELD, L. (1996). Domestic partner benefits: A bottom line discussion. *Journal of Gay & Lesbian Social Services, 4*(4), 53–78.

STEIN, T. J. (1996). Child custody and visitation: The rights of lesbian and gay parents. *Social Service Review, 70,* 435–450.

STEVENS, P. E., & HALL, J. M. (1988). Stigma, health beliefs and experiences with health care in lesbian women. *Images, 20*(2), 69–73.

SWIGONSKI, M. E. (1995). Claiming a lesbian identity as an act of empowerment. *Affilia, 10,* 413–425.

TEXTOR, M. (Ed.). (1989). *The divorce and divorce therapy handbook.* Northvale, NJ: Aronson.

USSHER, J. M. (1991). Family and couple therapy with gay and lesbian clients: Acknowledging the forgotten minority. *Journal of Family Therapy, 13,* 131–148.

VAN WYCK, P., & GEIST, C. (1984). Psychosocial development of heterosexual, bisexual, and homosexual behaviour. *Archives of Sexual Behaviour, 13,* 505–544.

VISS, D. C., & BURN, S. M. (1992). Divergent perceptions of lesbians: A comparison of lesbian self-perceptions and heterosexual perceptions. *The Journal of Social Psychology, 132,* 169–177.

VON SCHULTHESS, B. (1992). Violence in the streets: Anti-lesbian assault and harrassment in San Francisco. In G. M. Herek & K. T. Berrill (Eds.), *Hate crimes: Confronting violence against lesbians and gay men* (pp. 65–75). Newbury Park, CA: Sage.

WALLACH, J. (1989). AIDS anxiety among health care professionals. *Hospital and Community Psychiatry, 40,* 507–510.

WEINBERG, G. (1972). *Society and the healthy homosexual.* Garden City, NY: Anchor Press.

WEISSTUB, E. B., & SHOENFELD, H. (1987). Brief goal-limited couple therapy in the treatment of homosexuals. *American Journal of Psychotherapy, 41,* 95–103.

WESTON, K. (1991). *Families we choose.* New York: Columbia University Press.

CHAPTER TWELVE

Sophia F. Dziegielewski, Ph.D.
University of Central Florida

Dianne Harrison Montgomery, Ph.D.
Florida State University

Gender Issues in Family Therapy

This chapter reviews the construct of gender, how gender is viewed and developed in the cultural environment, and most important, how gender relates to the theoretical formulation and practice of family therapy by social work professionals. Gender is examined in terms of the traditional roots of theories central to the practice of family therapy, an alternate framework, practice applications, and special topics. In particular, women's issues and the subjugated role of women are discussed. Incorporating gender and women's issues into the foundation of family therapy is viewed as an essential ingredient for ethical and effective practice in today's practice contexts. Many times in the past, the importance of gender has been overlooked or ignored by traditional models and techniques of family therapy, including most of the models discussed in this book. The one exception is newer social construction and narrative models discussed in Chapter 6. Because family practice models traditionally have not given much attention to gender constructions and their effects on family problems, our discussion of gender in this chapter will help practitioners using the various models develop a more gender-sensitive practice.

The Concept of Gender in Society

The family is the unit that provides the basic environment for identifying, learning, and adapting the basic gender role orientations that will surround individuals through the rest of their lives. Family structure is a major dimension in the development of gender roles, even having been called the "cradle of gender roles" (Lipman-Blumen, 1984). To understand gender role development in the family, family structure and composition must be examined.

There is little challenge of the family's importance in shaping a child's own gender identity, the social and role expectations each gender is expected to exhibit, and the child's gender-specific social and emotional development. Williamson (1991) discussed this concept of family influence, concluding that the way an individual resolves family of origin issues will determine how he or she will handle all intimate relationships in later life. At the center of the family are the parents. The influence of parents (or primary caregivers) on the growth and development of their children has long been a subject for investigation; one study of 139 high school seniors reported that both boys and girls had enhanced self-esteem when their opposite sex parent was warm and supportive (Richards, Gitelson, Petersen, & Hurtig, 1991).

Note, however, that through the family is not the only way children learn, adapt, and absorb gender roles and gender identity. Gender roles are learned and relearned throughout the life cycle (Lipman-Blumen, 1984). As individuals take on new roles (e.g., marriage, parenthood), they are challenged to adapt new methods of adjusting to life's demands. Once a role or value is incorporated into the schema of the individual, it is not easily changed. "The experience of challenging personal beliefs and letting go of prior self-perceptions often provokes intense emotions" (Garcia & Van Soest, 1997, p. 119). C. S. Stoll (1978) claimed in her book, *Female and Male*, that there is no such thing as *sex roles*. Her objection to this term surrounded the simplicity often given the definition. She believed that in examining the term *sex role*, more must be considered than what makes girls females and boys males. It involves the complicated processes by which children are introduced to families at birth, as well as the subtle (and not so subtle) differences expected from each. Those who want to "fit in" will conform to the role-consistent stereotypes (Andrews, 1992).

For many years, there has been a struggle to understand how men and women relate to each other in all ways. The conventional definition used to measure this phenomenon of differentiation usually focused on understanding the *differences* between the sexes (Hare-Mustin & Maracek, 1988). In this chapter an emphasis is placed on the difference between men and women, how it has been used in the past, and how it can currently be used to overlook gender considerations in therapy or to further support gender superiority—males over females.

Theoretical Thought in Regard to Gender

Constructivism and deconstructivism are two postmodern movements that have influenced the ways individuals think about the meanings associated with life, and consequently, the ways life is represented. Constructivism challenges the scientific tradition of positivism—the basic premise that reality can be distinguished, observed, and measured. In the constructivism theories of gender, similar to other scientific theories, reality is organized by assumptive frameworks that reflect certain interests (Hare-Mustin & Maracek, 1988); language, the primary mode of communication, is considered to be biased in the presentation of information. In constructivism, there appear to be two means of approaching bias. The first is to exaggerate the differences between the groups; the second is to minimize or ignore the differences. Examples of current theoretical frameworks that highlight differences between the sexes are Freudian, Jungian, and Eriksonian theory. Several psychological theories do not pinpoint or highlight the differences between the sexes, resulting in possible minimizing or ignoring of the differences between them. Examples are the general systems theory and communications theories.

Deconstructivism, which is based on the philosophy of Derrida, denies the existence of a single fixed reality and claims that the language or text by which individuals communicate can be translated in many different ways. In deconstructivism, "just as the meaning of a word depends on what the word is not, the meaning of a text partly depends on what the text does not say" (Hare-Mustin & Maracek, 1988, p. 460). When Hare-Mustin and Maracek (1988) relate this theory to the action of the therapist in the therapeutic environment, the relationship is clarified. In the therapeutic situation, the therapist is influenced by his or her own background and beliefs. Therefore, each therapist approaches therapy from the cultural environment and the cultural biases he or she recognizes as natural or "normal" (Hansen, 1993; Jones, 1995; Sohng, 1994). These assumptions can keep us from seeing and/or discovering things that are essential to providing relevant, beneficial treatment (McHugh, 1993; Uehara et al., 1996).

In the therapeutic setting, the therapist is responsible for interpreting and finding meaning in what the client says, and this interpretation is not based solely on what the client has stated. The therapist must listen and respond by helping the client to solve the problems in what is determined to be the "real" situation. Further, therapists are expected to give clients permission to feel as they do, help them gain advice from family and friends, and provide encouragement and assistance to break current cycles of dysfunctional behaviors (Friedman, 1997).

In summary, early in a child's life, she or he is subjected to differential treatment and identification. Children will be dealt with differently based on their sex by both the parents and the larger societal network, and each child will be forced to model himself or herself after the appropriate gender lines. Research in this area has been difficult because of complications in isolating and defining the domain of behavior and the method of observation; also, parents and children appear to be influenced by the "formalized" laboratory rating process (Weitz, 1977).

Most of the inquiry made into gender has focused on the importance of outlining the so-called actual differences between male and female characteristics. Are there true physical, cognitive, and personality differences among the sexes? From a medical-biological perspective, most professionals would answer yes. There are obvious differences in physical structure, anatomy, and so on. More recently, an example has come to highlight this difference. When controlling for most factors (e.g., size, dose, etc.), therapeutic response to certain drugs can differ between males and females (Medical Economics, 1994, 1997).

When viewing gender divergence from a social-psychological perspective, differences that are more difficult to measure are often neglected. Based on this lack of attention, "broader social issues relating to sex and gender stereotyping and unfair practices of sexism" (Dziegielewski, Resnick, & Krause, 1996, p. 169) can be overlooked. Further, the term *gender difference* has picked up so much extraneous context that developing a definite construct for it in social work research remains difficult. One possible reason for this difficulty is explained by Hare-Mustin and Maracek (1988). After reviewing literature in the area, they reported that most differences between males and females tended to be culturally fluid. That means that defining the construct for measurement and the resulting differences between the sexes is complicated by changes in the environment in which the measurement occurs.

In regard to differential treatment, great strides have been made in acknowledging and recognizing sex gender bias. Writing now generally avoids the use of sexist language; written and oral communications about child rearing and child care (especially manuals) highlight the contributions and strides of each gender; the educational toys adults encourage children to play with are generally considered generic; there is increased acceptance of children using nontraditional toys for play; and in clothing, it is now possible for males to wear colored clothing that would have traditionally been considered unacceptable (e.g., pink shirts). However, given the reality that sex roles are woven so tightly into our beliefs, most professionals would agree that it is almost impossible to raise a child in this society without sex role bias. Even though parents and others may be more likely to recognize, identify, and acknowledge the importance of gender neutral influences, as products of the society at large, they seem to have definite ideas about sex role deviance (Weitz, 1977) and the importance of adherence to the "traditional" roles for future success.

Introduction to Family Therapy

The field of family therapy is a broad one that includes numerous theorists, schools of thought, and ways therapists can practice with their clients (Goldenberg & Goldenberg, 1994). In defining practice, one must include who is treated, how clients are treated, and the goals of the therapy itself. Many family therapists believe that the entire identified family does not have to be in the treatment session at the same time for successful family therapy to occur (Ferber, 1973; Bowen, 1978); others, however, believe they should (Satir, 1972). In general, though, the family unit is the primary interest of family therapy rather than how many people are in the room. The identified family is considered the focus of treatment.

How clients are treated is open to considerable variability because of the diversity found among those who call themselves family therapists. Some treat families from a psychoanalytic framework; they emphasize intrapsychic conflict as the cause of emotional distress, a focus that requires a concentration on history and development. Other therapists may focus on problem solving and restructuring, which requires that therapeutic emphasis be placed on the "here and now." Still others might focus on family behavior as it is maintained by reinforcement. Family practice models in this book all stress brief and systems perspectives, emphasizing the here-and-now orientation. Most family therapists, including those embracing the perspectives in this book, agree that the locus of pathology or pain to be addressed in treatment is the family system. How this situation or problem is to be addressed and who is to be involved in treatment is left open to the therapist. Most family therapists agree that the therapeutic goals that need to be developed within the family system include facilitating communication; modeling, educating, and strengthening the system; dispelling myths or changing meanings; strengthening the marriage; and helping to identify what the system needs, and to shift and adjust toward change or the maintenance of the family system equilibrium.

Treatment of Gender in Family Therapy

TRADITIONAL ROOTS

The *family* is considered the center for intervention in family therapy. The family is a naturally occurring group for both men and women, and this naturally occurring group should not, but often is, overlooked and underemphasized as to the impact it can have in the therapeutic environment (Gilligan, 1982; Hare-Mustin, 1986). Gilligan (1982) believed that women often gain their sense of identity within the context of relationships. The qualities that women often possess and contribute to these relationships (i.e., warmth and emotional expressiveness) are downplayed and characterized as indicative of the "weaker sex."

Hare-Mustin (1986) stated that family therapy is full of gender bias because the theoretical framework(s) that provide its roots either ignore or exaggerate gender. In the practice theories used to explore and examine family dynamics, gender issues are not always identified and recognized as a natural part of treatment; therefore, in many cases, gender differences have gone virtually unnoticed (Hare-Mustin & Maracek, 1988).

Most professionals would agree that psychoanalytic theory, social learning theory, the cognitive-development model(s), and the integration of systems and communications theory have impacted the foundation of family therapy. Further, the theoretical core of family therapy, regardless of the specific model of practice used, is primarily intertwined with general systems theory and communication theory. To understand how gender is addressed in family therapy, the roots of these theoretical frameworks are examined.

Earlier, the importance of differentiation in understanding gender was discussed. In addition to differentiation, the process of identification is considered equally important. Several of the theories that are considered basic in sex role development and in the origin of family therapy (psychoanalytic theory, social learning theory, and the cognitive-behavioral development models) highlight this concept of identification. Identification is considered necessary to both the development of a child's own gender identity and the social and role expectations each gender is expected to exhibit.

All three of these theories purport that a primary influence in this identification process is linked to two primary role model groups: the child's parents or identified caretakers, and other role models made accessible through the media, social contacts, and other sources. From a theoretical perspective, most of the influence is placed on the parents, making these models consistent with the societal base in which they were created.

Gender identification in psychoanalytic theory needs to be examined because psychoanalytic theory is the foundation underlying the training of so many social workers. This perspective is not discussed in this text because it is not thought to offer very much clinical utility for today's practice environments. In the psychoanalytic model of therapy, the roots of identification with the child's parents are clear. Freud focused primarily on the psychosexual development of the child. This development was considered an integral part of the child's social adjustment, influencing all present and future decisions in the child's life (Freud, 1939). Because sexuality is such an integral part of the child's life, there is overlap between the genders for the desire and love of the parent(s). The child undergoes many levels of adaptation to this love. The adaptation process as identified in psychoanalytic theory is very different for males and females, with the male considered to focus on the enjoyment of sex and women to be concerned with the interpersonal level of the relationship (Weitz, 1977). Most professionals agree that this view was consistent with attitudes in the Victorian Era in which Freud lived, and that his observations and subsequent writings were highly influenced by the societal climate of his time.

In the social learning model, as in the psychoanalytic model, role modeling, imitation, or learning through observation are thought to be basic ingredients in child development (Bandura, 1977). Social learning influences the cognitive-behavioral models covered in Chapter 4 as well as the family preservation perspective covered in Chapter 8. The social learning model of therapy, however, seems to focus on more discrete and measurable responses as opposed to the holistic and possibly inseparable nature of behavior learning and identification in psychoanalysis. In social learning theory, attention is placed on directly rewarding and punishing behaviors so as to shape new behaviors. The child learns what behaviors are directly appropriate to his or her sex by the immediate reward or punishment that follows. The biggest controversy over this model of explanation is its lack of emphasis on the personality, and how particular individuals might relate differently to environmental cues based on their personality differences (Weitz, 1977).

In the cognitive-developmental model theorized by individuals such as Kohlberg and Piaget, gender—the only fixed general category that individuals fall into—takes on significance in explaining a predetermined sequencing of development (Kohlberg, 1981; Piaget, 1965). Piaget's original interests were in biology and epistemology, and his four stages of cognitive development reflect the influence of both fields (Piaget, 1965). According to Piaget, a child in the *sensorimotor stage* (ages 0–2) does not establish object permanence or object concept (the ability to understand that objects continue to exist when they are out of sight) until the end of this stage. Therefore, the child cannot truly identify the differences between the sexes or know whether these characteristics are bound to one particular sex. For example, if a 2-year-old boy were dressed like a girl other same age children could see him and believe his sex had changed also. However, as children grow older (by approximately 6 or 7 years of age), they can abstract more information and they generally have a stated clear preference for their own gender identity.

Cognitive-developmental theory helps to explain how children identify sex roles by watching and modeling, considering also a child's physical size and strength as well as mental readiness; however, it does not take into account the significant influences of the social environment. A second disadvantage of this model is gender bias in the research used to support it. This research, like most studies prior to the last decade, has primarily used males rather than females as subjects. One can only guess how this cognitive developmental theory would relate to females. The problem is not unique to this particular developmental theory; most generalizations about human growth and development have been made after studying male subjects (Wood, 1994). Over the last 10 years, this trend has begun to diminish, but the vast amount of the research literature contains observations of "normal" human behavior based on male subjects.

Two further theoretical approaches that underlie much of family therapy are general systems theory and communications theory. In systems theory, the concept of *wholeness* (i.e., changes in one part can change the whole system) allows pathology to shift from one person to another. For example, if a one member gets well, another may take on the pathology. Wholeness can be particularly important in the therapeutic context because it allows the concentration to be removed from the individual (the identified problem) and placed on the family unit as a whole (the problem system). The concept of *non-summativity* simply means that the family has an identity of its own. The family system is more than the sum of its individual members. For treatment to be successful, this family entity must be treated as a whole. In family therapy, *equifinality* means that the same results can be obtained from different causes, and *equipotentiality (multifinality)* can occur when one cause can produce different results or behaviors in the individual. Last, central to systems family therapy is the concept of *homeostasis*, meaning that a system will try to maintain or restore the status quo in the event of any change. As the family system reacts, *negative feedback* is used to bring a family back into balance and maintain homeostasis (Goldenberg & Goldenberg, 1994). For example, if a woman wants to leave her young child at day care and go to work, her fear of her husband's disapproval may be enough incentive to change her mind. *Positive feedback,* on the other hand, is used to disturb or unbalance homeostasis by putting the flow of output back into a system (Goldenberg & Goldenberg, 1994). For example, if the same woman decided going to work outside the home was her choice, positive feedback would be used to get her family to redefine their roles for the changes that must occur in the family system. Positive feedback is often used by family therapists in the therapeutic relationship to allow a more functional family balance to emerge. These concepts are explored in more detail in Chapter 14 as they relate to advances in systems theory.

From a systems framework, family therapists are expected to be somewhat objective observers who help to interpret and reframe the situation. In the newer cybernetic systems models, however—sometimes called cybernetics of cybernetics—an observer cannot be objective as the observer cannot be totally separated from what is being observed (Becvar & Becvar, 1995). Traditional models did not acknowledge this lack of objectivity. In traditional models, gender differences were not formally acknowledged or considered in treatment, and the modifications utilized today are still deficient (Jones, 1995). Hare-Mustin (1987) noted that in family therapy from a systems perspective, therapists do not acknowledge the role definitions and expectations placed on individuals by the society and cultural environment in which we live. By virtue of living and growing in this environment, individuals are affected by these distinctions and therefore cannot be objective observers; they cannot view family dynamics as if gender and role distinctions do not exist. Lau (1995) warns that this is a particular problem for therapists working with ethnic minorities, who tend to be deeply influenced by religious values and patriarchal beliefs. Addressing multicultural issues remains essential (Van Soest, 1995; Atherton & Bolland, 1997).

The second major theoretical framework in family therapy rests in communications theory. Inclusion of this theoretical foundation is generally credited to Satir, Haley, and others who emphasized communication. Chapter 3 in this text covers Haley's model and other models that were influenced by communication theory. These professionals believe it is impossible not to communicate (Satir, 1972; Haley, 1971). Here emphasis is placed on *behavior as communication* and the message inconsistencies that can occur. To understand communication in this perspective, it must be observed from at least two levels. The first is the *surface level,* here, the communication is overt in its content. The message is given and the meaning is translated. For example, a mother may tell her child that he cannot eat a particular snack. The communicated message clearly says "Do not eat the snack." The second level is *metacommunication;* in this level, the first level is commented on. In metacommunication, emphasis is placed on the context in which the overt message is transferred. Individual characteristics are isolated and critiqued, including such characteristics as voice tone, gesture, and body posture. In the metacommunication, individuals communicate about their communications (Lazarus, 1977). As in the previous example, the child may examine the behavior(s) of his mother in transmitting this message. Does she seem distracted? The child may wonder, Is she really saying I cannot eat this now? The child interprets her words as he watches her lean forward and say not to eat the snack while placing it on the counter in his reach.

According to Hare-Mustin (1987), communication theory highlights the problem of ignoring gender. In metacommunication, a precise communication pattern is generally examined. In isolating this pattern, the views of the society at large and the way these beliefs and mores affect the communication process are not examined.

In summary, although these approaches have been extremely influential in the development of family therapy, they have tended to ignore the sociocultural aspects of gender in treatment (Hare-Mustin, 1987; Lau, 1995; Jones, 1995; Maracek & Hare-Mustin, 1991). When they are acknowledged, gender is viewed as experiential and uniquely defined by the relationship (Terry, 1992).

AN ALTERNATIVE THEORETICAL PERSPECTIVE

To help explain the necessity of including gender in family therapy, a feminist perspective is often cited (Burck & Speed, 1995; Jones, 1995). The majority of social work professionals who subscribe to this theory are females, and the males who support the theory are generally referred to as *profeminists.* Males are identified with a separate term because it is believed that by virtue of being male, they cannot truly know what it is to live as a female (Tolman, Mowry, Jones, & Brekke, 1986).

The feminist perspective first became popular in family therapy approximately 15 years ago, and it has been beneficial in highlighting the importance of gender in explaining family relations. Postmodern feminism is rooted in poststructuralism, postmodern philosophy, and French feminist theory (Sands & Nuccio, 1992). These theories generally became popular around the same time and many of their concepts overlap. Feminist writings and theory are helpful in the practice of family therapy just as in the broader society: They show that women are often placed in a degraded position by the sociocultural context in which they live (Concian, 1991). Many link this to the historical patriarchal belief system that is ingrained in our value and belief system; others simply attribute the devaluing of women to the past economic productivity and power of males (Hartman, 1995).

Feminist theory purports that taking into account a society's subscribed belief system makes it almost impossible to treat a family system without regard to the accepted role patterns and behaviors that have been typified as male and female. Feminism has been referred to as a form of oppositional knowledge (Maracek & Hare-Mustin, 1991) as it challenges this accepted dogma and warns the therapist not to fall into the stereotypic patterns. In these patterns, the male is generally viewed as the "doer" who is always rational, logical, and in control, the female is the "nurturer" who is often emotional, illogical, and needy. Women are therefore often viewed as suited to "caring" and expected to take a caregiver/caretaker role because of their child-bearing ability (Wilkes, 1995).

Unfortunately, these stereotypes have often been found in the family therapy literature (Hare-Mustin, 1986); many therapists may not realize the gender bias they are subscribing to because it is so natural to them. This bias may then go unnoticed in their practice. The feminists further warn that acknowledging this issue in therapy may not be enough actually to implement a change in practice. "The point being made here is that the politics of family life and the politics of family therapy are not necessarily susceptible to transformation by sheer clinical acumen" (Goldner, 1985, p. 45). Goldner's words may be the basis for one of the greatest criticisms of incorporating this feminist perspective into current practice principles: It isn't going to be easy.

To engage in a gender-sensitive practice, the therapist must reinterpret the whole concept of the family system to include gender as a naturally occurring phenomenon. Some professionals believe that gender inclusion must be taken even further than requested by the traditional feminists and to be accurately addressed, it must include the true epistemological ecosystemic constructs that remain relevant to the society (Auerswald, 1987).

In synopsis, recognition of the feminist perspective of gender and power relations is considered paramount to effective therapeutic research, intervention, and assessment. To summarize the methodology of feminism, five elements are generally considered: (1) In this society, gender inequality is highlighted, and many times women are oppressed by the society's patriarchal nature. (2) The individual experiences of men and women are considered the cornerstone of all social science understanding through research; here the use of interviews and ethnographies to validate feelings is highlighted. (3) This method has a social action component with the primary emphasis on improving the conditions that women experience. (4) Feminism questions the roots of traditional research and the ways gender bias exists in this research, noting that as products of the society, researchers cannot be objective observers. (5) Feminists feel that researchers and subjects should not be separated, generally favoring more interactive models for establishing information (Concian, 1991).

Whether one agrees with the feminist perspective or not, feminist contributions have clearly been a major force in stimulating and reformulating the traditional methods of counseling, and for developing new areas of inquiry and practice (Burck & Speed, 1995; Jones, 1995; Gilbert, 1991; Lott, 1991).

Current Status of Gender in Family Therapy

During the last 10 years, family therapy has come under attack for not including gender issues or concerns in treatment. Some have argued that in the practice of family therapy, gender concerns have been ignored, and that theories and interventions that disadvantage women have actively been taught (Coleman, Avis, & Turin, 1990). More recent family practice models, such as the social construction and narrative perspectives covered in Chapter 6, have highlighted the importance of gender and other sociocultural issues; but for the most part, gender has not been adequately addressed in family practice perspectives. In a study of 55 family therapy programs conducted by Coleman, Avis, and Turin (1990), only 27 programs either identified with a feminist perspective or seemed to have a clearly defined sense of gender awareness. Based on their results, these researchers suggested that the study of the role of gender in the training of family therapists was generally overlooked or absent. When gender was included, it was mostly discussed when gender topics were introduced in the classroom or supervision setting.

This chapter has reviewed family therapy from the following perspectives: (1) the introduction of the concept of gender to the individual, and therefore the importance of this concept in shaping the family system; and (2) how gender is addressed in family therapy, through both its traditional and alternate theoretical frameworks. Taking this information into account, the authors are left to contemplate why gender, with its ingrained importance in the family system, is not a fundamental organizing principle by which all family therapy is conducted.

It appears clear that "gender and gendering power are not secondary mediating variables affecting family life; they construct family life in the deepest sense" (Goldner, 1988, p. 280). Not only does the concept of generation (age) need to be part of the infrastructure with which all family practice models are based, but so does gender (sex). Family therapists are urged to advocate the inclusion of gender as an inseparable part of the family system and not just to emphasize its importance.

Gender and Brief Behavioral Family Therapy

Behavioral family therapy is rooted in social learning theory and classical and operant conditioning models. (The cognitive-behavioral perspectives in family practice are covered in more detail in Chapter 4.) This form of family therapy is generally characterized as viewing all behaviors as learned. It emphasizes the use of directive techniques and places importance on the ongoing assessment and evaluation of progress in therapy. A brief time-limited framework appears to be the future for practice in the field of social work (Dziegielewski, 1996, 1997), and in behavioral brief family therapy models, identification of specific behaviors and the brief format for service delivery are highlighted (Smyrnios & Kirkby, 1992).

Liberman (1973) cited the three main areas of technical concern for the behavioral family therapist: (1) creating and maintaining a positive therapeutic alliance, (2) making a behavioral analysis of the problem, and (3) implementing the behavioral principles of behavior reinforcement and modeling in the context of the therapeutic environment. Feminists have argued that in the traditional roots of behavioral family therapy, as well as in many other forms of brief family therapy, gender issues are not considered unless they come up in the therapeutic environment. For example, behavioral couples therapy implicitly emphasizes egalitarian relationships between men and women. Although this is a desirable relationship pattern in the view of most feminists, it was found to be ineffective in couples with patriarchally influenced gender roles (Jacobson & Christensen, 1996). Given this and other findings, it seems that gender inequities in therapy need to be addressed more directly so that these behaviors can be explored. Traditionally, behavioral therapy does not appear to have done this. However, brief behavioral therapy does appear to have the potential to adjust to this focus.

In traditional behavioral family therapy, two major areas have generally been considered. The first deals with identifying the behaviors that are adaptive or maladaptive (Liberman, 1973). Here the primary focus is placed on the actual behavior exhibited and the influences that affect it. When dysfunctional behaviors occur in the family system, they are generally viewed as learned, interactional responses. Therefore, if a difficulty arises in the family unit, it is generally explored in relation to how it has been reinforced. The parents or the primary caregivers are generally noted for having a strong influence on the development of child behavior problems whether they are aware of their influence or not.

The second area examines the particular environmental or interpersonal circumstances that currently support the problematic behavior. This examination is often referred to as a functional analysis (Liberman, 1973). It is here that the concept of gender is recognized. If gender issues are presented behaviorally and contribute to the social reinforcement of behavior patterns in the family, they will be addressed. For example, if a family's definitions of masculine and feminine role expectations affect the behaviors that each is expected to perform, they may block the therapist's ability to model more adaptive behaviors. Here the concept of gender will be clearly addressed, making the family unit more functional. Behavioral family therapy has always acknowledged the importance of societal reinforcers and learned behaviors (Smyrnios & Kirkby, 1992). It could be argued that all identified roles of male and female behavior are learned and reinforced within the societal and cultural climate in which individuals live. The difficulty, however, comes in knowing how to acknowledge this strong influence and adapt it for the therapeutic environment.

The feminists urge incorporating gender into the foundation of treatment. In modifying the behavior within a family system, the therapist will not be able to change society. In addition, this lack of ability to achieve societal and cultural change can be directly related to therapeutic outcome, resulting in the greatest limitation noted for brief, behavior-oriented family therapy as well as most traditional forms of family therapy. Stated simply, communication patterns in the family may change, but they are influenced by the society at large; the society may help to maintain the original patterns, no matter how much family system intervention is practiced. Nevertheless, therapists and families should not overreact and throw away the clinical progress they have made. It is clear that the feminist perspective is valid in the point that social workers and other family therapists must incorporate an understanding of gender role expectations and how these expectations will influence future therapeutic process. The recognition and anticipation of gender influences on the therapeutic gains cannot be underestimated. In current forms of brief behavioral family therapy, gender needs to be considered as a basic building block, along with such concepts as generation (age) and ethnic and cultural implications. Operating with this mind-set, therapists can look at the behavior patterns that are reinforced in this pattern. With a gender mind-set, the issue of gender can be addressed in regard to the treatment setting.

The effectiveness of brief behavioral family therapy has been well documented, especially in the areas of parent skills training, reducing dysfunctional behavior in children, problem-solving training, communication skills training, reduction of marital discord and treatment of sexual dysfunctions. Behavioral therapy is a successful form of intervention that would be enhanced by including the concept of gender. In using behavioral therapy to address family problems, treating gender as natural to the basis of interactions is strongly recommended.

Special Topics

Changing Role of Women

Women have been the primary child rearers and nurturers throughout history; however, this role is clearly in need of modification. Because of the patriarchal structure of society, women are expected to provide household services and emotional support whether they work in or outside the home (Bellas, 1992). As women continue to become more active in roles outside the home, sharing family labor and tasks has become essential. Women cannot do it all, and many of the traditional patterns of sex role behavior will be forced to change as they are no longer functional. The accepted role of women is slowly changing back to the role of the industrial revolution—that women do not belong in the home, they belong in the mill (Hare-Mustin, 1987). Women are now viable and necessary players in the labor market, as more than one-half of all women are employed outside the home (Hagen & Davis, 1992). Even so, they are still making much less money than their male counterparts (Perkins, 1992); and if self-worth is measured by the salary one makes, this wage gap could create additional stress and tension for women. (See Chapter 13 for a more detailed discussion of the lack of economic security of women and its effects on family life.) "While women have gained entry into virtually every arena in the American power structure, achieving equality with men in terms of economic power remains an elusive goal" (Wambach & Harrison, 1996, p. 116).

As women are having to change their roles, the family system will be forced to modify its existing role structures. The generation of *negative feedback* will become essential for women in generating change and reestablishing the homeostatic balance within the family system. The role of the therapist will become essential in helping and redirecting this energy into productive change, leading to homeostasis.

The therapist can help create this negative feedback. Therefore, therapists should realize that there are many different interpretations of gender. The therapist's interpretation of the "appropriate" or "ideal" sex role behaviors may differ from those of the individual family members and/or the family system. The therapist's gendered view has probably been altered by the context that surrounds it and filtered through a family therapy knowledge base that limits what and how things are perceived (Hare-Mustin & Maracek, 1988). Therapists need to explore the full range of gender interpretations as seen by members of the family system (Terry, 1992), and use this information to help the system establish enhanced family equilibrium (Frosh, 1995).

Women and Stress

Stress research in the past has tended to focus on the male, with the workplace often identified as the primary stressor (Baruch, Barnett, & Rivers, 1983). The home, which has largely been the domain of the woman, has been viewed predominantly as a private retreat or sanctuary. Approximately two-thirds of all women now work outside their homes, compared to approximately 34% in 1950 (Moorhead & Griffin, 1992). As women are forced to occupy more roles, both in the home and the workplace, role overload—too much to do—has been typically ignored in the stress-related research (Baruch et al., 1983).

In stress-reduction workshops conducted for women by the authors of this chapter, participant comments indicate that many women are torn by what they believe they are supposed to do (traditional housewife and mother roles), what they feel they must do to assist in supporting the family unit (outside work place responsibilities), and the conviction that their responsibilities within the home either couldn't be done as well or wouldn't be done at all by their male partners. This concept is supported in the research of Gunter and Gunter (1990), who examined 139 working couples and their division of labor. They found that women appeared to have more of an investment in the home and home duties than their partners; therefore, they often sacrificed personal freedoms to perform home-related duties. Although research does not appear to support the premise that the number of roles an individual is forced to accept directly relates to the amount of perceived stress the person feels (Baruch et al., 1983), family role and work role stressors need to be addressed in regard to their contribution to physical and mental health stress (Perry-Jenkins, Seery, & Crouter, 1992). Further research is needed in the area of marital distress and expression of affect, and how this can be related to mental and physical health problems.

Family therapy practitioners need to acknowledge that women and men may enter the therapeutic environment with preconceived notions of what the roles of each individual family member should be; the therapist must help to uncover these "underlying role behaviors" as the clients may be unaware of how they are affecting the dynamics of the family relationship. The effects of stress may be very different for males and females based on how they view "what is important" and "what must be done to feel complete."

If women's acceptance of responsibility for the household results in increased household strain, this situation could contribute directly to depressive symptomology found in women (Golding, 1990). It can also help to account for the increased prevalence of mental illness among women. Women willingly (or not so willingly) seem to accept more responsibilities beyond the workplace than do their male partners, and how this relates to female health risk factors remains an area to be researched.

Male and Female Stereotypes in Therapy

Family therapists need to be aware that sex-role stereotypes can affect intervention progression and success (Wambach & Harrison, 1996). In a randomized telephone survey of 100 respondents, Jussi, Milburn, and Nelson (1991) found that sex-role stereotypes appeared consistent with what would be expected in society, and women were generally expected to express their emotions more openly than men.

This result highlights two interesting areas that need to be considered. First, does this society consider women more expressive emotionally than men? If so, how will this perception affect the therapist's reaction to the male and/or female client in the session? In general, how can the therapist escape the ingrained biases that he or she may not even be aware of? To begin to address this, therapists should consider the following: (1) Individuals—including therapists—are products of their family, social, and societal context; therefore, therapists must make a conscious attempt to recognize their own behavior paradigms and the sexual stereotypes that they may consciously or unconsciously be fostering in the therapeutic environment. (2) Therapists should strive to be as objective and tolerant as possible of the uniqueness of clients, acknowledging that the behavioral paradigm of the therapist is not necessarily the correct or ideal one. (3) Therapists need to be aware of the literature that speaks to the importance of considering gender group composition and the ways that the sex of the facilitator can affect group intervention. (4) The personalities of those in the family can have a significant effect on how family members view and act on events in the family system.

Seibert and Gruenfeld (1992) conducted a study of the effective composition of groups and found that personality variables, such as sex-role classifications of masculinity and femininity, could have important consequences on group success. Participants who scored high on a measure of femininity (i.e., more positive interaction) were more likely to be less critical of suggestions generated within the group; those who scored high in masculinity (i.e., dominance) might work best with more structured techniques to keep from overpowering others during group decision making. For family therapists, assessing personality types of family members along the areas of masculinity and femininity may help explain family gender-based communications.

In summary, although there may be some differences between men and women, many of these perceived differences can be traced to the situations in which men and women find themselves; and in these situations, even if they behave identically, men and women may be judged by different standards (Aronson, 1988). Therapists must remember that they are products of their own social environments and are influenced by the culture that is natural to them. Thus, before declaring that one individual in therapy appears to be disturbing the homeostatic family balance causing system disequilibrium, therapists should examine the context within which these behaviors and communication patterns have occurred. They should be careful not to impose double standards of interpretation, or worse yet, interpret behaviors without realizing the influence of gender at all.

Is it possible that clients might see themselves as more expressive than other family members perceive them to be? For example, in a couple, the male genuinely may believe that he is as open to emotion in conversation as his female partner, and his female partner may believe that he is stoic and nonemotionally communicative, as most men are expected to be. This male may be genuinely showing what he believes to be adequate emotion when he refuses to "talk about it" with his female counterpart. However, based on the usual stereotypical behavior expected, his responses could be interpreted negatively as resistance to change by the therapist.

One therapeutic model used to treat couples and help them identify gender-sensitive communications is a technique called *relationship enhancement* (Snyder, 1992). This model emphasizes therapy as conversation. The goal of the therapist is to listen to the *story* told by the family member and interpret as accurately as possible what has been said. This meaning is then communicated in the session through the therapist, who doubles as the story-telling client. These stories may also have a different emphasis based on the way the genders perceive successful resolution of interpersonal conflict. Such an approach is compatible with social construction and narrative models, discussed in Chapter 6. In a study reported by Miller (1991), males placed more emphasis on establishing who initiated the conflict; females focused on the apology or on emotional resolution of the conflict. Taking these possible gender considerations into account, the therapist can intensify the feelings of the client in a more neutral manner, one that does not threaten the relationship. In this way, clients can more easily accept meanings.

Case Example

Mary and her daughter came to the shelter after a serious incident of domestic violence between herself and her husband. Mary had been married for 10 years to Mike. She described the marriage as difficult and troublesome. Many times their arguments ended in physical violence, with Mary being injured. Mary described her current marital situation as intolerable, and she was motivated toward change by her fears about the emotional and physical safety of her daughter. Mike had allegedly abused his 12-year-old stepdaughter, both physically and sexually. Mary was being forced by the state to find alternate arrangements for her daughter. If she did not separate from her husband, she was at risk of having her daughter taken from her and placed in foster care.

When Mary confronted Mike with the allegations against him, Mike hit her and accused her of instigating the entire situation. A neighbor called the police. After being taken to the hospital and receiving treatment in the emergency room, Mary was admitted to the domestic violence emergency shelter. On meeting with the counselor, Mary requested family counseling for herself and her daughter. During the admission interview, it was obvious that Ellen was angry with her mother and blamed her for much of what had happened. A referral for Mary and Ellen to begin family therapy was initiated.

Application

The first task for the social worker to ensure the inclusion of gender sensitivity in the practice of family therapy is to define the family or who constitutes the family system. In this case, Mary stated that she wanted to separate from and eventually divorce her husband, and Ellen agreed that this was necessary. The identified family system was, therefore, defined as Mary and Ellen. Based on this decision, therapeutic concentration was placed on establishing the wholeness of the family system while creating an environment conducive for the development of a positive homeostatic balance.

In establishing gender-sensitive practice, the therapist must first specify or identify what family system behaviors are adaptive or maladaptive (Liberman, 1973). Here, the primary focus is placed on the actual behaviors or events that have disturbed the general homeostatic balance of the system. Initial emphasis is always placed on ensuring the continued safety and security of the family system. Once safety issues are secured, the therapeutic process can begin.

In this case, Ellen had reported to a teacher that her father had abused her. The teacher subsequently reported the event to the state office for child protective services. Ellen was angry with her mother, her teacher, and her father. She had many conflicting feelings and felt trapped and lost in a system that was making all the decisions for her. It was clear that Mary and Ellen had ambivalent feelings toward each other, their extended family, the greater societal system, and their future.

Another step in the application of gender-sensitive family therapy is identifying the inter-family circumstances that have supported the problematic behavior. Here, gender issues are identified from a behavioral perspective and the way these issues contribute to the social reinforcement of behavior patterns in the family is explored. For example, in this case, Mary believed that she was expected to be an "all-knowing, all-seeing" mother, and by not meeting this expectation, she had failed her daughter and herself. Over the years, Mary had been continually told by Mike that she was useless and worthless, and that she was a poor mother. This pattern of repression was reinforced by her need to escape. Often, because of her employment commitments, Mary pressured Ellen to assume many of the traditional household duties and chores. This nontraditional role assumption caused Mary to feel guilty and Ellen to become confused as to what was truly expected of her. The resulting ambivalence made them both feel uneasy and may have contributed to the abuse of power allegedly assumed by Mike.

To begin the therapeutic plan, the family needs to determine the *expected* and *actual* roles of mother and daughter in this family and within the greater society. With the help of an objective therapist, shared family myths and dysfunctional assumptions can be identified. Once these are identified, they can be used to highlight the strengths of the family system and to facilitate family system communication. The concept and definition of gender roles and expectations need to be clearly outlined and incorporated into the foundation of treatment. Unfortunately, although the therapist may be able to modify behavior within a family system, she or he cannot generally bring about social change. Therefore, this limitation must be acknowledged within the family system. As a result, the discussion of how innovative internal family changes may be perceived by those external to the family unit becomes an essential therapeutic ingredient. Clients are taught rehearsal techniques and given opportunities to practice dealing with these reactions.

In brief, behavioral gender-sensitive family therapy, a definition of gender roles and expectations must clearly be identified. With these roles defined, the therapist can later establish the behavior patterns that will reinforce the newly defined roles. In the treatment process, dysfunctional behaviors that occur in the family system are generally viewed as learned responses. Therefore, the parents or primary caregivers are generally noted for having a strong influence on the development of child behavior problems whether they are aware of their influence or not. Even though Mike may no longer be an active part of the family system, his developmental influences continue to be felt.

To make the required role changes, this family system will be forced to modify its existing role structures. The therapist can help by facilitating communication, educating, modeling, role playing, and generally supporting the efforts that will be required to generate change and reestablish the homeostatic balance within the family system. In crisis, there is often energy for change. The primary role of the social worker is to redirect this energy into productive change that leads to homeostasis.

Summary

Social workers need to recognize the concept of gender when treating families from a family therapy perspective. Gender, with its ingrained importance in the family system, is a fundamental organizing principle for therapy. Including gender in the infrastructure of all family therapy practice models is essential. Family therapists are urged to advocate the inclusion of gender as an inseparable part of the family system, and not just to "emphasize"—or worse, ignore—its importance. Gender-informed family therapy requires that traditional and prescribed sex roles be examined as an essential ingredient for helping family systems to maintain homeostasis. This evaluation should be ongoing, as beliefs and values can change or shift (no matter how slowly) based on current economic, military, religious, or other societal and cultural concerns.

Process Questions

1. In family-based gender-sensitive practice, what is the first step (regardless of the therapeutic model used)?

2. In the case example, what are some important inter-family role changes that will be required? What are some important extended family and societal expectations that Mary and Ellen will have to contend with and plan for?

3. Once gender roles are clearly defined, how would you help bring about the needed changes?

4. According to Mary and her daughter, they no longer wish for Mike to be a member of their family system. Therefore, he will not be a contributing member within the therapeutic process. It is obvious, however, that he has greatly influenced family structure, beliefs, and future expectations within the family system. If you are the therapist in the intervention,

   A. Is it important to help Mary and Ellen to identify the gender roles and expectations that Mike supported in the past?

   B. What are the greatest influences Mike has had and will continue to have in the family system?

   C. What are some ways you can begin to address his influence in the maintenance of current behavioral patterns and as part of the change process?

References

ANDREWS, P. H. (1992). Sex and gender differences in group communication: Impact on the facilitation process. *Small Group Research, 23*(1), 74–94.

ARONSON, E. (1988). *The social animal* (5th ed.). New York: W.H. Freeman.

ATHERTON, C. R., & BOLLAND, K. A. (1997). The multiculturalism debate and social work education: A response to Dorthy Van Soest. *Journal of Social Work Education, 33*(1), 143–150.

AUERSWALD, E. H. (1987). Response to the problem of gender in family therapy theory. *Family Process, 26,* 29–31.

BANDURA, A. (1977). *Social learning theory.* Englewood Cliffs, NJ: Prentice Hall.

BARUCH, G. K., BARNETT, R. C., & RIVERS, C. (1983). *Life Prints: New patterns of love and work for today's women.* New York: McGraw-Hill.

BECVAR, D. S., & BECVAR, R. J. (1995). *Family therapy: A systemic integration.* Needham Heights, MA: Allyn & Bacon.

BELLAS, M. L. (1992). The effects of marital status and wives' employment on the salaries of faculty men: The (house) wife bonus. *Gender & Society, 6*(4), 609–622.

BOWEN, M. (1978). *Family therapy in clinical practice.* New York: Aronson.

BURCK, C., & SPEED, B. (1995). Introduction. In C. Burck, & B. Speed (Eds.), *Gender, power and relationships* (pp. 1–6). New York: Routledge.

COLEMAN, S. B., AVIS, J. M., & TURIN, M. (1990). A study of the role of gender in family therapy training. *Family Process, 29,* 365–374.

CONCIAN, F. M. (1991). Feminist science: Methodologies that challenge inequality. *Gender and Society, 6*(4), 623–642.

DZIEGIELEWSKI, S. F. (1996). Managed care principles: The need for social work in the health care environment. *Crisis Intervention and Time-Limited Treatment, 3*(2), 97–110.

DZIEGIELEWSKI, S. F. (1997). Time limited brief therapy: The state of practice. *Crisis Intervention and Time Limited Treatment, 3*(3), 217–227.

DZIEGIELEWSKI, S. F., RESNICK, C. A., & KRAUSE, N. (1996). Shelter-based crisis intervention with abused women. In A. R. Roberts (Ed.), *Helping battered women: New perspectives and remedies* (pp. 159–172). New York: Oxford University Press.

FERBER, A. (1973). *The book of family therapy.* Boston: Houghton Mifflin.

FREUD, S. (1939). *An outline of psychoanalysis,* Vol. 23. London: Hogarth Press.

FRIEDMAN, S. (1997). *Time-effective psychotherapy: Maximizing outcomes in an era of minimizing resources.* Needham Heights, MA: Allyn & Bacon.

FROSH, S. (1995). Unpacking masculinity: From rationality to fragmentation. In C. Burck & B. Speed (Eds.), *Gender power and relationships,* (p. 219–231). New York: Routledge.

GARCIA, B., & VAN SOEST, D. (1997). Changing perceptions of diversity and oppression: MSW students discuss the effects of a required course. *Journal of Social Work Education, 33*(1), 119–130.

GILBERT, L. A. (1991). Feminist contributions to counseling psychology. *Psychology of Women Quarterly, 15,* 537–547.

GILLIGAN, C. (1982). *In a different voice: Psychological theory and woman's development.* Cambridge: Harvard University Press.

GOLDENBERG, H., & GOLDENBERG, I. (1994). *Counseling today's families* (2nd ed.). Pacific Grove, CA: Brooks/Cole.

GOLDING, J. M. (1990). Division of household labor, strain and depressive symptoms among Mexican Americans and non-Hispanic Whites. *Psychology of Women Quarterly, 14,* 103–117.

GOLDNER, V. (1985). Feminism and family therapy. *Family Process, 24,* 31–47.

GOLDNER, V. (1988). Generation and gender: Normative and covert hierarchies. *Family Process, 27,* 17–31.

GUNTER, N. C., & GUNTER, D. G. (1990). Domestic division of labor among working couples: Does androgyny make a difference? *Psychology of Women Quarterly, 14,* 355–370.

HAGEN, J. L., & DAVIS, L. V. (1992). Working with women: Building a policy and practice agenda. *Social Work, 37*(6), 495–502.

HALEY, J. (1971). Approaches to family therapy. In J. Haley (Ed.), *Changing families: A family therapy reader.* New York: Grune & Stratton.

HANSEN, M. (1993). Feminism and family therapy: A review of feminist critiques of approaches to family therapy. In M. Hansen & M. Harway (Eds.), *Battering and family therapy: A feminist perspective* (pp. 69–81). Newbury Park, CA: Sage.

HARE-MUSTIN, R. T. (1983). Family therapy and sex role stereotypes. In D. R. Bardill & A. C. Kilpatrick, (Eds.), *Family therapy: A relational systems view.* Lexington, MA: Ginn Custom Publishing.

HARE-MUSTIN, R. T. (1986). The problem of gender in family therapy theory. *Family Process, 26,* 15–27.

HARE-MUSTIN, R. T. (1987). The problem of gender in family therapy. *Family Process, 26,* 15–25.

HARE-MUSTIN, R. T., & MARACEK, J. (1988). The meaning of difference: Gender theory, postmodernism, and psychology. *American Psychologist, 43*(6), 455–464.

HARTMAN, A. (1995). Family therapy. In *Encyclopedia of social work* (19th ed., Vol. 2, pp. 983–991). Washington, DC: NASW Press.

JACOBSON, N. S., & CHRISTENSEN, A. (1996). *Integrative couple therapy: Promoting acceptance and change.* New York: Norton.

JONES, E. (1995). The construction of gender in family therapy. In C. Burck & B. Speed (Eds.), *Gender power and relationships* (pp. 7–23). New York: Routledge.

JUSSI, L., MILBURN, M., & NELSON, W. (1991). Emotional openness: Sex role stereotypes and self-perceptions. *Representative Research in Social Psychology, 19*(1), 35–53.

KOHLBERG, L. (1981). *The philosophy of moral development.* San Francisco: Harper & Row.

LAU, A. (1995). Gender and power relationships: Ethnocultural and religious issues. In C. Burck & B. Speed (Eds.), *Gender power and relationships* (pp. 120–135). New York: Routledge.

LAZARUS, A. A. (1977). *Brief but comprehensive psychotherapy: The multimodal way.* New York: Springer.

LIBERMAN, R. (1973). Behavioral approaches to family and couple therapy. In J. Fischer (Ed.), *Interpersonal helping: Emerging approaches for social work practice.* Springfield, IL: Charles C. Thomas.

LIPMAN-BLUMEN, J. (1984). *Gender roles and power.* Englewood Cliffs, NJ: Prentice Hall.

LOTT, B. (1991). Social psychology: Humanist roots and feminist future. *Psychology of Women Quarterly, 15,* 505–519.

MARACEK, J., & HARE-MUSTIN, R. T. (1991). A short history of the future: Feminism and clinical psychology. *Psychology of Women Quarterly, 15,* 521–536.

MCHUGH, M. C. (1993). Studying battered women and batterers: Feminist perspectives on methodology. In M. Hansen & M. Harway (Eds.), *Battering and family therapy: A feminist perspective* (pp. 54–68). Newbury Park, CA: Sage.

MEDICAL ECONOMICS. (1994). *The PDR family guide to women's health and prescription drugs.* Montvale, NJ: Author.

MEDICAL ECONOMICS. (1997). *Physician's desk reference* (51st ed.). Montvale, NJ: Author.

MILLER, J. B. (1991). Women's and men's scripts for interpersonal conflict. *Psychology of Women Quarterly, 15,* 15–29.

MOORHEAD, G., & GRIFFIN, R. W. (1992). *Organizational behavior: Managing people and organizations.* Boston: Houghton Mifflin.

PERKINS, K. (1992). Psychosocial implications of women and retirement. *Social Work, 37*(6), 526–531.

PERRY-JENKINS, M., SEERY, B., & CROUTER, A. C. (1992). Linkages between women's provider-role attitudes, psychological well-being, and family relationships. *Psychology of Women Quarterly, 16,* 311–329.

PIAGET, J. (1965). *The moral judgment of the child.* New York: Free Press.

RICHARDS, M. H., GITELSON, I. B., PETERSEN, A. C., & HURTIG, A. L. (1991). Adolescent personality in girls and boys: The role of mothers and fathers. *Psychology of Women Quarterly, 15,* 65–81.

SANDS, R. G., & NUCCIO, K. (1992). Postmodern feminist theory and social work. *Social Work, 37*(6), 489–493.

SATIR, V. (1972). *People making.* Palo Alto, CA: Science and Behavior Books.

SEIBERT, S., & GRUENFELD, L. (1992). Masculinity, femininity, and behavior in groups. *Small Group Research, 23*(1), 95–112.

SMYRNIOS, K. X., & KIRKBY, R. J. (1992). Brief family therapies: A comparison of theoretical and technical issues. *Journal of Family Therapy, 13*(3), 119–127.

SNYDER, M. (1992). A gender informed model of couple and family therapy: Relationship enhancement therapy. *Contemporary Family Therapy, 14*(1), 15–31.

SOHNG, S. (1994, June). *Critical feminist research in a multicultural context.* Paper presented at the Global Society for International Social Work, Third Annual Conference, Chicago.

STOLL, C. S. (1978). *Female and male.* Dubuque, IA: William C. Brown.

TERRY, L. L. (1992). Gender and family therapy: Adding a bi-level belief systems component to assessment. *Contemporary Family Therapy, 14*(3), 199–210.

TOLMAN, R., MOWRY, D., JONES, L., & BREKKE, J. (1986). Developing a profeminist commitment among men in social work. In N. VanDenBergh & L. B. Cooper (Eds.), *Feminist visions for social work.* Washington DC: NASW.

UEHARA, E. S., SOHNG, S. S., BENDING, R. L., SEYFRIED, S., RICHEY, C. A., MORELLI, P., SPENCER, M., ORTEGA, D., KEENAN, L., & KANUHA, V. (1996). Toward a values based approach to multicultural social work research. *Social Work, 41*(6), 577–696.

VAN SOEST, D. (1995). Multiculturalism and social work education: The non-debate about competing perspectives. *Journal of Social Work Education, 31,* 55–66.

WAMBACH, K. G., & HARRISON, D. F. (1996). Social work practice with women. In D. F. Harrison, B. A. Thyer, & J. S. Wodarski (Eds.), *Cultural diversity and social work practice* (pp. 112–137). Springfield, IL: Charles C. Thomas.

WEITZ, S. (1977). *Sex roles: Biological, psychological, and social foundations.* New York: Oxford University Press.

WILKES, J. (1995). The social construction of a caring career. In C. Burck & B. Speed (Eds.), *Gender power and relationships* (pp. 232–247). New York: Routledge.

WILLIAMSON, D. S. (1991). *The intimacy paradox: Personal authority in the family system.* New York: Guilford Press.

WOOD, J. T. (1994). *Gendered lives: Communication, gender, and culture.* Belmont, CA: Wadsworth.

CHAPTER THIRTEEN

Diana M. DiNitto, Ph.D.
University of Texas at Austin

Nora S. Gustavsson, Ph.D.
Arizona State University

The Interface between Family Practice and Family Policy

There are numerous indices of family functioning. Practitioners select specific aspects of family life to examine in the assessment process. Depending on which school of family treatment practitioners follow, they may look at the way families envision solutions, the stories they tell within a cultural context, how they establish and maintain rules, how members communicate, how roles are assigned and performed, the permeability of boundaries, how both family and individual developmental stages are managed, the degree of family cohesion, and the composition of the family's subsystems (Berg, 1994; Haley, 1980; Minuchin, 1974; Bowen, 1978; Bateson, 1972). Most interventions in family treatment focus on changing processes within the family. For example, members may be encouraged to communicate more clearly or to change their worldview or narratives; or the family may be enmeshed and need help in establishing clearer boundaries.

This chapter reviews family policy from the viewpoint of family practice. Several programs and policies are summarized for the purpose of helping practitioners understand the macro context in which families live. The effects of various policies on families is reviewed. The plight of poor families is especially emphasized as well as a need for the United States to develop a coherent set of family policies that will support *all* families.

The Need for Family Policy Interventions

Because families have other needs that do not respond as readily to micro-level interventions by the therapist, social workers have encouraged family practitioners to consider an ecological perspective that views the family as an open system. (See Chapter 14 for a review of this perspective within family theory.) The ecological perspective requires practitioners to broaden the unit of assessment and intervention from the family alone to the family and its environment. Using this perspective, some needs of families can be met by public policies that foster nurturing environments. Many American families, however, struggle to survive in unfriendly and even hostile environments where there is little support for the family and its functions.

Social workers often blame this lack of support on the absence in the United States of a broad policy or a coherent set of policies that address family life. The need for therapists to intervene in the family policy arena is important if effective family practice is to be developed in today's changing practice context. Further hindering the establishment of supportive family policies is the lack of a simple definition of what constitutes a family. As suggested in case examples throughout this book, family practitioners serve "families" headed by a mother and a father, a single parent, or a gay or lesbian couple; they also serve nuclear, extended, and foster families. Family practitioners are also sensitive to the differences in family structure and processes based on ethnic background (see, for example, Sprenkle & Bischof, 1994).

From a social work perspective, a family may be best defined as those who consider themselves a family. Unfortunately, social welfare policies are rarely so generous in defining family boundaries. For example, federal regulations governing the Food Stamp Program contain five pages of small print that describe what constitutes a household (Ohls & Beebout, 1993)! One reason there is no coherent family policy in the United States is that the definition of family is fraught with political implications colored by the views of the religious right and other conservatives, the liberal left, libertarians, and those whose views fall along every other point on the continuum of political, religious, and moral beliefs (see, for example, Hartman, 1995). The diverse points of view on what constitutes a family are well illustrated by two pieces of legislation passed in 1996. One is the legislation passed in the state of Hawaii allowing marriage between two people of the same gender. The other is the U.S. Congress's passage of the Defense of Marriage Act, which denies the legitimacy (for federal purposes) of any union other than that between one man and one woman and allows states to disregard marriages between persons of the same gender performed in other states. Even among social workers and other family practitioners, there is often considerable disagreement on issues of vital importance to families.

Only the most naïve of human service professionals think they can escape the business of politics by choosing a career in family therapy. Most family practitioners are well acquainted with the impacts, both positive and negative, of public policy on the quality of life of the families they treat. They are also aware of the way public policy shapes who can provide services to families, what services family practitioners may provide and to whom, and the mechanisms available to pay for family services. Such impacts are illustrated by mental health and health care policies such as those associated with managed behavioral health care that were described in Chapter 1. Many family practitioners are involved in the political arena because they want a role in shaping policies that affect families. Even though it is often difficult to change existing policies or to influence new directions in public policy, family practitioners know they must try to help move the country toward a better family policy. Every day they see ways that existing policies both help and hurt families, and they want to use their knowledge to improve family functioning. They are also involved because they would prefer to work in a practice environment they have helped to shape rather than be subjected to policies with which they disagree but which they must follow in order to continue their practices. The role of social workers and other family practitioners in the policy arena has been hotly debated (see Abramovitz & Bardill, 1993; Way, 1993; McNeece, 1995; Franklin & Johnson, 1996), and family practitioners do not always agree on what family policy should look like. Even so, there seems to be no escaping an active political role to ensure that the United States moves toward policies that family practitioners believe are more supportive of the many constellations called families (see Pratt, 1995, and Way, 1993, for strategies to achieve this end).

The social work literature and the National Association of Social Workers reflect a long history of involvement in the political arena (see Monroe, 1995; Way, 1993). The current literature also indicates that marriage and family therapists have substantial interest in public policy (see, for example, the October 1992 and January 1995 Special Collections on family policy in Family Relations published by the National Council on Family Relations [NCFR]). The NCFR's Public Policy Committee and its *Action Alert* newsletter and the American Association of Marriage and Family Therapy's Family Impact Seminars also attest to the active role that family practitioners and family scientists are playing in shaping public policy (see Bogenschneider, 1995).

Virtually every government policy at the federal, state, and local level affects families. From national defense policies that dictate who will serve in wars to state and local environmental policies that determine the location of hazardous waste depositories, families are affected by choices in the political arena. In this chapter, we concentrate on the social welfare policies targeted directly at improving the quality of family life. These include income maintenance, child support enforcement, taxation, housing, health care, mental health care, chemical dependency treatment, nutrition, child neglect and abuse services and interventions into other forms of domestic violence, family planning, and family care. An understanding of current trends in family life and issues and policies affecting families is necessary if practitioners are to address a more progressive public policy agenda. This chapter covers a good deal of policy territory, territory that can change quickly in today's often turbulent political environment. Rather than offering a definitive view of what family policy should be, the chapter raises questions and issues that family practitioners are addressing and ones that individuals preparing for a career in family therapy and other aspects of family practice are also likely to face.

Income Maintenance

The most fundamental of the policies that support families are those that provide cash or goods for subsistence needs—food, shelter, clothing, and health care. Without adequate financial support, the family's ability to care for and nurture its members is gravely compromised (see Zimmerman, 1992); but as poverty figures indicate, even basic needs are inconsistently and poorly met for an increasing number of families (see Wisensale, 1992). Between 1970 and 1979, the percentage of all U.S. families living in poverty ranged from a low of 9.7% to a high of 10.9% (all poverty figures are based on Baugher & Lamison-White, 1996, Tables C-1 and C-3). Since 1980, poverty rates for families have ranged from 11.5% to 13.9%. In 1995, 12.3% of all families fell below the official government poverty line. Poverty is much greater for some ethnic groups and for female-headed households. In 1995, 28.5% of all African-American families and 29.2% of all Hispanic-American families lived in poverty, compared to 9.6% of white families. For families with children under 18 years of age headed by a single mother, the poverty rate was 41.5% compared to 7.5% for two-parent families. For African-American and Hispanic-American families with children under 18 years of age headed by single women, poverty rates were 53.2% and 57.3%, respectively. On the other hand, poverty among older Americans has decreased. In 1970, the incomes of 24.6% of Americans age 65 and older fell below the poverty line; in 1995 the figure was 10.5%, compared with 20.8% of children and 11.4% of those from 18 to 64 years of age. Many factors have combined to place our most vulnerable citizens (children) at the greatest risk of poverty. Some of these include the incidence of female-headed families, the changing nature and location of employment, and the uneven availability of quality educational and vocational programs (Gustavsson & Segal, 1994).

Policies that support healthy families are those that promote full employment, that provide a decent minimum wage, that afford equal employment opportunities to men and women, and that provide a basic income to those unable to earn it themselves (see DiNitto, 1995; Fine, 1992; Zimmerman, 1992). The federal minimum wage is not indexed to inflation, and only infrequently has the U.S. Congress raised it. In October of 1996, it was raised from $4.25 to $4.75 per hour, and again to $5.15 in September of 1997. Some states have set higher minimum wage levels, but many working families and individuals continue to struggle to make ends meet. Women continue to earn only 70 cents for every dollar earned by men. Inadequate income is a major source of family dysfunction. Without sufficient resources, families are rarely in a financial or emotional position to take advantage of family treatment, no matter how much they may need it. Putting first things first, family practitioners are generally knowledgeable about the federal, state, and local programs to which families can turn to meet their basic needs, and many family practitioners are involved in efforts to keep Congress and state legislatures from eroding these bases of support.

The United States has an array of income maintenance programs to help families, but these programs are complex and fragmented (see, for example, National Commission on Children, 1991). As was pointed out in Chapter 1, this fragmentation is one of the reasons there is a movement to integrate human services systems. In addition, many families do not qualify for income maintenance programs, and even families that do may remain in economic need. The Social Security Act of 1935 established the basic framework for income maintenance programs in the United States. These programs fall into two major categories: social insurance and public assistance. The Social Security Act has been amended many times, but policymaking is an incremental and piecemeal process that leaves much income maintenance policy out of date in light of the dramatic demographic, social, and economic changes of the past 65 years.

Social Insurance

Social insurance programs are designed to prevent poverty. They are financed from specific government trust funds. Workers or their employers must have paid into these funds to qualify for benefits, and the benefits are given regardless of recipients' financial need.

OLD AGE, SURVIVORS, AND DISABILITY INSURANCE

OASDI is a federal social insurance program that provides cash payments to former workers who are retired or who sustain permanent and total disabilities. Payments may also be made to their dependents or to the survivors of deceased workers. OASDI is the government's largest and most universal social welfare program. Almost all workers are required to pay Social Security taxes to insure themselves and their families. In 1997, workers and their employers each paid a 6.2% OASDI tax on the employee's wages up to $65,400. By December 1996, 43.7 million people were receiving OASDI benefits (Social Security Administration, 1997). Their average benefit was $673 per month. In 1995, OASDI payments amounted to $329 billion.

OASDI, or Social Security as it is usually called, was initially opposed on the grounds that it constituted socialism. Although everyone soon took it for granted as a source of support in old age, new issues have surfaced, perhaps none so important as that of intergenerational equity (Ozawa, 1984; Wisensale, 1992). Today's retirees are getting a substantial return on their investment in the program. Their payments are mostly financed by the contributions of current workers whose Social Security taxes have increased greatly in order to support a rapidly growing older population. The costs will be even greater when the baby boomers (those born between 1946 and 1964) move into the retirement years. Originally, Social Security taxes were quite modest, but today, they take a substantial bite from an employee's pay. Social Security taxes are regressive because everyone pays at the same rate, regardless of income. For young families, especially those with low and moderate incomes, the Social Security tax may be a real burden. It drains money that families may need for food, clothing, and shelter. Some argue that high Social Security contributions from individuals and families with modest incomes are going to support the growing elderly population, many of whom are in a better financial position than younger people. Individuals who emphasize these points may argue that wealthy retirees should not be entitled to Social Security benefits or that their Social Security retirement benefits should be taxed more heavily than current provisions allow.

The Social Security tax bite can be especially burdensome for the major ethnic minority groups in the United States (Gnaizda & Obledo, 1985). For example, because African Americans, Hispanic-Americans, and Native Americans tend to earn less than whites, Social Security taxes are more burdensome for them. Members of these ethnic groups also have shorter life spans than whites, so they are also less likely to collect retirement benefits or to collect them as long, even though they paid into the program at the same rate as others. Others, however, call these claims of inequity unfair. They argue that the payments at retirement, disability, or death made to lower wage earners or their families are proportionately higher than to other wage earners. They also point out that ethnic minority families make more use of survivors benefits (Kingson, 1989; Kingson, Hirshorn, & Cornman, 1986), but this may be of little consolation when weighed against the loss of a breadwinner (DiNitto, 1995).

Congress has taken some steps to promote greater intergenerational equity in the Social Security programs. For example, some benefits of more wealthy retirees are now taxed, and considering increased life spans and greater vitality, the full retirement age is rising slowly and will reach age 67 in the 21st century.

Gender equity is another issue, as women are more likely than men to have lower Social Security benefits than they anticipated. For example, if a couple divorces after fewer than 10 years of marriage, a spouse (generally the wife who may not have worked outside the home) cannot make a claim for Social Security benefits based on the ex-spouse's earnings.

Perhaps the major benefit of the OASDI program to younger Americans is that it provides income to elderly parents whom current workers might otherwise have to support. Many Americans would be hard pressed to provide much financial support to their parents, even though they may help elderly parents in many other ways.

OASDI does far more to reduce poverty than any other U.S. social welfare program (Committee on Ways and Means, 1994). It is part of the fabric of the country and a substantial source of income for many American families, particularly those headed by older people and younger people who can no longer work because of disabilities. It is also important for children who have lost a working parent. Without OASDI, many more families than the current number would face the stresses of inadequate income. In the years ahead, the country will continue to struggle with Social Security financing. Alarmists would have Americans think the program will be bankrupt at any moment or that it should be discarded and replaced with one that allows people to make contributions to private investments. However, family practitioners who have studied Social Security would probably agree that the real issues are how to modify the program so that current workers are taxed adequately but fairly and so that retirees receive a fair return based on their contributions and their financial needs. Social Security is not just an insurance program, it is a *social* insurance program that has served American families quite well.

UNEMPLOYMENT COMPENSATION

In addition to disability, unemployment is a serious threat to working families. Today, many workers consider themselves lucky to have a job in a rapidly changing work environment in which higher levels of education are required for employment and in which plant closings and work force reductions are everyday events. In a society that places such a high value on economic productivity, unemployment can bring feelings of worthlessness as well as economic insecurity.

Unemployment Compensation (UC) is another social insurance program established under the Social Security Act, but state governments rather than the federal government have the major role in administering these programs and determining eligibility requirements. Employers contribute to a UC trust fund to help their employees in the event of job loss. To receive benefits, unemployed workers must apply at the local unemployment insurance office, register with the U.S. Employment Services (USES), and seek work. Unemployment compensation provides only temporary assistance (generally a maximum of 39 weeks, although this can be extended during periods of severe unemployment). In 1994, the average, national, weekly benefit was $182 (amounting to only 36% of average weekly wages), and the average number of weeks for which benefits were received was 15.5 (U.S. Bureau of the Census, 1996, p. 378). In 1994, the maximum weekly benefit in the contiguous states ranged from $118 in Louisiana to $246 in New Jersey (U.S. Bureau of the Census, 1996, p. 378).

In addition, the majority of unemployed workers are not currently receiving any payments (Committee on Ways and Means, 1993, pp. 491–492) because they have exhausted their benefits, they did not work at their last job long enough, they left their previous job voluntarily, or they were fired for poor job performance. There have been many calls for reform of the unemployment compensation program; two of the suggested reforms are to provide more federal assistance to states with high unemployment, making it easier for areas with high unemployment to extend benefits to jobless workers (Pease & Clinger, 1985), and to provide benefits to those unable to find work initially (Committee on Ways and Means, 1994). Families may be forced into public assistance programs when their unemployment compensation runs out. Some countries have programs that cover unemployed workers until they are able to find work.

WORKERS' COMPENSATION

Another cash benefit program classified as social insurance is workers' compensation. It also provides medical benefits to workers hurt on the job. Advantages of this program are that it assists with temporary as well as long-term disability and with partial as well as total disability. Dependents of workers killed in job-related circumstances may also be entitled to benefits. Each state operates its own program, and employers insure their workers through private insurance companies, self-insurance programs, or state-insured options.

The social insurance programs are complex, and although many family practitioners may not have studied them in detail, they are the most far-reaching elements of the social welfare provisions in the United States. They deserve the vigilance of family practitioners to ensure that they are responsive to families' needs.

Public Assistance

Public assistance programs are financed from public general revenue funds. Although many recipients have paid income taxes that support general revenues, they need not have done so to qualify. Public assistance programs are remedial or ameliorative as they provide benefits after poverty occurs. These programs are also selective because only those in dire straits qualify, and eligibility is based on a means test. The primary public assistance programs that provide cash benefits are Supplemental Security Income (SSI), Temporary Assistance for Needy Families (TANF), and General Assistance (GA).

Supplemental Security Income

Supplemental Security Income used to be called Old Age Assistance, Aid to the Blind, and Aid to the Permanently and Totally Disabled. Today these categories of beneficiaries remain the same, but in 1973 the federal government took a number of steps to remove the inequities that existed among the 50 state-administered programs for these groups. It established the same minimum payment levels and basic eligibility requirements for all states. The Social Security Administration (which administers OASDI) now administers SSI in order to remove some of the stigma associated with receiving public assistance. Many states pay amounts greater than the federal minimums, and some also cover additional categories of beneficiaries.

To qualify for SSI an individual must be 65 years of age or older, have no better than 20/200 vision or "a limited visual field of 20 degrees or less in the better eye with use of eyeglasses," or be unable to work because of a physical or mental impairment that is expected to last at least 12 months or result in death (Social Security Administration, 1989). Although the first two criteria are clear, the last criterion has caused considerable debate and changes in the rules governing SSI. In addition to concern about ways to manage the rapidly increasing demands on the SSI disability program, there is dissension about what constitutes a legitimate disability, and these concerns color the way applicants and recipients are treated. For example, the extent to which drug addicts and alcoholics may qualify has been a point of contention, and rules governing their eligibility have become increasingly stringent. Under current program rules, alcoholism or drug addiction alone are not sufficient diagnoses, and individuals must provide evidence of other disabilities or impairments to qualify. Another contentious issue has been the requirements for children to qualify. Those under age 18 are supposed to qualify if their disability is of similar severity to that of an adult with the same condition, but the present trend is to scrutinize child cases closely. Medical and mental health professionals provide much of the evidence on which SSI decisions are based. Decisions to deny benefits are common, and mental health cases are among the most often contested.

SSI eligibility is also based on stringent resource and income limitations. For example, a family's assets (savings accounts, personal belongings, and so forth, but excluding their home and a car) cannot exceed $3,000. In the case of children, some allowances are made for their parents' work expenses and the family's living expenses. In 1997, the maximum federal SSI payment (not counting state supplements) for an individual was $484 and for a couple, $726. One-third of the SSI payment is deducted if the beneficiary resides with relatives or others who contribute to his or her support. This restriction may be unfair to families with limited incomes who are willing to care for members who are aged or disabled.

Other issues also inhibit the effective use of SSI and other policies and programs for people with disabilities. For example, cash assistance programs may discourage people with disabilities from performing whatever work they can because their benefits may be terminated when they earn even a small amount of income (see, for example, Berkowitz, 1987). In fact, civil rights legislation like the Education for All Handicapped Children Act of 1975 and the Americans with Disabilities Act (ADA) of 1990, which increase opportunities and support the efforts of people with disabilities to be part of the mainstream, may be the real policy achievements of modern times. Social, habilitation, rehabilitation, and other services also contribute to the policies and programs that assist people with disabilities and their families.

The political participation of people with disabilities and their families continues to grow. The independent living movement has gained added steam with the teeth given it by the ADA, and lawsuits and demonstrations aimed at forcing compliance with the law have increased. Knowledge of disability policy is useful to practitioners working with families experiencing a developmental or later stage disability of a member. Over the years, people with disabilities and their families have done a great deal to educate professionals on these matters. The former Association of Retarded Citizens, now called the ARC, was among the first to educate the community, professionals, and politicians. Professionals have also played important roles in legal actions supporting the rights of people with mental and physical disabilities. For example, a social worker was instrumental in bringing forward the case of *City of Cleburne, Texas v. Cleburne Living Center*, in which the U.S. Supreme Court found improper actions by the city when it refused to allow the establishment of a community home for people with mental retardation. A policy role that family practitioners fill more often is that of advocate, as a great deal of effort may be needed to help clients and their families to make their way through the maze of available services (which can vary considerably among states and communities) and to establish their eligibility or entitlement to them.

Temporary Assistance to Needy Families

As part of the conservative direction in which public policy has moved since the 1980s, the Personal Responsibility and Work Opportunity Reconciliation Act of 1996 replaced the 61-year-old federal guarantee of financial assistance to financially needy children under the former Aid to Families with Dependent Children (AFDC) program and made a number of other changes to public assistance programs. AFDC is the program that Americans have long associated with the word *welfare*, but in a bold move, the U.S. Congress abolished AFDC and replaced it with a program called Temporary Assistance for Needy Families. Whereas AFDC was a categorical program, TANF is funded through a block grant. Poor families could receive AFDC as long as they had children in the home and met other eligibility requirements; TANF places limits on the amount of time that payments can be received almost regardless of the family's situation. Furthermore, TANF gives states more discretion in determining program eligibility criteria.

Like the former AFDC program, TANF provides cash assistance to poor families so that children can be cared for in their own homes, but under TANF, the states will make many more decisions in shaping their programs. Prior to enacting TANF, the federal government had already approved many state waivers to AFDC program rules. For example, some states had already begun to institute time limits and other restrictive provisions, such as caps on the amount families could receive if they had more children while they were in the program.

Under TANF, the pressure on parents to go to work continues to increase because many Americans believe that a substantial number of parents receiving public assistance are capable of working and should be engaged in some type of productive activity outside the home. TANF payments will continue to vary widely across the states as they did under AFDC, and the states and the federal government will continue to share in the funding, with poorer states receiving more federal funding. Suffolk County, New York, has one of the highest payment rates; the maximum monthly payment for a parent and two children was $703 in 1996. Mississippi had the lowest payment rate, with a maximum monthly AFDC payment of $120 (Committee on Ways and Means, 1996, p. 442). Many states pay benefits that are far lower than what they estimate families' minimum financial needs to be. In Alabama, Mississippi, Tennessee, Texas, Arkansas, Louisiana, and South Carolina, benefits were less than 20% of the federal poverty level (Committee on Ways and Means, 1996, p. 437). Nationwide, cash benefits to AFDC families has dropped 51% in real dollar terms in the last few decades (Committee on Ways and Means, 1996, p. 435). Many family practitioners fear that child and family poverty rates will increase in the wake of TANF.

There are many misconceptions about those needy families who receive assistance, but it is true that most fathers are absent from these homes. In 1992, 89% of families receiving AFDC benefits had no father at home; in 53% of the cases, the child's parents had never married, and in another 30% of cases, the parents were divorced or separated (Committee on Ways and Means, 1994, pp. 400–401). The changing demographics of the American family mean that many children need more help from public sources at a time when political sentiments are causing serious program cutbacks.

Contrary to what many people may think, families receiving aid tend to be small; most contain one parent and one or two children. Similar numbers of whites and blacks have participated in the program, but blacks are overrepresented because of their higher rates of poverty. In 1993, the average monthly AFDC enrollment was nearly 5 million families (14.1 million individuals or 5.4% of the U.S. population) (Committee on Ways and Means, 1994, p. 325). Children receiving AFDC were 63% of all children in poverty, meaning that a substantial number of poor children received no AFDC benefits (Committee on Ways and Means, 1994, p. 399). Since 1995, the number of recipients has dropped; by the end of 1997, only 4% of the population was receiving family assistance benefits (U.S. Department of Health and Human Services, 1997, 1998). Much of the improvement was the result of a stronger economy, but some believed that the new requirements states had imposed were also contributing to the decrease.

Most families received AFDC payments for relatively short periods of time. Pavetti (1993) found "that 70 percent of all recipients who begin a spell of welfare will have spells that last for 2 years or less; only 7 percent of recipients who begin a spell of welfare will have a spell that lasts for more than 8 years" (cited in Committee on Ways and Means, 1994, pp. 441–442). Nevertheless, long-term welfare receipt (dependency) among the latter group was among the factors that caused Congress to make radical changes to the public safety net for children and their families. Now families may face termination of benefits even if they continue to need them.

Also of concern was the low incidence of working recipients of AFDC. Despite government rhetoric about getting AFDC parents to work under the Job Opportunities and Basic Skills (JOBS) program and its predecessors, in 1992, only 2.2% of AFDC mothers worked full time and 4.2% worked part time (Committee on Ways and Means, 1994, p. 402). Attempts to increase employment among these parents has been a concern of the program for more than three decades. Employment and training programs have generally not given parents the skills that would allow them to earn wages sufficient to put them over the threshold of poverty (see DiNitto, 1995, for a discussion of this issue). However, as more mothers in the general population have gone to work, there has been a growing sentiment that mothers receiving help from public assistance programs should do the same, no matter how young their children (see Ehrenreich, 1987) and no matter how low their wages. Whether single parents should have the opportunity to receive public assistance and remain at home to care for their children and whether this would be better for their children have become moot points.

Some of the major provisions of TANF include requiring adults to participate in work activities after 24 months of assistance (states may exempt a parent with a child one-year old or younger from this requirement), establishing a lifetime benefit limit of five years (states can set more restrictive time limits), allowing states to require adolescent parents to live in an adult supervised setting and attend school, permitting states to provide lower benefits to families moving into the state, and allowing states to deny TANF (and food stamps) to persons convicted of drug offenses (but not other crimes). States may also deny benefits to most noncitizens, even those legally admitted. In addition to the political stance on immigration that the Personal Responsibility and Work Opportunity Reconciliation Act takes, it also furthers a particular social agenda with other provisions such as offering states a bonus to reduce the incidence of out-of-wedlock births as long as the number of abortions does not increase.

Many people believe that states need flexibility to provide the best help to financially needy families, but advocates for children fear that the legislation will cause more children to enter the child welfare system as their parents face additional stressors and are unable to provide adequate care. Many other countries have much more universal financial assistance programs for young and single-parent families combined with more generous health and child care programs

(Kamerman & Kahn, 1988). The number of beneficiaries and the costs of AFDC have always paled in comparison to the social insurance programs, and they will do so under TANF, yet the devolution of social welfare programs, which can be particularly cruel to families with children, continues. Everyone wants policies that encourage productive activity and responsible parenting, but mothers and children in particular have become the targets of critics who do not seem to grasp the real issues at stake. AFDC rolls were already on the decline because of improvements in the economy before TANF was initiated. Many mothers receiving public assistance would prefer to work, and at least one study indicates that a substantial number have worked recently (Spalter-Roth, Hartmann, & Andrews, 1992). Poor parents are often thrown back on public assistance when child care and health care are not available and when their skills do not qualify them for decent jobs. In a highly competitive and individualistic society like that of the United States (see Hartman, 1995), it is a wonder that most families fare as well as they do (see Fine, 1992). Many child advocates worked tirelessly to stave off the onslaught on crucial public assistance benefits, but they have clearly lost this round in the political battle over the financial role of government in strengthening families. There are many questions about how states will implement TANF and other provisions of the welfare reform legislation and what the consequences of their actions will be. The role of family practitioners and other child advocates will be to document the consequences of Congress's and states' actions in the hope that the information will prove useful in encouraging a more satisfactory response to meeting the needs of families.

General Assistance

One consequence of reduced federal and state aid in the form of TANF is that there will likely be more requests for assistance from programs like General Assistance (GA), also called General Relief, or County Aid. GA is really a conglomeration of many small public assistance programs, but there is no federal involvement in GA. GA programs remain similar to many local and state efforts to provide governmental assistance to those in need prior to the Social Security Act of 1935. Some states have GA programs; in states that do not, local governments may choose to operate a program. GA programs differ widely in whom they serve and in the benefits they provide. Where they do exist, GA has been described as "the ultimate 'safety net' for low income individuals and families who are not eligible for federally-supported assistance programs," but these programs "are unusually sensitive to budget pressures . . . and change much more frequently than any other part of the welfare system" (U.S. Department of Health and Human Services, 1983, pp. 1–2).

Because many needy people fall through the cracks of federally supported assistance programs, family practitioners need to know whether there is a GA program in their area. Sometimes administrators of these programs have discretion over who can be served, especially in emergency situations, and family practitioners who take the time to establish relationships with individuals who staff these programs may have an advantage in securing resources for their clients. At the local level, family practitioners can also take an active role with city and county commissions and other public entities as well as private sponsors to see that families receive the maximum support their communities can provide.

Child Support Enforcement

Parents are legally obligated to support their children, but many noncustodial parents do not do so. One reason is that many of these cases never come before the courts; therefore, no child support order is issued. In 1991, no payments were awarded in 46% of all cases in which a parent was absent from the home; in the remaining 54% of cases in which payments were awarded, 51% received the full amount, 24% received partial payments, and 25% received no payments (U.S. Bureau of the Census, 1995b, p. 391). Never-married mothers are least likely to collect child support (Committee on Ways and Means, 1994, p. 465), and the number of out-of-wedlock births has risen dramatically among all the major ethnic groups in recent years. Despite increased government efforts and better methods of genetic testing, the Office of Child Support Enforcement reported that in 1993, paternity was established in less than one-third of cases in which the child's parents were not married (Committee on Ways and Means, 1996, p. 538). The Committee on Ways and Means (1993) reported that "a major weakness of the CSE [Child Support Enforcement] program is its poor performance in securing paternity" and emphasized the financial, social, psychological, and emotional benefits for families when paternity is established (p. 757). Many child and family practitioners assist children who have not had the benefits of the support of both their parents.

In 1974 and 1984, the federal government undertook substantial initiatives to increase pressure on states to enforce child support obligations. These efforts continue in order to establish CSE orders and increase collections. In addition to AFDC families, assistance with collecting child support is available to any family in which a noncustodial parent fails to meet obligations. States may garnishee a parent's wages if support payments are 30 days overdue, impose liens against the delinquent parent's income and property, report the parent to credit bureaus, and intercept federal and state income tax refunds. At the local level, judges have resorted to more frequent jailing of nonsupporting parents and some newspapers print the names of these parents. To ensure compliance, noncustodial parents are commonly subjected to automatic deductions of child support payments from their paychecks or required to make payments through law enforcement agencies or domestic relations departments of local governments.

As child support policies have employed more punitive approaches to forcing parents to meet their financial obligations, noncustodial parents have begun to organize to protect their rights. Some noncustodial fathers feel their rights are being violated because they must pay child support even though they may be denied the visitation privileges they would like to have or have little say if they feel the mother is not tending to the needs of the children. Hartman (1995) warns that "the aggressive pursuit of fathers for child support . . . may lead to a further break-down of family connections," because "fathers may be driven to terminate contact with their children out of fear of punitive action" (p. 189). Given federal pressures, however, states are intent on increasing collections and are using additional means such as revocation of driver's, professional, and other licenses if parents do not pay.

Family therapists address child support, custody, and visitation issues every day in their practices because these are highly emotional issues for all family members. They and other practitioners often find themselves on varying sides of the issues, depending on whether their client is a father, a mother, a child, or a family unit. Many family practitioners have acquired mediation skills to address these issues, as the adversarial nature of court proceedings often intensifies negative feelings, worsens relationships between parents, and causes further detriment to children. In fact, Piercy (1994) suggests that the number of failed marriages may be reduced "by requiring couples to undergo premarital counseling that focuses on communication skills and conflict resolution" (p. 164). Because improving family relations is the forte of family therapists, they may be the best advisers in developing policies that encourage both parents to provide the financial, social, and psychological support that children need.

Income Tax Policy

The poor are capturing a smaller share of all income generated in the United States. In 1993, the poorest one-fifth of families received 4.2% of all family income compared with 5.2% in 1980 whereas the richest one-fifth captured 46.2% of family income compared to 41.5% in 1980 (U.S. Bureau of the Census, 1995b, p. 475). Despite recent improvements in the economy, Duncan (1992) notes that "lower-middle-class families face an increasing threat of downward mobility. And low income families with children are less likely to rise into the middle class than before. The net result of these trends is a United States that is much more polarized economically now than at any time in the past" (cited in Committee on Ways and Means, 1993, pp. 1447–1448). The U.S. government's definition of a fair personal income tax policy changes frequently, but a more progressive tax structure would certainly help to increase the economic resources of low-income working families (see Zimmerman, 1992).

Several provisions of the federal income tax system do help boost the incomes of families with children or disabled members. Primary among them is the standard deduction that every family who pays income taxes is allowed to take for each dependent. Tax credits are also available for the care of dependent family members while adults in the family are at work. Also very important for low-income working families is the earned income tax credit (EITC). The EITC was substantially increased in 1990. In 1993, it was increased again and a smaller credit was made available to workers without children as part of the Clinton administration budget. The EITC operates like an income tax in reverse: The federal government pays it to low-income working families through the regular income tax system. The maximum credit in 1996 for a family with one child was $2,152 and for a family with more than one child it was as much as $3,556. The National Commission on Children (1991) "strongly endorse[d] the Earned Income Tax Credit . . . to encourage low-income parents to enter the paid workforce and strive for economic independence" (p. xxi). Writing for the American Association of Marriage and Family Therapy, Golonka and Ooms (1991) also hailed the EITC as "the largest single increase in any low-income program since 1977"; they also note that it reaches more low-income families than public assistance benefits (p. i). The EITC is especially appealing because it rewards work, yet even it has come under attack in congressional debates over how to balance the budget.

Although plans such as a guaranteed annual income proposed by President Nixon or a negative income tax proposed by economist Milton Friedman are far from viable in today's political climate, more could certainly be done through the tax system to help families. For example, the cost of long-term care for older Americans might be reduced if more tax incentives were made available to families to provide care. Currently, home care is not necessarily less costly than nursing home care because those receiving home care have more hospital costs, but older people, caregivers, service providers, and policymakers all preferred it to nursing home care, thus making it a better policy alternative (Weissert, Cready, & Pawelak, 1988). Family practitioners' knowledge of these "cost neutral" alternatives can also be used to persuade policymakers and their constituents to support policies that are more satisfying to the families they serve. The National Commission on Children (1991) considered many aspects of tax policy that might do a better job of benefiting families.

Nutrition Policies and Programs

Most Americans get enough calories to sustain life. In fact, the major nutrition problem in this country is obesity (Life Sciences Research Office, 1995). Some poor families, however, do not know where their next meal will come from. Malnutrition results "from failure to meet the total nutrient requirements of an individual" (Kotz, 1969); it may be reasonable to include in this definition those individuals who "for economic or other reasons beyond their control . . . experience repetitive periods of hunger, even though their total intake of nutrient is sufficient to protect them from symptoms of deficiency disease" (Bode, Gershoff, & Latham, 1975). In addition, the goal of "food security" includes obtaining food from normal channels (grocery stores, restaurants, and gardens) rather than sources that have become too common, such as food pantries, soup kitchens, and even trash bins ("Food Security," 1989). More Americans than some might think suffer from problems of undernutrition such as anemia. Poor individuals may eat adequately at the beginning of the month, but eating habits may change after a couple of weeks when food stamps, TANF, SSI, or other benefits run out (Bode et al., 1975; Physician Task Force on Hunger, 1985). Low-income individuals may have to decide between buying food or paying other bills, and children may rely on school meals for their major source of nutrition.

Food Stamp Program

The largest nutrition program in the United States is the Food Stamp Program administered by the U.S. Department of Agriculture (USDA) in conjunction with state and local welfare agencies. Stamp allotments are based on family size and income. To qualify, a person's gross income generally cannot exceed 130% of the poverty line. Although this requirement does not pertain to older and disabled recipients who are treated more generously, net income for all recipients cannot exceed 100% of the poverty line. The maximum monthly food stamp allotment for a family of four with no countable income in 1997 was $400 amounting to about $1.08 per family member per meal, which many people feel is inadequate. Some states have apparently relied on food stamps to make up for declining benefits under the AFDC, now TANF, program (Moffitt, 1990).

Food stamps or coupons are exchanged for food products in regular retail stores that choose to accept them. In the near future, "electronic benefit transfer" (EBT) will likely replace the stamps across the country. In a number of locations recipients are already using a plastic card, like those for automated teller machines, that deducts the amount of the purchase from their food stamp allotment. EBT may help to reduce the stigma and inconvenience associated with using stamps. Only food products may be purchased with food stamp benefits. Paper and cleaning products, which many people take for granted as grocery store purchases, are excluded.

As the Food Stamp Program covers single individuals and couples who are not aged or disabled or do not have minor children, it comes closer to covering all those in need than any other public assistance program in the United States. In 1994, participation in the Food Stamp Program reached an all-time high of nearly 28 million individuals (U.S. Department of Agriculture, 1997) or more than 10% of the U.S. population. Increased participation was primarily caused by economic recession and unemployment, but it also reflected population growth and several natural disasters that placed people in need. More recently, participation rates have dropped below 26 million as a result of improvements in the economy (U.S. Department of Agriculture, 1997). In 1994, a little more than half of all Food Stamp Program participants were children and 7% were elderly (U.S. Department of Agriculture, 1997). Ninety percent of food stamp households met federal poverty guidelines and only about 25% of recipients had income from earnings. The USDA estimates that in 1989, 41% of eligible individuals did not participate in the Food Stamp Program; however, the lower their income, the more likely they were to participate (Committee on Ways and Means, 1994). In addition, of those eligible, only 29% of households headed by an elderly person participated compared with participation rates of 78% for households headed by single mothers and 78% of households headed by disabled, nonelderly persons (Committee on Ways and Means, 1994). In 1995, Food Stamp Program costs were $24.6 billion (U.S. Department of Agriculture, 1997).

In its sweeping welfare reform of 1996, Congress spared the Food Stamp Program from being converted to a block grant. Perhaps the most serious change it made to the program with respect to families with children was eliminating households of most legally admitted immigrants from eligibility until such time as they may become U.S. citizens. Other changes included reducing food stamp benefit levels and freezing some of the income deductions that used to be adjusted for inflation. The Food Research and Action Center and other advocates continue to call for improvements in food stamps and similar nutrition programs at the same time that conservatives have called for merging the country's nutrition and other public assistance programs under block grants to the states. Congress takes a particular interest in the Food Stamp Program, and this attention has likely protected it over the years (Ohls & Beebout, 1993).

Special Supplemental Nutrition Program for Women, Infants, and Children

Among the other federally supported nutrition programs is the Special Supplemental Nutrition Program for Women, Infants, and Children, known as WIC. WIC's purpose is to prevent health problems by upgrading the nutrition of low-income women who are pregnant or breastfeeding, and infants and children up to age five who are at nutritional risk. The program is also operated by the USDA in conjunction with hundreds of local agencies, mostly health clinics and departments. Coupons are given to recipients for use in grocery stores. Only specified, nutritious products can be purchased. In 1995, nearly 7 million women and children participated, up from 4.5 million in 1990 (Food and Consumer Service, 1995). Seventy-seven percent of recipients are children.

WIC is not an entitlement program. Funds are divided among states according to a needs formula. When a state reaches its capacity of participants, vacancies are filled using a priority system. The program now reaches about 60% of all eligible participants; however, USDA estimates that 98% of eligible infants are reached and that the program now serves 45% of all infants born in the United States each year (Food and Consumer Service, 1995). WIC is associated with many positive effects, including better pregnancy outcomes (Rush, 1987) and decreased Medicaid costs (Devaney, Bilheimer, & Schore, 1992). Nutrition advocates continue to call for funding that would allow all eligible women, infants, and children to benefit.

Other Nutrition Programs for Children

Other programs that help children and their families are the National School Lunch Program, the School Breakfast Program, the Summer Food Program, and the Special Milk Program. The lunch and breakfast programs allow children to obtain meals at no cost if their family's income is 130% or less of the poverty line, or at a reduced price if family income falls between 130% and 185% of the poverty line. The cost of a reduced-price lunch cannot exceed 40 cents and a breakfast 30 cents. Children with family incomes over 185% of the poverty line may also obtain these meals, but the school district determines the price of the meals. The USDA provides cash and food commodities to state departments of education, which in turn distribute the funds and food to schools that operate breakfast and lunch programs.

Approximately 93,000 schools participate in the lunch program, including almost all public schools and many private schools (Food and Consumer Service, 1995). Approximately 25 million children participate in the lunch program each school day, and about half receive meals free or at a reduced price (Food and Consumer Service, 1995). In effect, the meals of all children are subsidized as the government also pays a small subsidy for the full-price meals.

Although all schools that have subsidized lunch programs may operate breakfast programs, many do not, probably because of the extra administrative responsibilities and personnel costs. About 65,000 schools currently participate (Food and Consumer Service, 1995). Nutrition advocates, including those in Congress and the USDA, are encouraging more schools to offer breakfasts. In 1995, about 6.3 million children received breakfasts daily, with about 5.5 million receiving them free or at a reduced price (Food and Consumer Service, 1995). The breakfast program has been associated with better academic functioning in students (Food and Consumer Service, 1995). Evidence also indicates that school meals can improve children's nutrition because of the control they afford in assuring an adequate diet (Clarkson, 1975).

The Healthy Meals for Healthy Americans Act of 1994 addressed calls for improvements in the National School Lunch Act and the Child Nutrition Act. In addition to increased funding for a number of the child nutrition programs, the bill makes it easier for some institutions and individuals to participate. The bill also requires that school meals meet the Dietary Guidelines for Americans. The idea of serving all school meals free will be tested as a result of the legislation.

During school vacations, the Summer Food Program provides lunches to children in impoverished areas. The Special Milk Program began in 1954 when the market was flooded with surplus dairy products; today it is restricted to schools and child care facilities not participating in other federal food programs.

Nutrition Programs for Older Americans

Under the 1972 amendments to the Older Americans Act, meals are provided to older persons at community sites (called congregate meals) or to homebound, older and disabled persons (known as Meals-on-Wheels). Shopping assistance can also be provided. The USDA and the Department of Human Services cooperate in administering these programs. Federal funds are channeled to the states, which then distribute them to local agencies that prepare and distribute the meals to participants. Participants may make a cash contribution for their meals, and food stamps can also be used. In some areas, community volunteers deliver the meals. An important spillover effect of these programs is that participants maintain contact with other community members who can alert appropriate individuals should an elderly or disabled person need other assistance. The programs also benefit families who might find it difficult to see that older or disabled members who live independently receive adequate nutrition each day.

Other USDA programs provide commodity foods directly to needy individuals or to facilities that serve children or older or disabled people. In addition, many not-for-profit groups fill gaps through food pantries and soup kitchens that help homeless and low-income individuals and families who lack the resources to obtain regular meals. Welfare reform has led to concerns that greater reliance will be placed on private resources to assist needy individuals, and it raises questions about what the proper balance between public and private responses might be. Critics of the federally supported public assistance program like Charles Murray (1984) believe that these programs should be abandoned in favor of reliance on private charities and state and local governments. Yet there are questions about how much private organizations can do and how social welfare responsibilities should be divided among the private sector and federal, state, and local governments. These are questions that many family practitioners have had to ponder.

Housing

A safe living environment is essential to families, but locating decent, affordable housing is a challenge in many areas of the country. For example, the Center on Budget and Policy Priorities (Hou & Lazere, 1991) reports that "46% of poor renter households nationwide spent at least 70% of income on housing in 1987" (p. xiii). In 1995, the U.S. Department of Housing and Urban Development (HUD) continued to report that housing costs were consuming more than half the income of 43% of very low-income renters. Lack of a secure home jeopardizes physical and emotional well-being (Bassuk, Rubin, & Lauriat, 1986; Boxill & Beatty, 1990). Estimates are that 1.3 to 2 million people are homeless each year (National Alliance to End Homelessness cited in Blau, 1992) and that family units may represent 25% to 40% of the homeless (Blau, 1992; Berlin & McAllister, 1992; Baum & Burnes, 1993; Burt, 1992). In the Housing Act of 1949, Congress recognized the need for a "decent home and suitable living environment for every American family," yet no policy assures that this need will be met. During the Reagan years, the number of affordable housing units dwindled, and throughout its history, the HUD has gone through scandals that have hampered efforts to increase the affordable housing supply. Federal housing policy has often been more of a boon to the housing industry than to those in need of a place to live.

Some HUD aid supports federal housing projects. Parents, however, generally want to avoid raising their families in "the projects," many of which are their own ghettos full of drugs, guns, and rodents. HUD also operates programs to help low-income households subsidize their rent under the Section 8 certificate and housing voucher programs. These subsidies allow renters to obtain housing in the private market, although there are often insufficient units to meet demand. Other programs help low- and moderate-income families purchase homes. Not-for-profit groups such as Habitat for Humanity help low-income households rehabilitate or construct housing. Rising housing costs and interest rates contributed to declining home ownership rates between 1980 and 1990 (U.S. Department of Housing and Urban Development, 1995). Not until 1997 did home ownership rates hit the 1980 peak of nearly 66% (U.S. Department of Housing and Urban Development, 1998). Lower interest rates are now helping to increase the ability of families, many of them first-time home buyers, to attain the American dream of home ownership, but there remains a substantial shortage of decent, affordable housing. The 1990 Cranston-Gonzalez National Affordable Housing Act authorizes block grants to states and local governments to fund a variety of options for providing housing assistance. Mulroy (1995) notes some of the provisions of this act that family practitioners might find especially encouraging: "affordable housing projects will be linked with social services, resources will be targeted to neighborhood and community development, and nonprofit community development corporations will be used as producers of affordable housing" (p. 1383).

In addition to attempts to respond to the need for individual housing units, Congress and the Clinton administration also developed a set of initiatives to revitalize economically depressed neighborhoods. In 1993, Congress provided funding for nine "empowerment zones" and 95 "enterprise communities." Funds were awarded competitively in both urban and rural areas across the country. The empowerment zones received tax incentives, and businesses that locate in the area and hire local residents also get tax breaks. The empowerment zones also received $100 million social service block grants for services such as job training, child care, and drug treatment. Each enterprise community received about $3 million dollars for these purposes. Pundits are watching these communities to determine whether this approach will work in light of the disappointments that often resulted from Great Society efforts to revitalize economically depressed areas (Lemann, 1994). The current grants will help only a small number of communities, but perhaps there will be more positive lessons to be learned this time around, given that the current mission of HUD is to "help people create communities of opportunity."

Health

Health care is another critical social welfare issue facing Americans because of spiraling costs that are just beginning to be contained and the number of people who have no health insurance at all, a number that may be increasing. Preliminary estimates by the U.S. Bureau of the Census (1995a) show that 39.7 million people or 15.2% of the population had no health insurance coverage at any time during 1994. People who were 14 to 24 years of age were more likely than other age groups to lack coverage during all of 1994; 26.7% of these young people had no coverage compared to 0.9% of those 65 years and older. The elderly are most likely to be covered.

Many uninsured adults are working at jobs that offer no health insurance. Of the major industrialized nations of the world, only the United States and South Africa remain without some form of universal health care plan, yet the United States spends the most on health care. In 1994, U.S. health care costs were 14.2% of the domestic national product (and this figure continues to rise) whereas the United Kingdom and Canada, which have national health plans (albeit different types), spent 6.9% and 9.8%, respectively (Organization for Economic Cooperation and Development, cited in U.S. Bureau of the Census, 1996, p. 834). Francoeur (1993) notes, "With the billions we pay for scientific research and health care, there is no justification for the United States ranking as low as we do in preventative medicine, basic prenatal and prenatal health care, and family support" (p. 152).

Health care is of particular concern to poor people because many have only limited access to health care services. It is also of concern to wealthier individuals, because a serious illness could bankrupt most Americans, even those with private health insurance. Family therapists often help families address the stresses associated with the serious illness of a member. Health problems like cancer and AIDS have increased the need for these services. Such stresses are exacerbated when families must also contend with the inability to obtain health care.

Health care in the United States is a two-tier system. The top tier is for those who have the financial resources to obtain health care privately; they are treated much differently from the uninsured and the poor who must rely on the second tier of services. Many in the second tier have to wait until their medical problems are severe before health providers will see them. Often they are treated in the overburdened emergency departments of public hospitals that must see them when other health care providers will not. Social workers, including family therapists, may spend hours trying to help clients with no coverage obtain desperately needed health care services. The strategy currently favored to provide coverage to more people and to contain health care costs is managed care (e.g., health maintenance organizations).

The two major, publicly administered health care programs available in the United States are Medicare and Medicaid. Public health services are also a component of government services.

Medicare

Medicare is a federal program that serves almost all people 65 years of age and older as well as individuals who have received federal disability payments for at least two years. Medicare is considered a social insurance program because it is financed from Social Security taxes. In addition to OASDI taxes, both employer and employee pay a 1.45% tax on *all* the employee's wages to finance the rapidly growing Medicare program. Medicare is a substantial source of help for individuals and families. Many people would otherwise be unable to afford health care in their older years, and their families would face a tremendous burden in trying to pay for this care. Even with increased Medicare taxes, demand for services has outstripped the funds generated for the program.

Another shortcoming of Medicare is that it does not cover all health care needs. These gaps in coverage, referred to as "medigaps," include the deductibles and copayments that beneficiaries must pay; they also include prescription drugs and eyeglasses. Some Medicare beneficiaries have joined health maintenance organizations (HMOs) to help cover medigaps. Many others purchase supplemental policies to cover some gaps. Perhaps the most serious medigap is that Medicare does not pay for long-term, custodial care in nursing homes or in one's own home. Families are the major providers of services to older persons (see Committee on Ways and Means, 1993, pp. 243, 257), but when the amount of care needed is substantial, the inability to purchase assistance or the older person's unwillingness to accept help from nonfamily members can be a major source of family stress. Medicare is strongly endorsed by older Americans, but a study of five countries showed that "while most elderly people worry about getting sick, only older Americans worry about how to pay for medical care" (Davis, 1993, p. 10).

Many social workers are involved in helping older people and their families negotiate the health care system. These practitioners may help ensure that people get all the care they need and to which they are entitled. Some function as case managers when an individual needs a number of health and social services. They may also play an important role when health care decisions and ethical dilemmas are involved, such as when to prolong life when the quality of life is at issue.

Medicaid

Medicaid provides assistance to some poor individuals and families who do not have other health insurance. Medicaid is an entitlement program—everyone who meets the eligibility requirements can receive benefits if they wish. It is also called an "in kind" program because patients receive their benefits in the form of services provided by physicians and other health care providers rather than the cash to purchase these services. About half the states use some type of program cost sharing; for example, recipients may have to pay small deductibles or copayments for services, but states cannot impose these requirements for emergency and family planning services. Certain recipients, like pregnant women and children are not required to share any costs. Although states' Medicaid eligibility requirements differ, they must cover certain groups—for example, all TANF and most SSI recipients. Remember, however, that states' eligibility requirements for TANF vary substantially, so many poor or near-poor families may be ineligible for Medicaid. States can cover individuals and families in addition to those mandated by federal requirements, and most do under a provision called "medically needy." Medically needy individuals and families are those with high medical expenses and low incomes as defined by the states. Some states extend coverage to individuals receiving unemployment compensation, even though the state may receive no federal reimbursement for this.

The federal government requires states to provide certain services under Medicaid (inpatient and outpatient hospital care; physicians' services; laboratory and x-ray services; nursing home and home health care for adults; family planning services; nurse-midwife services; and early, periodic screening, diagnosis, and treatment [EPSDT] for children). The majority of states offer additional services such as prescription drugs, eyeglasses, and dental care. Medicaid helps many low-income elderly persons cover costs that Medicare does not pay, and Medicaid has been expanded to cover more pregnant women and children, but many people in need clearly remain outside the program.

Both Medicare and Medicaid were instituted in 1965 and were a long time in coming. For much of the 20th century, the medical establishment fought such programs by branding them socialized medicine that would ruin the quality of health care in this country. Today, many physicians derive a substantial amount of their income from Medicare. Even Medicaid, which generally has low reimbursement rates, does not get much opposition from physicians, but many physicians refuse to accept Medicaid patients due to low reimbursement rates and the paperwork hassles involved. Despite low reimbursement rates, Medicaid is the United States's most costly public assistance program. In 1994, Medicaid costs were $144 billion (U.S. Bureau of the Census, 1996, p. 371). The federal and state governments share the costs of the Medicaid program. Approximately 35 million Americans received Medicaid benefits in 1994 (U.S. Bureau of the Census, 1996, p. 117). Families with dependent children receiving public assistance make up about 70% of Medicaid beneficiaries, but their medical bills amount to about 30% of the program's expenditures (Committee on Ways and Means, 1993). In 1992, the average amount of Medicaid funds spent on a child was $959, compared with $7,770 for an aged person, and $7,612 for a disabled person (Committee on Ways and Means, 1994, p. 804). Nearly 70% of Medicaid funds were used by elderly and disabled persons, and a substantial portion of these funds went to pay for long-term care for a relatively small percentage of beneficiaries (Committee on Ways and Means, 1993). Medicaid's ability to pay for long-term, custodial nursing home care is a blessing for those who might otherwise spend their last days, months, or years in squalor, but family practitioners often continue to invest substantial time in helping family members address their guilt at placing a relative and their concerns about quality of care. Therapists may also help family members entering a nursing home address their fears and concerns, including the anger that this transition may cause. Family practitioners are well advised to take an active interest in aging policy. This is a rapidly growing area of human service practice. Many family practitioners may find themselves working in this area in the years ahead.

Other Health Care Services

Additional health care services are provided through public health block grants. For example, the Maternal and Child Health Block Grant provides medical care to low-income pregnant women and young children. The Health Services Block Grant funds community health centers that provide medical care to low-income people in areas with few doctors or medical facilities; treatment for those with specific health problems, such as hypertension; health programs for migrant workers; rodent-control programs; and other services.

Health Care Reform

On taking office, President Clinton tried to make health care a high priority public policy issue. He proposed a national health care plan requiring most employers to contribute to the cost of employees' coverage with employees sharing costs. His plan also contained mechanisms for subsidizing the costs of care for unemployed persons. Many employers already subsidize health care benefits for their employees through traditional health insurance or through health maintenance organizations or other managed care alternatives. Employer-subsidized group plans are much less costly for workers than purchasing a plan as an individual. Many Republicans and many business owners, however, were concerned that the costs would be too great. Other concerns were that the president's plan focused on government control at the expense of private sector insurance and health care providers. Millions were spent in lobbying efforts by both proponents and opponents of the plan. Many other proposals were also offered, and all failed. The president and other advocates emphasized that in the long run national health insurance will reduce health care inflation by providing everyone with a regular source of health care so that preventive services and early treatment can be obtained. Even the American Medical Association now believes that steps should be taken to see that all Americans have health care insurance. National health insurance could be the best poverty fighter the country has seen in recent decades, but partisan politics is a major barrier to this type of health care reform. Even a universal program that would provide basic, preventive health care for children and could save many dollars in remedial health care costs has never been adopted, despite appeals from many child and family advocates in the country. As a result, states are taking the initiative to deal with the health care coverage problems at their doorsteps. For example, Oregon has instituted a program that offers a basic set of health care benefits to a larger number of residents even though it has been criticized as an example of rationing.

Mental Health and Chemical Dependency Services

During the family's life cycle, informal resources may be insufficient to help the family cope with stressors. A serious upset in family equilibrium requires effective services to help the family move through a crisis or cope with a member's serious mental illness (SMI) or chemical dependency problems. Like the health care system, the mental health care system is largely divided into two tiers even though there has been a blurring of the public, not-for-profit, and profit-making sectors. This blurring has occurred because governments now often contract with private service providers, and conversely, businesses may contract with public agencies such as community mental health centers to provide services to their employees. Although many dedicated practitioners work in public and nonprofit programs, the differences in treatment received by those with and without private resources to pay for services remains pronounced. Those without private resources have more limited choices. They are often referred to mental health and chemical dependency programs with long waiting lists and high caseloads.

Family practitioners who work in the top tier provide mental health services in individual or group practices or in outpatient clinics or hospitals in the private sector. Clients often pay through their insurance or managed care plans or from their own pockets, although Medicaid, Medicare, or other government programs may also pay for these services. Competition in the private sector and the constraints of working under managed care systems have put pressure on private providers to increase caseloads and has created a situation in which private and public providers are competing for the same dollars. In an attempt to control costs, insurers and other payers limit the amount of service to clients and determine which mental health professionals can provide services. The practice models in this book are aimed at preparing practitioners to work in today's practice, which involves managed care systems, although not all practitioners agree with the way managed behavioral health care structures mental health care or treats clients. In this section, we point out some of the limitations of managed care.

Borrowing from the medical model, managed care reimbursements for mental health services for families is usually based on diagnostic categories, with little recognition of the importance of family relationships. A client with a personality disorder, for example, may be entitled to fewer sessions than a client with a mood disorder. Clients and service providers are often placed in a difficult position when additional care is needed. Most people with private health insurance have plans that cover mental health and chemical dependency services as well as physical health services, but their mental health and chemical dependency coverage (now often called behavioral health care coverage) is generally inferior to their physical health care coverage. As a result, many family practitioners, especially those in the private tier, are working to encourage parity for behavioral health care services. In 1996, the U.S. Congress passed a bill that helps to improve parity in limited ways, but some states have already done better in this regard. Like improvements in physical health care, major reforms to improve behavioral health care coverage will likely come from state initiatives.

Many family practitioners practice in the second tier made up of the public and not-for-profit mental health care programs that serve people with no means of taking advantage of the first tier. The discussion in Chapter 1 showed that the first and second tiers are losing their distinct boundaries, but poor people still require public assistance to meet their mental health and chemical dependency needs, regardless of whether they are being served by private or public sectors. Second-tier individuals with SMI or chronic chemical dependency problems often deplete any insurance coverages they may have and end up at the mercy of public-funded services. The large caseloads that practitioners in the second tier often carry may not afford them the opportunity to serve clients as well as they or the client and the client's family would like.

In both tiers, as discussed in Chapter 1, the focus has become brief interventions. Fortunately, there is evidence that brief treatments are effective for a large number of individuals (see Chapters 2 through 9). However, managed care and brief treatments are models better suited for clients with acute rather than long-term problems (Miller & Hoffman, 1995; Prezioso, 1994). This fact suggests that clients with SMI or chronic chemical dependency problems often go without continuous care. Family therapists are paying close attention to behavioral health care reform as it affects them and their clients directly. Sprenkle and Bischof (1994) noted that mental health care reform in the United States "is likely to include downward pressure on fees, an emphasis on brief treatment, a reduced role for solo private practitioners, and an increased emphasis on accountability. MFTs [marriage and family therapists] will, no doubt, be caught between the merits of the system (better coverage for the less fortunate) and issues of professional survival" (p. 8).

Originally, the hope was that managed care would provide a more individualized approach to treatment, tailored to the client's need, but evidence indicates that insurance providers of various types are taking a "one approach fits all" model. Many health care experts are disappointed with the response of managed care organizations to mental health and substance abuse treatment because most evidence is that they have not "moved beyond traditional services" (Mechanic, Schlesinger, & McAlpine, 1995). Apparently, insurers are approving the same length of stay or outpatient services regardless of clients' needs. For example, in a study by Wickizer and his colleagues (1996) of utilization management practices, inpatient psychiatric treatment (including substance abuse treatment) was approved for nearly all (99%) of the patients for whom it was requested, but on average, only one-third (6.9 days) of the 19 days initially requested were authorized, and on average a total of 16.8 days were approved compared with the 23.5 days requested. Perhaps no recent issue has mobilized mental health practitioners politically so solidly as have the effects of managed care on mental health treatment.

Managed care has also raised issues about confidentiality and patient privacy. Questions are being raised about the number of clients who are paying for substance abuse treatment out of their own pockets rather than asking their insurance carriers to pay, out of fear of stigma and privacy concerns. Payers are now asking more and more questions about the details of patients' lives as they make decisions that were once left between patient and health care provider. In addition, Iglehart (1996) says that "the behavioral health care companies are forming integrated delivery systems, thus linking the functions of direct provision of care and plan management. . . . These companies increase their vertical integration . . . [but] create potential conflicts of interest by combining the roles of providers and manager in one for-profit enterprise" (p. 132).

At the federal level, the Substance Abuse and Mental Health Services Administration (SAMHSA) is primarily responsible for implementing mental health and chemical dependency treatment policy and assisting states in providing services, but the states play the most important role in determining the number and types of publicly supported facilities that will be available to citizens. States also set the laws that govern voluntary and involuntary commitment of people with severe mental disorders. Mental health laws are of concern to families with members who have serious mental illness. Families often ask mental health service providers, law enforcement agencies, or the courts to intervene when a member with SMI experiences a relapse but refuses treatment. Involuntary commitment is usually restricted to those who present a serious danger to self or others, including the lack of ability for self-care. There may be a fine line between preserving civil liberties and contributing to neglect when a person with SMI is not hospitalized (see Krauthammer, 1985; Mechanic, 1989; Szasz, 1974). Sometimes the family believes a member requires hospitalization but authorities disagree, based on their interpretation of the law. Family therapists must exert considerable skill to negotiate the different wishes and decisions of the parties involved, or they may face a dilemma in deciding who is their client when rifts occur with a family.

Family therapists must understand the many mental health policies that govern their practices. These are often state laws, but sometimes they are policies that have emanated from court decisions. In cases that involve issues of confidentiality or duty to warn, state laws and court decisions may differ and they may also conflict with a professional's code of ethics. Knowledge of mental health policy is important, but it may not contain the answers that practitioners need to solve ethical dilemmas.

Mental Health Problems and Mental Health Care

The youngest members of families are at high risk for psychiatric neglect (U.S. Department of Health and Human Services, 1990). SAMHSA (1995a) estimates that 20% of children have emotional problems that interfere with functioning and that only one-third are receiving help. It is often quite difficult for parents to obtain psychiatric care, especially long-term residential care, for children with SMI. In some instances, parents of children with a severe disturbance have transferred custody to the state in order for their child to receive the residential care the family could not afford (SAMHSA, 1995b). One of the public efforts to assist is the Child and Adolescent Service System Program (CASSP) of 1984 that allows states to apply for grants to develop local community-based continuums of care for children with severe emotional disturbances. Another important initiative is the Child and Family Mental Health Services Demonstration Program of 1993.

One reason that children have received comparatively little interest from the mental health industry may be that childhood is a time of rapid, nonlinear development marked by temporary regressions. The more serious mood and thought disorders observed in adults are not as easily recognized in children. For example, the major features of depression in adults include feelings of sadness, worthlessness, and hopelessness. Children rarely admit to long-lasting feelings of sadness (Glasberg & Aboud, 1982), and other symptoms of adult depression, such as eating, sleep disturbances, and crying are not uncommon among children.

The *Diagnostic and Statistical Manual of Mental Disorders (DSM)* of the American Psychiatric Association provides a common tool for diagnosing mental disorders. The codes assigned to each diagnosis are used by many mental health practitioners, including marriage and family therapists, to request third-party reimbursement for the services they render. Accountability and uniformity can be enhanced when mental health providers use the same criteria for diagnosing disorders, criteria such as the *DSM* affords. However, psychiatric labels in the *DSM*, which are based on individual dysfunctions, are often little help to family therapists. Between the first edition of the *DSM* in 1952 and the fourth edition in 1994, a number of changes and additions were made to the diagnostic criteria for childhood disorders. In the second edition published in 1968, six behavior disorders for children were added. In 1980, the third edition departed dramatically from earlier editions; it included more disorders of childhood and adolescence and introduced the use of axes to examine multiple facets of the client and his or her environment (American Psychiatric Association, 1980). The clarity of some of the diagnostic categories for children and their ability to distinguish among clusters of problem behaviors remains problematic (Costello, Edelbrock, Dulcan, Kalas, & Kloric, 1984). Children may meet the criteria for multiple disorders such as depression, attention deficit hyperactivity, conduct disorder, and anorexia nervosa (Carlson & Cantwell, 1980). In addition, there is concern about applying a label from a psychiatric manual to children experiencing difficulty mastering reading or math. Requiring mental health practitioners to use labels to obtain reimbursement may result in a self-fulfilling prophecy for the client and a tag that follows the individual for a life-time (e.g., see Sprenkle & Piercy, 1992). In addition, clients may be "overdiag-nosed" or otherwise inappropriately diagnosed in an effort to get them services when other means fail.

Other factors that can have a profound impact on the emotional well-being of children and adolescents are not included in the *DSM*. There are no specific codes for the effects of racism, sexism, homophobia, or poverty. Although, in the most recent addition of the manual (*DSM-IV*, APA, 1994), there have been improvements in recognizing the importance of ethnicity on mental health diagnosis. In fact, the *DSM-IV* includes sections on these issues. Contextual variables that impact the well-being of children and families include race or ethnicity, social class, and the impact of family relationships; these may be listed under Axis IV—psychosocial and environmental problems—to allow the practitioner to provide a broader pic-ture of the client's functioning. Lyman Wynne and other family therapists also worked diligently to get the American Psychiatric Association to adopt the Global Assessment of Relational Functioning Scale (GARF), which assesses the function-ing of the family or other ongoing relationships. Fortunately, the GARF was in-cluded as an appendix in the *DSM-IV* manual. Perhaps diagnostic categories spe-cific to families will become part of the *DSM*.

The mental health industry still has much to learn about the identification and manifestation of emotional disturbances in children. There is little research on the outcomes of intervention with children, especially when compared to outcome studies focusing on adults. Without this understanding, effective interventions and public policies cannot be developed. Much knowledge about adult mental health is the result of research funded almost exclusively by the federal government. Re-search is expensive, and support for child mental health research remains meager. The lack of funding perpetuates a cycle that slows the development of knowledge on which better policies could be based. Researchers interested in children may feel forced to pursue interests in better funded areas.

Another group often underserved by mental health professionals is older peo-ple. Their symptoms, such as poor appetite and sleep disturbances, are often mis-taken by family members and even by professionals as signs of age rather than of mental disorders such as depression or alcohol abuse. Other misdiagnoses occur when the effects of too much medication or the interactions of medications are mistaken for mental disorders. Service providers may see older family members as too advanced in age to benefit from mental health treatment (Hooyman & Kiyak, 1993), or providers may prefer younger patients who are closer to their own age.

As the life span continues to increase, more individuals are developing de-mentias (organic brain syndromes) such as Alzheimer's disease. Clients with these disorders require constant supervision that families often find difficult to provide. There are also stresses involved in juggling the needs of older and younger family members. Those in the "sandwich generation" can be overwhelmed by family de-mands, and many rifts can develop within nuclear and extended family members in trying to work out solutions to caregiving. This is especially true when public policies fail to provide a viable range of options to meet the needs of the family members involved.

Chemical Dependency Problems and Treatment

As family practitioners have come to realize, a family member with an alcohol or other drug problem challenges the effective functioning of both the individual members of the family and the family unit. Since the early 1970s, private chemical dependency treatment has become a profitable business; however, there remain few guidelines to help practitioners match clients with appropriate treatment. Evidence indicates that outpatient treatment, especially for alcoholics, is generally as effective as inpatient treatment, and that success rates are influenced more by marital, job, and psychiatric stability than by treatment modality (National Institute on Alcohol Abuse and Alcoholism, 1994).

Most substance abuse research and treatment models are based on the needs of men. Sexism has inhibited the development of treatment models appropriate for the special needs of women (Reed, 1987; Wellisch, Prendergast, & Anglin, 1994). Men and women bring gender- and role-specific issues to treatment. Improvement in parenting skills is a typical goal for women in treatment but is a less common goal for men. Concern about family functioning encourages women to enter treatment whereas men are more likely to enter treatment as a result of arrests for driving under the influence or because of referrals from employers (Wellisch et al., 1994). In recent years, agencies such as the National Institute on Alcohol Abuse and Alcoholism (NIAAA) have amended their grant processes to ensure that women as well as members of various ethnic groups are included in research that expands knowledge of chemical dependency and its treatment.

During the 1980s, arrests for drug offenses increased more dramatically than for any other crime. From 1983 through 1986, arrests increased by 52%, convictions increased by 71%, and sentences to incarceration were up 104% (U.S. Department of Justice, 1989). In 1965, the adult arrest rate (per 100,00 inhabitants) for drug violations was 36.4; by 1992, the rate was 554.7 (Bureau of Justice Statistics, 1994a). While arrests for drug offenses were increasing, the incidence of drug use was actually decreasing. In 1979, 27% of youth ages 12 to 17 had used an illicit drug in the past year; by 1992, this figure had dropped to 12% (Substance Abuse and Mental Health Services Administration, 1995c). Among young adults ages 18 to 25 in 1979, 50% used an illicit drug; by 1992, this figure had dropped to 26%. Among those age 26 and older, 10% used an illicit drug in 1979; this figure dropped to 8% by 1992. However, the percent of youth ages 12 to 17 who used an illicit drug in 1994 rose to 16% (Substance Abuse and Mental Health Services Administration, 1995d). Among those ages 18 to 25, the number who used an illegal drug in the previous year has remained fairly constant at 25% in 1994. Among those ages 26 and older, there is a considerable disparity between the 26 to 34 group and those who are 35 and older. In 1994, 15% of those ages 26 to 34 and 6% of those age 35 and older had used an illicit drug in the last year.

Parental chemical dependency is a serious risk factor for families. The intergenerational transmission of alcoholism, especially from fathers to sons, is well known (Cloninger, Bohman, & Sigvardsson, 1981; Cloninger, 1983). Another consistently identified risk factor for child mental health problems is maternal drug use. While drugs have been used for centuries, the recent interest has been in the use of mood altering chemicals by women, especially pregnant women. The consequences of using alcohol and tobacco during pregnancy have been studied most extensively. The negative effects of alcohol were identified more than 20 years ago when Fetal Alcohol Syndrome (FAS) was established (Jones & Smith, 1973). Infants born with FAS suffer from growth deficiency, central nervous system impairment, and distinctive facial features. Mental retardation is the most debilitating impairment. Fetal Alcohol Effect (FAE) is a more common condition in which the infant suffers impairment but does not have all the characteristics of FAS. Tobacco use is linked with premature birth, more frequent miscarriages, and low birth weight (Office of Smoking and Health, 1988).

Methodological problems have raised questions about estimates of the number of children born prenatally exposed to chemicals. Which drugs are included, where the data are collected (e.g., private or public facilities), and how the drugs were detected have resulted in varying estimates. Most drugs are used in combination, making it difficult to attribute effects to any single drug. It is also difficult to control for variables that can occur with drug use, such as poor maternal nutrition, inadequate prenatal care, and the effects of living in a stressful environment. In the most comprehensive study to date (data were collected between 1992 and 1993), 6% or 221,000 women used an illicit drug one or more times while pregnant, 19% used alcohol, and 20% smoked cigarettes (National Institute on Drug Abuse, 1996). With respect to illicit drugs, 2.9% used marijuana, 2% used psychotherapeutic medication without prescription, and 1% used cocaine (including crack). Rates of other substance use were considerably lower. Consistently reported results of maternal drug use are an increase in preterm birth and the subsequent low birth weight that accompanies early birth (Gustavsson, 1992). Although it is difficult to separate drug use from other factors that may result in negative pregnancy outcomes, it is clear that chemical use can compromise the well-being of both the fetus and the mother.

Much of the debate over maternal drug use focuses on what the appropriate public response should be. Beliefs that maternal drug use is widespread, causes serious harm to the fetus, and results in high medical costs to the public have been used to justify punitive approaches. Some states and communities have attempted to criminalize maternal drug use during pregnancy and have modified child abuse reporting laws to include prenatal exposure (see Blank, 1993; Swenson & Crabbe, 1994). Criminal prosecutions of women based on prenatal exposure have generally not been upheld by the courts as a result of constitutional rights to privacy and Supreme Court decisions that place the rights of the mother above those of the fetus. In addition, criminalization fails to recognize the complicated issues associated with maternal drug use such as limited social support, lack of access to services, history of physical and sexual abuse, and relationship problems, including drug-using and sometimes violent male partners (for a review of this literature, see Davis & DiNitto, 1998). Child abuse statutes have been used more successfully to take children from their mothers by deeming them unfit parents. Family practitioners may struggle with their feelings about what the appropriate public policy response should be to pregnant women's use of drugs during pregnancy. They are likely to favor social services and treatment approaches, but they may disagree about what the appropriate response should be when these approaches fail to help the woman terminate drug use, as is sometimes or even frequently the case.

SAMHSA estimates that 48% of those who need drug treatment are not receiving it (see Office of National Drug Control Policy, 1996). Others feel that this "treatment gap" is even larger. The services available to women, especially mothers and pregnant women, with chemical dependency problems are especially limited. Mothers who want treatment face multiple challenges. Long waiting lists are typical. Half the drug treatment agencies in New York City refuse to admit pregnant women and some states have only a handful of beds for pregnant women (U.S. General Accounting Office, 1990). Few residential treatment programs allow women to bring their children, especially older children. Many women fail to enter treatment when it means separation from their children. Such fears are realistic when one considers that child welfare authorities may place the children in foster care and that there is always a threat that the children will not be returned in a timely manner. Rehabilitation can take a long time and relapse is common. In the meantime, children may remain in placement.

The effectiveness of the federal policy response to drug use in general (see McNeece & DiNitto, 1998) and to maternal drug use in particular is highly questionable if the goal is rehabilitate rather than punish. About two-thirds of drug control funds are used for law enforcement and interdiction efforts and one-third for treatment, education, and prevention (Office of National Drug Control Policy, 1996). On the supply side, stopping the flow of drugs into the United States has been a futile effort. On the demand side, not all states require insurers to offer coverage for drug treatment, so even those with health insurance may be unable to afford treatment if they can find it. Medicaid coverage for drug treatment is complicated and varies by state (Horgan, Larson, & Simon, 1994), and insurers are cutting the length of stay in intensive treatment. Wickizer and his colleagues (1996) found more limitations placed on care for alcohol or drug dependent patients than for patients with mental disorders; for example, compared to patients with mental disorders, alcohol or drug dependent patients were more likely to get approvals for outpatient care when inpatient care was requested. Practitioners are often heard complaining about the time they spend haggling with managed care providers about what treatment will be approved for the client. Even more discouraging is the conclusion of Mechanic and his colleagues (1995) "that the probability of treatment for substance abuse is certainly no higher and may be significantly lower under prepaid care" (pp. 35–36). For example, in studies they reviewed, outpatient care was not substituted for inpatient care for substance abusers in a number of cases, or insurers were covering detoxification services as the only inpatient service even though detoxification alone is generally ineffective in preventing relapses.

Shulman (1994) points to some other problems that are being encountered in this era of managed care, such as insurers requiring that a patient have "failed" in outpatient treatment as a condition of admission to inpatient treatment. Whereas treatment in the least restrictive environment should be a standard, when an individual clearly needs inpatient care, it should not be denied. Shulman (1994) also notes that even if patients do not use the maximum number of inpatient treatment days allotted for a treatment episode, they may not be allowed to use the unused days later. Also, a provider may cover only some of the types of care on the continuum and sometimes these are more rather than less expensive types of care. For example, residential or supported living may not be covered, causing use of hospital care when intensive outpatient treatment with supported living arrangement may be at least as helpful and less costly.

In terms of how managed care is affecting the lives of substance abusers, a McDonnell Douglas study of mental health and substance abuse services found that more HMO enrollees lost their jobs than those in traditional fee-for-service plans (Mechanic et al., 1995). It is also dismaying to hear about managed care organizations that do not explain to providers and patients what their guidelines and conditions of treatment are (Peele, 1996; Garnick, Hendricks, Dulski, Thorpe, & Horgan, 1994), or to wonder whether those who determine the treatment to which the insured is entitled have the proper credentials in the area of substance abuse and dependence.

In many ways, the United States is less progressive than other countries like the United Kingdom and Australia in its response to drug use and dependence. For example, chemical dependency professionals in this country have been reluctant to consider treatment such as moderate drinking programs, and federal and state governments have been reluctant to provide readily accessible needle exchange programs for IV-drug users to prevent the spread of HIV and to provide access to health and social services. Drug users are also denied the benefits and protections of important government policies that people with other disabilities may claim. For example, drug use by residents in public housing can result in eviction, and many employment protections in the Americans with Disabilities Act of 1990 are denied to drug users.

Relatively little federal money (less than 1%) is directed to drug treatment programs for women (Gustavsson, 1991). Child welfare agencies have had to respond to this gap in services because of the large numbers of children entering care resulting from parental substance abuse issues (Azzi-Lessing & Olsen, 1996). Their response has been to develop collaborative arrangements with drug treatment agencies to serve these vulnerable families.

Although many family practitioners support a biopsychosocial model of chemical dependency, much of the public views the problem in more moralistic terms. There is much that family practitioners can do to educate families about alcohol and drug problems and to promote improved treatment policies to assist the many families affected by alcohol and other drug problems. What is less clear is whether family practitioners agree on the "demand" and "supply" side issues posed by the "war on drugs" (e.g., legalization) to a degree that will allow them to present a united front to policymakers.

Intervention in Violence

Living in an environment characterized by violence is a reality for too many families. More than 25% of the murders committed in the United States occur when one family member kills another, and spouses are the primary perpetrators and victims of such violence (Shamsie, 1985; Craven, 1996). The home and neighborhood are the primary location for crimes of violence such as rape, assault, and robbery. In 1992, more than half the victims of intimate violence were attacked by a boyfriend or girlfriend, 34% were attacked by a spouse, and 15% were attacked by ex-spouses (Bureau of Justice Statistics, 1994b). Each year, women experience more than one million violent victimizations committed by an intimate compared to about 143,000 for men (Craven, 1996). Homicide is the second leading cause of death for 15- to 24-year-olds, and for African-American youth, it is the primary cause of death (Committee on Ways and Means, 1991). Suicide, another manifestation of violence, is the third leading cause of death among the 15- to 24-year-old population.

The United States leads the world in rates of incarceration. In 1989, the number of women in prison reached a record high of 40,556, and 41% were in prison for violent offenses (U.S. Department of Justice, 1991a). Between 1995 and 1996, the number of incarcerated women increased another 6.4% (compared to 5.6% for men)—from 69,161 to 73,607 (Bureau of Justice Statistics, 1997). According to a study published in 1991, three-fourths of the female inmate population were mothers (U.S. Department of Justice, 1991a). A third of the women convicted of a violent crime victimized a relative or intimate, and 25% were convicted of homicide of a relative or intimate. Incarcerated women are likely to have been victims of violence, and courts are beginning to accept the "battered women's syndrome" as a defense in some of these cases. Forty-one percent of incarcerated women reported that they had previously been sexually or physically abused (U.S. Department of Justice, 1991a). These figures attest to the fact that many women feel helpless in trying to escape violence before irreparable harm is done.

Estimates are that as many as 10 million children are at risk of witnessing abuse of women each year, and half of these children have also experienced abusive treatment (Schecter, 1995). For some children, depression, conduct disorders, developmental delays, and low self-esteem accompany their observing parental violence (Silvern & Kaersvang, 1989). There is some evidence to suggest the intergenerational transmission of violence. Children who observe parental violence often have feelings of anxiety and helplessness. Identification with the violent parent helps the child to cope with these intense feelings (Green, 1984). Violence may become a typical method of conflict resolution and a family norm.

Violence is also a characteristic of some communities. Too many young children become familiar with violence at school. Violent and criminal behavior, especially in urban schools, has become common (National Institute of Justice, 1986) and shows no signs of abating. Metal detectors and armed guards are standard security measures at some schools. One survey reported that 40% of a group of 500 grade school children had seen a shooting and 34% had observed a stabbing (Children's Defense Fund, 1990). In other areas, as many as 25% of teenagers had witnessed a murder and 75% knew someone who had been shot (Zinsmeister, 1990). The ready availability of firearms adds to the risk.

The fastest growing arrest category for adolescents in New York City is gun possession (Pooley, 1991). Quick and easy access to firearms is an invitation to violence. Attempts to enact even minor restrictions on access to handguns have been met with fierce opposition by organizations such as the National Rifle Association, but states such as New Jersey have taken the lead in trying to reduce the supply of automatic weapons. Ronald Reagan's former press secretary, James Brady, was seriously wounded during an assassination attempt on the president. The efforts of Brady and his wife finally resulted in the "Brady Bill," which provides a modest federal effort at gun control, but efforts to overturn it continue.

There is a lack of consensus on how to respond to violence, especially to violence in the home and neighborhood. President Carter established an office of Domestic Violence within the Department of Health and Human Services, but it was abolished in 1981 and its duties were assigned to the National Center on Child Abuse and Neglect. Shelters for victims of domestic violence and prosecution of their attackers has been the primary response to family violence. Because domestic violence is not a federal crime and there is no comprehensive federal policy that addresses prevention of family violence, the effectiveness of responses varies by locality. Some communities have taken the initiative and developed high profile programs. Minneapolis, for example, was among the first to institute mandatory arrests of batterers. This law has removed the choice of whether to arrest the perpetrator from both the victim and the police officer. Some states have enacted mandatory arrest laws. By 1992, 14 states and the District of Columbia had such laws and almost half of local law enforcement agencies had units to deal with domestic violence (Bureau of Justice Statistics, 1994b). The 1994 Violence Against Women Act shows Congress's increased concern by providing funding for judicial and social services to help prevent domestic violence, to enforce the laws and punish perpetrators, and to offer more help to women who have been victimized.

Concern about violence on television and in the movies has also prompted congressional hearings. On average, young people will see on television more than 180,000 murders, rapes, armed robberies, and assaults (Comstock & Strasburger, 1990). Some studies suggest that viewing violence can encourage the expression of aggression (Comstock & Strasburger, 1990; Singer & Singer, 1981). There is some debate about the relationship between viewing violence and subsequent aggressive behavior, but there is substantial support for the notion that exposing children to multiple acts of violence is not in their best interest. Concerned citizens and child welfare professionals have lobbied Congress for years to enact legislation to address TV violence. The television industry is well organized and has presented attempts at regulation as censorship. Perhaps in anticipation of federal regulation, the industry has promoted voluntary compliance. In 1993, it began to issue advisories about violent content during prime time hours.

Violence is a learned behavior and thus amenable to prevention and change. Individual communities are experimenting with strategies such as teaching conflict resolution in the schools and organizing public education campaigns to alert citizens to the dangers of and solutions for violence. Viewing violence as a public health issue provides guidance for policy development.

Child Abuse and Neglect Policy

When the caretaking abilities or actions of parents fail to meet community expectations, the state can forcibly intervene through the public child welfare system. This challenge to the integrity of the family and the authority of the parents occurs with increasing frequency, especially for poor families. However, what constitutes maltreatment is subject to debate. Particularly troublesome to define is child neglect. Each state establishes its own definition of maltreatment. Intentional injury, failure to provide for a child's basic needs, and sexual contact between the caretaker and child are included in most definitions of abuse. The parent who is homeless or does not obtain the services of a physician when the child is ill is defined in many states as neglectful. The fact that the parent is poor, unemployed, and without medical insurance or access to social services may not alter the assignment of blame.

The number of reports of child maltreatment has stabilized in the last few years, but prior to this time there were substantial increases. Greater awareness of child abuse probably accounted for much of the increases, but there may also be a real increase in child maltreatment. A few organizations, such as the American Humane Association (AHA) and the National Center on Child Abuse and Neglect (NCCAN), collect statistics on maltreatment. In 1980, NCCAN tallied 652,000 reported incidents of maltreatment; six years later the number had increased to over one million (NCCAN, 1988). When a more encompassing definition of maltreatment was used, the number of cases increased to 1.7 million. In 1992, child protective service agencies in the United States received 2,920,000 reports of suspected abuse or neglect (about 45 per 1,000 children), an increase of 50% since 1985 (National Committee for the Prevention of Child Abuse, 1993). In 1993 and 1994, there were about 2,940,000 reports each year (National Center on Child Abuse and Neglect, 1996). Of reports investigated in 1994, 33% were substantiated, 8% were indicated (there was reason to suspect, but insufficient evidence to confirm, maltreatment), 54% were unsubstantiated, and the disposition of the remainder was either unknown or handled in another way (National Center on Child Abuse and Neglect, 1996). Since 1990, data show that about 48% of cases are classified as neglect. About 21% are physical abuse, 13% are sexual abuse, 5% are emotional abuse, and the remainder are medical neglect, another type of abuse, or the type is unknown (NCCAN, 1996).

These figures demonstrate that many children are living with caretakers who have seriously deficient parenting skills and are dangerous to their children. The state has two basic strategies for such families. One is to remove the children and place them in substitute care. The other is to help families remain together by offering services.

The types of services that the federal government funds determine the types of services that states offer, and federal funds for foster (substitute) care are substantially greater than for services to keep families together. From 1986 to 1989, the foster care population increased 29%—from 280,000 to 360,000 (Committee on Ways and Means, 1991). In 1992, about 429,000 children were in foster care, an increase of 50% since 1986 (Ingram, 1996). The national placement rate is approximately 4.8 children per 1,000, but rates vary considerably by state. New York and California account for one-third of the nation's foster care population, yet less than 20% of the nation's children live in these two states. The reasons for this disparity are not known. There may be a unique constellation of variables that serves to subject some families to an elevated level of scrutiny such as a more ethnically and racially diverse population combined with a large child welfare industry.

Poor and minority children are at an elevated risk of placement. Minority children make up 46% of the foster care population (Committee on Ways and Means, 1991). A survey by the National Black Child Development Institute (NBCDI) of more than 1,000 children in care in five cities in 1986 reported that 65% of the children came from families supported by AFDC and the leading reason for placement was neglect. The caretakers of the children faced multiple problems. Drug use was reported in 36% of the population, 30% had inadequate housing, 8% were homeless, and 41% suffered from mental illness (NBCDI, 1986).

Children pay a high price when their family is disrupted. Removal from the home can mean multiple changes and losses for the child. Contact with extended family, siblings, friends, teachers, and neighbors may be diminished or lost. Foster children are at an elevated risk of academic problems. Less than 30% of adolescents in placement graduate from high school, and 30% of foster children are at grade level by the 12th grade compared to 70% of children living at home (Cook & Ansell, 1986).

Foster care can be a lengthy experience, and it is fraught with insecurity. National data for 1985 indicated that 27% of the children had been in care more than two years, 15% had been in care more than five years, half of the children experienced at least two placements, and about 35% of the children who were in care at the end of 1987 had been in placement more than two years (U.S. General Accounting Office, 1990). About 27% of foster children who were in care in 1987 had experienced three or more placements (Committee on Ways and Means, 1991).

The federal government enacted the Adoption Assistance and Child Welfare Act of 1980 to improve the child welfare system. The principle of permanency planning was a cornerstone of this legislation. The act requires states to make reasonable efforts (reasonable is not defined) to keep families together, place children near their parents, and have a permanent plan for the child after 18 months in care. The permanent plan consists of one of four options: reunification with the parents, adoption, guardianship, or long-term foster care placement. Another attempt at improving child welfare policy is the Family Preservation and Support Services Program enacted in 1993, which provided $930 million over five years for child welfare services. Each state receives an allocation based on the number of its children receiving food stamps, and 90% of funds must go to services. The act is largely aimed at offering more services to keep families together. However, permanency as a social policy has not been achieved for many children. Of the children reunited with their families in 1986, 27% reentered care (U.S. General Accounting Office, 1990). Adoption is a more stable permanent plan with a reported disruption rate of about 11% (Barth & Berry, 1990). In 1990, long-term foster care was the "permanent" plan for 12% of the youngsters in care (Committee on Ways and Means, 1996, p. 750), but it is the least stable arrangement, with reported disruption rates in excess of 50% (Stone & Stone, 1983).

Separating children from their families is an expensive policy and one that creates new problems. One such problem involves reconstituting the family. The process of successfully reintegrating the child into the family is poorly understood. Once the child is returned to the family, services are frequently terminated because funding for aftercare is scarce. This lack may help to explain the high recidivism rate among parents involved with child protective services. Preventing the removal of the child would seem to be less costly on multiple levels, especially when most children are removed because of neglect, not abuse.

States have few incentives to work with families to preserve the family unit, but exemplary programs in various parts of the country are providing intensive services to vulnerable families. These programs are referred to as home-based service models or intensive family preservation programs. In these programs, services are offered quickly for a short period of time. The goals include protecting the children, stabilizing the crisis, preventing placement of the children, increasing the family's skills, strengthening the bonds within the family, and helping the family to use both formal and informal resources (Trace, Haapala, Kinney, & Pecora, 1991). There are two main types of family preservation programs. The family systems model is based on the structural family therapy ideas of Minuchin (1974) and focuses on such issues as enmeshment, coalitions, isomorphic sequences, and hierarchy. In contrast, the Homebuilders model (described in Chapter 8) is ecological and based on cognitive-behavioral ideas. It is more eclectic, requiring considerable flexibility on the part of the therapist. Most current-day models that have evolved use a mix of systems and cognitive-behavioral approaches. (See Chapter 8 for a discussion of the family preservation model.)

Evaluations of family service programs using multiple measures of success indicate that with these programs, family relationships, the emotional climate in the home, and children's school performance all improve (National Resource Center on Family Based Services, 1988). Child placement rates can be reduced substantially. In a study using matched groups, families in the intensive group had a placement rate of 44% compared with an 85% rate for families receiving traditional services (Pecora, Fraser, & Haapala, 1990). However, there are questions about the durability of the gains, as placement rates apparently increase with time (Matthews & McKee, 1993). Not all children's advocates embrace family preservation. For example, a spokesperson for a Texas organization called Justice for Children stated that "CPS [Child Protective Services] has adopted the unproven social theory that it is more important to 'save the home for the child' than to 'save the child from the home'" and that "CPS is making unreasonable efforts to keep unhealthy families together, causing further risk to the child and jeopardizing the criminal case against the abuser" (Burton, 1991, p. 10). Permanency planning has also been criticized for creating impermanence for some children (Bryant, 1993). Professional judgments generally weigh heavily in the decisions that agencies and courts make about family preservation and child placements. CPS workers often find themselves criticized by parents who believe their child has been unjustly removed. At other times, they are criticized by community members for failure to intervene. Balancing the rights of parents and the rights and needs of children makes work in this field difficult.

When home-based services work, they are relatively economical. The Home-builders model has an average cost of $2,600 for handling one family case. Rates vary by state, but foster care providers generally receive a few hundred dollars a month per child. At an average of $300 per month, taxpayers spend $3,600 per year for a child just in the direct costs of care (*Keeping families together*, 1985). The indirect costs (those associated with child welfare agencies, courts, law enforcement, health and social services) add significantly to this amount.

The federal government provides funding for foster care (Title IV-E) and more modest funding for family preservation programs (Title IV-B). These two titles were not substantially altered by the federal welfare reform legislation of 1996. Family preservation programs remain underfunded at the state level whereas foster care expenditures have increased.

State legislatures have been encouraged to adopt family preservation programs as a method of reducing placement costs. However, the ever-increasing number of families referred for services as well as the intractable problems facing families (such as poverty and homelessness) suggest that cost savings may be temporary. From a social work perspective, immediate cost savings should not be the primary motivation for keeping families together. Although the emotional and social costs of disrupting families are difficult to calculate, they provide additional justification for both preventive services and aftercare. Family treatment is critical in assisting children who have experienced child abuse or neglect and in improving the functioning of their families.

Another provision of the Adoption Assistance and Child Welfare Act of 1980 requires all states to offer financial support to adults willing to adopt special needs children. This group includes older children, sibling groups, children of particular ethnic backgrounds, and children with physical, emotional, and mental problems. The 18-month dispositional hearing that is supposed to be afforded to all children in the system requires courts to impose a permanent plan, and adoption is the second plan to be considered after reunification with the child's biological parent(s). The law alters the relationship between child protection agencies and adoption agencies by encouraging more coordination and cooperation among them. Adoption agencies had been struggling because of a reduced supply of healthy white babies at the same time the demand for these children was increasing. The federal law gave new life to some adoption agencies, but it also required the agencies to change their definition of the adoptable child. In addition, agencies are now allowing adults to adopt who previously did not meet agency standards, such as single adults or adults with restricted financial resources. In some states, lesbians and gay men are seen as viable adoptive parents. All these changes have contributed to the evolving definition of family.

This discussion illustrates some of the dilemmas in trying to develop a rational policy to ensure the protection of children. In fact, there are questions about the extent to which children are entitled to protection. In 1989, the U.S. Supreme

Court ruled 6 to 3 that public employees could not be held liable for failure to protect citizens from harm by other private citizens. The case in question was that of Joshua DeShaney who suffered severe and permanent brain damage as a result of abuse by his father after the Winnebago County, Wisconsin, department of social services failed to remove the child from the home. Protective service workers carry a grave responsibility even though state personnel policies may allow people with little relevant education to be hired as child protective service workers. Among the concerns of professional groups such as the National Association of Social Workers are that states adopt policies requiring qualified personnel be hired for these positions, yet it is very difficult to find qualified individuals who are interested in these jobs in many areas of the country. Family practitioners might focus attention on policies and other avenues that would make work in this field more attractive to qualified individuals.

Family Planning and Reproductive Rights

Assistance with family planning is available from a number of sources such as the family doctor. Local health departments and organizations such as Planned Parenthood also offer services, especially to low-income individuals. A variety of family planning methods are available, although some countries make more birth control options available than the United States does. The recent arrival in the United States from France of an oral medication, RU486, commonly referred to as the "abortion pill," may make surgical abortion less frequent. Although "pro-life" groups opposed making this pill available, the Food and Drug Administration approved the drug. Some private clinics include RU486 in their repertoire of pregnancy termination techniques.

Concern over sexually transmitted diseases and births to unwed parents have caused some individuals to demand the distribution of free condoms, especially to young people, but others argue that the focus should be on abstinence for young people and monogamy for adults. Many people with the best intentions for families disagree over what public policy should be in this regard, or whether such matters are better left to private, family decisions about the type and extent of education on sexual matters. This point is well illustrated by the work of the National Commission on Children (1991). Nine of the 32 commissioners disagreed with key recommendations contained in the chapter on health care of the commission's final report. As a way of recognizing these differences, a "minority" chapter on health care was included in the report. Among the recommendations of the minority was "increased support for abstinence education . . . as a means of reducing the spread of sexually transmitted diseases (STDs) and AIDS, as well as the rate of unwed teenage pregnancies" (National Commission on Children, 1991, p. xxiv).

No part of the controversy over family planning has gotten more attention than that of abortion. In 1973, in *Roe v. Wade* and *Doe v. Bolton,* the U.S. Supreme Court upheld a woman's right to an abortion when it ruled that the Fifth and Fourteenth Amendments to the Constitution, which guarantee all persons "life, liberty, and property," did not include the life of the unborn fetus. The First and Fourteenth Amendments guaranteeing personal liberties were also said to extend to child-bearing decisions. The states can, however, prohibit third trimester abortions except to save the mother's life.

Divisiveness over abortion has affected the use of public funds for this purpose. Federal Medicaid funds can be used only to provide abortions for poor women in a few circumstances, such as when the mother's life is in danger. States can use their own funds to help low-income women obtain abortions, and several do. Among the many ironies of public policy is that caps are being placed on the payments made to TANF recipients at the same time that public funds are often unavailable for abortion, even if the mother wishes to have an abortion.

Abortion rights top the list of the country's most contentious issues. Whether based on biological, religious, or moral and ethical grounds, some people believe that abortion should never be allowed, even in cases of rape or incest. Many of these individuals believe that life begins at conception and that abortion is murder. They believe that allowing abortion shows the most base disregard for human life and underlies much of the violence that is found in society. Others believe just as strongly that the government should stay out of this very personal decision: It should be a woman's right to choose.

Challenges to *Roe v. Wade* and *Doe v. Bolton* have survived the U.S. Supreme Court, but with changes on the bench, there has been some erosion of abortion rights in recent years. In 1986, the Court upheld state laws that require notification of one or both parents of minors as long as these laws have a judicial bypass provision that allows minors to ask the courts for permission to obtain an abortion. In 1989, the Court upheld a Missouri law that prohibits the involvement of public hospitals and public employees in performing abortions and in counseling a woman to obtain an abortion unless her life is in danger; requires physicians to determine whether a woman who is at least 20 weeks pregnant is carrying a fetus that is viable (able to survive outside the womb); and declares that life begins at conception. The ruling opened the door for states to consider more restrictive provisions. Several other states also passed or attempted to pass stricter abortion laws.

By 1992, the battles that ensued over these laws led the Supreme Court again to hear an abortion case, this time Pennsylvania's new abortion law. The justices in a 5 to 4 decision protected the right to an abortion, but in a 7 to 2 decision upheld Pennsylvania's parental consent provision for women under age 18, 24-hour waiting periods for almost all those requesting an abortion, and requirements that physicians inform women of their options, but it struck down provisions that required notification of husbands.

Given the changing moods of the U.S. Supreme Court, pro-choice advocates believe that the best way to protect abortion rights is for Congress to pass a law providing these protections. The proposed Freedom of Choice Act is intended to do this. The legislation would prevent states from enacting their own restrictions on abortion prior to fetal viability.

Various professional organizations have addressed abortion rights. In *A National Social Agenda for American Families*, the National Association of Social

Workers (1992) asked Congress to "ensure a woman's right to choose to have an abortion or not through passage of legislation codifying *Roe v. Wade*" (p. 3). In March 1992, the board of the American Association of Marriage and Family Therapy (AAMFT) met to consider abortion but did not reach a consensus on the issue. Some AAMFT members have organized groups such as the Texas Feminist/Gender Caucus, which describes itself as "a group of feminists dismayed at the alienation . . . from our national leadership in Washington—AAMFT" (Way, 1992, p. 10). As Way (1992) noted, "The message is that many of us will not rest easy when the national organization to which we have pledged allegiance refuses consistently to take political stands around issues that affect women's lives" (p. 10).

The composition of American families has also been affected by the decisions of many unmarried women to keep their babies. Less than 3% of single mothers surrender their infants for adoption, and for every available infant, there are 40 couples waiting to adopt (Hermann & Kasper, 1992). The number of healthy white babies available for adoption has diminished while infertility rates have increased. Waiting for years for an infant placed through a child welfare agency is common (Silin, 1996).

International adoption is another option. In 1986, there were more than 10,000 foreign adoptions by Americans (Hermann & Kasper, 1992). Romania has become a recent source of children, with more than 2,800 adopted between 1990 and 1993 (Groze & Ileana, 1996). Many children come from Asia, especially South Korea, and increasing numbers are from Central and South America. In some cases, questions about how these children were obtained and whether their parents voluntarily relinquish them for adoption have been raised (Hermann & Kasper, 1992). In all adoptions, there is increased concern about knowing the medical and psychological histories of the children. As open adoption has become more common, and as more adopted children and birth parents seek to reunite, these issues have affected the caseloads of family practitioners.

More than four million couples experience difficulty in conceiving or carrying a baby to term (Hermann & Kasper, 1992). The small number of children available for adoption in the United States and the strong desire of many couples and individuals to bear their own children has led infertility technology to become a booming business. Many of the procedures are expensive, and third-party payment for these services is inconsistent among insurance providers. The technology has raised new challenges to the definitions of parent, sibling, and family. It is now possible for a child to have five parents: one party may provide the egg, another party provides the sperm, a third party rents her body to carry the baby, and another couple pays for these services and rears the child. The ethical and social implications of this technology are now beginning to be realized.

There are many ramifications of family planning policy for family therapists. They may help clients decide whether to pursue an abortion, an adoption, or treatment to increase their likelihood of conceiving a child. In the near future, clients and therapists will likely be faced with more difficult moral and ethical dilemmas. Genetic screening and testing can already reveal the likelihood of passing certain genetic diseases to children (Francoeur, 1993). The rights of all parties—parents, children, and society—must be weighed in determining who should have the option to decide about bearing a child who may have painful, fatal, and expensive medical conditions (see Francoeur, 1993, for a discussion of future issues in contraception and reproduction). Technology is leading the way to other difficult dilemmas such as gender selection at conception or through selective abortion and reproduction outside the womb.

Family Care

With so many households headed by a single parent and with so many households in which both partners work outside the home, the demand for child care and for care of members who are elderly or disabled continues to grow (Fine, 1992; Wisensale, 1992; Zimmerman, 1992). This care is difficult for many to afford, and concerns continue about the quality of care that is provided (Committee on Ways and Means, 1992, p. 935), including ways to monitor the services effectively.

Child care may be needed throughout the work day, after school, and during school vacation periods. This care is offered by various types of providers. Some are for-profit organizations (such as private day care centers) that generally charge parents at the current market rate. Not-for-profit organizations (such as those run by local governments or churches) may charge more modest fees or use a sliding scale fee based on parents' ability to pay. There are also cooperative child care arrangements in which parents may pay for services or share child care responsibilities. Child care is also provided in private homes or in the child's home for a fee, or it may be provided by friends or relatives on a more informal basis. Some parents prefer not to use day care or cannot afford it, and they arrange their schedules so that one parent is always available to care for the children. In other cases, older siblings care for younger siblings. Finally, there is no care at all. "Latchkey" children are left at home with no supervision for periods of time. In 1991, 36% of children under 5 years of age whose mothers worked were cared for in their own home by their father, another relative, or another person; 31% were cared for in the home of another (a relative or other party); 23% were cared for in child care facilities; 9% were cared for by their mother while she worked, and the remainder were cared for in other arrangements such as at school activities (U.S. Bureau of the Census, 1995b, p. 390). A 1987 study found that .3% of children under age 5 were left unsupervised, and of children 5 to 14 years of age, 4.1% were unsupervised while their parent or parents worked (Committee on Ways and Means, 1992, p. 939).

Burud, Aschbacher, and McCroskey (1984) discuss four ways that employers assist with child care: personnel policies, information and education, financial assistance, and direct child care. Personnel policies include flexible working hours that allow parents to schedule their work time to accommodate their child care needs and job sharing that allows two people to split the responsibilities of one full-time position. Maternity and paternity leave also falls under this category. Information and education include services that help parents locate appropriate child care and programs that help parents learn about what constitutes good child care services.

Employers who provide financial assistance reimburse parents for child care expenses and support child care services in the community. Reimbursement may be made directly to parents, who purchase their own child care, or to the child care providers. Employers who provide financial assistance may allow parents full discretion in selecting child care or they may restrict the centers or types of individuals they will reimburse. Some companies prefer to use community child care programs they designate. Depending on the level of support provided by the company, employees may obtain free or reduced-cost child care or simply a slot for their child in the center.

Employers may provide child care directly. Some operate their own centers; others contract for these services. Depending on arrangements, the financial contributions of employees and employers vary. Company-operated child care centers may be located at the work site or off site. Some of these centers are organized as not-for-profit corporations with employees and company officials serving as board members. They may serve other community members in addition to employees. Some parents like the on-site centers because they can see their child during breaks and lunch or dinner hours. Another direct service option is family day care homes subsidized by the employer; this option allows homes within employees' neighborhoods to be used for child care.

Employees may also need help with care when children are ill and when other needs arise, such as employee travel. Few employers offer much help in these cases, but Burud and her colleagues (1984) remind us that working parents need care that is "dependable, affordable, congruent with their work schedules, conveniently located, suitable to their children's ages, and compatible with their child-rearing philosophy" (p. 40). According to the Texas Child Care Resource (n.d.) of firms that provide child care and other dependent care, 95% report that benefits outweigh costs, 90% report better employee morale, 85% report improved employee recruitment and retention, and 53% report less absenteeism. Employers also benefit from the tax breaks they receive and savings in all these areas can be used to offset the costs of child care (Burud et al., 1984). Obviously, employees who are not constantly worried about the safety of their children or distracted by phone calls to check on their children can be more productive, and all children deserve the protection offered by adequate child care. In 1987, only 11% of public and private employers with 10 or more employees operated their own day care centers, assisted with day care expenses, or provided information and referral services, counseling, or other child-care benefits (Committee on Ways and Means, 1992, p. 947).

Given that many parents do not have private means of meeting child care and child development needs, governments have chosen to intervene. The federally supported Head Start program prepares children to enter school, provides an array of social services, and encourages parental participation in child development activities (Golonka & Ooms, 1991). In 1993, about 714,000 children were enrolled in Head Start (Committee on Ways and Means, 1994, p. 835). At least 90% of the children served must be from low-income families and 10% of the slots must be available for children with disabilities. Research indicates that as they grow older, children who participate in the program are more likely to complete high school and to become employed and less likely to be delinquent and to receive welfare (*Newsweek*, 1980). There have been many calls to expand Head Start so that all eligible children can participate. Since the 1960s, the federal government, by subsidizing the cost of child care, has also made efforts to encourage parents receiving public assistance payments to work. However, the supply of adequate and affordable child care has been insufficient to meet demands.

Some responses to the need for increased child care were included in the federal Economic Recovery Tax Act of 1981 and the Tax Reform Act of 1986. Employers may receive tax deductions for dependent care services they provide; child care costs up to certain limits paid by a company are not treated as income to the employee; there are tax benefits associated with depreciating the costs of establishing new child care facilities, and up to 10% of a business's taxable income can be deducted from taxes if the center is a local one serving all community children; IRS codes allow employers to create flexible child care options for their employees; and salary diverted to employee reimbursement accounts for child care is tax exempt from Social Security, unemployment, and federal income taxes (Texas Child Care Resource, no date).

In 1990, Congress passed several pieces of legislation that further increase the federal government's participation in child care. Among them were two block grants aimed at providing more child care and increased expenditures for the Head Start program. Begun in 1991, the Child Care and Development Block Grant (CCDBG) was designed to increase the ability of low-income families to obtain child care on a sliding fee basis, improve the quality of child care, and give families more choice in selecting child care providers, including relatives who may be paid for their services (see Vinet, 1995). Vinet's (1995) analysis is that CCDBG improved the quality and availability of child care, but that overall public expenditures for child care only scratch the surface of need. The second block grant was an expansion of child care services provided by the JOBS program under Title IV-A of the Social Security Act; the purpose was to help families obtain child care so that they can maintain employment rather than run the risk of joining the public assistance rolls. As part of the major federal welfare reform legislation of 1996, Title IV-A child care funds and the CCDBG were consolidated. The bulk of funds will again go to welfare recipients, to encourage them to work and to reduce their dependence on public assistance, and to those at risk of receiving public assistance. Nearly $14 billion has been allocated for fiscal years 1997 to 2002 (see American Public Welfare Association, 1996).

In addition to helping families consider child care needs and options, family practitioners may also become involved in decisions about care of other family members. Community day centers assist with care of members who are elderly or disabled, and many families purchase some type of home care from their own pockets for expenses not covered by Medicare. For those who cannot afford these services, Medicaid may cover some costs. Cooney (1993) emphasizes the growing need for families to consider all the options, especially as more of the financial burden for care will be transferred from public to private means.

Congress and the Bush administration battled over whether employers must allow workers to take leave when a new baby arrives, a child is sick, or another family member needs care. Congress twice passed a family leave bill that would have required some employers to provide 12 weeks of unpaid leave to family members when a new baby arrived or when a spouse, parent, or child had a serious illness. The same benefits would have been extended to employees with an illness. Despite strong public support, Bush vetoed both bills, saying that although he favored family leave, the bills were too restrictive on business because of the need to hire replacements and that implementation of the bills might result in a net job loss. On taking office, President Clinton signed the Family and Medical Leave Act. However, businesses with fewer than 50 workers (thereby including only 50% of workers and 5% of businesses) are exempt, and covered businesses are not required to provide leave to upper-echelon employees. Evidence indicates that employers in states with such laws have had little difficulty in complying and that the costs of compliance amount to just over $7.00 per year per employee ("Family leave bill deserves," 1991). Many other industrialized countries have government policies that provide for substantial periods of paid family leave. For example, Finland allows 35 weeks of fully paid employment leave, and Japan allows 12 weeks at 60% of pay (Cooper & Dewar, 1993).

Case Example

The McClintock household consists of Angela, age 36, and her three children, fraternal twins Ryan and Amber, 16, and Roy, 10. Mrs. McClintock contacted the Mesa Family Resource Center saying she was frustrated and exhausted. She appeared wan with a depressed affect. She had been a single parent for the last nine years and had received sporadic and inadequate child support payments. The payments stopped completely about seven months ago when her ex-husband moved to Australia. The children have had infrequent contact with their father since the divorce. Mrs. McClinock generally worked outside the home. She used AFDC to support the family when she was between jobs. Three months ago, Mrs. McClintock lost her job in the clerical section of a freight company. She was hired as a temporary employee, had not received any benefits, and had been employed less than 26 weeks. The electric company was about to disconnect service for nonpayment, and the landlord had served notice of eviction.

Although Mrs. McClintock was not pleased with her living arrangements, she could not afford to move. The plumbing was often inoperable, the paint was peeling, and the monthly visits from the exterminator were not adequate. Most of her neighbors did not speak English, and her church had closed a year before. As an English-speaking Anglo, Mrs. McClintock felt isolated in her neighborhood.

When asked about her children, Mrs. McClintock stated that the high school wanted Ryan removed. He had not been attending classes and was in trouble for fighting other students. Ryan was active in Queer Nation, a gay and lesbian political group. He wore shirts to school that read, "I'm here. I'm queer. Get used to it." Ryan had come out to his family two years earlier. Roy was also having trouble and seemed unable to pay attention in class. He was diagnosed six months before with a heart condition that requires expensive medication. Amber was doing well in school and hoped to attend college. She was viewed as quiet, shy, and well behaved; however, Angela commented that Amber had seemed "moody" lately. Amber had always been reserved and reluctant to engage in conversation with Angela. Angela volunteered that her father abandoned her family when she was six, that she was never close to her mother, and that she rarely had contact with relatives. She had hoped for a closer relationship with her own daughter.

This was the first time Mrs. McClintock had sought the services of a social agency. On the intake form she listed her problems as "lack of money and I am really tired." When asked what she would like to get from her contact with the agency, Mrs. McClintock replied that she wanted money for her bills.

Discussion

This case illustrates some of the dilemmas faced by family practitioners. Contemporary families face multiple stressors and often function in inhospitable environments. Depending on the school of family therapy, the practitioner might ask when Mrs. McClintock did not feel tired, examine the permeability of the boundaries among family members, or explore the strength of the executive system. These explorations might prove to be informative but they would do little to address the serious systems problems facing this family. Mrs. McClintock identified at least 10 problem areas. Prioritizing these problems, developing a plan for addressing them, and assessing the effectiveness of interventive efforts all within six sessions requires both commitment and skill.

At the intake staffing, the decision was made to intervene in the environment. Mrs. McClintock was eligible for six sessions at the agency. Some staff felt she needed extensive work on her unresolved issues in her family of origin. As she could not afford to pay for additional sessions, environmental work seemed most appropriate. Problems were defined as lack of fit between the needs of the family and the community, with community defined broadly. The family was viewed as having strengths and resources that were being overtaxed. Intervention efforts included encouraging existing systems and organizations to meet the needs of the family and identifying barriers to effective service delivery. The family was to be engaged as partners in the change process. A team approach was selected, and the agency participated in a community-based assessment team. Representatives from the school, medical, and religious community participated in monthly meetings.

Summary

This chapter reflects the diverse elements that make up family policy in the United States. These policies range from governing the conditions under which a woman may terminate a pregnancy, to addressing child care, to providing income to older persons in retirement and relieving the financial burden on younger family members. Each of these policies and programs addresses stressors that families may face at some stage of the life cycle. Even so, increased demands on family therapists and other family practitioners indicate clearly that (1) the conglomeration of policies that do exist are inadequate to prevent many families from experiencing the problems that lead them to need family treatment; (2) many gaps in policies and programs remain, and political issues and lack of resources prevent the development of an integrated framework for addressing family stressors; (3) family practitioners must integrate the provision of therapeutic services with knowledge of policies and programs in order to help families achieve the most optimal functioning; and (4) the active involvement of family practitioners and family scientists in all stages of the policy process is important.

There is ample evidence that a more comprehensive, universal, and integrated system of policies has been successful in reducing poverty and achieving a higher quality of life for older Americans (also see National Commission on Children, 1991, p. 80). These accomplishments are reflected in reduced poverty rates and greater access to health care for older Americans, changes that have come about largely through the country's social insurance system. For example, the Social Security retirement program has done more to reduce poverty than any other social welfare program, and virtually all those 65 years of age and older in the United States know they can count on Medicare to meet many of their health care needs. These programs are not perfect, but they represent the country's most successful response to social welfare needs.

The goals achieved for older Americans can also be achieved for younger families. In addition to their face-to-face work with families, more family practitioners are becoming involved in the development of policies and programs that shape the environment in which families function. This increased political activity has resulted from alarm about the conditions that families face. Family practitioners are in an excellent position to help policymakers understand the human costs of failing to support families. The constant taxing of the family's ability to manage life tasks places vulnerable members at increased risk of negative outcomes. These negative outcomes frequently require expensive remedial services. It would be less costly, financially and emotionally, to support families, but family practitioners often have difficulty finding the time to be politically active. Large caseloads and long working hours can leave little time to become involved in the political arena, yet family practitioners often make the effort for several reasons. First, they want to see that families, including their own, are afforded the kinds of environments that help them to thrive. Second, they want to ensure that the families on their caseloads have access to the kinds of resources that will help them solve the problems they face. Third, it is much more satisfying to practice in an environment in which professionals have the tools, including policies, that can be tapped to help families. Fourth, family practitioners often see their work threatened by policies that undermine their professional practices, including their livelihood.

Even busy family practitioners with little time to carve out of the day can become competent policy practitioners by setting aside a little time to do some of the following:

1. Become knowledgeable about the many facets of family policy, especially those that have the greatest impact on the clients they serve
2. Become active in national, state, or local coalitions that address policy issues of particular interest
3. Participate in and organize policy forums at local and regional levels to discuss family policy issues and to set directions for political action

4. Support the efforts of professional groups to which they belong as these groups work to improve policies that help families
5. Communicate regularly with elected officials to inform them of the therapist's positions on policy issues
6. Provide data and case examples from their practices about the ways in which policies positively or negatively affect the clients they serve
7. Be available to educate concerned individuals and groups about policy issues with which they are especially knowledgeable
8. Support candidates whose views support strengthening families

Perhaps most important in this era of contention over family values and family policy is that family practitioners with different points of view come together to work toward mutually agreeable policy alternatives that will promote the kinds of healthy, happy families that all envision as part of the American dream.

Process Questions

1. Identify four systems that are negatively impacting the family in the case example. Explain how these systems are failing to meet the needs of this family. What systems are meeting the needs of this family?

2. Explain how you would address these oppressive systems from your position as a practitioner in the family service agency. Identify two strategies you could use to alter these systems. If you select a case advocacy approach, explain how that will help the next family facing similar problems. If you select a class advocacy approach, explain how that will help the McClintock family.

3. How would you assess the effectiveness of your system interventions? How would you collect data and from where? What variables would you isolate and measure?

4. How do your interventions support the status quo? What could you do to challenge the status quo? What is the goodness of fit between your actions on behalf of this family and your personal political and social opinions? How do you deal with the variability (if any)?

References

ABRAMOVITZ, M., & BARDILL, D. R. (1993). Point/counterpoint: Should all social work students be educated for social change? *Journal of Social Work Education,* 29(1), 6–18.

American Psychiatric Association. (1952, 1968, 1980, 1987, 1994). *Diagnostic and statistical manual of mental disorders (DSM)* (1st ed., 2nd ed., 3rd ed., 3rd ed. rev., 4th ed.). Washington, DC: Author.

American Public Welfare Association, National Governor's Association, and National Conference of State Legislatures. (1996, August 22). *The Personal Responsibility and Work Opportunity Reconciliation Act of 1996, Analysis* [On-line]. Available: http://www.apwa.org/reform/analysis.htm

AZZI-LESSING, L., & OLSEN, L. J. (1996). Substance abuse-affected families in the child welfare system: New challenges, new alliances. *Social Work,* 41(1), 15–23.

BARTH, R. P., & BERRY, M. (1990). Preventing adoption disruption. *Prevention in Human Services,* 9(1), 205–222.

BASSUK, E. L., RUBIN, L., & LAURIAT, A. (1986). Characteristics of sheltered homeless families. *American Journal of Public Health,* 76(9), 1097–1101.

BATESON, G. (1972). *Steps to an ecology of mind.* New York: Ballantine.

BAUGHER, E., & LAMISON-WHITE, L. (1996). *Poverty in the United States: 1995.* Bureau of the Census, Current Population Reports, Series P-60-194. Washington, DC: U.S. Government Printing Office.

BAUM, A. S., & BURNES, D. W. (1993). *A nation in denial: The truth about homelessness.* Boulder: Westview Press.

BERG, I. K. (1994). *Family-based services: A solution-focused approach.* New York: Norton.

BERKOWITZ, E. D. (1987). *Disabled policy: America's programs for the handicapped.* Cambridge, England: Cambridge University Press.

BERLIN, G., & MCALLISTER, W. (1992). Homelessness. In H. J. Aaron & C. L. Schultze (Eds.), *Setting domestic priorities: What can government do?* (pp. 63–99). Washington, DC: Brookings Institution.

BLANK, R. H. (1993). Maternal-fetal relationship: The courts and social policy. *The Journal of Legal Medicine, 14*(1), 73–92.

BLAU, J. (1992). *The visible poor: Homelessness in the United States.* New York: Oxford University Press.

BODE, B., GERSHOFF, S., & LATHAM, S. (1975). Defining hunger among the poor. In C. Lerza & M. Jacobson (Eds.), *Food for people, not for profit* (pp. 299–304). New York: Ballantine.

BOGENSCHNEIDER, K. (1995). Roles for professionals in building family policy: A case of state family impact seminars. *Family Relations, 44,* 5–12.

BOWEN, M. (1978). *Family therapy in clinical practice.* New York: Aronson.

BOXILL, N., & BEATTY, A. (1990). Mother/child interaction among homeless women and their children in a public night shelter in Atlanta, Georgia. *Child and Youth Services, 14*(1), 49–64.

BRYANT, B. (1993, Summer). Panacea watch: Permanency planning. *Focus* (Foster Family-based Treatment Association Newsletter), p. 11.

Bureau of Justice Statistics. (1994a). *Sourcebook of criminal justice statistics.* Washington, DC: U.S. Department of Justice.

Bureau of Justice Statistics. (1994b). *Violence between intimates.* Washington, DC: U.S. Department of Justice.

Bureau of Justice Statistics. (1997). *Prison and jail inmates at midyear 1996.* Washington, DC: U.S. Department of Justice.

BURT, M. R. (1992). *Over the edge: The growth of homelessness in the 1980s.* New York: Russell Sage.

BURTON, R. (1991, March). Testimony cited in *Justice for Children Newsletter,* p. 10.

BURUD, S. L., ASCHBACHER, P. R., & MCCROSKEY, J. (1984). *Employer-supported child care: Investing in human resources.* Dover, MA: Auburn House.

CARLSON, G., & CANTWELL, D. (1980). Diagnosis of childhood depression: A comparison of Weinberg and *DSM-III* criteria. *Journal of the American Academy of Child Psychiatry, 21,* 247–250.

Children's Defense Fund. (1990). *S.O.S. America: A children's defense budget.* Washington, DC: Author.

CLARKSON, K. W. (1975). *Food stamps and nutrition.* Washington, DC: American Enterprise Institute for Public Policy Research.

CLONINGER, C. R. (1983). Genetic and environmental factors in the development of alcoholism. *Journal of Psychiatric Treatment and Evaluation, 5,* 487–496.

CLONINGER, C. R., BOHMAN, M., & SIGVARDSSON, S. (1981). Inheritance of alcohol abuse. *Archives of General Psychiatry, 38,* 861–868.

Committee on Ways and Means, U.S. House of Representatives. (1991). *1991 green book: Background material and data on programs within the jurisdiction of the Committee on Ways and Means* (Committee Print 102–109). Washington, DC: U.S. Government Printing Office.

Committee on Ways and Means, U.S. House of Representatives. (1992, 1993, 1994, 1996). *Overview of entitlement programs: 1992 green book, 1993 green book, 1994 green book, 1996 green book.* Washington, DC: U.S. Government Printing Office.

COMSTOCK, G., & STRASBURGER, V. (1990). Deceptive appearances: Television violence and aggressive behavior. *Journal of Adolescent Health Care, 11*(1), 31–44.

COOK, R., & ANSELL, D. (1986). *Study of independent living services for youth in substitute care.* Rockville, MD: Westat.

COONEY, T. M. (1993). Recent demographic change: Implications for families planning for the future. *Marriage & Family Review, 18*(3/4), 37–55.

COOPER, K. J., & DEWAR, H. (1993, February 4). House OKs bill pledging 12 weeks of family leave. *Austin American-Statesman,* pp. A1 & 8.

COSTELLO, A., EDELBROCK, C., DULCAN, M., KALAS, R., & KLORIC, S. (1984). *Report on the diagnostic interview for children.* Pittsburgh, PA: University of Pittsburgh.

CRAVEN, D. (1996). *Female victims of violent crime.* U.S. Department of Justice, Bureau of Justice Statistics, Washington, DC.

DAVIS, D. R., & DINITTO, D. M. (1998). Gender and drugs: Fact, fiction, and unanswered questions. In C. A. McNeece & D. M. DiNitto (Eds.), *Chemical dependency: A systems approach* (2nd ed.). Boston: Allyn & Bacon.

DAVIS, K. (1993, October–November). Cited in *Modern Maturity, 36*(5), 10.

DEVANEY, B., BILHEIMER, F. L., & SCHORE, J. (1992). Medicaid costs and birth outcomes: The effects of prenatal WIC participation and the use of prenatal care. *Journal of Policy Analysis and Management, 14*(4), 573–592.

DINITTO, D. M. (1995). *Social welfare: Politics and public policy* (4th ed.). Needham Heights, MA: Allyn & Bacon.

DUNCAN, G. (1992, February). Testimony before the House Select Committee on Children, Youth and Families, based on Greg J. Duncan, Timothy Smeeding, and Willard Rodgers, "W(h)ither the Middle Class: A Dynamic View?" University of Michigan, Survey Research Center, 1991, cited in Committee on Ways and Means, U.S. House of Representatives. (1993). *Overview of entitlement programs: 1993 green book.* Washington, DC: U.S. Government Printing Office.

EHRENREICH, B. (1987). A step back to the workhouse? *Ms., 16*, 40–42.

Family leave bill deserves high level of support. (1991, June 29). *Austin American-Statesman*, p. A22.

FINE, M. A. (1992). Families in the United States: Their current status and future prospects. *Family Relations, 41*, 430–435.

Food and Consumer Service. (1995). *Nutrition program facts.* Alexandria, VA: U.S. Department of Agriculture.

Food security and methods of assessing hunger in the United States. (1989, March 23). *Hearing before the Select Committee on Hunger, House of Representatives, 101st Congress.*

FRANCOEUR, R. T. (1993). Technological change, sexuality, and family futures planning. *Marriage & Family Review, 18*(3/4), 135–154.

FRANKLIN, C., & JOHNSON, C. (1996). Family social work practice: Onward to therapy and policy. *Journal of Family Social Work, 1*(3), 33–47.

GARNICK, D. W., HENDRICKS, A. H., DULSKI, J. D., THORPE, K. E., & HORGAN, C. (1994). Characteristics of private sector managed care for mental health and substance abuse treatment. *Hospital and Community Psychiatry, 45*(12), 1201–1205.

GLASBERG, R., & ABOUD, F. (1982). Keeping one's distance from sadness: Children's self-reports of emotional experience. *Developmental Psychology, 18*, 287–293.

GNAIDZA, R., & OBLEDO, M. (1985, Spring). 1983 Social Security reforms unfair to minorities and the young. *Gray Panther Network*, p. 12.

GOLONKA, S., & OOMS, T. (1991). *Child care in the 101st Congress: What was achieved and how will it work?* Washington, DC: The Family Impact Seminar, the AAMFT Research and Education Foundation.

GREEN, A. (1984). Generational transmission of violence in child abuse. *International Journal of Family Psychiatry, 6*, 389–403.

GROZE, V., & ILEANA, D. (1996). A follow up study of adopted children from Romania. *Child and Adolescent Social Work Journal, 13*(6), 541–565.

GUSTAVSSON, N. (1991). Chemically exposed children: The child welfare response. *Child and Adolescent Social Work Journal, 8*(4), 297–308.

GUSTAVSSON, N. (1992). Drug exposed infants: Facts, myths, and needs. *Social Work in Health Care, 16*(4), 87–100.

GUSTAVSSON, N. S., & SEGAL, E. A. (1994). *Critical issues in child welfare.* Thousand Oaks, CA: Sage.

HALEY, J. (1980). *Leaving home.* New York: McGraw-Hill.

HARTMANN, A. (1995). Ideological themes in family policy. *Families in Society, 76*, 182–192.

HERMAN, K., & KASPER, B. (1992). International adoption: The exploitation of women and children. *Affilia, 7*(1), 45–58.

HOOYMAN, N. R., & KIYAK, H. A. (1993). *Social gerontology: A multidisciplinary perspective* (3rd ed.). Needham Heights, MA: Allyn & Bacon.

HORGAN, C., LARSON, M. J., & SIMON, L. (1994). Medicaid funding for drug abuse treatment: A national perspective. In G. Denmead & B. A. Rouse (Eds.), *Financing drug treatment through state programs.* Services research monograph No. 1 (pp. 1–20). Rockville, MD: National Institute on Drug Abuse. NIH Publication No. 94-3543.

HOU, J., & LAZERE, E. B. (1991). *A place to call home: The crisis in housing for the poor.* Washington, DC: Center on Budget and Policy Priorities.

INGRAM, C. (1996). Kinship case: From last resort to first choice. *Child Welfare, 75*(5), 550–566.

IGLEHART, J. K. (1996). Managed care and mental health. *The New England Journal of Medicine, 334*(2), 131–135.

JONES, K., & SMITH, D. (1973). Recognition of the fetal alcohol syndrome in early infancy. *Lancet, 2*(7836), 999–1001.

KAMERMAN, S. B., & KAHN, A. J. (1988). *Mothers alone: Strategies for a time of change.* Dover, MA: Auburn House.

Keeping families together. (1985). New York: Office of Communications, Edna McConnell Clark Foundation.

KINGSON, E. R. (1989). Misconceptions distort Social Security policy discussions. *Social Work, 34*(4), 357–362.

KINGSON, E. R., HIRSHORN, B. A., & CORNMAN, S. M. (1986). *Ties that bind: The interdependency of generations.* Washington, DC: Seven Locks Press.

KOTZ, N. (1969). *Let them eat promises: The politics of hunger in America.* Englewood Cliffs, NJ: Prentice Hall.

KRAUTHAMMER, C. (1985, December 2). When liberty really means neglect. *Time*, 103–104.

LEMANN, N. (1994, January 9). The myth of community development. *New York Times Magazine*, p. 27.

Life Sciences Research Office, Federation of American Societies for Experimental Biology. (1995). *Third report on nutrition monitoring in the United States* (Vol. 1). Washington, DC: U.S. Government Printing Office.

MATTHEWS, M., & MCKEE, E. (1993). Family preservation programs may benefit legal services clients. *Youth Law News, 14*(3), 1–5.

MCNEECE, C. A. (1995). Family social work practice: From therapy to policy. *Journal of Family Social Work, 1*(1), 3–16.

MCNEECE, C. A., & DINITTO, D. M. (1998). *Chemical dependency: A systems approach* (2nd ed.). Boston: Allyn & Bacon.

MECHANIC, D. (1989). *Mental health and social policy* (3rd ed.). Englewood Cliffs, NJ: Prentice Hall.

MECHANIC, D., SCHLESINGER, M., & MCALPINE, D. D. (1995). Management of mental health and substance abuse services: State of the art and early results. *The Milbank Quarterly, 73*(1), 19–55.

MILLER, N. S., & HOFFMAN, N. G. (1995). Addictions treatment outcomes. *Alcoholism Treatment Quarterly, 12*(2), 41–55.

MINUCHIN, S. (1974). *Families and family therapy.* Cambridge, MA: Harvard University Press.

MOFFITT, R. (1990, June). Has state redistribution policy grown more conservative? *National Tax Journal,* 123–142.

MONROE, P. A. (1995). Family policy: Introduction to the special collection. *Family Relations, 44,* 3–4.

MULROY, E. A. (1995). Housing. In R. L. Edwards (Ed.), *Encyclopedia of social work* (Vol. 2, pp. 1377–1384). Washington, DC: NASW Press.

MURRAY, C. (1984). *Losing ground: American social policy, 1950–1980.* New York: Basic Books.

National Association of Social Workers. (1992). *A national social agenda for American families.* Washington, DC: Author.

National Black Child Development Institute. (1986). *Who will care when parents can't?* Washington, DC: Author.

National Center on Child Abuse and Neglect. (1988). *Study findings: National study of the incidence and prevalence of child abuse and neglect.* Washington, DC: U.S. Department of Health and Human Services.

National Center on Child Abuse and Neglect. (1996). *Child maltreatment 1995: Reports from the states to the national child abuse and neglect data system.* U.S. Department of Health and Human Services, Washington, DC: U.S. Government Printing Office.

National Commission on Children. (1991). *Beyond Rhetoric: A new American agenda for children and families.* Final report of the National Commission on Children. Washington, DC: U.S. Government Printing Office.

National Committee for the Prevention of Child Abuse. (1993). *Current trends in child abuse reporting and fatalities: The results of the 1992 annual fifty-state survey.* Chicago: Author.

National Institute of Justice. (1986). *Violence in schools.* Washington, DC: U.S. Department of Education.

National Institute on Alcohol Abuse and Alcoholism. (1994). *Eighth special report to the U.S. Congress on alcohol and health.* Rockville, MD: U.S. Department of Health and Human Services.

National Institute on Drug Abuse. (1996). *National pregnancy and health survey.* Rockville, MD: U.S. Department of Health and Human Services.

National Resource Center on Family Based Services. (1988). *Family based services: A national perspective on success and failure.* Iowa City: Author.

Newsweek. (1980, December 11), p. 54.

Office of National Drug Control Policy. (1996). *The National Drug Control Strategy: 1996.* Washington, DC: Executive Office of the President.

Office of Smoking and Health. (1988). *The health consequences of smoking: Nicotine addiction.* A report of the Surgeon General (CDC 88-8411). Washington, DC: U.S. Government Printing Office.

OHLS, J. C., & BEEBOUT, H. (1993). *The food stamp program.* Washington, DC: Urban Institute Press.

OZAWA, M. N. (1984). Benefits and taxes under Social Security: An issue of intergenerational equity. *Social Work, 29*(2), 131–137.

PAVETTI, L. A. (1993). The dynamics of welfare and work: Exploring the process by which young women work their way off welfare. Cambridge, MA: John F. Kennedy School of Government, Harvard University. Cited in Committee on Ways and Means, U.S. House of Representatives. (1994). *Overview of entitlement programs: 1994 green book* (pp. 441–442). Washington, DC: U.S. Government Printing Office.

PEASE, D. J., & CLINGER, W. F. (1985, January 29). Reform unemployment insurance. *The Wall Street Journal,* p. 26.

PECORA, P., FRASER, M., & HAAPALA, D. (1990). Intensive home based family preservation services: Client outcomes and issues for program design. In D. Biegel & K. Wells (Eds.), *Family preservation services: Research and evaluation* (pp. 3–32). Newbury Park, CA: Sage.

PEELE, R. (1996). Letter to the editor. *The New England Journal of Medicine, 335*(1), 56–57.

Physician Task Force on Hunger in America. (1985). *Hunger in America: The growing epidemic.* Middletown, CN: Wesleyan University Press.

PIERCY, K. W. (1994). Reforming the revolution: Responses to the consequences of divorce law reform. *Family Perspective, 28*(3), 155–167.

POOLEY, E. (1991). Kids with guns. *New York Magazine, 24*(30), 20–29.

PRATT, C. C. (1995). Family professionals and family policy: Strategies for influence. *Family Relations, 44,* 56–62.

PREZIOSO, F. A. (1994, March/April). Preserving inpatient care. *Behavioral Health Management,* 22–23.

REED, B. G. (1987). Developing women-sensitive drug dependence treatment services: Why so difficult? *Journal of Psychoactive Drugs, 19,* 151–164.

RUSH, D. (1987). *An evaluation of the special supplemental food program for women, infants, and children (WIC).* Research Triangle Park, NC: Research Triangle Institute.

SCHECTER, S. (1995). *In the best interest of women and children: A call for collaboration between child welfare and domestic violence constituencies.* Iowa City, IA: The National Resource Center for Family Centered Practice.

SHAMSIE, J. (1985). Violence and youth. *Canadian Journal of Psychiatry, 30*(7), 498–503.

SHULMAN, G. D. (1994, May/June). Costs: Don't blame them all on providers! *Behavioral Health Management,* 63–65.

SILIN, M. (1996). The vicissitudes of adoption for parents and children. *Child & Adolescent Social Work Journal, 13*(3), 255–269.

SILVERN, L., & KAERSVANG, L. (1989). The traumatized children of violent marriages. *Child Welfare, 68*(4), 421–436.

SINGER, J. L., & SINGER, D. G. (1981). *Television, imagination, and aggression: A study of preschoolers.* Hillsdale, NJ: Lawrence Erlbaum.

Social Security Administration. (1989, January). *SSI.* Washington, DC: Department of Health and Human Services. SSA publication no. 05-11000.

Social Security Administration. (1997). [On-line]. Available: http://www.ssa.gov/

SPALTER-ROTH, R. M., HARTMANN, H. I., & ANDREWS, L. (1992). Combining work and welfare: An alternative anti-poverty strategy. Washington, DC: Institute for Women's Policy Research.

SPRENKLE, D. H., & BISCHOF, G. P. (1994). Contemporary family therapy in the United States. *Journal of Family Therapy, 16,* 5–23.

SPRENKLE, D. H., & PIERCY, F. P. (1992). A family therapy informed view of the current state of the family in the United States. *Family Relations, 41,* 404–408.

STONE, N., & STONE, S. (1983). The prediction of successful foster placement. *Social Casework, 64,* 11–17.

Substance Abuse and Mental Health Services Administration. (1995a, Spring). Children's mental health information campaign launched. *SAMHSA News, 3*(2), 19.

Substance Abuse and Mental Health Services Administration. (1995b, Spring). Children with emotional disturbances: One family's story. *SAMHSA News, 3*(2), 11, 20–21.

Substance Abuse and Mental Health Services Administration. (1995c). *National household survey on drug abuse: Main findings, 1993.* Rockville, MD: Department of Health and Human Services. DHHS Publication No. (SMA) 95-3020.

Substance Abuse and Mental Health Services Administration. (1995d). *National household survey on drug abuse: Population estimates, 1994.* Rockville, MD: U.S. Department of Health and Human Services. DHHS Pub. No. (SMA) 95-3063.

SWENSON, V. J., & CRABBE, C. (1994). Pregnant substance abusers: A problem that won't go away. *St. Mary's Law Journal, 25*(2), 623–673.

SZASZ, T. S. (1974). *The myth of mental illness: Foundations of theory of personal conduct* (rev. ed.). New York: Harper & Row.

Texas Child Care Resource. (n.d.). Employers reaping benefits of child care. *Clearinghouse News,* special edition, p. 2.

TRACE, E., HAAPALA, D., KINNEY, J., & PECORA, P. (1991). Intensive family preservation services: A strategic response to families in crisis. In E. Tracy, D. Haapala, J. Kinney, & P. Pecora (Eds.), *Intensive family preservation services: An instructional source book* (pp. 1–14). Cleveland: Mandel School of Applied Social Sciences.

U.S. Bureau of the Census. (1995a). Census Bureau releases information on income, poverty, and health insurance coverage in 1994. [On-line]. Available: http://www.census.gov/

U.S. Bureau of the Census. (1995b). *Statistical abstract of the United States: 1995.* Washington, DC: U.S. Government Printing Office.

U.S. Bureau of the Census. (1996). *Statistical abstract of the United States: 1996.* Washington, DC: U.S. Government Printing Office.

U.S. Department of Agriculture. (1992). *Food assistance programs.* Alexandria, VA: Author.

U.S. Department of Agriculture. (1997). *Some food stamp facts.* [On-line]. Available: http://www.usda.gov/fcs/fs.htm

U.S. Department of Health and Human Services. (1983, May). *Characteristics of general assistance programs, 1982.* Washington, DC: Author.

U.S. Department of Health and Human Services. (1990). *Research on children and adolescents with mental, be-*

havioral and developmental disorders. Rockville, MD: Author.

U.S. Department of Health and Human Services. (1997) *Percentage of the U.S. population on welfare since 1960.* [On-line]. Available: http://www.acf.dhhs.gov/news/6090_ch2.htm

U.S. Department of Health and Human Services. (1998). *Temporary assistance for needy families (TANF): 1936-1966.* [On-line]. Available: http://www.acf.dhhs.gov/news/3697.htm

U.S. Department of Housing and Urban Development. (1995, June). *Why America's communities need a Department of Housing and Urban Development.* Issue Brief #10 [On-line]. Available: gopher://huduser.org:73/00/2/briefs/issbr10a.txt

U.S. Department of Housing and Urban Development. (1998). Cuomo says 1997 annual home ownership rate hit record annual high of 65.7%, breaking 17-year record. Press release, HUD No. 98-15. [On-line]. Available: http://www.hud.gov/news.htm

U.S. Department of Justice. (1989). *Criminal cases in five states.* Washington, DC: Author.

U.S. Department of Justice. (1991a). *Special report: Women in prison.* Washington, DC: Author.

U.S. General Accounting Office. (1990). *Drug abuse, the crack cocaine epidemic: Health consequences and treatment* (HRD 91-55FS). Washington, DC: Author.

VINET, M. J. (1995). Child care services. In R. L. Edwards (Ed.), *Encyclopedia of social work* (Vol. 1, pp. 367-375). Washington, DC: NASW Press.

WAY, A. (1992, July). Who are we? *Texas Feminist Gender Caucus,* pp. 10-11.

WAY, A. (1993). Social policy issues: Awakening your inner activist—A guide for socially responsible MFTs. *Contact, 20*(2), 6-7.

WEISSERT, W. G., CREADY, C. M., & PAWELAK, J. E. (1988). The past and future of home- and community-based long-term care. *The Milbank Quarterly, 66*(2), 309-386.

WELLISCH, J., PRENDERGAST, M. L., & ANGLIN, M. D. (1994). *Drug abusing women offenders: Results of a national survey.* Washington, DC: U.S. Department of Justice, Office of Justice Programs, National Institute of Justice.

WICKIZER, T. M., LESSLER, D., & TRAVIS, K. M. (1996). Controlling inpatient psychiatric utilization through managed care. *American Journal of Psychiatry, 153*(3), 339-345.

WISENSALE, S. K. (1992). Toward the 21st century: Family change and public policy. *Family Relations, 41,* 417-422.

ZIMMERMAN, S. L. (1992). Family trends: What implications for family policy? *Family Relations, 41,* 423-429.

ZINSMEISTER, K. (1990). Growing up scared. *The Atlantic Monthly, 265*(6), 49-66.

PART FOUR

New Directions in Brief and Systems Family Theory and Practice

Social workers and marriage and family therapists believe that it is important to change systemic patterns and family environments in order to change individuals. This mutual emphasis on environmental change gives social work practitioners and marriage and family therapists similar values and goals in working with clients to change social environments, whether these social environments be families or larger institutions. Systems theory has been the guiding therapeutic model for changing social environments for the past 20 to 30 years. Chapter 14 provides future directions for work with families using systems theories. It also provides some thoughts on how brief therapies may be further developed through the use of new advancements in systems theories such as the sciences of chaos and complexity. This chapter further addresses the importance of environmental change from the viewpoint of systems theory and social work practice. Implications for how newer systems theories may affect family practice are reviewed.

CHAPTER FOURTEEN

Cynthia Franklin, Ph.D.
University of Texas at Austin

Keith Warren, MSSW
University of Texas at Austin

Advances in Systems Theory

Social workers have long believed that it is important to place the individual in a broader context to assess and work with both the person and the environment. Marriage and family therapists also believe that it is important to change systemic patterns and family environments in order to change individuals. Laird (1995) discusses different venues of emphasis on environmental change in family practice through the advent of different types of systems thinking. Interest in systemic and cybernetic theories grew in the 1950s, and during the 1960s there was an interest in systems and ecological theories. The 1990s have brought a further shift in thinking about environmental change. In recent years, family therapists have emphasized the importance of changing larger environments such as social systems (Franklin & Johnson, 1996) and are developing interests in influencing social policies and political trends that maintain those systems (see Chapter 13). This mutual emphasis on environmental change gives social work practitioners and family therapists similar values and goals in working with clients to change social environments, whether these social environments be families or larger institutions.

All the clinical approaches in this book have emphasized environmental changes from three perspectives:

1. *Cognitive-interpersonal.* Focusing on changes in meanings or in ways clients think about their social environments. These types of cognitive changes are illustrated in the postmodern, cognitive-behavioral, and strategic-Milan perspectives.

2. *Behavioral-interactional.* Focusing on changes in repetitive behavioral patterns and social interactions. These types of changes are illustrated in the solution-focused, cognitive-behavioral, and strategic therapies.
3. *Structural changes in social relationships.* These types of changes are illustrated through approaches such as structural family therapy and the family preservation models.

This book has further discussed the importance of understanding the institutional relationships, such as gender, ethnicity, and alternative family lifestyles, in which families exist. Such institutional relationships also affect the treatment of families.

Systems theories, which have undergirded the approaches discussed in this book, have influenced the clinical perspectives of traditional social work and family therapy practice and have served as the dominant therapeutic paradigm for the past 20 or 30 years (Franklin, DiNitto, & McNeece, 1997). Systems approaches focus on environmental change and interfacing between environments as an important vehicle for individual change. Recently, however, systems theories have fallen into some disfavor (e.g., Anderson & Goolishian, 1988; Wakefield, 1996a, 1996b, 1996c). Some family therapy theorists express concern that the traditional systems approaches are too authoritative and directive, and they have offered therapist-centered instead of client-centered interventions (Laird, 1995). While calling systems theories an important theoretical advancement for social work practice, Wakefield (1996a, 1996b, 1996c) questions the utility of systems theories and their empirical basis. Despite these concerns, systems theories continue to offer important theoretical and methodological advancements that provide brief and effective interventions into the person-environment matrix.

We offer this chapter as a capstone to the book because it provides future directions for work with families using systems theories. It also suggests how brief therapies may be further developed through the use of new advances in systems theories. The chapter is highly theoretical but offers examples of uses of theoretical developments for family practice. Specifically, we review new advances in systems theory in the contexts of chaos and complexity and discuss how these advances are leading to new ways of looking at the processes of change and new methods for studying change. Our focus is to emphasize the importance of environmental change from the viewpoint of systems theory and social work practice. We provide a detailed discussion of environment, different types of environments, and how both persons and environments influence each other in a transactional view. Finally, we offer implications for how newer systems theories may affect family practice.

Environmental Change and Brief Therapies

Environmental change is important to brief therapies and managed behavioral health care practice environments. For example, most brief therapies carry assumptions that either address or imply the importance of environmental changes, like an emphasis on working in the present to help the client discover options for coping, new learning, and behavior. Change is something that can happen quickly and can be lasting, but it usually happens outside the therapy session. The natural process of life that takes place in interactions with social systems is the main force of change, and even very small differences in relationship patterns and circumstances may cause significant life changes. Once change is started, it will continue forward and gain momentum even without the aid of the therapist. Because of these characteristics of change, many believe that long-term therapy has no advantages over time-limited approaches and in fact may not be as effective as using the present moment and life circumstances to facilitate changes (Hoyt, 1995; Hoyt, Rosenbaum, & Talmon, 1992; Koss & Shiang, 1994).

In a recent review of the psychotherapy research, Miller, Duncan, and Hubble (1997) discuss effective therapy components. Forty percent (40%) of change can be accounted for by interventions that take place outside the therapy session in the informal support systems and naturally occurring life processes and social environments of individuals. In comparison, 30% of change happens as a result of the helping relationship and only 15% as a result of the practitioner's model or style. This conclusion may seem a little disheartening for proponents of specific therapeutic models and techniques, but it may point to common characteristics across models that facilitate change. In this regard, the conclusions hold considerable implications for the power of the environmental context and how a practitioner should focus on changing this context to help clients change.

Social Work Practice and the Social Environment

The history of social work practice has left a legacy of belief in the power of social-environmental change. Settlement house workers provided education and vocational training to help the poor take advantage of whatever opportunities their environment offered them, organized cultural events to improve that environment, and engaged in political activism around issues of local—and sometimes national—importance. Charity workers in the late 19th and early 20th centuries have been described as "experts on urban survival"; their activities included extensive brokerage of resources for their poverty-stricken clients (Katz, 1986).

Moreover, even those case workers (later called clinical social workers) whose primary aim was to induce change in the individual cognitions, emotions, and behavioral patterns of clients believed that the person could not be separated from the environment and that intervening in the environment could be a key to bringing about change. In *Social Diagnosis* (1917), for example, Mary Richmond wrote about the "wider self" of which each of us is a part:

> A man [sic] really is the company he keeps plus the company his ancestors kept. He is "coextensive with the scope of his conscious interests and affections." . . . many of the more thoughtful case workers of today are learning to study the relations of individual men in the light of this concept of the wider self—of the expanding self, as they like to believe. In so doing, they are allying themselves with the things that "move, touch, teach"; for where disorders within or without threaten a man's happiness, *his social relations must continue to be the chief means of his recovery.* (p. 369, italics added)

In recent years, there has been a continued dual focus on the person and the environment, drawing from both the sociological and psychological perspectives. This social-psychological perspective emphasizes the growth of individuals and their ability to cope with the environment and constitutes the basic frame of reference for social work (Gordon, 1983). A number of social work theorists have elaborated ecosystemic models that emphasize a dual focus in social work practice (Germain, 1991; Germain & Gitterman, 1980; Hartman & Laird, 1983; Maluccio, 1981; Meyer, 1983). These theorists work from an ecological metaphor—or frame of reference—that promotes a holistic view of people and environments as units that cannot be fully understood without each other (Germain, 1991). Hartman and Laird (1983) have specifically placed family therapy within a larger ecological context, discussing the effects of such factors as government policies toward the family and agency constraints on the practice of family therapy.

At the same time, doubts about the usefulness of an ecological approach have persisted. Even strong advocates of the ecological metaphor admit that, by itself, it does not tell us very much about practice and that it needs to be supplemented with other models (Greif, 1986). One of the most noted ecological theorists believes that ecological theory, though useful for framing case situations, does not imply any particular social work interventions; interventions are drawn from other sources, and the choice of where, when, and how to use them must arise from the practitioner's own values and thought (Meyer, 1993). In family therapy literature, *ecosystemic* sometimes refers to therapy conducted in a narrative/constructivist mode (Becvar & Becvar, 1994). One social work clinical theorist, herself a constructivist, has argued that a view of mental health as a good adaptation to the environment implies a somewhat authoritarian relationship between the social worker and the client, as it puts the social worker in a position to judge what is good adaptation; she suggests a mode of clinical social work in which social workers try to understand the meaning system of both the client and her or his environment (Saari, 1991).

Advances in Systems Theory

At the same time that there are doubts concerning the utility of systems theories, social scientists are arriving at the best understanding they have ever had of how people interact with and within their environments. Environmental psychologists have delineated the effect of movement from one environment to another in great detail; individuals, as we know from our own lives, will behave very differently depending on where they are behaving (Schoggin, 1989). General systems theory and its intellectual descendants provide theoretical guidelines for how systems, such as human social environments, behave (Bertalanffy, 1968; Martin & O'Connor, 1989). New developments in the fields of chaos and complexity studies indicate ways in which complex systems emerge and change (Lewin, 1992; Nicolis & Prigogine; 1989, Kauffman, 1993). Social scientists use complexity theory as a lens through which to examine the growth of, and changes in, human social systems (Chen, 1993; Harvey & Reed, 1994). These theoretical and empirical developments call for a reexamination of the potential usefulness of an ecosystemic view in family therapy practiced by social workers. We look first at the current understanding of environments, their construction, functioning, and impact, and then ask what this understanding might imply for social work and for family therapy.

What Is an Environment?

At first glance, this would appear a simple question. Glance up from this book, look around, breathe deeply, perhaps speak to the person next to you. You have seen, smelled, and interacted with your environment. With a bit more thought, we might ask ourselves how this particular environment came about, how it changes or does not, what our own role is in maintaining it, and how it maintains us. This last question has an odd ring to it—my environment maintains me?—until we realize that we are always in an environment of some sort, and the environment is always giving us messages about who we are and how we should behave. We, in turn, have a certain tendency to conform to those messages (Schoggin, 1989). Anyone who worked while he or she was in school will realize that classroom and workplace elicit very different behaviors. How does a complex world of multiple environments, which collectively we think of as our environment, arise and then exert influence on our behavior?

To begin on a rather abstract level, an environment is the cocreation of a group of actors in a situation in which the actions of one actor will influence and constrain the actions of other actors. If there is a sufficient number of actors with a sufficient level of contact between them, a global structure emerges that influences each of the actors in ways that cannot be explained simply by the impact of one individual on another; the whole is greater than the sum of the parts and cannot be explained completely by breaking it down into parts (Kauffman, 1993; Lewin, 1992). Thus, a system is born.

An example of such a birth familiar to most social workers and marriage and family therapists is the process of group formation in group therapy and group work in general. The role of the social worker is to foster an environment in which clients will help each other with their problems (Gitterman & Schulman, 1994; Schwartz & Zalba, 1972; Yalom, 1985). Two aspects of group formation illustrate the formation of complex systems in general. First, a group structure naturally tends to arise from the interactions of the group members (Yalom, 1985). The worker does not need to impose such a structure, and an authoritarian attempt on the part of the worker to structure the group process from the center is likely to impede the development of the group (Yalom, 1985). Group work necessitates a strong element of democracy (Cox & Parsons, 1994; Lee & Swenson, 1994). Second, the emergence of a group structure involves a period of conflict, anger, and anxiety, in which group members struggle for power and are likely to be harshly critical of one another and of the group worker (Corey, 1995; Toseland & Rivas, 1984). Serious conflict may recur at various times in the life of the group (Yalom, 1985). Not surprisingly, these periods can be quite stressful for both group members and the worker. However, it is generally agreed that a group that does not go through such a time is unlikely to evolve into an effective helping group (Corey,

1995; Yalom, 1985). In terms of emergent systems, before this period of storm and stress occurs, a group is not a group; it is merely a collection of individuals. After this period of conflict, a group acts as a system, exerting influence on its individual members.

The chemist Ilya Prigogine has dubbed such self-organizing systems, which are capable of increasing their complexity over time, "dissipative systems"[1] (Harvey & Reed, 1994; Nicolis & Prigogine, 1989; Prigogine & Stengers, 1984). Harvey and Reed point out that dissipative systems share two fundamental characteristics:

> First, they have the capacity to import energy from their immediate environment and transform that energy into increasingly more complex, internal structuration. By dint of their ability to increase metabolically their structural and functional complexity over time, we can say that dissipative systems are "information accumulating" and "information preserving" configurations. Second, although all thermodynamically ordered systems naturally accumulate increasing levels of random disorder, dissipative systems have the capacity to offset this tendency toward organizational decay by transporting their internal disorder out to their environment. Hence, the dual ability of dissipative systems to increase and store information in the form of internal structuration, on the one hand, and to export disorganization to their immediate environment, on the other, are their essential characteristics. (pp. 377–378)

By this definition, both biological entities—such as individual human beings—and human social entities—such as families, communities, and entire societies—are dissipative systems (Cambel, 1993). They have the capacity to import energy, matter, and information from their environment and export the entropy that inevitably results in their use of the imports. Thus, it should be possible to gain insight into human social systems from an examination of the characteristics of dissipative systems.

Whereas the sorts of clockwork systems emphasized by Newtonian physics are time reversible (in theory, it is possible to reverse the motions of a frictionless pendulum and run it backward through its previous positions), dissipative systems are not. They cannot simply recreate the energy that they have used in maintaining themselves and moving to a higher state of complexity (Cambel, 1993; Nicolis & Prigogine, 1989). Harvey and Reed (1994) point out that dissipative systems show the characteristics of deterministic chaos. Prigogine himself appears to agree and has worked with colleagues at the University of Texas at Austin to apply the concept of deterministic chaos to the social sciences (Chen, 1988; Nicolis & Prigogine, 1989; Prigogine, 1993). Researchers working with complex systems often refer to the systems as operating at "the edge of chaos" (Kauffman, 1993, 1995; Lewin, 1992). For the past 15 years, family theorists have used these ideas in discussing how families work. Borrowing from the work of biological and cognitive theorists such as Maturana, Varela, and Prigogine, family theorists describe families as self-organizing, dissipative systems with the properties to transform them-

---

[1]Social workers are doubtless more familiar with Bertalanffy's phrase "open systems" (Bertalanffy, 1968). Bertalanffy was familiar with Prigogine's work—he cites Prigogine a number of times—and his definition of open systems as those that continuously exchange energy with the environment and show emergent levels of complexity appears synonymous with the definition of dissipative systems used in this chapter.

selves spontaneously, given the correct sorts of conditions. (See, for example, Chubb, 1990; Dell, 1982, 1985; Elkaim, 1981; Elkaim, Prigogine, Guattaris, Stengers, & Denenbourg, 1982; Elkaim, Goldbeter, & Goldbeter-Merinfeld, 1987; Hoffman, 1981; Varela, 1989.)

Chaos and Complexity Theory

New developments in systems theory include knowledge from the expanding sciences of chaos and complexity theory just now starting to be adapted into family therapy practice (e.g., Butz, Chamberlain, & McCown, 1997; Chamberlain, 1995). However, understanding families through the lens of chaos and complexity theory may be interpreted as an extension of the work of the early theorists mentioned above who discussed self-organizing and dissipative structures and who borrowed heavily from cybernetic systems theories and biological and cognitive sciences as a basis for their family systems formulations. In second-order cybernetics, for example, there was an understanding of the role of positive feedback and the belief that systems could change rapidly. Interventionists borrowing from the ideas advanced by Maturana and Varela (1987), Prigogine and Stengers (1984), and other theorists advancing "cybernetics of cybernetics" (Becvar & Becvar, 1996) believed that it was possible to insert a strategic intervention into a family system to produce rapid change. The family theorist Keeney (1983), for example, thought of family systems as being in a constant state of change and that any intervention could serve only as meaningful Rorschach (later called noise) that could perturb or reverberate through the system in a manner that produced self-organizing change.

For us to understand how rapid change in a family system can occur, we need to know what is meant by the term *chaos*. Chaos refers to unpredictable, long-term behavior arising in a deterministic dynamical system due to sensitivity to initial conditions, sometimes referred to as the "butterfly effect" (Gleick, 1987). In essence, sensitivity to initial conditions means that even small changes in situational contexts, such as the historical and maturational conditions of people or the tiniest change in environmental conditions, may radically alter the trajectories of a person's life. The idea of incremental change or one-to-one correspondence between small changes in initial conditions and outcomes is therefore undermined in chaotic or complex systems.

Most clinical practitioners are familiar with the idea of nonlinear or recursive change, but the precise mathematical definitions of these terms are used in chaos theory. Linear change is *straight line* change and includes simple cause-effect relationships, in which a change in A causes a proportional change in B: If an adolescent shouts at her father, he may respond by shouting back. A one-decibel rise in the adolescent's voice leads to a one-decibel rise in the father's voice, and that relationship stays the same no matter how loud the adolescent gets. We could map this as a straight line, with a slope of 1. Nonlinear changes do not follow a straight line; a one-decibel change in the adolescent's voice may lead to no change in the father's voice or to a ten-decibel change in his voice, depending on how loud her voice was in the beginning. Of course, the simple cause-effect relationships described above do not apply. Family relationships involve feedback, and cause and effect are free to act recursively on one another in a way that reverberates through the system in an unpredictable manner that may cause very rapid change.

Family systems theories have used many metaphors from the physical, biological, and mathematical sciences to describe how family systems function and change. Cybernetic systems theories (first-order and second-order cybernetics) that propose complex mechanisms for change that are systemic, circular, nonlinear, and recursive have been used extensively (Becvar & Becvar, 1996). Family therapists, for example, discussed and illustrated the notions of reiterative or recursive feedback loops that are mathematically demonstrated in chaos theory. Recursive feedback within family systems theory is believed to amplify behavior in families. That is, person A reacts to person B, who in turn reacts to A, and this produces a new and amplified reaction to person B, who further reacts to person A, and so on. As these interactions work their way through the family, they may grow in intensity and be self-perpetuating. Thus, in an "enmeshed" family system, it is not uncommon to see sensitivity to initial conditions and sudden amplifications of behavior patterns.

In solution-focused family therapies, change is viewed as a naturally occurring process and a dynamic flow. Practitioners are taught that small changes in patterned behavior may bring forth quick and dramatic changes in the system (O'Hanlon & Weiner-Davis, 1989). As discussed in some detail by Fraser (1995), process, in solution-focused therapy, is a continual flow of patterned constructs (concepts) of the actor and related actions (behavior). "Change is a continual process . . . evolution or positive feedback is primary, and change is often quite rapid" (p. 266). These ideas are consistent with views concerning "chaotic" change processes that are described in chaos and complexity theory—particularly the idea of sensitive dependence to initial conditions.

This combination of nonlinearity and feedback seems to give a more intuitive depiction of the patterns one observes in families than does a linear model. In the earlier example, a slight increase in the intensity of the adolescent's shouting, which she might not even notice, might lead to an unexpectedly large increase in the intensity of her father's shouting. In his eyes, she has crossed the line and now he's really mad. Because the adolescent had no way of knowing just where "the line" was, his reaction is likely to surprise her. Perhaps she runs out the door of the house. Her father calls the police. An initially small difference in the loudness of the adolescent's shouting has escalated into a crisis. Without that difference, the whole confrontation might have decreased (Warren, Franklin, & Streeter, in press).

Chaos emerges in complex, nonlinear systems (discussed in more detail later) as a result of highly iterative (repeats itself), recursive (feeds back upon itself), and dynamic (changing) structures. Chaotic behavior exists in some part of the system's domain, making the system prone to highly discontinuous behavior and sudden changes in behavior, such as is sometimes experienced in organizations (i.e., sudden shifts in policy or downsizing) (Gregerson & Sailer, 1993). Note, however, that a social system may be both chaotic (nonorderly) and nonchaotic (orderly) at the same time. This paradox leads to the suggestion made earlier, that social systems exist on the edge of chaos. Butz, Chamberlain, and McCown (1997) explain why chaos is important and how self-organizing change occurs in systems:

> During the past 15 years, extensive research has occurred regarding the capacity for the self-organization of complex systems that are on the verge of chaos. In many systems the following predictable pattern occurs: Order begins to transition into a state known as bifurcation, otherwise described as oscillation or wildly fluctuating behavior. Following this there is a further transition into a period of apparent randomness or more complete chaos, where everything seems to break down. Eventually, the system seems to slow down, as if drained of energy into a period of stability. Often, though not always, there may be a superior organization following this period of chaos. Systems do not have to become completely chaotic to self-organize into more sophisticated functioning, and there is actually greater chance of self-organization if the system stays on the edge of chaos. Stuart Kauffman (1993), the renowned biologist, believes that this capacity of systems on the verge of chaos to self-organize into a higher, more superior level of functioning is what is responsible for both consciousness and the process of evolution. (p. 133)

Complexity Theory

Warren, Franklin, and Streeter (1997) provided an explanation of complexity theory for social workers. According to these authors, the study of complex and nonlinear systems may be understood as an extension of systems theory. Complex, nonlinear systems theorists, however, have developed a very different understanding of the way social systems and other complex systems behave. Previous theories suggested that systems or social organizations are quite orderly, rational, and somewhat predictable. Proponents of these theories elaborated on processes such as boundaries, homeostasis, and equilibrium that in various ways indicated the stability of social systems (Harvey & Reed, 1994). Practice theories such as the structural family therapy of Minuchin (1974), the systems perspectives of Pincus and Minahan (1973), and the ecological systems perspectives of Germain (1979) borrowed from the notions of general systems theory (Warren, Franklin, & Streeter, in press).

Nonlinear, complex systems provide a new way of looking at these systems. Nonlinear dynamics, for example, mathematically models a different process from what has been proposed previously in understanding how systems change. They go through an evolutionary change process that is both orderly and disorderly. This process of change is sometimes called "discontinuous change" versus "continuous change." The concept of discontinuous change is not so foreign to social workers and marriage and family therapists because many developmental theories have proposed this type of change. For example, common stage theories of development propose that individuals and families reach a certain point in their development followed by a rapid developmental burst or growth spurt that changes the developing organism (Lerner & Tubman, 1991). Developmental stage theories also propose a type of linear unfolding (epigenesis) toward these discontinuous changes, but complexity theory would differ, emphasizing instead more unpredictability in developmental sequences and leaning more toward compatibility with developmental approaches such as contextualism (Lerner, 1993).

Another difference is that traditional behavioral science theories such as those found in ecological systems theory often emphasized equifinality—the idea that systems that start at different states will end up in the same state. Complexity theorists, however, emphasize path dependence. Path dependence is a result of the sensitivity nonlinear systems show to initial conditions. It implies that systems that start in a nearly identical state can develop in completely opposite directions as the system amplifies initially minor differences. To put this in family therapy terms, complexity theorists privilege multifinality over equifinality (Warren, Franklin, & Streeter, in press). Moreover, once a system has developed along a given path, it cannot go back again; the changes in the interrelationship between the various individual components of the system are far too complicated and interwoven simply to reverse (Cowan & Gunby, 1996). Again, marriage and family therapists will note the resemblance to the work of other systems thinkers, specifically Maturana and Varela's idea of autopoesis and the group of cognitive scientists known collectively as connectionists (Davis, 1992). Complexity theorists, however, base their assumptions on the mathematics of nonlinear dynamics and seek more detailed explanations of the manner in which sudden change in complex systems occurs (Thelen & Smith, 1994).

Complex systems may exhibit order for a time, but this order is never very predictable or linear in regard to how long it may last and how it may unfold. As a part of their processes of self-organization, complex systems sooner or later will exhibit a pattern of disorder or chaos that unfolds into a new organization more complex than their previous state. The presence of a new organization assumes a process of evolution or achievement of a higher order functioning than was previously achieved. Thus, the concept of hierarchy is maintained in complex systems theory, but this theory emphasizes the independence of emerging hierarchical organizations from previous structures. This does not mean, however, that this organization is necessarily more functional in a social sense. When a system enters a state of disorder (chaos), there is no way to predict what may be the outcome, although it can be assumed that some type of organizational change is forthcoming (Mahoney, 1991).

To put it more simply, complex systems often exhibit erratic changes in behavior, but these fluctuations usually occur within a certain set of parameters that allow deviation without change. Barton (1994) notes that nonlinear systems usually settle into one of four patterns: (1) point attractor (converging around a single point), (2) cyclical or oscillating attractor (converging around a cyclical pattern), (3) quasiperiodic attractor (converging on a periodic pattern), and (4) chaotic attractor (converging on an irregular and unpredictable pattern). These patterns are all nonlinear and take on a nonlinear appearance when mapped. At a certain point in the development of a complex system, often called a bifurcation, the changes or deviations in the system fluctuate beyond the set parameters and push the system into disorder, or chaos. From this disorder emerges a new type of order or structure more complex than the previous organization. The new organization, however, is a "new life form," to use a metaphor from science fiction, and the emergent properties have their own new order that exists independent from the properties of the previous structure. Thus, the science of complex systems observes and mathematically models the development of those systems (Warren, Franklin, & Streeter, 1997).

Applications of Chaos and Complexity to Brief Therapies

Contemporary trends in brief therapy models offer parallels to chaos theory. For example, clients come for help during life upheavals, times of increasing demands for developmental changes, or when their current lifestyles or cognitive constructions no longer work very well. During these periods, families in a state of chaos or on the "edge of chaos" may change rapidly, even if only small behavioral changes or meaningful information are positioned to transform social constructions. Simple techniques such as reframing can make dramatic effects on family functioning. Changes in meanings and beliefs may produce rapid second-order (fundamental) changes in the system's structure and functioning. On the other hand, families who are stuck and are not able to change quickly may be thrown into a state of chaos or crisis that will facilitate their change. Thus, paradoxical interventions, or the introduction of radically new ideas into narratives may facilitate a shift from a stable pattern to a more chaotic pattern where change is easier to initiate.

These ideas are not foreign to family therapists in that they are central to the assumption of brief family therapies. These therapies draw inspiration from second-order cybernetics and the work of theorists and practitioners such as Gregory Bateson and Milton Erickson, who subscribed to a nonlinear epistemology. Many clinical techniques discussed in this book, such as circular questioning, miracle questions, reflecting teams, use of paradox, prescribing rituals or ordeal tasks, and counterparadoxical interventions, are used to put information into a client system for the purpose of producing self-organizing and rapid changes (de Shazer, 1988, 1991; Fraser, 1995; Keeney, 1983; Ray & Keeney, 1993; Selvini-Palazzoli, Cirillo, Selvini, & Sorrentino, 1989; Weakland, Fisch, Watzlawick, & Bodin, 1974). Chaos theory and nonlinear dynamics differ from the historic roots of the systems approaches discussed in this book because they do not rely on cybernetic machine models but rather on biological and organismic models. Like the ecological-systems models in social work, chaos theory emphasizes the properties of living systems. Chaos theory, however, goes further than cybernetics and ecological models in emphasizing the transformative states of living systems (Butz et al., 1997). As mentioned previously, chaos and complexity focus practitioners on the multifinality of systems.

We believe that chaos theory may provide a more detailed understanding of processes involved in systems change and may aid the development of effective interventions for brief therapy models. The effectiveness of small perturbations in bringing about large change is dependent on the presence of sensitivity to initial conditions, which in turn depends on deterministic chaos. We might be able to identify clinical situations that show evidence of deterministic chaos and might therefore be better candidates for brief and apparently minor interventions that can bring forth transformative results.

Chaotic systems, for example, include numerous stable, periodic orbits within the overall chaotic regime, and physicists have been able to stabilize such systems along these periodic orbits by using tiny nudges as they begin to drift away. Conversely, physicists have been successful in inducing major changes in chaotic systems using tiny perturbations; sensitivity to initial conditions (the butterfly effect) allows these initially tiny differences in the system to grow to major proportions in brief periods of time. Thus, chaotic systems actually have a flexibility that more orderly systems lack: It would take a much larger perturbation to move a periodic system off its track (Ott & Spano, 1995; Shinbrot, Grebogi, Ott, & Yorke, 1993). Clinical practitioners can use this information by becoming aware of the developmental level of families and where they are in the process of change. Butz and colleagues (1997) point out that some families may be chaotic and need to find a way to self-organize out of chaos back to a more stable orbit/state whereas others may be too stable and need to be moved toward more chaos.

Paradoxically, intrusive interventions will not help families in a state of chaos self-organize, but less intrusive interventions, such as guiding the families' own interactions and giving information, may achieve the goal of self-organization. If a family is in chaos and it is desirable to stabilize them, specific interventions may also be employed. Butz and colleagues (1997) discuss the work of chaotician A. B. Cambel, which has applications for stabilizing chaotic systems. The two best ways to stabilize a chaotic system are to introduce directed feedback when the system is beginning to bifurcate or to introduce more chaos, which acts as a stabilizing chaotic energy. One way to introduce directed feedback is critical feedback stabilization, in which the clinician allows the family to go in any direction they want during a crisis and brings them back only when they are at risk of escalating further into an unmanageable crisis situation. To introduce more chaos, the clinician can adopt such provocative techniques as acting "crazier" than the family system, which may have the paradoxical effect of bringing the system back into order.

Some families who are sometimes termed *rigid* may need help in moving toward a chaotic state so that they can find a new level of adaptation. Introducing crisis in a family destabilizes a dysfunctional system. Chapter 9 discusses the circumplex model, a standardized method for assessing the degree of rigidity in a family system. To help rigid families, it may be necessary to disrupt homeostasis and stability. Paradoxes, counterparadoxes, enactments, and many other directive interventions described in this book are aimed at disrupting repetitive dysfunctional family patterns. There has been increasing concern, however, that interventions aimed at destabilization may be dangerous or even unethical. These methods should be used with caution. Based on chaos theory, the following guidelines may help practitioners know which families *not* to destabilize (Butz et al., 1997). Families with a history of terminating therapy prematurely should not be treated with chaos-inducing methods because they are likely to leave therapy. It is also risky to facilitate a crisis with families in perceptual crisis, such as those who do not experience a precipitating event but still perceive that their lives are in a crisis. According to chaos theory, it is impossible to know what the effects of an intervention might be. It is best to act to stabilize these systems. Destabilizing families is also likely to have an adverse effect if the system is in a period of moving from one state to the next. This is called a "critical developmental bifurcation." When families are moving from one state to the next or are already in chaos, they have energy to help them change. Destabilizing interventions are too aggressive for these families. There is already a lot of change and energy going on in these families, and they can use this energy to self-organize on their own. Conversely, family systems that show signs of stability, such as the rigid families mentioned above, also show signs of being stuck in the same behavior patterns over time and can handle—and may even need—destabilizing interventions.

Chaos Theory and the Social Environment

Chaos and complexity are large and rapidly growing fields; a number of books provide introductions at varying levels of difficulty (Cambel, 1993; Gleick, 1987; Peak & Frame, 1994; Stewart, 1989). For this chapter, we have emphasized several aspects of deterministic chaos. In a chaotic regime, systems with a small number of variables can exhibit complex and unpredictable behavior (Stewart, 1989). Although this behavior is unpredictable, it is not truly random. As described above, its unpredictability comes from sensitive dependence on initial conditions; an extremely small change at one point can lead to an enormous difference after a while (Cambel, 1993). There is no way of predicting ahead of time how small such a difference might be, and thus no way of anticipating the future—at least not very far in advance—based on our knowledge of the present (Peak & Frame, 1994; Stewart, 1989). This is the "butterfly effect" mentioned above, a name that comes from the idea that the fluttering of a butterfly in Africa can set off a chain of events that will culminate in a hurricane in the Caribbean a few months later (Gleick, 1987). Family practitioners have used the butterfly effect to explain the rapid changes that can be achieved in solution-focused brief therapy (O'Hanlon & Weiner-Davis, 1989). Sensitive dependence on initial conditions arises because chaotic systems typically consist of a number of interrelated elements, each of which influences the other again and again over time. Under such conditions, small changes can grow as they bounce back and forth through the system (Barton, 1994; Chubb, 1990).

If human social systems are indeed dissipative systems, an examination of the characteristics of dissipative systems could be expected to shed light on the way in which human social systems influence their members. This has been a long-held belief by some family theoreticians. General systems theory, developed by Bertalanffy (1968) as an attempt to study systematically a wide variety of physical, biological, and social systems, describes some relevant aspects of such systems. Systems can be seen as a hierarchy of organizational levels. Thus, a family consisting of a number of individuals is a more complex system than any of those individuals alone, and a community consisting of a thousand families is a more complex system than any of those families alone (Martin & O'Connor, 1989). Levels *emerge* from the interaction of a number of individuals or smaller systems and are thus sometimes called *emergent levels*. Emergent levels include emergent properties (i.e., properties that can be understood only with reference to that level of the system). A family cannot be understood simply by reference to its individual members, a principle basic to family therapy; and a society cannot be understood simply as an aggregate of its individual members, a principle basic to sociology (Simmel, 1950). Also, higher levels of the organizational hierarchy tend to constrain lower levels (Harvey & Reed, 1994; Martin & O'Connor, 1989). These constraints are not absolute, but they can be formidable. A social service agency is free to ignore state-mandated paperwork requirements, but a loss of funding followed by disbanding of the agency is likely to follow.

However, there is a flip side to hierarchical constraint. Dissipative systems, as we have mentioned, tend to increase in complexity over time. They are not at equilibrium; rather, they are moving away from it, away from an entropic state, toward greater levels of complexity (Harvey & Reed, 1994; Nicolis & Prigogine, 1989). Thus, dissipative systems test their boundaries, push out into their environments, and seek new sources of energy, matter, and information. It is probably true that, more often than not, they return to where they began after failing to find sufficient inputs from the environment, but the impulse to explore and expand remains (Harvey & Reed, 1994).[2] Any dissipative system, however, is also part of a larger and hierarchically more complex dissipative system, which serves as its environment and which constrains its actions. We see the resulting tensions every day. An adolescent girl develops an interest in art, but her parents want her to be an engineer. Meanwhile, her mother has accepted a promotion at work and is dealing with the uncertainty of learning a new job. Because of sensitive dependence on initial conditions, such boundary testing can at times produce rapid leaps of development (Harvey & Reed, 1994). However, such progress requires an environment that yields enough matter, energy, and information to allow the system to maintain itself and increase its level of complexity. Harvey and Reed (1994) refer to such environments as "free energy environments" (p. 384), and Germain (1991) has written about the nutritive value, or lack thereof, of different human environments, metaphorically including economic and information resources among the necessary nutriments. Again, examples immediately suggest themselves. Life arose on earth in part because the energy flow from the sun is sufficient for life to maintain itself and increase in complexity.

Now we are in a position to answer our initial question, "What is an environment?" For any individual or family, the environment is composed of systems. The individual is part of the family system but is also likely to be part of a workplace, school, social organization, and so on. The family system is likely to be part of a neighborhood (itself part of a town or city, and so on up the organizational hierarchy), and also part of a school system, a church, and so on. Individuals and families will tend to use the resources of material, energy, and information in the

---

[2]At this point, some of our readers may cry foul, pointing out that we have shifted from general systems theory back to dissipative systems theory, and arguing that Bertalanffy placed much greater emphasis on equilibrium and homeostasis. In fact, Bertalanffy sharply distinguished between homeostasis through feedback, which he saw as applying only to certain fairly mechanical maintenance functions in open systems, such as the working of bodily organs, and what he referred to as the operation of a steady state, the far more dynamic process by which the open system maintains a steady flow of energy, materials, and information between itself and its environment. Bertalanffy (1968) writes, "In brief, we may define our viewpoint as 'Beyond the Homeostatic Principle'" (p. 107). Bertalanffy also emphasized the tendency of open systems to increase in complexity over time.

environment to reach higher levels of complexity. To accomplish higher order, they must maintain a continuous exchange of resources with the environment. The resources available in the environment will constrain the ways individuals and families can seek to increase their complexity. However, because the system as a whole exhibits deterministic chaos, movement toward a higher level of complexity is possible and can occur very quickly. Not every exploration results in such a movement, and not every movement toward greater complexity is successful. Thus, it is good to have plenty of options for change, so that if some fail, there will be others to try. In addition to a possible lack of resources, higher levels of the system will impose some direct constraints on actions. Some actions will go contrary to established norms and be frowned on by other members of the system. The play between systemic constraints and individual members of a system exploring possible routes to higher levels of complexity creates tensions that have been the subject of many novels and movies.

How Does the Environment Exert Its Influence?

In this section, we separate out several aspects of the environment for examination. Such a separation is fundamentally artificial; the parts of any system influence each other in complex and often unexpected ways. It seems increasingly likely, for instance, that waste from human economies, in the form of carbon dioxide, is raising the average temperature of the world climate system—the so-called greenhouse effect (Kerr, 1995). Likewise, what we refer to as the *built environment* is an outgrowth of the human socioeconomic system and is, as Germain (1991) has pointed out, just as natural as the nests of birds and squirrels. Nevertheless, it is conceptually far more convenient to refer separately to various aspects of the system, while dropping occasional reminders of their interrelatedness. We start with the natural environment, the system of geology, living things, and energy from the sun that includes us all.

The Natural Environment

By *natural environment* we mean simply those physical, biological, and climatic systems that would exist even in the absence of human beings. It is surprising how little those of us who work indoors notice about the natural world around us, and also how little outdoors activity is required before we begin to notice details that had previously escaped us. Even drying clothes outside on a clothesline rather than in a dryer will alert one to changes in wind conditions, humidity, and cloud cover that had previously passed unnoticed.

In fact, it could be argued that the environment of walls, houses, air conditioning, and rapid transportation that we have built for ourselves has buffered us so effectively from the vicissitudes of nature that it has largely isolated us from nature. This is disturbing for two reasons. First, such isolation is likely to make it far more difficult to take political action to solve problems of ecological decline. People are far less likely to act to save a species of bird that they have never noticed or an endangered marsh that they have always passed at 60 miles per hour in an automobile. Second, it has been argued both with eloquence and with persuasive reason that people need contact with nature if they are to live happily. The biologist Edward O. Wilson has pointed out that when compared to the age of Homo sapiens as a species, and particularly to the age of the genus Homo, agriculture is an extremely recent development, and industrialization, of course, even more so. Wilson has coined the term *biophilia* for what he believes is a subconscious human desire to seek a connection with nature. Manifestations of such a desire include the human proclivity to spend time outdoors in recreational pursuits and the preference shown for living in rural areas and close to water (Wilson, 1992). A considerable body of psychological research supports the importance of involvement with nature at some level for mental health (Kaplan & Kaplan, 1989).

The ecologist and deep ecology thinker John A. Livingston has pointed out that the price of our isolation from nature is a simplification of our experience of the world. He writes, "Nature is complex and multispecific; the human environment is essentially simple and monospecific" (1994, p. 135). Livingston refers to this as "urban sensory deprivation" (p. 136). This is particularly striking in light of our above description of dissipative systems, including families and individuals, as seeking higher levels of complexity. Nabhan and Trimble (1994) have written a book of eloquent essays on the importance of nature in the lives of children. They emphasize the significance of specificity and detail to children—the presence of nature as a complex environment, offering many opportunities for learning, and far more intricate than the planned and manicured playgrounds that adults create for them.

One result of the altered rhythm of contemporary human life in the industrialized nations may be the cyclical depression referred to as seasonal affective disorder (Gallagher, 1993). Seasonal affective disorder involves depression that arrives in fall or winter, in response to the shorter and darker days. Some symptoms of depression, such as lack of energy and an increase in sleep, would not present much of a problem if they were to occur in the winter in a society of hunters and gatherers. In such a society, most of the work involved in obtaining food happens in the warm summer months, and people live off stored food in the winter. In fact, under these conditions, a certain level of lethargy might even be adaptive, as a lowered activity level would allow one to live on less food. However, the same level of lethargy is far from adaptive in today's high-paced economy (Gallagher, 1993).

The Built Environment

Social work theorist Carel Germain has written about the "built world" (Germain, 1981), composed of the structures we live in and work in, the roads we drive on, and the neighborhoods we traverse. Clearly, most contemporary Americans spend most of their time in this built world. Authors who write about the built environment tend to distinguish two broad categories of effects (Germain, 1981; Rubinstein, 1989). First, the built environment often imposes physical constraints on human actions. Second, it carries a weight of meanings, emotional associations, and messages.

Physical constraints are perhaps most obvious when we work with those who are disabled. One example that will be familiar to most social work students is the impossibility of negotiating stairs in a wheelchair, and thus the necessity of ramps leading to the entrances of buildings—a necessity that became a legal mandate with the passage of the Americans with Disabilities Act in 1991. However, the simple existence of a ramp is not necessarily enough to allow a person in a wheelchair to enter a building. If a ramp is too steep, negotiating the entrance may be impossible for a person in a wheelchair. The same strictures apply to home environments. In a longitudinal study of a small group of elders, Rubinstein (1989) found that as they grew older, his participants tended to use less of their houses, consolidating their activities into the more accessible areas. In institutional settings such as nursing homes, Gutheil (1992) has pointed out that the common furniture arrangement of lining chairs against walls makes it more difficult for residents to talk with each other. Simply arranging the chairs in circles will increase communication between them.

The built environment imposes other restraints. For instance, the transportation infrastructure in the United States is largely built around the automobile. If you don't own an automobile, it will probably take you longer to get to work or appointments, and if you live in an area with a poor or nonexistent mass transit system, the lack of an automobile can severely constrain your opportunities. Computer literacy has become a central factor in employability; clearly, those children who attend schools with fewer resources to invest in computers will have a harder time developing their computer skills. On a micro level, there is evidence that children who are raised in highly crowded and noisy conditions can be impaired in their early cognitive development (Van Vliet & Wohlwill, 1985).

As Germain (1981) has pointed out, such differences in allocation of resources carry an implicit message as to one's personal worth. Germain refers to this as "symbolic identification" (p. 113) and calls attention to the differences in location, interior and exterior design, and furnishings between many public and private social welfare agencies. Germain argues that this is not only a matter of client self-worth; staff in poorer agencies, receiving the same messages, are likely to doubt their own competence. Some have argued that the design and meaning of the built environment have an effect on the health of those who live in it, just as do safety hazards—which are, of course, also part of the design and meaning of the built environment (Raffestin & Lawrence, 1990).

Built environments also hold a wealth of purely personal meanings that arise from long-term human interactions with and within them. Germain (1981) has pointed out that people sometimes experience their environment as part of themselves, as when one is at home in a room full of personal items, each of which has some story that is in turn part of the larger narrative of one's life. Germain is surely correct in asserting that part of the horror most people evince in leaving home for an institutional environment comes from the sudden ripping of this web of associations. Similarly, in his study of the home environments of elders, Rubinstein (1989) found that his participants saw their homes and the objects in them as the expression of their life courses. One of his subjects admitted that she was carrying on a 70-year love affair with her home, which she refused to leave despite its location in a decaying neighborhood and her own increasing physical frailty.

One area of human experience that may encompass both the physical and the built environments, and both public and private places, is that of sacred space. A sacred space might be a church, a natural area such as Mount Shasta in California, or a private shrine space in one's home. Eliade (1959) describes sacred space as forming the center of the world, the fixed axis around which the ordinary, the profane, world swirls. Such a space connects the ordinary world to both heaven and the underworld. One of the striking things about the contemporary built world is that it offers little access to sacred spaces. Church doors are locked except when services are going on, and sacred spaces are not built into contemporary residential architecture. Mazumdar and Mazumdar (1993) believe that modern apartments cause distress to Hindu families and make it difficult for those families to socialize their children into the Hindu religion because they lack appropriate spaces for the traditional family altar. At least in the contemporary West, natural features such as streams and springs have been thoroughly desacralized.

The Social Environment

The built environment also influences individuals because of the implicit understanding that certain actions will happen in certain settings. It is unlikely, for example, that a volleyball game will suddenly break out in an office suite. Ecological and environmental psychologists refer to the combination of a physical place and the behaviors that are expected there as a behavior setting (Barker, 1968; Schoggen, 1989). Within the setting, both physical and social forces act to encourage some forms of behavior and discourage others. The absence of chairs in a high school hallway discourages sitting down and encourages motion, whereas the rows of chairs in a classroom have the opposite effect. Social forces, in the form of both authority figures such as teachers and peer pressure, also encourage "appropriate" forms of behavior in behavior settings (Schoggen, 1989). Similar dynamics apply in homes. Different areas of the home are defined by the activities that occur there and whom those activities are shared with. Living rooms are seen as being appropriate for social functions whereas bedrooms are considered to be more private spaces (Oseland & Donald, 1993). Ecological psychologists have observed that behavior often varies more between different behavior settings than it does between individuals (Schoggen, 1989).

Behaviors go along with roles as well as with physical settings. William Foote Whyte's classic *Street Corner Society* (1943), a participant-observation study of the young men in a Northeastern slum that Whyte named Cornerville, is largely concerned with the ways social roles influenced the behavior of his subjects. Whyte largely focused on a single gang, the Nortons, and their leader, Doc. One of the most striking aspects of the book is the way social standing within the gang affected members' scores in bowling, their favorite recreational activity for a period of several years. The leadership of the gang, Doc and several of his close friends, typically won when the gang members bowled together on weekends, even when they bowled against followers who had beaten them in individual matches during the week or who were demonstrably superior athletes. Moreover, leadership was not determined by athletic ability, although it certainly did not hurt; a combination of verbal and diplomatic skills and self-confidence seemed to be more important. Whyte also observed that the members of the gang were bound by a net of reciprocal obligations. Whyte conducted his study in the late 1930s at the end of the Depression, and unemployment rates in Cornerville were high. As the leader of his gang, Doc was expected to lend money to others; attend social functions such as movies, dances, and bowling contests; and sometimes pay for others. It was considered inappropriate for him to take loans from others, although he would sometimes accept money from the small number of close friends who shared the leadership of the group with him. When he became unemployed, he was unable to lend money or pay for others and was often unable to attend social gatherings himself. His leadership in the group began to decline.

Implicit in much of our discussion of behavior settings and roles is the idea that the human social environment is largely a world of meanings—both the meanings an individual gives to his or her actions and the meanings a larger system attaches to them. Such meanings can be found in the stories we tell ourselves and each other. Becvar and Becvar (1994) have gone so far as to write, "Thus, the stories we tell ourselves constitute our experienced reality" (p. 24). They argue that the task of the therapist is to help clients to become aware of the ways in which the stories they tell themselves define their relationships with people, both themselves and others, and the living and nonliving creatures and things that also constitute their environments. Stories also exist on a family level and can be passed down from one generation to the next; one of the challenges we all face in intimate relationships is integrating the stories we have learned in our families of origin with the stories of our friends and partners (Van Heusden & Van Den Eerenbeemt, 1987). This focus on the world of meanings is consistent with the cognitive, solution-focused, and narrative family models discussed in this book.

How Does the Individual Affect the Environment?

To say that meaning is central to the interaction between person and environment is to imply that people can alter the interactive process. After all, it is possible to explore one's own meanings and stories. Such exploration is an iterative, recursive process that will tend to lead to change in the meanings and therefore change in the interactions.

People also help create their environments. This is perhaps most obvious in the built environment, as we decorate our houses and work spaces with objects we find beautiful or meaningful (Rubinstein, 1989). We also help to create the social environment in which we live, through our interactions with others. This is illustrated by the way we all deal with roles. Roles carry certain expectations of behavior, demeanor, dress, and so on. If, however, you wish to be rewarded for fulfilling a role in a social setting, it is not enough to fulfill those expectations; others must know you are fulfilling them. So the role itself becomes something of a performance (Giddens, 1988; Goffman, 1959). In fact, one might improve one's credibility in the role by joking about the role itself, or by consciously failing to meet some minor expectation that you know will do no harm—for instance, when a surgeon makes small talk during an operation rather than maintaining silence. In this case, the underlying message is that the role is so completely familiar and under such complete control that the individual can afford to distance himself or herself from it (Giddens, 1988). "Spin control" does not occur only in politics; it is a feature of the daily lives of each of us.

Sometimes we pursue longer term goals as well. Wicker (1991) has discussed this pursuit. The attainment of any long-term goal invariably involves attaining numerous shorter term goals that together lead to the long-term goal. If a family wishes to move from an apartment to a house, they will need to estimate how much per month they can afford to pay, find out about which neighborhoods they would like to live in, learn which banks will be willing to lend to them and how terms will differ, and so on. Family members may first need to work toward job promotions in order to have the money. Each step of the way will bring feedback, and members will need to adjust their plans and actions as they go along. Thus, the process is more of a search for the destination than a journey to it.

In the case of a family hoping to buy a house, the goal being pursued is a new environment. Earlier, we said that open systems will seek to explore their energy-rich environment and to exploit new sources of energy. Pervin (1991) quotes Baron and Boudreau's (1987) metaphor for individuals searching for new environments:

> Personality, in this metaphor, is a key in search of the "right" lock, whereas the environment, including other people, is the lock waiting to be opened so that its affordances can be realized. Viewed in this manner, personality and environment are interactive in that each is incomplete without the other. (p. 1227)

Pervin (1991) adds,

> To continue with this metaphor, individuals may be restricted and rigid or differentiated and flexible in their goals and plans, and environments may be varied or constricted in the range of affordances offered. What is important is that one of multiple keys (plans) fits one of multiple locks (environment affordances). (p. 81)

This view, of a world in which people influence their current environment while exploring new environments and at the same time are influenced by their environments in a circular process, has come to be known as a transactional view of person-environment relations.

The Transactional View

The transactional view of person-environment relations, sometimes called an interactional view (Magnusson & Torestad, 1991), rests on the idea of circular causality. Consider the simple case of a conversation between two people. Each person will have to be aware of the other, of what the other is saying, and the rhythm of the other's conversation in order to carry on the conversation in a coherent manner. Each person will, to some extent, look to the other for cues— waiting for a pause in order to speak, choosing words so as not to provoke an unnecessary argument, and so on. In such a situation, it is inaccurate to say that either person is causing the conversation. Rather, the conversation is an emergent level of organization that requires the ongoing and modulated participation of both people. Within the conversation, the two individuals influence each other over and over again, in a reciprocal manner. Causality runs both ways. Germain (1991) remarks, "Whereas in linear relations one entity changes the other, in transactional relations *both entities are changed with consequences for both*" (p. 16, italics in the original). This reciprocal process extends through most of our relations with the social environment and even the way in which we create our built environment and are in turn created by it.

As the reciprocal process of person-environment transaction continues, a person will develop a niche (Germain, 1991; Brower & Nurius, 1993). A niche

> defines the set of environmental and internal forces that are mutually interdependent: Within it we are sustained, and within it we can take advantage of our strengths and allow for our weaknesses . . . the development of a niche is . . . a fluid, lifelong process, where the person and environment change and accommodate to one another, where each becomes dependent on the other, forming, ideally, a delicate dynamic balance. (Brower & Nurius, 1993, p. 35)

It is clear from our earlier look at chaos and complexity theory that within such a system of person and environment—multiple environments including home, work, school, each in turn composed of social contacts, roles, expectations, and multiple physical settings—some degree of continual change is certain to be the rule, and that sudden and discontinuous change is a possibility, even in the absence of a plan for change. However, as Brower and Nurius (1993) point out, for one who is highly adapted to a particular niche, change is likely to be difficult. The drive and work habits that go into business success are likely to make retirement a challenge. They may even make a vacation unpleasant!

Thus, the well-being of a person or a system is not only a matter of the traits typical of that person or system. Rather, well-being is the outcome of a good fit between the traits of the person or system and the traits that the larger system requires. For instance, it has been demonstrated that the concept of person-environment fit serves as a predictor of job performance as well as which employees are likely to leave a job and which are likely to stay (Caplan & Van Harrison, 1993). There is evidence that one source of burnout among social work interns lies in the struggle to understand the actual rules under which their agencies operate, and the ways in which those rules often differ from the standards of social work they have learned in school and the stated rules and goals of the organization (Um & Brown-Standridge, 1993). It also seems likely that person-environment fit affects school performance and attrition, a frequent concern of family therapists (Caplan & Van Harrison, 1993).

Implications for Family Practice

In this chapter we have covered a lot of ground concerning advances in systems theory and the relationships between people and their environments. In this last section we discuss some of the implications for the field of social work and marriage and family therapy practice. If family therapists are to use advances in systems theory such as those discussed in this chapter, they will have to give considerably more attention to the environments families inhabit and to the fields of chaos and complexity systems theory. Notions from ecological theory and chaos and complexity will affect how family practitioners work. We offer some suggestions concerning the basic assumptions and guiding philosophy a practitioner may use in applying the ideas discussed in this chapter.

1. Human Beings Are Deeply and Inextricably Connected with Each Other

The sorts of surprising jumps and changes that have been documented in such large-scale human systems as stockmarkets (Chen, 1988), which can be seen in political systems in times of revolution and which family therapists have noted in families (O'Hanlon & Weiner-Davis, 1989), are only possible in systems in which individuals are intricately connected through multiple feedback loops and thus constantly interacting and reacting to each other (Briggs & Peat, 1989). This is one of the reasons for the excitement about chaos and complex systems theory: It is revealing a world of interconnections.

It may be that even in ecosystemic models of social work and family therapy we have underestimated the interconnectedness of human beings. For instance, a typical ecomap will show a family marked off by a circle with lines connecting the individuals in the family and other lines leading from individual family members to various people, places, and social situations outside of the family. It is striking that the authors of genograms seldom draw connections between any of these outside people and places. For instance, an ecomap might include one line leading from the mother of a family to a box marked "Work" and another to a circle marked "Friends." It is possible that "Work" and "Friends" influence each other, and that the two boxes should be linked. For instance, some of her friends may have come from work. Alternatively, the hours that she works may make it difficult for her to get together with her friends, or her friends may have influenced the work she does, perhaps through advice or because she was looking for co-workers who would be like her friends.

2. Focus on Process

Family practitioners will focus on process instead of content in helping families change. For example, patterned behavior and responses will be mapped from the beginning to the end to get a full understanding of the system and its current state of functioning and rate of change. The context of behavior will be important to include in mapping these processes as well as the meanings that human systems impose on these patterned responses.

3. Change Is Inevitable

Family practitioners will focus on the fact that change is inevitable and that very small changes in a system may result in a major reorganization of that system. In this regard, however, introducing a change within a system is always fraught with multiple and unpredictable outcomes. Because of sensitivity to initial conditions, all one can know is that the change will iterate through a system and result in an exponential change. The exact result of that change, however, may only be observed and not predicted. Systems are always in the process of change, and those systems that exist on the "edge of chaos" may be prime candidates for accomplishing quick and spontaneous changes without moving into a state of chaos if the right conditions are maintained. In addition, practitioners will use the metaphor of the logistic curve from mathematics to keep in mind that systems are always going through growth spurts and may change rapidly. Rapid change is always followed by a slowing of change, but the change process itself never stops. During the process of slowed change, change in systems may look more linear, but during the next growth spurt the system will again follow the overall pattern of nonlinear change.

4. Small Changes Can Turn into Big Changes

The optimistic implication is that small changes can make a difference, not because they add up to large changes but because they can expand through systemic interactions.[3] So take heart; a small change in behavior may be a harbinger of larger things to come. Such changes are more likely to expand if people notice them and think about them, so it is often a good idea to point them out.

The pessimistic implication is that prediction of anyone's behavior, except for possibly in the short term, is theoretically impossible. This is because the passage of time allows tiny initial differences to build up into major changes. One of the earliest descriptions of this phenomenon came from meteorological research and earned the sobriquet "the butterfly effect" described earlier. Meteorologists cannot possibly keep track of every butterfly in the world, so the weather is inherently unpredictable in any time frame longer than about five days or possibly a week (Gleick, 1987; Lorenz, 1963; Stewart, 1989). By the same reasoning, it is not possible to control the weather; one can institute changes, but beyond a very short time frame, there is no way of knowing what new changes your changes will lead to. This would seem to indicate that the therapeutic ideal of "curing" clients so that they need never again return to therapy is probably unattainable. It is probably more reasonable to look at therapy as a resource available to people when they need it, and to understand that they may need it occasionally through their lives. This probability has also been suggested in the brief therapy literature, on experiential rather than theoretical grounds (Budman & Gurman, 1988).

5. Disequilibrium Is Normal

Disequilibrium, including unpredictable reactions, sudden changes in thinking and behavior, distressing emotions, and life circumstances that mirror crisis and reorganization, are normal processes that accompany adaptation and change.

---

[3]Solution-orientated therapists have suggested that therapists should aim for extremely small initial changes in client behavior patterns, which they can then work to amplify. They have also argued that chaos theory implies such an approach (O'Hanlon & Weiner-Davis, 1989).

Distressing emotions should not be treated as dysfunctional but as information on the state of the human system as it seeks greater complexity and organization. This promotes a nonpathological view of human distress. This view of distressing emotions is different from the view in many theories of psychotherapy that emphasize stamping out irrational beliefs and uncomfortable subjective feelings that are often seen as pathological. Instead, nonlinear dynamics would suggest that all humans may experience these types of reactions on their road to self-organization.

6. Self-Organization Is the Key to Transformation

All that is needed for change is present in the current system, and the best practitioners use the self-organizing changes and resources already present. If a system has reached a resource limitation and is no longer meeting its potential, perhaps the system needs to be helped to obtain more resources, or more energy needs to be imported from the environment. On the other hand, if a system is in a state of chaos, the system may need to be supported through this state of fluctuation until it reaches its new level of organization. This is a different orientation from the interventionist strategy common to therapy practice. Interventionists may seek to stabilize someone who is in distress, for example. This would be the typical path taken in crisis theory. Chaos and complexity theory, however, suggests that the distress is a positive and normative sign that more complex development is trying to emerge. What is needed is not for the distress to stop but for the person to be helped to use this information to change and to reach a new level of complexity. Nonintervention, Socratic instruction, and reflexivity may be the best responses to support this type of self-organization process.

7. Context Matters

It is increasingly clear that one cannot separate an action from its physical setting and from the social role of the actor. This is important in family therapy, as many family therapy models make the implicit assumption that therapy happens in an office, at a set time, for a period of an hour or so, and at regular intervals. Family therapists, however, are often expected to "deal with the families" in settings that differ greatly from a middle-class office setting—as in a nursing home, which involves frequent interactions with the families of residents, often in hallways or in the residents' rooms. As Germain (1981) has pointed out, the context of any practice includes the physical characteristics and the culture of the place where it is carried out.

8. The Larger System Matters

Classic systems theory holds that the larger system matters. Systems are hierarchical entities in which the higher levels of the hierarchy constrain the lower. Losing sight of this is easy, however, and can result in blaming individuals for problems that are in part or in whole systemic effects. Following are a few examples.

In a study of families in northern Iowa, Elder, Conger, Foster, and Ardelt (1992) found that economic pressure in the form of low income, loss of income, and unstable work led to an increase in the number of hostile interactions between parents and increased the likelihood of depressed affect and externalizing behavior for children. If hostility in the family does appear to be the result of adverse economic circumstances, employment counseling and education in stress management and possibly in the economic roots of the family's difficulties might be a more appropriate response than family therapy.

As another example, there is considerable evidence that Americans are, on average, spending more time at work than they did 20 years ago, working more hours per week, and taking fewer weeks off. Millions are working two jobs (Schor, 1992). In addition to the toll this is likely to take on family life, as parents spend less time with their children while spending more time at work, the value to them of their leisure time will tend to increase. As most of the time people put into family therapy comes out of their leisure time, it will in effect become more costly to go to therapy sessions and to do homework outside of therapy. A family member who does not seem to follow through with homework for which he or she has contracted may simply not have the time.

Finally, Crittenden (1992) has examined an attempt to improve the functioning of child protection teams in the state of Florida. She states, "Even simple changes in microsystems can have major ramifications in the network of related micro-, meso-, exo-, and macrosystems. These ramifications can greatly impede the process of change or can speed and facilitate it, as in the case of an idea whose time has come" (p. 31).[4] Crittenden concludes that in those states lacking a consensus on values, policies, and public resources, it may be necessary to work on the macro-systemic level before changes in the micro-system of clinical practice can be successfully implemented.

9. Mathematical Tools Can Transform Our Understanding of How Families Change

Mathematical tools are available to allow practitioners and researchers to study nonlinear change in human systems. Through the applications of mathematics, such as the logistic equation, fractal geometry, and other forms of nonlinear math, it becomes possible not only to talk about the concepts of nonlinear dynamics and complexity as metaphors but to demonstrate empirically how systems work using these new mathematical tools. The new mathematical tools bring systems theories such as the presence of deterministic chaos outside the realm of the speculative and the theoretical and cast them into the world of the empirical where these systemic processes may be mapped. Thus, with the use of the new math, the validity of systems theories, which have been some of the favorite theories of social

---

[4]Readers will doubtless have noted that this could be seen as an example of sensitive dependence on initial conditions. Note that Crittenden does not reference any of the chaos literature in her bibliography; she appears to have noticed sensitive dependence in the course of her observations of the system.

workers and marriage and family therapists, may at last be shown to be applicable to human systems.

Process Questions

1. What is the importance of systems theory in social work?

2. What is meant by environment and environmental change?

3. Chaos and complexity theory offer theoretical advances in systems theory. What are some of the main ideas that these theories suggest?

4. How would an application of chaos and complexity theory influence the way we conduct family practice?

References

ANDERSON, H., & GOOLISHIAN, H. (1988). Human systems as linguistic systems: Preliminary and evolving ideas about the implications for clinical theory. *Family Process, 27,* 371–394.

BARKER, R. G. (1968). *Ecological psychology: Concepts and methods for studying the environment of human behavior.* Stanford: Stanford University Press.

BARON, R., & BOUDREAU, L. (1987). An ecological perspective on integrating personality and social psychology. *Journal of Personality and Social Psychology, 53,* 1222–1228.

BARTON, S. (1994). Chaos, self-organization, and psychology. *American Psychologist, 49*(1), 5–14.

BECVAR, R., & BECVAR, D. (1994). The ecosystemic story: A story about stories. *Journal of Mental Health Counseling,16*(1), 22–32.

BECVAR, D. S., & BECVAR, R. J. (1996). *Family therapy: A systemic integration* (3rd ed.). Boston: Allyn & Bacon.

BERTALANFFY, L. VON (1968). *General system theory: Foundations, development, applications.* New York: George Braziller.

BRIGGS, J., & PEAT, F. (1989). *Turbulent mirror: An illustrated guide to chaos theory and the science of wholeness.* New York: Harper & Row.

BROWER, A. M., & NURIUS, P. (1993). *Social cognition and individual change: Current theory and counseling guidelines.* Newbury Park, CA: Sage.

BUDMAN, S., & GURMAN, A. (1988). *Theory and practice of brief therapy.* New York: Guilford.

BUTZ, M. R., CHAMBERLAIN, L. L., & MCCOWN, W. G. (1997). *Strange attractors: Chaos, complexity, and the art of family therapy.* New York: Wiley.

CAMBEL, A. (1993). *Applied chaos theory: A paradigm for complexity.* San Diego: Academic Press.

CAPLAN, R. D., & VAN HARRISON, R. (1993). Person-environment fit theory: Some history, recent developments, and future directions. *Journal of Social Issues, 49,* 253–275.

CHAMBERLAIN, L. L. (1995). Strange attractors in patterns of family interaction. In R. Robertson & A. Combs (Eds.), *Chaos theory in psychology and life sciences.* Mahwah, NJ: Erlbaum.

CHEN, P. (1988). Empirical and theoretical evidence of economic chaos. *System Dynamics Review: The Journal of the System Dynamics Society, 4*(1–2), 81–108.

CHEN, P. (1993). China's challenge to economic orthodoxy: Asian reform as an evolutionary, self-organizing process. *China Economic Review, 4*(2), 137–142.

CHUBB, H. (1990). Looking at systems as process. *Family Process, 29,* 1669–1675.

COREY, G. (1995). *Theory and practice of group counseling.* Pacific Grove, CA: Brooks/Cole.

COWAN, R., & GUNBY, P. (1996). Sprayed to death: Path dependence, lock-in, and pest control strategies. *The Economic Journal, 106,* 521–542.

COX, E., & PARSONS, R. (1994). *Empowerment-oriented social work practice with the elderly.* Pacific Grove, CA: Brooks/Cole.

CRITTENDEN, P. M. (1992). The social ecology of treatment: Case study of a service system for maltreated children. *American Journal of Orthopsychiatry, 62*(1), 22–34.

DAVIS, S. (1992). *Connectionism: Theory and practice.* New York: Oxford University Press.

DELL, P. F. (1982). Beyond homeostasis: Toward a concept of coherence. *Family Process, 21,* 21–41.

DELL, P. F. (1985). Understanding Bateson and Maturana: Toward a biological foundation for the social sciences. *Journal of Marital and Family Therapy, 11,* 1–20.

DE SHAZER, S. (1988). *Clues: Investigating solutions in brief therapy*. New York: Norton.

DE SHAZER, S. (1991). *Putting differences to work*. New York: Norton.

ELDER, G. H., CONGER, R. D., FOSTER, E. M., & ARDELT, M. (1992). Families under economic pressure. *Journal of Family Issues, 13*(1), 5–37.

ELIADE, M. (1959). *The sacred and the profane: The nature of religion*. New York: Harcourt, Brace, Jovanovich.

ELKAIM, M. (1981). Non-equilibrium, chance, and change in family therapy. *Journal of Marital and Family Therapy, 7*, 291–297.

ELKAIM, M., GOLDBETER, A., & GOLDBETER-MERIN-FELD, E. (1987). Analysis of the dynamics of a family system in terms of bifurcations. *Journal of Social and Biological Structures, 10*, 21–36.

ELKAIM, M., PRIGOGINE, I., GUATTARIS, S., STENGERS, I., & DENENBOURG, J. L. (1982). Openess: A round-table discussion. *Family Process, 21*, 57–70.

FRANKLIN, C., DINITTO, D. M., & MCNEECE, A. (1997). In search of social work theory. In D. M. DiNitto & A. McNeece (Eds.), *Introduction to social work practice: Issues and opportunities for a challenging profession*. Boston: Allyn & Bacon.

FRANKLIN, C., & JOHNSON, C. (1996). Family social work practice: Onward to therapy *and* policy. *Journal of Family Social Work, 1*(3), 33–47.

FRASER, J. S. (1995). Process, problems, and solutions in brief therapy. *Journal of Marital and Family Therapy, 21*, 265–279.

GALLAGHER, W. (1993). *The power of place: How our surroundings shape our thoughts, emotions, and actions*. New York: Poseidon.

GERMAIN, C. (1979). *Social work practice: People and environments. An ecological perspective*. New York: Columbia University Press.

GERMAIN, C. B. (1981). The physical environment and social work practice. In A. Maluccio (Ed.), *Promoting competence in clients: A new/old approach to social work practice*. New York: Free Press.

GERMAIN, C. B. (1991). *Human behavior in the social environment: An ecological view*. New York: Columbia University Press.

GERMAIN, C. B., & GITTERMAN, A. (1980). *The life model of social work practice*. New York: Columbia University Press.

GIDDENS, A. (1988). Goffman as a systematic social theorist. In P. Drew & A. Wootton (Eds.), *Erving Goffman: Exploring the interaction order*. Boston: Northeastern University Press.

GITTERMAN, A., & SCHULMAN, L. (1994). *Mutual aid groups, vulnerable populations, and the life cycle* (2nd ed.). New York: Columbia University Press.

GLEICK, J. (1987). *Chaos: Making a new science*. New York: Viking.

GOFFMAN, E. (1959). *The presentation of self in everyday life*. Boston: Northeastern University Press.

GORDON, W. (1983). Social work revolution or evolution? *Social Work, 28*, 181–184.

GREGERSON, H., & SAILER, L. (1993). Chaos theory and its implications for social science research. *Human Relations, 46*(7), 777–802.

GREIF, G. (1986). The ecosystems perspective "meets the press." *Social Work, 31*, 225–226.

GUTHEIL, I. (1992). Considering the physical environment: An essential component of good practice. *Social Work, 37*(5), 391–396.

HARTMAN, A., & LAIRD, J. (1983). *Family-centered social work practice*. New York: Free Press.

HARVEY, D. L., & REED, M. H. (1994). The evolution of dissipative social systems. *Journal of Social and Evolutionary Systems, 17*(4), 371–411.

HOFFMAN, L. (1981). *Foundations of family therapy*. New York: Basic Books.

HOYT, M. F. (1995). Brief psychotherapies. In A. S. Gurman & S. B. Messer (Eds.), *Essential psychotherapies: Theory and practice* (pp. 441–487). New York: Guilford.

HOYT, M. F., ROSENBAUM, R., & TALMON, M. (1992). Planned single-session therapy. In S. H. Budman, M. F. Hoyt, & S. Friedman (Eds.), *The first session in brief therapy* (pp. 59–86). New York: Guilford.

KAPLAN, R., & KAPLAN, S. (1989). *The experience of nature: A psychological perspective*. Cambridge: Cambridge University Press.

KATZ, M. B. (1986). *In the shadow of the poorhouse: A social history of welfare in America*. New York: Basic Books.

KAUFFMAN, S. A. (1993). *The origins of order: Self-organization and selection in evolution*. New York: Oxford University Press.

KAUFFMAN, S. A. (1995). *At home in the universe: The search for the laws of self-organization and complexity*. New York: Oxford University Press.

KEENEY, B. P. (1983). *Aesthetics of change*. New York: Guilford.

KERR, R. A. (1995). Studies say—tentatively—that greenhouse warming is here. *Science, 268*(5267), 1567–1568.

KOSS, M. P., & SHIANG, J. (1994). Research on brief psychotherapy. In A. E. Bergin & S. L. Garfield (Eds.), *Handbook of psychotherapy and behavior change* (4th ed., pp. 664–700). New York: Wiley.

LAIRD, J. (1995). Family-centered practice in the postmodern era. *Families in Society, 76*, 150–162.

LEE, J. A. B., & SWENSON, C. B. (1994). The concept of mutual aid. In A. Gitterman & L. Schulman (Eds.), *Mutual aid groups, vulnerable populations, and the life cycle*. New York: Columbia University Press.

LERNER, R. M. (1993). Human development: A developmental contextual perspective. In S. C. Hayes, L. J.

Hayes, H. W. Reese, & T. R. Sarbin (Eds.), *Varieties of scientific contextualism*. Reno, NV: Context Press.

LERNER, R. M., & TUBMAN, J. G. (1991). Developmental contextualism and the study of early adolescent development. In R. Cohen & A. W. Siegel (Eds.), *Context and development*. Hillsdale, NJ: Erlbaum.

LEWIN, R. (1992). *Complexity: Life at the edge of chaos*. New York: Collier Books.

LIVINGSTON, J. (1994). *Rogue primate: An exploration of human domestication*. Toronto: Key Porter Books.

LORENZ, E. (1963). Deterministic nonperiodic flow. *Journal of the Atmospheric Sciences, 20*, 130–141.

MAGNUSSON, D., & TORESTAD, B. (1991). The individual as an interactive agent in the environment. In W. B. Walsh, K. B. Craik, & R. H. Price (Eds.), *Person-environment psychology: Models and perspectives*. Hillsdale, NJ: Erlbaum.

MAHONEY, M. J. (1991). *Human change processes: The scientific foundations of psychotherapy*. New York: Basic Books.

MALUCCIO, A. N. (Ed.). (1981). *Promoting competence in clients: A new/old approach to social work practice*. New York: Free Press.

MARTIN, P., & O'CONNOR, G. (1989). *The social environment: Open systems and applications*. New York: Longman.

MATURANA, H., & VARELA, F. (1987). *The tree of knowledge*. Boston: New Science Library.

MAZUMDAR, S., & MAZUMDAR, S. (1993). Sacred space and place attachment. *Journal of Environmental Psychology, 13*, 231–242.

MEYER, C. H. (Ed.). (1983). *Clinical social work in the ecosystems perspective*. New York: Columbia University Press.

MEYER, C. H. (1993). *Assessment in social work practice*. New York: Columbia University Press.

MILLER, S. D., DUNCAN, B. C., HUBBLE, M. A. (1997). *Escape from Babel: Toward a unifying language of psychotherapy practice*. New York: Norton.

MINUCHIN, S. (1974). *Families and family therapy*. Cambridge: Harvard University Press.

NABHAN, G., & TRIMBLE, S. (1994). *The geography of childhood: Why children need wild places*. Boston: Beacon Press.

NICOLIS, G., & PRIGOGINE, I. (1989). *Exploring complexity: An introduction*. New York: W. H. Freeman.

O'HANLON, W., & WEINER-DAVIS, M. (1989). *In search for solutions: A new direction in psychotherapy*. New York: Norton.

OSELAND, N., & DONALD, I. (1993). The evaluation of space in homes: A facet study. *Journal of Environmental Psychology, 13*, 251–261.

OTT, E., & SPANO, M. (1995). Controlling chaos. *Physics Today, 48*(5), 34–40.

PEAK, D., & FRAME, M. (1994). *Chaos under control: The art and science of complexity*. New York: W. H. Freeman.

PERVIN, L. (1991). Transversing the individual-environment landscape: A personal odyssey. In W. B. Walsh, K. B. Craik, & R. H. Price (Eds.), *Person-environment psychology: Models and perspectives*. Hillsdale, NJ: Erlbaum.

PINCUS, A., & MINAHAN, A. (1973). *Social work practice*. Itasca, IL: Peacock.

PRIGOGINE, I. (1993). Bounded rationality: From dynamical systems to socio-economic models. In P. Chen & R. H. Day (Eds.), *Nonlinear dynamics and evolutionary economics*. New York: Oxford University Press.

PRIGOGINE, I., & STENGERS, I. (1984). *Order out of chaos: Man's new dialogue with nature*. New York: Bantam Books.

RAFFESTIN, C., & LAWRENCE, R. (1990). An ecological perspective on housing, health and well-being. *Journal of Sociology & Social Welfare, 17*(1), 143–160.

RAY, W. A., & KEENEY, B. (1993). *Resource focused therapy*. London: Karnac.

RICHMOND, M. E. (1917). *Social diagnosis*. New York: Russell Sage Foundation.

RUBINSTEIN, R. L. (1989). The home environments of older people: A description of the psychosocial processes linking person to place. *Journal of Gerontology: Social Sciences, 44*(2), S45–S53.

SAARI, C. (1991). *The creation of meaning in social work*. New York: Guilford.

SCHOGGEN, P. (1989). *Behavior settings: A revision and extension of Roger G. Barker's* Ecological psychology. Stanford, CA: Stanford University Press.

SCHOR, J. B. (1992). *The overworked American: The unexpected decline of leisure*. New York: HarperCollins.

SCHWARTZ, W., & ZALBA, S. (1972). *The practice of group work*. New York: Columbia University Press.

SELVINI-PALAZZOLI, M., CIRILLO, S., SELVINI, M., & SORRENTINO, A. M. (1989). *Family games: General models of psychotic processes in the family*. New York: Norton.

SHINBROT, T., GREBOGI, C., OTT, E., & YORKE, J. A. (1993). Using small perturbations to control chaos. *Nature, 363*, 411–417.

SIMMEL, G. (1950). *The sociology of Georg Simmel*. New York: Free Press.

STEWART, I. (1989). *Does God play dice? The mathematics of chaos*. Cambridge, MA: Blackwell.

THELEN, E., & SMITH, L. (1994). *A dynamic systems approach to the development of cognition and action*. Cambridge, MA: MIT Press.

TOSELAND, R. W., & RIVAS, R. F. (1984). *An introduction to group work practice*. New York: Macmillan.

UM, M. Y., & BROWN-STANDRIDGE, M. D. (1993). Discovering organizational "rules" that contribute to student stress in social work field placements. *The Journal of Applied Social Sciences, 17*(2), 157–171.

VAN HEUSDEN, A., & VAN DEN EERENBEEMT, E. (1987). *Balance in motion: Ivan Boszormenyi-Nagy and his vision of individual and family therapy.* New York: Brunner/Mazel.

VAN VLIET, W., & WOHLWILL, J. F. (1985). *Habitats for children: The impacts of density.* Hillsdale, NJ: Erlbaum.

VARELA, F. J. (1989). Reflections on the circulation of concepts between a biology of cognition and systemic family therapy. *Family Process, 28,* 15–24.

WAKEFIELD, J. C. (1996a). Does social work need the ecosystems perspective? Part 1. Is the perspective clinically useful? *Social Service Review, 70*(1), 1–32.

WAKEFIELD, J. C. (1996b). Does social work need the ecosystems perspective? Part 2. Does the perspective save social work from incoherence? *Social Service Review, 70*(2), 183–213.

WAKEFIELD, J. C. (1996c). Does social work need the ecological perspective: Reply to Alex Gitterman. *Social Service Review, 70*(3), 476–481.

WARREN, K., FRANKLIN, C., & STREETER, C. (in press). New directions in systems theory: Chaos and complexity. *Social Work.*

WARREN, K., FRANKLIN, C., & STREETER, C. (1997). Chaos theory and complexity theory. *Encyclopedia of social work.* (19th ed.) Washington, DC: NASW Press.

WEAKLAND, J., FISCH, R., WATZLAWICK, P., & BODIN, A. M. (1974). Brief therapy: Focused problem resolution. *Family Process, 13,* 141–168.

WHYTE, W. F. (1943). *Street corner society: The social structure of an Italian slum.* Chicago: University of Chicago Press.

WICKER, A. W. (1991). Making sense of environments. In W. B. Walsh, K. B. Craik, & R. H. Price (Eds.), *Person-environment psychology: Models and perspectives.* Hillsdale, NJ: Erlbaum.

WILSON, E. O. (1992). *The diversity of life.* Cambridge, MA: Harvard University Press.

YALOM, I. D. (1985). *The theory and practice of group psychotherapy* (3rd ed.). New York: Basic Books.

GLOSSARY

analogical messages Communications between family members that have symbolic meaning.

autopoiesis Literally, the process of self-generation; the way that parts of systems relate to one another in order to maintain the system.

behavioral and cognitive-behavioral family therapy Therapies that emphasize the importance of family members' interactions with each other and with the environment. The action-oriented approach of these therapies focuses change on learning new skills, modifying behavioral functioning, and reframing or altering cognitive perceptions.

boundaries Invisible lines of demarcation in a system that function to distinguish parts of the system from other parts or to distinguish the system itself from its environment.

chaos theory Based on the assumption that order can exist without predictability, chaos theory can be used in the study of social systems. For example, mathematical techniques may show an underlying order in social systems, but social systems, as iterative, recursive systems, are unpredictable in detail. See also **complexity theory**.

circular causality An idea from systems theory that suggests that an individual's behavior is understood within the familial context, and one person's behavior is a reaction to and influences the behavior of others.

closed systems Systems that become depleted because of a lack of interaction with other systems.

complexity theory A theory that assumes that complex systems exhibit order, but an order which is not predictable. A complex system will eventually exhibit a pattern of disorder or chaos and develop into a new, more complex system. Some theorists consider chaos theory a subdiscipline of complexity theory. See also **chaos theory**.

cybernetic systems theory (cybernetics) Theory that emphasizes ecology and whole systems and assumes that it is not possible to assign one part of a living system as a causal influence on another; rather, influence is a recursive process of circularity.

dissipative systems Self-organizing systems that are capable of increasing their complexity. This term, sometimes used interchangeably with "open systems," describes systems that are able to import energy, matter, and information from their external environments and export the entropy inherent in these types of systems. See also **system**.

ecological systems theory Theory that describes the reciprocal relationship between an organism and its environment.

equifinality Literally, equal ending; implies that no matter where one begins in a system, the end will be the same.

family preservation An intensive practice model that focuses on strengthening the family and preventing placement of children into substitute care. The model is home-based and family-centered, requiring the social worker to work effectively within the family's ecological system.

feedback See **negative feedback** and **positive feedback**.

first-order change Small adjustments in a system within the parameters of the system's own rules and structure.

functional family therapy Integrating concepts from systems theory, behavioral therapy, and cognitive therapy, this therapy focuses on the family over the individual, and recognizes circular causality and how relationship functioning and roles maintain dysfunctional behavior patterns.

hierarchies Ordered levels within a system or subsystem.

homeostasis Tendency of a system, such as a family, to try to maintain the system's equilibrium or status quo, even at the expense of making a positive change.

integrated services delivery systems Service delivery systems that integrate health, mental health, and social services through forming collaboratives and partnerships.

integrative couples therapy Combining traditional behavioral couples therapies and emotional change strategies, this therapy focuses on couples' acceptance of each other and their letting go of the struggle to change one another.

managed behavioral health care A system of financing health, mental health, and social services, which emphasizes cost containment, accountability, and increasing the quality of services.

miracle question An intervention strategy used in solution-focused therapy that is intended to help the client envision a new way of behaving. The therapist asks the client to imagine what will be different when a miracle occurs and the problem that brought them to therapy has disappeared.

modeling A component of social learning that indicates how people learn behavior by watching the behavior of others.

multifinality Literally, multiple endings; different end states may be accomplished through the same beginnings. This term is used interchangeably with "equipotentiality."

mutual influence (reciprocal causality) The theory that describes how each element of a system influences every other element, in contrast to the belief in a simple cause-effect relationship between select elements.

narrative therapy A postmodern therapy that views problems as stories that people tell themselves. Though the amount of direction by therapists varies, the narrative therapist listens to client-generated stories and helps the client to restructure the stories or to explore new possibilities for the stories. See also **postmodern therapies**.

negative (attenuating) feedback Feedback that helps maintain the status quo of a system by keeping it within a limited operating range or eliminating performance fluctuations around a norm or standard.

network therapy A therapy model developed in work with Native Americans, which recognizes the interdependency of family and community members and mobilizes the community to engage in group problem solving.

nonlinear change As opposed to linear change, which is a simple cause-effect change, nonlinear change occurs when cause and effect recursively act on one another, causing unpredictable changes in a system.

open systems Systems that are open to interaction with other systems.

paradoxical interventions A technique of providing information or giving instructions which the client does not expect, such as instructing the client to continue or exaggerate a problem behavior.

positive (amplifying) feedback Feedback that forces the system to change by reinforcing its operation.

postmodern therapies A broad spectrum of therapies based on the postmodern assumption that there is no universal reality but many possible interpretations of events and that language is the primary vehicle for the transmission of possible meanings. See also **narrative therapy**.

preferred provider network A network of collaborating service professionals set up by a managed care organization.

psychoeducational family practice A brief therapy approach that combines didactic presentations on the nature of mental illness with other techniques, such as cognitive-behavioral techniques and social skills training.

recursion Each element in a system mutually influencing other elements in a manner that is more complex than linear causality, or simple cause-effect influence.

reflecting team A team of therapists that observes the therapy session either from behind a one-way mirror or by sitting quietly in the room with the therapist and clients. Differing from the Milan-style team, the therapist does not confer with the team privately to discuss possible directions therapy with each client may take. The reflecting team method, developed by Tom Andersen in Norway, allows clients to listen to the team's discussion of the therapy session.

reframing/relabelling Redefining the client's behavior in a way that helps the client and/or family develop a more positive understanding of the behavior.

scaling technique The therapist helps the client anchor problem descriptions and resolutions at either end of a Likert scale and then asks where the client currently is on the scale.

self-anchored scales An ordinal scale (1–10) used by therapists to anchor a wide variety of individualized client behaviors, emotions, thoughts, or other experiences in order to monitor the effectiveness of practice interventions.

second-order change A major transformation of a system's rules and structure.

single-case design Research design in which each participant serves as his or her own control by developing a baseline of behaviors that are the focus of change.

social construction theory A postmodern theory that asserts that it is impossible to receive an exact replica of objective reality in the mind without structuring it according to one's cognitive structures, subjective or linguistic meanings, and unique social experiences. This theory emphasizes language, narratives, and sociohistorical and cultural processes as primary factors in understanding one's constructions.

solution-focused therapy A strengths-based therapy model that stresses respect for clients' capacities to solve their own problems and charges the therapist with creating a context in which this can happen.

strategic family therapy A present-focused therapy model that emphasizes the importance of understanding the client's construction of reality and focuses intervention on alteration of the dysfunctional interactional patterns that are believed to maintain the client's presenting problem.

structural family therapy A therapy model that defines the family as a system whose structure consists of predictable patterns that govern the family members' interactions. The goal of this therapy is to change the family structure by reinforcing healthy hierarchies and clarifying boundaries.

subsystem   A subunit of a system, defined in a family system by generation, sex, interest, or function.

system   A group of individuals, objects, or forces that interact to serve a particular function.

systems theory   A spectrum of theories utilizing a systems framework for therapeutic models, including general systems theory, ecological systems theory, cybernetic models, and complexity and chaos theory.

tracking   A way of assessing family interactions to discover the systemic pattern that maintains the problem. Assessment involves learning when and where the problem occurs, who sees the problem as a problem, what attempts have been made to solve the problem, and so on.

AUTHOR INDEX

SUBJECT INDEX